MOVEMENT EXPERIENCES FOR CHILDREN

Third Edition

MOVEMENT EXPERIENCES FOR CHILDREN

A Humanistic Approach to Elementary School Physical Education

EVELYN L. SCHURR

State University of New York College at Brockport

PRENTICE-HALL, INC., Englewood Cliffs, New Jersey 07632

Library of Congress Cataloging in Publication Data

SCHURR, EVELYN L.
    Movement experiences for children.

    Includes bibliographies and index.
    1. Movement education. I. Title.
GV452.S38 1980   372.8'6   79-18932
ISBN 0-13-604553-7

© 1980, 1975 by Prentice-Hall, Inc., Englewood Cliffs, N.J. 07632

Printed in the United States of America

10   9   8   7

Editorial/production supervision by Frank J. Hubert
Interior design by Emily Dobson
Cover design by R L Communications
Manufacturing Buyer: Harry P. Baisley

PRENTICE-HALL INTERNATIONAL, INC., *London*
PRENTICE-HALL OF AUSTRALIA PTY. LIMITED, *Sydney*
PRENTICE-HALL OF CANADA, LTD., *Toronto*
PRENTICE-HALL OF INDIA PRIVATE LIMITED, *New Delhi*
PRENTICE-HALL OF JAPAN, INC., *Tokyo*
PRENTICE-HALL OF SOUTHEAST ASIA PTE. LTD., *Singapore*
WHITEHALL BOOKS LIMITED, *Wellington, New Zealand*

Dedicated to MY FATHER and MOTHER

CONTENTS

x

PREFACE

As in previous editions of *Movement Experiences for Children,* an effort has been made to synthesize contemporary educational theories and practices in a practical and scholarly manner for elementary school physical education teachers. The central theme is learning how to help children become skillful movers. In this edition, there is an increased emphasis on a humanistic curriculum with more examples of how to plan and implement a more individualized, personalized program. The affective goals of physical education are more specifically identified, and practical suggestions are made for helping children attain them.

Stress is not only placed on knowing how to plan learning experiences to help children achieve *literacy in movement* but *also* on how to help children go *beyond literacy in movement.* Literacy is defined as competence in basic skills and activities, basic motor fitness, and basic understanding of the fundamentals of human movement structure. A humanistic curriculum takes the child beyond literacy in movement by providing opportunities to use these basics to do the following: develop high levels of skill in various structured activities and creative movements; develop processes necessary for self-directed learning in movement; reach new insights into self and others in movement; appreciate movement; experience joy in the movement experiences themselves; and have better access to the beauty of movement.

The book is presented in five parts. An overview of the book and major changes and improvements in this edition will be noted here.

Part I presents an overview of the curriculum and methods of physical education in the elementary school. It serves as the basic framework for the rest of the book. Discussions of cognitive, social, emotional, and motor development have been expanded to provide a better basis for understanding why certain activities, organizations, approaches, and methods are more suitable at certain stages of development than at others.

Chapter 3 includes an explanation of the hierarchy of goals, purposes, and objectives and stresses the relationship of what is done in the daily lesson to the whole of the child's education and, more particularly, to movement education. The addition of program objectives at different levels of development should give the teacher a better basis for understanding the more specific suggestions in future chapters. Greater attention is given to clarifying affective and process objectives as well as activities for helping to actualize purposes and objectives in these areas.

Sandefur's generalizations on good teaching and the characteristics of good teachers—reached after an extensive review and study of the results of the major research on teaching—serves as the basis of Part II, which deals with what a teacher does and therefore has to learn. The characteristics of good teachers are of course attitudinal and personal behaviors, which may or may not already be evident in the student and might be difficult to achieve as the result of studying any one book or taking any single course. However, learning more about children, their needs, the subject matter, the use of different tools and techniques to become a more creative teacher, and, in general, becoming more comfortable and confident can have a positive effect on personal attitudes and behaviors and move one toward becoming a good humanistic teacher.

Part II focuses on what the teacher does to implement the curriculum. It deals with teaching approaches, methods, and techniques based on a knowledge of how children learn. Basic considerations underlying the long-term and short-term planning necessary for implementation are discussed, as well as how to evaluate the progress of children. Stress is placed on learning to use an indirect approach and insure that quality or attainment of skill is reached. Many more practical suggestions and examples of ways to individualize and humanize learning are included in this part than were previously. Emphasis is placed on ways to present experiences in the affective and process areas.

Part III provides background information about the structure of movement and the foundations of the movement education of children. This part is particularly vital to the elementary classroom teacher who has had less opportunity to study these foundational areas in the context of movement. Many suggestions are given for implementing and organizing basic movement lessons in an indirect manner which will help insure skill development. A Basic Movement Glossary is included in the introduction to Part III and is a summary of terms and concepts which children should know and understand and skills that they should be able to perform as a result of the elementary school phase of their total movement education. Each chapter in Part III contains definitions and explanations to help children acquire this movement vocabulary in thought and in action.

Part IV introduces to the student a wide variety of movement experiences, the activity content through which the broader skills and concepts are developed. New activities and ideas have been added. The section of self-designed games has been expanded.

Part V, Programs for Special Needs and Interests, is new in the organization of the book. The concept of mainstreaming and suggestions for meeting the needs of exceptional children and those with learning disabilities are included in Chapter 18. Chapter 19 deals with extraclass activities and the use and construction of tournaments.

The Appendix contains supplementary information for the teacher. A new addition is the American Alliance for Health, Physical Education and Recreation paper, *Essentials of a Quality Elementary School Physical Education Program*. This gives the teacher a source of professional guidance and support in developing and refining curriculum and in requesting additional funds, time, staff, and support from administrators and parents.

The college instructor may wish to change the sequence in which parts or chapters are studied. I find it helpful early in the course to concentrate on the movement experiences themselves. This enables one to study experientially the theory and ideas found in the other chapters. The book is a basis for study, and field experiences or simulated teaching and learning experiences should accompany its use. Throughout the book, application and enrichment experiences are suggested.

Since this is a comprehensive book for those planning to teach physical education as a classroom teacher or as a specialist and those already teaching, each topic cannot be covered with the detail it deserves. Contemporary, in-depth resources are identified in the Suggested Readings for each chapter. Many references and quotations from publications of the American Alliance for Health, Physical Education and Recreation, the major representative organization of the profession, appear throughout the book. The dimension of Dance was added to the name of the organization just as the book went to press—too late for changes to be made in the text.

I hope that you will find the contents helpful as you help children become skillful movers and take them *beyond literacy in movement.*

E.L.S.

Part I
Overview

The chapters in Part I provide an overview of the physical education curriculum in the elementary school. Chapter 1 is a brief historical review of the growth and development of physical education in the school curriculum, with a focus on the contemporary shift to a humanistic philosophy. To emphasize the urgent need for a good physical education program in the elementary school, the chapter includes a review of research that supports the value of activity in the social, emotional, physical, and cognitive development of children. Chapter 1 also contains a list of the characteristics of good teaching. You should use this list to evaluate yourself and your abilities. In this way you will be able to identify the areas in which you need work, and thus personalize your education.

Chapter 2 examines growth and development stages in terms of the child's readiness for certain movement experiences. In Chapter 3 this information is used as a base for a discussion of curriculum development.

1 / PHYSICAL EDUCATION IN THE ELEMENTARY SCHOOL

- **Physical education in the school curriculum**
- **Values of physical education to the child**
- **The elementary school physical education teacher**

The physical education program in today's elementary school curriculum provides a continuity of movement experiences for children. These experiences will help children to acquire the skills of movement, to understand the structure and concepts of human movement, to utilize the processes of movement, and to employ and enjoy the products of movement. Through experiences in play, exercise, games, sports, and dance, children learn about themselves. They become better able to control their bodies, to adapt and relate to the world around them (space, people, and inanimate objects), to communicate feelings and ideas, and to maintain a state of well-being. Children begin to find movement experiences significant and meaningful. A good physical education program helps children build a foundation for present and future success in all life activities.

There is a wide spectrum of study and experiences in physical education. Teachers must be familiar with the skills, knowledge, activities, experiences, processes, and interactions a child should encounter during the formative years in the elementary school. Teachers must be able to encourage children to use their abilities productively. It is the teacher's responsibility to diagnose movement patterns, and to organize the environment so that children may choose appropriate ways to meet their individual needs.

Years of study and research have resulted in many changes in the philosophy, content, and method of preparing children to move and live effectively in the complex modern world. In the following section we will discuss the progress of physical education in the school curriculum.

Physical Education in the School Curriculum

The spontaneous play of children and the more organized efforts of adults in various forms of games, sports, exercises, and dance are an important part of all civilizations. Early in the history of American education, leaders recognized that physical exercise is specifically valuable to health and welfare. Many colleges, universities, and public school systems introduced instruction in health and physical exercises after programs were initiated at the Round Hill School in Northampton, Massachusetts in 1825 and at Harvard University in 1826. The state of California passed legislation in 1866 regarding programs of physical education that would increase the health and vigor of the mind and body. Since that time, most states have enacted laws that make physical education a vital part of the public school curriculum.

Physical education in the curricula of the 1800s was primarily corrective in nature, with an emphasis on formal exercises. Various systems of physical education were borrowed from European and Scandinavian countries and adapted for use in American classrooms and gymnasia.

As our society expanded and changed economically, politically, and culturally, so did the nature of education and physical education. Educational curricula began to reflect the values and needs of the democratic system. The nature of physical education became preventive and broad in nature rather than corrective and primarily one of formal exercises. Content emphasis has changed periodically along with the changes in education attendant to major political, social, and economic forces of the time.

In recent years American education has been based on a developmental concept, whose ultimate goal is helping the individual achieve his/her fullest capacity as a functioning, self-actualized being. The focus today is on understanding basic concepts of disciplines and development of processes and using these concepts in a meaningful way.

Most recently the focus has shifted from subject matter per se to the development of the fully functioning person. This has brought about changes in organization and methods to allow for more student responsibility and choice. There is more emphasis on the affective aspects and values of education, in which the skills or processes of *valuing* are stressed.[1]

Physical education has followed this trend, and today there is far more emphasis on developmental and lifetime activities and pupil participation in planning and goal setting. Many people describe this departure from the traditional activity-centered program as "the new physical education."

Professionals in the field of physical education, through increased concern, services, and responsibility, have developed a concept of movement education ranging from early childhood to mature adulthood. The concept of movement education has been translated into the physical education programs planned and implemented within all levels of schools. Programs in the elementary school that focus on developing concepts and skills of basic movement are often referred to as "movement education." However, this is a rather narrow interpretation of the concept, since learning in movement, about movement, and through movement is a lifelong process and venture. The elementary school physical education program is the foundation of lifelong movement education. Learning *in* movement is the unique and primary experience of physical education. To learn *about* movement is to learn about the world of movement, the feeling of movement, and the significance of movement to oneself. Learning *through* movement enhances the individual's appreciation of many related disciplines and aesthetic experiences; this knowledge stimulates the basic learning processes.

Recently, educators and child development specialists have paid an increasing amount of attention to the significance of the motor dimensions of development. The recognition of the interrelationships among all aspects of development has led to better understanding and acceptance of physical education programs in the preschool and in the elementary schools. Hence physical education programs have become an integral part of the total curriculum. Today's movement education of the elementary school child is based on a vast knowledge of the values of a wide range of movement experiences, and is supported by research in the fields of child development, medicine, psychology, sociology, education, and physical education.

Values of Physical Education to the Child

To emphasize the potential value of the elementary physical education program, this section presents a brief review of known facts and recent research findings in the areas of physical, intellectual, social, emotional, and affective development. College students and teachers should be aware of these values as they assess their own interests in teaching, and as they plan objectives and experiences for children. Moreover, this review should be helpful in explain-

---

[1] Kirschenbaum identifies five dimensions of the valuing process as thinking, feeling, choosing or decision making, communicating, and acting (using academic, professional, and personal-social skills competently). Howard Kirschenbaum, "Values Education: 1976 and Beyond," in R. Freeman Butts, Donald H. Peckenpaugh, and Howard Kirschenbaum, *The School's Role as Moral Authority* (Washington, D.C.: Association for Supervision and Curriculum Development, 1977).

ing the importance of the physical education program and in some cases justify its existence to administrators, parents, legislators, and pupils.

Physical Growth Heredity determines physique or basic body build. Intrinsic factors and environment control growth. Physical exercise stimulates growth of body tissues, organs, and bones, and is essential to optimum physical development.

The physiological law of use and disuse implies that exercise promotes growth, and a cessation of exercise or disuse results in atrophy or retardation of growth. Muscle tissues are especially influenced by this law. Much evidence has been gathered from research to indicate that muscles increase in size and strength as a result of repeated exercise; however, the reverse is true if exercise is discontinued or withdrawn. Mineralization of bone tissues increases as greater stress due to exercise is placed upon bones. Exercise affects the lateral growth of bones but does not affect the length. Lack of function, as is evidenced by paralysis of some nature, causes bones to remain small and undeveloped. Inactivity due to long illnesses or immobility due to broken bones stabilized in casts causes demineralization. Subsequent exercise over a period of time will restore loss of calcium.

Healthy, normal growth of the organs of the respiratory and circulatory systems is also stimulated by vigorous exercise. The demands of exercise require the heart to pump more blood to supply more oxygen to the working muscles. Consequently, the breathing mechanism is accelerated, and the lungs must increase in capacity to provide greater amounts of oxygen. The ability to do this work depends upon the strength of the musculature of the organs. Thus, the law of use and disuse is applicable as well to the condition of the organic muscles and the efficiency of the systems they control. Flabby skeletal muscles in children are an indication of a poorly developed cardiorespiratory system. Gordon R. Cumming, M.D., summarizes definite medical reasons that support the need for a physical activity program in children:

> Physical exercise is important during childhood for the proper development of the functional capacity of the heart, the lungs and the strength of bones and muscles. If [these remain] underdeveloped during the growing years, the opportunity for optimal development of these organ systems has likely been lost.[2]

The human body has an inherent need for activity. Gardner Murphy stated that "activity needs are indeed as fundamental as the nutritive need. We are provided with a set of complex organic equipment and if it is not allowed to function something happens to us, just as in using it we find joy."[3] Children satisfy this need in play. Adults satisfy much of it in work. In many instances the "American way of life" has inhibited the opportunity for fulfillment of the urge for activity. Most adults once met activity needs through the demands of their vocation, but today many jobs are sedentary. The working day is short, and many recreational pursuits are also sedentary. Urbanization, and the apartment living that results, curtail space in which children may play. Congested traffic makes it hazardous for small children to walk to and from school. The consolidation and integration in urban schools often requires

[2] "The Child in Sport and Physical Activity—Medical Comment," in J. G. Albinson and G. M. Andrew, *Child in Sport and Physical Activity* (Baltimore: University Park Press, 1976), p. 67.

[3] In *Human Potentialities* (New York: Basic Books, Inc., 1958), p. 339.

long bus rides for even very young children. The necessity of going directly home and waiting inside for one or both working parents to come home certainly restricts vigorous play after school. Lawrence Rarick states that "observations of pre-adolescent school age children indicate that they need four to five hours of physical activity each day; adolescents need a minimum of one and one-half to two hours each day."[4] Therefore, one can easily understand that children's natural activity must be supplemented in order to satisfy their normal urge and need for activity. A good physical education program will partially fulfill this need. It will also improve motor skills and promote a good attitude toward the necessity for and the enjoyment of physical activities in present and future leisure time.

Physical Fitness   A child is able to function in his environment according to the level of physical fitness he possesses. Physical fitness is the condition of the body necessary for a person to carry out daily tasks without undue fatigue, yet have enough energy to pursue leisure activities and meet emergency situations requiring additional exertion. This definition implies that a person must develop and maintain muscle strength, endurance, and cardiovascular efficiency; he must be free from disease, make compensation (adjustments) for chronic physical handicaps, and maintain optimum weight. Of course, all of these factors are interrelated and are all dependent upon physical exercise. They are also basic elements which underlie the capacity for learning motor skills.

Overweight or obesity in children has increased a great deal in the last decade. The inactive habits of many children combined with an availability of rich foods are the major reasons for this situation. Most overweight youngsters encounter social and emotional problems in school, and most are antagonistic toward exercise. Obese children find it difficult to exercise and play vigorously; therefore they become less active, and the resulting frustration often makes them eat more. Thus a never-ending circle of problems is set up—and it becomes even more difficult for an obese child to become fit as he or she gets older.

The role of inactivity as a factor in the increasingly alarming incidence of heart disease has caused doctors to look at childhood activity patterns. Kenneth Rose[5] traced the developmental history of arteriosclerotic disease and found that earliest signs appear at the age of 2. The disease process is reversible until the age of 19, but after that it is essentially irreversible; at about age 40, it becomes clinically obvious. Autopsies of children have shown fatty deposits in blood vessels which would eventually lead to heart attack. Proper diet and exercise are essential in childhood.

D. A. Bailey[6] presents a number of studies completed and underway which indicate that functional capacity in adults appears to be related importantly to activity during the growing years. Physical activity is necessary not only to support growth in children and provide a healthy childhood but also as a long-range preventive medicine. Because attitudes and activity habits are

[4] "Research Evidence on the Values of Physical Education," *Theory Into Practice,* 3, no. 3, Ohio State University (June 1964), 109.

[5] "To Keep the People in Health," *Journal of American College Health Association,* 22 (February 1973), 80.

[6] "The Growing Child and the Need for Physical Activity," in J. G. Albinson and G. M. Andrew, *Child in Sport and Physical Activity* (Baltimore: University Park Press, 1976).

formed early, stress is placed on understanding the effects of good nutrition and exercise and on encouraging many activity opportunities in the growing years. If children are physically unfit, a well-designed program can be undertaken to develop acceptable standards of fitness in a short time.

Acquisition of Motor Skills

As was discussed earlier, most behavior is based on motor skills. The child begins to develop motor skills in the prenatal stages, and consequent skill development follows a sequential pattern. Children have acquired patterns of performance in the basic locomotor and nonlocomotor skills before they enter school. Because these basic skills form the foundations of the everyday work tasks and play skills of children, it is important that an instructional program is started in the first grade or earlier to ensure proper acquisition and refinement of the more difficult skill patterns. Unfortunately, many children enter first grade with a very low level of locomotive and manipulative skills. Although maturation provides them with the equipment or readiness to learn, they must have the opportunities to practice and refine their skills. It is true that some progress can be made through the trial and error process; however, constant analysis of errors and suggestions for correction can reduce the number of repeated failures.

Many studies support the hypothesis that specific instruction in skill will result in learning. Repeated practice is the essential element in acquiring proficiency, and greater retention of skills is promoted by overlearning. However, in the primary grades maturation may exert a greater influence on new skills than does learning. *Opportunity* for general practice through game play, and exploration with certain skills, will prove more productive at this stage than emphasis on extended practice and direct skill teaching.

Sports are an important element of the American culture today, and they exert influences on the populace in many ways. The acquisition of a certain level of proficiency in traditional American sports is beneficial to both girls and boys, and a knowledge of the conduct of sports is also valuable, whether one participates as a spectator or as a player. Since most adults tend to select leisure activities in which they have already achieved skill, guided practice in learning sports skills is essential so that people will have a variety of sports activities to enjoy.

Sport skills are combinations of various fundamental (basic) movement patterns adapted to specific sports implements, boundaries, rules, and strategies. Consequently, a good foundation can be established for sport skills in the instruction and generalized practice that takes place in the primary grades.

Motor skills also provide avenues of expression for creative and aesthetic efforts. Only by learning through experience what the body can do can the child explore this mode of self-expression. The learning and practice of motor skills is essential in order for a child to acquire the tools to achieve desirable goals of physical fitness, recreation skills, scholastic achievement, and social efficiency.

Intellectual Development

Physical education activities are valuable in the intellectual development of the school child, usually measured by scholastic achievement. The child's level of achievement is primarily dependent upon his intellectual capacity, but whether or not his potential is realized depends a great deal upon his physical development.

Throughout history, philosophers and educators have stressed the importance of a sound body and good health as a framework for optimum mental effectiveness. As physical exercise contributes to the physical fitness level and the social and emotional adjustments, it is also setting the stage for the child to learn well academically. Generally, if children are well-adjusted socially and emotionally, they will have a good self-concept, be self-assured, and will desire to work well in school.

Recently, results of research and study on the relationship of motor patterns and academic achievement have indicated that the type of movement experiences a young child has may influence academic achievement. Despite the empirical and observed evidence that perceptual-motor development and academic success are correlated, the evidence is not yet conclusive. Perceptual-motor development as a vital part of normal child development has long been considered a sequence of learning stages; however, research indicates specific cases in which the correction of delayed motor patterns resulted in improved performance and apparently improved capacity for intellectual achievement.

Most children develop the ability to monitor proprioceptively through their play experiences before beginning school, but for those who do not, primary school programs stressing work with the fundamental motor patterns in an exploratory setting increase orientation of the body in space and development of the muscle-sensor system. Many schools have incorporated perceptual motor activities into existing programs for children under various titles; Perceptual-Motor, Sensorimotor, Motor Facilitation, Motor Perception, etc. A close look at the objectives and activities of many of these programs reveals that they are very similar to a well-developed elementary physical education program as recommended in this book. Inclusion of many activities designed to foster enrichment of the sensory-motor mechanisms will facilitate perceptual-motor development in the preschool and primary years; however, this should be within or in addition to the regular physical education program, not in place of it. For children who demonstrate retardation or deficiencies in this area, there should be additional personalized work. In severe cases a specialist should be involved as well as the classroom teacher. Bailey reports an interesting study undertaken in France relating to academic achievement and intellectual development with longer periods of the school day devoted to physical education.[7] In a ten-year study of children who spent one-third of the school day in physical education activities, it was found that these pupils matured more quickly, and were more independent. Their intellectual tools were much keener than those who did not participate in as much physical education. As a result of this Vanves study, the Ministries of Education, and Youth and Sports of France specified "1/3 time" physical education for elementary schools in France, and five hours for secondary schools, dependent on personnel and equipment.

The motor learning process itself is, in part, an intellectual one. Successful performance is dependent on a knowledge of the component parts of the skill, an understanding of how the skill is to be utilized, and insight into actions and results. As the skill is performed repeatedly, the physical action must be accompanied by reflective thinking in terms of what students have

[7] *Ibid.*, pp. 89–91.

observed from demonstrations or observations of the actions and directions of others, as well as of their own past trials.

Children are gaining a knowledge of how the body operates and what it is capable of doing when they are exposed to good teaching in physical education—a program which stresses a problem-solving approach and emphasizes acquiring good basic movement skills at the primary level. An understanding of the cause-and-effect relationship of exercise and fitness is essential to the maintenance of fitness throughout life and the selection of active leisure activities in adulthood.

Efficiency of movement is the ultimate goal in all play and work skills. The mechanical principles of movement are learned by children, and the concepts are applied to the learning of new play or work skills. Before the complete understanding of principles and identification by definition, concepts or generalized applications of these principles can be made in the exploration and problem-solving phases with basic movement skills in the primary grades. As the student matures intellectually, and physical laws and principles are introduced in the classroom, direct analogies can be made as to how these operate in the body.

Development of process skills are desired outcomes of every discipline. Development and use of the processes of discovery, exploration, experimentation, analysis, critical thinking, divergent thinking, creative thinking, and problem solving are all critical to success in physical activities. This applies to the sense of good execution of skills and the appropriate use of them; strategy in game play; safety decisions; expressive performance; and logical choices of activity. In order to develop process skills related to efficient, safe, and satisfying performance in movement, a child has to have opportunities to *use* these skills in the activity setting.

Social and Emotional Growth and Development

Physical education contributes to the child's social growth and development, because it provides an opportunity for the acquisition of social skills and moral values. Frequently, physical education is referred to as a laboratory in which children experience social interactions. Varied activities provide excellent opportunities for children to interact with individuals, small groups, large groups, and authority figures. Concepts of courtesy, modesty, cooperation, honesty, dependability, and respect for authority and rules can all be developed through active participation in realistic, demanding situations.

The mere experiences of social interactions do not insure the development of social skills and moral values. The skills must be taught. The teacher must plan situations in which children have responsibilities—friendly rivalries, where the cooperation of each group member is important to success—and where there is the chance to make decisions involving honesty. The teacher must make the most of the "teachable moments" when problems arise, and must guide the children in their value judgments and social behavior.

Most of a child's social contacts are in a motor skill setting. Therefore, good play skills are of major importance in the social life of a child. In writing about the movement experiences of young children, Mary Gutteridge states:

> Skill in bodily activity has deep-rooted social significance. It is to be ranked first among factors that lead to a child's acceptance among his peers. Approval raises

for him the value of an activity and leads him to put forth to reach acceptable standards and to compete successfully with others.[8]

Because most children value success in physical performance, "distinguishing oneself in this area of competence may lead to increased social acceptance."[9] Further, "for the educator to ignore the marked influence that game success has on the social acceptance of children and adolescents is to ignore an important dimension of the value system with which youngsters are surrounded."[10]

A number of research studies (Clarke and Greene,[11] Nelson,[12] Hagberg,[13] Buchanan et al.[14]) have found that there is a positive relationship between social status, leadership, and popularity and athletic ability and sport skill in elementary school children. These and many more studies indicate that a good level of motor skill performance is important to a child's status and his or her relationship with the peer group. However, we must be careful about making generalizations in these areas, as many variables play a part in the social development of children in and through play activities. Implications of research results of group size and structure must be more clearly interpreted for the teacher of physical education.

Physical education contributes to the development of emotional control, since play periods are filled with emotionally charged situations. Games are demanding whether or not there is an emphasis on competition. Dance and gymnastic performances are exciting in themselves. Anxieties build up. Both losing and winning produce strong emotions. Learning to control these emotions can only come about through experiences and careful guidance. Team competition teaches the discipline of accepting defeat. Children can adjust better to a defeat when they share it with teammates.

Children's successes and failures provide them with a self-concept which, in turn, influences personality development and approach to new tasks and experiences. As children grow in size and age, they begin to make judgments and comparisons of other children and relate their perceptions to their own body images. In Larry Kehres' words, "the degree to which an individual has met the physiological needs for movement directly influences the development of his self-concept."[15] Play skills and games are common activities to all children, and success in them is highly prized. Children recognize that success in

[8] In "A Child's Experiences in Bodily Activity," 46th Yearbook, Part II (National Society for Study of Education, 1947), p. 108.

[9] Bryant Cratty, *Perceptual and Motor Development in Infants and Children* (London: Macmillan, 1970), p. 228.

[10] *Ibid.*

[11] Harrison Clarke and Walter Greene, "Relationships between Personal-Social Measures Applied to 10-Year-Old Boys," *Research Quarterly,* 34 (1963), 288.

[12] Dale Nelson, "Leadership in Sports," *Research Quarterly,* 37 (1966), 268.

[13] S. J. Hagberg, "A Study of the Relationship between Social Popularity and Physical Fitness of Boys and Girls Grade 3 through 5, in a Selected Illinois Community," unpublished Master's Thesis, University of Illinois, 1963.

[14] Hugh Buchanan, Joe Blankenmeyer, and Doyice Cotten, "Academic and Athletic Ability as Popularity Factors in Elementary School Children," *Research Quarterly,* 47, no. 3 (October 1976), 320-25.

[15] In "Maslow's Hierarchy of Needs Applied to Physical Education and Athletics," *The Physical Educator,* 30, no. 1 (1973), 25.

skills comes only through their own repeated efforts to achieve their goal. When the goal is initially too difficult, the attendant failures reduce enthusiasm and confidence in approaching other new experiences. If in the primary grades the physical education program is conducted on a developmental basis and the teacher utilizes an approach in which children can experience a sense of achievement in control of their bodies over the environment, children will learn to develop a positive self-concept.

Many people believe that there is a decay of moral values in our society; consequently there is a reemergence of efforts to stress moral education in schools. The physical education setting and natural interactions necessitated by playing, working, and sharing physical education activities provide many opportunities for teaching values. Kirschenbaum identifies two overall goals of teaching moral values and good citizenship as "(a) to help people become more fulfilled and satisfied with the quality of their lives, and (b) to help people become more constructive members of the groups of which they are a part—that is, in their relationships, families, task groups, social groups, and societies."[16] (See the Suggested References at the end of this chapter for additional readings in value/citizenship training through physical education.)

What Movement Means to Children

The last few pages have discussed the values of activity and physical education for children in terms of what educators have found meaningful. It seems appropriate also to look at what movement means to children. In a speech at a joint conference of the American Alliance for Health, Physical Education and Recreation and the National Association for the Education of Young Children, Katurah Whitehurst said that movement, to the child, means:

1. Life—not only does he experience life in his own movements but he also attributes life to all moving things.
2. Self-discovery.
3. Environmental discovery, both physical and social.
4. Freedom . . . from the restrictions of narrow physical confinements and . . . to expand oneself through creative body expression.
5. Safety—in a basic sense it has survival value.
6. A method of establishing contact and communication.
7. Sheer enjoyment and sensuous pleasure.
8. Acceptance.[17]

The Elementary School Physical Education Teacher

The primary functions of the elementary school physical education teacher are to provide appropriate situations for children to learn the concepts of movement and to acquire skill in movement. In order to do this, teachers must have a good understanding of movement theory, child growth and development factors, a wide range of movement activities, physiological principles,

[16] In "Values Education: 1976 and Beyond."

[17] "The Meaning of Movement to the Child," in *Echoes of Influence for Elementary School Physical Education*, Washington, D.C., 1977.

and, as with teachers of any subject, a knowledge of learning and curriculum theory. In addition to these knowledges and understandings they must also have an interest and desire to work with children, an attitude that physical education is a vital part of the curriculum, a love of movement, and a willingness to study new materials and ideas in the field of physical education and education.

Because teachers who have taken an undergraduate major in physical education have the most extensive preparation in movement theory and generally a broader interest and knowledge in physical activities, it is most desirable to have them teach physical education at all levels. However, owing to a number of reasons, many classroom teachers are also teaching physical education. Unfortunately, many school districts find it financially impossible to hire all the specialists they would like.

Where specialists are not available, various staffing patterns have developed. Most often, school districts have a consultant who assists classroom teachers with planning, demonstrations, curriculum guides, and in-service sessions. A specialist may work with children once a week and then help the classroom teacher plan the physical education activities. A most exciting pattern has developed where schools have reorganized on a nongraded system or a team teaching arrangement. Here the specialist has often become a member of a multidisciplinary team. The latter organizations have also stimulated an interest in and a need for classroom teachers with a resource area in physical education when no specialist can be hired as part of the team. Many elementary education professional preparation programs are including electives in physical education as a minor for the classroom teacher or, as already mentioned, a resource area. Frequently where there is no specialist, classroom teachers adopt a team teaching plan for physical education wherein each teacher concentrates on teaching the activity area in all or several grades in which he or she feels most competent or has the most interest. Most state departments of education provide consultative services to local schools that are not fortunate enough to be able to hire specialists.

Characteristics of Good Teaching and Good Teachers

In order to develop a model for evaluation of teachers, J. T. Sandefur, after an extensive review of research on teaching and teacher characteristics, established three major generalizations and several subgeneralizations about good teaching and the characteristics of good teachers:

1. Good teaching utilizes maximal involvement of the student in direct experiential situations. Good teachers
   - Attempt to foster problem-oriented, self-directed, actively inquiring patterns of learning behavior in their students.
   - Elicit pupil-initiated talk and allow more pupil-initiated exploration and trial solutions.
   - Try to elicit independent thinking from their students.
   - Involve students in decision-making processes in active, self-directive ways.
   - Are interested in student involvement and try not to dominate the classroom through lecture and other teacher activities.

2. Good teaching encourages maximal freedom for the student. Good teachers
   - Use significantly more praise and encouragement for the student.
   - Accept, use, and clarify student ideas more often.

- Give fewer directions, less criticism, less justification of their own authority, and less negative feedback.
- Use a relaxed, conversational teaching style.
- Use more divergent questions, do more probing, and are less procedural.
- Are more inclined to recognize the "affective climate" of the classroom and are responsive to student feelings.
- Are more likely to use indirect methods exhibiting open-mindedness.

3. Good teachers tend to exhibit identifiable personal traits broadly characterized by warmth, a democratic attitude, affective awareness, and a personal concern for students. They are
   - Able to exhibit characteristics of fairness and democratic behavior.
   - Responsive, understanding, and kindly.
   - Stimulating and original in their teaching.
   - Responsible and systematic.
   - Poised and confident, and emotionally self-controlled.
   - Adaptable and optimistic.
   - Well-versed in subject matter and give evidence of a broad cultural background.[18]

The first two generalizations are what a teacher does and can learn. These methods and techniques are discussed at length in future chapters. The third generalization concerns what a teacher *is*. These characteristics are somewhat harder to develop or change; however, they are mostly environmental personality characteristics and can be changed by education, desire, conscientious effort, and modeling. Hopefully you will study these characteristics and see how well you match; then throughout your teacher education experiences work to become a good teacher.

SUGGESTED REFERENCES FOR FURTHER STUDY

AMERICAN ALLIANCE FOR HEALTH, PHYSICAL EDUCATION AND RECREATION, *Echoes of Influence for Elementary School Physical Education.* Washington, D.C., 1977.

————, *Essentials of a Quality Elementary School Physical Education Program.* Washington, D.C., 1970.

ASSOCIATION FOR SUPERVISION AND CURRICULUM DEVELOPMENT, *Humanistic Education, Objectives and Assessment.* Washington, D.C., 1978.

————, *The School's Role as Moral Authority.* Washington, D.C., 1978.

GORDON, T., *Teacher Effectiveness Training.* New York: Peter Wyden, 1975.

KIRSCHENBAUM, HOWARD, and SIDNEY B. SIMON, *Readings in Values Clarification.* Minneapolis: Winston, 1972.

KOHLBERG, L., Development of Moral Character, in *Developmental Psychology Today.* Del Mar, Calif.: Communications Research Machines, 1971.

RATH, L., M. HARMIN, and S. B. SIMON, *Values and Teaching.* Columbus, Ohio: Merrill, 1966.

[18] *An Illustrated Model for the Evaluation of Teacher Education Graduates* (Washington, D.C.: American Association of Colleges for Teacher Education, 1970). Used with permission of the American Association of Colleges for Teacher Education and the author.

2 / UNDERSTANDING AND FULFILLING THE NEEDS OF CHILDREN

- Motor development
- Physical development
- Social and emotional growth
- Cognitive development

Children come to school in various states of readiness; with different backgrounds, different abilities, different interests, different needs, and many other dissimilarities. In order to face the challenge of helping children reach their fullest potential, the teacher must know as much as possible about the characteristics of all children. Studying the natural and social factors that either inhibit or promote the child's ability to learn should help the teacher plan a good method and program as well as to better understand the child with whom he or she is working.

Although all children are basically very much alike and follow much the same sequence of growth and development, each is an individual and the time schedule of this sequence varies for each. Some children develop faster or slower in one area of development than in another. Owing to environment, accident, or other causes, some children do not follow the typical sequence; therefore we have many exceptional children in our schools.

There are identifiable stages of development during which children's learning and behavior tend to follow more or less predictable patterns. At these stages their readiness for certain behaviors is expected and/or anticipated. These are often associated with age groups for convenience; however, it must be remembered that chronological age is not the determinant of readiness. Although today many schools are organized on the basis of development (usually cognitive), the majority of schools still group according to age and grade. Grade levels in which children appear to be more alike than different are most often termed Primary (K–2), Intermediate (3–4), and Upper (5–6).

The remainder of this chapter is devoted to an examination of some basic stages in the areas of physical, motor, perceptual, cognitive, and social/emotional development. There are many good sources that describe in detail the developmental characteristics in each of these areas and the reader should study these. The purpose of this brief discussion is to highlight selected aspects and to stress the interrelationships of these characteristics and their implications in learning and teaching physical education in the elementary school. Knowing the stages and sequences gives the teacher a base for understanding and analyzing where children are in their development and readiness for learning. We sequence learning experiences in respect to children's readiness to learn.

Motor Development

The acquisition of motor skill patterns is dependent upon an orderly progression of development from simple gross movement to more complex movement patterns. Movement begins with the unborn child in the early fetal stages— approximately at the eighth week—and continues into the first year in the form of *reflexive behavior* or involuntary movements. The reflexive movements are usually associated with survival or protective mechanics for the newborn; they include sucking, grasping, postural reflexes, etc. At the next stage, called the *rudimentary stage,* voluntary movements develop with increasing control of head, neck, and trunk muscles and include first attempts to stand and the elementary locomotor movements of creeping and crawling, walking, and the basic manipulative movements of reaching, grasping, and releasing. Generally by the end of the second year these patterns have emerged and children have achieved a certain level of control and development.

Operative in early and later development is the principle of cephalocaudal and proximo-distal trends. The former implies that development proceeds longitudinally from head to foot; the latter implies that development of muscles close to the trunk precedes those farther away from the center of the body—i.e., arms, then hands. Early movements are those of the trunk, legs, and arms, with later control of smaller muscles of the hands, fingers, and feet.

Once the rudimentary movements have developed at about the end of the second year, the *fundamental movement* patterns of the walk, run, jump, hop, leap, push, bend, stretch, twist, turn, fall, and crude throw, catch, and strike develop concurrently. The hop, skip, and gallop are more difficult, because they are combinations of other basic patterns and sometimes are not fully developed until after the child enters school. The child learns and refines these patterns before school through exploration of the environment, necessity, and imitation. The degree to which they are refined before school age varies considerably, according to the environmental conditions in which the child lives. By the time a child enters kindergarten, he or she has encountered all of the basic movement patterns. The focus and responsibility of the physical education teacher in the primary grades is to help the child further develop and refine basic movement patterns through guidance and provision of opportunity for use of the skills in respect to various environmental factors which cause one to make adaptions of the basic movements.

The next stage of skill development is in the further *refinement of fundamental patterns* into mature form and development of combinations of movement patterns. During the eighth and ninth year, or approximately grades 3 and 4, the child's skill patterns and control increase in respect to continued development of physical growth in size and strength; development of small-muscle control; greater endurance; balance; and perceptual qualities of hand-eye, foot-eye coordination, tracking, etc. More complex combinations of the fundamental patterns are developed, with the stress on greater accuracy, control, coordination, and performance in the beginning activities of the various movement forms of dance, games, gymnastics, and aquatics. Improvement in skill is also accompanied by changes in cognitive and social development. The increased ability to understand, reason, and see relationships helps youngsters to better understand principles of movement and begin to associate cause and effect. Social development also increases children's interest in refining skills.

The next stage of skill development and learning focuses on the combinations of fundamental skill patterns as they are used in *specific sports, dance, gymnastics, aquatics*. For example, once having gained the control and ability to bounce the ball repeatedly, the child can now concentrate on using this general skill as a dribble in basketball. The child works on the ability to move and to change directions while advancing the ball, maintaining control of it while another person is using defensive strategies to take it away. Adapting one's ability in using general skills to rule limitations and varying relationships of space, objects, and players in structured activities and creative aspects of the movement forms becomes the challenge of 10- and 11-year-olds (grades 5 and 6). Children's interests and awareness of the traditional sports are met through an emphasis on lead-up games modified to meet their readiness at this time. At this age level they are capable of learning complex motor skills if the equipment, space, and demands are modified.

As children continue to grow in all respects beyond the age of 11, the emphasis is on *specialized skill development*. The stage of motor development and an understanding of one's capacity and limitations, interests, significance of various movement experiences, and an opportunity for choices both within instructional settings and enrichment opportunities govern development of selected skills to a high degree of proficiency, and learning of new skills specific to a personal specialization. Youth of this age will still be learning new skills; however, their capacity is to develop a high degree of proficiency in those of their choice.

Children continue to grow in strength from the first grade on. Boys at all ages have a slight advantage in this respect over girls. This difference increases markedly at puberty and increases for both sexes after the postpubescent stages. At puberty the shoulder width of boys continues to grow in size, and likewise the throwing ability becomes greater. Hip width increases just before puberty, much more so for girls than boys. This greater width may produce some mechanical inhibition in running as a girl matures. Boys tend to have a greater energy level than girls at all ages. The arm length of boys is greater than that of girls from the age of 2 on. Although these differences between boys and girls are slight before puberty, achievement in skill performance has been greater at all grade levels for boys in most gross skills except in stunts requiring balance.[1]

Generally, girls enter puberty in the fifth, sixth, or seventh grades and boys enter approximately two years later. A period of rapid growth and changes in the body system characterize pubescence. Because boys generally begin to mature later than girls, there will be considerable differences between the two in their stature, interests, emotions, and needs during the upper grade years. There need be no large gap of performance achievement due to physiological or anatomical differences. Cultural expectations for boys and girls have been a primary determinant in the gap between performances. As girls are increasingly given more opportunity and are encouraged to participate and excel in sport activities, primarily due to federal legislation (Title IX), they will more likely achieve their potential. Discontinuing the heretofore persistent practice of separating boys and girls for instruction in physical education classes should enhance their development and interests.

The body build of a child helps determine his or her success in motor performance. One's basic body build is established approximately between the ages of 6 and 7. As early as first grade, variations in physique among both boys and girls are noticeable. Some will be tall and slender, with small bones and light musculature (ectomorphs); some will be stocky and muscular (mesomorphs); and others will have a tendency to be round, flabby, and accumulate fat easily (endomorphs). These characteristics change very little throughout life.

Mesomorphs are usually stronger, excelling in activities requiring gross strength and stability. Ectomorphs may move more quickly, and be better at games requiring running and jumping. Endomorphs usually display less muscular strength and have a more passive attitude toward activity. Naturally, there are gradations and combinations of these three types of basic body

[1] Robert D. Johnson, "Measurement of Achievement in Fundamental Skills of Elementary School Children," *Research Quarterly,* 33, no. 1 (March 1962), 94; Robert Malina, "Ethnic and Cultural Factors in the Development of Motor Abilities and Strength in American Children," in R. L. Rarick, *Physical Activity: Human Growth and Development* (New York: Academic Press, 1973); D. Sinclair, *Human Growth After Birth* (London: Oxford University Press, 1973); Conrad Milne, Vern Seefeldt, and Phillip Reuschlein, "Relationship between Grade, Sex, Race, and Motor Performance in Young Children," *Research Quarterly* 47, no. 4 (December 1976), 726.

builds. Recent studies indicate that the type of body build does play an important part in determining the nature of motor activities in which a child will have most success. From the descriptions given, it is obvious that the endomorphs cannot be expected to do as well in most activities as the others, and that a child with this type of body build must be encouraged to be active.

Normal, healthy children abound with energy during all the elementary grades. Some teachers have an unfounded concern that too much vigorous activity will cause children to become fatigued and will be harmful. Most young children will rest or change their activity when they become tired. They recuperate quickly. Children in the middle and upper grades may have to be watched for signs of fatigue or overexertion because the development of a highly competitive spirit may allow them to push beyond the point of fatigue.

Repeated exercise results in improved organic development of both the heart and respiratory system. Too often the physical education period does not require enough strenuous exercise. Recent studies show that the young child's tolerance for exercise is greater than was once thought to be true.

Elementary school children continue to grow increasingly long-legged; therefore, the ability to run and jump increases with each year of growth. Balance improves rapidly in the primary years. At the third-grade level most children can control balance reasonably well; however, practice in this area will improve the development of this quality measurably. This is evidenced by better body control, which can be expected in games and activities requiring quick changes of direction and sudden stops and starts in the middle and upper grades.

Changes in vision also take place in the process of growth. Great accuracy cannot be expected in primary grades. Activities requiring much fine hand-eye coordination should not be stressed before late second or third grade. Most activities involving accuracy in the primary grades should utilize a large stationary target. Throwing at moving targets may be stressed in the late second grade, and obviously, should also involve large objects. Practice and experience opportunities are necessary for the development of sensorimotor coordination necessary for accuracy, but expectations by the teacher should be geared to the level of maturity of the individual child.

Reaction time improves progressively with age. Intermediate grade children can be expected to react to movements of other objects, people, and signals much more quickly than those in the primary grades. At both levels there is great variability in reaction time between individuals; therefore, a great number of speed or timed events should not be stressed. Opportunities for practice in activities requiring quick reactions and movement in relation to others help children move more easily and time their actions better so that they develop more control and coordination.

Sport skills involving combinations of movement patterns must be introduced in a progressive fashion commensurate with the growth pattern of children. Children in the upper grades are capable of learning highly complex motor skills. Often sport skills and activities are not introduced until high school because of the mistaken assumption that they are too difficult for elementary school children to learn. It is the size of the equipment and the complexity of the rules of the official games that are too difficult for children, not the skills. Lead-up games are available in which the skills can be used and practiced until the child is physically and socially mature enough to play the official sports.

Social and Emotional Growth

Young children are usually quite egocentric and prefer to play alone or in the same space with someone else, yet concentrating on their own play task. The latter is usually called parallel play. Preschool and kindergarten children are not ready for small- or large-group play or organized games as such. Six- and seven-year-olds (first and second grades) continue to enjoy solitary or parallel play activities, but begin to enjoy cooperative play and will work productively with a partner and in small groups of two to four people. They must learn how to share equipment, space, and ideas. They must also learn to listen, not just to the teacher, but to other pupils as well. Listening skills are not developed just for politeness' sake, but to focus on what is said, relating what is said to what is being done, and on recalling what is said.

The drive to be active is characteristic at this age and the attention span is short. Long practice periods on specific skills are impractical. Working on skills or activities that are too complex or with equipment that is too small or too heavy or large to handle creates frustration and disinterest.

Although young children want to be "first," little stress should be placed on competition. These children are discovering themselves and what they can do, so have little competence to compete. The push to win, coupled with their natural desire to be first, may lead to poor social habits of making alibis, cheating, and lying. Individual challenges, simple goal setting, and self-evaluation should be utilized. Young children are capable of working at tasks set either by the teacher or, with help, by themselves. Games and relays with a focus on the team or group winning are neither desirable nor successful at this stage.

Children at ages 8 and 9 (third and fourth grade) become less egocentric and enter a stage of more cooperative play. They become increasingly interested in becoming proficient in skills, and they will work hard and long to improve these. Their interest in games with more concrete rules grows. They can work with a greater number of people at one time in a more cooperative manner, and interest in group success becomes more important. Simple team games appeal to them, because there is a chance to use skills in exciting ways and an opportunity to use strategy. They are capable of understanding more complex rules and resent games that are too simple. When activities are not challenging they become bored quickly, and behavior problems often arise. Their background of skills and experiences gives them a better base for simple problem-solving experiences and creative productions.

Because of increased social and physical maturity, the organization of the class may change somewhat, and more group-work may be undertaken. Self-control is improved to the extent that many small groups may be working independently. Focus may be put on one major lead-up game for a period of time, since interest is sustained longer when the team spirit is stronger. Folk dances with more complex steps, formations, relationships, and longer sequences become more appropriate.

Intermediate-grade children are ready to compete and need challenges, but the challenges must be reasonable and attainable. Competition is motivating only as long as there is a chance to win. The child's experiences of winning and losing must be balanced with an overbalance on the winning. According to Hilgard, "tolerance for failure is best taught through providing a backlog of success that compensates for experienced failure."[2] However, there is a danger in tailor making experiences in such a way that a child will *always* encounter success. At some point he or she needs to learn the values of working hard to achieve success. Achievement without any effort encourages an unrealistic attitude toward accomplishments.

In the upper grades, children continue to grow in all respects. Their ability to concentrate improves; consequently, they are interested in longer practice periods. Interest in team play is high. Also, their ability to learn more complicated rules and to understand and use simple strategy expands. They are better able to abstract and reason; they need more opportunities to design their own games, routines, and dances. They can take more responsibility for their own learning and begin to make choices, set goals, and follow through on those goals with more independent station or task work. They are also interested in peers and will work hard in small groups and in self-directed team activities. Peer instruction is productive at this age.

Cultural factors play a large role in the interest and success in skills of boys and girls at this age. Proficiency in skills and games is important to both sexes, and social acceptance is often related to it at this age, particularly for boys. Although in-class instruction in skills, knowledges, and strategies should be the same for boys and girls, it may be desirable to have separate competitive experiences for games that involve body contact. Because boys at this age sometimes are more exuberant and intensely interested in certain activities, the teacher should be sure to use an organization that does not allow stronger and more aggressive boys to dominate the game and exclude girls. This is a time to use some value clarification tools to deal with interests and differences and similarities. Many girls may express the same interests and feelings about activity as boys, yet without the opportunity to discuss them, they may mask their feelings in participation.

Cognitive Development

A thorough discussion of cognitive development is beyond the scope of this book; however, a cursory review of the stages of cognitive development will help the reader keep in mind the general ranges of ability for children at various ages. Too often teachers expect too little or too much of children. For example, problem solving is a desirable goal for learning, but first-graders are not capable of using the problem-solving process. Any mention of mechanical principles at first-grade level seems out of place to some people, yet in reality first-graders can and do utilize basic concepts of, for example, gravity and stability, through experiences of self-discovery and the need to use the principles to keep balance. They cannot verbalize and truly understand the con-

[2] Ernest R. Hilgard, *Theories of Learning,* 2nd ed. (New York, Appleton-Century-Crofts, 1948), p. 407.

cepts, but nevertheless, the concepts can be broken down to the children's experiential comprehension.

The cognitive development theories of Jean Piaget are widely used in studying child development. Piaget has identified stages of development within an evolutionary process of growth wherein certain cognitive processes emerge and develop in a sequence. Again, these stages are identified with approximate ages, yet all children will not follow the same timetable. The *sequence* of expected development is what is important. Piaget's developmental stages are:

Sensorimotor Stage (0-2 years)   During this stage the infant develops gradually from purely reflexive action to meaningful experimentation with objects and a sense of purposeful and goal-directed movements. At the end of this period the child is able to recall past experiences rather than repeat through trial and error.

Preoperational Stage (2-7)   During this stage the child is still egocentric, but begins to interact with the environment, objects, people, etc. Symbolic language appears and begins to replace identification of objects by direct contact. Within this stage the child moves from a *preconceptual* stage (2-4), in which he/she begins to discover his or her environment and self through movement and play (mostly imitative) to an *intuitive stage (4-7)*, in which the child begins to generalize mental experiences. Now the child uses language without really understanding the meaning of it; he/she discovers basic concepts of distance, time, numbers, area, speed, but has no sense of quality. Although the child remains egocentric, he/she is beginning to relate to and play with others. He/she does not yet think in terms of the whole, and cannot usually entertain two ideas at the same time.

Concrete Operational Stage (7-11)   During this stage children begin to think in a logical way; they cannot yet abstract, but think in terms of the concrete or the actual experience; they can see relationships between parts and wholes; reversibility develops (children can add and substract or put things together and then take them apart into their original wholes); they can order or seriate objects according to different dimensions; they can think in terms of past, present, and future; they can find solutions by rational thinking and understand cause-and-effect relationships. Each of these operations develops slowly and sequentially. At the end of this stage the child can use the process of problem solving.

Formal Operational Stage (11-15)   In this last stage, children begin to think more like adults, and enter the age of adolescence. They can think and reason beyond the realistic or the concrete and present; thinking is logical and systematic; the true problem-solving process is used; concepts are developed; they can think about consequences of decisions and/or actions; they can reflect on experiences. Adolescents act and interact with other people and can see themselves as others see them.

The teacher must study each class and child in relation to the cognitive stage of development described here in order to assess readiness for process learning and for specific methods and techniques that can be used. Careful selection of activities and their demands on perception, complexity of numbers of parts, rules, seriation, etc. should be appropriate to the expectations of development of the individuals in the class. The child should be involved in his or her own learning through the teacher's guidance. Opportunities for repetition, discovery, verbalization, additive experiences, etc., must be carefully and sequentially planned. Children need time and guidance in developing the steps of the complex problem-solving process. Most children of elementary school age are in the preoperational and concrete operational stage.

Growth and development characteristics and their implications for the physical education program are summarized in Table 2-1 by grade groups. Although some of this material may be repetitious, the table will help the prospective teacher to better understand the pattern as a whole.

Table 2-1. Summary Chart of Growth and Development Characteristics and Implications for Physical Education Program Content

KINDERGARTEN, GRADES 1 AND 2

Characteristics	Needs	Types of Experiences
1. Spurt of growth of muscle mass	1. Vigorous exercise requiring use of large muscles	1. Running, chasing, fleeing-type games; hanging, climbing, supportive-type exercises
2. Gross movement skills becoming more refined	2. Exploration and variations of gross motor skills; opportunities to refine skills	2. Self-testing activities of all types; dance activities; movement tasks
3. Manipulative skills still unrefined, but improving; will catch balls with body and arms more so than hands	3. Opportunities to manipulate large- or medium-size objects; throw small balls	3. Ball-handling activities; work with beanbags, wands, hoops, progressing from large to smaller objects
4. Imaginative, imitative, curiosity	4. Opportunities for expression of ideas and use of body	4. Creative dance, story plays, creative stunt and floor work; exploration with all basic skills and small equipment
5. Very active, great deal of energy	5. Ample opportunities for vigorous play, particularly at the onset of the physical education period; recess needed in other half of day	5. Running, games, stunts, large apparatus; need locomotor work each period
6. Short attention span	6. Activities which take short explanation and to which some finish can be reached quickly; frequent change in activities or tasks	6. Simple games; class organized so activities can be changed quickly; conversations in movement
7. Individualistic or egocentric	7. Need experiences to learn to share or become interested in others; engage in parallel play alongside other children rather than with them	7. Much individual, some small-group work, self-testing activities, exploration of movement factors, few relays

Table 2-1. Continued

	GRADES 3 AND 4	
Characteristics	*Needs*	*Types of Experiences*
1. Gross motor patterns more refined and graceful	1. Use of skill for specific purposes	1. Refinement of basic skills and combinations; introduction to specific sport skills in grades 3 and 4; expressive-style skill utilized in dance; traditional dance steps
2. Hand-eye coordination improved; growth in manipulative skills	2. More opportunities to handle smaller objects; more importance placed on accuracy; throw at moving targets	2. Ball-handling activities, use of bats, paddles, target games
3. See need to practice skills for improvement of skill and to gain social status	3. Guided practice sessions, self-testing problem situations	3. Drills, skill drill games, self-testing practice situations; task setting
4. Balance more highly developed; better body control	4. Opportunities to work on higher beams, bars; more activities requiring static balance	4. Large apparatus work, tumbling, stunts
5. Increased attention span	5. Activities with continuity, more complex rules and understandings	5. Lead-up games to sports, low organized games with more complex rules and strategy
6. More socially mature, interested in welfare of group	6. Make a contribution to a large or small group, remain with one group for a longer period of time, help make and accept decisions with a group	6. Team activities, dance compositions with small groups; problem solving with small groups
7. Greater sex differences in skills; some antagonism toward opposite sex (grade 4)	7. Ability grouping	7. Combative-type stunts; folk dance; after-school activities for grade 4
8. Great interest in proficiency and competitive spirit (particularly boys) may drive to fatigue	8. Recognition of symptoms of fatigue and place of rest, relaxation and moderation in competition	8. Self-testing activities; relaxation techniques; interval training with developmental exercises
9. Spirit of adventure high	9. Activities requiring courage, adventure, initiative; recognition of safety factors	9. Self-testing activities of all types; use of large apparatus; low organized games demanding courage; creative dance compositions, adventure games

Table 2-1. Continued

GRADES 3 AND 4

Characteristics	Needs	Types of Experiences
10. Tendency toward poor posture	10. Understanding of body mechanics, development of endurance and strength	10. Developmental exercises, vigorous running games, large apparatus, and fitness activities; individually planned program for those below average in posture and fitness
11. Intellectually curious	11. Learn mechanical principles of movement, similarities of movement patterns, and physiological principles	11. Self-testing activities of all types; problem-solving method used in analyzing own skill patterns; creative dance; developmental exercise programs; set own goals; create games, dances; self-evaluate

GRADES 5 AND 6

Characteristics	Needs	Types of Experiences
1. Coordination highly developed, keen interest in proficiency in skills	1. Need to learn more difficult skills; more coaching on refinement of skills; use of skills in games, routines, and compositions	1. Lead-up games to sports in season; instruction and practice in sport skills; more advanced dance step patterns and folk dances; track and field; apparatus routines; intramurals
2. Greater sex differences in skills, interests; some prefer to play and compete with own sex; boys may play more vigorously and roughly than girls	2. Separation of sexes within classes for competitive contact activities	2. Dance; swimming, gymnastics, activities, recreational games; sexes separate in contact sports; fitness activities; intramurals for both sexes
3. Goods skills and physique important to social acceptance, particularly for boys	3. Instruction and practice sessions in skills, understanding of fitness elements, understanding of changes in growth and abilities due to puberty	3. Fitness tests; developmental exercises; work with apparatus; classroom discussions and movies about puberty (may be done in cooperation with nurse or parents)
4. Group or gang spirit high, allegiance to group is strong	4. Need to belong to a group with some stability; make rules, decisions, and abide by group decision; longer term of membership on a squad or team	4. Team games, tournaments, group dance compositions, gymnastic squads with student leaders, gymnastic meets, track and field meets

Table 2-1. Continued

GRADES 5 AND 6

Characteristics	Needs	Types of Experiences
5. Social consciousness of need for rules and abiding by rules; assumption of greater responsibility	5. Participate in setting rules, opportunities for squad captains or leaders; make choices in activities	5. Student officials; plan and conduct tournaments in class and after school; students plan own strategy, line-ups, etc.; contracting, goal setting
6. Flexibility decreasing	6. Need to maintain flexibility within structural limitations	6. Stunts, tumbling, apparatus, developmental exercises
7. Muscle growth of boys increasing; most girls in puberty	7. Interest in maintaining good posture, fitness level; build good attitudes toward activity and proficiency for girls; knowledge of methods of increasing strength and endurance	7. Apparatus, developmental activities, track and field, more individual and dual activities, intramurals

GRADES 7 AND 8

Characteristics	Needs	Types of Experiences
1. Coordination very highly developed; skill level increasing more rapidly for boys than girls; skill level for girls reaches a plateau	1. Learning more advanced sport skills; opportunities for refinement and use of skills in sports, routines, compositions	1. Modified team and individual sports, more demanding dance skills and composition work, intramurals for both sexes and individuals
2. Sexes differ in skills and interests; boys' muscle strength much more than girls'	2. Separation of sexes in classes illegal and undesirable; male and female teachers for both sexes; sexes separate for competitive contact sports	2. Team sports for both; recreation in individual sports, volleyball, gymnastics, social, folk, and square dances
3. Most girls in puberty and some in grade 8 reaching full stature, some boys starting puberty, less sex antagonism, boys' interest in opposite sex increases	3. Understanding of changes due to puberty, better understanding of body mechanism	3. Fitness activities; body mechanics; focus on body building and shaping
4. Prestige associated with good skills for boys; lack of interest in activity for some girls due to cultural influences	4. Many opportunities for individual coaching and practice of skills; girls need to be encouraged to maintain fitness and an interest in activity	4. Much game play and individual coaching in class and in intramurals; interest clubs

Table 2-1. Continued

GRADES 7 AND 8		
Characteristics	*Needs*	*Types of Experiences*
5. Intellectually very capable and knowledgeable; ability to deal with the abstract	5. Opportunities for logical reasoning and creative thinking	5. More emphasis placed on strategy in game play; creative dance composition work; more involved routines in gymnastics; goal setting; selective programming; contracting
6. Feeling of insecurity, unsure of self in group (particularly 7th-graders); great desire to be a part of group	6. Need to have feeling of acceptance by teacher and other members of class; great understanding and patience needed by the teacher (especially in grade 7); children need recognition	6. Involved in selecting teammates; work in small groups; expected to produce in group work projects; involved planning special events and after-school tournaments and play days; social service projects related to movements; peer teaching

It is impossible to designate the grade at which these characteristics will appear for each child. Owing to individual differences in rate of growth, there will always be overlap from grade to grade. The grades have been grouped together in periods of time in which the characteristics and needs will most likely first appear and be resolved before changing into another stage.

SUGGESTED REFERENCES FOR FURTHER STUDY

ALBINSON, J. S., and G. M. ANDREW, *Child in Sport and Activity.* Baltimore: University Park Press, 1976.

CORBIN, CHARLES A., *A Textbook of Motor Development.* Dubuque, Iowa: Wm. C. Brown, 1973.

FLAVELL, JOHN H., *The Developmental Psychology of Jean Piaget.* New York: Van Nostrand and Reinhold, 1973.

MILNE, CONRAD, VERN SEEFELDT, and PHILLIP REUSCHLEIN, "Relationship between Grade, Sex, Race, and Motor Performance in Young Children," *Research Quarterly,* 47 (December 1976), 726–30.

RARICK, G. LAWRENCE, *Physical Activity: Human Growth and Development.* New York: Academic Press, 1973.

RIDENOUR, MARCELLA, ed., *Motor Development: Issues and Applications.* Princeton, N.J.: Princeton Book Co., 1978.

STONE, L. JOSEPH, and JOSEPH CHURCH, *Childhood and Adolescence,* 3rd ed. New York: Random House, 1973.

Understanding and
Fulfilling the Needs of
Children

3 / THE CURRICULUM

- **Physical education design: goals, purposes, and objectives**
- **Goal of humanistic education**
- **Primary goal of physical education**
- **Purposes of physical education**
- **Program objectives of physical education**
- **Program content of physical education**
- **Activity areas**

The focus on humanism in education today appears to be a manifestation of a social need and force that is permeating our thinking and feelings. The world around us is not always a humanistic world, but in our personal interactions and inner selves there is a yearning to live in a humanistic environment. People are searching for ways to improve the quality of life after years of emphasis on quantity. Since most people look toward schools as the source of learning in our society, school programs must provide for this need.

Because the term "humanism" is nebulous and used in many contexts, it is appropriate to set forth a definition that will serve as the basic framework for an elementary physical education program and for all the other ideas, beliefs, suggestions, and feelings included herein to implement a humanistic curriculum. Humanism appears to defy a specific definition; in reality it is a concept of moral conviction. The word "concept" denotes that an individual has organized understanding and meaning from what he or she has perceived and experienced and uses these as valuing dimensions in developing attitudes, opinions, and personal behaviors.

A *humanistic concept* implies a reverence for the individual person, with a focus on a genuine concern for the growth and fulfillment of the individual. The humanistic approach to education is concerned with the psychological or emotional aspects of the learning environment.

Morrel J. Clute identifies a definition of humanistic education and seven major goals through which it may be more explicitly approached:

> Humanistic education is a commitment to education and practice in which all facets of the teaching-learning process give major emphasis to the freedom, value worth, dignity, and integrity of persons. [It]
>
> 1. Accepts the learner's needs and purposes and develops experiences and programs around the unique potentials of the learner.
> 2. Facilitates self-actualization and strives to develop in all persons a sense of personal adequacy.
> 3. Fosters acquisition of basic skills necessary for living in a multicultured society, including academic, personal, interpersonal, communicative, and economic proficiency.
> 4. Personalizes educational decisions and practices. To this end it includes students in the processes of their own education via democratic involvement in all levels of implementation.
> 5. Recognizes the primacy of human feelings and utilizes personal values and perceptions as integral factors in educational processes.
> 6. Develops a learning climate which nurtures growth through learning environments perceived by all involved as challenging, understanding, supportive, exciting, and free from threat.
> 7. Develops in learners genuine concern and respect for the worth of others and skill in conflict resolution.[1]

In summary, the long-term goal of a humanistic curriculum is self-actualization, with equal emphasis on developing attitudes, feelings, and processes as legitimate program purposes along with subject-matter mastery. This is not a new concept of education, but it seems that there is more commitment to actualizing concern for the individual with more concrete ideas and ways to implement humanistic curricula.

The major elements in developing and implementing a humanistic curriculum for children are the teacher, who must embody the concept in belief and in behavior; the goals, purposes, and objectives; the content; the teaching and learning processes; and the evaluation process.

---

[1] "Humanistic Education: Goals and Objectives," in *Humanistic Education: Objectives and Assessment,* a report of the ASCD Working Group on Humanistic Education (Washington, D.C.: Association for Supervision and Curriculum Development, 1978), pp. 9–10. Reprinted with permission of the Association for Supervision and Curriculum Development and Morrel J. Clute. Copyright © 1978 by the Association for Supervision and Curriculum Development.

All too often the student and novice teacher have difficulty relating the daily planning of experiences for children to the ultimate or long-term developmental goals of education, or they lose sight of the goals entirely. In order to help you better understand the basis of curriculum development and to better relate your contributions to the development of the whole child, this section presents a short discussion of the relationship of goals, purposes, and objectives in program planning. Figure 3-1 shows the sequence of this relationship.

Goals

It is important to remember that teachers of all subject areas have basically the same goals and objectives for children. It is the uniqueness of each subject, particularly the acquisition of skills of that subject, and the way a child learns to use those skills to reach the ultimate goal of education, that are different.

As a basis for curriculum development within a school or school district, a general philosophical statement is established. This statement is philosophic in nature and reflects the broad aim or goals of education as accepted by the particular school district. These goals are influenced by the values and beliefs of all of the constituents of the school—i.e., the students, parents, community, teachers, and administrators.

Educational goals are broad in nature and are usually theoretical and idealistic. They portray the desired ultimate characteristics of a person after learning opportunities throughout the school experience. They most often relate to the individual as he or she will function as a citizen in our democratic

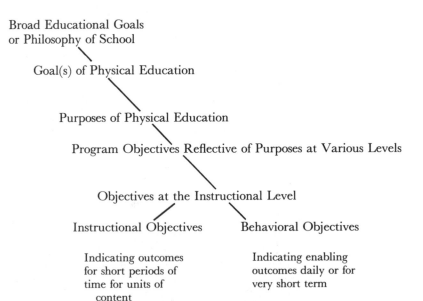

Figure 3-1 Relationship of goals, purposes, and objectives in curriculum design.

society. Often a statement of philosophy is accompanied by a series of goal statements which reflect various areas in which development is most appropriately accomplished by specific disciplines. This is a basis for the development of goals, purposes, and objectives of the various programs of subject areas within the total school curriculum.

The broad goal(s) statement of physical education may follow the same pattern as that of general education, but must reflect the unique contribution of movement in the person's life as enhanced by the physical education program throughout his or her school years. Again, these are idealistic and long-term. All teachers or prospective teachers should identify their own beliefs through the development of a personal statement of philosophy and periodically review it as they gain more experience and knowledge about the subject matter and the students.

Purposes

Derived from goals are purposes which provide statements of intent that indicate guides to actualize the goals. They represent beliefs and values held by the curriculum designers with respect to each area of development in their subject matter. Determining purposes helps in the understanding, verbalization, and knowledge of what it is the designers are attempting to do to help learners. All goals, purposes, and objectives should be written in terms of what the student will gain through learning experiences, not what the school or teacher will provide or do. The latter should be implied by the expectations for the learner.

Each purpose is a guide to action, and each consequent stage of curriculum planning should relate to a stated purpose. Specifically, purposes should be directly related to the knowledges, understandings, skills, and values of physical education as generally accepted and proposed by the profession. They must reflect sound understanding of the child as an individual learner, and of his/her interests and needs. They should serve as the basic framework of the program and yield objectives to be emphasized and realized at appropriate levels of the curriculum. They allow for development of behaviors in the domains of the *cognitive* (knowledges, concepts, understandings, problem solving, judging, creating, evaluating), *affective* (attitudes, interests, values, appreciations), and *psychomotor* (motor skills, and physical development).

Program Objectives

As the purposes are broken down into objectives of emphasis at the various organizational levels of the program, they serve as the basis for: expected student behaviors, selection of content, organization of content, organization of students, and evaluation. Up to this point goals, purposes, and objectives are developed from a true idealistic, value-centered approach without regard for administrative constraints, facilities, equipment, and personnel restrictions.

INSTRUCTIONAL OBJECTIVES Program objectives are further broken down into objectives at the instructional level for the purpose of implementation of curriculum. They represent short-term expectations within a level and for specific units or themes of content. For example, in the first grade for an instructional theme on space; in the second grade for a unit of ten lessons on development of ball-handling skills. At this point, as one selects and plans the modalities (organization, teaching styles, specific content, instructional aids, evaluation) through which learning opportunities are actually implemented, the facilities, time allotted, equipment, abilities of personnel, etc., may cause some modifications, but these should be in modalities and emphasis, not in the true purposes and the goals.

BEHAVIORAL OBJECTIVES Instructional objectives are further reduced to specific objectives which indicate more specific outcomes that can be attained in a short time, perhaps in one lesson, and thus are considered enabling objectives to reach the broader objectives and purposes.

Goal of Humanistic Education

The broad goal of humanistic education is to help each child become a fully functioning or self-actualizing person. The traditional goals of education have involved the transmission of the culture, the preservation of the past and the present, and the development of the intellect. The more recent humanistic goal of education emphasizes the individual. This does not really contradict the traditional goals, since it is individuals who make up the culture and the quality of the individuals who collectively determine the quality of the culture.

What is a fully functioning or self-actualizing person? Earl Kelley identifies the following characteristics of a fully functioning person:

1. He thinks well of himself.
2. He feels able or *competent* through being aware of his limitations.
3. He also thinks well of others, and sees their importance to him as opportunities for self-development.
4. He is always changing and developing.
5. He holds human values and lives by these values.
6. He is a creative person.[2]

Arthur Coombs, writing in the same book, says that self-actualizing persons seem to be characterized by the way they perceive or see themselves and the world around them. Characteristically, they tend to:

1. Have a positive view of self.
2. Identify with others in a feeling of unity or oneness, a feeling of sharing a common fate or of striving for a common goal—an extension of oneself to include one's fellows.
3. Have an openness to experience and an attitude of acceptance.
4. Have a rich and available perceptual field (i.e., tools to see, understand, feel, act with, etc.), this being a product of the kind of opportunities and experiences to which an individual has been exposed.[3]

Since all of these ways of perceiving are learned, they can be taught. Each subject-matter program has a part in supplying experiences to enhance these perceptions.

---

[2] "The Fully Functioning Self," in *Perceiving, Behaving, and Becoming: A New Focus for Education,* Arthur Coombs, ed. (Washington, D.C.: Association for Supervision and Curriculum Development, 1962).

[3] "A Perceptual View of the Adequate Personality," in *Perceiving, Behaving, and Becoming: A New Focus for Education.*

Although the emphasis in both of these descriptions and in most educational literature is on the individual, we must keep in mind also the references to the concern and involvement of others. Since everyone lives in a society composed of other individuals, one can only actualize oneself in interaction with others. People live in cooperative relationships with people around them. A cooperative atmosphere is one of involvement and responsibility. A fully functioning person is independent and free to act upon his or her own decisions and needs, but must also act responsibly with respect to the consequences of those decisions for himself/herself *and* those affected by the decisions.

Primary Goal of Physical Education

Throughout the school curriculum there is an emphasis beyond learning specific subject-matter concepts and skills. There must be equal emphasis on the development of individuals who are self-directive, self-disciplined, self-responsible, and capable of making intelligent choices. Thus the primary goal of physical education is that of contributing to the broader goal of education by helping each person reach one's *movement potential*.

To realize one's movement potential, one has to know and understand the structure of movement while learning to move efficiently, effectively (within one's own limitations), and in terms of one's own needs. One must also learn process skills appropriate for learning to move and to become self-directive, self-disciplined, responsible, and capable of making intelligent choices.

Purposes of Physical Education

The following purposes of physical education support the realization of the primary goal of physical education—reaching one's movement potential. As a result of individual learning experiences in physical education, each person should be able to

1. Understand the structure of movement.
2. Move competently and confidently in a wide variety of structured and unstructured movement activities.
3. Develop and maintain fitness.
4. Meet and solve new movement demands.
5. Communicate through, about, and in movement.
6. Interact positively with others through, about, and in movement.
7. Find personal meaning and significance in movement.

Each of these purposes is broad and is broken down to program objectives, with the emphasis relative to the needs, interests, and abilities of each educational level. These objectives then become more specific at the instructional and behavioral level.

The purposes of physical education have implications and give direction for content, organization, materials, experiences, process (teaching and learning), and evaluation.

The Curriculum

Purpose one, *understanding the structure of movement,* involves the understanding and development of concepts of the basic body actions, skill patterns, the elements and dimensions of movement, movement in relationship to objects and other people, body awareness, the mechanical principles and laws that affect movement, body capacity, the effects of movement on the body, and health facts related to exercise and movement. Obviously the expectations of understanding will relate to cognitive development. Understanding movement patterns in primary grades will focus on recognition of the pattern, basic mechanics of how to do it, variations, combinations of the patterns, and development of a movement vocabulary. In more advanced grades emphasis will be on analyzing patterns of self, peers, opponents; selecting appropriate patterns; adapting patterns of self, peers, opponents; selecting appropriate patterns; adapting patterns to new demands; seeing relationships of patterns and factors in more complex movement skills and specific activities within games, sports, dance, gymnastics, and aquatics.

Purpose two, *moving competently and confidently in a wide variety of activities,* refers to the actual performance of movement. This includes refinement of basic movement patterns, combinations of patterns, perceptual skills and use of skills in unstructured and structured activities in the primary grades. In the upper grades emphasis is on developing specialized skills for dance, games and sports, gymnastics, and aquatics and playing or performing and creating new aspects in the traditional forms of activity. A wide variety of activities in the elementary schools is stressed as a base from which individuals will seek high competency in one or more activities in which they find significance for themselves at the high school level and beyond.

Purpose three, *developing and maintaining fitness,* is a traditional aim of physical education, and for some the only purpose. In a humanistic curriculum it is vital, but not the sole purpose. Being fit and healthy is a prerequisite for reaching one's movement potential.

The emphasis on fitness at all levels of the elementary school involves the attitude toward fitness—understanding the role of fitness as it relates to success in movement performance, understanding the effect on the body and psyche of poor fitness, and attaining a feeling of enjoyment of vigorous activity. In the upper grades additional emphasis is placed on analyzing one's own fitness, and on designing plans for exercises and activities to meet one's own needs. Building skills so that there is enthusiasm and joy in participating in activity in class and out of school builds a positive concept toward lifelong fitness. Activities should be taught with the aim of helping children develop a desire to play and be active, as well as to continue to learn new activities throughout life.

Purpose four, *meeting and solving new movement demands,* refers to process development. It is sometimes called "learning how to learn." This involves learning how to explore, discover, solve problems, set goals, diagnose, create, make decisions, relate similarities of movements, and evaluate and manage one's own study of movement. In organizing and presenting learning experiences, teachers will have to include opportunities for practice of these processes so that people will be able to learn and meet new movement problems without the direct help of professional teachers and also will know how and where to seek help if it is needed. Additionally, pupil involvement is implied in goal setting, selecting ways of learning activities, creating games, dances, movement routines, and peer teaching as individuals grow progressively more capable at each state of development.

Purpose five, *communicating through, about, and in movement,* is primarily but not exclusively focused on nonverbal aspects of communication. Children tell us a great deal about themselves as they engage in play or structured activities by their actions and postural approaches. Their joy, security, confidence, hostility, awareness, and acceptance of others are readily evident in manner and play and performance in activities as well as in choices of activity. Avenues of expression, creativity, and feeling are expanded through opportunities in the expressive forms of dance, movement, and gymnastic routines and aquatic arts. Creative opportunities afford the communication of ideas as well as feelings. Communication may be through movement itself, verbally through writing, speaking, pictures related to movement, or through other art forms.

The media and activities are the same for all the levels, but the expectations are different. Children have to develop the tools of communication and creativity. Their experiences and ability to abstract give them the background for communication and creativity. The teacher must provide opportunities and give encouragement and keep the lines of communication open.

Purpose six, *interacting positively with others in and through various movement forms,* reflects the necessity for interdependence in order to become self-actualized. Most movement experiences occur with other people; with or against or in the presence of another person, a small group, large groups, and/or authority figures. Opportunities abound for the development of interaction skills—a member of a partnership or group must try to analyze, solve problems, share responsibility, defeat, success, frustration, encourage others, and achieve excellence together to reach a common goal. The nature of the activity may be cooperative or competitive or a combination of both. An attitude of achieving and contributing to excellent group performance must be fostered, rather than an emphasis on beating or humiliating opponent(s).

Inherent in this purpose of developing interaction skills is awareness and acceptance of other's strengths, weaknesses, and values. Accepting, understanding rules and regulations and roles of officials and other people, can be accomplished only through experiences designed specifically for that purpose.

In primary grades, children are naturally egocentric; however, they must learn gradually to work and play with others. Again the teacher must plan progressively freeing, responsible, cooperative, and leadership roles, more pupil-dominated activities, and give guidance as children learn interaction skills.

Purpose seven, *finding personal meaning and significance in movement,* is one major distinction of a truly humanistic curriculum. In the sense that education is humanizing, education must enable individuals to discover and expand their own meanings. Movement is a mode of human experience in which body and mind efforts and awareness are coordinated. Participation in activities has personal relevance and becomes a source of meaning for individuals. Various activities are meaningful in diverse ways and to varying degrees.

Phillip Phenix explains the self-expressive role of meaning in movement:

> No other instrument is as elaborate, sensitive, and immediately responsive as the human body. This is why the arts of movement are so important for the expression and perception of human meaning. . . . The union of thought, feeling, sense and act is the particular aim of the arts of movement—nowhere else is the

coordination of all components of the living person so directly fostered, nor the resulting activity so deeply rooted in the unitary existence of the person.[4]

Teachers must help children analyze movement experiences which they find significant so they can raise their perceptions to the conscious level, thus becoming aware of the experience and being able to identify the components to maximize the potential for significance. They then can place themselves in other experiences with high potential for significance.

Recognizing the values inherent in movement, learning what one values in or about movement, and experiencing joy in movement—all these must begin early in life. According to Phenix, reflective mediation is the basis of meaning. Therefore, we should provide children the opportunity to analyze, reflect, and articulate on the meaning of their movement experiences. It is important to help children learn to share ideas about values and recognize and respect those held and prized by others.

In the primary grades, the emphasis is on awareness through simple discussions and opportunities to talk and write about movement experiences—in drawings, poems, and stories about them. More sophisticated tools may be used with older children. There are many techniques designed to help children clarify values, identify interests, make choices, set goals, and make decisions based on personal values and meanings. Examples are given in Chapter 6.

Program Objectives of Physical Education

Once the purposes of the physical education program have been selected and/or accepted, they must be broken down into subcomponents—program objectives—which reflect emphasis of development of a purpose consistent with the developmental level of the child. In reality, objectives are very specifically programmed or school-oriented and are the responsibility of individual teachers and/or schools to develop. They will indicate the biases, priorities, interests, and values of the planners and of the locality, and the readiness of the children of that locality as a result of the cultural background and school structure.

The objectives included here (Table 3-1) offer a breakdown of the purposes presented earlier and are those deemed viable in view of needs of the general population of children at varying stages of growth and development, the nature of the content of physical education (taken from the Schema of Areas of Development of Understandings, Concepts, and Skills, Table 3-2), and the needs of individuals in today's humanistic-oriented society. Each objective may be realized in many different ways through many different activities.

The objectives are stated in terms of student outcomes in the psychomotor, cognitive, affective domains at four levels. If a school is organized on a grade basis, K-1 might be considered as Level I; 2 as Level II; 3-4 as Level

Overview

36

[4] In *Realms of Meaning* (New York: McGraw-Hill, 1964), pp. 165-66.

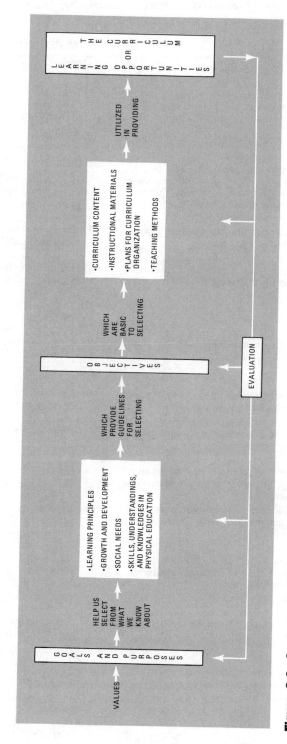

Figure 3-2 Curriculum Design in physical education.

Table 3-1. Program Objectives for Elementary School Physical Education

<hr>

OBJECTIVES IN THE PSYCHOMOTOR DOMAIN

<hr>

The child will demonstrate:

Level I

1. Refinement and combination of fundamental movement patterns

2. Good body control for safe play in starting, stopping, moving on signal, changing directions, moving through general space without touching anyone or any obstacle
3. Basic postural control in sitting, walking, and standing

4. Awareness of body parts and subsequently the range of uses of various body parts

5. Awareness of body parts and positions in various manipulative skills

6. Use of various dimensions of space, both personal and general

7. Basic awareness of laterality and directionality

8. Minimal control of objects when rolling, throwing, striking, and catching them
9. Use of basic movement patterns in relation to large pieces of apparatus

10. Continued increased strength in large muscles of body (legs, arms, abdomen, back)

11. Increased endurance for longer periods of uninterrupted activity

12. Increased flexibility in large muscle joints

Level II

1. Execution of all of the basic locomotor and nonlocomotor patterns with mature form

2. Execution of the basic movements in various combinations with respect to various dimensions of time, space, force in relation to self, other people, and objects
3. Some consistency in repetition of movement patterns

4. Mature underhand and overhand throwing patterns

5. Increased control and accuracy in throwing at stationary targets

6. Beginning control and accuracy in throwing at moving targets

7. Increased catching ability in the horizontal and vertical planes

8. Increased control of ball while bouncing and kicking it with body

9. Earlier perception of oncoming objects and of those coming from greater distances and different directions

10. Control when manipulating objects with large striking instruments

11. Control of body balance on increasingly smaller bases of support

12. Increased control while moving along, over, on, off, under, large apparatus

38

Table 3-1. Continued

OBJECTIVES IN THE PSYCHOMOTOR DOMAIN

The child will demonstrate:

Level III

1. Increasing ability to combine different movement patterns and to vary movement patterns with respect to given environmental, spatial, temporal, and force-related dimensions
2. Increased motor memory and ability to replicate own movement designs and patterns with consistency
3. Increased control of movement flow in executing sequences of movement
4. Execution of basic sport skills with minimal form
5. Mature jumping form and ability to jump farther and higher from different takeoff positions
6. Ability to catch balls coming at greater speed, from different directions, and with different trajectories
7. Ability to kick with preliminary force, kick through ball, and maintain balanced position
8. Ability to avoid objects and people coming from different directions at greater speeds
9. Increased accuracy in throwing at or toward moving targets
10. Increased control of an object while propelling it with body and other instruments
11. Increased control and accuracy in manipulating objects having various surfaces, sizes and shapes
12. Basic tumbling and stunts on the floor and on apparatus in sequences

Level IV

1. Application of basic movement concepts to approach and analysis of new skills learned in dance, gymnastics, lead-ups to sports, aquatics, and other activities
2. Utilization of good movement mechanics for efficient performance
3. Performance of a greater number of sport skills with increased proficiency
4. Development of movement memory to the point where practice and repetition result in increased control and confidence in using skills in various activities both structured and creative
5. Ability to vary performance of skills to meet demands of new problems and challenges within various activities
6. Game sense and use of strategic maneuvers in lead-ups to sports
7. Increasingly complex stunt, tumbling, and apparatus skills
8. Employment of safe spotting techniques while helping others in gymnastic events calling for spotting
9. Good body management skills in the creation and performance of sequences on various pieces of apparatus and in floor exercise
10. Continued physical growth with attending increased fitness elements of strength, endurance, power, balance, and agility, and productive use of fitness elements in performance
11. Correct performance of traditional dance steps in various folk, square, and recreational dances calling for more complex formations, group, and partner relationships
12. Expressive and extemporaneous responses in rhythmic movement to various stimuli (poems, music, words, feelings, work and play experiences)

Table 3-1. Continued

OBJECTIVES IN THE PSYCHOMOTOR DOMAIN

The child will demonstrate:

Level I

13. Beginning ability to move to an imposed rhythm while using locomotor and nonlocomotor movements

14. Free improvisation of movement patterns in response to various rhythmic stimuli

15. Good body management in shallow water with beginning breath control, basic floats

Level II

13. Balance control and good body position in landing from a jump

14. Continued body growth patterns in size and in attending strength, power, flexibility, agility, and speed of movement

15. Correct response to a rhythmic beat while moving, using various movement patterns

16. Self-expressive movement in response to various rhythmical accompaniments, poems, stories, words, props, etc.

17. Basic floats, drownproofing skills, and elementary swimming strokes and techniques in deep water

OBJECTIVES IN THE COGNITIVE DOMAIN

The child will demonstrate:

Level I

1. Concept of dimensions of personal and general space

2. Understanding of basic environmental directions (over, under, above, below, around)

3. Understanding of direction in relation to oneself and other objects (right, left, in front, behind)

4. Ability to identify body parts and their relationship to one another in response to verbal and nonverbal cues

Level II

1. Differentiation between various locomotor, nonlocomotor, and manipulative patterns

2. Understanding of basic dimensions of space and time as they relate to basic movements

3. Understanding of basic mechanical principles of stability; control of force in stopping and starting; absorbing force in catching an object, or self, such as, in landing from a jump or a fall

4. Identification of various body parts and positions for bases of support

Table 3-1. Continued

OBJECTIVES IN THE PSYCHOMOTOR DOMAIN

The child will demonstrate:

Level III

13. Endurance for longer periods of time in vigorous activities

14. Continuous growth pattern with productive use of attending increased strength and power in movement performances

15. Correct responses to changes in patterns and rhythmic tempo while executing locomotor movements and while handling objects

16. Correct performance of basic dance steps and use of time in structured dances

17. Use of various spatial patterns, formations, steps, and relationships in self-made dances

18. Ability to perform elementary swimming strokes, elementary dives, and water safety skills

19. Limited ability to vary swimming strokes and skills while participating in water games and stunts

Level IV

13. Ability to create and perform own dances showing good use of dance structure and unique combinations of spatial design, relationships, and movements

14. Ability to perform more advanced swimming strokes, dives, and water safety skills

15. Increased ability to vary swimming strokes and skills while participating in water games, stunts, and synchronized or rhythmic swimming

16. Utilization of skills acquired and refined in class in activities of choice and in after school activities conducted by the school and other agencies

OBJECTIVES IN THE COGNITIVE DOMAIN

The child will demonstrate:

Level III

1. Appropriate use of a good verbal movement vocabulary

2. Selection of appropriate movements or adaptations of movement patterns to demands of various combinations of dimensions of time, space, force

3. Recognition of fundamental movement patterns inherent in specific beginning sport, gymnastic, dance skills

4. Knowledge of basic principles related to control of propulsion and reception of objects

Level IV

1. Application of knowledge of elements and dimensions of movement structure to solve movement problems and to create unique games, contests, gymnastics, and dances

2. Use of basic mechanical principles in learning new skills and refining known ones

3. Identification and performance of skills and game play within rules and procedures of lead-up games to sports taught in class

4. Knowledge and understanding of strategies of each activity taught

Table 3-1. Continued

OBJECTIVES IN THE COGNITIVE DOMAIN

The child will demonstrate:

5. Ability to identify basic movement skill patterns and terminology associated with them

6. Skills of listening and thinking while moving

7. Understanding of rules and procedures of games taught in class

8. Ability to solve simple movement problems

9. Ability to identify basic rhythmic elements of underlying beat, tempo, intensity

10. Ability to minimally assess own movement performance, e.g., How did I do? Was it easier than before? Why?

5. Recognition of various body shapes and basic forms

6. Ability to choose relevant movements to solve increasingly difficult movement problems

7. Knowledge of rules of various games played in class

8. Knowledge of safety rules related to class procedures, use of equipment, traffic patterns

9. Ability to participate in formulating class safety and behavior expectations

10. Recognition of the rhythmic elements of tempo, phrasing, rhythmic pattern, and accent

11. Ability to make simple choices of activities, stations, partners, equipment quickly and within given limitations

Table 3-1. **Continued**

OBJECTIVES IN THE COGNITIVE DOMAIN

The child will demonstrate:

Level III

5. Ability to solve more complex movement problems and tasks

6. Understanding of space through use of strategies in simple games and lead-ups to sports

7. Knowledge of structure of games and dances through creation of dances and games

8. Application of principles of absorption of force, production of force when learning new sport skills and gymnastic skills

9. Knowledge of rules and strategy of games played in class

10. Recognition of safety hazards of improper use of equipment, hitting into groups, running through playing groups, arrangements of space for play and practice

11. Understanding of basic principles of exercise to development of strength and endurance, e.g., intensity of exercise, number of bouts

12. Recognition of relationship of size, strength, endurance to good performance

13. Recognition of performance expectations due to difference in size, weight, body build, and experiences

14. Recognition of how to care for specific equipment and apparatus

15. Understanding of principles of buoyancy

16. Beginning ability to use facts, skills, previous experiences as basis for solving movement problems and/or analyzing new movement situations

17. Beginning ability to choose between alternative solutions that which is best for limitations set for task

18. Ability to evaluate self or a peer in relation to correct movement pattern or form with some guidance

19. Beginning ability to make choices of activity, when quality of performance demands practice rather than game play, which skills need practice, etc.

Level IV

5. Ability to determine rules to avoid injury when creating games

6. Selection of game strategies appropriate to opponent's abilities

7. Ability to design more complex sequences of movement, games, and dances

8. Recognition of basic formations, sequences, relationships, rhythmic structures of dances taught in class and/or designed by classmates

9. Ability to discriminate between poor and good execution of skill

10. Increased knowledge and understanding of fitness concepts, effects of exercise on heartbeat, overload principle, feeling tone, selection of exercises for own needs

11. Ability to draw relationships with respect to previous knowledge and similarities of new skills

12. Improvement in inventing or improving solutions to new situations

13. Ability to make choices about activities, direction of practice, partners, groups, with increasingly fewer limitations*

* Combined affective and cognitive skill

Table 3-1. Continued

OBJECTIVES IN THE AFFECTIVE DOMAIN

The child will demonstrate:

Level I

1. Basic listening skills, attending to directions, explanations, requests

2. Play and work with another child sharing space, equipment, simple ideas while maintaining emotional control and interest

3. Consistent assumption of responsibility for taking care of equipment, getting it out, and returning it to designated place when finished using it

4. Assumption of self-responsibility for safe play, i.e., not running into walls, wearing gym shoes if required, staying in personal space when working with equipment, etc.

5. Ability and willingness to follow directions and rules set by teacher or inherent in game itself

6. Willingness to share responses, exploratory and discovery tasks with classmates

7. Free movement responses to various sensory stimuli, done willingly

8. Verbalization at a simple level of his or her feelings about a movement experience

9. Joy in movement experience

Level II

1. Awareness of own behavior and acceptance of responsibility for it

2. Increasing responsibility for sharing and use of equipment

3. Cooperative play and work with another person, a small group, and the large group

4. Willing, confident, exuberant responses to activities asking for imaginative responses

5. Willing participation in group decisions about rules of games, safety rules, and consequent allegiance to those rules

6. Ability to make choices of activities, stations, equipment, when to do certain things quickly and within given limitations

7. Ability to follow through on choices

8. Ability to set a simple goal and verbalize about reaching that goal

9. Increasing willingness and interest in talking about and sharing feelings about movement experiences

10. Joy in movement experience

Table 3-1. Continued

OBJECTIVES IN THE AFFECTIVE DOMAIN

The child will demonstrate:

Level III

1. Cooperative participation with others in various relationships where joint effort is necessary to reach a common goal
2. Understanding of need for rules and officials' roles in game play

3. Willingness to develop own ideas through self-designed games, dances, routines

4. Constructive choices of activities, practice efforts, space, and time based on some identifiable criteria

5. Concern and consideration of safety factors in relation to self and others

6. Recognition and acceptance of individual differences (of self and others) due to various limitations

7. Appreciation and respect for peers' values and performances
8. Ability to compare present self-performance with the past and to identify needs and interests in future performances
9. Acceptance of constructive criticism of peers and teacher

10. Willingness to participate in activities to derive physiological benefits (fitness)
11. Ability to set realistic short-term goals and to follow through on evaluating progress toward goals
12. Willingness to discuss basic values of self and others in respect to sharing, sportsmanship, competition, cheating, helping others, activity interests
13. Expression of emerging value system about exercise, choice of activities, and own limitations in movement

Level IV

1. Greater responsible, cooperative attitude in working with others in dual and/or team cooperative-competitive situations
2. Responsibility for planning and presenting ideas or activities in class and out of class

3. Wholesome attitude toward the compatibility of cooperative and competitive attitudes

4. Continued, free, enthusiastic, and expressive response in creative and unstructured movement activities

5. Awareness of movement activities as an avenue of self-expression, self-realization, and socialization

6. Ability to set goals, select learning experiences, and follow up on assessment of goal achievement with consistently more logical reasons commensurate with abilities and limitations

7. Interest in learning new movement activities as well as traditional ones
8. Measurable results through more self-directed learning modalities

9. Ability and willingness to critically evaluate own performance and needs

10. Respect for limitations of others

11. Appreciation of performance of peers and skilled performers as a spectator or observer

12. Awareness of the values of the physiological effects and benefits of exercise

13. Assumption of responsibility developing fitness aspects as needed and wanted by self

Table 3-1. Continued

OBJECTIVES IN THE AFFECTIVE DOMAIN

The child will demonstrate:

Level III	*Level IV*
14. Expression of feelings about personal meaning of movement experiences	14. Willing participation in some movement activities of own choice outside of the class situation
15. Joy in the movement experience	15. Beginning value system regarding movement choices, interests, and participation
	16. Desire to participate in movement experience that is intrinsically motivated
	17. Appreciation of cultural aspects of movement of own and other countries
	18. Joy in the movement experience

III; 5-6 as Level IV. Even with a graded system, levels may be used within grades to determine readiness and achievement for more advanced objectives and experiences. Remember, each child varies in rate or extent of development in each of the domains and in prior and concurrent experiences outside the class experience.

The objectives are not at all inclusive or exclusive, but are meant to serve as a framework to help teachers and students in developing an elementary curriculum. These may also serve as the basis of a laboratory experience in which students further develop instructional and specific objectives enabling purposes and objectives to be actualized through various activities and experiences. From that point they can further project alternate learning experiences, modes of presentation, media needs, and evaluative techniques from which to select to meet individual school and pupil needs.

Figure 3-2 (on page 37) is a flow chart of all the aspects considered in the design of the physical education curriculum. The curriculum as used in this book is defined as the plan for instructional action and the learning opportunities or experiences supported by the school for the child. In general, there is a chapter in the book to clarify and expand on each aspect as it relates to the elementary school child and the physical education program.

Program Content of Physical Education

Table 3-2 provides a schema of areas of development of understandings, concepts, and skills that provide the basis of the learning experiences that teachers should include in their program planning—i.e., the *content* of the program. The unique major content of the discipline of physical education lies in the areas of movement mechanics, elements and dimensions of movement, body capacity and effects of movement, and the traditional cultural activities or forms of movement (games, dance, sport, gymnastics, and aquatics). However, if we support a humanistic curriculum and thus a respect for the development of the whole child, then we must also consider those aspects of social-psychological behavior in the child's life which can affect or be affected by the unique skills, understandings, and concepts of movement.

Learning experiences designed to present this content will help children actualize the purposes and objectives presented earlier. Actualizing the *fundamentals* of the first three purposes (understanding the structure of movement, moving competently and confidently in a wide variety of movement forms, and developing motor fitness) and experiencing the unique content implied for them is developing *literacy in movement.* Enrichment opportunities and content related to these purposes, and opportunities and experiences to actualize the other purposes, prepare a child to cultivate and deepen his/her skill and appreciation. Information, facts, knowledge, and basic skills are all important—in fact, imperative—to the study and teaching of physical education or any other subject. Their value lies in how they enhance increased appreciation, new insight into self and others, feeling in movement, and better access to

Table 3-2. Schema of Areas of Development of Understandings, Concepts, and Skills in Physical Education

MOVEMENT SKILLS AND ACTIVITIES	ENVIRONMENTAL FACTORS	BODY CAPACITY AND EFFECTS OF MOVEMENT	SOCIAL-PSYCHOLOGICAL
LOCOMOTOR SKILLS Walk Run Jump Hop Leap Skip Slide Gallop Various combinations	*MECHANICAL PRINCIPLES* Equilibrium Motion Gravity Force Levers	*MOTOR FITNESS* Strength Endurance Flexibility Power Agility Speed	*TRADITIONAL CULTURAL ACTIVITIES* Sport Dance Gymnastics Games
NONLOCOMOTOR SKILLS Twist Turn Stretch Bend Push Pull Swing Roll Various combinations	*MEDIA* Water In flight Floor Grass *SPACE* *FORCE*	*HEALTH HABITS* Posture Weight control Preparation for exercise Relaxation Fundamentals of exercise	*INTERPERSONAL RELATIONS* *COMMUNICATION* *CREATIVE – EXPRESSION* *LEARNING PROCESSES*
MANIPULATIVE SKILLS Throw Catch Strike Kick Trap Roll	*TIME* *FLOW* *BODY SHAPE* *RELATIONSHIPS*		*VALUES* *KNOWLEDGE OF MOVEMENT OF OTHER CULTURES*
WEIGHT BEARING *INITIATING MOVEMENT* *RECEIVING WEIGHT*	*Persons* Partner Small group Large group Team or side		*MEANING AND SIGNIFICANCE OF MOVEMENT TO SELF*
TRANSFERRING WEIGHT *FORMS OF MOVEMENT* Dance Gymnastics Games Aquatics Sports	*Objects* Small and large apparatus		
UNSTRUCTURED MOVEMENT			

the beauty of movement, thus taking one *beyond literacy in movement.* This is the goal of a humanistic program. Thus the social-psychological content takes on added importance in such a program. At the primary level, the major effort is on acquiring the basic skills and knowledges; however, opportunities for social-psychological development must be provided concurrently at the onset of the instructional program.

Each entry in the schema of content may be considered a concept to be developed or considered as a theme upon which to build instructional objectives, resource units, and/or long-term unit plans and ultimately daily lessons. The actual learning experiences may be in many modes—unstructured movement activities, the various traditional activities of movement (games, sports, dance, gymnastics, aquatics), discussions, readings, etc. The traditional activities, which to many people have always been the subject matter and content of physical education, are used as learning experiences for two purposes: as vehicles through which to teach and reinforce the understandings of skills, feelings, and attitudes in each area of the schema, and as activities to be learned and in which to participate as a cultural facet of physical education.

Process and affective learning opportunities are provided through the teacher's selection and use of teaching methods, techniques, and organizational strategies which allow children to explore, discover, solve problems, set goals, communicate, interact, create, express, establish values, make choices, identify and clarify feelings, etc.

Classroom teachers who also teach physical education will see in the schema similarities and relationships of concepts with those of other subject-matter areas and common learning and life skills—for example, mechanical principles, spatial elements, health knowledges and habits, social-psychological aspects. Learning those concepts and use of them in the context of one's own body movement reinforces the acquisition of the concepts. Beyond the primary purpose of learning about and in movement, integrating other subject-matter learning through movement is important to both the child and the teacher. If a specialist is responsible for teaching physical education, he or she should become familiar with the curricula of other areas and work closely with the classroom teacher with respect to integration of subject matters, and of course vice-versa.

Deciding *what* to teach is probably one of the most persistent and fundamental questions that both inexperienced and experienced teachers face. Actually, what should be taught is determined by the goals of education as expressed by society in general. The goals that reflect the values of a society are translated into content and objectives of education by professional educators. The teacher translates goals into specific objectives and makes them operational.

What is actually taught in the daily lesson is up to the teacher. This is a very important decision, affected by several forces. Figure 3-3 diagrams these forces. What is actually taught should be consistent with the goals and needs of all those the teacher serves, the students being the most important group. Although those forces external to the teacher become modified by internal forces—his or her own values, self-concept, and knowledge of the subject matter—critical and responsible decisions must be made on the basis of the best interests of all involved. There must be a congruence of input by the external and internal forces.

Figure 3-3 Internal and external forces that influence teacher decision about what will be taught.

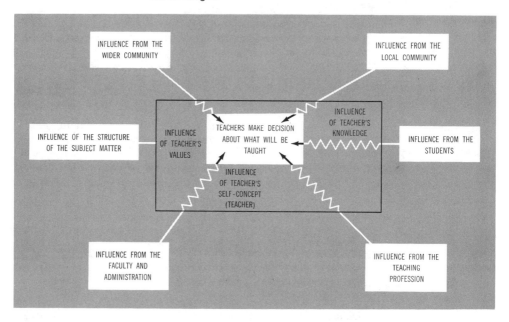

Depending on the size and organization of the school, the curriculum is designed by a group representing the external influences and compromises of the internal forces of the individual members of the group. Where only one person is responsible for designing the curriculum, he or she must be accountable to the external forces while making decisions potentially overridden by personal internal forces.

Curriculum designers develop the *basic organization* and *plan of action* for what is taught. The teacher puts the plan into action.

The planners are responsible for organizing the basic subject matter of physical education (Table 3-1) into sequences of program objectives on the basis of a logical conceptual hierarchy (see, for example, Table 3-2). Each of these sequences must then be broken down into instructional objectives by the teacher. In turn, these have to be analyzed in terms of what a student is able to do, know, or feel before the broader objective can be realized; what kinds of learning experiences will help students learn and use what is learned; and what criteria indicate that students have indeed reached the objective or, in essence, learned. The latter is the development of the specific or behavioral objectives.

Organizing Content

To insure continuity in learning, it is necessary to select some type of organizational pattern or organizing center of content—i.e., concepts, activities, purposes and objectives, needs, integrated approach with other subject-matter areas, or a combination of these. Which you use is a matter of preference and the situation in which you are operating. For purposes of illustration in this book, a conceptual approach is used for Levels I and II, and the basic concepts are the elements and dimensions of movement, basic movement patterns, body awareness, and relationships, with appropriate elementary concepts of mechanical principles and physical attributes affecting performance. The Basic Movement Glossary presented in the Introduction to Part III should serve as the source of concepts and subconcepts and skills upon which to build themes and behavioral objectives.

These should then be studied, explored, and refined separately and in various combinations from the aspect of each domain. They should further be studied, refined, and used in developmentally appropriate structured activities of games, dance, gymnastics, and aquatics.

At Levels III and IV, a combination of concepts and activity areas themselves serve as the organizing centers, with a dual emphasis on drawing on those concepts of basic movement that children have formed as the basis of learning and understanding new activities and in learning the activities in and of themselves. The teacher must consciously plan experiences which allow development of behavioral concepts in the social-psychological area—i.e., communicating and expressing in and about movement, values, recognition of meaning and significance of movement, etc. (see Table 3-1).

Where one makes the change from organizing content around the basic concepts of movement to that of an activity approach is dependent upon the organization of the school program and the readiness of children to move in this direction. Realization of the program objectives designed for the different levels should be a decision point in the latter.

Activity Areas

In order to better acquaint the reader with the many and varied activity areas, this section provides a brief description of them, as well as appropriate types of emphasis within the activity areas at different stages of development.

Basic movement is not usually categorized as a traditional activity area; however, the elements and dimensions of basic movement provide a large share of the movement activities for the primary grades. The basic locomotor skills, nonlocomotor skills, and manipulative skills, and combinations of these, will be explored and refined. Tasks and experiences to help children understand, and to adapt movements to the environmental factors which affect movement, are designated as a major part of the curriculum at the primary grades. At the same time they are used and studied in appropriate structured activities of games, dance, gymnastics, and where possible, aquatics. Basic movement is the foundation of the entire program, with constant reference made to foundational skills and concepts as more complex skills, strategy problems, relationships, and creative opportunities are encountered. See Part III for the Basic Movement Glossary, a discussion and explanation of each concept as well as suggested movement experiences to enhance their development.

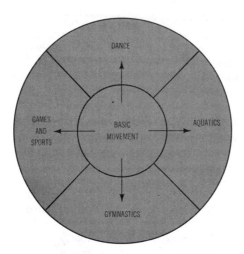

Figure 3-4 Relationship of basic movement to all activities.

Gymnastics

This area of activities is broad and inclusive. Most of the activities are of a self-testing nature, which implies an opportunity for children to prove themselves, to discover their abilities, and to achieve success by their own efforts. The challenge of success is individual according to each child's body build and skill. In this book, the forms of gymnastic activities are developmental exercises, stunts, tumbling, activities using small equipment, and activities on large apparatus.

Guided developmental experiences in all these forms provide for development of large-muscle groups, strength, muscle endurance, agility, balance, flexibility, and coordination. Work in this area affords excellent opportunities for the development of perseverance, courage, initiative, resourcefulness, and understanding of individual differences.

The term "educational gymnastics" is widely used in elementary school programs where the approach to the various forms of gymnastics is child-centered rather than formal-stunt-centered. Early experiences are exploratory in nature and emphasize performance within the individual's abilities, readiness, and interest. Stress is placed on exploration, selection, refinement, and originality. Traditional and specified stunts are included in the program, but the process of learning them and the flexibility required for doing them are less formal than is the case in "Olympic gymnastics."

Olympic gymnastics is an approach in which the emphasis is on everyone learning and performing set traditional tumbling and apparatus stunts, using a prescribed form. For the advanced performer, creative routines are included wherein the performer sequences Olympic stunts and moves. Obviously, educational gymnastics allow more opportunity for some of the process objectives to be realized, as well as meeting more individual abilities.

Some elementary programs focus on educational gymnastics in primary and intermediate grades and on Olympic gymnastics in upper grades. Frequently there is a combination of approaches for those interested and ready for the Olympic stunts in both class and the voluntary after-school program.

DEVELOPMENTAL EXERCISES For the most part, developmental exercises call for combinations of basic movement that may require use of isolated parts of the body or gross body movement. This type of exercise lends itself to work with the whole group where the teacher may pose challenges to be met, ask for original or creative exercises, or introduce new concepts in a more direct manner. Many basic maneuvers used on apparatus may be practiced first on the floor—such as landing techniques, balance stunts, weight bearing, etc. What are sometimes referred to as "fitness activities" fall into this category. Exercises that help develop strength (such as push-ups, sit-ups), those that help develop endurance (such as jumping jacks, running in place), and many others are developmental. This form of gymnastic activity may be used profitably in all grade levels and may very well be utilized at the beginning of every lesson for loosening-up purposes, introductory activities, or for a whole lesson.

STUNTS There is some overlap of stunt activities and developmental exercises. Traditional stunts are usually set feats that require certain elements of flexibility, strength, balance, agility, or combinations of these. Original stunts may be created by children at all ages. When children cannot perform a stunt on the first try, they are challenged and motivated to work until they master it. A series of stunts as a challenge to be accomplished over a period of time provides valuable opportunities for social growth as well as physical growth.

TUMBLING Tumbling activities include rolling, balancing, supporting one's weight when inverted, and springing. The elements of agility, flexibility, strength, balance, and coordination are developed through tumbling activities. As with stunts, there is always the element of challenge involved in trying to develop good form as well as accomplishing the initial tasks. Most tumbling activities build one upon another, so a definite progression must be followed whether tumbling activities are initiated in the second grade or in the seventh grade.

SMALL EQUIPMENT In the primary grades, exploratory work with small objects and equipment of all types is stressed. Children develop manipulative ability, hand-eye coordination, and foot-eye coordination. They experiment with a variety of shapes, sizes, and weights of small equipment—balls, beanbags, hoops, wands, jumping ropes, stilts, rings, paddles, bats, etc. In this way they gain a familiarity and confidence in using their bodies in a variety of relationships which each object demands. They also may experiment and invent many different ways to use equipment in a nonprescribed manner.

In the intermediate grades, work with sport implements and balls is related to the basic skills of the specific sports. It is important that the size of the equipment be appropriate to the size of the children. Children may invent new ways to use different kinds of small equipment or invent games in which to use them.

LARGE APPARATUS Work on apparatus is largely exploratory in the primary and intermediate grades. The emphasis is on learning how to get on, over, and off objects, and learning the application of basic principles of mechanics and movements to many different apparatus situations. Confidence and familiarity with various pieces of apparatus are developed before formal set patterns of specific exercises or routines on apparatus are initiated. The former is accomplished in the primary grades in combination with exploratory work in adapting basic movement skills to apparatus. This is *educational gymnastics*. Informal work can and should be continued throughout the school years in addition to or to the exclusion of formal gymnastics. The latter type of work is begun in the upper grades. As with all of the other forms of gymnastic activities, strength, balance, coordination, and flexibility can be developed through apparatus work. Developing shoulder girdle strength is one of the major values of apparatus work. The hanging and supporting opportunities are more numerous than in any other activity area.

Games and Sports

Games and sports have been an important part of most cultures from the beginning of civilization. Children and adults play games for fun and for the satisfaction they provide. Most after-school and leisure activities of both children and adults are drawn from the game and sports activity area. In the physical education program there is a type of evolution process from games of simple organization to official sports. This evolution may be likened to a pyramid, where the basic movement skills serve as the base and official team and individual sports as the apex of the pyramid (Figure 3-5).

At the same time work in basic movement is underway in the primary grades, games of low organization in which skills are used in a variety of ways are introduced. In this way children begin to recognize the purposes and values of good skills. The more confining game situation demands a cognitive process in the use of skills as well as physical prowess. Most games provide vigorous activity; however, there are games designed for inactive relaxation and confined spaces.

The value of games in promoting good social development cannot be overemphasized. Games may be selected for the primary child which help promote good habits of taking turns, following directions, recognizing bound-

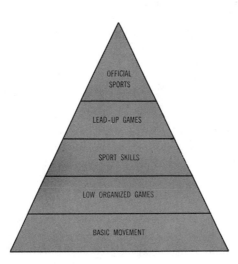

OFFICIAL SPORTS

LEAD-UP GAMES

SPORT SKILLS

LOW ORGANIZED GAMES

BASIC MOVEMENT

Figure 3-5 Evolution of games and sports in the elementary school.

aries, working together, being a leader, etc. There are many forms of games, each of which can make a contribution to the development of a specific type of social behavior.

Games are cooperative or competitive in nature. In cooperative games, everyone works together to achieve a common goal. In competitive games, everyone on one side or team works together in order to achieve more excellence than the other side or team.

There is danger that a teacher may include too many games or not select games for specific outcomes. To the children, the game may be played just for fun, but to the teacher every game that is played should be a means of producing definite developmental outcomes. Each game presented should reveal a progression of difficulty in use of skills, rules, and strategy. (The various forms of games and specific learning experiences for each are presented in Chapter 13.)

Starting in third grade, special attention is given to exploration with balls and implements specific to team and individual sports. At this point the primary purpose is to help children develop competence in the basic skills which serve as the foundation for specific sport skills. Basic mechanical principles are stressed as new combinations of movements are introduced for use with different sizes of balls, implements, and the particulars of each sport. These skills are then used in lead-up games.

Depending on the sport, lead-up games are introduced as early as third grade. A lead-up game may be defined as a game within itself; however, it must include one or more skills, similar rules, and simple strategy of an official sport. Lead-up games range from one of utmost simplicity to an increasingly complex game that is almost identical to that of the official sport.

Through careful selection from grade to grade, progression can be developed while the sport skills, rules, and strategy are learned cumulatively to a point at which those of the official parent game can be learned with ease. Therefore, children can enjoy games that are planned for their level of skill, size, understanding, and interest, from the middle elementary years to junior high school when they become ready for the official rules of each sport.

The social values gained from team games or sports are many. In these games there are great opportunities for teaching valuable social responses through both competition and cooperation. All of our democratic traits are emphasized with the need of teamwork and personal sacrifices in the pursuance of team play. The satisfaction that children derive from their small contributions to the part of a winning team will help build unselfish adults. The understanding of the inevitability of having to lose at times can forestall the development of a "sore loser" and encourage the recognition of the need for improvement in the next quest.

An important phase of the games program is the inclusion of opportunities for children to design their own games and to modify known games. In order to do this they have to understand game structure. This phase is the predominant aspect of low-organized games in the upper grades.

As children mature, they naturally become more interested in group activities, vigorous activity, and improvement in skills. The percentage of time spent in low-organized games decreases proportionately until in the upper grades practically no amount of time is assigned to them. It must be remembered that children at these ages still like to play simple games for sheer enjoyment, but not too long or too often. Beginning skills and lead-up games related to individual sports are given more attention. It is this type of game that will be utilized most by the individual for leisure activities.

Dance Activities   People have danced for pleasure and purpose throughout the recorded history of humanity. Dance can serve as a means of communication of ideas and expression, creativity, and as a recreative activity.

"Dance activities" is an inclusive term, for there are several forms of dance. In the elementary school four major aspects of dance are generally studied: fundamentals, creative, folk, and recreational. All dance activity is based on movement affected by the elements of space, force, and rhythm. The fundamentals include basic locomotor and nonlocomotor movement skills, rhythm skills, and space elements.

Actually, the movement skills are the same as those taught and explored as basic movement skills; however, in dance the expressive form of the skills is stressed. More emphasis is given to the coordination of the movements and rhythmic elements. It is difficult to separate the two activities as far as attention to fundamental skill work is concerned. The basic difference is in the application of skills.

In the primary grades, work with dance fundamentals is usually associated with a dramatic purpose and has some type of rhythmic accompaniment. The creative area takes the form of portraying incidents or telling a story in movement, or pretending to be an object or animal within the children's realm of experience. Primary children enjoy singing games and very simple folk dances. Since today in many schools the latter two forms are taught in conjunction with the music lessons, the classroom teacher has an opportunity to integrate the music and dance lessons quite productively.

Once children have explored the fundamental skills of locomotion and rhythm, they are ready to learn the traditional dance steps which are combinations of various basic locomotor movements. These are then the basic steps for the various folk dances which are learned throughout the school years and form the basis of most of the recreational dance forms.

Creative work is continued in all the grades. As children grow older, their experiences and interests expand, and consequently their needs and desires to express themselves grow. Making one's own dance is extremely vital and exciting to children of all ages. The complexity of the dance, the refinement of the skills involved, and the length of time for the preparation of the dances increases proportionately by grades.

The introduction of social dance skills and etiquette is dependent on the social needs of children in their respective communities. Most frequently there are school or community parties or dances that require some dance skills by eighth grade. Because boys particularly may not be interested in this phase of dance unless they have a tangible need to learn, it is foolish to force social dance on groups before they can use their skills in a social situation.

Aquatics   Although swimming and water sports are an integral part of American recreation and pose many safety hazards, a minority of children learn how to swim. The cost of building and maintaining pool facilities is prohibitive for many school systems. It is unfortunate that most pools are found in the secondary schools, because children learn to swim quickly and easily and could engage in water activities safely at a very young age.

When community pools are available, the school personnel should seek a way to include swimming instruction for children starting at least in the third grade. Children learn to swim quite rapidly at this age, and fear of the water appears to be overcome more quickly by younger children than by older ones.

Whenever aquatics is introduced, the initial emphasis should be on water orientation skills and basic breathing techniques. Safety rules must be initiated immediately. Drownproofing skills and elementary swimming strokes should be introduced next, with basic diving skills following. There should be a variety of water games, advanced strokes, dives, and rhythmic swimming available in upper grades. Often when aquatics is introduced early, the program consists only of swimming strokes that everyone must conquer. As in every activity, all children may not be interested in or adept at swimming, and a repetition of working on the same strokes every year may become very demoralizing.

If swimming is included in the elementary school program, usually qualified swimming instructors are hired rather than having the classroom teacher responsible for the instruction. Content for an aquatic program is not included here; however, source books are recommended for reference.

Every activity area has specific applications for contributing to the various phases of the development of the child. Because the goal is one of a well-balanced individual, the content must also be well balanced. The description of the forms of activities in each area has indicated the implications of the various stages of growth and development and cultural influences as related to emphasis and time spent at the different levels. Consistent with this information, Table 3-3 (p. 58–59) portrays schematically the scope and emphasis in time and nature of activity content as an aid to program planning. Table 3-4 (p. 60) portrays affective and pupil process experience emphasis.

SUGGESTED REFERENCES FOR FURTHER STUDY

AMERICAN ALLIANCE FOR HEALTH, PHYSICAL EDUCATION AND RECREATION, *Aquatics for All.* Washington, D.C., 1978.

———, *Echoes of Influence for Elementary School Physical Education.* Washington, D.C., 1977.

———, *Essentials of a Quality Elementary School Physical Education Program.* Washington, D.C., 1970.

———, *Guidelines for Middle School Physical Education.* Washington, D.C., 1977.

———, *Knowledges and Understandings in Physical Education.* Washington, D.C., 1973, rev.

ASSOCIATION FOR SUPERVISION AND CURRICULUM DEVELOPMENT, *Humanistic Education: Objectives and Assessment,* a report of the ASCD working group on humanistic education. Washington, D.C., 1978.

JEWETT, ANN and MARIE MULLAN, *Curriculum Design: Purposes and Processes in Physical Education,* Washington, D.C.: AAHPER, 1977.

MOLNAR, ALEX, and JOHN ZAHORIK, eds., *Curriculum Theory.* Washington, D.C.: The Association for Supervision and Curriculum, 1977.

SIEDENTOP, DARYL, *Physical Education-Introductory Analysis,* 2nd ed. Dubuque, Iowa: Wm. C. Brown Co., 1976.

Table 3-3. Scope and Emphasis Sequence of Activity Content in Elementary School Physical Education

Activities	Level I	Level II	Level III	Level IV
Basic Movement Patterns				
Locomotor				
Nonlocomotor				
Manipulative				
Elements and Dimensions of Movement				
Space				
Time				
Force				
Flow				
Relationships				
Person to person(s)				
Person to large apparatus				
Person to small apparatus				
Body Awareness				
Specific Perceptual-Motor Activities				
Fitness Activities				
Low Organized Games				
Predesigned				
Teacher designed				
Pupil designed				
Sports Skills Lead-up Activities				
Basketball				
Volleyball				
Soccer				
Softball				
Field hockey				
Floor hockey				
Flag football				
Speedball				
Field ball				
Tennis—Paddle tennis				
Badminton				
Track and field				
Winter sports				
Wrestling				

Table 3-3. (Continued)

Dance				
Rhythmic elements				
Creative				
Folk				
Singing games				
Recreational				
Gymnastics				
Floor exercise				
Stunts				
Tumbling				
Apparatus				
Aquatics				
Drown-proofing skills				
Safety skills				
Strokes				
Dives				
Water games				
Rhythmic swimming				
Minicourses in New or Timely Events				
Teacher led				
Community resources				
Pupil led				

KEY

Very Light Emphasis   Light Emphasis

Heavy Emphasis   Not Appropriate

Table 3-4. Scope and Emphasis Sequence of Process and Affective Experiences in Elementary School Physical Education

Process Experiences	Level I	Level II	Level III	Level IV
Explore				
Discover				
Solve Problems				
Set goals				
Make choices-decisions				
Alone				
In concert with others				
Create-Design				
Games				
Dances				
Floor exercise/routines				
Apparatus routines				
Rhythmic rope, ball routines				
Evaluate				
Self				
Peer				
Teach Others				

Affective Experiences	Level I	Level II	Level III	Level IV
Creative-Expressive				
Communicative				
Cooperative				
Competitive				
Self				
Others				
Study of Activities of other cultures				
Goal Setting				
Accepting and Respecting				
Self				
Others				
Leading				
Values Clarification				
Reflective mediation on meaning of movement experiences				

KEY

- ⧄ Very Light Emphasis
- ⧅ Light Emphasis
- ▨ Heavy Emphasis
- □ Not Appropriate

Part II
The Teaching-Learning Process

Each chapter in Part II contributes to the teacher's role in making decisions about what is to be taught, how the content will be organized, how it will be presented, and determining if the child has learned. Many alternatives are offered. You must select from these alternatives on the basis of knowledge gained from Part I and from Chapter 4 on how children learn.

After studying Part I and Part II, you should be able to substantiate the following basic assumptions and principles underlying a humanistic physical education program. If you can and do, you are on your way to becoming a good humanistic elementary school physical education teacher.

The Humanistic Physical Education Curriculum: Basic Assumptions and Principles

. . . ABOUT THE FOUNDATIONS FOR DESIGN

1. The physical education curriculum is an essential part of the total school curriculum.
2. It should reflect the nature and needs of a democratic society with high emphasis and respect and concerns of the individual as he/she interacts within the total society.
3. It should be based on a well-conceived statement of goals and purposes.
4. The broad societal goal of education is to develop the self-actualized individual who can function as an effective family member and citizen. This implies an emphasis on the development of individuals who are self-directed, self-disciplined, self-responsible, and capable of making intelligent choices. (Self-actualized means being independent.)
5. The primary goal of physical education is to contribute to this broader goal by helping every child realize his/her movement potential.
6. It should be based on the most generally accepted basic structure of physical education and/or human movement.
7. It should include a concern and provision for all children and youth in the school—including those with mental, physical, and cultural limitations.
8. It should be organized into a continuous, sequential flow of experiences with basic competencies identified for everyone, with subsequent opportunities for in-depth study and enrichment.
9. It should offer a varied program with provision of choice for students and attendant counseling.
10. Whatever the nature of the curriculum, it must provide each individual with a number of different ways of learning and with an opportunity to cultivate his/her potential for excellence.

11. Out-of-class experiences (intramurals, clubs, interscholastic activities, community centers) should be considered a part of the total curriculum and receive the same concern and planning as the regularly scheduled instructional activities. These should provide for the whole range of interests, abilities, and needs of all children and youth.

12. All who are involved in the support and implementation of the curriculum should be involved in its planning and evaluation (parents, students, administrators, teachers).

13. Community resources should be utilized in the planning, implementing, and evaluating of the physical education design (people and facilities).

14. It should be evaluated continuously with respect to demonstrated necessary changes.

15. Any large-scale plan for curriculum change must include provisions for an effective transition from the existing program.

. . . ABOUT CHILDREN

1. Children learn at different rates, and have differing needs to achieve.
2. Children have different interests and values.
3. Children can conceptualize movement.
4. Children can create their own games and movement patterns.
5. Children need time to *play* with skills both newly acquired and internalized.
6. Children demonstrate steady growth and rapid skill acquisition.
7. Children are capable of utilizing resource material in cooperative planning of activities.
8. Children can teach children.
9. Children learn more rapidly when the sequence is logical and clear and when there is flow from one area of instruction to the next.
10. Children learn more rapidly when what they are to learn is relevant to them.

. . . ABOUT CONTENT DESIGN

1. Content may be organized around the *conceptual approach,* with various movement elements and factors isolated for study.
2. Content may be organized around the *integrated approach,* which incorporates study from the areas of language arts, music, art, math, science, etc.
3. Content may be organized around the *activity-centered approach,* which is typified by units such as football, basketball, gymnastics, etc.
4. Content may be organized around the *need-to-know approach,* which is initiated by questions to identify interest areas in physical education. (Example: What would you need to know to play volleyball?)
5. Content may be organized around the *core curriculum,* in which specific movement patterns are identified and then studied in the context of various activities such as the general patterns of striking used in softball, soccer, racquet games.

... ABOUT SELECTING CONTENT

1. Content should relate to purpose.
2. Content should reflect the basic structure of physical education.
3. Content should allow alternatives for meeting purposes and/or objectives.
4. Content should be appropriate to developmental needs, abilities, and interests of the students involved.
5. Content should be sequential. It should reveal some progression of difficulty—i.e., simple to complex—so that a person may proceed to learn sequentially or enter a sequence at a point of suitability to meet his/her needs or experiences and exit at a point to meet his/her needs (continuous progress).
6. Content should fit cultural and social norms of the students and the community.
7. Content should be contemporary in nature.
8. Content should be reasonable in both breadth and depth.
9. Content should be varied and provide for a wide range of objectives.
10. Affective aspects and processes, as well as skills and knowledge, should be considered as content.
11. Children should have a part in selection of content.
12. Results of studies by nationally recognized groups or innovative projects may be a base for selection of content.
13. The content that is offered should be continuously studied for its effectiveness and relatedness. Some content should be added, some eliminated and/or emphasis changed as students' interests and needs change.

... ABOUT YOU (THE TEACHER) AND YOUR RESPONSIBILITIES

1. You understand the contribution of physical education to development in the cognitive, affective, and psychomotor domains.
2. You have the ability and knowledge to use both direct and indirect teaching methods and a variety of teaching techniques.
3. You can select and construct a variety of modalities to utilize in presenting content.
4. You adapt your teaching style to the learning styles of your students.
5. You are responsible for the design, implementation, evaluation, and redesign of your program.
6. You see the necessity for effective interaction, communication, and coordination with others in the school and community.
7. You provide vital support in terms of morale, budget, scheduling, facilities, and equipment.
8. You consider alternative grouping patterns (by grade, interest, ability) in designing programs.
9. You are a model for children.
10. You are humanistic.

4 / HOW CHILDREN LEARN MOTOR SKILLS

- • **Motor learning**
- • **Factors that affect learning**
- • **Stages of learning**

Children learn within the framework of their own abilities, capabilities, and efforts. The teacher provides the setting, the opportunities, the feedback, and the encouragement for each child to succeed within his/her own limitations. Good teaching depends upon both artistry and scientific applications—upon what a teacher is and does. Successful learning as described by Madeline Hunter is

the result of an appropriate behavioral objective implanted by teaching decisions and actions that reflect the teacher's personality and style but are consonant with principles of learning. A lesson with an inappropriate objective or teaching that violates these basic principles is unsuccessful no matter how dramatic or scintillating the teacher or his teaching performance.[1]

Motor Learning

An understanding of how a child learns and an ability to apply principles of learning are prerequisites to the "how" of teaching. Learning is usually discussed in terms of the specific nature of the type of learning to be accomplished—i.e., cognitive, verbal, affective, perceptual, or motor. Of course all these, to a certain degree, are interdependent. Since a *primary* concern of the physical educator is motor learning, most of the following discussion will be directed toward the concepts and principles relating to the learning of motor skills. The terms "perceptual-motor skills," "sensorimotor skills," or "psychomotor skills" would be appropriate also; however, for the sake of convenience, the shorter terms of "motor skills" and "motor learning" will be utilized in the discussion.

Motor learning is defined by Bryant J. Cratty as "the rather permanent change in motor performance as observable, voluntary, goal-centered movement."[2] The focus is on gross motor or large-muscle movements rather than fine-muscle movements.

It must be remembered that in working with young children the emphasis is on motor skill development and refinement of fundamental movement patterns, and that maturation is a factor in improvement. Normal development and maturation provide the *potential* for skill to be developed. Improvement and proficiency in skills can only come about as the result of practice and experience. Therefore the teacher must structure the environment and provide guidance for best learning to occur at all age levels.

Our knowledge of how one learns is based on theories derived both empirically and experimentally. There is no one simple explanation of how motor skills are learned. The process of learning is the same regardless of the type of learning—cognitive, affective, or motor. There are many theories of learning, including the traditional learning theories and the more recently proposed neurological theories, information theories, and system development through study of educational psychology or experimental psychology. A number of physical educators have recently contributed theories and models of motor learning. Several references are included at the end of the chapter so that the reader may further study this topic. Because space does not permit discussion of them here, a very simple model of learning and a discussion of selected generally agreed-upon variables or factors which affect motor learning at various stages are presented, with some examples and implications for the physical education teacher. These should serve as criteria for organization of content, method, materials, and evaluative procedures.

Figure 4-1 presents a very simple learning model that will provide a framework for discussion of factors that inhibit or enhance the learning of a

[1] Madeline Hunter, "The Teaching Process," in *The Teachers' Handbook* (Glenville, Ill.: Scott Foresman, 1971), p. 146.

[2] In *Movement Behavior and Motor Learning* (Philadelphia: Lea & Febiger, 1964), p. 26.

Figure 4-1 Simple learning model.

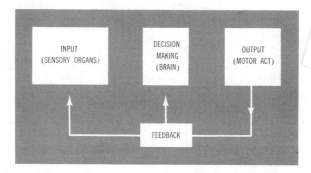

skill; these are things teachers must consider as they set and maintain a favorable environment in which students can learn. Descriptively, in the simplest sense, learners must know or receive what it is they are to learn (input). They must send this information to the central decision-making center (brain) where it is monitored or translated, and make a decision about action—the output is the motor act itself. This act or the results of it in relation to the goal are then evaluated and some form of feedback or error information sent back to the sensory mechanisms and the decision-making center.

Crucial at the *input* state is the nature of the input, the description of the goal itself, the information and how well it is received by the sensory mechanisms, and the encoding or transmission of it to the brain. The information transmitted to the brain is organized, stored, coded, or translated for the subsequent muscle actions. The actual decision making is influenced by past experience or knowledges (memory), and consequent transfer of learning, new information, and the predicted consequences of the act. Feedback is information as to how the skill was performed in relation to the goal; this is sent back to the receptors and the decision-making center.

Many variables contributing to success or lack of success in achieving the goal are operative at each stage. These variables have different levels of importance at different stages of learning skill.

Factors That Affect Learning

Sensory Input

What is to be learned in seeking to achieve a goal is received by the learner through the sensory organs of the body. The teacher presents the information through auditory, visual, or tactile stimuli. Learners have varying degrees of sensory capacities that may inhibit or enhance their ability to receive stimuli. The teacher must be aware of these as he or she learns the student's best mode of perception. Equally important is the learner's *perception* of the sensory stimuli—his interpretation of the sensory information. Individuals perceive quite differently. How one perceives is based on previous experience, interest, or motive as well as the directions given by the teacher, but a teacher's directions are more adaptable to change. Most perceptual abilities are the result of integration of sensations from more than one modality, and the development of this integration may be more advanced for some children in lower grades than others. Therefore the teacher must be aware of the variations in sensory capacities and in individual perceptual abilities, and utilize a variety of sensory cues within one sequence of input.

At the time of sensory input, the important factors for the teacher to be aware of are the understanding, the sensory abilities, and perceptual processes of individuals; therefore, presenting information through various modalities, helping learners focus on the most important aspects of the skill to be learned, filtering out unnecessary stimuli in the environment, and getting learners interested and motivated are of primary concern to the teacher.

Attention

The teacher must set an environment that helps the learner attend to the most pertinent and relevant stimuli he or she can process or encode and subsequently transmit to the brain for decisions and action. For best learning, the physical environment should be free of distraction such as noises, visual displays for other purposes, equipment not being used for the task at hand, etc. Many teachers find that children often have difficulty concentrating on learning when classes are held outside. Frequently, playgrounds are near streets where such things as passing cars, birds, dogs, wind noises, and interesting cloud patterns, to name a few, easily distract children.

Instructions or directions in any form must be clearly and concisely formulated so that they emphasize the most pertinent points to be processed. Beginners can handle only so much information and are apt to filter out most of a lengthy description. A sheer overload of information often causes them to fail to receive the most important information. Teachers should repeat and help the student focus on key words or use cue words for emphasis. When using visual input the teacher should have the learner focus on specific relevant acts, with the demonstration repeated several times. Often the student focuses on the results of the demonstration rather than the parts and sequences of the act itself.

Motivation

Motivation is often described as a state of need or desire to learn that prompts a person to do something that will satisfy that need or desire. This need is intrinsic—therefore, the teacher doesn't really motivate the learner; he or she manipulates environmental factors that may result in an increase or decrease of motivation. Examples of this kind of manipulation are the reward of a grade for good performance in the broad jump, or even giving no grade at all for a performance, thus reducing the tension or anxiety evoked by grades in some students. Some of the motivational factors that can be manipulated by the teacher to meet class or individual needs are the degree of arousal elicited, the feeling tone related to the task, interest in the activity, degree of success encountered, meaningfulness of the task, knowledge of results, goal setting, etc. Some of these will be discussed as they are commonly met within the physical education class.

AROUSAL LEVEL Sometimes the terms "arousal" and "motivation" are used synonymously, as are "anxiety," "stress," "tension," "level of aspiration." They all have something to do with motivation and are related via the learner's emotional state. It is obvious that an individual has to be "aroused" or at least have an "intent to learn." The degree of arousal itself may actually inhibit a person's learning because too much anxiety or stress may increase muscular tension when relaxation is needed. But if the learner is not aroused or has no intent to learn at the input stage, attention to the input will be minimal. Too often students present at a demonstration don't even perceive what it is they are supposed to do because of a lack of intent to learn.

Sometimes a state of anxiety elicited by factors other than the task itself are operative and therefore have a negative effect on learning. For example, a child's fear of water must be reduced before active instruction in swimming is begun. Even if the student wants to learn, muscle tension will inhibit the relaxation needed for an unsupported position in the water. Similarly, if children are afraid of heights, plans to reduce this fear must be initiated before they are given tasks to do on high pieces of equipment.

Actually, arousal level is too specific to the individual and to the task and situation for generalizations to be made. It is important for the teacher to recognize the importance of monitoring it for the sake of learning, safety, and enjoyment. Individuals tend to have arousal characteristics which the teacher should learn to identify, consequently modifying the instruction and environment to help the child adjust it toward the optimal.

INTEREST IN LEARNING   Students learn best and fastest when they have a purpose and interest in what they are learning. The teacher must recognize students' interests and incorporate them in planning. Very often teachers plan activities merely because they like them, assuming the students will also. Interest inventories can be made for even very young children, providing a base for later opportunities for choices in activities, use of pieces of equipment, themes for compositions, and programmed materials related to these interests. Teacher-pupil planning evokes more interest. Very often children introduce new activities to both their classmates and their teachers. Unrestricted choices may result in repetition, because some children, feeling comfortable and confident in a familiar situation, want to repeat what they know or do well. New interests and purposes can be formulated as an outgrowth of new experiences.

At the input stage pupils should identify purposes in learning specific activities—for example, in relating practice of skill to improvement of game play. Demonstration and explanation should include the ultimate purpose of the skill as it relates to game play, as should rules. Individualizing learning and responsibility for one's own practice and evaluation of results usually makes learning much more meaningful to the student. Interest and purpose are important at the input and decision-making stage.

GOAL-CENTERED LEARNING   Learners should know the goal toward which they are working. The goal should be reasonable and within the abilities of learners, yet challenging. Goals of varying degrees of achievement may be set so that students can select one and move at their own pace. If learners participate in setting the goal, they are more apt to understand it and work toward achieving it. Frequently when a new skill or game is introduced, teachers set goals that are actually the ultimate goals of the high performer in the game itself. Perhaps a film is shown of champions performing. This is often overwhelming for beginners or students who have little aspiration to be a champion but would like to learn well enough to enjoy playing the game at their own level. Even very young children can set goals with the teacher's guidance.

(All too often the teacher does not even mention goals!) Behavioral objectives are valuable for both students and teachers; if stated well and graduated in difficulty, they give students a clear picture of what they will be expected to do. Designing behavioral objectives also forces the teacher to analyze what is to be taught and helps focus on the important aspects of what he or she expects to be done. A good, clearly defined goal helps a person focus better on the most important and relevant inputs related to achieving the goal. It also helps in the decision-making process as the learner predicts the consequences of the action and uses prior knowledge related to the goal.

TRANSFER OF LEARNING Speed of learning new skills is somewhat dependent on how well one adapts and applies previous learning to the new task. Transfer of learning is not automatic; research has shown that skill learning is specific. Thorndike's identical elements theory suggests that when there are identical elements in a learning situation that are similar or identical to elements in a skill already learned, learning will be enhanced; dissimilar elements will hinder the learning. Gestalt theory supports the idea that a knowledge of basic fundamentals of movement will help one understand and learn new skills. This approach, however, still does not have conclusive research evidence. But theories have been proposed and research is continuing in the effort to discover the general and specific factors that affect skill acquisition.

Each specific skill may be unique, and only repeated practice and specific guidance may help one learn; however, there are also general perceptual, motor, and motivational factors that will help one learn a specific skill more efficiently and effectively. The importance of the concept of "learning to learn," or the process element of movement education, can only enhance the learner's ability to learn motor skills.

The teacher must help learners utilize the possibilities of transfer by drawing attention to similarities in known and new patterns and the basic principles operative in the new skill. Hopefully, as the teacher supplies the guidance to learners that enable them to draw on their memory banks, they will begin to "learn to learn" at the same time they are solving new motor tasks or problems. The teacher must analyze skills carefully to discover similarities and dissimilarities with other skills; suggesting similarities when they do not exist only interferes with learning.

SCHEDULING AND DISTRIBUTION OF PRACTICE Many research studies have shown that skill learning is best at the beginning stage, when practice periods are short and frequent. Often teachers plan to spend a whole period working on one skill. Beginners tire easily when the same movement pattern is repeated for very long. Sheer muscle fatigue sets in, making a student uncomfortable and promoting less chance of success and even the possibility of injury resulting from fatigue. At early stages of learning, many extraneous movements are used that cause early fatigue. Short rest periods seem to enhance learning. Age, maturation, and motivation also play a part in how long one can practice before fatigue or boredom sets in. The nature of the task plays a part as well. Tasks that call for a great deal of accuracy are learned more easily with frequent rest periods between practices. Once a skill is learned and at the refinement stage, the learner can practice longer, because he/she no doubt moves more efficiently and has more success.

If a new skill or concept is introduced one day, both practice and application of the concept or principle to similar but different tasks should follow within the next few lessons. Too often something new is introduced and then new tasks added to that with little opportunity allowed for practice or refinement; therefore, little actual learning occurs. Physical education programs often schedule a different activity every day or every lesson, ignoring this principle. Some teachers seem to feel that they must teach everything every year, thus failing to help children really learn and retain any one thing well—this might be called a smorgasbord approach.

WHOLE AND PART LEARNING   Educators have long wrestled with the problem of when it is more efficient to work with a *whole* activity and when it is more efficient to break it down into parts. A commonly accepted generalization is that instruction should begin with teaching the whole and then working on parts if necessary. Learning should be concerned with complete, meaningful units. Again, the real decision is dependent on the complexity of the task itself, the organization of the task, and the learner.

The task or skill must be analyzed to see what subparts of the whole are present, as must the dependency of each part and each succeeding part, and the temporal aspect of the skill. If the proper execution of a whole skill depends on proper execution of various parts, then each part must be practiced until it can be done efficiently and will no longer cause errors in the execution of the other parts. An obvious example of this is a swimming stroke in which there are independent arm actions, leg actions, and breathing actions which must be learned separately and then coordinated in order that the whole stroke may be done.

Some learners can perceive wholes better than others and can learn by the whole method much more quickly than others. To dwell on parts for long periods of time may inhibit learning for these people. If the task is presented as a whole and the learner has difficulty, the teacher should analyze performance and isolate the part wherein the error(s) occur and provide guidance in correction of the error and practice of that part.

Dance, sports, and games consist of many skills that are wholes in themselves. Many of the skills are learned as wholes long before they are used in the game or dance; however, the nature and demands of the game or dance dictate a new way in which the skill is utilized. In this instance, isolating a skill as a part is not necessary. It should be used in the situation or practiced in a simulated game situation rather than taught as a new skill.

FEEDBACK   Many people believe that feedback is one of the most important factors affecting learning. Fitts and Posner theorize that feedback has three functions: (1) to motivate, (2) to change immediate performance, and (3) to reinforce learning.[3] The importance of understanding its relationship to learning and the necessity for the teacher to make definite provisions for it cannot be overemphasized.

Feedback can be described as error information, the discrepancy between the learner's performance and the goal. It is more than knowledge of results.

[3] Paul Fitts and M. Posner, *Human Performance* (Belmont, Calif.: Brooks/Cole Publisher, 1967).

A learner can see when the ball misses the basket; hence, he or she has knowledge of results. However, he/she needs to know where the error occurred in the shooting pattern that resulted in the missed basket.

Feedback can be received internally or externally. Internal feedback is that which is provided by the receptors (proprioceptors) which provide the learner with information regarding the action. This is often called kinesthetic sense. The learner may say "that felt right" or "that felt good." Advanced players usually have better control of internal feedback than beginners. However, the teacher must be alert to a situation in which a student may think the action is wrong because he/she *thinks* it feels bad when in effect he/she has been doing it wrong so long that the correct action feels so different or bad.

Most feedback in physical education is external in nature and is usually augmented by the teacher, a partner, or some media after the act is completed (terminal feedback). More valuable might be error information given concurrently or during the action. The latter might be provided by verbal cues, manual guidance. In tumbling, the use of a belt allows the instructor to give feedback to the performer while he/she is in the air by pulling ropes that create pressure on the body part that should be bent or extended. More teaching aids are on the market now which apply pressure when body action or muscle tension is applied incorrectly.

The learner and whoever gives the feedback must first establish a reference point of correct performance so each has a source of comparison when the discrepancy between the desired patterns and the actual performance is assessed. Usually this is done through demonstration, pictures, movies, loop films. Videotape instant replays in physical education provide a quick, good source of augmented feedback and self-evaluation. Students can learn to use the TV equipment rather easily.

READINESS TO LEARN   The activities presented to children must be appropriate to their maturation level. Learners should have achieved the strength, endurance, and coordination necessary to do a task. They must be intellectually able to understand the purpose of the activity and the relationship of movements. If the activity involves other people, the social maturity of the learner must be consistent with the interpersonal relationships the activity demands.

The teacher must select content in terms of a continuity of experiences so that children within a class may tap in at their own point of readiness. Asking all children in the class to walk on their hands would be ridiculous if a number of them didn't have the shoulder strength to support their own weight. This should point out the need for the teacher to analyze the task in reference to pupils' abilities and readiness.

RETENTION   The best retention of a motor skill results from good initial learning and thereafter from overlearning. Overlearning is additional or continual practice after one reaches a level of performance set as the initial point of learning. The teacher should provide many opportunities for using skills in games and dance situations. Practice should simulate the game as much as possible. Practice should be encouraged outside of the gym period. Often students are not really given a chance to experience overlearning because the teacher introduces a skill one day and goes on to another the next day without ever returning to the first one. Conversely, many teachers do not recognize degree of retention and each year start an activity reviewing each skill pattern as if it were new. Skill patterns or sequences are seldom forgotten after a period of nonuse, but it does take some time and practice to regain the timing in use of the skill.

Stages of Learning

Recently theorists and researchers in motor skill learning have stressed the importance of understanding the stages or phases of learning skills. Fitts,[4] Gentile,[5] Lawther,[6] and Robb[7] have all contributed to this aspect, using different terms and emphasizing slightly different aspects of the stages. Full treatment of these ideas is not possible here, but some generalizations seem important so that a teacher can be aware of the relationship of some of the various factors already mentioned in relation to the stages of learning.

In the first phase of learning a new skill, the focus should be on helping the learner understand the sequence of the task or getting the gross general framework of the skill. Here the teacher's attention to task analysis, sensory input, awareness of the individual's perceptual abilities, clear, correctly executed demonstrations, concise, pertinent explanations, and the accompanying motivational factors regarding interest, attention, etc. must be very acute. This stage may not be lengthy, although of course some learners will grasp the idea more quickly than others. Once the learner has the general idea and understanding of the movement he/she moves into the next stage, that of practice of the skill. This is often called the fixation phase. This is when the learner refines the pattern and smooths out the temporal factors of the skill and the skill takes on a coordinated or controlled aspect. At this stage error information is extremely important, as are meaningful relevant practice opportunities. Practice periods can gradually be extended; verbal directions made more specific or detailed, with attention given to refining specific parts in order to smooth out the wholes; there can also be more self-analysis. This stage should last longer than the first stage. How long it will be will depend on the capacities and the interests of the learner. Too often the teacher does not allow enough time for this stage and many students have only a gross idea of a skill and actually gain very little proficiency in it.

The final stage is more of an automatic execution of the skill or diversification of the skill. The learner has fixated the skill to the point where he/she can more easily expect consistent performance and more easily adapt and diversify it to meet a variety of environmental factors. More attention can be given to detailed analysis of errors and more specific practice patterns. This

[4] Paul Fitts, "Factors in Complex Skill Learning," in Robert Glaser, ed., *Training Research and Education* (New York: John Wiley, 1965), p. 172.

[5] Ann Gentile, "A Working Model of Skill Acquisition with Application to Teaching," *Quest,* XVII (1972), 3–23.

[6] John Lawther, *The Learning of Physical Skill* (Englewood Cliffs, N.J.: Prentice-Hall, Inc., 1968).

[7] Margaret Robb, *The Dynamics of Motor-Skill Acquisition* (Englewood Cliffs, N.J.: Prentice-Hall, Inc., 1972).

advanced stage is seldom reached in physical education classes except in advanced classification courses. Often children gain experience outside classes and are at more advanced stages, but unless the teacher truly individualizes instruction, they are forced to start at stage one. With good elementary school programs, most high school physical education programs should be having instruction at the advanced stage.

The review of selected principles of motor learning with accompanying implications for planning, organizing, and implementing learning experiences only emphasizes the need to assess pupil readiness both in terms of maturation and in immediate terms. The physical/social/emotional relationship of individual differences and these learning principles accentuate the need for as much individualized learning as possible.

SUGGESTED REFERENCES FOR FURTHER STUDY

KNAPP, BARBARA, *Skill in Sport*. London: Routledge & Kegan Paul, 1967.

ROBB, MARGARET, *The Dynamics of Motor Skill Acquisition*. Englewood Cliffs, N.J.: Prentice-Hall, Inc., 1972.

SINGER, ROBERT, *Motor Learning and Human Performance*. New York: Macmillan, 1974.

STALLINGS, LORETTA, *Motor Skills Development and Learning*. Dubuque, Iowa: Wm. C. Brown, 1973.

5 / ALTERNATIVE TEACHING APPROACHES AND METHODS

- **Direct approach**
- **Indirect approach**
- **Insuring progress and quality in learning**
- **Communicating with the learner**

The terms "method," "approach," "style," and "strategy" seem to be used interchangeably to denote the procedure teachers employ to help students learn. For the purposes of this book, the word "approach" is used to designate a general way, mode, or style of teaching. One's approach reflects an attitude toward teaching and an understanding of how different children learn, as well as a procedure for teaching. The term "method" refers to a more specific procedure chosen to meet certain conditions and outcomes. "Techniques" refers to details of procedure and skills used to enhance execution of chosen methods. Many teaching techniques may be used in implementing each method or approach. They relate to organization, communication, diagnosis, etc.—for example, ways of asking questions, ways to give choices, ways to expedite distribution and collection of equipment, observing, designing tasks.

The particular approach and methods one chooses to use must be very specific for each teaching-learning situation. More than one method may be utilized within a single lesson. There are a number of factors, as shown in Figure 5-1, which must be considered before a method is selected: namely, the learning goals (teacher- and/or student-determined), the students' best learning styles, the students' readiness, the task itself, the teacher's values, the teacher's ability and knowledge, and the students' and teacher's personalities. How most of these relate to learning has been discussed previously, indicating that all of these factors exert more or less influence at any one time. It is imperative that the teacher have knowledge and skill in using a number of methods.

One does not learn *a* method, nor should one adopt a single method. We learn methods long before we actually become teachers. As learners we observe others teach; we know the types of teaching methods which help or hinder us; we reject or accept certain practices as we watch other students react to teachers. As each child is unique, so is each teacher, and each experiences greater or lesser success with different teaching methods.

This author believes that to denote a number of categories of specific teaching methods is unnecessary. In essence, teaching method is really a strategy of organization, presentation, and communication. A teacher preplans how she/he will organize content, teaching materials, and aids; what she/he will communicate and how; and what will be the role of the student and the teacher in the subsequent presentation.

Basically, there are two general types of approaches—direct and indirect—with varying degrees in between. The terms "teacher-centered" and "pupil-centered" might also be utilized, because they represent the ends of a scale that indicates the amount of dominance each has in determining roles and organization of the learning process. Figure 5-2 shows a continuum of alternate methods ranging from the extremes of directness and indirectness. It does not imply least desirable to most desirable, since appropriateness of method or approach depends on many variables.

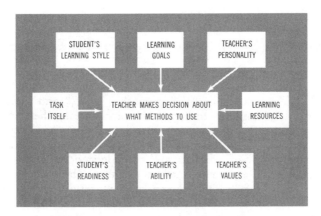

Figure 5-1 Factors that influence teacher's decisions as to what approach or method to use.

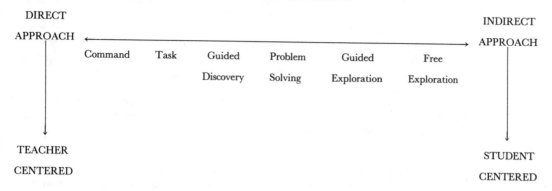

Figure 5-2 Continuum of alternate methods.

DIRECT
APPROACH

Command   Task   Guided   Problem   Guided   Free

            Discovery   Solving   Exploration   Exploration

INDIRECT
APPROACH

TEACHER
CENTERED

STUDENT
CENTERED

Direct Approach

The direct approach can be effective or ineffective, depending upon the teacher's knowledge of the learning principles previously presented and the factors (illustrated in Figure 5-1) that are operative in a particular situation. As indicated earlier, the distinguishing factor of the direct approach is the direct dominating role of the teacher. Personality, or what a teacher *is*, plays a big part in the success of this approach. Many teachers can employ this method successfully because their warmth and personal style turn students on to learning. But a teacher can turn off learning with a drill-sergeant type of barking commands directed to the group rather than to individuals.

There are advantages and disadvantages to a direct approach. The greatest disadvantage is that it does not allow for as much inventiveness and creativity on the part of the students. The goal rather than the learning process is the most important aspect of this approach. It allows little diversity of performance—yet we know that when working with young children, in whom the rate of maturation is so varied, one has to expect diversity. In its purest sense it certainly does not allow the objectives of self-actualization and self-responsibility to be realized. A direct approach is best employed when one particular skill is being learned, rather than many general knowledges and understandings in relation to a skill. Direct methods provide security for the beginning teacher, because children are working on the same aspect of a skill and are thereby easier to control and study as a group. It is also easier for a beginning teacher to establish a good progression from one aspect of a skill to the next. Some children respond better to the security of knowing exactly what they are to do and where they are going. At some stages of skill and movement learning, children do not understand how or what is to be done. Then a direct method is the most expedient way to help them. It aids some teachers who may at times have difficulty phrasing problems or questions that will lead to correct application of principles for safe and efficient performance.

It should be obvious that within this approach there could be many modifications and combinations of degrees of teacher control and modes of presentation; verbal, nonverbal, to an individual, or to a group. The teacher can give students increasing roles in organizational and temporal decision making, still retaining the key decisions of what is to be learned, the reference point of correct performance, specific directions, ways to practice, and feedback. Until he or she allows more freedom and responsibility for decisions about choices of content, diversity in performance level, goal setting, and self-evaluation, the teacher is still in this realm of directness and teacher-centered operations.

Descriptions and examples of a few selected methods should help a teacher see the move from very direct to less directive procedures and a more open, student-centered environment.

Command

The most direct method is that of command, wherein the teacher makes all the decisions: what is to be learned, how it is to be executed, all the organizational and temporal controls, and the quality expected. Students are expected to follow the directions and perform as the teacher has directed with no variations.

The following pattern describes teaching a specific skill using the command method. In physical education this has usually been termed the "traditional method" and in the past has been the one most commonly used.

The teacher briefly describes the skill and its use and then shows the class what the skill looks like in the context in which it is used. These two processes may be reversed. The verbal description should be extremely brief. The students then try to do the skill several times before any errors are pointed out or more explanations or directions are given. This step is then followed by more demonstrations and, if necessary, verbal explanation to enhance the student's observation. Then more time is given for practice. The teacher gives coaching hints to individuals who are in need, by pointing out and correcting errors. If the skill involves an object or an implement, demonstration, and/or explanation should be preceded by an opportunity for the students to become familiar with the object or implement to be utilized. Usually, a drill formation is set up so students can practice the skill in a prescribed manner. Before completion of the first learning session, some provision should be made for using the skill in a situation as close as possible to that expected when the skill is mastered.

A similar pattern may be followed in the presentation of games, dances, rules, and concepts, whether to a large group or to one student.

Task

In the task method, the teacher still determines what and how something is to be done. He or she releases some of the organizational decisions, such as location of where to work, temporal decisions about when to stop working, and at what pace to work. This allows pupils more freedom and responsibility in their work and practice and more social interaction in the class, but it does not allow them freedom of choice in what they do, or diversity in performance.

The teacher may verbally give a task to the whole class and each child responds at his/her own pace. Feedback may be given to the group as a whole or to individuals as they are working on a task. The teacher may design tasks and present them to the class or to individuals in written form. Tasks of varying degrees of difficulty may be designed wherein pupils may choose or be assigned those to meet their readiness. When a student is allowed to choose because of interest or makes his or her own judgment about readiness, the teacher is moving toward a more indirect style.

Task work can be undertaken by the individual who works alone and evaluates himself as the task directions indicate; or partners may work together with one doing the task and the other evaluating (reciprocal style or peer teaching); or a few students may work in a small group. Either the teacher presents the task to the group through demonstration and explanation and then the student works on the task, or the directions are written on a task card with appropriate visual aids available for resources. When the teacher designs a series of tasks to be completed by the learner over a long period of time and the student is more responsible for assessment, it becomes an individual program. This is a way of individualizing learning and does shift more responsibility and independence for learning to the pupil.

Tasks can be designed just to be completed, or to be assessed quantitatively or qualitatively. However, the teacher sets the standards for performance. (*Task cards* are described in Chapter 7.)

EXAMPLES OF TASKS

I. Tasks given to the whole class at the same time. Pupils execute in response to the task. The teacher may interject group feedback.
Teacher:
Jump on both feet, up and down, up and down.
Jump and turn.
Jump high, jump low.
Jump like a bouncing ball; bounce high, bounce low.
Jump forward—jump backward—jump in a circle.

II. Verbal tasks set for the whole class, each individual to complete task at own rate. Teacher moves around, giving feedback to individuals.
Teacher:
Task 1. Bounce the ball with your right hand 10 times; then switch to your left and bounce it 10 times.
Task 2. Bounce the ball with your right hand 5 times as low as you can, then 5 times as high as you can.
Task 3. Bounce the ball as many times as you can without losing control of it. Sit down in your space and remember how many times you bounced it before losing control.

III. Verbal tasks set for the whole class participating as partners. Pupils respond in movement at own speed, then wait for next task. Feedback and discussion may take place between tasks. Pupils get own partners, choose space to work in, and monitor own speed.
Teacher: Take a partner, find a space large enough to move freely and largely. One partner get down on hands and knees and make a bridge. The other person stand 10 feet away, facing partner's side.
Task 1. Run and jump over your partner without touching. Try it three times, using a standing 2-foot takeoff, then three times using a 1-foot takeoff.
Task 2. Run and go under your partner without touching. Try it three times.
Task 3. Run, jump over your partner without touching, come back by going under your partner without touching. Repeat three times.

When you have finished Task 3, change places and repeat the whole sequence. You may change partners when you are ready until a 5-minute signal is given. Try to improve your speed without touching your partner.

IV. Task presented on written card pasted to the Perception Box. Pupils are at different stations. They follow the tasks set at each station.

Task 1. Go through the box; go in red and out green.

Task 2. Using one hand and one foot, go in the diamond shape and come out the circle shape.

Task 3. Go through with a partner and repeat Tasks 1 and 2.

V. Task presented to be done in order as a floor exercise routine. Pupil repeats task sequence, trying to improve flow and quality of each task. *Sequence:*

1. Run four steps.
2. Do two forward rolls to a 2-foot balance.
3. Jump from 2 feet, do a 180-degree turn in the air.
4. Go into a headstand.
5. Do a forward roll.
6. Finish with a good two-point balance.

VI. Tasks presented on task card for each pupil. Pupil works to complete and record achievement at different levels. Card may be used during several class periods.

TASK CARD—ROPE JUMPING

	Level 1	Level 2	Level 3
1. Two-foot basic jump forward consecutively.	15	25	35
2. Two-foot basic jump backward consecutively.	15	25	35
3. Rock step (alternate landing on each foot) for 15 seconds.	15	25	35
4. Single hop for 15 seconds.	15	25	35
5. Go 10 yards skipping rope in less than	30 sec.	25 sec.	20 sec.

(When you have completed one level, go to the next. Cross lines through those you have completed.)

Guided Discovery

In the guided-discovery method, the teacher decides what skill or movement task is to be learned. He or she guides the student through a carefully planned sequence of tasks or questions oriented to each student's discovering a single predetermined answer or movement response. There may be diversity in how students discover the right answer as they make decisions concerning their responses, rather than the teacher telling them how to do it. Evaluation is built into each step, because students can't proceed from sequence to sequence unless each step is done correctly; this allows no failure. The teacher leads incorrect decisions back into the correct channel by redirecting questions or giving new tasks. This method encourages the important process of inquiry and allows diversity through exploration and experimentation to find, at last, a congruent answer.

Using the guided-discovery method is difficult for some teachers because it calls for careful analysis of the task and a carefully designed sequence of tasks or questions to help students discover the correct answer or response. The teacher must also have a great deal of patience because the answer must not be given to the pupil, but instead guidance and encouragement to *find* the answer. Sometimes this takes longer than expected.

EXAMPLES: GUIDED DISCOVERY

MAJOR FACTOR TO BE STUDIED   Development of the jump for height.

MAJOR CONCEPTS OR PRINCIPLES TO BE LEARNED OR REINFORCED   Landing on balls of feet to absorb shock, bending knees as you start the jump so that you can push off harder against the floor, a swinging upward with the arms to help you gain height.

PROCEDURE

1. *Teacher's questions and challenges:* Bounce up and down . . . lightly. . . . Point your toes as you go up. On what part of your feet do you land? . . . Jump up and land on your heels . . . now on the balls of your feet. . . . Which was the most comfortable? Do you bend your knees before you jump? Try it. . . . Did you go higher? Try again. . . . Do you bend your knees when you land? How does that help? How can you use your arms to help go higher? . . . Swing arms down and up! Does it help if your arms go high? How high? Stretch. . . . Does it help if you look at your hands high above your head? . . . Jump and reach as high as you can. . . .

2. *Discussion:* Summary of concepts that help increase height in jump, and absorbing force in landing.

The teacher may make references to the principles throughout this session through his questions and challenges. There need be no discourse between the teacher and the students except through movement. Carefully planned challenges, questions, and observations are required in order to correct errors in the use of force and direction.

OBJECTIVE OF LESSON   To learn to lift the ball to self using only one foot.

PROCEDURE

Teacher   With the ball on floor in front of you using one foot, lift the ball up in the air so you can catch it. With what part of your foot can you lift it up? Try it!

Expected Answer   Top part of the foot or behind the toes.

Teacher   How do you get the ball to that part of your foot if it is sitting still?

Expected Answer After Experimentation   Pull it back with bottom of foot.

Teacher   Where in relation to your body does the ball have to be?

Expected Answer After Experimentation   Right in front of the leg or foot you are using.

(Note that the teacher redirects answers or asks more questions until the expected answer is given or done.)

Teacher   Try to draw the ball back and then lift it straight up in the air. How do you cause the ball to come up high enough in the air to catch it? What other body parts do you use? . . . Experiment. . . .

Expected Answer   Ankle has to snap up quickly, knee bends.

After children try the skill some more, the class stops and the teacher asks the children to summarize the steps in getting the ball up to self. Body position, draw ball back so there is a backspin as the ball rolls onto foot, quick ankle snap, knee flexes, lift ball up and reach out and catch. Each one works on his/her own skill as the teacher encourages each to remember the steps they found.

Indirect Approach

The indirect approach at the extreme gives freedom and responsibility to pupils to set their own goals; to make a selection of content; to work on the content in their own way, at their own pace; to self-evaluate; and to select assistance from whatever resources, human or media, available to them. Limitations in each of these areas can be placed on the child as he/she learns how to handle this freedom and to use the necessary procedures. One disadvantage of this approach is that learning may not be immediately forthcoming, particularly learning of specific skills. Structuring good clear problems is a difficult task and requires a thorough analysis of what is to be studied. This takes time and practice on the part of the teacher.

Care must be taken that continuity and progress is built into a child's program. Sometimes using an exploratory or a problem-solving method seems easy to some teachers, because the pupils appear to do all the work. Actually, the teacher is much more involved because he/she must constantly be observing and alert for children who need guidance. Planning and preparing resources takes a great deal of pre-class time and work. When pupils have many choices, they sometimes prefer that which they know they can do well and like best. The teacher must be very aware of this tendency and encourage pupils to try new things or alternate ways. If children are not challenged or become frustrated because they do not have the tools or understandings to solve problems, behavior difficulties often occur.

The advantages of this approach are many. It does allow pupils freedom of choice along with responsibility and accountability. It gives them practice in problem solving and decision making. If process, development of self, and knowledge of one's body potential are major objectives of a program, one has to give pupils the opportunity to experience these things. The indirect methods do these much better than the direct ones. The teacher is freer to get to know individual students better and give students more attention. In addition, children can work within their own capacities and move at their own pace.

The terms "exploration" and "problem-solving method" are used interchangeably by some people, particularly those who work with young children in studying movement structure and in more generalized movement factors. Although they are both basically indirect and have some of the same characteristics, they also are unique in themselves. Their differences basically revolve around the limitations, extent of expected refinement, extent of freedom in seeking answers, and readiness of children to use the more complex problem-solving process.

Indirect methods are designed so that children can use a problem-solving approach to learning—that is, to have the opportunity to invent and improvise alternate responses to problems rather than coming up with a single predetermined answer, as occurs with direct methods.

Problem Solving   In the problem-solving method, the teacher designs a problem for a pupil, who is expected to come up with one or more solutions. The pupil uses the processes of exploration and experimentation in an independent manner as strategies to solve the problem. He/she uses known facts, skills, concepts, as he/she discovers relationships between them which will help find solutions. Problems may be of varying degrees of difficulty and have several subproblems. There may be alternate solutions; however, there may be one most appropriate solution with respect to the limitations of the situation in which the solution will be used or that which is best for the performer. Completing the problem-solving process by selecting the most appropriate solution further involves self-evaluation.

When designing problems, the teacher must carefully analyze the pupil's readiness both developmentally and experientially. Pupils must have the tools to solve the problem—i.e., facts, knowledges, skills. They must be ready cognitively to formulate possible solutions, then test them, and finally select appropriate solutions. First- and second-graders are not ready for the true problem-solving process. Problems should be those for which the pupil has no known solutions. When pupils choose between alternate solutions which are already known to them, they are practicing decision making and not problem solving.

Problems vary in complexity according to the number of elements or dimensions involved, number of people involved, and degree of open-endedness. "How many ways can you throw the ball into the basket?" does not provide for a true problem-solving method. It is exploration. It may precede a more limiting problem, such as, "Using one hand, select the way to get the ball through the hoop so that it hits on the backboard before going through the hoop." Perhaps the initial exploration will help a learner more quickly find the most expedient way to generate enough force to get the ball up to the backboard, decide on the angle of release of the ball, the point of contact on the board which will most likely result in the ball going through the basket.

The teacher's role beyond setting problems is to give help to the pupil, provide learning materials or resources for help when asked, have subproblems formulated to help those who cannot work as independently as others, help as best solutions are selected, and provide feedback and encouragement throughout the process. Obviously this method moves toward the indirect end of the continuum. When pupils are involved in self-analysis and goal setting, they may set their own problems or set them with the help of the teacher so that the method takes on an even more indirect nature.

Almost anything can be discovered through problem solving; specific skills, concepts, relationships, variations of known or specific skills, strategies, preferences of style, etc. Problems may have various limitations which make pupils refine and test the validity of their solutions. Limitations may be in the form of spatial demands, time factors, use of specific body parts, force, rules of games, equipment, etc.

A generalized pattern for teaching a new skill using the problem-solving approach is as follows. The skill is introduced by the teacher, who presents the problem in terms of what has to be accomplished by the skill. The class then experiments with solving the problem. After experimenting, the class and teacher observe classmates' performances, and discuss the progress. This provides a basis for evaluating one's own performance. Everyone practices in order to refine his/her skill while the teacher circulates and gives individual coaching.

The observation phase may vary according to the skill and the age level of the students. There is no reason why a movie or a demonstration by someone with previous knowledge of the skill cannot be utilized in a problem-solving approach. The important factor is that it be shown *after* the students have experimented with the skill and can therefore study the performance in relation to their own concepts and problems. The demonstration may be as provocative a stimulator as the teacher's questions.

While the class is experimenting with the skill, the teacher may structure a series of experimental experiences wherein the students will proceed to learn in the same manner as described earlier. Students are encouraged to discover the correct way for them to accomplish the goal and solve the problems rather than being given the solution. The teacher makes suggestions in questions and in comparisons gained from doing things in a variety of ways. Observation of others aids each child in evaluating his or her own performance and provides a basis for improvement or refinement of his/her skill.

EXAMPLES: PROBLEMS OF VARYING DEGREES OF DIFFICULTY

PRELIMINARY EXPLORATION

Teacher:
See how many ways you can get from one end of the beam to the other. Select three ways which are the *fastest* for *you* to use.
If you had to take a large ball with you, which would be the fastest?

PROBLEM   Throw the ball up straight, sit down and catch it while staying in your own space.

Subproblems or questions to help solve problem: Does the height of your throw have anything to do with it? What type of throw will help you control it most?

PROBLEM: MAKING A FLOOR ROUTINE   Select stunts or moves that fit the following limitations and those that will make a smooth transition between each move.

1. An inverted sideward movement
2. Two rolls
3. Flight
4. Inverted hand support
5. One-leg balance

6. A flexibility movement into
7. Roll
8. Locomotor movement on feet
9. Flight to
10. A high landing

MAJOR FACTOR TO BE STUDIED   Learning a specific sport skill for the game of floor hockey.

TASK   Receiving a pass on the run from a partner in hockey.

PROCEDURE

1. *Give challenge or problem* (Could be verbal or written on a task card or a program): With partner, experiment in receiving the ball on the stick when it is coming from backward left; from backward right; from in front of you.

2. *Teacher's questions:* Do you move to meet it? Where is your attention directed? Where is your stick in relation to your body? Where do you attempt to contact the ball?

3. *Pupils experiment and respond in action and verbally:* If the ball is traveling slowly, go to meet the ball without turning your back to the direction in which you are going to run. Keeping to the right of the ball, look over your left shoulder; keep the stick on the right side of the body, allow the ball to cross in front of your feet onto your stick on the right of the body. Look over your right shoulder, twist the body, and place your stick slightly behind and to the right of it, keeping it near the ground; angle the blade so that it faces the ball; "give" on contact and redirect the ball with a series of taps so that it does not cross to your left but goes ahead. Move to meet the oncoming ball, keeping your stick close to the ground and to the right of the body, with the blade squarely facing the ball. The body should be reaching forward slightly but on contact with the ball there should be a "give" in the body including your arms, which draw the stick toward you, keeping the ball slightly ahead and to your right.

Exploration

Exploration as a method takes advantage of the intrinsic interest in exploring and experimenting. The curiosity, joy, and involvement in self-discovery can lead a child into learning concepts and a better understanding of her/himself and movement. The teacher uses exploration when introducing new concepts, ideas, generalized skill experiences, in using new equipment, when eliciting original responses and ideas from students. When designing exploration experiences the teacher should design movement tasks that are broad in nature and open-ended. Pupils are encouraged to explore a variety of responses. Exploration falls into two categories: *free* and *guided*.

GUIDED EXPLORATION   As the word "guided" implies, some limitations are put on the responses, but for each limitation a variety of responses is encouraged. Usually the purpose is to institute exploration of broad movement factors, patterns rather than specific skills, or use and manipulation of movement factors. This method is used predominantly with primary-age children before they are able to truly use the process of problem solving. Through guided exploration, the teacher helps children discover with more individual results and freedom than in guided discovery, in which a predetermined answer or way to do something is predominant. For example, in studying and exploring general space, the task may be to "move about in any fashion, touching all the boundaries of the general space in a room." The pupil is free to use any type of locomotor action. Another example: "Move about the room, changing your base of support often." This implies a choice of ways to move and use of a variety of bases of support.

Exploration of a factor in this fashion may precede a more structured task with more limitations, or a problem for which the student will have to select the most appropriate use of the factor. For example, after exploring general space while moving in any way, a problem may be set up to follow a specific pattern in general space with the limitation of moving at a very low level. The student would need to experiment and select the best way. Previous exploration may have provided him/her with ideas and actions with which to further experiment and from which to start adapting to the situation.

EXAMPLE: STUDYING CHANGES IN LEVEL

Teacher:

Move anywhere in the room changing the level at which you move (the basic concept of level has already been explored).

In what way can you move across the room and be very close to the floor?

This time see how close to the ground you can move with only two parts of your body supporting you. . . . Can you change levels and using the same body movement be as far from the ground as possible? . . . Can you change from high to low or to a middle level as you move? . . . Change on the accent of the drum. . . . Is it hard to change levels without stopping your movement?

A demonstration and discussion follows of the various ways the children have explored and found the activity easier or harder to do. This is followed by a more specific limitation where they can still explore but can use some of the ways they have found in their exploration.

Teacher: Can you move like a machine that moves at a low level as it operates?

FREE EXPLORATION   When using free exploration, the teacher designs a task that allows pupils to work in any way they wish. The only limitation imposed may be for safety purposes. This is to encourage an endless variety of responses and the enjoyment of free, spontaneous movement. The task may be to "take a ball and a paddle and play with them together in any way you wish"; or "select a piece of apparatus and move across it as you wish." This allows pupils to get acquainted with various pieces of apparatus and equipment or with their own bodies as they try out various body actions. It also allows them to do things they may have learned before, perhaps varying them freely.

The teacher's role is to observe how children are moving, and determine if they are actually exploring or doing the same thing all the time. Some children need to watch others or have some pertinent questions asked of them to inspire their own thinking.

Creating routines, games, dances, or one's own tasks without limitations is a mode of free exploration. In the process of creating, one explores modifications of known things, varying relationships, trying out new ideas in a free atmosphere. In this sense students explore in a more sophisticated manner with encouragement from the teacher to try things out and come up with a unique product, process, or feeling after having the freedom to explore their own thoughts, interests, and desires.

Insuring Progress and Quality in Learning

When using an indirect approach, teachers must carefully sequence the type of learning experiences presented to children. Too often the indirect approach is interpreted incorrectly as all exploration or freedom to do what one wants to do. Progress and quality of performance is not always achieved, simply because there was no planning for it to happen.

Each time you plan a lesson, you must assess the particular stage of learning children have achieved, with respect to what is about to be taught. You must assess variables of the particular aspect of whatever it is you are going to teach, consider learning principles operative in the situation, and thereafter plan so that the present experience is an extension of what has gone before and further, will lead to something more challenging and fulfilling within the lesson and the lesson to come. In other words, you must sequence the types of learning experiences.

The information about learning taxonomies in relation to designing objectives (see p. 105) will give you a better background for understanding the concept of sequencing. A *sequence of types of learning experiences* in the context of using the indirect approach is described in the following paragraphs.

1. Exploratory Experiences

These are usually planned when something new is presented or something old is revisited and new ideas or ways of doing it are sought. Time must be allotted and tasks presented in an open way so that pupils get a *feel* for the idea or skill. When new equipment is used, time must be given to *explore* with it. Adjustments in how to hold it, the weight of it, what to do with it, usually occur only after the freedom to experiment, and no specific results are expected. At this stage variety and experimenting are encouraged.

2. Limitation-Discovery Experiences

After the exploratory or orientation experiences, guided exploration or guided discovery tasks with limitations are given by the teacher. Tasks should allow children to discover different ways to do the same thing and to adapt the way it is done to different limitations—perhaps in respect to time, space, direction—or to move with different variations. More specific limitations may be accompanied by observations and contrasts or comparisons of how the task can be done. Children can also begin to get a concept of how something can be done more efficiently and effectively as they begin to make some choices based on their understanding of how to do something.

3. Selective-Refinement Experiences

More limitations are set by the teacher, and emphasis is placed on improvement and refinement through repetitive and selective experiences. Tasks are made more challenging by the addition of more combinations of movements adapting to more and varied dimensions of movement; more relationships; different variables that make the task harder (e.g., different distances, angles, greater number of repetitions); selecting preferred solutions to meet personal interests and needs; selecting preferred solutions to meet demands of more specific problems, equipment, apparatus, rules. Learning experiences of this type may be quite a few in number and last longer than the previous ones. One may also return to this stage after the next stage.

4. Performance Experiences

Skills, ideas, and concepts are used in more challenging environments. Solutions to problems must be selected within structured games, dance activities, and gymnastic stunts and routines as well as self-designed games, dances, and gymnastic routines. More difficult movement problems may be given as a challenge. The emphasis is on using, adapting, and selecting from what one has learned. After this, the teacher could return to #3 for further refinement.

Not all of these types of experiences would necessarily be used within one lesson. Some would occur in the same lesson quite naturally—i.e., 1 and 2 and 3 and 4 together. It is possible that all four may occur in one lesson, but the degree of difficulty of the combination experiences and performance experiences would not be as great as usual, nor would the expectations of results. To stay at one level for a long period of time would indicate poor planning and low expectation levels of achievement or learning for children. Within one class, children may be working at different levels and could easily move back and forth from refinement or combination experiences and performance levels. Can you identify each of the stages in the following examples?

MAJOR FACTOR TO BE STUDIED   Quality of movement—running fast and stopping quickly.

MAJOR CONCEPTS OR PRINCIPLES TO BE LEARNED OR REINFORCED   Acceleration and maintenance of balance.

PROCEDURE

1. *Initial problem:* "Run anywhere in the room and stop when you hear the drum." (Allow several experiences of this.)
2. *Possible responses in movement:* Many children will take several steps forward before coming to a full stop; some will lose balance and fall; some will fall forward onto hands; some will shuffle feet to keep balance; some will use arms and body sway to keep balance; some will start slowly and anticipate beat of drum; some will have picked up speed just as drum sounds.
3. *Possible questions by teacher:* "What is our problem in stopping?" or more directly, "We seem to have a problem in coming to a full stop without taking some extra steps. What can we do about that?"
4. *Anticipated responses:* Bring weight back, lean back, keep feet under body, use arms to help, etc. Here the teacher may tell everyone to try some of these suggestions; or rephrase a few of the suggestions and tell everyone to try these; or be somewhat more direct and ask, "Can you stop with one foot ahead of the other? Can you bring your weight directly over your feet? Can you keep the upper part of your body erect?" Class then experiments with these suggestions. Some of the more direct questions might be asked only of those who indicated a need for them.
5. *Demonstration:* Select a few children who are stopping quickly with good balance. While others are observing, direct their attention to the position of the feet and the bent knees.
6. *More experimentation by children.*
7. *New problem:* "You want to get to the other side of the gym as quickly as possible, but you must stop every time the drum beats."
8. *Experimentation.*
9. *Teacher's questions:* "How can you get started more quickly? Will taking small quick steps and pushing hard against the floor help you start to run faster? Try it."

10. *More experimenting, practicing, and demonstration if necessary.*

11. *Summary of concepts about starting and stopping drawn from the children.*

12. *Introduction of game:* Red Light (p. 318).

It is obvious that before the lesson the teacher must analyze the two actions of stopping and starting as well as the skill of running. He or she must know what principles control the actions and be able to summarize concepts of starting and stopping, if he or she expects to help children learn to control this aspect of movement and learn the concepts of acceleration and balance.

MAJOR FACTOR TO BE STUDIED   Development of a jumping-rope routine with music (use a march recording).

PROCEDURE

1. *Initial problem:* "Everyone listen to the music then jump the rope trying to stay with the music. . . . Everyone jump with two feet together . . . moving forward. . . . Jump with alternate feet moving forward. . . . This time try going backward. . . . Can you go to the side and keep jumping in time with the music? Sit and rest. Let's listen to the music and listen for the changes of phrases. Clap when the phrase changes. . . . This time jump, and when you hear the phrase change your jump in a different direction. . . . Can you change level while you are jumping? This is pretty hard, but try it. . . .

2. *Demonstration and observation:* Watch Joe, Jane, and Jerry change level as the phrase changes.

3. *Setting of problem for individual routine:* "Everyone must make up his own routine. You must jump rope and include changes in direction, style of jump, and at least one change of level in your routine. You can work out and practice your routine for four minutes, then we'll watch the routines."

4. *Work period.*

5. *Presentation of routines:* Three or four at a time.

6. *Discussion and evaluation:* Were all factors included? Did changes occur as phrases changed? What routines were particularly interesting, why?

The preliminary work should have given children ideas for changes in direction, in level, and style of jump as well as the idea of changing as phrases change. Often it is helpful to give everyone the challenge of the same short routine prior to the assignment of individual routines. This gives them an understanding of the format of a routine. Rope jumping is quite exhausting, so discussion should be held frequently to allow a rest period.

This sequence of learning experience is comparable to a logical sequence when the direct approach is used: step 1 would be the orientation through explanation/demonstration; step 2 and 3, working on tasks or practice drills of increasing difficulty; then in step 4, playing the game, doing the dance, or performing the set stunts or routines. The advanced skills and practice of step 3 and performance of step 4 would be interchanged.

In teaching skills, there are several things the teacher should look for to learn whether or not the quality of the skill is improving. Does it appear that the child makes fewer errors? Does accuracy improve? Does control improve? Can the learner do the skill faster? Does the skill look smoother, have better flow? Is there consistency in execution? Is the child more relaxed? Are there fewer extraneous movements? Does the child express (verbally or nonverbally) satisfaction or pleasure in how he or she is doing?

While children are working at any of these types of learning experiences, the teacher works to help improve the quality of learning by motivating individual children through encouragement and praise; by stimulating variety in the exploratory and discovery stages, particularly; by having observations and demonstrations; by letting the children know that he/she knows what their limitations are and by acknowledging accomplishments no matter how small; by expecting improvement; by giving help; by redirecting tasks and questions.

Both the direct and indirect methods have advantages and disadvantages and various degrees of latitude toward the extreme. To use the direct methods is not wrong; but to use them exclusively is wrong. Because this book proposes that process (here defined as the ability to think and act autonomously) is content as students learn about both movement and themselves as movers, and that the major purpose of education is to develop a self-actualizing individual, methods which allow pupils to learn how to think and act autonomously and how to be responsible for their actions must be used. In other words, if learners are to learn to use problem solving, they must be given problems to solve; if they are to make decisions, they must be given decisions to make; if they are to be responsible, they must be given freedom and be held accountable for their actions.

The reader must be cautioned that pupils must "learn how to learn" when indirect methods are used, just as the teacher must learn how to use them. In the past, direct methods have been prevalent in both the classroom and the gymnasium. Many children have not had the opportunity to make decisions or to take responsibility for their own freedom. For some it can be a frightening and chaotic experience. Therefore the teacher may have to proceed slowly and cautiously as both he/she and the pupils experiment with new styles of teaching and learning.

The reader is encouraged to read Muska Mosston's book *Teaching Physical Education*,[1] in which he gives a theoretical analysis of teaching based on the concept of individualization. Mosston's analysis has made a fine contribution to physical education, identifying very specifically all the decisions that must be made within a lesson. He describes seven different styles of teaching that shift decision making from teacher to student in a progressive fashion. Each style is described in its own pure and perfect form (though it is doubtful that styles are ever used as specifically as they are described). Mosston also includes a large number of excellent examples of how to teach physical education activities using each style. His later book, *Teaching—From Command to Discovery*,[2] is also excellent in its descriptions of the teaching styles as they are related to all subject areas.

The teacher must be cautious in using indirect methods with retarded, emotionally disturbed, hyperactive, and learning-disabled children who may be mainstreamed into the regular classroom. These children most often have difficulty coping with a great deal of choice and freedom, and may function better in a structured environment. Smaller increments of freedom and more

[1] Columbus, Ohio: Merrill, 1966.

[2] Belmont, Calif.: Wadsworth, 1972.

gradual involvement in making choices and decisions will have to be planned for them in their individually prescribed programs.

Teaching and learning both are a continuous relationship between the learner, what he/she is trying to learn, and the teacher's guidance. In order to maintain this relationship, there must be communication. The teacher must communicate what is to be learned, how the learner can proceed to learn it, how it is done, what the quality of the performance is to be, how well the student has done, errors that have been made, encouragement, reinforcement, acceptance, etc. Students communicate their interest in learning, their understanding or lack of understanding of what they are supposed to do and how it is done, how well they can do it, when they want help, their satisfaction, their joy, etc. Obviously in most of these there has to be a sharing, a direct interaction in some mode of communication. Both student and teacher must be able to deliver and receive. Both communicate verbally and nonverbally. Teachers and students can converse directly or through media. In any event, both have to give input to the media and receive through the media.

Recently much attention has been given to the analysis of interaction between the teacher and pupil. Most research has been done with verbal interaction, yet there is growing recognition that nonverbal communication (conveying information without words) is as important to learning as verbal. Because space does not permit a lengthy discussion of verbal and nonverbal communication here, several references are suggested for more in-depth reading about the topic and the use of some of the systems of analyzing verbal and nonverbal interaction between the student and teacher in the classroom and the gymnasium. Guidelines for use and practice of verbal and nonverbal techniques as they usually operate in the physical education class are discussed in the following pages.

Guidelines for Verbal Communication

When using an indirect approach, the teacher should phrase tasks in an indirect manner through questions, challenges, etc. He/she should use approaches that will challenge the children without giving them the feeling they are being commanded. Actually, the same is true of some of the direct methods also. Some phrases appropriate to shift the direct statement "*Throw* the ball so it hits the center of the target on the wall" to indirect are:

- Can you throw the ball so . . .
- Who can throw . . .
- How can you . . .
- Try to . . .
- What other way can you . . .
- Will you . . .
- If you . . .
- With two hands can you . . .
- Could you . . .
- How often can you . . .
- Find a way to . . .
- How else can you . . .
- How many times can you . . .
- Can you add more?

Using words that convey action pictures helps the learner better understand specific acts—for example, swish the racquet, reach for the sky, land like a kitten, shake hands with the racquet, spring like a jack-in-the-box, blast off, etc.

The quality of the teacher's voice is important. The voice is a teaching tool—not in the sense of what is said, but *how* it is said, including the tone and the inflections used. We can attract as much attention by speaking very softly as by speaking loudly. Sometimes teachers overstimulate children in their own excitement as revealed through their voice. Fear is often conveyed by the pitch of the voice, as is calmness and enjoyment.

Regardless of the method utilized, there is some verbalization in every lesson; however, it should be kept to a minimum. The explanation sets the stage for the kinesthetic concept of the particular skill or activity to be taught. A few considerations concerning length, use, and timing of directions are discussed here.

Be sure that everyone is listening before proceeding. A definite signal should be established which signifies, "Stop, look, and listen!" This may be the use of: a command such as "freeze" or "statues"; a beat on a drum; a chord on the piano; or a whistle. The use of the latter is discouraged, since the whistle is also used for starting signals and indication of infractions in games. Do not expect children to be absolutely quiet immediately. It takes a few seconds to complete a sentence, to catch one's breath, and to sit down. Beginning teachers might practice counting to 20 before starting to speak.

Teachers should stand in a position so that everyone can see and hear them and so that they can see every student. Teachers should use a vocabulary that is meaningful to the students, without "talking down" to them. If a new term is introduced, explain it, have pupils repeat it, and then use it.

Be familiar with what is to be said, so it is not necessary to repeat or say something another way in order to be sure everything is included. Summarize and repeat only key phrases or words that children need to use and remember in the skill. Be sure to do this after getting responses from children, since frequently they do not speak loudly and clearly enough for the others to hear.

The initial introduction to a skill or activity should be brief but inclusive enough so that it is preparation for what is to come. Detailed explanations or directions before students have tried a skill are useless, as they have no reference point for understanding. Include only the key words or actions that are essential to starting the activity. A demonstration may accompany a few words of explanation. Other visual aids may also be helpful, such as diagrams of foot positions or of step patterns, pictures, etc.

Watch and analyze the initial experimentation with the skill or task. If a large percentage of the class is having problems with the same things, ask a question or make a suggestion that will help everyone. If problems seem to be of an individual nature, help those children to analyze the sources of their errors.

Guidelines for Nonverbal Communication

Nonverbal communication is talking without words or using body language instead of words. The old adage "actions speak louder than words" is often true because our facial expression and body gestures often get the message across more strongly than words. For example, we may praise a youngster, but if our expression or posture is one of disinterest, the insincerity of the praise comes across to the child. In a crowded class little signs of recognition of praise or just awareness of one as an individual by a smile, a nod, or a body gesture can establish rapport, motivation, and reinforcement.

With our facial expressions, gestures, dress, postures, and body gestures we convey feelings and attitudes. An absence of these when they are expected also conveys feelings and attitudes. Teachers should learn how to use these in a positive manner to communicate to students; they should also learn how to read these same actions in the students.

We can use nonverbal communication to get specific information across to students. Most often, demonstration of some type is utilized in teaching movement activities. This can take many forms.

Some people learn better from a visual input than a verbal input. This is often reflected in children's cries of "show me how to do it." In the popular play *My Fair Lady*, Eliza Doolittle, in frustration, sings to Professor Higgins, "Words, words, words, all I hear is words. *Show* me, show me *now!*"

A demonstration may take various forms and be essential at various times. The major difference between the traditional and the problem-solving approach is the placement of initial demonstration. In the former it precedes the student experiments and in the latter it follows them. The latter may include choices of which form of demonstration the student wishes to view and when he or she needs or wants to view it. The demonstration used in the exploration method must be contributed by the class, not by the teacher.

A demonstration is used for a variety of reasons:

1. It may serve as a model from which a student gets the original conception of what is to be done.
2. It may be used to illustrate the use of the skill in a game, dance, or routine.
3. It may serve as a motivating factor.
4. It may be used to compare similarities of skill patterns, or to portray varying forms or styles.
5. It may show what has been learned.
6. It may be used for self-evaluation and making comparisons.

Demonstrations may come from a variety of sources including:

1. The teacher.
2. A student or several students in the class.
3. A highly skilled performer.
4. Someone in the process of being taught a skill or stunt if no one is able to do it before the instruction takes place.
5. A group or squad showing how skills are used to advantage in specific games, dances, etc.
6. Movies, loop films, filmstrips, pictures, posters, and diagrams.

Emphasis should be placed on the technique involved rather than the results of the skill, unless the purpose is to see the results. For example, if demonstrating a throwing pattern, throw the ball to the wall so students will not become more interested in how far the ball goes rather than how it is thrown.

Since each child will notice something different in the demonstration, it should be done several times, and immediately after the demonstration, opportunities for practice and participation should be provided, unless the demonstration was that of learned material and is a culminating event of the class session.

There is no advantage in having a highly skilled person demonstrate for those who are learning a skill for the first time, since their concept of the skill will be quite general. However, any demonstrator must be adept enough to *employ the correct mechanics,* and the skill must be performed at the tempo normally used. When children are asked to demonstrate, do not ask the same ones to perform repeatedly.

Guidelines for Asking Questions

The use of questions for either verbal or nonverbal responses can be a powerful teaching tool. How valuable they are depends upon how well they are formulated, how appropriate they are to the intended purpose, and how they are presented. We use questions for

1. Clarification of directions
2. Getting attention
3. Reinforcement of facts, knowledges, ideas, concepts
4. Evaluation
5. Helping pupils construct knowledge
6. Encouragement of expression
7. Helping children find personal meaning and relevance in movement

There are a number of common errors teachers make in asking questions:

1. Giving indefinite or vague questions ("Are there any questions?" rather than "Are there any questions about the starting procedure?")
2. Asking questions requiring only a yes or no ("Was that hard?" "Did that feel good?") rather than adding a *why* to each.
3. Asking questions in succession without giving students time to answer, or asking run-on questions with no time given to answer one before the next two or three are given, thus losing students' interest and/or attention ("Did you have any problems . . . if not, we'll go on to the next step.").
4. Evaluating each answer rather than leaving answers *open-ended* so other children can add to them or disagree.
5. Asking only low-level thought questions.

Questions should be formulated to elicit responses at different thought or learning levels. Following is a taxonomy of levels of questions related to levels of learning.

LEVEL I: KNOWLEDGE—MOTOR MEMORY Simple recall and/or recognition of facts, directions, terminology, rules, patterns; recognition and reproduction of patterns or skills.

Examples What are the dimensions of personal space? General space? What are the violations in basketball? What does the schottische pattern look like?

LEVEL II: CONVERGENT THINKING—ACTIONS Applications of knowledge, integration of facts and principles from game to game, applying concepts to a similar movement. Leads to one expected answer.

Examples What fundamental movement pattern is used for the volleyball serve? What is the most stable base of support? Show me.

LEVEL III: DIVERGENT THINKING—ACTION   Use of knowledge to generate own idea, change knowns, and create own patterns or sequences.

Examples   What ideas do you have about making a Christmas dance? How could you change the game to make it more challenging?

LEVEL IV: EVALUATIVE THINKING—ACTION   Deals with matters of judgment, value, choice.

Examples   What position do you think you should play based on what your best contribution to the team would be? What do you think our next step should be? What would happen if . . .?

There are a number of ways in which teachers may elicit responses both verbally and in movement:

- *Solitary response*—Designate pupil by name, then ask pupil the answer.

- *Controlled response*—Pose question, then designate pupil to answer.

- *Uncontrolled response*—Present a question with no designated responder.

- *Spontaneous response*—No questions are asked or any designated to answer. Pupils freely comment or ask questions in direct response to teacher's comment or an activity. Usually follows an uncontrolled response.

- *Mass response*—A number of pupils respond to a question simultaneously (used most often when expecting answers in movement if using guided discovery or exploration).

The teacher asks many questions when using indirect methods. Each individual responds in movement with his or her own answer. These may be a discourse between class members. To insure progressive learning, questions and learning experiences must be designed at each of the learning levels. Only in this way can the teacher help children *construct knowledge about and of movement.*

Guidelines for Observations

Both teachers and students must learn to observe the performance of others accurately and fairly. The teacher's observation throughout the lesson permits him or her to evaluate the work on current problems, and the general progress of the class, and helps in setting up new problems and planning for future tasks. Considering each child's performance gives the teacher an idea of his or her readiness to learn and provides a base from which to alter expectations and individualize objectives and practice opportunities.

Keen observation is based on prior knowledge of what is valued in performance. The teacher must have a standard established which concerns quality, efficiency, and variety. He or she may recognize potential problems in the way a skill is performed, for example, or by the fact that certain necessary steps are omitted from the performance.

Since demonstrations are designed to improve understanding of skills and movement patterns, children need guidance in their observations. Specific factors to be aware of may be stated before the demonstration and then discussed afterward, or the demonstration may precede the questions, and in this way observational powers may be checked. As the demonstration is underway, the teacher may ask questions or give cues to focus attention on specific phases of performance.

Following the observation, a short discussion may be held, or children may immediately practice what they have learned from the observation. Comparisons of styles and quality may be made. Discussion of the latter must be guided discreetly.

Observation of others may give the shy or slower youngster a springboard for action. A new variation of a task may stimulate further exploration or experimentation by the rest of the class. An opportunity to return to the task or skill should be given immediately after the observation and/or discussion unless the purpose was to see culmination of efforts in performance.

Guidelines for Group Evaluation

Evaluation within the daily lesson is a vital part of the teaching/learning process. The teacher's role is to involve individuals in self-analysis, and the students in a critical analysis of the status and progress of the class as a whole.

The group evaluation need not be long or involved. The critical aspects are timing and the teacher's ability to focus attention on the most important facets of the matter. Most frequently, the last few minutes of the lesson are reserved for group evaluation. This also serves as a culmination of the lesson, a period to relax, a group-unifying process, and a planning period for the next lesson.

The teacher may prepare for the evaluation by making a comment regarding the purposes of the lesson or emphasizing what was to be accomplished in the working period. He/she may ask a pertinent question, or make comments to provoke leading questions from the students. Through class discussion based on personal participation and observation of others during the working period, the class members can appraise their progress or lack of it, and agree on what must be done to improve.

As stated, a demonstration may precede or accompany the evaluation. It is possible that no discussion is necessary when self-evaluation is the primary purpose of the demonstration. The teacher may offer a few pertinent questions or remarks to guide individuals in making comparisons of various performances. Afterward, pupils should be free to put their analyses to work in improving their own tasks.

Immediately following the lesson, the teacher should do a self-evaluation of the lesson. Following are a few questions that may be asked:

1. Were the objectives of the lesson accomplished? If not, why?

2. Were all of the students actively involved in the lesson?

3. What resulted from the lesson and the student's evaluation that should be incorporated in the next lesson?

4. Was there any particular behavior or improvement in an individual of which I should make special note?

SUGGESTED REFERENCES FOR FURTHER STUDY

ASSOCIATION FOR SUPERVISION AND CURRICULUM DEVELOPMENT, *Perceiving, Behaving, Becoming,* 1962 Yearbook. Washington, D.C., 1962.

BARRETT, KATE, "The Structure of Movement Tasks," *Quest,* XV (January 1971), 22–26.

BILBROUGH, A., and P. JONES, *Physical Education in the Primary School.* London: University of London Press, 1963.

COPE, JOHN, *Discovery Methods in Physical Education.* London: Nelson and Sons, Ltd., 1967.

DIEM, LEISLOTT, *Who Can.* Washington, D.C.: American Alliance for Health, Physical Education and Recreation, 1977.

GALLOWAY, CHARLES, *Teaching Is Communicating: Non-Verbal Language.* Washington, D.C.: The Association for Student Teaching, Bulletin #29, 1970.

GILLIOM, BONNIE CHIRP, *Basic Movement Education for Children: Rationale and Teaching Units.* Reading, Mass.: Addison-Wesley, 1971.

LANDERS, DONNA, "How, When, Where to Use Demonstrations: Suggestions for the Practitioner." *Journal of Physical Education and Recreation* (January 1978), pp. 65–66.

MOSSTON, MUSKA, *Teaching—From Command to Discovery.* Belmont, Calif.: Wadsworth, 1972.

———, *Teaching Physical Education.* Columbus, Ohio: Merrill, 1966.

6 / ORGANIZING FOR LEARNING AND TEACHING

- Individualized instruction
- Concept learning
- Objectives
- Practice of skills
- Effective use of equipment and space
- Grouping within the class
- Facilities, equipment, and supplies

Once the program objectives and scope and sequence of the general content for the program are established or identified, planning and organizing for implementation begins. The teacher will have to sequence specific activities to be taught, develop alternative learning experiences, develop materials and resources, plan use of facilities and space, decide on the evaluative criteria and the means by which the child's needs and readiness for tasks are ascertained, and determine whether or not the child has achieved the objectives after the learning experiences. However, there are a few things that must be considered before the teacher goes ahead with the selection of specific content and the organization for the program.

Since the primary goal of education is in essence the development of individuality, the need for individualized instruction is well-supported. All educators accept the fact that children vary tremendously in their biological constitution and mental and physical capacities; they come to school with different experiences, interests, motivations, behavior patterns, and styles of learning. If children are to become competent and self-actualized, they must have experiences which allow them to think independently, to make choices, to plan, and to evaluate. The ends and the means are interwoven.

Few teachers would deny the desirability of individualizing learning; however, most do not know how to accomplish this, especially in situations in which the pupil–teacher ratio is high, materials and facilities for individual choices are not readily available, and the teachers themselves may not have encountered this type of learning situation.

The teacher must know what individualized instruction *is* and what it is *not*. Individualizing is not a method of instruction. It is a way of managing or organizing children, materials, equipment, and facilities so that each child can learn at the peak of his or her potential in a manner that is productive, appropriate, pleasant, and rewarding. It can have varying degrees of structure. It is a process of adjusting learning to the student. It is not, as is commonly thought, a one-to-one ratio of teacher and pupil or tutorial situation. Individualized learning can and does take place in such a setting, but it more often takes place in a small- or large-*group* setting. Each child is different, but children also share some characteristics; some will need and want to do the same things in the same way at the same time.

A few key elements distinguish individualized instruction. Because of differing abilities, interests, and past experiences there will be different activities and diversity of expectations within the same class period. The teacher must plan a continuity of experiences in which the activities are open-ended—in relation to the time in which they are performed, the speed at which learning must take place, and the ways in which learning is presented and evaluated. Planning allows continuity, a continuous progress in a direction that accommodates increasingly challenging and demanding tasks, although the steps may be small or large, depending on the individual.

Essentially, individualizing requires the teacher to encourage individual interests, learning styles, and responses. Teachers take on new roles as they become less directors and dispensers of knowledge and more diagnosticians, facilitators, arrangers of space, materials, groups, and tools. They should become co-designers, contributors, reactors, guides, helpers, and a resource to the pupils.

Since the thrust of this book is toward a humanistic curriculum, we will assume that the teacher will employ humanistic philosophies in the conduct of these roles. Frequently the terms "humanistic" or "personalized instruction" are used rather than "individualized instruction." The ideas and suggestions for implementing individualized instruction in a humanistic and/or personalized manner are especially workable for teachers who meet children in large diversified groups in which organizing for various stages of self-directed learning becomes a real challenge.

"Learning to learn" is a commonly used term implying an emphasis on teaching children basic skills and basic tools to learn—i.e., processes. It takes children a long time to acquire these skills. The term also implies that teachers must patiently design learning experiences that require children to *practice* and *use* these skills. Children learning how to learn as they move toward becoming *self-directed* and self-actualizing will be able to

1. Set goals for themselves—sometimes alone, sometimes with the help of teachers and/or peers.
2. Determine what they need to do to reach goals.
3. Determine what resources will help them.
4. Know where to find resources and how to use them.
5. Accept help and guidance from others.
6. Try out new ways of learning and working with others.
7. Evaluate progress toward goals.
8. Recognize if goals are realistic or unrealistic and reset them if necessary.
9. Evaluate end results and total process.
10. Gain new insights into self and become further able to set new goals or projects to be completed.

Giving Students Choice

If the goal of education is for children to become self-actualized individuals, then the stress in school programs must be upon independence or freedom. Responsibility accompanies freedom. Responsibility and self-direction are learned, and are acquired only through experiences. It is the teacher's role to see that children learn to handle their independence in an increasingly responsible manner. They must be given choices.

Self-selection of *program content* does not imply *random* selection, but *responsible* selection. Providing students the opportunity to make choices of content without self-evaluation or teacher-evaluation and subsequent goal setting would not be responsible teaching. Deciding on what game to play, what topic to pursue, questions to study, or skills to practice should be a result of self-diagnosis, or one-to-one pupil/teacher or group/teacher discussion and evaluation. Thus alternatives may be available rather than authoritarian decree or arbitrary assignment, yet a continuity of learning is assured.

We know that students learn more readily when they see purpose and meaning in what they learn. If they set learning goals, they can also select what to learn in order to achieve these goals.

When one refers to student choices in learning, one must remember that there are different *types* of learning, and students make choices in each type in varying manners. Some of the different types of learning follow.

1. Learning in which students have no real choice of *what* they learn—i.e., the tools of learning—basic concepts, fundamental movement patterns, processes, strategies. The teacher or more likely a curriculum committee decides what is essential for everyone to know. Specifically, one must look to the structure of movement and include opportunities for children to *learn* and to *use* the elements of movement, the physical laws of motion, the

principles of human movement, the principles of exercise, and the great variety of efficient and creative ways of moving and communicating with others. The actual activities used are vehicles for learning this content and are many and varied. In this type of learning students do not select basically *what* they learn but provisions should be made for their selection of how they learn, at what rate they learn, how well they learn, and through what activities they learn.

2. Learning in which students choose to *expand* and *enrich* their knowledge, skill, and appreciations. This may be in the order of choices within a class, of advanced courses, intramurals, interest clubs, electives, learning labs, etc.

3. Learning in which students choose to *use* their tools and knowledges as they see fit. This may be in the nature of recreational choices, teaching others, competitive experiences, outside of school experiences, etc.

In the second and third type, learners select what they learn as well as the how, when, where, why, how well, etc. They are interested in learning more about many things, in expanding their knowledge or skills, improving, creating, using, sharing with someone else. They may choose to work alone, in a group, with a partner, against someone, or for someone. These various types of learning can occur in a regular class, after school, in independent study, in a learning lab, or in the community.

Even at an early stage in the acquisition of concepts about movement structure or fundamental skill patterns there can be student selection of content. For example, if the broad concept of weight bearing is being studied, students could decide to work on this through experimenting on the horizontal bar, the floor, on ropes, with objects of various weights, or dual stunts such as the angel balance. The gym could be arranged so that all this apparatus is available at different stations or locations. Even with this variety, the same concept is being explored.

There is no best structure in any of the disciplines nor one best sequence in skill development. As has already been mentioned in the discussion of concept learning in physical education, there is no universally prescribed set of concepts or necessary order of presentation. Facts, principles, and related aspects basic to physical education are identified. There is a multitude of activities through which these can be studied and learned.

Teachers must be able to diagnose each student's position in a continuity of concept and skill acquisition and differentiation of movement tasks. They must be alert to each student's status, and where they encourage choices, be a guide or a partner-consultant in the student's choice. Self-selection of program content eventually may be manifested in elective courses, interest clubs, after-school activities, open labs, advanced courses in selected activities, participation in community activities, independent study, and so forth.

Learning is very personal. Although many people believe that the teacher is responsible for learning, it is truly only the learner who is responsible for his/her own learning. Perhaps it is more true to say that the teacher is responsible for helping the learner *become responsible for* his/her own learning.

Learning theory has provided us with a knowledge of individual differences in learning styles and patterns. We know that the sensory modalities influence the learning styles; in addition, each learner has different motivational patterns. Because we know that children have different learning styles, that most people become more interested in doing something when they have a chance to make their own choices of what and how to do it, and because a primary objective is to develop decision-making ability, it is imperative that alternate ways to learn be offered. This may involve identifying what is to be learned, goal setting (behavioral objectives), and then a choice of ways to learn. The teacher should have available different materials and equipment such as audiovisual aids and library resources; groups may be formed on the basis of mutual interests and help—human resources. Most of these alternatives can be provided within each lesson.

What the teacher does to help students see what it is they need to know *before they make a choice* is of utmost importance. Before a truly "open gymnasium" is possible, both the teacher and the student should develop the skill and personal security needed for independence. The teacher's responsibility is to make students aware of alternatives when they make their decisions and to provide a variety of ways to do things. For example, if the task is to develop a sequence of movement on a piece of apparatus using an approach, mount, flight, balanced position, change in body shape, and a low dismount, the following things may be available: various pieces of apparatus, the teacher for help or evaluation, loop films of a variety of stunts, videotape for self-analysis, work with anyone else in the class, books with pictures, and the help of an older student or more experienced gymnast.

Where children have not had earlier opportunities to make choices, they will have to *learn* to do so. The teacher may begin to initiate choices by allowing choice between two things, and gradually introduce more and more opportunity for student independence. A small portion of a period or one day a week may be set aside as a time for choices. (The reader is referred to Dick Hurwitz's article entitled "Give Students a Choice" for more ideas and practical suggestions for a variety of ways of providing choices.[1])

Concept Learning

"Concept" means many different things to people. Here, the term will be used as described by Ashel D. Woodruff, denoting that individuals have organized understanding and meaning from what they have perceived and experienced.[2] It may be that they synthesize and draw conclusions about something after a number of related experiences. Concepts vary in degree of depth and value for individuals; they may be at a very simple and concrete level or at a highly abstract one. For example, the concept of endurance as experienced through pain or inability to continue an activity is very concrete; but the concept of the feeling of exhilaration from a particular experience of movement is very abstract.

Concepts function in many ways: as shortcuts to communication; as essentials to true comprehension; as aids to transfer of learning; as valuing

[1] In *Journal of Physical Education and Recreation*, 48, no. 5 (May 1977), 28.

[2] "The Use of Concepts in Teaching and Learning," *The Journal of Teacher Education* (March 1964), pp. 81, 84, 89.

dimensions in developing attitudes, opinions, and personal behaviors; and as aids to anticipating and avoiding problems. It must be emphasized that one does not teach concepts as such. Because the actual acquisition of concepts is based on personal perception and organization as a result of experiential interactions between learners and their environment, one teaches *toward* the *acquisition* of concepts. Vincent C. Arone lists several points the reader should keep in mind in working with concept development:

1. Concept development requires the reorganization of experiences; concepts therefore are constantly open to change.

2. They develop slowly from facts and information moving from specifics to abstractions.

3. They develop at different rates for different individuals.

4. Varied experiences do more to promote concept development than does repetition of the same experience.

5. Concepts vary in degree of depth, accuracy, emotion, and value.

6. They develop from noting similarities and differences of known concepts.[3]

Concepts may serve as unifying themes for instructional modules or the basis of resource units. The concepts may serve as instructional objectives or objectives may be defined from concepts. Where specific concepts are utilized as unifying themes, behavioral objectives, appropriate content, learning materials, learning experiences, and evaluative tools may arise as one insures a continuity of learning in physical education.

Even when concepts are not the basis of selection of activities, the teacher should stress concepts inherent in the specific activity being learned. For example, there are certain concepts of strategy inherent in field hockey, ice hockey, soccer, floor hockey, basketball—yet the games vary considerably. The basic concept of defense in basketball is much the same whether it is zone, one-to-one, or a specific play utilizing one type or the other. There are basic concepts about passing in the above-mentioned games, yet there are many *styles* of passing. Students should be taught to identify the basic concepts inherent in each style and to make selections using each based on these concepts. As children develop patterns of social behavior, the emphasis should be on making choices and behaving on the basis of concepts about personal and societal values.

As the teachers plan long-term and/or short-term, they should study the specific activities in view of concept development and use and provide a variety of learning experiences all aimed at the same objective rather than having rote repetition of the same experience. For example, in catching activities, rather than having two people standing still and throwing the ball back and forth, the teacher can ask for varying speed of throw, varying level and direction from which the ball comes, varying ball size. Basic concepts of body position, hand position, etc. may be stressed in each experience for successful catching. Unfortunately, many drills for passing and catching in fifth and sixth grades still emphasize the traditional stationary position of partners, and

[3] "The Nature of Concepts: A Point of View," *Theory Into Practice*, X, no. 2 (April 1971), 102.

the same back-and-forth repetitive throwing that is practiced in the first grade.

Developing objectives for learning is the "what" in the process of teaching. When making long-term plans for specific content, teachers analyze what is to be learned and design instructional objectives. These provide them and subsequently the students with "conceptual handles" which will prove useful in further organization of learning experiences and evaluation.

Daily objectives make it possible to evaluate achievement or progress so that after a class or lesson the teacher and pupils are able to make valid decisions to

1. Redo an unsuccessful lesson.
2. Drop what seemed irrelevant or unnecessary from the lesson.
3. Practice or extend the learning from this lesson.
4. Move to the next appropriate learning experience.

This reflective process insures a better continuity of relevant, progressive learning.

Objectives are essential for individualization of learning. When pupils are working independently they need reference points for direction and self-assessment of their program in learning. Task style of teaching and learning depends on objectives, which in essence *are* the tasks. When the teacher makes known directions in learning through specified objectives, pupils, as they undertake more of their own decision making about learning, will develop more purposeful planning and learning patterns.

Writing or designing objectives sometimes proves to be difficult at first. One of the most perplexing things is to actually verbalize and pin down what it is you think pupils *should learn* and *can learn* (therefore exhibiting some change in behavior) through the learning experience you provide, in the time available and with your guidance. This of course makes you accountable for knowing your subject matter and being able to analyze and organize it with respect to the pupils you are teaching. This will be a result of your conceptualization of all the materials in this book; however, the major purpose of this discussion is to deal with the process of designing objectives at the instructional level.

Several excellent references dealing with more detailed instruction in writing objectives are included at the end of the chapter. The reader should extend his or her knowledge about the taxonomy of the various domains if these have not already been studied in educational psychology courses.

Guidelines for Writing Objectives

1. State the instructional objectives as expected learning outcomes in terms of the students' behavior.
2. For each instructional objective design a set of specific learning outcomes that describe the terminal behavior students are to demonstrate when they have achieved the objective. These may be identified as different levels of

achievement showing incremental steps toward the realization of the instructional objective. (For example: Level I—Using the overhand throw pattern, hit the target 4 out of 10 times; Level II—Using the overhand throw pattern, hit the target 6 out of 10 times; Level III—Using the overhand throw pattern, hit the target 9 out of 10 times.)

a. Begin each specific learning outcome with a verb that specifies definite observable behavior.

b. List several specific objectives for each instructional objective to describe sufficiently the expected behaviors for learners who achieve the objective. There may be alternate objectives for pupils to select.

c. Be sure the specific learning outcomes are truly relevant to the instructional objectives.

3. Revise the objectives periodically after assessment and review with pupils.

4. Do not omit complex objectives (i.e., critical thinking, appreciation, specific sportsmanship behaviors) simply because they are difficult to define in behavioral terms.

5. Do not use other people's lists of objectives—make them specific to your students. But do consult reference materials for assistance and examples of behavioral objectives.

Learning taxonomies describe classification levels or types of learning. These provide the teacher with a base for developing objectives and consequently learning experiences which insure that pupils learn at increasingly higher levels. For example, the discussion on page 94 about asking questions relates to the acquisition of learning at different levels.

The types of learning which we expect of pupils falls into three major classifications or domains: the cognitive, the affective, and the motor area. (The reader who has not studied the taxonomies of educational objectives in educational psychology courses is urged to read Bloom,[4] Krawthwohl et al.,[5] Simpson,[6] Clein and Stone,[7] and Corbin.[8]) Included here is a brief review of the cognitive and affective domains, with more detail about the motor domain.

The *cognitive domain* includes objectives that deal with content and processes and are intellectual in nature. These are learnings of *knowledge* of facts (parts, names, law and order concepts, or information); *understandings* (comprehension, principles, generalizations, high-order concepts, or the use of information and ideas); and *processes,* or transformational skills used in learning, communicating, or using knowledge and understanding in solving problems (synthesizing, associating, conceptualizing, creating, perceiving, evaluating, analyzing, etc.).

[4] Benjamin Bloom, *Taxonomy of Educational Objectives: Handbook I—Cognitive Domain* (New York: David McKay Co., 1956).

[5] David Krawthwohl, Benjamin Bloom, and Bertram Masia, *Taxonomy of Educational Objectives: Handbook II—Affective Domain* (New York: David McKay Co., 1956).

[6] Elizabeth Simpson, "The Classification of Educational Objectives, Psychomotor Domain," *Illinois Teacher of Home Economics,* 10, no. 4 (Winter 1966-67).

[7] Marvin Clein and William J. Stone, "Physical Education and the Classification of Educational Objectives: Psychomotor Domain," *Physical Educator* (1970), pp. 34-35.

[8] Charles Corbin, *Becoming Physically Educated in the Elementary School,* 2nd ed. (Philadelphia: Lea & Febiger, 1976), Chapter 6.

The *affective domain* includes objectives dealing with the emotions. These are *attitudes* (feelings, values, mood, acceptance or rejection of ideas or a person); *appreciation* (perception of a worth or value to something, recognition of aesthetic value of something); and *interests* (desires, curiosity, attentiveness to something, manifested voluntary participation, involvement, degree of involvement). Objectives in the affective area are more difficult to describe behaviorally; they are also difficult to observe and measure. Yet learning in this area must be planned or provided for, because it does not automatically occur.

The *motor domain,* often termed "psychomotor," includes objectives dealing with movement skills and movement processes. Jewett and Mullan[9] present a taxonomy of movement process categories through which one learns movement. These provide a basis for sequencing learning experiences. They can be used in designing objectives in a progressively facilitating manner. The authors say, "If the learning of movement process skills is viewed as an important outcome, the student may be expected not only to improve his performance, but also to increase his range of movement abilities. Learning movement process is as important to achieving a liberal education today as achieving competence in particular subjects of a movement education, perhaps more so."[10] Descriptions and definitions of the categories follow:

1. *Generic Movement:* Those movement operations or processes which facilitate the development of characteristic and effective motor patterns. They are typically exploratory operations in which the learner receives or "takes in" data as he or she moves.

   a. *Perceiving:* Awareness of total body relationships and of self in motion. These awarenesses may be evidenced by body positions or motor acts; they may be sensory in that the mover feels the equilibrium of body weight and the movement of limbs, or they may be evidenced cognitively through identification, recognition, or differentiation.

   b. *Patterning:* Arrangement and use of body parts in successive and harmonious ways to achieve a movement pattern or skill. This level is dependent on recall and performance of a movement previously demonstrated or experienced.

2. *Ordinative Movement:* The process of organizing, refining, and performing skillful movement. The processes involved are directed toward the organization of perceptual-motor abilities with a view to solving particular movement tasks or requirements.

   a. *Adapting:* Modification of a patterned movement to meet externally imposed task demands. This would include modification of a particular movement to perform it under different conditions.

   b. *Refining:* Acquisition of smooth, efficient control in performing a movement pattern or skill by mastery of spatial and temporal relations. This process deals with the achievement of precision in motor performance and habituation of performance under more complex conditions.

[9] Ann Jewett and Marie R. Mullan, *Curriculum Design: Purposes and Processes in Physical Education Teaching-Learning* (Washington, D.C.: American Alliance for Health, Physical Education and Recreation, 1977), p. 9.

[10] *Ibid.*

3. *Creative Movement:* Those motor performances which include the processes of inventing or creating skillful movement which will serve the personal and individual purposes of the learner. The processes employed are directed toward discovery, integration, abstraction, idealization, emotional objectification, and composition.

   a. *Varying:* Invention or construction of personally unique options in motor performance. These options are limited to different ways of performing specific movements; they are of an immediate situational nature and lack any predetermined goal or outcome which has externally imposed on the mover.

   b. *Improvising:* Extemporaneous origination or initiation of personally novel movement or combination of movement. The processes involved may be stimulated by a situation externally structured, although conscious planning on the part of the performer is not usually required.

   c. *Composing:* Combination of learned movements into personally unique motor designs or the invention of movement patterns new to the performer. The performer creates a motor response in terms of the movement situation.

The categories are described as processes. Obviously they are in a hierarchy of difficulty, yet all can be sought and achieved at any age level in the content of the stage of learning by the learner; i.e., one must have tools (basic skills) in order to create. The creative product can be very simple.

Teachers must design objectives and consequent learning opportunities whereby these processes can be learned at each stage.

To help the reader better understand and be able to design objectives in the motor domain, some examples of objectives in each of the areas are described below.

EXAMPLE

GENERIC MOVEMENT

Perceiving

1. Recognize a 2/4 beat and use a locomotor movement following that tempo.
2. Watch your partner, identify a high and low movement.
3. Identify your own body part as leader identifies his/hers.

Patterning

1. Execute a forward roll.
2. Demonstrate the overhead serve.

ORDINATIVE MOVEMENT

Adapting

1. Adjust the force needed to throw a ball 30 feet to a target to that needed to throw a ball to a target 10 feet away.
2. Jump rope with a 2-foot jump 15 times while on a trampoline.

Refining

1. Perform a specified sequence of stunts on the balance beam in a flowing, rhythmical manner.
2. Serve the ball into a specified target on the other side of the net, 7 out of 10 times.

CREATIVE MOVEMENT

Varying

1. Alter the rules of Toss-Up Basketball so that there may be three team-mates on the playing floor at one time.
2. Change your lead foot occasionally as you gallop across the floor.
3. Diversify your dribbling pattern so your opponent will not be able to "read" your intention of direction.

Improvising

1. Extemporaneously respond in movement to the recording of "Let's Fly a Kite."
2. Pass the soccer ball to a teammate while moving down the floor on a scooter.

Composing

1. Design and perform a sequence of movement on the balance beam which shows different levels, changes of support, and both free and bound flow of movement.
2. Make up a dance to "Jingle Bells" using the schottische step as a basic step.

Following are some specific objectives in various activity areas, levels of learning, and in the various domains. Can you identify the domain, the level, and type of learning?

The pupil will demonstrate the ability to:

1. Replicate two balances which classmates design on the beam.
2. Move the length of the beam using a different base of support each time (minimum of 4).
3. Assist a classmate on the vaulting box.
4. Chart the fouls of a volleyball game.
5. Analyze the amount of force needed to hit the target from 4 feet versus 25 feet.
6. Design a sequence of movements utilizing the stunts which allow each body action to flow into the next.
7. Describe the body shape most conducive to quick rotary movements.
8. Design an offensive pattern of play to offset the 2–2–1 defensive pattern of opponents in basketball.
9. Replicate the rhythmic patterns of the arm movement for the overhand pass in volleyball.
10. Break down opponents' defensive strategy into individual players' moves.
11. Prepare an exercise program for gaining strength in the biceps.

12. Appraise a free exercise routine of a classmate.

13. Design a new game using only a ball and a base for equipment.

14. Select the level of exercise routine that is personally appropriate.

Practice of Skills

The instructional sport and games unit may be approached by teaching the skills first, followed by the game (part-whole), or by introducing the game first and then the skills (whole-part). Proponents of the latter approach feel that initially children are interested only in playing the game. A need and desire to improve skills grows from action in the game itself. Others feel that the logical progression is to teach skills first, since playing without skill leads to frustration and subsequent disinterest in the game. Obviously, both of these methods have advantages and disadvantages.

If children have acquired a rich background of fundamental skills in the lower grades, and the teacher has provided them with opportunities to develop beginning sport skills, they can easily begin to play games suited to their ability level with just a cursory introduction to the skills involved. The danger in teaching skills first is an overemphasis on skill for skill's sake, resulting in a lack of opportunity for children to see the relationship of the skill and its use in a game situation. Practice of skills is *essential;* however, practice drills and games can be selected which children will enjoy while still developing and perfecting techniques. The danger of placing the major emphasis on the game might result in the pupils' lack of understanding of the need for good skills. It is evident that proficiency in skill performance depends on practice which will enable individuals of all levels of ability to improve.

Practice drills or tasks are organized activities which involve a repetition of a specific skill or combination of skills but involve no elements of game rules or team scoring. In their simplest form, practice drills may consist of individual work, with the teacher setting a task with provisions for individual stages of progress. When a child achieves a relative degree of competency and confidence, the instructor designs tasks which involve other people and are as nearly like the game situation as possible. Too often drills are static, slow, and unrealistic; consequently, the transition from drill to game is frustrating, and the drills prove to be valueless.

Practice drills must be progressive, as are games. Just as in the developmental progression of games, the teacher must allow time and practice at each stage of drill for the students to gain confidence and proficiency in skills.

Recently some teachers have looked upon drills as used in the traditional sense as too structured and inhibiting for students. The term "drill" implies fixed procedures and much repetition. The repetition is essential for skill acquisition and cannot be discarded. The procedures can be changed and less fixed. The important thing is that each pupil have many opportunities to practice skills in tasks that are constructed so that there are progressively more challenging and diverse ways to do them—at the *fixation stage of learning.* The author prefers the term tasks. It is up to the teacher to think very carefully about constructing the tasks and making them relevant, progressively challenging, and interesting. Allowing for an element of play and making them gamelike makes learning more probable and fun.

Small-Group Task Formations

As an aid to the teacher, a few set group-task-formations are diagramed. Most of these are quite versatile and may be modified to fit specific needs. These also provide good formations for relays of various types. Children can learn the formations by name and get into action quickly.

1. MASS OR GROUP (Figure 6-1a) This drill is useful for individual work in which directions or demonstrations are given by a leader. Pupils should make a quarter turn to face teacher so that all will have an unobstructed view of him or her.

2. SINGLE CIRCLE (Figure 6-1b) The object may be passed around or across a small circle. If a ball is passed around, pivoting may also be practiced. When giving directions the teacher should break the circle. He or she should never stand in the center when addressing the whole group.

3. CIRCLE AND LEADER (Figure 6-1c) This formation may be used for a stationary drill in which the leader throws the ball to circle players, and they throw it back. In a moving drill, a player may follow the ball back and forth, changing with the leader. A player may move around the circle catching or throwing the ball from gaps between other players.

4. LEADER AND CLASS (Figure 6-1d) The squad is spread in a semi-circle with the leader centered in front of them.

5. ZIGZAG (Figure 6-1e) This task provides practice of throwing, catching, and kicking from an angle. Two groups face each other, but the object follows a zigzag pattern. A pupil may follow the object.

6. SHUTTLE (Figure 6-1f) This is a moving drill where the first person in one line throws, kicks, or dribbles to the other line and then takes a new place at the end of the opposite line.

7. SHUTTLE AND TURN BACK (Figure 6-1g) The object is passed back and forth, but person moves to the end of his own line when his turn is over.

8. DOUBLE COLUMNS (Figure 6-1h) This is a moving task which is useful when two players practice a skill where they pass an object back and forth as they move down the field. Another column may be added if multiple play is demanded, as in forward line play in soccer, hockey, lacrosse, etc.

9. SQUARE OR CORNER (Figure 6-1i) This drill can be used with players who are running, dribbling, or carrying an object around the square, then returning to the end of their own line. It may be a stationary drill with the object going around the square and players moving to the end of their own line. The player may move to another line. The object may also be passed across the square.

10. TRIANGULAR (Figure 6-1j) This drill is similar to the square or corner formation. The object may go in any direction.

11. STAR (Figure 6-1k) This drill is much like that of the triangular formation but is more effective in the practice of deceptive passing where no set pattern is required. The pupil may move with the object and exchange places with someone else.

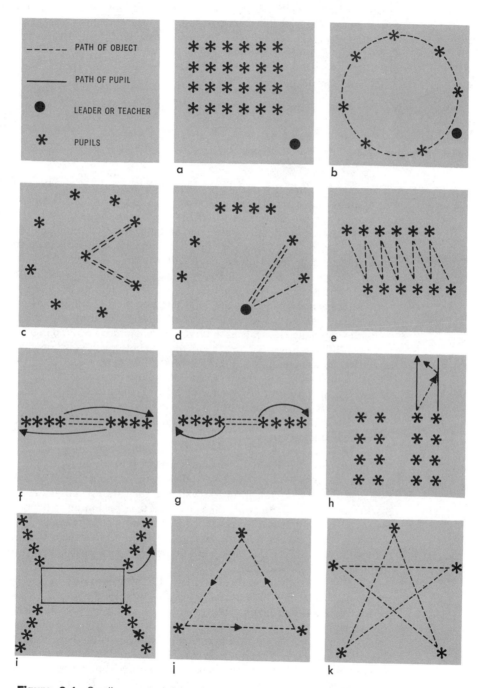

Figure 6-1 Small-group task formations.

Skill games are games which principally involve the use and practice of one or two skills. A game element of competition is involved, but the rules are simple and the game can be started and completed very quickly. This is a means of giving children an extensive opportunity to use the skill currently being stressed under game conditions. An example of this would be the game of Keep-Away (p. 382) where the skills of passing and intercepting are practiced much as they are used in the game of basketball.

Effective Use of Equipment and Space

The values of practice tasks are somewhat dependent on effective use of equipment and space. How much time is spent on skill practice is subject to how many opportunities each child has to execute the skill. If there is a ball for every two children rather than one ball for many, the time allotted to skill practice may be less. Of course, the same amount of time may be spent but greater results in terms of improvement in skill would be expected. Often teachers organize drills by squads and fail to see opportunities to break into smaller units in order to utilize all the available equipment.

The teacher should not overlook the values of a wall as a teaching aid. Much time can be saved with younger children in throwing and catching activities by using the wall as a target or rebound object. Younger children have a difficult time catching small balls; consequently, when throwing is practiced, much time is spent on chasing the ball. This is especially true when work on the overhand throw is started. Children can concentrate on the throwing pattern and need not be concerned about catching a hard thrown ball. As the ball rebounds off the wall, it loses some of its force. Everyone may start relatively close to the wall, and as an individual's skill improves, he may move farther away.

The wall is extremely helpful when teaching beginning volleyball skills. Beginners can more easily hit the ball thrown up in the air by themselves than they can hit a ball which has been volleyed by someone else. The ball should be caught as it rebounds from the wall and then thrown up again. Repeated volleys returned off the wall do not simulate a beginning volleyball game; however, strength and timing can be developed in this manner. Much time can be saved when learning the serve if the ball is hit into the wall rather than across the net. This enables the pupil to concentrate on the skill pattern rather than on where the ball goes.

Children can learn the skill pattern of batting earlier than they can learn to pitch accurately. The use of a batting tee enables them to practice batting or to play a game utilizing batting without waiting for a good pitch to cross the plate.

When children are practicing ball-handling skills, there is no need for them to use the exact type of ball specified for the game at hand. For example: in a basketball unit, soccer balls, volleyballs, and playground balls may be used for practicing shooting, dribbling, and passing. If a limited number of balls and baskets are available, one group of children can be practicing a skill requiring one type of equipment and another group a skill that requires different equipment or no equipment at all.

Balls and implements that are related to the size of the children involved are essential to their success. When purchasing equipment, intermediate-size footballs, basketballs, bats, protective devices, and goals should be ordered. Playground balls of various sizes are inexpensive and can be used as substitutes for many official types of balls.

When equipment for practicing skills is minimal and there must be sharing, waiting in line, etc., it is better to divide the class and have some of the pupils engage in a different activity which requires no equipment or an entirely different type of equipment. Everyone in the class need not be learning the same thing at the same time. In fact it is desirable for different activities to be available. This makes for more efficient use of space and equipment, and pupils will also have a chance to develop more responsibility in their freedom to choose activities, pace themselves, and proceed at their own speed to other tasks. For example, half a class could be working on archery, using the twelve available bows and four targets, and the other half could be engaged in track and field activities. Task cards for the track and field activities could be designed, or group instruction could precede individual work at the high jump, broad jump, and throw for distance. The teacher may wish to spend all the class time with the archery group, with students rotating within one class period or by days or weeks.

Many teachers feel stymied when they teach stunts and tumbling and only one or two mats are available. They frequently have long lines of ten or twelve children waiting to try stunts on the mat. Chaos may result as boredom and restlessness set in. It is far better to have a small group at each mat with other task stations set up for activities not needing mats; i.e., jumping ropes, work with wands, hoops, etc. Given responsibility, even very young children can work independently.

Grouping Within the Class

Grouping students into small working units aids both the students and the teacher in many ways. The units may be termed squads, groups, teams, units, or anything you wish to call them. They may be established for a long time or may be very temporary. Whenever different pieces of large equipment are used, use of groups is invaluable. Track and field and gymnastic activities demand small working groups, since several work stations are needed owing to the nature of the equipment and the space needed. Teams can be formed easily by combining groups, and games and relays requiring small teams may be started quickly by utilizing existing groups.

Assignments of responsibilities for equipment and student planning can be given to groups. The teacher can spot some social behaviors more readily as a child reacts to an intact group for a period of time. Evaluating progress and analyzing errors is easier if one watches a small group work, rather than watching a large, scattered group.

Groups offer children stability and a close working relationship with other children. They learn to work and plan together. In many instances they must share responsibilities. If one child in the group is given leadership responsibilities, each of the others learns how to follow a peer member. Group membership develops teamwork, group spirit, interdependence, commitment, and sharing of interests.

Forming Groups   There are several ways groups may be formed. The nature of the activity and objectives of the unit usually determine the method. Children may be grouped according to abilities, characteristics, interests, at random, by the teacher, or selected by the students themselves. If the teacher makes the decision, such things as results of skill tests, fitness tests, sociometric tests, height, weight, body build, and observation of skill and social behavior may serve as the basis for assignment to groups.

There are advantages and disadvantages to homogenous grouping on the basis of ability. Whenever progress on the part of either the highly skilled or the less skilled is likely to be retarded, the two levels should be separately grouped. This situation is more likely to occur when equipment is used and the activity is highly progressive. For example, in high jumping, the bar is usually raised after each successful jump. If one or two pupils cannot jump 16 inches they certainly are discouraged if the bar has to be lowered for them each time their turn comes. Often the bar is raised each time everyone has a turn at the same height, successful or not. The poor jumper is definitely doomed for defeat in this instance. Separate groups might be more encouraging.

In game play the highly skilled need the challenge of playing against others of comparable ability. For example, the good hitter needs to hit against good pitching; he or she needs the challenge of having to beat out a hit, rather than getting a free trip around the bases because the fielders are not capable of fielding the ball and throwing it accurately to the basemen.

Some poorly skilled youngsters are easily discouraged as they watch those who are consistently successful. However, they need to watch others in order to get a concept of how skills are done well and how skills are used in a physical activity situation. The teacher can forestall discouragement on the part of the poorly skilled by using a variety of organizations, by having better skilled youngsters help those who are less skilled, by giving guidance during the observation of demonstrations, and by making provisions for many self-testing activities.

IDEAS FOR FORMING GROUPS

1. Homogeneous ability, size, fitness qualities
2. Heterogeneity, with each group having equal numbers of students of high and low ability, size, fitness qualities
3. Sociometric questionnaires
4. Social behavior
5. Random selection from class list
6. Counting off within the class
7. Similar needs to develop skills or specific qualities

The Teaching-Learning Process

Pupil participation in selecting groups can be done in the following ways:

1. Electing four leaders, leaders choose members (selection of members should be done in a cooperative closed session of leaders and teachers)

2. Electing leaders, student goes to leader of his choice (maximum number of squad members must be stated)
3. Participation in sociometric questionnaire
4. Drawing numbers, colors, or places
5. Selection on basis of activity interest
6. Selection on basis of self-assessment of needs

Facilities, Equipment, and Supplies

The quality and effectiveness of any physical education program depends to a great extent upon the facilities and equipment available. Facilities are the permanent structures within and on which the program takes place, such as the gymnasium and playgrounds. Equipment includes items that are usually movable and rather durable, but must be replaced periodically. Items such as mats, net standards, basketball baskets, record player, etc. are considered equipment. Items that are less expensive and expendable within a few years time are usually called supplies. Balls, bats, wands, records, etc., fall into the supply category.

Few teachers have an opportunity to plan facilities or make many changes in existing ones; however, they do need to know how to make the best use of what is available. Occasionally when new buildings are planned, teachers are asked to make recommendations to a building committee. Sources of information pertaining to recommended specifications are available for those planning the construction.[11]

Most teachers have an opportunity to make recommendations for the purchase of new equipment and supplies. All should be aware of minimum needs and the approximate price of most items.

Facilities

OUTDOOR SPACE The National Council on Schoolhouse Construction[12] has recommended that an elementary school provide a 10-acre site with an additional acre for every 100 pupils, for play space. The junior high school should provide a minimum site of twenty acres, plus an additional acre for every 100 pupils of predicted ultimate enrollment. Many older schools have less space than this and where open space is at a premium some newly built schools do not meet these requirements.

Where streets run adjacent to the play space, a fence should be constructed for reasons of safety. A portion of the play space should be hard surfaced so play may be held in inclement weather, and games may be played where a good bounce on the ball is desirable. It is preferable to have this area adjacent to a windowless wall of the building so that balls may be safely hit or

---

[11] *Planning Facilities for Physical Education and Recreation* (Washington, D.C.: American Association for Health, Physical Education and Recreation, 1974); and National Council on Schoolhouse Construction, *Guide for Planning School Plants* (East Lansing, Mich.: The Council, Michigan State University, 1964).

[12] *Ibid.*

thrown against the wall. Lines forming boundaries for popular games should be permanently painted on the hard-top surface. Suggested line markings are:

- Paddle tennis courts
- Four square courts
- Bases, 30 feet apart
- Tether-ball courts
- Safety line, 6 feet from edge of entire area
- Rectangular area with center line for low organized games
- Hopscotch courts
- Circles

The majority of the area should be well turfed, free from holes and rocks, and suitable for field games and track and field activities. A back stop should be available for softball. One or two jumping pits filled with sand or tanbark should be to one side.

A separate area for placement of apparatus should be set aside. A soft surface of sand, tanbark, or wood shavings should be under and around the apparatus. Listed below are some developmental pieces of equipment which should be permanently installed in this area.

- Climbing structures
- Horizontal bars, multiple sizes
- Horizontal ladder
- Parallel bar
- Monkey rings
- Climbing poles
- Turning bar
- Old tree trunks laid horizontally on ground
- Rails or beams
- Creative commercial equipment as available

Traditional playground equipment such as swings, teeters, slides, and merry-go-rounds are being replaced by creative and developmental equipment. The latter provides opportunities for children to develop strength, balance, skills, and to be imaginative in the use of their skills.

A separate play area may be designated for preschool and primary grade children so that no balls from older children's games are hit or thrown into an unaware group. If space and finances permit, separate apparatus areas may also be set up. Portable equipment for outdoor use should include:

- Standards for net games
- Tether-ball poles and balls
- Jumping standards
- Bamboo crossbars
- Portable basketball goals
- Hurdles
- Bases
- Goal stands
- Field markers

INDOOR SPACE Available indoor play space varies in every school. A gymnasium 50 feet by 75 feet with a 20-foot ceiling is recommended. The floor should be wooden and treated with a nonskid wax. Windows and lights should be covered with protective screening. There should be no sharp edges protruding from the walls or objects along the walls. The latter must be carefully checked if there is an all-purpose room rather than a separate gymnasium.

An equipment storage room should be located off the gymnasium. Ideally, locker rooms for changing clothes and showering should be available for children above fourth grade.

As much wall space as possible should be left free and clear for target games and skill practice. There should be several electrical outlets on each wall. Provision must be made for attachment of nets to the wall and climbing ropes to the ceiling. Basketball backboards which may be adjusted for height should be installed at both ends of the floor.

Permanent lines which will serve many games should be painted on the floor. A safety line painted 6 feet from the wall all around the play area may also serve as the outside boundary for many games. Two parallel lines painted one foot apart in the center of the floor can serve to divide the room into two play spaces, and also provide a buffer space for games where each team or side occupies one half the court. Large circles may be painted on both halves of the floor. When temporary lines are needed, poster paint serves well, because it will not rub off immediately but can easily be removed with a wet cloth.

When an all-purpose room serves as the cafeteria, auditorium, meeting room, community room, and gymnasium or any combination of these, careful scheduling must be supervised by the administrator, with priority given to physical education classes. If classes are interrupted or cancelled frequently when other groups wish to use the room, a good physical education program cannot be ensured. It is imperative that careful attention is given to the proper cleaning of the floor, if the room is used for many purposes other than classes.

Frequently, the only indoor play space available is the classroom. Many activities with the exception of running and throwing games can be conducted in a satisfactory manner in the classroom, if necessary. This calls for ingenuity and good organizational techniques on the part of the teacher. Movable furniture is essential if anything but quiet or semi-active games are to be played. Most dance activities can be conducted if the floor is cleared. If mats and small equipment can be moved into the classroom, all gymnastic activities with the exception of those requiring large apparatus can take place. Doorway gym bars, heavy library tables, sturdy boxes, and small-sized vaulting boxes can be moved from room to room.

If possible, some space should be set aside for a learning lab or resource center where books, loop films, notebooks, charts, tape recorders, tape decks, learning packages, individual programs, and the like can be stored and used. If a school has a resource room used for these purposes for all subject areas, it would be most desirable if it were located near the gym. Some schools have converted closets or small storage rooms near the gym for this purpose. In some instances unused corners of corridors or parts of equipment rooms or the gym itself have been screened off to provide a quiet and/or separate nook for individual and independent study.

Some teachers have used shelves on wheels as portable resource centers, having space for books, tapes, pictures, task cards, learning package files, etc.

SWIMMING POOLS   The construction and maintenance of a swimming pool for each school in a district seems to be prohibitive in most communities. Some schools use community public pools or private pools. Some concentrate swimming instruction in spring or early fall and use city outside pools. Plastic air bubbles or structures are being put over many outside municipal pools, thus making them inside pools for the winter and much more functional for maximum use.

A relatively new practice gaining much popularity is to have portable pools. These can be erected at one school for a few weeks, then moved onto another site and thus around the district.

Use of Community Resources

Where adequate playground space is not available around the school, use is frequently made of nearby park areas. More and more school and recreation authorities are joining forces and sharing the building and maintenance of community facilities whereby the school and school grounds are used day and night and in the summer for recreation and formal education. The savings in cost when duplicate facilities are avoided is tremendous.

Owners of commercial recreation facilities are usually very cooperative with schools in renting their facilities or contracting for usage, and will often provide instructional help. For example, for many years bowling alley proprietors have charged minimal fees for the use of alleys and shoes and have provided instruction. Many winter sports areas are very cooperative in this type of service.

The trend toward making the community a learning setting for the school has eased some of the caution and reserve about transportation, legal liability, supervision of students, etc. There is a way to solve these problems and enrich the experiences of the pupils. Where community people are more involved in education, there is more support and pride taken in the schools. Businessmen know they are dealing with tomorrow's customers and are making a business investment as well as assuming civic responsibility.

Equipment

Recommended equipment and supplies for an elementary school with an average class size of twenty-eight pupils are listed in Appendix B. Although the prices are approximate, they may help the teacher recognize the need for teaching pupils to take care of equipment. It is most economical to have all equipment stored in a central storage room and shared by all classes. Adequate containers, shelves, and hooks should be placed in the room so that children can learn to replace equipment neatly and safely. A plan for care and distribution must be worked out with all school personnel so that it may be used to the best advantage. Equipment should be inspected frequently to see that it is in good repair. It should be cleaned periodically.

In some schools each room has its own equipment and supplies, and they are stored in the classroom. This may be more convenient, but it frequently limits the variety and number of pieces available at one time. Frequently, each room has a few balls which are used at recess time so that no items need be wanted by more than one group at the same time. Equipment for quiet games in the classroom is usually purchased out of the classroom supply budget.

If individual schools cannot afford large or expensive equipment, the school district can purchase it and rotate it among schools. This is a valuable plan when starting a gymnastics program. Each school may sign up for a particular period of time when it wishes or prefers to have the equipment.

It is wise to purchase high-quality equipment. Usually it will last longer and be safer. When balls are to be used outside, they should be rubber rather than leather. The latter wear out faster on blacktop surfaces and absorb water from wet grass, which makes them heavy and unmanageable.

Many items may be improvised. School shops, maintenance departments, fathers of pupils, and/or PTA groups can often make or install some large apparatus equipment at less cost than that purchased and installed commercially. A few suggestions for improvising equipment are listed below.

OUTDOOR APPARATUS

1. Turning bars, horizontal bars, parallel bars, climbing poles—made from used pipe and set in concrete.
2. Tree trunks set horizontally or supported on an angle; used for vaulting, balancing, climbing.
3. Railroad tracks and ties; used for balancing.
4. Concrete culverts, large cement blocks, large packing boxes (painted and any protruding nails removed), ladders set between two sturdy supports; used for exploratory climbing, crawling, and jumping.

SMALL EQUIPMENT AND SUPPLIES

1. Color identification bands, made from pieces of muslin.
2. Bowling pins acquired from bowling alley proprietors.
3. Old bicycle and automobile tires and tubes from service stations.
4. Pins or boundary markers made from large plastic bottles filled with sand.
5. Batting tee made from pipe covered by garden hose.
6. Standard for nets and tether ball made from pipe set in a tire filled with cement.
7. Jumping ropes made from 16-pound sash cord cut into varying lengths with ends dipped in paint.
8. Wands made from broom handles or 1-inch dowels.
9. Paddles of various type made in shop from ¾-inch plywood.
10. Beanbags made from old denim and filled with corn or beans.
11. Medicine ball made from an old basketball filled with sand.
12. Jumping boxes, vaulting benches, made from sturdy old tables or boxes.
13. Yarn balls and/or papier-mâché balls.
14. Scoops for throwing and catching objects made from plastic or bleach bottles.

Most equipment and supply items can be purchased from a local sporting goods store or through a sporting goods company representative, who may deal with the school principal or purchasing agent. Sources of supplies are listed in the Appendix. Suggested references are listed giving detailed plans for making equipment quite inexpensively.

SUGGESTED REFERENCES FOR FURTHER STUDY

AMERICAN ALLIANCE FOR HEALTH, PHYSICAL EDUCATION AND RECREATION, *Personalized learning in Physical Education.* Washington, D.C., 1976.

————, *Planning Facilities for Athletics, Physical Education, and Recreation.* Washington, D.C., 1974.

CHALRES, C. M., *Individualizing Instruction.* St. Louis: Mosby & Co., 1976.

HOWES, VIRGIL, *Individualization of Instruction.* New York: Macmillan, 1970.

KRYSPIN, WILLIAM J., and JOHN F. FELDESEM, *Writing Behavioral Objectives.* Minneapolis: Burgess Publishers, 1975.

SEIDEL, BEVERLY et al., *Sport Skills: A Conceptual Approach to Meaningful Movement.* Dubuque, Iowa: Wm. C. Brown, 1975.

WERNER, PETER H., and RICHARD A. SIMMONS, *Inexpensive Physical Education Equipment for Children.* Minneapolis: Burgess & Co., 1975.

7 / PLANNING AND MODALITIES FOR PRESENTATION

- **Long- and short-term planning**
- **Modalities to enhance individualization**
- **Open laboratory/open gymnasium**
- **Actualizing affective and process objectives**

Long- and Short-Term Planning

There are several stages of planning the teacher must undertake before actually presenting lessons to children. In order to make sure learning is progressive, sequential, varied, and balanced, some long-term planning is necessary. Figure 7-1 shows stages of planning, with indications of what is considered long-term or short-term and who is involved. The size and organization of the school and/or school district are major factors in the long-term stages. The individual teacher must always be responsible for the instructional unit and lesson planning. At various times during these two stages pupils should also become involved in planning.

Figure 7-1 Long- and short-term planning stages.

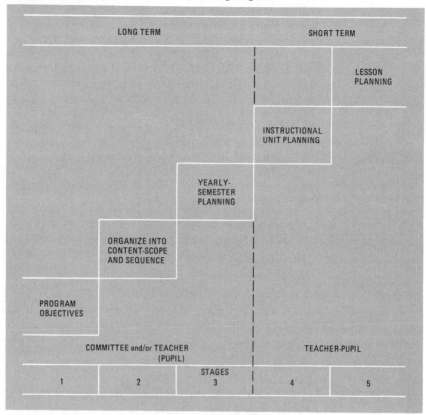

Stages one and two have been discussed earlier in the book; they are usually planned in committee if more than one teacher is involved. There definitely should be articulation between elementary, middle or junior high, and secondary programs at these stages. At stage three the individual teacher usually is free to plot for the year approximate time and duration of various movement themes and specific activities for the semester or year, for each level or grade. Students are often involved in this phase also, through discussions, activity interest inventories, questionnaires, and of course through demonstrated needs.

Planning at this stage translates the program objectives and scope and sequence of content into a logical balance of types of activities, variety of activities, and needed emphasis at various levels. Organizationally, this stage may also reflect necessary preplanning for the sharing of equipment, facilities, staff, and for some seasonal aspects of outdoor activities. The amount of instructional time available for physical education will influence how many activities are taught and how long can be spent on each phase of the program. There is no established formula for how long planning periods should be. Although many schools determine the length of units of instruction by reporting periods, weeks, months, etc., the main considerations should be developmental needs and abilities, stages of learning, and the nature of the activity. This phase of the planning should be flexible so that changes can be made without undue problems.

Where there are two or three days of instruction per week it is best to continue learning on the same general topic for a period of time rather than scheduling some different activity every day. If there is a five-day program, one type of activity should be on Monday and Tuesday and another should be on Wednesday, Thursday, and Friday, or Friday may be a special day such as Open Lab, Interest Day, or Interdisciplinary Day. Of course more than one type of activity can be taught within a class period; however, this pattern should also have consistency over a long enough period of time so that children can develop some continuity in their learning and have a chance to develop familiarity and skill. (Refer to learning principles from Chapter 4.)

Unit Planning

For each unit of instruction (activity, theme, or whatever) the teacher must do some preplanning. For beginners this may be more detailed than for more experienced teachers. In order to have sequence and continuity you must consider the following questions:

- Who is going to be learning?
- What is to be learned?
- How can it be learned?
- What experiences will enhance learning?
- What materials will enhance learning?
- How will the student and teacher know to what extent the objectives have been realized?
- What will be the appropriate timetable of the total plan?

Flexibility will have to be built into each of these because of the uncertainty of time schedules and the learning process.

Adjustments in objectives and procedure can be made in respect to the amount of student involvement in goal setting the teacher and student are prepared to handle. The initial planning will insure that the learning is progressive, sequential, and inclusive. It will allow the teacher to prepare new learning materials, revise old ones, order films, check equipment, schedule facilities, schedule outside resources, etc. Children may be involved in some of the preliminary preparation also. If teachers realize their own need for review of rules for task analysis, etc., they then have time for research and seeking help.

Teachers must consider, before the planning begins, facilities available for use, equipment available, length of class period and number of times a week it meets, amount of previous instruction or previous experience the learners have had in this particular activity or knowledge area, and the range of ability or achievement level of the students.

If using a teacher-centered or direct style of presentation, teachers must develop learning materials or resources that will help them introduce, explain, demonstrate, or supplement their teaching. If using a more student-centered or indirect style of presentation, materials have to be developed that are more self-instructional and self-contained in nature—in other words, objectives, directions, self-evaluation, and reporting systems have to be built into the materials. More materials will have to be developed that are designed to teach the same objectives through optional tools. Materials dealing with different levels of achievement will be needed for each class. Worksheets, programs of instruction, notebooks, filmstrips, loop films, TV tapes, movies, tape recordings, and charts can all be utilized. Examples of some of these materials are included in later pages. All of these instructional materials may be supplemented with guidance from the teacher, peer teachers, teacher aides, or volunteer aides. After dealing with these considerations, the teacher is ready to start.

The actual plans can be looked upon as a unit plan, a resource unit, a syllabus, a module of activity, or a teaching-learning unit. Following is an outline that may be utilized in planning for a unit of learning. Depending upon the focus of the learning and the style of teaching, many variations of each topic can be expected. Alternatives and examples are given in this chapter and others.

OUTLINE FOR AN INSTRUCTIONAL UNIT PLAN

MAJOR FOCUS OF THE UNIT: e.g., ball-handling activities, folk dance, beginning paddleball.

1. *Instructional objectives:* These are expected learning outcomes to accrue after instruction and experiences in this term of work in the unit. Outcomes should be appropriately related to cognitive, affective, and motor domains.

2. *Specific objectives:* These are more specific learning outcomes that describe the terminal behavior that students are to demonstrate when they have reached the instructional objective (these can further be defined or modified in respect to the learners after pre-assessment or pupil-teacher discussion and thus become short-term objectives).

3. *Development of the activity:*
   a. List of skills or techniques to be learned or refined, in progressive order, if appropriate.
   b. Lead-up games, skill games, or dances to be used.
   c. List of knowledges to be gained, such as concepts or principles, *use* of specific skills, strategies, rules, dance formations.

4. *Plans for general class organization:* Decision of how students will be organized for instruction and practice, small groups, independent study, programmed instruction, tasks, out-of-school settings, electives: e.g., station work in gymnastics, levels for swimming.
   Plans for forming small groups, alternate activity choices, leadership responsibility, rotation charts for sharing equipment, etc.

5. *Equipment and facilities needed:* Plans for scheduling or procuring that which is not permanently assigned to the class.

6. *Learning materials or resources needed* (examples follow):
   a. Movies, filmstrips to be ordered, sources, costs, dates needed.
   b. Loop films.
   c. TV tapes.
   d. Posters, charts.
   e. Tournaments, track meets, gymnastic meets to be planned and scheduled for space, officials, etc.
   f. Demonstrations by outside specialists (who, when, where?).

g. Field trips to plan.

h. Assembly programs.

i. Demonstration for parent, other classes.

j. Programs to be observed.

k. Task cards to be made.

l. Notebooks of source pictures and directions.

m. Books to be ordered for library or gym.

n. Learners or aides to be trained.

7. *Health or safety precautions:*
   Anything specific to this unit or activity—e.g., helmets, face guards, long socks, leotards.

8. *Evaluation:*
   a. Plans for ongoing daily feedback and evaluation.

   b. Achievement:
      1) Skill performance, choice of pre-test, post-test, rating charts, incidence charts, student self-evaluation.
      2) Knowledge, written tests.
      3) Social responsibility or citizenship.
      4) Student evaluation of course or unit and teacher.
      5) Plans for necessary input for report to parents and student or for grade cards.

9. *Block plan:* Timetable of *approximate* days or lessons in which specifics are introduced, resource people brought in, schedule of movies, any testing, tournaments, field trips, etc. This must be flexible but also plausible in terms of the time available.

10. *Reference list:*
    a. Sources of information for the teacher.

    b. Books or materials for the student.

This type of unit plan is most appropriate for structured types of activities. When using themes as an organizing base or planning themes for teaching basic movement, it is best to follow the format found on p. 263.

Lesson Planning

At stage five, lesson plans grow out of the long-term plans. Although one anticipates a general timetable of introducing, refining, and completing specific topics, specific lessons cannot be planned in advance because each lesson is the springboard for the planning of the next one. Plans for lessons vary considerably in view of the nature of the unit, the stage of the learner, the style or method of teaching, etc. Obviously, a plan for a lesson with an open lab and one for a teacher-directed lesson on learning a new sport skill would be quite different.

Actually, the teacher must look at the same general aspects of each lesson and ask these questions before planning:

- *Why* do I teach this lesson? What will students learn as a result of this lesson? (Objectives)
- What materials and learning activities will I use to help pupils attain these objectives? (Content)

- *How* shall I present and organize these materials and experiences to help pupils attain the objectives and have pleasant, relevant, productive, significant experiences? (Procedure, method)
- How will the pupil and I know to what extent *learning has taken place?* (Evaluation, concurrent and terminal)

Planning the lesson in written form helps one to think through each phase of the lesson and make provisions for the many things the teacher or student must do within a lesson. As Muska Mosston indicates, teaching is a series of decisions, and someone must make those decisions.[1] The teacher must decide who will make them. They may be as simple as where to stand, when to move, when to stop, etc. As one gains experience and works with a class, many of these decisions seem to become automatic and routinely done. Teachers learn to think on their feet, have many things going at one time, be able to handle the whole group yet communicate with individuals. Writing down the plans at first helps teachers to develop a way of thinking about the lesson so that eventually the planning can be done mentally. If teachers are held accountable for what goes on in a lesson, they will find it advantageous to write detailed plans at first. Each beginning teacher will have a different pace of acquiring the ability to recall details, develop an ability to visualize a lesson, see when changes need to be made; he/she soon will not need to write in such detail. Each person should develop an individual format that proves most helpful. A suggested format for a lesson plan is offered here for a starter:

OUTLINE FOR A LESSON PLAN

CLASS

NATURE OF LESSON

DATE

OBJECTIVES   These should be stated in learning outcomes for the student. The objective would not be to play a game but what is learned through the game. There may be only a few objectives attainable in one lesson.

PROCEDURE   How will the class be started? How will it be organized? How will groups be formed? What will be explained? What are key points of explanation? What will be demonstrated? Who will demonstrate? What will be the formation for practice, game, dance, etc.? What are key questions to be asked?

MAJOR COACHING OR TEACHING POINTS   Cue words or coaching phrases that will be repeated; concepts to be stressed or reinforced or applied; notes to self about individuals needing special help.

EVALUATION   During class: (1) concurrent feedback to individuals and group; (2) summary of lesson plan for next lesson. After class: self-evaluation of lesson, objectives accomplished, notes about individuals—progress, help needed, things to praise in the next lesson.

Figure 7-2 is a suggested format for a lesson plan. Figure 7-3 is an instructional model for teaching and learning. It should indicate to the teacher areas of concern for organizational planning, long- or short-term, and the possible involvement of pupils.

[1] In *Teaching Physical Education* (Columbus, Ohio: Charles E. Merrill, 1968).

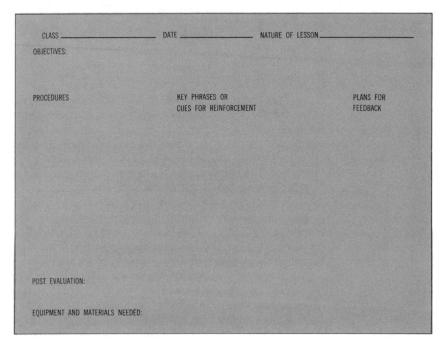

Figure 7-2 Suggested format for a lesson plan.

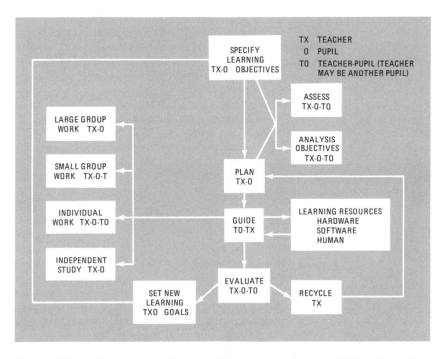

Figure 7-3 Instructional model for teaching and learning: possibilities for involvement of pupils.

In order to implement a program that stresses individualization, actualizes process, affective, interaction, communication objectives as well as develops competencies in movement skills and activities, it is necessary to use a variety of instructional modalities (*ways* to organize and present) that may not be familiar to you. The remainder of this chapter contains many ideas and examples that should act as a springboard for developing many more that will be appropriate for your classes. Before using one of these ideas you must consider yourself, your pupils, and your situation and modify the idea to meet your needs. Don't try to use someone else's ideas; you may be disappointed. And don't be disappointed if yours don't work the first time. Analyze why there were problems, then change and try again. Discuss the problems with the children and let them help you. A good learning experience for college classes is to examine one or more of these examples and analyze it in view of selected learning principles, child growth and development principles for selected age groups, objectives, and appropriateness for various age groups.

Modalities are presented to serve the following purposes: learning something new, refining something, enrichment, motivation, self- and/or peer evaluations, goal setting, independent study, teacher-pupil planning, actualizing affective objectives. Some of these ideas serve more than one purpose. Note also that terms are used differently by different people; the terms are not as important as the concept.

TASK CARDS

PURPOSE   The use of task cards should not be confused with the *task method* of teaching. In the task method the teacher sets tasks for children to do, thus establishing a particular relationship with the learner. Task cards are used to *communicate* with the learner about the subject matter; what is or can be done, directions, a problem to be solved, a choice of what to do, etc. Task cards may be used with any teaching method; therefore, the relationship with the learner may vary as may the way in which the learner learns.

Task cards can be used to learn new things, refine skills; they can be used in partner work, with a group, with a learning package; they can be used over a series of lessons, or for one day; they can be used for peer or self-evaluation, for station work, or to record work done. Instruction or orientation to new material may be given before work with the cards, or all instruction may be on the card. Cards may be given to each child or posted on the wall.

Designing the Cards

1. Analyze what is to be learned in respect to the objectives (chosen by the teachers or by pupils).
2. Break what is to be learned into logical variables so that each becomes a major task—each skill within an activity may be a source for a set of tasks to be on separate cards; or the different ways skills are used may become a source of a set of tasks.
3. Differentiate for each variable a quantitative scale (minimum or maximum times, bouts, hits, etc.) or qualitative scale (degree of finesse or form).

4. If directions are to be included, break them down into simple, short, progressive steps.
5. Study each variable and design appropriate tasks.
6. Design a card and format for each task or sequence of tasks to be done by pupils. Try to allow for different ranges of readiness and abilities. The size of the card will depend on the age level, how it will be used, where it will be displayed and later stored. Large cards and print are more easily read if posted on a wall. Cover them with plastic if they are to be handled a lot or used more than once and are not to be written upon. If child is to write on them, be sure to allow adequate space. Directions must be brief and simple for young children. Pictures and symbols are used for primary grades.

INCLUDE ON CARD

- If task is related to a learning package, is one in a sequence, or one of a series, identify it as such.
- If child is to write on card or keep it, allow space for name.
- Include directions for using the card.
- Allow space for recording or checking off items completed. If qualitative judgements are to be made, include a key for symbols and their meanings.
- Write in the task(s).

Examples of Task Cards

TASK CARD—PERCEPTUAL SKILLS

Making Forms

WITH ROPES   *WITH YOUR BODY*

Make a △
Make a O
Make a □
Make a ◇
Make a M
Make a W
Walk around the W
and see what else you see!

TASK CARD—FOOTBALL PASS, TIRE TARGET

Name	CHECK WHEN COMPLETED	COMMENTS
1. Hit the target from 10 feet 4 out of 10 times; tire stationary.		
2. Hit the target from 10 feet 8 out of 10 times; tire stationary.		
3. Hit the target from 10 feet 4 out of 10 times, tire moving.		
4. Hit the target from 15 feet 7 out of 10 times; tire stationary.		
5. Hit the target from 15 feet 7 out of 10 times; tire moving.		

```
┌─────────────────────────────────────────────────────────────────┐
│                    TASK CARD—SQUAT VAULT                          │
│   Name_____          EVALUATION               │
│   Work on each step in order. Have teacher    FORM    WHAT NEEDED │
│   check.                                      E G F   IMPROVEMENT  │
│   1. Five-step approach and a hurdle step                         │
│      (using no vaulting box).                                     │
│   2. Five-step approach, hurdle from spring-                      │
│      board (using no vaulting box).                               │
│   3. Five-step approach, placing hands on box take weight         │
│      on hands, squat on box, hold, jump off.                      │
│   4. Approach, hurdle from springboard, squat                     │
│      vault over box.                                              │
└─────────────────────────────────────────────────────────────────┘
```

STATION LEARNING

PURPOSE   The use of stations for teaching and learning in physical education is not new, but you can add new twists. Usually learning and practice of specific components of movement are done at stations or specified areas in the gym while the teacher gives individual help. A game or dance or some other type of small- or large-group activity that contains the skills practiced at the stations summarizes the lesson. Frequently part of the class is involved in the group activity while individuals work at stations, then rotate into the group. Task cards may be used at stations. Pupils may have to complete certain tasks before they can join the group activity. When they come into the gym, pupils may go directly to a station of their choice and rotate at their own pace; therefore, the activity time is extended. A limit may be set for numbers at each station. When you are beginning station work, groups may be given a signal that tells them when to rotate, until the students learn to work more independently.

Stations are used in *circuit* learning, in which each child must complete tasks at each station and complete the whole circuit of tasks in order. This insures the practice of each skill. Frequently circuits are used in perceptual motor improvement programs and in fitness development. (See page 218 for an example of a fitness circuit.)

Examples of Station Teaching—Learning

MATCHING MOVEMENTS—CHANGING SHAPES

Station 1 (with partners)
1. Try a three-point balance. Have your partner match it.
2. Do several rolls. Have your partner match it.
3. Using different body parts, make a set of three movements. Have your partner match the set.

Station 2 (with partners)
1. Walk like a soldier. Have your partner match you.
2. Select an animal walk to mimic. Have your partner match your animal.
3. Make the letters of your name. Have your partner make your name.

Station 3
1. Experiment with small shapes you can make with your body.
2. Make a large shape with the lower half of your body and a small shape with the top half.

Planning and Modalities
for Presentation

129

3. Make eight different shapes with your body, holding each for a count of 4 before making the next one. Vary small and large shapes.

Station 4 (with partners)
1. Using one arm only, make different shapes and see if your partner can mirror (using opposite arm) your movements.
2. Do sliding movements and have partner mirror your movements.
3. Make a pattern of various movements with your arms and legs and see if your partner can mirror these.

After each pupil has worked at each station, have the class break into groups of six for games of Simon Says (page 354); the leader is to make different body shapes and specify mirror or match. The whole group may play together with one leader.

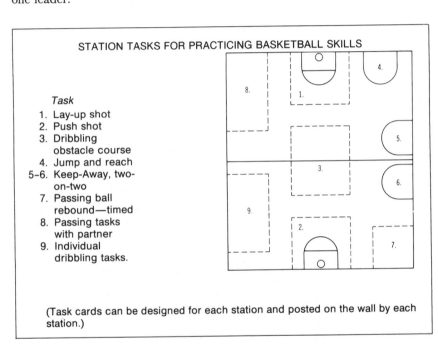

STATION TASKS FOR PRACTICING BASKETBALL SKILLS

Task
1. Lay-up shot
2. Push shot
3. Dribbling obstacle course
4. Jump and reach
5-6. Keep-Away, two-on-two
7. Passing ball rebound—timed
8. Passing tasks with partner
9. Individual dribbling tasks.

(Task cards can be designed for each station and posted on the wall by each station.)

There should be a sign at each station giving directions for tasks. Individual task cards may be used so that pupils can record the number of successful trials. A ball-throwing game like Guard Ball (page 331) might be used at the end of practice. Children might be asked to design a game using a combination of the factors.

LEARNING PACKAGES

PURPOSE Learning packages are self-contained programs for self-directed study. They are usually designed to provide for individual pacing in learning a particular activity or skill. There may be a package for each skill within an activity, a series of similar types of skills (e.g., balance stunts, tumbling stunts, partner stunts) or a package for each competency level of the activity. Pupils may select the activity they wish and learn that activity at their own pace, or they may be permitted to learn at their own pace within a required activity. A contract may be made for achievement or grading purposes. Packages may

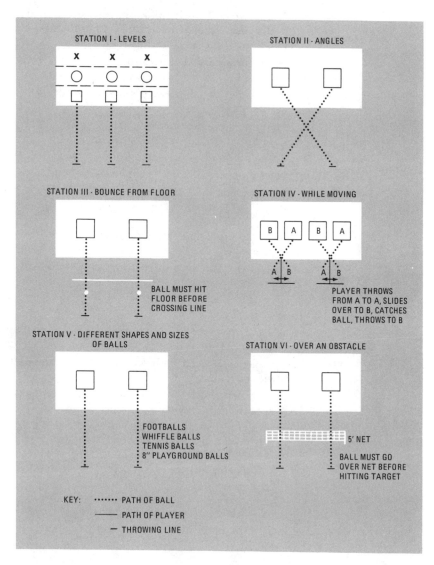

STATION I - LEVELS

STATION II - ANGLES

STATION III - BOUNCE FROM FLOOR

BALL MUST HIT
FLOOR BEFORE
CROSSING LINE

STATION IV - WHILE MOVING

PLAYER THROWS
FROM A TO A, SLIDES
OVER TO B, CATCHES
BALL, THROWS TO B

STATION V - DIFFERENT SHAPES AND SIZES
OF BALLS

FOOTBALLS
WHIFFLE BALLS
TENNIS BALLS
8" PLAYGROUND BALLS

STATION VI - OVER AN OBSTACLE

5' NET

BALL MUST GO
OVER NET BEFORE
HITTING TARGET

KEY: ••••••• PATH OF BALL
——— PATH OF PLAYER
— THROWING LINE

STATIONS FOR DIFFERENT FACTORS AFFECTING THROWING ACCURACY

be very simple and designed to take one lesson, several lessons, or an entire instructional unit. If facilities can be arranged safely, pupils may work on packages from different activities within any one class.

Developing a Learning Package

1. Analyze the topic to be developed.
2. Divide the topic into major subcategories; identify skills, concepts, knowledges, appreciation to be gained.
3. Construct instructional goals from #2.
4. Write behavioral objectives as transitional objectives leading to the realization of the instructional goals.

5. Identify which behavioral objectives are minimal or should be mastered by all; which should be learned for those above minimal level; which should be for the advanced learner.
6. Locate resource materials through which the behavioral objectives may be learned.
7. Identify learning activities from which students may select to help reach alternate objectives.
8. Plan large group instructional activities which may or may not be appropriate for all students at the same time.
9. Plan small-group experiences from which students may select.
10. Plan for peer evaluation experiences.
11. Plan alternate final evaluation.

If students are to contract to complete learning packages:

1. Discuss the learning goals and objectives. Assess students' status, interest, and needs.
2. Redesign with students the behavioral objectives or have them agree that they will complete as stated.
3. Give students copies of package. Have them select experiences and media resources they will use.
4. Have students agree on form of evaluation they will use. (This may include contracting for a specific grade in view of specified level of learning.)
5. Let students proceed with learning activities; be available as resource/provider of resources.
6. Evaluate periodically with students—recycle objectives, activities, grade goal if necessary; provide continuous feedback.
7. Assess final evaluation projects with students.

Example of a Learning Package

SKILL   Volleyball overhead pass, Level I, Learning Package #4.

OBJECTIVES

1. Attain a minimum score of 180 points on the overhead pass test.
2. Describe the pattern of the overhead pass skill.
3. Identify fouls related to the execution of the overhead pass when used in a volleyball game.

LEARNING EXPERIENCES

1. Check out task cards for volleyball overhead pass practice
2. Read as you need:
   • *Volleyball*, Schaafsma and Heck, pp. 19–26.
   • *Physical Education for Life*, Bucher, pp. 12–18.
   • *Fundamentals of Physical Education*, Hall et al., pp. 42–49.
3. View the loop film on:
   • Overhead pass skill analysis, #16.
   • Overhead pass in game play, #17.
   • Volleyball ball-handling fouls, #26.
   • Overhead pass skill test, #28.

4. Have partner or leader rate you on checklist for form and execution of overhead pass.

5. Ask leader or teacher for help in reviewing the checklist if it is not easily analyzed by you (ask for further help if you wish).

6. When you feel you are ready, ask leader or teacher to score your performance on the overhead pass. (You may practice this test before you do this. A partner or the leader will administer this test.)

7. Ask for the written test for this skill. This will include questions relative to the description of the skill and a place to check the fouls committed when using the overhead pass as seen in a tape of a segment of a volleyball game.

8. Play in a volleyball game in class whenever you are ready to or wish to. If you complete the objectives at this level ask for the Learning Package for Level II. You may work on another skill before going on to Level II. If you have difficulty with meeting the objectives, discuss the evaluation with the teacher and plan how you will work further to reach the objectives.

The instructor will have designed individual learning packages like this for each skill or knowledge or strategy area in Level I Volleyball. The loop films will have been made from students' performances in former classes. Books will be available in the resource center. A projector will be available in one corner of the gym. Task cards encased in plastic covers will be filed in the resource center. A supply of checklist forms for skill analysis and scoreboards for the skill tests will be on file where students may check them out themselves when ready. The teacher will keep alternate written tests and game-play tapes in his office. The directions for the test are on loop films and readily available to the students. Provision for game play is made for those who wish to play each period and during open lab periods.

LEARNING CONTRACTS

PURPOSE A learning contract is an agreement between the pupil and the teacher and/or a promise students make to themselves about what they will learn, perhaps within a specified time period, and how well they will learn it. For older children, a grade or competency level to be reached is most often attached. Contracts may be made for an instructional unit over a long period of time or for just one lesson or for a short period of lessons.

PROCEDURE The teacher may design contracts and specify what must be done to reach certain competencies or grade levels; pupils may have some input by making choices between alternatives set by teacher, or may choose their own things to do, with the help of the teacher.

Many contracts just list certain skills to be achieved, or experiences to be encountered, or tests to be taken, with a number of points given for accomplishment. Several, such as the learning package, are associated with instructions and help in achieving the goals.

For younger children contracting must be simple. For example, a contract may be used in an open lab—pupils write down what they intend to accomplish that day, what pieces of apparatus they will work on. At the end of class they may show or write on the contract what they have accomplished. Goal setting accompanied by identification of what one will do to complete the goals is an informal contract with oneself (see page 140).

Obviously, contracting makes one think about what is to be learned, and calls for some self-assessment and self-accountability in working toward the contract goals. Teacher guidance and explanation of alternatives and responsibilities should precede the actual agreement. The teacher should provide for a change in the contract halfway through, if this seems advisable.

Open Laboratory/Open Gymnasium

Since these terms are used quite differently in literature and in practice, clarification of our meaning is necessary. Open education/open physical education/open gymnasium is a *concept* that denotes a learning environment in which there is an openness—sharing, freedom, choice, responsibility—in general, a humanistic atmosphere. In specific *practice* sometimes the gym is open certain periods, before school, after school, or during lunch hour and everyone is free to participate in specified activities or in activities of their choice. The emphasis might be on improving skills, enrichment, and/or recreation. The examples given here are more concerned with employing the concept or attitude within the instructional class than with simply the physical openness of the gym. *Self-study is the primary goal.*

OPEN LABORATORY

1. Balls of all sizes and shapes may be set out in the gym. The task is written on the blackboard. For example, "Select any ball, set your own goal regarding some task or level of skill you hope to achieve with the ball by the end of the class. Be able to tell if you reached your goal or what progress toward it you made."

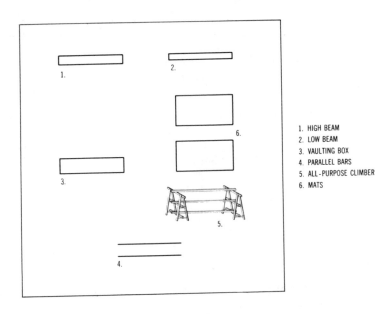

1. HIGH BEAM
2. LOW BEAM
3. VAULTING BOX
4. PARALLEL BARS
5. ALL-PURPOSE CLIMBER
6. MATS

2. Small equipment of all kinds is set out in the gym. The task is written on the blackboard. For example, "Using any two pieces of equipment, work out with a partner a game that you can teach to someone else at the end of the period."

3. Floor hockey lesson (verbal announcement): "Those who wish to play a game may do so in the area marked off for a game. Those who wish to work on individual skills may do so anywhere in one space outside the game boundaries. Those who wish to work in a one-on-one, or two-on-two situation meet over in north corner and then select free space for work. You may join the game when ready, or leave the game if you wish to practice skills."

4. Various pieces of apparatus are set up. The verbal announcement is "Free play or practice is allowed. No more than five people on one piece at a time. Rotate when you are ready and when there is room at a piece of apparatus."

USING A COMMON TASK FOR ALL   Using all the same equipment or stations as diagrammed above, assign common tasks for all to work on during the period. Your directions might be as follows:

1. Move across apparatus, changing base of support twice.

2. Find three different ways to mount each piece of equipment.

3. Mount and change your body position before getting off.

Rotate groups so they can try each of the tasks on the different pieces of equipment. They could choose to go to either of the balance beams.

SELF-STUDY CLASS OF STUNTS AND TUMBLING   Three sets of mats are laid across the gym, with one designed for new stunts, one for practice and evaluation of basic stunts, and one for work on routines. On the wall is a chart with a list of stunts classified by levels indicating difficulty. Students must select twelve in Level I to complete before going to Level II, in which they select eight; at Level III, six. Each is expected to design and practice a routine also. Each may elect to do more than a minimum as bonus stunts.

There are notebooks describing and illustrating each listed stunt available on a table at one end of the gym. In an equipment room is a projector and a set of short loop films depicting each stunt. (These were made by the teacher of students in previous classes.) Students are free to leave the gym and view the films when they wish. They have learned to use the projector and file the films for storage. The instructor is free for individual help and evaluation. Two students from other classes who are proficient in stunts and tumbling come in periodically to help.

INTEREST DAYS   One afternoon each week is set aside for interest groups. A panel of students polls classes and designs areas of interest that can be studied. Students work with each special teacher and the classroom teacher. Many parents, high school students, and students from nearby colleges assist in this program. Often what results is a series of mini-courses—for example, Star

Gazing, Outdoor Cooking, Rocketry. In physical education some of the areas may be fly casting, bicycling, judo, backpacking, scuba, horseback riding, fencing, or skiing. Some of these become appreciation courses with films, demonstrations, reading resources, etc. Very often community resources are utilized when the students can be gone all afternoon. Purposes and length of each unit or course vary. Open labs in all areas may be held for those who wish to pursue already existing interests and do not want to commit themselves to another at that particular time.

OPEN PHYSICAL EDUCATION Each child has physical education, art, and music three times a week. Two of these are scheduled by class groups. All the teachers have agreed that one day a week will be an open day for these activities. The specialist in each of these areas draws up a list of times and special activities which will be offered during the day. Those lists are circulated to the classrooms and children indicate to what subject area they wish to go. A limit of numbers is set by each specialist in respect to the space and equipment available for the activity being offered. Sometimes the activities offered are those requested by the pupils through an interest inventory; sometimes a guest teacher or specialist is there for the day; sometimes two of the specialists plan a joint activity; sometimes an open lab is planned. Children from different grades may very well be together, although often the choices are designated "lower" or "upper."

Those not going to pool may go to the gym and plan their own activity under the supervision of the classroom teacher. Volunteer aides accompany students to the pool when the physical education specialist is teaching.

Examples of Activities Scheduled.

Friday, February 16

TIME	ACTIVITY	LIMIT
8:30– 9:35	Balance activities	25
9:35–10:10	Ball-handling skills	25
10:10–10:45	Folk dance—intermediate	30
10:45–11:20	Open lab practice for gymnastic routine	35
11:20–12:30	Open lab practice for gymnastic routine	35
1:30– 2:05	Creative dance	35
2:05– 2:40	Rhythmic ball handling (Brief demonstration by a group of sixth-graders who have designed their own routine)	35

Friday, February 23

TIME	ACTIVITY	LIMIT
8:30– 9:30	Plot a design with fingerpaint in art room—then go to the gym and do a movement design to accompany the painting	20
9:30–10:30	Same, but new group	20
10:30–11:30	Same, but new group	20
1:00– 2:00	Water games at nearby YWCA Pool (4th grade)	25
2:00– 3:00	Water games at nearby YWCA Pool (5th grade)	25

Although processes are cognitive tools children must develop, they frequently are used with overtones of affective aspects of development. In goal setting, which requires self-assessment of skill and knowledge needs, there is an attitude and feeling about oneself and an awareness of importance to oneself regarding what one needs and wishes to do. This is true for some of the evaluative processes also. Although children need to be guided to evaluate objectively, they need also to reflect upon their values as they make decisions. At times teachers may use some process techniques with more emphasis on the affective than the cognitive.

Everyone acknowledges the importance of affective objectives, but we don't always purposefully include experiences designed for that purpose. The examples given here are to help you with this dilemma. All of these modalities may be done within a short period of time. Many may be done in written form and/or in verbal form; with a group or individually; within the class period or outside it. Some people think that when you use paper and pencil techniques in physical education classes you waste precious activity time. This is not necessarily true. The brief time that most of these suggestions take will improve the quality of the activity time. Experiences such as these will help take the child *beyond literacy in movement.*

MOVEMENT JOURNALS

PURPOSE   The purposes of a movement journal may be many, but the focus is on providing a way for children to consciously record some things that concern their experiences in movement. These may be collections of records of things they have done, original ideas, feelings, anecdotes about their experiences in movement. Some are cumulative, some are started and ended each year. Children usually design and keep their own journals. They may or may not be shared with parents, teachers, or friends; however, the teacher should have some discourse with the child about the journal. Contents may include goals, tests, drawings, newspaper and magazine articles, evaluation reports, original games and dances, fitness scores, vocabulary lists, etc. The contents should include an emphasis on original reflection about one's feelings and the significance of one's experiences in movement.

Teacher-Pupil Planning

ME CHART

PURPOSE   A "Me Chart" is a tool to help the child assess his or her needs, abilities, and interests in a certain activity. It allows pupils to do some reflective thinking about themselves, about their current abilities, what they would like to learn, what they can share with others. It can be used as a basis for pupil planning, goal setting, and for the teacher's use in planning class content.

Planning and Modalities for Presentation

PROCEDURE   Two examples accompany this description. One is a Me Chart that is used for preplanning for a specific activity and one can be used for preplanning for a long period of time.

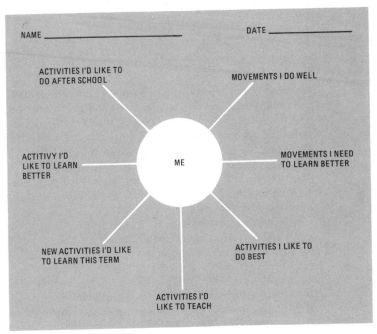

NAME _____   DATE _____

ACTIVITIES I'D LIKE TO
DO AFTER SCHOOL

MOVEMENTS I DO WELL

ACTITIVY I'D
LIKE TO LEARN
BETTER

ME

MOVEMENTS I NEED
TO LEARN BETTER

NEW ACTIVITIES I'D LIKE
TO LEARN THIS TERM

ACTIVITIES I LIKE TO
DO BEST

ACTIVITIES I'D
LIKE TO TEACH

ME CHART

Pupils are given a paper with the center circle and divisions or topics identified, as are the samples. The ME could be a drawing, it could be a picture, the pupil's name, or whatever they would like it to be. Young pupils' drawings of themselves can be indicative of body image. The topics to be completed (activities they want to learn) could be in pictures cut from magazines, words printed or cut out of paper, drawings, or paintings. Depending on the purpose of the chart, newsprint or large posterboard may be necessary.

The construction of the chart can be done at home, in the classroom, in the art room, or in the gym class. Some teacher-pupil discussion should precede the construction. The chart can be shared with teacher, peers, or no one. It can be filed in a class file or the pupil's movement journal. It may be posted in the gym or classroom. The teacher may refer to the charts for planning for an activity; individuals may design action plans or specific goal sheets, contracts, etc. from the charts. They may be referred to periodically or at the end of the time period for evaluation. A large class chart could be designed for a focus on class planning.

LEARNING CENTERS

PURPOSE   Learning centers are designed to help children "learn to learn" and to learn or improve specific skills, knowledges, and/or activities independently. Learning centers are sometimes confused with resource centers. A resource center is primarily a place where resources are available for learning a variety of things. Ideally, each school has a resource center in which physical education materials are included. At or in *learning centers,* the focus is on one self-contained particular theme or topic with objectives, learning experiences, resources, evaluation tools. Physical education learning centers may or may not include the space and equipment with which to do activities.

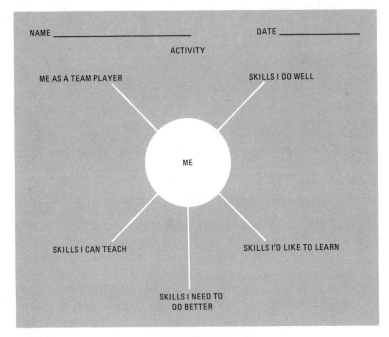

NAME _____ DATE _____

ACTIVITY

ME AS A TEAM PLAYER

SKILLS I DO WELL

ME

SKILLS I CAN TEACH

SKILLS I'D LIKE TO LEARN

SKILLS I NEED TO
DO BETTER

ME CHART

PROCEDURE   Centers are set up wherever space permits and are intended for use by one or a few children at a time. They may include some required experiences, but should always allow for different levels of learning, choices, and enrichment opportunities. The center itself may be very small—a corner of the gym, a closet, corner of the locker room, on the stage, etc. It may be on a mobile cart, mounted on a wall, or in a corner set off by a cardboard screen. The focus may be on any one of the learning domains or any combination of them. If activity is included, it may be done on the spot, in the gym, or outside school. Centers are usually designed by the teacher or may be a team effort. Children may also contribute ideas and resources. Electric outlets should be available to use for audiovisual equipment. Bulletin-board space should be included. Directions and resources for learning experiences and evaluation materials should be housed in the center. They may take a form much like learning packages or task cards. If they are colorful and attractive, they are more motivating.

INDEPENDENT STUDY

PURPOSE   Independent study is for children who have reached a fairly advanced stage of self-direction. It gives children a chance to identify interests and needs, to select what they want to study, set goals, plan experiences, carry through on them, and evaluate the results. The child has the initiative for planning, with the help and approval of the teacher. The teacher helps locate and provide resources and has periodic pupil-teacher reviews of progress.

PROCEDURE   In its simplest form, independent study may be for a day in which free choice of activity is allowed but pupils must identify goal objectives, preplan what they are going to do, and evaluate realization of the goals at the end of the period. It may be for a span of several years or it may be for a longer period of time along with other activity in the regular class period. A simple outline and perhaps a written contract may be drawn up with the teacher to include:

INDEPENDENT STUDY PLAN

Name _____ Date _____

Nature of content: _____

What I expect to learn: _____

What kind of things I will do to learn: _____

What kind of resources I will use: _____

What kind of help I will need from others: _____

How I will know and show what I have learned: _____

When I will complete study: _____

Signed: Pupil _____

Teacher _____

Date of midway evaluation:

List any changes of plans:

Final evaluation of study (refer back to objectives):

Signed: Pupil _____

Teacher _____

Pupil Goal Setting

WHAT I'D LIKE TO LEARN OR DO BETTER IN _____

PURPOSE   To have students set their own goals for a lesson or a long-term learning sequence in a particular movement activity.

PROCEDURE   This technique may be used with pupils who are going to learn something new, or who are learning more advanced skills or knowledges in a particular movement activity. Pupils may write their goals in class or take the goal sheet to their classroom or home and complete it. The teacher should read the goal sheet and make comments on it or discuss it with the pupil. If the activity is new, there should be some description, discussion, film, demonstration, or story read about the activity. If the pupils have engaged in the activity before, some provision should be made for reflective thinking about past experiences and performance. This could be done through large-group, small-group, or partner discussion; review of the goal sheets or evaluation forms; review of the last experience, or via some type of visual presentation. This technique can be used for affective learning also—e.g., What I'd Like to Do Better as a *Team Player* in Alley Soccer.

WHAT I'D LIKE TO LEARN OR DO BETTER IN ___Striking-Kicking___

Name ___Julie Lynn Exter___

	SKILL	FIRST STEP	WHO OR WHAT CAN HELP ME
1.	Kick ball into goal	Mark a spot on wall - move back farther each time I hit spot	Myself Wall
2.	Drop, kick ball into goal	Practice dropping ball straight down in front of leg	myself or teacher
3.	Hit ball with head to a partner	Hit easy up in air first then partner toss it easy	Book Partner
4.	Dribble faster	Practice around cones slow first for control	Self
5.			

141

The form can be kept in the student's file or movement journal and referred to occasionally, if it is a long-term experience, and at the end. Second steps may be added. Self-evaluation regarding meeting the goal may be done on the same sheet or form, or separate goal evaluation forms can be used, or a verbal self-evaluation with peers or teacher can be done.

GOALS I WANT TO ACHIEVE

PURPOSE   Same as "What I'd Like to Learn to Do Better In."

PROCEDURE   In a preliminary discussion, ask the pupils to think (within the content of the activity under consideration) of what they would like to accomplish within a specified time. Select one goal and complete the chart. This should be preceded by some orientation or previous experience in the activity.

CROSS-AGE AND/OR PEER TEACHING

PURPOSE   A number of teachers and researchers have found that children learn from other children, sometimes better than with the regular teacher. Having peers teach others is a technique that can be used at every level. Having older children teach or assist in teaching younger children helps youngsters learn and helps the pupil teachers gain more insight about understanding others and themselves. It is a technique that increases self-confidence and enhances motivation and a feeling of contribution to others, thus providing a source of process and affective development.

PROCEDURE   This teaching procedure presupposes that the pupil-teacher knows what he or she is teaching, knows what to look for, given a model of acceptable performance, and has a resource to the expected outcome. Muska Mosston describes the method of reciprocal teaching which outlines this very well.[2] Using cross-age teachers necessitates some organization or planning with other teachers for time arrangements. In elementary schools with flexible time schedules, children from upper grades can arrange to come to the gym at a certain hour for a period of time to work with the teacher. High schools frequently make elementary school teaching one of the electives in a selective physical education program. This meets experiences in social-affective development. High school students interested in working with children and/or in teaching physical education find this particularly helpful in their career planning and study. In either case, the teacher must take some time to orient pupil-teachers to working with younger children and to the subject matter under consideration.

MINI-WORKSHOPS

PURPOSE   This process recognizes the value of having children learn from one another; share the unique knowledge, skills, and interests of others; and make selections or choices of what they want to do. It also gives children the responsibility of planning.

PROCEDURE   The teacher should set aside certain days or times within a lesson during which pupils may choose to be teachers, to share with other pupils

[2] *Teaching Physical Education* (Columbus, Ohio: Charles E. Merrill Co., 1968).

GOAL I WANT TO ACHIEVE

STEPS I MUST TAKE	PROBLEMS I MIGHT HAVE	HOW I CAN MEET PROBLEMS	WHAT OR WHO CAN HELP ME	WHEN I HOPE TO FINISH STEP
1. Learn how to put feet right	Not getting rope on the right spot between feet	Watch someone else	Look at picture teacher Some other kid	Monday first thing
2. When to move hands up then legs	Move my hands when I should move my feet	Watch loop film	Loop film book Teacher	Monday second thing
3. I need to get stronger	Takes long time	Hang every day Do push ups	Just me	Long time two weeks may be
4.				

what they know. Conversely, it is an opportunity for pupils to choose something they want to learn that is usually not taught by the teacher in class.

A sign-up sheet may be posted asking those who want to plan or teach a mini-workshop to indicate what they want to teach. The teaching may range from a demonstration to a full participation lesson, the latter being preferable. It may be fly casting, a dance step, juggling, backpacking, etc. There may also be a list of what pupils would like to learn. A schedule is set; the teacher may help the pupil-teacher with plans or resources (two persons could plan together); the size of the learning group may be set. More than one workshop may be planned at the same time. Sign-up sheets may be posted for each workshop. The workshop may be held during class or during an open lab period, during lunch hour, or after school. It is best not to start with too many at the same time. Alternative activity centers may be scheduled at the same time for those who are not interested in the workshops or for those beyond the number that can be accommodated. The teacher may prepare with the pupils the parameters for the workshops—i.e., time limits, space limits, teacher responsibilities, etc. Too many rules destroy the purpose of having pupils plan and take responsibility. Workshops may be repeated. A simple evaluation form may be designed for use by pupils to aid pupil presentations in the future and to determine repeat performance needs. The same procedure may be followed for mini-workshops to be given by parents, other teachers or pupils, or people from the community.

Values Clarification

"I CAN" STATEMENTS

PURPOSE   To let pupils express what they feel they can do. For some shy or slow children, this affords a chance to build confidence. Voluntary and spontaneous one-sentence statements allow very small accomplishments to become larger.

PROCEDURE   This technique may be used at the beginning of an instructional unit, at the end of a lesson, or at the end of an instructional unit. The teacher should ask the students to think of one new and/or small thing they can do related to the activity, perhaps giving them an example (I can hop across the beam; I can bounce the ball with one hand). If children have trouble thinking quickly, let them have a minute or two to write something down or discuss it with another pupil (during class the teacher may casually say to a shy child, "That's an 'I Can' for you today"). Pupils may be allowed to call out one "I Can" statement or you can go around the circle, giving students the option of contributing or passing. This should be done quickly and take only a few minutes. A list of students' "I Can" statements may be kept in their movement journals.

MOVEMENT ESSAYS

PURPOSE   To have children reflect on their feelings about themselves and a particular activity. This will help children become more aware of their values and/or help them clarify their values.

PROCEDURE   Identify some topics and ask children to write a short essay or position paper on a topic of their choice. You might limit it to two pages or so many words. You may give the same topic to everyone. The follow-up may be a discussion about topics: this can be in a teacher-pupil conference, or with the group.

Suggested Topics

- The activity in which I like to be as highly skilled as possible.
- Everyone should be physically fit.
- How I feel when I play_____ . . .
- What new activities would I like to learn.
- The best positions to play in softball, soccer, . . .
- The responsibilities of a team captain.
- My preference of playing activities alone, with a partner, or with a team.
- How I feel about cheating to win a game.

SENTENCE COMPLETION

PURPOSE   Sentence completions may be used for a variety of purposes. They can help pupils reveal, explore, or state their attitudes, beliefs, interests, desires, goals, or value indicators. They can provide feedback or evaluative tools. They can be used as diagnostic tools. The stem of the sentence can be designed to elicit the desired type of information or expression.

PROCEDURE   Pupils may be asked to finish the sentences in written form. They may be asked to read one or more of their sentences to the group; or to share them with a partner, a small group, the teacher, the classroom teacher, parents, or no one. They may keep them in their movement journals to be reviewed later; or they may complete the same set and compare them with former completions. This exercise may be done orally as a class group, with the teacher going around the room asking each student to complete aloud any one sentence with whatever comes to mind. A discussion may or may not follow. Pupils should understand they may pass if they wish. There are no right or wrong answers. Some examples follow (all of these would not be used at one time):

SENTENCE COMPLETION

Name _____   Date _____

When I don't follow the rules . . .
When I make a mistake and we lose the ball . . .
When I make a goal . . .
When I reach the goals I set for myself . . .
When I help my partner . . .
When I run I feel . . .
When we have to sit and wait for other kids to get quiet . . .
When there are not enough balls for everyone . . .
If I were the teacher . . .
When our group gets the answer quickly . . .
When three people ask me to be their partner . . .
The next time we do this I'll . . .

MOVEMENT AUTOBIOGRAPHY

PURPOSE   To help children recall and reflect movement experiences and to use to help clarify the importance of experiences, feelings, and projections.

The "movement autobiography" also helps students gain better insight, better interpersonal relations, as well as enabling them to trace the development of some skill or interest.

PROCEDURE   The autobiography may be written in essay form; as a chronological listing of developments of a certain aspect; in book form in chapters; in pictures, drawings, song, or dance. This is a good modality to plan in conjunction with the art, music, and/or dance teacher. It could be done in and out of the activity setting—or perhaps at home. The movement autobiography is best used in the upper grades, because older children have more and broader movement experiences to reflect upon. The teacher should first discuss writing the autobiography, giving some suggestions of things to think about—or, for some groups, an outline, depending on the major reason or further use of autobiography and the abilities of the individuals. This may be cumulative or added to within a year or two.

READING CLUBS

PURPOSE   To enrich and broaden knowledge of certain activities or concepts through reading historical or contemporary novels, biographies, and nonfiction concerning movement activities or related topics such as the Olympics. It is an activity that may be planned with the reading teacher.

PROCEDURE   With the help of the librarian, a list should be compiled of movement-related books available in the school library, or those available in the lending library. Pupils should be encouraged to read a book a month, so many a year, one about each activity, etc. A chart may be made listing book club members with the names of the books read. A book review session may be held periodically on Interest Days or in after-school activity time. Each pupil may contract to read so many books a semester or year. Some provision should be made for the pupils to discuss what they have read. The emphasis is not necessarily on quantity, but on enjoyment and learning more about movement.

Self-Evaluation and Feedback Tools

"I LEARNED" STATEMENTS

PURPOSE   This tool serves to elicit verbal feedback and self-evaluation about what students have learned from a recent experience or long-term unit. It helps pupils clarify and reinforce what they have learned. "I learned" statements help children set new goals and can also be used for future planning. Learning in each of the domains can be clarified or questioned, depending upon the stems the teacher has designed. This is very similar to using sentence completion as a tool.

PROCEDURE   The teacher may distribute a ditto sheet for each pupil to complete the "I learned" statements. These can later be read aloud or kept and shared with the teacher, with a partner, small group, or parent. They can become a part of the child's movement journal.

The teacher may make a large chart with the sentence stems and post it when an evaluative session is to be held. Pupils should be given a few moments to think about their completions, then the teacher may ask for volunteer answers or go around the room. No discussion need follow or selected items may be used for large-group, small-group, or partner discussion. Certain statements may be used as a basis for group or personal planning for future content or experience. These may also be used as a takeoff point for teacher-pupil conferences.

Examples of "I Learned" Stems

- I learned that . . .
- I learned to . . .
- I learned about . . .
- I was surprised that . . .

- I learned that I could . . .
- I learned that I could not . . .
- I learned that others . . .

"HOW I FEEL ABOUT PHYSICAL EDUCATION"

PURPOSE To help children learn to develop awareness of how they feel about some of the things they do in physical education. This may consider princi-

HOW I FEEL ABOUT PHYSICAL EDUCATION ACTIVITIES

	Everyone has fun.	It's too hard for me.	It's easy for me.	I would like to do much better in it.	Makes me feel good all over.	It's good for all of us.	Super!	It's a challenge for me.	I like it.	I'm the best.	
Fitness Circuit											
Folk Dance											
Diving											
Soccer Games											
Gymnastics											
Four Square											
Parachute Play											
Ball-Handling Activities											
Volleyball Games											

Place a check in the column that best describes how you *feel* about these activities and participating in them. In the last column you may write any feelings that are not listed. You may check more than one feeling for each activity.

Name_____ Date_____

pally activities with values related to self-concept, group awareness, progress, interest. You may talk with the group or with individuals about some of the responses or use the process just to make the children become aware of their feelings. The exercise could be a group verbal experience. Procedures and processes—learning centers, movement journals, grades, open gym, etc.—may be the focus of the technique.

PROCEDURE   An example is given in which the focus is on activities and personal feelings about participation in these activities. If this is a paper and pencil form, it can be done outside the class period as well as during class. A brief discussion about feelings gained from playing or doing the activities may precede this. The completed form may be kept in the movement journal.

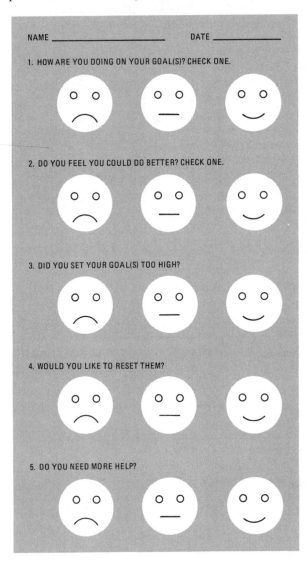

NAME _____   DATE _____

1. HOW ARE YOU DOING ON YOUR GOAL(S)? CHECK ONE.

2. DO YOU FEEL YOU COULD DO BETTER? CHECK ONE.

3. DID YOU SET YOUR GOAL(S) TOO HIGH?

4. WOULD YOU LIKE TO RESET THEM?

5. DO YOU NEED MORE HELP?

PERIODIC GOAL EVALUATION

Goal Evaluation Activities

Two examples of self-evaluation forms in terms of personal goals are included which can be used with rather young children. They may be used midway in some project, at the end, with some modifications, or at the end of a one-lesson project. The use of the faces is always popular with any age group. For young children, the questions can be asked verbally and children asked to check the appropriate face. They may be used with a number of other types of tools to encourage children to learn to evaluate their goals.

GOAL EVALUATION

Name _____ Date _____

1. Did you complete your goal(s)?
2. Did you do as well as you expected?
3. If not, why not?
4. Would you like to try longer to reach them?
5. Would you like to leave this goal now and work on it at a later date?
6. What or who helped you most in reaching your goal(s)?

These examples and ideas are only a few you may use to help individualize and personalize your teaching and work with pupils. You will want to adapt them to your own pupils and your own situation.

SUGGESTED REFERENCES FOR FURTHER STUDY

AMERICAN ALLIANCE FOR HEALTH, PHYSICAL EDUCATION AND RECREATION, *Organizational Patterns for Instruction in Physical Education.* Washington, D.C., 1971.

————, *Personalized Learning in Physical Education.* Washington, D.C., 1976.

BAILEY, DOT, and NANCY MARTI, "Elementary School Interest Centers," *Journal of Physical Education and Recreation* (September 1974), p. 93.

BLAKE, HOWARD E., JOSEPH G. FLEISCHUT, and RICHARD J. WESTERVELT, "Open Up," *Journal of Physical Education and Recreation* (April 1975), p. 48.

DAVIS, ANN E., "Station Teaching," *Journal of Physical Education and Recreation* (April 1975), pp. 49–50.

DUANE, JAMES E., ed., *Individualized Instruction—Programs and Materials.* Englewood Cliffs, N.J.: Prentice-Hall, Inc., 1973.

DUNN, RITA, and KENNETH DUNN, *Practical Approaches to Individualizing Instruction.* New York: Parker Publishers, 1972.

HUYCKE, DONALD F., JR., and L. MIGNON LESTER, "Skills Circuit with Music for Fun and Fitness," *Journal of Physical Education and Recreation* (November–December 1973), p. 69.

KLEIN, M. FRANCES, *About Learning Materials.* Washington, D.C.: Association for Supervision and Curriculum Development, 1978.

MILLAN, ANNE, "An Open Gym," *Journal of Physical Education and Recreation* (May 1972), p. 59.

RAVITZ, SUSAN, "Play Cards," *Journal of Physical Education and Recreation* (February 1975), p. 56.

SUPERKA, DOUGLAS P., CHRISTINE AHRENS, and JUDITH E. HEDSTROM, *Values Education Sourcebook.* Boulder, Col.: Social Science Education Consortium, 1976.

8 / EVALUATION

- Formative and summative evaluation
- Evaluating the child
- The program
- Facilities and equipment
- The teacher
- The lesson

Evaluation is a constant procedure of determining where an individual, a group, a program, or a process is in relation to established values and or goals (established by self, teacher, or norms), and the subsequent use of this information in redirecting efforts to reach the values or goals. In simple terms, teachers or pupils utilize evaluation to see if they have accomplished what they set out to do, and if they have not, to determine how they can succeed in future efforts.

Evaluation in physical education involves measurement of the progress and status of the child, facilities, equipment, program, teacher, and daily lesson. The measurement process involves many techniques and types of tests and can be both quantitative and qualitative. The value of the results of measurement lies in the completion of the evaluative process where the results are studied and plans are made to implement the findings in the future. The process and the interpretation of results involve the teacher, student, and parents.

The tools of evaluation are many. The most widely used, reliable, and valid are the objective written and performance achievement tests. Because some desirable qualities of performances cannot be measured by objective tests and must be measured subjectively, careful observation of performance and behavior must be made and recorded in the form of rating scales, performance charts, anecdotal records, checklists, and questionnaires. Group and individual discussions, conversations, and conferences are also tools of measurement.

Because children are the focal point of the educative process, most of the evaluation centers about them. Their status and progress must be evaluated in terms of the primary goal of physical education; that is, for each child to develop his or her fullest capacity to function as an individual, with primary emphasis on movement potential. The specific goals involve development and growth in the physical, mental, social, and emotional areas. These goals suggest that both subjective and objective measurements must be made of status and achievement in the areas of physical development, skill performance, knowledge, and social behavior. Specific tools yield information that should enhance learning and teaching in each of the areas. When results of specific measurements are analyzed and interpreted in relation to other test results, a broad evaluation can be made of children and the contribution of the program to them.

Contrary to what many people think, the term "evaluation" does not mean grading. It is a much broader concept. Even if grades are not used or assigned, evaluation is essential in any learning situation. It must be both continuous and long-range, and be a cooperative process between the pupil and the teacher.

Formative and Summative Evaluation

Evaluation in the program is summative or formative in nature. *Summative* evaluation is that which occurs at the completion of some aspect of learning—i.e., at the end of an instructional unit or semester or year—and denotes the level of achievement reached. A score or status may then be compared to normative standards or previous achievements. Usually this provides the basis for grades. *Formative* evaluation is that which occurs within each lesson; it is related to short-term objectives. In essence it is ongoing. Assessment may be objective but, in the elementary grades particularly, it is usually subjective and becomes the basis for adjustments within the lesson and for the plans for individuals and for the next lesson.

Both types of evaluation are necessary; each complements the other. However, at the elementary level, particularly in the primary grades, there is an emphasis on development and refinement of basic skill patterns and emerging sport patterns in unstructured settings; initial group and partner interactions (both cooperative and competitive); beginning awareness of values and significance; and process development. At this level there must be a preponderance of formative evaluation.

Evaluation in the program should contribute to:

a. Motivating the child.
b. Giving guidance to the child in understanding and in self-acceptance and awareness.
c. Reporting to parents.
d. Diagnosing strengths and weaknesses of the child and the program.
e. Helping children to appraise themselves.

Motivation

Children are motivated to varying degrees and in various ways by testing. Almost all children want to do their best, and when their best is measured in an objective manner they will work hard to achieve. The frequency with which they are tested and the way the test results are used determine the values of testing in terms of positive motivation. If where a child stands in relation to the group is always stressed and the child is always at the bottom, the tests may prove to be more frustrating than motivating. If the emphasis is on self-improvement and the goals are in small enough steps so that improvement is possible, testing is a positive motivating factor for most children.

Informal measurement in the primary and intermediate grades is an important part of the learning and teaching process. The evaluation that follows and/or accompanies the observation of performance should be structured so that children will assess their own performance and then try to improve it in the subsequent time allowed for practice.

Many self-testing activity situations should be set up where there is a sliding scale of evaluation of performance. Following is an example of a self-directed activity where a child works at his own rate and progresses to the next stage of achievement after he has mastered the first stage.

THE PROBLEM (AS STATED TO THE CHILD)   Using an overhand pattern, throw the ball against the wall, and catch it as it bounces back. When you can do this fifteen times without dropping the ball, move back to the next line. Each time you can do this successfully at one line, you may move back to the next line.

GENERAL SET-UP   Draw lines at varying distances from the wall to designate different stations. Each student is free to go to the space that fits his or her stage of throwing proficiency and to move to the next space consistent with his or her progress.

Guidance

A down-to-earth approach should be used when you explain expectations of improvement and success in skill performance. Children should be helped to understand that some will always do better than others. When they are long jumping, they should know that people with longer legs usually will be able to jump farther than those with short legs. Those who are taller and stronger probably will be able to throw a ball farther if they throw it correctly. In most instances, children who have had instruction and experiences outside school will score higher than those who are learning skills for the first time.

In items in which equal levels of performance may be gained, children should be told how to improve scores. For example, if strength is a key ingredient to success in a skill, they should learn how strength is gained. They should learn that practice is the indispensable element for improvement of skills. Often children want to know if they will be credited for their effort even if their scores are not high. They should learn that true effort is revealed by the personal comparison of the results of several administrations of the test. The important thing to children should not be how well they perform compared to others, but how much they improve their own performance.

Reporting Progress to Parents

Parents deserve to know how their children are doing. Measures of status and achievement in three basic areas should form the basis of the report in the primary grades. The first is whether the child's status in learning and refining basic motor skill patterns is characteristic of his/her age group and whether or not his/her skills and use of them are improving steadily. Second, the report should include some indication of general fitness level. Third, an indication should be made of the child's social behavior as it affects his or her relationship with others in the physical education setting. The report should be cumulative so that progress or decline will be evident from one reporting period to the next.

The procedure of reporting progress to parents varies considerably. Today in many schools all reporting occurs in conferences between parent and teacher. Often a written descriptive report of general progress in all areas is made. Seldom is the single letter-grade used for assessment in the elementary years. Physical education is often recorded as satisfactory or unsatisfactory in play skills, or a checklist of excellent, fair, poor is utilized. One report form usually serves all subject areas in a school system.

Table 8-1. Progress Report in Physical Education for Primary Grades

MIDTOWN ELEMENTARY SCHOOL PROGRESS REPORT IN PHYSICAL EDUCATION

Name _____ Grade _____

Period 1 Date _____ Period 2 Date _____

AREAS	REPORT PERIOD 1	COMMENTS	REPORT PERIOD 2	COMMENTS
Motor skill typical of age group				
Fitness level				
Social behavior				

Key

1—Excellent.
2—Better than average for age level.
3—Typical of age level.
4—Slightly below that expected for age level.
5—Atypical of age level. Needs more individual help.

Teacher's Signature_____

Parent's Signature_____
Comments:

Descriptive comments should accompany reports that utilize a checklist or S or U in order to explain the check or define strengths or weaknesses. A child may be satisfactory in one area and unsatisfactory in another. Progress in a subject with as much diversity of content as physical education can hardly be assessed in such a dichotomous way as S or U. Report forms for the intermediate and upper grades should include the same basic information as those for primary grades, but progress in specific types of activity should also be indicated (see Tables 8-1 and 8-2 for suggested forms). Ideally, the report should be verbal or in a written description for each child; however, many schools have yet to master the logistics of the heavy pupil–teacher ratio in physical education classes and the amount of time conferences and completing report forms take.

Table 8-2. Progress Report in Physical Education for Grades 4 through 8

MIDTOWN ELEMENTARY SCHOOL PROGRESS REPORT
IN PHYSICAL EDUCATION

Name _____ Grade _____

Period 1 Date _____ Period 2 Date _____

ACHIEVEMENT IN ACTIVITIES	REPORT PERIOD 1	COMMENTS	REPORT PERIOD 2	COMMENTS
1.				
2.				
3.				
4.				
5.				
6.				
7.				
8.				
9.				
10.				
Fitness level				
Social behaviors				

Key

1—Excellent.
2—Better than average for age level.
3—Typical of age level.
4—Slightly below that expected for age level.
5—Atypical of age level. Needs more individual help.

Teacher's Signature _____

Parent's Signature_____
Comments:

In some schools the contract system of evaluation and/or grading is being utilized in the upper grades. There are two types of contracting; in one, the teacher sets definite expectations for each mark and students select the mark for which they will work; in the other students make their own contracts for a mark with the agreement of the teacher. They set their own goals and the ways in which they will reach these goals. In each, students know exactly what is expected of them. This reduces anxiety over marks and decreases the impact of competition. It usually provides more objectivity in the grading process. Too often though, contracts yield specified quantities of work but little provision for assessing quality of work.

Ideally, the physical education program should be discussed at a parents' meeting early in the year. The evaluation plan should be described and explained so that parents will understand the report.

Reporting Progress to Students

When progress reports are sent home to parents, students usually see them or hear about them. However, many teachers fail to report progress to students personally. The need for concurrent feedback has been stressed repeatedly in this book, as has the need for stating goals and expectations, either by the student and/or the teacher. However, at this point it is well to stress that if parents need planned progress reports, so do students. Evaluation with the student should be seen as both feedback and guidance.

If possible, the teacher should try to have individual conferences or at least some written communication with students in which the following information is shared:

1. Clearly defined goals and objectives for what is to be studied.
2. Communication about the student's progress toward reaching these goals with emphasis on strengths and weaknesses and plans for improvement.
3. Student input into evaluation in respect to progress and feelings about the teacher-designed objectives and personal goals.
4. A conversation about the commonalities or divergencies of the teacher and student evaluations.

(The movement journal is a good way to communicate these items regularly.)

Diagnosing Strengths and Weaknesses

The study of the results of tests can serve as a diagnostic tool for assessing the needs of individuals and of the group. There are standardized tests of fundamental skills which include test items of the basic skills of running, throwing, catching, jumping, kicking, as well as of general coordination. Usually norms have been established on a large group of children and reported in percentile scores of T-scores.

These tests, or a teacher-constructed battery of selected items, can be administered at the start of the year. Teachers may study the group results in comparison to other similar groups and therefore assess program emphasis needs. They may study individual scores within the group and identify low achievers and high achievers. This may serve as one basis for grouping for class work. Results of fitness tests may be utilized in the same way. Some of the same test items are found in both fitness and achievement test batteries. A follow-up test may be given at the end of the year to assess progress. Perhaps only the items that indicated great weaknesses may need to be tested the second time. Unless specific practice and instruction are done with the skills in question, a great deal of progress cannot be expected. Subjective assessments of quality of performance should be made also.

An individual teacher can construct school norms if he or she collects scores for two or three years. These may be revised periodically thereafter. In this way teachers can objectively assess comparisons of children, the program, and their teaching from year to year.

Physical Measurements

Because the unique contribution of physical education is in helping the child through the medium of motor activity, most measurement is involved with assessing motor performance and the physical factors which affect the child's level of performance. The status of the physical qualities of health, posture, nutrition, and the specific elements of physical fitness is directly related to how efficiently and effectively a child can function in motor skills. Periodic testing in these areas must be done before expectations or standards of performance can be set or comparisons of achievement are made.

HEALTH An evaluation of the child's health status must be made periodically by a physician. The results and implications should be made known to the physical education teacher so that he/she is aware of the child's limitations and needs for exercise. This information is usually disseminated to the teacher by the school nurse. Schools vary in their requirements of medical examinations before entrance to school and at specified grade levels.

The teacher should develop a daily practice of observing children for minor deviations in appearance, habits, and energy level. Signs such as inflamed eyes, flushed face, poor color, sneezing, coughing, listlessness, rashes, itching, fatigue, restlessness, complaints of headaches, sensitive reactions to criticism—all these bear investigation and referral to the school nurse or the parent.

POSTURE Poor posture and poor physical and mental health are interrelated. Observation of posture habits and periodic posture exams are important in forestalling undesirable posture habits, which become increasingly difficult to overcome if neglected. (A simple posture test is suggested in Chapter 10, p. 204.)

HEIGHT AND WEIGHT Usually the classroom teacher or the physical education teacher must weigh and measure children two or three times a year. These records not only give an indication of a normal or abnormal growth pattern but also serve as a rough basis for classification or grouping in the physical education class.

Height, weight, and age have a relationship to performance in physical education. As children grow older they gain in height and weight. These gains are generally accompanied by growth in strength, power, and coordination. If one assumes that gains in height and weight are related to physiological maturity, then the child who is taller and heavier can be expected to be more mature and therefore have added advantages in the accompanying elements of strength, power, and coordination. Expectations of performance level for the short, light child then would be different than for the heavy, tall child. Thus, these measures may be criteria for grouping for activities and indications of readiness for certain activities.

PHYSICAL FITNESS The components of physical fitness and tests to measure status in physical fitness are discussed at great length in Chapter 10. Assessment of fitness is important at the beginning of any school year so that teachers know in what areas their classes are weak, and therefore can plan the program in order to best correct weaknesses. Individuals with low fitness scores need to be identified so that a plan for correction can be undertaken. Parents should be notified of their child's fitness status early in the year so they can help out at home.

The greatest value of fitness testing comes in a retest in the middle of the year and/or at the end of the year so that changes in status can be measured. Once again, the results should be useful in planning programs, helping children understand their status, motivating children, and reporting to parents and administrators.

Skill Performance

Since the majority of the time spent in physical education involves learning and improving skills, it is only logical that improvement in skill performance would be the best measure of the results of instruction in physical and motor skills. Just as the teacher constructs or uses standardized written achievement tests to measure attainment or improvement in academic subjects, so should performance tests be used as objective evidence of achievement in skill learning.

Because the emphasis in the primary grades is on work with basic skill patterns to increase adaptability, variability, flexibility, and variety in the use of them, few objective skill tests are used in the evaluation of skill improvement. Most evaluation is done through observation; however, the teacher should make a systematic observation of each basic skill pattern and record a child's progress in adaptability, variability, flexibility, and variety in their use. Too often the teachers are unaware of progress and status of individual students because they do not critically analyze the child's solution to movement problems.

In the intermediate and upper grades, skill tests should be given, and the results recorded. Some standardized tests constructed for the basic sport skills may be used, or the teacher may construct his or her own. Stunts usually can be evaluated on the basis of whether one cannot or can do them; gymnastics and dance skills can only be judged subjectively. In addition to giving individual skill performance tests, the teacher should also plan to assess the use of the skills in game play, in a dance, or in a gymnastic routine. Learning the basic concepts of how to use skills properly is as important as learning how to do them.

Basic Movement Patterns

Progress in the development of efficient basic movement patterns should be monitored and evaluated by the teacher. Too often teachers misinterpret the indirect approach for teaching basic movement as primarily exploratory—"however one does it is correct"—and thus no judgment is made on how *well* a child does things. Don't forget that the purpose is to learn to move efficiently and effectively and that basic patterns are being developed by children. Free exploration is used either at the beginning phase of learning or at the advanced phase. The teacher must include limitations and tasks that help children develop good patterns. Frequent observations and ratings of performance of basic skill patterns are essential. Results provide a basis of further limitations or tasks so children can discover and refine elements of good movement patterns.

Checklists or rating scales may be used to do this while children are working on tasks alone or with a partner. Barbara Godfrey and Newell Kephart[1] have compiled checklists for eighteen different movement patterns (Figure 8-1 shows a checklist for skipping). Teachers can devise their own by using the key teaching phrases or common faults identified for each of the basic skills described in Chapter 11.

SPECIFIC SPORTS SKILLS   Few tests to measure achievement in the specific sports skills have been designed for the elementary grades. Recently, the Research Council of the American Association for Health, Physical Education and Recreation conducted a project of developing and establishing skill tests and norms for all sports taught in schools to help teachers effectively evaluate the skill performance of boys and girls 10 to 18 years of age. A manual containing the directions for the skill tests, directions for administration of the tests, norms for ages 10 to 18, suggestions for interpreting results, and suggestions for the use of the results is available from the AAHPER, 1201 16th St., N.W., Washington, D.C., for volleyball, archery, basketball, football, and softball. These tests also serve as good practice tasks and most can be self-administered. Every school library should contain a copy of the skill tests manual for the sports that are conducted in its physical education program. If these manuals are not available or if skill tests can't be found to suit the needs or ages of children, teachers may modify an existing test or design their own.

MOVEMENT PATTERN CHECKLIST—SKIPPING.

Date _____ Age _____ Sex _____ Name _____

PATTERN ELEMENTS PRESENT	DEVIATIONS NOTED
___Combines step then hop	___Not "true" skip (step-hop)
___Alternation of feet	___"True" skip one side only, ___L, ___R
___Opposition arm & leg (up)	___Jerky
___Moves in direct or straight path	___Extraneous arm mvts, ___doesn't use arms
___Maintains balance easily	___Heavy step or landing
___Can skip fwd, ___circle	___No elevation, shuffles
___Can skip str line, ___circle	___Trips or, ___hits feet, ___foot
___Ease and flow of movement	___Uses one arm better, ___L, ___R
	___Feet cross in front

REMARKS: Examiner _____

Figure 8-1   Example of evaluation form for a basic movement pattern.

[1] *Movement Patterns and Motor Education.* New York: Appleton-Century-Crofts, 1969, p. 163.

SELECTING SKILL TESTS   There are a few criteria which should be observed when the teacher is selecting, modifying, or constructing a sport skill test.

1. The test should measure as accurately as possible what it is supposed to be measuring—that is, the ability to perform a skill basic to the sport.
2. The test should yield dependable and consistent scores.
3. Only skills basic and important to the sport should be tested.
4. The test should simulate how the skill is used in the sport.
5. The test should be of suitable difficulty for the group taking it. If not, it will not be motivating or educationally sound.
6. It should be possible to score the test objectively.
7. The administration of the test should be simple: require few complicated directions, require no elaborate or expensive equipment, require a minimum amount of space and time, require as few people as possible to administer it.
8. Only one person should be involved in a test at one time. For example, when testing batting ability, if one relies on a person to pitch the ball so it may be hit, reliability of the test will be reduced, because the speed, height, and accuracy of the throw may vary with each pitch.
9. Scores on the test should be variable enough so that skill level can be differentiated.

In an attempt to obtain objective achievement scores, many teachers spend proportionately more time on testing than on teaching. The length of a unit and the amount of time spent on learning the skill are factors to consider in selecting tests. The inclusion of a test of a skill that has been practiced only once is unfair to children and is of little assistance in assessing pupil progress or the teaching process. Plans for evaluating both the student and the unit should be made in the initial planning stages. In that way, testing will be done with a purpose and will be a vital part of the teaching-learning process. Skill tests, as a rule, are good practice drills also. (Specific suggestions for skills that should be tested are included in each activity chapter.)

SUBJECTIVE RATINGS   When a skill is evaluated regarding its use in a game situation or a skill does not lend itself to an objective test, observation must serve as the measurement tool. The skills of dancing, swimming, and gymnastics fall into this category. Attitudes and social behavior must also be measured by observation techniques.

Naturally, observations are very subjective and are based on opinion and personal judgments. Both teachers and students can and should learn how to make observations as objective as possible so that they will be valuable evaluation tools.

Students must have criteria on which to base their observations. The teacher should suggest that the students watch for certain things. Children in the primary grades need guidance to look for a few particulars and then a follow-up of their observations with questions and summaries that will reinforce them. In this way their powers of observation are developed.

When rating students, the teacher needs a rating scale or checklist in order to guide observation. A few suggestions for making and using a rating scale follows. (A sample rating scale is shown in Table 8-3.)

Table 8-3. Rating Scale for the Overhead Volley

PHASE OF SKILL	SQUAD _____ Student							
	1	2	3	4	5	6	7	8
1. Judges flight of ball accurately, is in line with ball.								
2. Flexes knees, shoulders, wrists in preparation for hit.								
3. Contacts ball with fingers and thumbs.								
4. Extends hips, knees, ankles which results in forward, upward motion of body.								
Total Points								

Directions: Observe each student's performance and place number of category which best describes the performance of the student in each phase of his skill.

Key
0—Failed to execute skill at all.
1—Poorly executed, inadequate performance, results of hit poor.
2—Acceptably executed, adequate results of hit, inconsistent pattern.
3—Well-executed, good results of hit, confident movement, consistent pattern.
4—Outstandingly well executed, effective results of hit, smooth consistent pattern, little room for improvement.

1. Plan for the rating in the original unit plan. Decide upon the purpose of the rating. This may determine the form of the scale, the time necessary to rate, and the discrimination power of the scale. If teams are to be made from the ratings, the discrimination will not have to be as fine as if grades are to be based on the rating.

2. The skill or trait to be rated must be decided upon. Then the qualities or factors of the skill or trait should be broken down into just what will be rated. Frequently, teachers try to rate too much. Break the skill down into only the most important elements.

3. Decide on the number and type of categories to be used; i.e., descriptive words, letter scale, point scale, or whatever. Each category should be defined so that the rater looks for the same trait with the same standards in mind. This is particularly important if more than one person is rating. For instance, the term "average" may be interpreted diversely if it is not defined clearly.

4. Rate each student under the same conditions. It is best to make observations during activity, but all must have the same opportunity to perform under similar conditions. For instance, if passing is to be rated in soccer, each child must have an opportunity to play a position in which he or she will have a comparable chance to pass. The forward line affords more opportunity to pass than would the goalkeeper's position, so all positions must be rotated periodically.

5. Equalize competition when ratings depend upon two people or a team in a competitive situation. In couple stunts and balances, equal abilities and sizes must be assured. In a couple dance, one partner's performance may influence the appearance of the other's performance.

Table 8-4. Checklist for Overhead Volley

	SQUAD _____						
	Student						
	1	2	3	4	5	6	7
1. Judges flight of ball accurately, is in line with ball.							
2. Flexes knees, shoulders, wrists, in preparation for hit.							
3. Contacts ball with fingers and thumbs.							
4. Extends hips, knees, ankles, which results in forward, upward motion of body.							

Directions: Observe performance and check those phases of the overhead volley which the student performs correctly.

6. Rate everyone on the same quality at one time, rather than rating one person on all qualities and then rating the next person on all qualities.
7. Don't make rating scales too long or too complicated or the process will be too time-consuming.

Checklists (Table 8-4) help to objectify observations by providing the observer with a list of items to be aware of as the observation is made. They do not provide for an estimate of quality, but usually are checked as "yes" or "no" in regard to presence. An incidence chart (Table 8-5), on which the number of times an incident occurred or a skill was used is recorded, serves

Table 8-5. Volleyball Incidence Chart

Date _____ Team Name _____

FOULS	SKILLS	SUCCESSFUL	UNSUCCESSFUL
Pushing	Serve		
Holding	Receive serve and set		
Catching	Key set		
Net	Spike		
Line	Block		
Foot fault	Recover from net Dig		
Totals			

Place tally (1) mark beside type of foul called against team.
Place tally in proper column every time a skill is executed.

much the same purpose as the checklist in organizing observation. Checklists and incidence charts are frequently used in studying social behavior and attitudes. The rating scale and the checklist may be utilized for self-practice and self- or peer evaluation.

The teacher and pupils may review a series of rating scales or checklists and make summary statements about progress or achievement, or use the summary for future planning and/or goal setting. The charts themselves may be kept in the child's movement journal.

KNOWLEDGE TESTING   Since the acquisition of specific knowledges and understandings is one of the objectives of every unit of instruction in physical education, measurement of the child must also be made in this area. Starting in the third or fourth grade, teachers should construct tests to measure learning of what was stressed as a specific concept, rule, procedure, or principle. Classroom teachers may integrate measures of spelling and vocabulary with words and terms learned in the classroom and in the gymnasium.

As with skill tests, the time taken for knowledge tests must be in balance with the time spent on instruction. Provision for the test should be made when the unit is planned so that it is an integral part of the teaching-learning process. Rules, scoring procedures, terms, basic principles, strategies, and understanding lend themselves to testing.

Tests may be administered verbally or in written form. They may be given to a group, or, depending on what type of organization is used, individuals may take them when they are ready for them.

Affective Behaviors

Every activity affords the opportunity for the development of certain social and emotional behaviors. Provisions for providing learning experiences in the area of these behaviors should be made when the unit is planned. Development of some particular traits is a major objective of certain units, whereas development of other traits is a constant objective, and equally possible through the majority of activities. In the case of the former, a special evaluation may be made of the trait as a youngster manifests it throughout play or work in the unit. Periodically, teachers may wish to make a checklist of traits so that they will be aware of the social behavior of each child. If they have a difficult time determining whether or not a certain child behaves in a way that is consistently good, bad, or indifferent, they should make a systematic study of the child's behavior in order to assess the overall progress. Various forms for measuring behavior may be utilized, and they usually take the form of a rating scale or checklist. Children may fill out some forms in a self-evaluation.

Suggested here are some of the social behavior items that may be evaluated regarding expected behavior (as indicated by child growth and development factors) as a child participates in physical education activities. (Note the similarity to affective program objectives on page 44 .) Does the child

1. Share equipment readily?
2. Take turns in order?
3. Make contributions of ideas in group problem-solving?
4. Accept suggestions and criticism from peers?
5. Express ideas that are his or her own, or are they ideas that are similar to those of someone else?

6. Accept suggestions and criticism from adults?

7. Accept decisions of others when they are officials or leaders?

8. Exaggerate, cheat, or alibi in order to be first or to win?

9. Abide by the rules even if no one is watching?

10. Appear tense or anxious when practicing or playing?

11. Appear happy or confident in the movement experience?

12. Work to improve skills or learn new ones?

13. Carry out assigned responsibilities?

14. Show leadership ability?

15. Help others willingly?

16. Make activity choices based on what he or she believes is significant for or to him/her?

17. Verbalize readily feelings about a movement experience?

18. Show respect and appreciation for peers' performance and values?

19. Recognize and accept individual differences and limitations of others?

(See examples of a few modalities one may use to look at different affective aspects in Chapter 7.)

Self-Evaluation

The point that pupils need to be involved in evaluation cannot be overemphasized. People learn most effectively when they have a part in planning for their own learning needs. In other words, if people are *involved*, learning will be enhanced; if they are not involved in some diagnostic evaluation process, chances are they will not truly know what they need to learn. Therefore, evaluation must be both continuous or immediate and long-range.

For pupils to evaluate themselves effectively, they must have help from the teacher. Actually the evaluation process as well as the goal setting or objective setting should be an interactive process between the pupil and teacher. The follow-up of assessing progress or status in respect to goals must include a look at what the individual can do next to better reach the goals. Self-evaluation should imply not only assessment, but responsible planning, self-direction, and self-pacing toward further attainment. Some of the examples of pupil goal setting in Chapter 7 contain self-evaluation opportunities and processes. Use of the skill profiles as shown in Figure 11-3 also involves the child in self-evaluation.

The Program

The program is measured against the objectives of physical education in general, those of the particular school, those of the physical education curriculum, and those of the teacher, through a study of the results of measurements of the items listed below. Some of the measurements may involve statistical evidence, some involve subjective judgments, some are made by the student, teacher, parent, and the administrator. All of these are discussed, results are synthesized, and the program as a whole is evaluated. Future plans for improvement should be made and implemented in order to complete the evaluation process. Suggested below are some of the items that may be considered in the evaluation of the program:

1. Objectives of program clearly defined, and sequential experiences outlined for the year.
2. Physical fitness status of the children.
3. Achievement in skills by children.
4. Knowledge gained by children.
5. Social behavior of children.
6. Daily class period allotted to physical education.
7. Activities suited to maturation level of children and provision made for individual differences.
8. Variety of activities offered in the program.
9. Adequacy of facilities and equipment.
10. Utilization of existing facilities and equipment to best advantage.
11. Adequate after-school activity program.
12. Adaptive measures for exceptional children.
13. Integration of physical education with other subjects in the curriculum.
14. Interests of the children being met.

Many state departments of education, state universities and colleges, and professional organizations assist local schools in evaluation of programs. A specialist or team of specialists may facilitate eveluations by means of visitations, provision of evaluative forms, and/or follow-up consultative service to interpret the results of the evaluation. Materials for evaluating the physical education program may be obtained from several sources listed in the bibliography.

Members of the Association for Supervision and Curriculum and Development Working Group on Humanistic Education devised a checklist for humanistic schools. This is a compilation of teacher and pupil behaviors and procedures and environmental aspects that are indicators of humanistic school practices. The list may be used to evaluate present programs, or to plan or revise the curriculum, in-service training, etc. There is no scoring procedure; however, you may wish to make a column for yes and no answers, or a scale (always, sometimes, never, etc.). Basically the list should give guidance and be a reminder of practices, procedures, and opportunities that should exist in a school or in classrooms of teachers who consider themselves humanistic educators.

Checklist for Humanistic Schools[2]

Items are listed in rank order as arranged by educators, teachers, and high school students.

1. Teachers who are genuine, warm, and empathic.
2. Student mistakes not resulting in a damaged self-concept.

[2] Association for Supervision and Curriculum Development, *Humanistic Education: Objectives and Assessment,* a report of the ASCD Working Group on Humanistic Education (Washington, D.C., 1978), pp. 52–55. Reprinted with permission of the Association for Supervision and Curriculum Development and the Members of the Checklist Task Force, Doris M. Brown, Chairperson; Sarah Caldwell, Shirley King, George Pressey, and Shirley Salmon. © 1978 by the Association for Supervision and Curriculum Development.

3. Policies aimed directly at maintaining personal worth, dignity, and rights of students.

4. Staff treating students with same courtesy and respect accorded peers.

5. Students listening to each other.

6. Necessary disciplinary treatment tempered with compassion and understanding.

7. Staff emphasizing positive rather than negative consequences in guiding behavior.

8. A library with an abundance of books and other materials.

9. Principal truly using the staff and students in making decisions which affect them.

10. Teachers conveying through action that they trust the students.

11. At least once a day, teachers finding the time and incident to indicate to each student "I care who you are."

12. Activities which encourage divergent thinking and other forms of creative effort.

13. Teachers using objectives for humane teaching rather than against it; student choice, pacing; teacher time management for greater individual attention.

14. Teachers showing competence in subject-matter content.

15. Developmental characteristics of students taken into consideration more than age and grade when planning learning experiences.

16. Staff able to detect and respond appropriately to signs of personal problems of students.

17. Free access to counselors, nurses, tutors, and other special personnel.

18. Teachers making verbal or nonverbal responses to students to indicate "I hear you."

19. All students receive some "ego-builders," honors status, roles, "happy grams," positive comments by others.

20. Teacher giving observations as feedback, not judgment.

21. Small group field trips and excursions which make in-school learning relevant.

22. Students readily assisting and sharing with other students.

23. Students involved in discovery and "hands on" activities.

24. A school philosophy, including values and attitude concerns, being used by teachers in planning classroom activities.

25. Free discussion of questions and issues not covered in the text.

26. Teachers motivating students with intrinsic value of ideas or activity.

27. Teachers having greater concern for the person involved than for task achievement.

28. Curriculum materials accurately reflecting our multiethnic society and varying family structures.

29. Evidence of well-planned lessons.

30. Access to activities regardless of sex, age, personality, and other characteristics.

31. Interest or learning centers being used with purpose.

32. Students talking enthusaistically about what they are doing in school.

33. Teachers making comments during a dialogue with students: for example, "tell me more," "that sounds interesting."

34. New students and family members given a tour of the building and an explanation of the program.

35. A student attitude of, "I've chosen this hard thing. Learning is challenging, stretching, sometimes hard, but oh so worth it!"

36. Wide variety of courses and special events from which to choose.

37. Staff seeking training in communications and human relations.

38. Evaluation of student work emphasizing correct responses instead of errors.

39. Planned school interactions which foster appreciation of human differences.

40. Students questioning accuracy, applicability, and appropriateness of information.

41. Spontaneous discussions being encouraged.

42. Principals and teachers seeking suggestions from parents.

43. An entrance area with a friendly decor which displays students' work.

44. Students involved in self-evaluation.

45. Students, teachers, and parents displaying symbols of school pride.

46. Students sharing classroom and school responsibilities.

47. Teachers knowing specific things each student likes and dislikes, as well as personal tragedies and successes.

48. Adults laughing with students; lots of smiling.

49. Learning organized around students' own problems or questioning.

50. Community volunteers assisting in learning centers, libraries, teaching technical skills, and serving as special resources.

51. Opportunities for students to be involved in career exploration or job location through out-of-school work.

52. A resource center in which students are free to use projectors, filmstrip viewers, and cassette tape recorders.

53. Teachers who view teaching as "freeing" rather than controlling.

54. Class meetings held to discuss solutions to problems which arise.

55. Space outside where people can run.

56. Teachers seeking parents' evaluation of child's progress.

57. Student records which note student's strengths and interests more than limitations.

58. Playground with grass as well as asphalt.

59. Teacher stopping to talk to parents in the school.

60. Teachers questioning misconceptions, faulty logic, and unwarranted conclusions.

61. Teachers working, playing, learning along with the students.

62. Evaluations as important in areas of personal-social development as in academic progress.

63. Spontaneous laughter.

64. Representative student governments dealing with relevant school problems.
65. Utilization of available non-classroom space for activities, learning centers, tutoring.
66. Teachers building student ideas into the curriculum.
67. Teacher disclosing aspects of own experience relevant to the teaching-learning.
68. System for students accepting responsibility for movement within the school, and to other places of learning.
69. Outsiders feeling welcome in the classroom.
70. Classes working outdoors when it is appropriate to the experience.
71. Student access to materials for on-going projects.
72. Principal spending some of his or her time working with students.
73. Space to "move around" in every classroom.
74. Availability of tools and scientific instruments for use by the students.
75. Staff and students sharing resources.
76. Student sub-groupings based on special interests, social preference, as well as skill needs.
77. Parents welcomed as a member of instructional team.
78. Classwork evolving from out-of-school events in the lives of students.
79. A brief period each day to do "fun things."
80. Teacher talk supplemented with some friendly physical gestures.
81. Presence of alternatives to traditional grading systems.
82. "I'll help with that" actions by teachers.
83. Students working independently on what concerns them.
84. Secretary providing a positive greeting when meeting visitors, students, and faculty.
85. Presence of human development and study of humankind as a regular part of the curriculum.
86. Teacher not always expecting students to come up with answer he or she has in mind.
87. An absence of negative comments to students by teachers.
88. Students working independently in small groups.
89. Teachers greeting students entering and leaving classroom.
90. A setting for student dramatic and musical productions.
91. Students having time to sit, think, and mull things over.
92. All students evaluating the classroom and school instructional program.
93. Senior citizens involved with students, at school, in their homes, and in care homes.
94. Students doing some of the teaching and other leadership tasks.
95. Student task-oriented committees.
96. Students able to go to the school resource center whenever needed.
97. Teachers spending some of their unscheduled time with students.
98. Libraries, laboratories, shops, and recreational areas available to students after school hours.

99. Surprise exhibits such as a litter of pups, white rabbits, unusual type plants.

100. Students engaged in community service.

Facilities and Equipment

Facilities and equipment are evaluated in terms of safety, adequacy, appropriateness, and efficiency. A yearly evaluation in all of these aspects serves as the basis for budget requests for the entire program. When requests for annual budget monies or additional funds are made, a well-organized, precise statement of conditions, needs, and requests is much more impressive and workable than a vague request for a certain sum of money or number of items. The teacher's report furnishes the principal with tangible evidence of need when he or she requests money from the school board.

The Teacher

Teachers are generally evaluated by the supervisor, the principal, the students, and themselves. The supervisor and principal usually evaluate teachers on the basis of observation of one or more lessons. This procedure varies from school system to school system. Formal evaluation of the teacher by the students is most often reserved for older students, and informal evaluation is evidenced by the general atmosphere and attitude of the class itself.

The most important evaluation of teachers is their own. After leaving the student-teaching situation, few teachers encounter the opportunity to discuss their lessons, planning, and techniques with anyone. This may seem like a relief, temporarily; however, it soon leaves a void in the teacher's growth. Periodically, teachers must evaluate their practices in working with students, the experiences which they provide for their classes, the growth of their classes, and their own professional growth. The daily lesson evaluation with the class should provide a measure of planning and efficiency. In discussions, the type of responses and participation of the class will indicate the degree of involvement in the learning process. The students' understanding or lack of it will also be revealed.

If at all possible, teachers should have a TV tape made of themselves while teaching a lesson. They can analyze their own teaching by watching the tape. They may look at it several times, each time looking for some specific behavior—e.g., communication techniques, verbal and nonverbal; feedback provisions (who talks most, student or teacher?), enthusiasm, and so forth.

Evidence of good teaching practices, accomplishment of objectives, and degree of student progress seen in careful consideration of each lesson must be further studied by a consideration of broader aspects. Listed here are a number of questions which teachers can ask themselves periodically.

1. Can I verbalize what I intend for my students to learn each day?

2. Do I plan units of work?

3. Do I plan each lesson carefully? Is it a contributing part of the whole unit?

4. Do I consider each child and his or her abilities in my planning and teaching?

5. Am I democratic in my organization and conduct of the class?

6. Do I help individuals learn to identify their own problems and guide them in solving them, or do I just tell them what to do?

7. Are the experiences that I plan challenging?

8. Do I evaluate student progress fairly and consistently?

9. Do I build lessons upon the evaluation of the previous lessons?

10. Do I consider relating and integrating learning experiences of the students from other areas of the curriculum?

11. Do I allow for student expression and evaluation?

12. Do I make the best use of facilities and equipment?

13. Is there a good learning atmosphere in my class?

14. Do I cooperate with other teachers and the administration in respecting time schedules, care of equipment, and proper use of space assigned?

15. Do I enjoy teaching each class?

16. Do I improve my knowledge and skills of teaching physical education through reading current literature, attending meetings, or taking part in in-service training when it is available?

17. Do I ask for help from the supervisor, consultant, principal, or other teachers when I need it?

The Lesson

The daily lesson is the basic unit of the physical education program. Teachers must evaluate each preceding lesson before they plan for the next one. The following questions synthesize information that has been discussed in earlier chapters about teaching methods, learning principles, organization, individual differences, discussion, and demonstration into practical terms as one evaluates and plans a lesson. These are questions that supervisors or supervising teachers may ask as they read a lesson plan or observe a lesson.

1. Were objectives formulated for the lesson?

2. Do the activities meet the objectives of the lesson?

3. Are the activities within the range of ability and interests of the pupils?

4. Does the selection of activities show progress from the last lesson?

5. Does the selection of material show a recognition of need of review and clarification, as revealed in the evaluation of the last lesson?

6. Do the activities provide a balance of big-muscle activity with lighter activity?

7. Does the selection of activities provide for maximum participation of the entire class?

8. Is some provision made so that those not actively participating can have an active part and interest in the lesson?

9. Are there plans for a good system of the distribution and collection of equipment? Is there an awareness of the proper type and number of pieces of equipment needed for this lesson?

10. Are there any plans to utilize student leadership?

11. Is there a clear understanding of the points the demonstration should stress?

12. Are the explanations and directions clear, concise, and to the point?

13. Are questions that are to be asked formulated well?

14. Are questions from the class anticipated? Are weaknesses and coaching hints anticipated?

15. Are there definite provisions for continuous feedback for individuals?

16. Are students given responsibility for self-directed learning?

17. How much freedom and choice do students have?

18. Are any provisions made for class evaluation?

19. Were objectives met?

SUGGESTED REFERENCES FOR FURTHER STUDY

BARROW, HAROLD M., and ROSEMARY MCGEE, *A Practical Approach to Measurement in Physical Education*. Philadelphia: Lea & Febiger, 1979.

CALIFORNIA STATE DEPARTMENT OF EDUCATION, *Criteria for Evaluating the Physical Education Program. Kindergarten, Grades One Through Six*. Sacramento, Cal.: State Department of Education, 1960.

FRANKS, B. DON, and HELGA DEUTSCH, *Evaluating Performance in Physical Education*. New York: Academic Press, Inc., 1973.

KIRSCHENBAUM, HOWARD, SIDNEY SIMON, and RODNEY NAPIER, *Wad-ja-get? The Grading Game in American Education*. New York: Hart Publishing Co., 1971.

LOGSDON, BETTE, et al., *Physical Education for Children*, Chapter 10. Philadelphia: Lea & Febiger, 1977.

SAFRIT, MARGARET J., *Evaluation in Physical Education*. Englewood Cliffs, N.J.: Prentice-Hall, Inc., 1973.

SIMON, SIDNEY, and JAMES A. BELLANCA, eds., *Degrading the Grading Myths*. Washington, D.C.: Association for Supervision and Curriculum Development, 1976.

WILHELMS, FRED, ed., *Evaluation As Feedback and Guide*. Washington, D.C.: Association for Supervision and Curriculum Development, 1967.

Part III
Foundations of Movement

Materials in Part III are in essence the foundations of movement: the analysis of the basic movement patterns, the elements and dimensions of movement, an analysis of the components of fitness and the fundamentals of exercise, and the mechanical analysis of movement. The analyses are presented in a manner which will help the teacher understand them or review them, and apply them to actual learning experiences for children. These are the knowledges, skills, and concepts which children need as the foundation of their movement education. Suggestions for content and ways to convey the concepts and skills are included in each chapter.

The Basic Movement Glossary forms the movement vocabulary that children should acquire in both action and understanding. The definitions of the terms and concepts about each are contained in appropriate chapters. This list is also a source if concepts are used as an organizing center for content, as suggested earlier for the primary grades. (Note the same can be used at all levels; however, the understanding, use, and performance would be more in-depth or advanced.) This is the source for planning Movement Themes and lessons. All physical education teachers should know well the terms and concepts included in the glossary.

Glossary of Terms for Basic Movement Structure

BASIC MOVEMENT PATTERNS

Locomotion	Nonlocomotion or Stability	Manipulation
Even	Bend	Throw
Walk	Stretch	Underhand
Run	Pull	Overhand
Jump	Push	Sidearm
Hop	Lift	Catch
Leap	Swing	Kick
Uneven	Twist	Trap
Slide	Turn	Strike
Skip	Stand	With Implement
Gallop	Roll	With Body
	Land	Bounce
	Stop	Roll
	Dodge	
	Support on other body parts	

ELEMENTS AND DIMENSIONS OF MOVEMENT

Space

DIVISIONS OF SPACE
Personal or Self
General

DIMENSIONS OF SPACE

DIRECTION	Forward
	Backward
	Sideways
	Upward
	Downward

LEVEL	High
	Medium
	Low

PATHWAY	Straight
	Curved
	Zigzag

BODY SHAPE	Curled
	Long
	Straight
	Wide
	Short
	Asymmetrical
	Symmetrical

Time
Slows
Medium
Fast

Force
Strong
Light

Flow
Bound
Free

MOVING IN RELATIONSHIPS

*One Person to Another
or Others*

Moving with—side by side
Leading
Taking Weight
Moving Alternately
Moving Simultaneously
Contrasting Movements—Mirroring
Matching Movements—Shadowing
Following
Parting

*Person to
Large Apparatus*

On
Off
Over
Under
Around
Along
Across
Above
Below
Through

Person to Small Objects

BALLS	Bouncing	Beanbags
	Tossing	Ropes
	Throwing	Hoops
	Catching	Wands
	Striking	Scooters
		Balance Boards
		Etc.

Foundations of
Movement

BODY AWARENESS

Body Parts
Head
Neck
Arm
Etc.

Body Surfaces
Front
Back
Sides

Body Shapes
Curled
Long
Straight
Wide
Twisted

Body Supports
Feet
Knees
Hands
Back
Shoulders
Head
Etc.
Combinations

Body Leads
Shoulder
Hips
Head
Foot
Etc.
Combinations

Body Controls
Starts
Stops

MECHANICAL PRINCIPLES AND LAWS AFFECTING MOVEMENT

Equilibrium
Motion
Gravity

Levers
Force
    Absorbing Force
    Creating Force
    Degrees of Force
    Qualities of Force

PHYSICAL ATTRIBUTES AFFECTING MOVEMENT PERFORMANCE

Strength
Endurance
Flexibility

Power
Speed
Agility

9 / UNDERSTANDING THE BODY MECHANISM

- **Mechanical principles of movement**
- **Actions of the body joints**
- **Muscle action**
- **Fundamentals of exercise**
- **Relaxation**

In earlier discussions of the purposes, aims, and values of physical education in the elementary school, repeated references were made to movement skills as the medium through which physical education contributes to the optimum development of the child. Therefore, acquisition of good movement skills is essential to each child. The teacher's responsibility is to help each child understand and learn a wide variety of skills. In order to do that, the teacher must have an understanding of skills and be able to analyze performance.

To analyze performance, teachers must know and understand how skills are executed. Mechanical principles regulate all movement and dictate how the body moves most efficiently and effectively. These principles are basic to the effective performance of all skills, play and utilitarian. If teachers understand how the physical or mechanical laws relate to human movement, they will be able to apply them to all skills and be better able to recognize and correct errors. All skills have common elements, and the ability to perceive these will help teachers plan skill-learning experiences for children which involve transfer of learning to related skills.

There are other factors which determine how effectively a child can utilize these principles and knowledges. These include physical limitations of body build, strength, endurance, and flexibility. Teachers should know the basic principles of improving and maintaining the physical components that are necessary in varying degrees to perform certain tasks. External and internal factors of the child's environment also affect efficient movement. (The mental and emotional factors prerequisite to good skill learning were discussed in Chapter 4.)

Through trial and error and incorporation of concepts gained from observation of others, most children have learned to utilize movement principles in their skills at an early age. For instance, when children are learning to walk, their biggest problem is maintaining balance. In their initial attempts they immediately sit down at the first indication that they are losing balance. They walk on the full sole of the foot with feet widely separated, and they take small steps to maintain a wide base of support. They also raise their arms to a position where they can be helpful in maintaining balance. They are actually applying the mechanical principles of stability or balance by widening their base of support and keeping their weight low.

As children grow, they develop concepts of movement principles. However, some children have difficulty in making observations, and few see the relationships between principles and various movement patterns. Fewer make applications when learning new skills unless the teacher directs their attention to them.

Teachers must make an effort to teach children the basic principles of movement and supply meaningful situations in which the children can understand and see their application in a variety of forms. When introducing new skills, teachers should relate similarities in patterns and principles to those that children already know. A problem-solving approach lends itself to the discovery and application of the principles by the children themselves. Attention can be drawn to the way they are utilized even before children can understand the principles or verbalize about them. Observance of the principles should be stressed in all movement experiences.

All these principles are studied in science units at some time in the elementary grades; however, they are not always related to the body, and therefore some children have difficulty understanding them. A child is surrounded by examples of how the principles work. What better teaching method could there be than to relate them to the working of the child's own body in play activities?

In the following pages essential principles of stability, motion, force, and leverage as they affect movement skills are presented. One section discusses how they specifically apply to sports skills in which objects are handled. An attempt has been made to present principles in a way that will be meaningful to the student or teacher who has not had the advantage of a course in kinesiology (analysis of movement). For the student who has had such a course, this should serve as review or summary.

The laws or principles are explained for the teacher, and examples given which are found in the play experiences of children. Suggestions are given for movement activities that will help children understand certain principles better. The ideas alone are stated, for teachers can implement them through any method they wish. Basic concepts that children should gain are summarized.

Mechanical Principles of Movement

Gravity

Everything on earth is subject to forces that affect the motion or equilibrium of the body. A push or pull exerted against an object is called a force. Forces are man-made or natural. Gravity is a natural force that pulls everything toward the center of the earth. Gravity always pulls through the center of weight or mass of an object. Therefore, the center of weight of the body is known as the *center of gravity,* or the point about which all of the body parts exactly balance. The center of gravity of balls or cubes is in their exact center. Depending upon body structure and distribution of weight, this point in the human body usually lies near the top of the hips and a little to the rear, between the front and the back of a person's trunk. This point changes as the position of the arms and legs changes, or an external weight is added to any one part of the body (Figure 9-1). The line passing vertically downward through the center of gravity to the center of the earth is the line of gravity.

Figure 9-1 Changes of the location of center of gravity as body position changes.

Stability is an important factor in all movement skills. Depending on the action involved, one may wish to maintain balance, upset balance in order to move quickly, or regain balance. A stable position is also important for the production of force. When all the forces acting upon a body are equalized, the body is in a state of equilibrium. When the center of gravity is directly over the base of support, a body is balanced.

The base of support is that part of a body which is in contact with the supporting surface, which is holding the body in vertical equilibrium against the force of gravity. Whenever there are two or more points of contact, the base also includes all the space between the contact points. Although the usual base is the feet, activities present themselves where various body parts become the base. In a headstand there is a three-point base, the head and the two hands. When a person is lying flat on the back, the whole area of the body that is touching the floor is the base.

The nearer to the center of the base of support the center of gravity is, the more stable the body. Therefore, the body weight should be in the center of the stance. This is why many directions for skills say to distribute the weight evenly. If the purpose of the skill is to make a quick move in a predetermined direction it would say "weight back or weight forward," so the body could be thrown off balance quickly.

ACTIVITY   Partner A straddles a line with weight centered over base of support. Partner B tries to push A over the line by pushing shoulder against shoulder. Still straddling the line, A shifts weight to the left foot. B tries to push A over the line by pushing against his right shoulder. After doing this, the students can see how much harder it is to dislodge someone from a position if that person's body weight is centered over the base of support rather than at the edge of the base.

The larger the base of support, the more stable the body. A wider base allows more room for movement before the center of gravity moves outside the base.

ACTIVITY   Partner A stands on one foot on a line. B tries to push him across the line by pushing shoulder against shoulder. A stands with feet close together with weight on both feet on the line. B tries to push A off the line in the same manner. A stands with feet about 16 inches apart on the line. B tries to push A over the line. The students then can understand the ease of pushing one off balance with the size of the base.

A foot position that allows for a larger base in the direction of the movement gives added stability. When a person is running and must come to a stop, the feet should be in a forward stride position with the weight centered over both feet. This position allows room for more forward movement before the center of gravity passes outside the base of support. When receiving a force, or a fast-moving object, the base should be spread in the direction of the oncoming force for the same reason.

ACTIVITY   Partner A stands in a side-stride position (feet side by side but apart) on a line. B tries to push A forward across the line. Then A stands with line between the feet. B tries to push A forward or backward across the line. When they contrast foot positions and stability, they should see that the forward stride position was the most stable.

The closer the center of gravity is to the base of support, the greater will be the stability. A position with knees bent lowers the center of gravity; consequently, in many activities when a force is to be received, the directions state to bend the knees.

ACTIVITIES   Partner A gets into a position on all fours. B should try to displace A from that position by pushing shoulder against shoulder or hip against hip. A stands up tall, and B tries to displace A from this position. They should contrast the feeling of stability from the low to high positions.

SENSORY CONTROL OF STABILITY   There are sensory organs which control stability also. The sensory control center of balance is located in the inner ear where the semicircular canals are the mechanisms of equilibrium while the body is in motion, and the otoliths are the mechanism of stability while the body is static. Proprioceptive endings are found in muscles, tendons, and ligaments. They contribute to the development of a kinesthetic sense, or what is commonly referred to as the feel of correct body position.

Visual perception also plays a part in maintaining balance. With the eyes focused upon an object to help determine relative position of the body, an individual can usually control his or her position better than if the eyes are closed or allowed to wander with the movement.

In general, the eyes should be focused in the direction of the intended movement. Actually, the head tends to move or assume a position in the direction in which the eyes are looking. If the eyes look downward, the head will undoubtedly move forward and downward, thus changing the center of gravity and throwing the body off balance. It is especially important to focus on a spot about 20 feet straight ahead when walking on the balance beam or when on a trampoline, unless, of course, one wishes to change position.

BASIC CONCEPTS ABOUT STABILITY THAT CHILDREN SHOULD LEARN

1. For greatest stability, the center of weight should be directly over the base of support.
2. When receiving a fast moving object or a heavy force, widen the base of support in the direction from which the force is coming.
3. When applying a force, widen the base in the direction in which the force is to be applied.
4. To stop quickly, bend the knees (drops weight closer to base of support) and place feet in a forward stride position.
5. When falling or leaning to one side, raise and lower arms or legs or some other body part on the side opposite the direction of the fall or lean.
6. When carrying or lifting a heavy object, keep object close to body.
7. When moving in a rotary manner, keep eyes focused on one spot straight ahead.

Motion

Motion implies movement. The body may move as a whole, some parts or one part of the body may move, or the body may move some other object. Everything that moves is governed by the laws of motion, which describe under what condition and how things move.

Newton's Laws of Motion

Understanding
the Body Mechanism

Law 1: An object at rest will remain at rest, and an object in motion will remain in motion at the same speed and in the same direction unless acted upon by a force.

The tendency for an object to remain at rest or continue in motion is called inertia. Force can be the pull of muscles or the force caused by gravity, air resistance, or friction. This simply means that a ball will remain stationary until it is kicked or pushed, and it will continue to move in a straight line at the same speed until a wall, or someone's body stops it. If nothing gets in its way, the force of gravity, friction, and/or air resistance will cause it to cease moving.

Once a body movement is begun, the inertia of the body is overcome by the work of the muscles. If the movement is continued, the effect of inertia is overcome. Therefore, in performance for which repeated body actions are required, much less energy is expended if the movement is continued rather than if the body comes to a dead stop and inertia must be completely overcome again. For example, when a person is doing sit-ups it is much easier if the up-and-down motion is continuous than if the body comes to a complete stop in the down position and inertia must be overcome again when the upward motion is made.

ACTIVITIES

1. Children can place a soccer ball in front of them and see that it will not move until a force is applied to it. When they apply a force as they kick it, it moves. If they kick it toward a wall, the direction of the ball will change as it hits the wall.

2. Children can experiment with sit-ups or pull-ups as described in the example above. They can contrast the amount of work or energy expended if the movement is continuous or if they stop between the sit-ups.

Law 2: The amount of acceleration (change in speed and/or direction) of an object is directly proportional to the force acting on it and inversely proportional to the mass. If unequal forces are applied to objects of equal mass, the greatest force will cause the greatest acceleration; if equal forces are applied to objects of unequal mass, the greatest mass will have the smallest acceleration.

Given a certain box to move, a child must push to make it move and push harder to make the box go faster, but if two heavy weights are put into the box, he must push even harder to make the box move as fast. The greater the force applied to an object, the greater the change of speed and direction will be. The greater the mass (weight), the greater the force must be to reach a certain change of speed.

ACTIVITY Children can throw balls toward a wall from increasingly farther distances and compare the amount of force and strength needed to throw from the farthest distance as opposed to the shortest distance. Balls of extremely different weights can be used to compare the differences in the amount of force needed in relation to greater mass. A soccer ball and a plastic ball would afford a contrast. Perhaps a bowling ball could be brought into the gym for use in a demonstration.

Law 3: For every action there is an equal and opposite reaction (counterforce).

When a foot pushes against the ground, the ground pushes back, and the body is propelled forward. When a person is swimming, the arms push back against the water, and the body is driven forward.

ACTIVITY   Jump and reach. Have students relate bending their knees and pushing down hard on the floor to the distance that they can jump and reach. The harder one pushes against the floor, the higher one goes in the air. If scooters are available, relate pushing against the floor with one foot while rest of weight is on the scooter to discovering that the floor pushes back against the foot and makes the scooter go.

BASIC CONCEPTS ABOUT MOTION THAT CHILDREN SHOULD LEARN

1. Anything that is standing still will stay still until someone or something exerts a force against it.
2. Things that are moved or are moving will keep on moving unless a force stops them.
3. Whenever one object moves, another object moves too. When you push on something, it pushes back. When you pull on something, it pulls back.
4. The greater the force against an object, the faster it moves.
5. The heavier an object, the greater must be the force exerted to move it.

FACTORS THAT AFFECT MOTION   *Mass* is an important factor that affects motion. Mass is the measure of quantity of matter (anything that occupies space) in an object. Although some people think of mass as weight, this is not true, since weight is the gravitational pull on the mass of an object. For example, objects here on earth have the same *mass* as they would have in outer space, but they are *weightless* in space because there is no pull exerted by gravity in space. Some balls are much the same size, such as a soccer ball and a volleyball, but one has greater mass than the other and appears to be heavier. A balloon may be much larger but have less mass than a tennis ball. Mass may be the same, but shape may be different. A football has approximately the same mass as a basketball. *The mass of an object affects an object's motion.* The greater the mass, the more difficult it is to move an object.

ACTIVITY   Children may push a bowling ball and a volleyball with one finger and compare the force needed to push each. They should try to stop each ball with the palm of the hand and decide which ball is harder to stop. Any two balls with considerable differences in weight but similar size may be used. The children can see that the shape of a football and a basketball are different, but the mass is similar. By throwing them, they will realize it takes the same amount of force to throw each.

BASIC CONCEPTS ABOUT MASS THAT CHILDREN SHOULD LEARN

1. Mass is the quantity of matter in an object.
2. Two objects may be the same size but have different masses.
3. Two objects may have different shapes but have the same mass.
4. More force is needed to move objects with greater mass.

Momentum is the quantity of motion. It is a measure of both speed and mass. The greater the speed of a body, the greater the momentum. The greater the mass of a body, the greater the momentum. If two balls have the same mass, the one with the most speed will go the farthest. If one object has greater mass than another the same size and they are propelled at the same speed, the one with the greatest mass will go farthest. The more momentum an object has, the longer it will remain in motion. When jumping for distance, a person runs very fast before taking off so enough momentum will be built up to allow the jumper to go farther horizontally in the air before gravity pulls the body down to the ground.

When a moving body hits a stationary body or object, the one that is moving may stop and transfer its momentum to the other object, or both objects may move. The total momentum of the two bodies before impact equals the total momentum after impact.

ACTIVITY

1. By playing the game of Stop and Go (p. 318), running and stopping on signal, children may compare how much longer the body will remain in motion after the stop signal when they run at different speeds.

2. Children can roll one ball at a stationary ball and see the reaction as the balls meet. In the game Poison Ball (p. 332) this factor can be further studied.

BASIC CONCEPTS ABOUT MOMENTUM THAT CHILDREN SHOULD LEARN

1. Momentum is affected by both speed and mass.
2. The greater the speed of an object, the greater the momentum.
3. The greater the mass of an object, the greater the momentum.
4. Momentum may be transferred from one object to another.
5. The total momentum remains constant when one object strikes another.

A push or pull exerted against an object is called a *force*. Everything one does is subject to one or more forces which affect the motion or equilibrium of the body.

Gravity, explained earlier, is a natural force that affects the body in relation to balance. Gravity will be discussed in greater detail in relation to how it affects projectiles.

Air resistance is a force that is always present; it slows the fall of moving bodies. The effects of air resistance on bodies or objects is dependent upon their size, shape, and form; these factors determine the air flow around the objects.

The velocity at which an object is moving is also a factor in amount of air resistance. A light object with a large surface area falls more slowly than a small object with great mass. This is why a badminton shuttle and a tennis ball, when dropped from a height, do not fall to the earth at the same rate of speed. They also have a different flight pattern when they are hit. Have students compare, as well, the fall of a balloon and a golf ball.

Acceleration is the rate of change of velocity (speed). A reduction in velocity is usually spoken of as *deceleration*. The higher one wishes to jump vertically, the greater the vertical acceleration has to be before the downward acceleration, due to gravitational force, becomes greater than upward acceleration.

Friction is the resistance to the forward motion of one surface or object moving over another. The force resulting from the friction between two surfaces depends upon the type of surfaces and the force pushing them together.

There must be friction if there is to be motion. There must be some friction between the surface of shoes and the surface on which one walks, or

Foundations of
Movement

there would be no traction. Traction is the adhesive friction and is the reason why tennis shoes are worn on gym floors and cleated shoes are worn on grassy surfaces. In some instances it is desirable to reduce the amount of friction. Sharpening ice skate blades reduces friction between the blade and the ice.

There are three forms of friction: starting, sliding, and rolling. *Starting friction* is present in the instant between the time the force is applied and the time the object starts to move. This type causes the greatest resistance to motion and is the hardest to overcome. When one body slides or is dragged across another, it is called *sliding friction*, and when a wheel rolls across a surface, it is *rolling friction*. The latter is the easiest to overcome. Therefore, any heavy object that can be put on wheels will be easier to move than if it is resting flat on the floor.

The force that results from friction slows or stops the forward motion. This opposition to movement is called a *frictional force*. The amount of the frictional force that opposes the motion of an object is dependent on its shape. The less surface area in contact with another object, the easier it is to move. Frictional forces opposing the motion of rough surfaces are greater than those opposing the motion of smooth surfaces.

ACTIVITY   Using a partially deflated soccer ball and a normally inflated one, let children kick each ball alternately and help them compare the difference in the roll of the balls and the amount of force needed to kick each ball the same distance. If a ball can be kicked or rolled in grass that needs cutting and then kicked or rolled on grass that has just been cut, children will see the effect of friction in regard to surfaces. They will see the need to kick the ball harder on a rough surface as opposed to a smooth one. In softball the need to run up to field a ground ball in the outfield should be apparent as the children see how the speed of the ball diminishes as it rolls through the grass as opposed to the smoother surface of the infield.

The heavier an object, the more friction there is to be overcome. If an additional downward force is added to the object, friction is increased. Therefore, if anything heavy is to be moved, the push should be made horizontal to and a little below the center of weight of the object.

Centripetal force is the name given to any force directed toward the center of a circular path of motion. There is an opposing force which works against this inward pull. For example, an object that is moving in a circular motion must have this inward pull to keep it going in a straight line; if a ball is attached to the end of a rope and the rope is swung around the head, one can feel a great force pulling outward. This is *centrifugal force*. Centrifugal force is the inertia tendency of a body in motion to travel in a straight line and is the reaction to centripetal force.

ACTIVITY

1. Using the game Jump the Shot (p. 331), relate the principles of centripetal and centrifugal force as the children learn how to turn the rope around the circle. In this game a strong rope with a ball or a deck-tennis ring tied to the end may be used. The leader stands in the center and turns the rope so the "shot" swings around the circle just under the feet of the people standing in the circle. The circle players must jump as the rope passes under them. If they touch it, they are eliminated from the game. Children often have trouble getting the rope to swing out and maintain a steady swing. They should understand, by actually trying to swing the rope, that it takes

a few turns before the shot will travel in a complete circle above the ground, as inertia must be overcome (Newton's first law). As they pull the rope toward the center and feel the outward pull, relate the force needed to keep the ball from flying off into the air to centripetal force. As they feel the ball pulling away from their hand, relate this to centrifugal force which is the reaction of the inward pull exerted by the child to keep the ball from going off in a straight line. After the game, one child may demonstrate turning the rope and then letting go of it. As the shot flies straight out and down from the point of release, relate the principle of inertia that the ball will tend to move forward in a straight line. The friction of the air and gravity will cause it to drop down to the ground.

2. If the children have good body control, a game of Crack the Whip may be played on the grass. In this game everyone stands in a line and holds hands and runs. When everyone is running, the leader turns quickly and stops. Everyone else should stop, but it will be evident that those closest to the leader will stop first and those out toward the end of the line will circle around the leader and as momentum picks up, the line will probably break as the "whip is cracked." Those on the end will continue running in the same direction as they were going when the line breaks or the "whip is cracked." Children can relate their flight to centrifugal force.

BASIC CONCEPTS ABOUT FORCES THAT CHILDREN SHOULD LEARN

1. A force is a push or a pull.
2. Gravity pulls downward.
3. Acceleration is the rate of change of speed.
4. The greater acceleration that is desired, the greater the force must be.
5. Air resistance pushes against an object and slows down its flight through air.
6. The larger the surface area of an object the more air resistance will affect its movement.
7. Friction is the resistance to the forward motion of one surface or object moving over another.
8. The amount of friction depends upon the surface area in contact between two bodies.
9. Friction must be overcome to move an object.
10. There must be some friction between the surface one walks on, runs on, or pushes against.
11. Rolling friction is the easiest to overcome.
12. An object that moves in a circle has a force on it that pushes the object to the outside of the circle; therefore, it must have an inward pull against it to keep it from flying off on a tangent.
13. If an object that is moving in a circular path is released it will go off in a straight line from the point where it was released.

Types of Motion

Motion is of two types, *linear* and *rotary*. Linear motion is that which is in a straight line. In linear motion the body as a whole moves the same distance, in the same direction, at a constant rate of speed. The body is usually carried by another object such as a sled, skis, car, or bus. The body acquires the same motion as the object that carries it. An object, such as a ball, when carried by the hand acquires the same motion and speed as the hand. After it is released, it continues to move at the same speed until it is acted upon by another force.

Rotary motion consists of movement of a body around a center of rotation or an axis. Most human movement is a combination of rotary and linear motion. Most movement patterns involve rotary movement to a point where the rotary speed is converted into linear speed to propel the body or object into a linear path or forward movement. The resultant linear force is dependent upon the weight of the object and speed and the length of the radius of the circle of rotation (the distance between the center of gravity and the axis of the rotation). In a forward roll this would be from the center of gravity to a point near the knees. Throwing patterns are examples of this combination of linear and rotary motion. A ball that is thrown takes the direction of a straight line tangent to the arc in which it was moving when it was released.

In rotary motion, the shorter the radius of the circle of rotation, the greater will be the rotary speed, and conversely the longer the radius, the lesser the speed. When a person is turning around in a circle, the closer the arms and legs are to the body in a tucked position, the quicker the turn can be made. As an ice skater twirls around he draws his arms in toward the body as speed is built up. When he wishes to slow down, he extends his arms away from the body. If great linear speed is desired the radius should be lengthened. In throwing and striking activities where speed is desired, the arm should be fully extended at the moment of release or impact; therefore, the ball will travel at a faster rate of speed than if the elbow were bent.

ACTIVITY   When working on rolling and tucking, help children compare how much faster they can roll if their body is all tucked in a tight ball than if their arms and legs are out to the side or if their body is straight. They can observe how other children straighten their body in order to stop rolling.

Leverage

Body movements are possible through a system of levers. A lever is a mechanical device to produce turning about an axis. It is used to gain a mechanical advantage for speed or so that less effort is necessary to accomplish work. A lever has a fulcrum, which is the axis or center point; a force arm, which is the distance from the fulcrum to the point of application of the force; and a resistance arm, which is the distance from the fulcrum to the resistance upon which the force is acting.

The bones of the body are levers. The force to move the levers is produced by muscles and the fulcrum is the joint where a specific movement takes place. The resistance is the center of gravity of the part of the body part to be moved plus the weight of any object held or placed on the body.

There are three types of levers, and each is classified by the relative position of the fulcrum, force, and resistance (Figure 9-2). In a first-class lever the fulcrum is located between the resistance and the force. A second-class lever has the resistance between the fulcrum and the force. It is a third-class lever when the force is between the fulcrum and the weight (resistance).

The mechanical advantages of the lever are either in producing speed or strength. The first-class lever may do either or both. Second-class levers favor force, and third-class, speed. The decision of advantage is in terms of the ratio

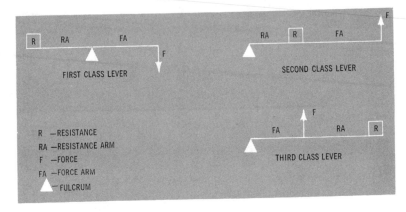

Figure 9-2 The three different classes of levers.

of the length of the arm force to the resistance arm. If one wants to exert great force, the force arm should be as long as possible. If one wants to create great speed, the force arm should be as short as possible and the resistance arm as long as possible.

Most movements of the body are made through third-class levers (Figure 9-3). Note that in the third-class lever the force arm is short in relation to the longer resistance arm. The force arm of the body's levers is short due to structure—the muscles insert close to the joint and most of the weight is far from the joint. Therefore the body can do tasks which require speed or handling of lightweight objects better than heavy tasks. Usually some type of machine must be utilized for the heavy tasks.

Most sports movements usually require the action of many levers. When it is desired to give speed to an object to be thrown or hit, or if the speed is transferred by an instrument held in the hand, many levers function in sequential order so there is a buildup of force and speed. Implements held in the hand such as racquets, bats, and paddles are an extension of the body and

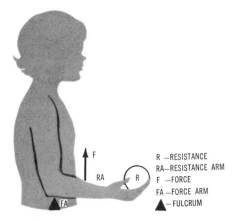

Figure 9-3 Utilization of a third-class lever in the body.

lengthen the body's levers. Applications of this can be seen in the discussion on production of force.

BASIC CONCEPTS ABOUT LEVERS THAT CHILDREN SHOULD LEARN

1. Levers are used to gain a mechanical advantage for speed or so that less effort is necessary to accomplish work.
2. The mechanical advantage of a lever is the ratio of the length of the force arm to the resistance arm (the distance between the effort and the fulcrum and the distance between the fulcrum and the weight or object to be moved).
3. The longer the force arm, the greater the force produced.
4. The longer the resistance arm at the time of release, the faster the action can be. In throwing, the straighter the arm the faster the ball may be thrown. A racquet, bat, or paddle adds to the length of the lever, and therefore the object can be propelled faster.

The Body's Force

It is obvious that force and motion are closely associated, since it is only through force that motion is initiated. Therefore, it is important that the teacher understand how force is developed and how it is used. The source of force in the human body is strength derived from a muscle or a combination of muscles. Force is needed to move the body itself, or to move another body or object with one's own body. The factors concerned with force will be discussed in terms of production of force, application of force, and receiving and absorbing force.

PRODUCTION OF FORCE The amount of force that needs to be produced depends upon the purpose of the movement. Since the muscles supply force, one should recognize certain facts about them and their operation in order to use them efficiently for specific purposes.

Naturally, strong muscles will exert more force than weak ones. The muscles of the legs, hips, and thighs are larger and stronger than those of the arms and back. Several muscles or muscle groups working together will supply more force. If a heavy object is to be moved, force should be exerted directly on the object by all of the large muscles of the legs, hips, thighs, shoulders, and arms simultaneously. Muscles exert more force when they are extended or stretched before they contract. This is why a windup is used before pitching a ball or a backswing is taken before throwing any ball.

The most effective total force is developed when the force from each contributing part of the body is applied in a single direction in a sequential order. The greater the mass of the muscles or number of muscles supplying the force, and the longer it is applied to an object, the greater the force will be. Therefore, the greater the length and the number of levers that are brought into action in successive fashion, the greater the amount of time will be provided for force to develop.

There is a summation of forces as each body part contributes its share until momentum reaches its maximum at the point of application of the force or the release of an object. The momentum developed is imparted to the object which is hit or propelled.

If the momentum is stopped immediately after release of an object or at impact, a jerking motion results, the arc of the movement is shortened, and the speed of the hand is slowed before the object actually leaves the hand. A follow-through motion insures that the center of the arc of the throwing movement is at the point of release, and the maximum speed or force generated is transferred to the object. The follow-through is also a safety factor in terms of reducing possible strain of the shoulder and arm if momentum were stopped immediately.

Production of maximum force can be seen in the proper mechanics of an overhand throw. A forward stride position enables the thrower to rotate the body over the back foot in order to have a great number of muscles contribute to the subsequent forward motion. The ball is brought back to a position well behind the body by a full extension of the arm and hand. In this manner the lever is the whole body and allows a greater distance over which momentum may be developed in the forward motion. As the ball is carried forward, the full weight of the body is behind the forward movement. Each contributing muscle and body part is brought into action in a sequential manner. All of this force is then transferred to the ball, and it acquires the same rate of speed at which the hand is moving at the time of release.

APPLICATION OF FORCE   The force should be applied to an object as directly as possible in the direction in which it is to go. To move the body upward, the body must be erect and all the force directed upward. To move an object forward, the force should be applied through the center of the weight of the object in the desired direction. If force is applied away from the center of weight, a rotary motion will result. Any force applied in a direction other than that which an object is to go is a hindrance and waste of effort. For example, in running, if the arms are swung from side to side the forward motion is retarded.

The direction a body or object takes is a line tangent to that which the arm or implement is moving at the point of release or impact. This means that an object can be released or hit only at the point where the arc is tangent to the desired target, if accuracy is to be achieved (Figure 9-4). The follow-through movements after the object is released do not change or alter the direction of the object.

ABSORPTION OF FORCE   When it is necessary to absorb or receive the force of a thrown object, as in catching a ball, a fall, another body, or a kick, there should be a gradual reduction of force. The shock should be spread over as

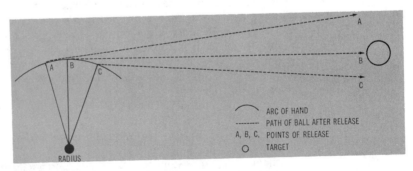

ARC OF HAND
-------- PATH OF BALL AFTER RELEASE
A, B, C, POINTS OF RELEASE
o   TARGET

RADIUS

Figure 9-4 Path of ball after different points of release.

large an area as possible and over as long a distance as possible. When landing from a jump, the bending at the hips, knees, and ankles gives more time for momentum to dissipate. A softball glove helps disperse the impact of a ball over a large area of the hand, as well as lengthening the time it takes for the ball to slow down. If when falling or sliding, one tries to land on a large portion of the body, the force of the impact will be absorbed more gradually and there will be less chance for injury.

Since a force applied anywhere other than through the center of weight sets up rotary motion, balance or stability becomes a problem in receiving or absorbing force. Hence, one should get in line with the oncoming force and assume a balanced position with the body weight low and over the base of support.

BASIC CONCEPTS ABOUT THE BODY'S FORCE THAT CHILDREN SHOULD KNOW

1. To push or pull heavy objects, big muscles of the legs, hips, and thighs should be used. All of the muscles should be used at the same time.
2. Push should be applied to the center of the weight of the object and in the direction the object is to go.
3. As more muscles are used, more force is produced.
4. As the muscles act faster, more force is produced.
5. As a greater number of body levers or parts are used, the amount of time available to build force becomes greater.
6. Each body part should act in order. The throwing pattern follows the order of: trunk rotation, upper arm, lower arm, hand, fingers, release.
7. In kicking, the order is: upper leg, lower leg, foot, contact.
8. The more fully each working muscle is stretched, the more force it can supply.
9. As large an area as possible should be used in order to absorb force.
10. Each joint should give when landing from a jump, or when catching a ball.
11. A follow-through in all hitting and throwing activities ensures maximum application of force and allows time for gradual reduction of momentum.

Principles Related to Projectiles

Since many physical education activities require projection of the body or objects of some type into the air, a few mechanical principles will be related directly to projectiles. A projectile is any object that is sent in motion into space. The body is a projectile as it moves through space in a jump, dive, or a rebound in trampolining. Of course any ball, ring, or shuttle as it is thrown or hit becomes a projectile. The flight a projectile travels in space is affected by gravity, air resistance, angle of release (or angle at which it was struck), spin, and the degree of initial force that launched it.

INITIAL FORCE The way in which the force to project an object is generated in the body was discussed earlier in the chapter and is related to specific skill patterns of throwing, striking, and jumping in Chapter 11. The amount of force imparted to an object is dependent on the mass of the object and the distance and speed necessary for the purpose of the flight.

It is important to remember that whenever an implement is used, it actually becomes an addition to the arm as a longer resistance arm. The longer the resistance arm, the greater the resulting momentum. The momentum acquired from the shift of weight and rotation of the body all are transferred to the implement, which in turn transfers it to the ball or other object.

When the implement or lever is longer, greater velocity can be achieved, but a long lever is often difficult to control. Weight and size of implements such as bats, racquets, and clubs should be determined by the size and weight of the person using them. For this reason, when children first learn tennis and badminton skills, use of short paddles or racquets rather than regular racquets is recommended.

GRAVITY Gravity will exert a downward pull on an object. In the absence of any air resistance or any upward force, any objects dropped from a height will fall to the ground at a standard rate of speed (32 ft/sec/sec). If an object is thrown horizontally with no upward force and at the same speed, it will fall to the ground in the same amount of time and will land a slight distance from the thrower. If the same object is thrown straight up (90-degree angle) its speed will gradually diminish until the upward force and the force of gravity are in equilibrium, then it will fall to earth. When it reaches the point at which it was initially projected it will be traveling at the same speed with which it was projected.

If a ball is given a diagonally upward force, the vertical force is decelerated by gravity until the two are in equilibrium, then it starts its downward path. It takes the same amount of time for the object to reach the height from which it was projected as it did to reach its high point.

The distance an object travels depends upon the initial speed and angle at which it was released. As the angle is lower, the horizontal component is greater and the resistance to gravity is less; therefore, the ball does not stay in the air long enough to go very far. If the angle is large, the object will be in the

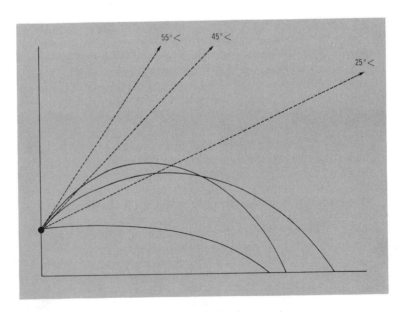

Figure 9-5 Path of objects projected at various angles.

air longer but will go only a short distance. Usually, the greatest distance is obtained when the object is projected approximately at a 45-degree angle (Figure 9-5).

AIR RESISTANCE   Air resistance has little effect on the type of activities usually engaged in by the elementary school child. However, shuttlecocks may be observed as their flight is affected by air resistance. The pattern of flight will be that of almost a vertical descent after the shuttle has reached the top of its ascent (Figure 9-6). The teacher should remember that larger and lighter objects are most affected by air resistance. The influence would be a slight decrease in height and distance that larger and lighter balls would travel.

If a ball has spin on it, there will be an effect on the flight by air resistance. If a ball has no spin, the air resistance is the same on the surface that meets the wall of air through which the ball must pass. When it is spinning, the side that is turning into the wall of air meets greater resistance. The resistance on the opposite side, turning away from the original direction of the ball, is diminished. The ball then tends to move where there is less resistance and the direction of the ball changes. It will curve in the direction of the least resistance. When the ball has a right spin, the flight will curve to the right, and the ball will bounce to the right. When it has a left spin, the flight will curve to the left, and the ball will bounce to the left when it hits the ground.

If there is spin on the top (forward spin), the ball tends to drop faster, as the least resistance is on the bottom of the ball. This type has a long and low bounce. If there is backspin, the resistance is greater on the back, so the ball tends to rise and remain in the air longer. This type has a shorter, higher bounce (Figure 9-7).

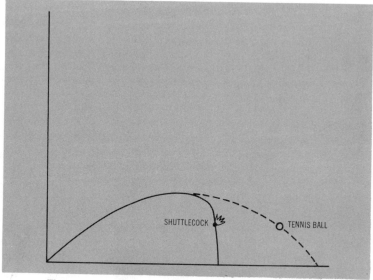

Figure 9-6 Path of a shuttlecock as compared to a tennis ball projected at the same angle.

Figure 9-7 Effect of spin on path of ball.

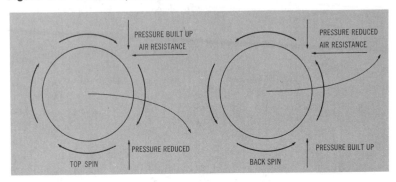

ACCURACY The most important factor in accuracy is the point of release or the point of impact on the object. This must be that point in the arc of the arm or implement at which the ball is tangent to the target. Since the throwing and striking movements are rotary, the arm is moving in an arc; however, it is slightly flattened just before release or impact on the object. This requires timing, concentration, and practice. The trunk should be rotated forward only as far as necessary to allow the arm to remain in a straight line toward the target. The hand or implement should travel in as straight a line as possible toward the target on the backswing and on the follow-through. Focusing on the target until the ball is in flight helps retain concentration on the straight line.

ANGLE OF REBOUND Usually a ball will rebound at an angle equal to that at which it strikes a surface (Figure 9-8). Spin, elasticity of the ball, and the firmness of the surface affect the angle of rebound. Spin was discussed previously. All balls are flattened somewhat by the force of the impact against a hard surface. A hard or properly inflated ball is restored to its original shape very quickly, and the angle of rebound affected very little. A soft or old ball allows some of the force to be absorbed, and the rebound is lower. The same is true if the striking surface is not firm. If the striking implement is not held firmly or is allowed to "give" when it contacts the ball, the rebound or projecting force is considerably less, and the direction of the rebound may also be changed.

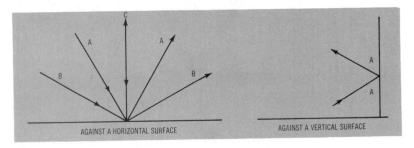

Figure 9-8 Angle of rebound.

BASIC CONCEPTS ABOUT PROJECTILES THAT CHILDREN SHOULD LEARN

1. A projectile is anything that is sent into space by some force.

2. A sport implement (bat, racquet, paddle) becomes a part of the body.

3. A ball that is projected at a large angle at the time of release will travel high in the air a short distance and be in the air longer than a ball released at a small angle.

4. To throw the ball as far as possible the ball should be released at approximately a 45-degree angle.

5. To project the body into the air and to have it go the greatest forward distance, the takeoff from the ground should be at a 45-degree angle.

6. If a ball spins to the left, the path of the ball will curve to the left, and the ball will bounce to the left.

7. If a ball spins to the right, the path of the ball will curve to the right, and the ball will bounce to the right.

8. A ball with topspin will drop faster and have a long and low bounce.

9. A ball with backspin will rise in the air and travel farther and it will have a high and short bounce.

10. A ball must be released at a point when the hand is tangent to the target.

11. Eyes should be focused on the target.

12. The throwing arm should be brought straight back and straight forward in the throw.

13. A ball will bounce back from the floor, wall, racquet, bat, or paddle at the same angle at which it hit.

14. A bat, racquet, or paddle must be held firmly when contact with the ball is made.

The mechanical principles presented here are those that are most essential to basic skills. When working with highly skilled individuals, the teacher may wish to refer to more detailed resource material. The fundamental skill patterns are analyzed in Chapter 11. The basic mechanical principles relative to the understanding of the different factors involved in each movement pattern are described. The reader will find that the material in this chapter is the background for Chapter 11.

The teacher should help children understand the principles of force, balance, motion, and direction as each skill is introduced. Naturally, the vocabulary and depth of detail should be commensurate with the maturity level of the students. (Remember—the principles are described using the vocabulary of the reader, not that of elementary school pupils.) First-graders can learn *how* to use the body to gain more force and *how* to retain balance. Concepts about levers and force are usually introduced in the third-grade science curriculum. Thereafter, additional information about work and machines is presented in subsequent years. It would be wise for the teacher to relate body movement and the physical principles as the concepts are learned in the classroom.

Movement of the body actually starts from specific joints, which are where two or more bones join or come together. Joints are classified by their potential for mobility. A few joints are immovable. The greatest number are classified as freely movable, and these are the ones involved with body actions. Within these are varying degrees of movement due to limitations imposed by the muscles, tendons, and ligaments that hold the joints together.

Children should be aware of the joints and their fullest range of movement which can be achieved. The degree to which one can use joints throughout their fullest range is called *degree of flexibility*. The way to increase and maintain flexibility is to use the joints and stretch the connective tissues within the muscles.

Joint Movements

There are a few terms which describe the movements of body parts due to action within the joints. As many body actions are described in these terms, both the teacher and the students should include them in their vocabulary.

Flexion takes place when adjacent bones of two body parts are brought together and the angle between the two diminishes. With young children the terms "bend," "shorten," and "make small" are often used.

Extension takes place when the adjacent body parts are returned to their original position or when they are in a standing position. With young children the terms "straighten," "stretch," "reach," and "make tall" are often used.

Hyperextension refers to a continuation of movement beyond the original or standing position. Most commonly, and in this book, the term "extension" is used in reference to body action, even though the action moves beyond the original position into hyperextension.

Rotation refers to a movement of a segment around its own longitudinal axis. The body part may be turned inward or outward (medial or lateral rotation, respectively). With children this usually is referred to as "twisting."

Circumduction refers to a movement where the end of a segment or body part as a whole describes a circular pattern. The shape of this movement is similar to that of an ice cream cone; the point is the joint where the action takes place, and the wide end of the cone is the area where the circle is made. With children this is usually referred to as "turning."

Abduction is a sideward movement away from the midline of the body. *Adduction* is a sideward movement inward toward the midline of the body. The major joints and their actions are summarized below.

1. *Spine* (as a whole): flexion, extension, adduction, abduction, rotation, and circumduction.

2. *Head and neck:* flexion, extension, abduction, rotation, circumduction.

3. *Shoulder:* flexion, extension, abduction, rotation, circumduction.

4. *Elbow:* flexion, extension; no hyperextension, circumduction, or rotation (except at radio-ulnar joint).

5. *Wrist:* flexion, extension, abduction, adduction, circumduction, rotation.

6. *Hip:* flexion, extension, abduction, adduction, circumduction, rotation; little hyperextension.
7. *Knee:* flexion, extension; slight rotation in free-standing position.
8. *Ankle:* flexion (dorsal), extension (plantar), hyperextension, circumduction; no abduction, adduction, or rotation.
9. *Foot:* flexion, extension, abduction (pronation), adduction (supination).

It should be remembered that this is a very general description of joint movements and that within each of these there are varying degrees of movement. There is an interrelation of all of these joint actions as the body parts move. Children should be encouraged to experiment with the range of motion. They will learn to appreciate the varying ranges and uses of the body parts. They should note the greater mobility and range of the shoulder, arms, and hands than that of the spine, hips, knees, ankles, and feet. At the same time, they should realize the strength and the stability for supporting the body weight which the latter afford. Suggested movement experiences to explore these actions are given in Chapter 11.

With younger children the common terms "bend," "stretch," "sideward," "twist," and "turn" may be used, but should be associated with the feelings and actions of the joint. As children study and learn about the structure and functions of the body in health classes, the terms and movements should be related to action in the physical education classes.

Muscle Action

Our ability to move is dependent upon the action of muscles and their control by the nervous system. Through a complex interrelationship of the nervous system and sensory devices, messages concerning various external stimuli and needs for muscle action and movement are coordinated. The development of the nervous system determines the efficiency and quality with which the muscle system is controlled.

Because there is a continuous relay of impulses from the nervous system to the muscles, the muscles are in a constant state of partial contraction called *tonus.* When a muscle is not used because of neglect or immobilization of some type, there is less nerve supply to a muscle and it loses its tonus. Muscles with good tonus are firm and smooth; those which are flabby and weak have poor tonus. Muscles must be exercised to retain shape and strength.

When a muscle is stimulated by the nervous system, tension is developed and movement is produced. When activated muscles pull or contract, the muscle shortens. Muscles are arranged in pairs and counterbalance the joint which they cross. As one muscle contracts, the paired muscle relaxes. Efficient movement is sometimes hampered by the inability of the paired muscles to contract and relax in a coordinated manner. Movement is then jerky and wasteful. This problem can be eliminated through learning the techniques of relaxation and through much practice of movements in order to coordinate the actions.

The sources of energy for the muscle to contract are oxygen and other substances, which are brought to the muscle by the blood supply. There is a ready supply of these in the muscle, but if action is sustained for any length of time, the muscle becomes fatigued unless the blood supply is supplemented and maintained. Certain by-products of action are produced and must also be removed by the blood supply.

Whether or not there is an adequate supply of oxygen and blood to the muscles depends upon an individual's state of endurance. There are two types of endurance, *cardiovascular* and *muscular*. The latter is related to the individual muscle, which enables the muscle to contract over a period of time. Physiologically, the recovery rate of the muscle is increased due to a greater number of functioning capillaries in the muscle. This increase comes about through use and exercise.

Cardiovascular endurance is related to work or contractions of large muscle groups over a long period of time. Stress is placed on the respiratory and circulatory systems of the body because they must supply adequate blood and oxygen to the muscles when they are called upon to work over a period of time.

Fundamentals of Exercise

The condition of a muscle is dependent on the amount of exercise it gets. When a muscle is not used, it atrophies or deteriorates, strength decreases, capillary function decreases, size decreases, and it becomes limp. If the muscle is used regularly, hypertrophy will result. In this event, all of the conditions just mentioned will increase rather than decrease. This is the *law of use and disuse*. However, it is possible to increase the strength of a muscle three times or more without a proportional increase in size; therefore girls or women need not worry that exercise will produce bulky, masculine-looking muscles.

In order to maintain the desired amount of strength, regular exercise is essential. It is a physiological fact that a muscle will increase in strength only if it is called upon to increase its workload beyond what is ordinarily required of it. This is called the *principle of overload*.

Providing an overload can be done in two ways: by increasing the *duration* of an activity or by increasing the *intensity* of it. This simply means that a pupil must lift something heavier or do something over a longer period of time than he usually does. Obviously the term is relative to the individual. Asking a pupil who can do only one sit-up to do three more would be a heavy overload and would, therefore, be unrealistic. Asking one who can do thirty-five to do two more would be a small overload and probably not a difficult undertaking.

The development of strength is specific to the muscle or muscles involved in a particular exercise or activity. Therefore, in order to maintain or build strength in general, a school program must include a wide variety of activities that necessitate use of all muscle groups. Specific exercises are available which will aid strength building in isolated muscles or muscle groups.

There are two types of exercise, *isotonic* and *isometric*. In isometric exercises the muscle contracts against a resistance that is greater than the force the muscle can produce. There is no actual work done, no shortening of the muscle, no movement, but within the muscle itself tension is created and values gained from the increased tension. Pushing against an immovable object and holding the contraction for a few seconds provides a simple isometric exercise. The values of isometric exercises are that little time is needed for them, because few contractions at any one time are necessary, and very little space or equipment is necessary.

In isotonic exercises the muscle contracts against a resistance less than the force in the contraction, and the body part to which the muscle attaches moves. The tension within the muscle is constant throughout the period of contraction. Lifting a weight, which may be a brick, a book, or the body weight itself, is an isotonic exercise. Most exercises for children are isotonic, since usually there is a joint movement involved. These exercises can be made more interesting than the isometrics, and greater endurance is developed through isotonics.

There are three basic points to remember when plans are made to build strength.

1. There must be an overload on a muscle. The resistance must increase as the capacity of the muscle increases. The overload may be an increase in degree of repetition, duration, speed, and intensity of contraction of the muscle.

2. There must be regular practice.

3. Muscle strength is specific. Exercises or activities should be planned to localized effort in order to build up weak areas.

Muscular endurance is highly related to strength. The more a muscle is used, the more functioning capillaries there will be. Building muscle endurance is dependent on the overload principle. Continued contractions of the muscle beyond the point of apparent fatigue will enhance both the development of endurance and strength of the muscle.

In building general cardiovascular endurance, large-muscle activities have to be extended over a long period of time during which the respiratory and circulatory systems can build a tolerance for more work. It is difficult to build endurance if an activity or exercise is used in which a child has little skill, because there is a great deal of wasted effort in his uncoordinated movements. One must build skill first, then endurance. As with strength, the development of cardiovascular endurance is dependent upon the overload principle.

Running is an excellent activity through which to develop endurance. The distance run must be increased gradually and regularly. After increasing the distance, the overload may be applied in terms of speed in which the distance must be covered.

Each child starts out with a different tolerance level for exercise, and each should have a varying degree of intensity and duration added daily or periodically. There are five basic points to remember when plans are made to build endurance:

1. Build skill first.

2. All work should be done near one's limit.

3. Increase workload first in terms of duration of time, then tempo.

4. Practice should be regular.

5. Endurance activities should be individualized and graduated.

Teaching the techniques of relaxation to elementary school children is extremely important from two standpoints. Relaxation of muscles is essential in all movements owing to the paired nature of muscle arrangement, where the antagonistic muscles relax while the opposing muscles are contracting. Clumsy, awkward, inefficient skills are a result of an imbalance between relaxation and contraction. The ability to relax is an important asset to maintaining good physical and mental health. There are many pressures, real or imaginary, in our society today which lead to frustration, tension, fatigue, and ultimately to poor health. The ability to relax at will can relieve some of those tensions and prevent possible illnesses or breakdowns.

Relaxation is the release of tension in a specific muscle, or more generally, a number of muscles. It is a motor skill and must be learned. The basis of learning it is a recognition of a state of feeling of tension or tonus in the muscle. One must be able to differentiate between the feeling of tension and relaxation.

In addition to teaching the techniques of relaxation, the teacher should create an atmosphere in the classroom and the gymnasium in which pressures and resulting tension will be at a minimum. Undue emphasis on competition for grades and academic success should be avoided. The teacher should help parents understand realistic goals for children in terms of their ability. Both the academic program and the physical education program should be geared to individual abilities. Schedules should be planned so that the most demanding academic subjects do not follow one another. Planning should allow enough flexibility so that short activity breaks may be taken when needed.

Teaching Relaxation Techniques

In order to differentiate between contraction and relaxation, children must experiment with the feel of the two as they use their muscles. When children are sitting down, suggest that they make one of their arms like a baseball bat, then like a piece of loose rope. They should compare the feeling of the muscles within that arm and also the feel of it as they touch it with the opposite hand. The terms "contract" and "relax" should continually be associated with the action and the feel. The terms "tense" and "tension" should also be related to contract and contraction.

Suggest extending the arm and contracting the upper part and the lower part of it at the same time. As the children do this, ask if they can move the arm. They will find that if muscles in both parts are contracting with the same amount of force there will be no movement. This is an isometric contraction. Suggest relaxing the bottom part some and contracting the top. It will be apparent that there will be movement toward the muscle that is pulling the hardest.

Further exploration such as this with various body parts may be pursued. Experiences that help students to control relaxation of muscles in each body part, or one part of a part, or one leg and the opposite arm, or a hand or a foot, or one side of the body, etc., should be structured. Some of these should take place when children are in a standing position or when they are moving; for example, they should be asked to "walk with the legs stiff and the arms limp."

Most of the suggestions have been related to differential relaxation of specific parts of the body. Experiences should be provided for general relaxation where one tries to relax the whole body. This is usually done in a reclining position and involves relaxation in breathing also. The expiratory phase may be passive as the air is let out. At first this may be accompanied by a loud sigh or noise. Gradually there will be a slower rate of respiration due to passive expiration.

Imagery may be utilized as a technique to acquire a relaxed state. Following are a few suggestions that can be made to the class to encourage general relaxation:

1. Melt like an ice cream cone on a hot day.

2. Be a rag doll.

3. Be a balloon that has burst.

4. Be squashy.

5. Be a soft fluffy cloud.

6. (*Contrast*) Be a tin soldier, then a rag doll.

7. (*Contrast*) Be a piece of steel, then a feather pillow.

Similar ideas may be used to induce differential relaxation.

1. Be a mast on a sailboat and let your arms be sails in a stiff wind. What happens to the sails when the wind stops blowing?

2. Let your body be a tulip stalk and your head be a tulip flower that has been snapped partially off the stem.

3. Be a bird that has one wing broken.

Relaxation must also be taught in relation to specific skills. Once children recognize the difference between contraction and relaxation and their relationship to movement, they must apply this in their skill performance. Teachers must be alert to opportunities to point out the need for relaxation in specific skills. They should watch for tenseness in individuals as they perform and encourage free-swinging movements, particularly in striking events. The feel of correct position and tension of body parts during movement should be stressed as new skills are learned.

Summary

The information in this chapter should provide the teacher or prospective teacher with a better understanding of how the body operates in relation to movement. The majority of the material has been presented to the teacher as information about the mechanical laws that govern movement, the movement possibilities of the body, and the fundamentals of exercise. Teachers, in turn, must teach this information to children through body movement. They must use this information in order to understand why, what, and how they can utilize the activities presented in the latter part of this book to help children successfully realize the movement potential of their bodies.

**SUGGESTED
REFERENCES FOR
FURTHER STUDY**

BROER, MARION, and RONALD ZERNICKE, *Efficiency of Human Movement.* Philadelphia: Saunders, 1973.

DUNN, LOIS, *Motion, Investigating Science with Children,* Vol. 4. Darien, Conn.: Teacher's Publishing Co., 1964.

UBELL, EARL, and ARLINE STRONG, *The World of Push and Pull.* New York: Atheneum, 1964.

WALLIS, EARL L., and GENE LOGAN, *Exercise for Children.* Englewood Cliffs, N.J.: Prentice-Hall, Inc., 1966.

WICKSTROM, RALPH H., *Fundamental Motor Patterns.* Philadelphia: Lea & Febiger, 1977

Foundations of
Movement

10 / PHYSICAL FITNESS

- **Factors of physical fitness**
- **Assessing physical fitness**
- **Improving physical fitness**

In recent years there has been much attention and concern about the fitness status of the children and adults of America. Most of this concern was touched off by the discovery that children of some foreign countries scored higher on certain fitness tests than American children. A review of history indicates that there have been periods of concern over fitness whenever America has been exposed to the threat of war. The combination of the need for military preparedness during the "cold war" period and the revelation of the low fitness level of American children in 1956 sparked a national interest in improving the fitness level of all Americans.

President Dwight D. Eisenhower originated a committee on the fitness of youth in 1956. John F. Kennedy supported the cause for fitness and enlarged the original committee to the President's Council on Youth Fitness. This council sought cooperation from professional physical educators, medical and health groups. With further encouragement from successive presidents, this council has continued to supply information, materials, and guidance in promoting fitness testing, standards, programs, and interest throughout the country.

The profession of physical education has long accepted the responsibility for development of physical fitness of school children as one of its prime objectives. When studies showed that many American young people were not as physically fit as the youth of other nations, the profession took up the challenge and opportunity to study and promote programs designed to improve the fitness level of all children and adults.

Physical fitness involves the development of the physical qualities needed to enable individuals to function efficiently and effectively in their environment. This includes provisions for guidance in posture, health habits, strength, endurance, flexibility, power, agility, balance, and motor skills.

Some people wrongly believe that the *only* job of physical educators is to provide and structure exercise and activities to develop fitness. They must also encourage a positive attitude toward the importance of fitness. The child should understand the values, the need for, and the skills related to acquiring and maintaining physical fitness. Thereafter, the provision of opportunities for exercise will be of more long-lasting value. All attitudes are developed and/or acquired through knowledges, experiences, and insights into particular learnings. The more positive and rewarding the experiences in the physical education program, the more appreciative of physical fitness young people will become, and their habits and expectations of good physical fitness will be more positive. The development of these attitudes is reserved not just for the gymnasium. Parents and teachers must relate knowledge and appreciation to total fitness.

A good attitude toward the need to acquire and maintain physical fitness can be gained best through a good developmental physical education program. Starting in the primary grades children should be taught not only the skills of fitness but the *qualities* of physical fitness. They should discover that vigorous activities are fun. Some realization of fitness should be inherent in every activity presented in the daily lesson. Provided with a program planned for maximum participation for all, most children in the elementary school should have few deficiencies in fitness qualities.

There is a growing trend for physical educators and health educators to join forces to plan cardiovascular intervention programs (CVI). Heart disease is the number one cause of death in America; it is related to lifestyle and may be correlated between parents and children, so early study of health and exercise habits as related to prevention of cardiovascular disease is essential. The emphasis in health education programs today is on good nutritional habits and on drug use and abuse patterns. In physical education programs the emphasis is on the cardiovascular aspects of strength and endurance and attitudes toward play and exercise. In fact the term "CVI program" is replacing the term "fitness" in many programs.

Many factors contribute to the development of physical fitness. A child must have the basic equipment in terms of health, energy, body structure, and opportunity before the activities of physical education can be very effective. Everyone has some degree of fitness, and all can improve upon their present status. Teachers must know how to determine and interpret status before they can set expectations of ultimate attainment.

Factors of Physical Fitness

The areas of physical fitness which are of greatest concern to the elementary school teacher will be described and suggestions will be given for development and maintenance in the areas of health, posture, and components of physical fitness.

Health

The health status of children provides the limits or extent of the minimum fitness level that we can expect of them. Expecting a child with health problems to achieve a high level of physical fitness is as unrealistic as expecting a racing car to win a race without fuel. The classroom and the physical education teacher have two major responsibilities in regard to the health status of each pupil. One is to identify pupils whose health level or habits appear to be below normal and then refer them to the proper authorities for examination and treatment. The authorities may vary in any one school system from a school nurse, physician, principal, or parents. Teachers are in a good position to notice deviations from the norm in appearance, behavior, or energy level of children. Listlessness, fatigue early in a game, poor color, hypersensitivity to reactions of other children in give-and-take situations, inability to react quickly enough to required activity responses, and lack of interest in activities all indicate a need for further investigation.

The second responsibility is to be acquainted with and understand the health status of each child. This also includes an understanding of the limitations and fitness needs of children who have physical defects that are not remediable, such as structural malformations, deafness, partial loss of sight, and heart conditions. Modifications of exercise and activities may have to be developed for a child with a particular handicap. Children returning to school from absences due to prolonged illnesses have suffered from a loss of physical fitness and must rebuild muscle strength and endurance. The inactivity induced by even a brief confinement in bed results in a depreciation of strength and endurance.

The school administration has the responsibility for requiring or providing periodic medical examinations for each child. The classroom teacher may be expected to assist with some phases of this examination, such as screening of visual and hearing defects, and weighing and measuring. The administration also has the responsibility for providing a healthful environment for children. Naturally, the teacher plays a vital part in daily routine provisions of a healthy environment through attention to proper ventilation, rest periods, seating, etc.

Posture

It is extremely difficult to ascertain the cause-and-effect relationship of good or poor posture to fitness, health, nutritional status, or psychological factors. There is no one ideal posture. In the course of a day a child is in many postures—sitting, running, standing, and walking. Generally, good posture is judged when one is in a standing position and the body is in good alignment, with the body segments well balanced over the base of support. The body line

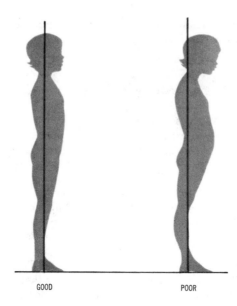

Figure 10-1 Examples of good and poor body alignment.

GOOD   POOR

should be vertical with a nearly vertical line running from a joint just in front of the ankle joint, through the middle of the kneecap, the middle of the hip joint, the edge of the shoulder, and up through the middle of the ear (Figure 10-1).

When maintaining this position, the body is constantly fighting the downward force of gravity. The anti-gravity muscles must have enough strength and endurance to hold this position. If poor posture is prolonged over a long period of time, muscles adapt both in length and function to the faulty position, and it becomes increasingly difficult to correct the fault. The teacher should remember that the physical environment of the classroom contributes to posture defects. As children grow, the size of their desks needs to be increased. Also, adjustments to see the blackboard from an awkward position or because of inadequate lighting can cause poor habits of sitting posture, which may be hard to remedy.

Although there is little evidence from research to substantiate it, there is a common belief that there is a relationship between posture and health. When the body segments are out of line, vital internal organs are possibly pushed out of the proper position, pressure is placed upon them, and as a result, proper growth and functioning is impaired.

Improper diet and fatigue affect the amount of energy that one has to exert upon good posture. Emotional stresses or depression affect the mental attitude toward a good self-image. An alert teacher will notice a sudden change in posture and should then look for any deviations in the child's habits or attitudes. A child with a slight hearing loss may strike a posture, which enables him to lean closer to what he is trying to hear. In this and similar cases one can easily see the interrelation between poor health and poor posture.

ASSESSING POSTURE Usually, the teacher's responsibility for assessing posture is limited to mere observation for deviations from the normal. There are posture tests available from different sources; however, teachers may devise their own checklists and look for the signs of good posture which are listed below.[1]

STANDING

1. Feet parallel and about 6 inches apart.
2. Head high, as if balancing a book on the head.
3. Chest out.
4. Stomach and hips firm.
5. Abdomen and back as flat as possible.
6. Knees very slightly flexed—not locked.
7. Weight evenly distributed on each foot. Most of the body weight on balls of feet.

SITTING

1. Sit back in the chair, so that hips touch the back of the chair.
2. Sit tall.
3. Keep chest out and neck in line with upper back.
4. When writing, lean forward from the hips. Keep head and shoulders in line.

WALKING

1. Knees and ankles limber and toes pointed straight ahead.
2. Swing legs directly forward from the hip joints.
3. Lift feet off the ground; don't shuffle.
4. Shoulders and arms swing free and easy—no pulling or tension.
5. Head and chest high.
6. The heel touches the ground first in each step.

The terms used in this list may also be used for cue words when making suggestions for good posture. Observation of standing posture is enhanced if a long mirror is utilized. A piece of tape running down the mirror will aid the teacher in checking body alignment as the child stands in front of the mirror. A plumb line or string with a weight on one end can be hung in a doorway and used to check body alignment as the child stands next to the line (see Figure 10-1 for proper alignment).

Recently, physicians have found a high incidence of mild *scoliosis* (3 to 4 percent) in young adolescents. Scoliosis is a lateral curvature of the spine, generally associated with rotation of the spine and rib cage. If undetected and thus untreated, curves may lead to severe cosmetic deformity or eventually cardiopulmonary decompensation. They also cause back pains and disability in adulthood.

Some cases are congenital and progress rapidly; some are secondary to a neurogenic problem such as polio, neurofirmatosis, meningomyelocele, or paralysis; some are genetic or familial, probably owing to a genetic trait. The latter are most common (50 percent) and usually develop at the prepubertal

[1] From the President's Council on Youth Fitness, *Youth Physical Fitness* (Washington, D.C.: Superintendent of Documents, 1973), p. 94.

age (9 to 13), then progress rapidly until skeletal maturity and afterward more slowly. Early cases of genetic scoliosis are largely asymptomatic and hard to detect, because the children appear healthy.

Mild and moderate cases can be treated nonsurgically through exercises and use of the Milwaukee brace or Boston module. Severe curves are usually treated surgically. If surgery is required, the best results usually occur during adolescence rather than in adulthood. With the high incidence rate at ages 9 to 13, the asymptomatic condition and the better prognosis if detected and treated early, it is imperative that screening for scoliosis be conducted in the upper elementary and/or middle school years. A number of states now require screening in the schools at these ages.

While the incidence is not as high as with scoliosis, the onset of conditions of *kyphosis* and *lordosis* is also at the same ages, and screening for these should be done at the same time. Kyphosis (round shoulders) is a structural deformity of the thoracic spine in which the normal rounding of the back as seen from the side is increased. Sometimes this may be increased by slouched posture, in which the rounding is fixed in the kyphotic spine due to wedging of the vertebrae; in this case severe deformity develops. If detected early, it too can be treated by exercise and bracing.

Lordosis (swayback) is an increase in the normal forward curve of the lumbar spine and prominence of the sacrum and buttocks. It may be postural due to weak and droopy abdominal muscles and/or unusually large buttocks or it may be a fixed structural deformity—a manifestation of an underlying structural defect of significance, such as spondylolisthesis, a slipping of the vertebrae forward over one another.

Many young children will exhibit a protruding abdomen, a slight hollow in the back, and protruding shoulder blades but not have marked posture deviations. These are signs of immaturity and naturally resolve themselves into a more mature contour in later years if proper activities are provided for natural growth and strength.

Each of the above conditions may be detected by a screening exam, which should take no more than 30 seconds and identify those children who need to be further tested and possibly treated by a physician. The school nurse usually coordinates a screening program with the help of the physical education and the classroom teacher in the fifth, sixth, and seventh grades; she notifies parents if a physician's help is needed.

Following are suggested screening procedures. For all of the tests children should wear leotards, halter and shorts, or anything that will allow the bare back and the contour of the spine to be easily seen.

SCREENING FOR SCOLIOSIS   The child should stand erect with the back toward the examiner, who will look for these signs (see Figure 10-2).

1. Balance—does the head and the base of the neck line up over the center of the sacrum? (Use plumb line if necessary.)

2. Is one *shoulder* higher or longer than the other, or is there a fullness on one side of the neck?

3. Is the "wing" of one *shoulderblade* higher or more prominent than the other?

4. Is there a deeper crease over one side of the waist than the other, or is there a greater distance between the arm and flank on one side or the other? Is there a deeper crease over one side of the waist?

Figure 10-2 Screening steps for scoliosis.

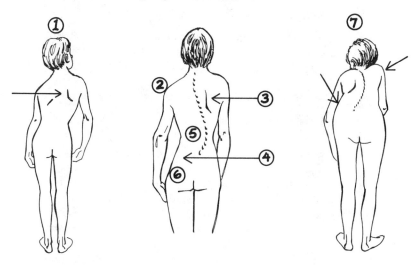

5. Does the spine appear to curve?
6. Is there an asymmetrical contour of the flanks and hips?

The child should then bend forward with the back parallel to the floor and the hands clasped.

7. Is there a prominence or bulge on one side of the back or flank?

Any one of these findings suggests an underlying scoliosis curve and needs further evaluation.

SCREENING FOR KYPHOSIS Have the child turn so as to be viewed from the side, standing relaxed and erect (see Figure 10-3).

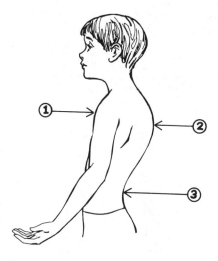

Figure 10-3 Screening steps for kyphosis and lordosis.

1. Do the shoulders hunch forward excessively?
2. Is there excessive prominence of the dorsal spine?

If the child cannot correct the above postural defects when he/she is asked to stand as straight as possible, then a fixed postural deformity should be suspected and a physician should make further examination.

SCREENING FOR LORDOSIS   Have the child in the same position as above.

3. Is there an increased angle between the lumbar spine and the sacrum, and unusual prominence of the sacrum?

Have the child bend forward. If the lumbosacral angle does not flatten out and if the child has difficulty touching his toes, there may be a structural lordosis present and further evaluation is necessary.

When marked deviations are found, the child should be referred to the proper authorities and the parents. Corrective exercises must be given by the physical education specialist under the prescription of the doctor. Exercises to maintain good posture and improve some poor posture habits of a minor nature due to a lack of muscle strength and control are found in Chapter 17 under "Developmental Exercises." Provision for many climbing, hanging, and swinging activities will help build good posture. Most running games and dance activities do not provide enough vigorous use of the upper trunk, shoulder, and arms.

Components of Physical Fitness

There are a number of components that contribute to the attainment of efficient work habits. Actually, these components are basic to all good movement. Some of them contribute more than others to physical fitness. A person may possess a high degree of one and not of another. The most fit person attains a high degree in most of the components.

Some people maintain that physical fitness reflects cardiorespiratory fitness; other include the motor fitness aspects of strength, muscular endurance, muscular power, flexibility, agility, speed, balance, and coordination. Some refer to the former as health-related aspects and the latter as performance aspects. For the purposes of this book, no differentiation will be made because every teacher should know what these are and how each is affected by exercise and movement.

STRENGTH   One of the most basic components to success in all movement is strength. Muscular strength is defined as the amount of force that can be exerted by a particular muscle. The strength of a muscle is dependent on its size and quality. Muscles grow in size in relation to general growth, nutrition, and amount of exercise. Varying degrees of strength needed in muscles are dependent upon the type of work or activity that is to be done beyond the ordinary daily needs.

Physiologically, the muscle will increase in strength only if it is called upon to increase its workload beyond what is ordinarily required of it. This is called the principle of overload. Muscle strength is just maintained, not increased, if no additional effort or intensity is added to exercises or activities.

The development of strength is specific to the muscle or muscles involved in a particular exercise or activity. Consequently, the teacher must plan a variety of activities which will necessitate use of all of the muscle groups. Many of our popular games and sports require the use of the muscles of the legs, lower back, arms and hands, but not much use of the upper back and shoulder girdle muscles. Opportunities should be provided for hanging and inverted activities where shoulder area muscles must help support the weight of the body.

ENDURANCE There are two types of endurance: cardiovascular and muscular. The latter is related to the extent to which the individual muscle can continue to contract over a period of time. This is highly related to strength.

Cardiovascular endurance is related to work or contractions of large-muscle groups over a long period of time. Stress is placed on the heart and the respiratory and circulatory systems of the body when they must supply adequate blood and oxygen to the muscles. Certain adjustments are made in these systems as the use of the overload principle demands them. Generally children will not overexert themselves. In order to develop both types of endurance and strength they must be pushed to do a little more or try a little harder than they did the time before. The amount of extra effort needed will vary for each child in relation to his or her present status.

AGILITY Agility is the ability of a person to change direction or body position quickly and regain poise or control to proceed with another movement. Agility is highly dependent upon or interrelated with speed, strength, balance, and coordination. It is developed through practice and confidence in movement. The acquisition of agility is not only important to success in games and sports requiring quick changes of direction and dodging of objects or other people, but also to safety outside of the play situation. Instruction and opportunities to participate in activities requiring fast starts, stops, and changes of direction should be included in the daily program.

FLEXIBILITY Flexibility is the range of movement in a joint. The degree of flexibility determines the extent of extension and flexion of a joint and consequent body action in terms of bending, reaching, twisting, and turning. The degree of flexibility is first determined by the nature of the joint itself and then by the ligaments and muscles related to the joint. Flexibility is very specific to each joint. One may be quite flexible in one area but not another. Within the limitations of the bone structure and the condition of the ligaments, range of movement can be expanded through exercises of stretching the muscle.

A high degree of flexibility not only enables a child to perform some activities more efficiently, but it also provides a safety factor in terms of absorbing sudden shocks or blows around vulnerable joint areas. The knee and ankle joints are prone to sudden jolts in everyday activities.

POWER Power is the capacity of the body to release maximum force or muscle contraction in the shortest possible time. Power denotes explosive movements, a release of maximum force at maximum speed. Obviously, power is highly dependent upon the elements of speed and strength. Power is important to success in performance of jumping, kicking for distance, throwing for distance, charging an object or opponent, starting a run with a fast takeoff or sudden bursts of speed, or pulling away from an assailant. It can be improved through gains in strength and practice of the activities just mentioned.

SPEED Speed is the rapidity with which one repeats successive movements of the same pattern. Great speed in muscle contraction is not always conducive to the greatest efficiency of movement. It seems that there is an optimum speed at which muscles contract with the greatest conservation of energy for the amount of work done.

Success in some activities is highly dependent upon how fast one can move body parts or the whole body from one place to another. This need is also inherent in some occupations or in the face of imminent dangers. Speed of movement can be improved through practice for good technique and efficiency of movement.

BALANCE Balance is the ability to maintain a desired position of the body whether in a static or held position or in a dynamic or moving state. It denotes a degree of stability and ease in control of the body in a specific position.

Balance is an important factor in most games, sports, dance, and gymnastic activities. Most life and work activities require good balance in order to prevent falls and accidents. The balance of children can be improved through exposure to and practice of balance activities.

COORDINATION Coordination is the ability to integrate muscle movements into an efficient pattern of movement. Coordination makes the difference between good performance and poor performance. The efficiency of skill patterns depends upon the interrelation of speed, agility, balance, and muscle movements into a well-coordinated pattern. The child must understand the movement to be performed and see the relationships of each movement to the total pattern. Development of kinesthetic perception usually allows movements to become rhythmical and efficient.

Good coordination is not only essential to good performance in sport and skill games, but it is also vital to all daily and vocational tasks where efficient movement and conservation of energy are important. Only a great deal of guided practice of specific skills will produce well-coordinated movements.

Assessing Physical Fitness

Because the components of physical fitness are specific and not necessarily interrelated, the teacher must select a variety of tests to determine specific areas of weakness in individuals. The selection must be prudent, because the administration of a great number of tests can be very time-consuming. The results of the tests may be used to diagnose the physical status of each child, to identify those needing special help, to measure achievement, and to aid in planning of program activities.

Primary Grades   In the first and second grades, children do not always exert maximum effort in performance, and it is difficult to assess fitness status. Their attention is easily diverted, and often they become curious about the test itself, the mea-

suring instr▒ ▒ore do not concentrate on
their per▒

Most ▒ ▒mely interested in testing. Typic▒ ▒ir own performance. It is
productive ▒ ▒uity to begin some assessment of
fitness at this ▒ ▒peed, power, and endurance will help to
identify the u▒ ▒nd will also prove highly motivating.

There are ▒ew physical fitness test batteries recommended for use
with children below the fourth grade. Some of those that are available and
have norms are listed on page 214. A few tests that may be administered to
primary grade children are described. The teacher may select one or all of
them to use as a screening device to identify the underachievers. Minimum
levels of achievement are suggested for both boys and girls in grades 1 through
3. If a child scores below these levels, a concentrated effort should be made to
plan a remedial or special exercise program for the individual and to inform
and involve parents in planning an individualized program.

TESTS FOR GRADES 1, 2, AND 3

- ### *Sit-up*

Purpose: To measure abdominal strength, endurance, and speed.
Directions: Page 548.

- ### *Standing Broad Jump*

Purpose: To measure leg strength and power.
Directions: Page 550.

- ### *30-Yard Dash*

Purpose: To measure speed.
Directions: Page 551. Reduce the distance to 30 yards for the first three
grades.

- ### *Seal Crawl*

Purpose: To measure arm and shoulder girdle strength, endurance, speed.
Directions: Mark two lines 20 feet apart. Child starts behind starting line with
weight held on hands on the floor with elbows straight, legs out behind and
dragged along the floor (Seal Crawl, p. 474). On the signal "Go," he moves

Table 10-1. Minimum Levels of Performance

GRADE	SIT-UPS (NO.)		BROAD JUMP (IN.)		DASH (SEC.)		SEAL CRAWL (SEC.)	
	B	G	B	G	B	G	B	G
1	3	3	36	32	9	9	20	26
2	5	5	40	36	8.5	8.6	18	20
3	8	7	42	38	7	7.5	13	17

forward and to the finish line 20 feet away as fast as possible. If he falters, he should assume the starting position and continue until he crosses the line. While he is moving, the knees may not touch the floor, and the subject may not push with the feet. To do either of these constitutes a mistrial, and the test must be repeated.

Scoring: The time is taken from the signal "Go" until the hands cross the finish line. Score is recorded to nearest tenth of a second.

Intermediate and Upper Grades

Children in grades 4 and above become quite interested in measurement of their skills and their fitness level. They are capable of producing an all-out effort when tested. Children are particularly interested in acquiring strength and prowess. Deficiencies in certain aspects of fitness begin to emerge now, as well as interest in physique and figure.

The President's Council[2] recommends that a screening test be given to all children. This will help identify the very lowest children in a short time. This test may be administered quickly at the start of the year, or it may be used as the only fitness test if it is not feasible to administer a whole series of tests. The test consists of three items:

1. Flexed arm-hang (Girls)
   Pull-ups (arm and shoulder strength) (Boys)
2. Sit-ups (flexibility and abdominal strength)
3. Squat thrusts (agility)

INSTRUCTIONS FOR THE SCREENING TEST

• *Pull-up (Boys)*

Directions: Page 546.

To Pass: Boys must complete one pull-up.

• *Flexed Arm-hang (Girls)*

Equipment: A stopwatch and a sturdy bar, comfortable to grip and adjustable in height (height should be approximately the same as that of the student tested).

Starting Position: Using an overhand grip, the pupil hangs with chin above bar and elbows flexed. Legs must be straight and feet free of floor.

Action: Hold position as long as possible.

Rules: Timing should start as soon as pupil is in position and released from any support other than her own. Timing should stop when the pupil's chin touches or drops below the bar. Knees must not be raised, and kicking is not permitted.

To Pass: Hold position for 3 seconds.

Note: In case an adjustable bar is not available, different-size boxes can be used to position the girls. Another method is to have someone lift each girl into hanging position.

² *Ibid.*

- *Sit-up (Boys and Girls)*

Directions: See page 548.

To Pass: Boys (ages 10 to 17) must complete fourteen sit-ups. Girls (ages 10 to 17) must complete ten sit-ups.

- *Squat Thrust (Boys and Girls)*

Equipment: A stopwatch, or a watch with a sweep second hand.

Starting Position: Pupil stands at attention.

Action:

1. Bend knees and place hands on the floor in front of the feet. Arms may be between, outside, or in front of the bent knees.
2. Thrust the legs back far enough so that the body is perfectly straight from shoulders to feet (the push-up position).
3. Return to squat position.
4. Return to erect position.

Scoring: The teacher carefully instructs the pupils how to do correct squat thrusts. The teacher tells the pupil to do as many correct squat thrusts as possible within a 10-second time limit. The teacher gives the starting signal, "Ready! Go!" On "Go" the pupil begins. The partner counts each squat thrust. At the end of 10 seconds, the teacher says, "Stop."

To Pass: Girls (ages 10 to 17) must complete three squat thrusts in 10 seconds. Boys (ages ten to seventeen) must complete four squat thrusts in 10 seconds.

There are a number of physical fitness test batteries designed for boys and girls in grade 4 through high school, and, for that matter, for adults also. Many states and organizations have combined specific tests of fitness elements and developed norms for their respective populations. The most widely used battery is that of the American Association for Health, Physical Education and Recreation, which was designed for use by teachers all over the country. The test was planned to be comprehensive in nature, to be easy to administer, to require little equipment, and to yield norms based on a sampling of children from all parts of the United States. (The directions and latest norms for the AAHPER Youth Fitness Test may be found in the Appendix.)

Included in Table 10-2 is a list of names of test batteries, test items in the batteries, age levels for which the test is suitable, and addresses of sources of the various tests. Many of these may be secured free of charge or for a small fee. Manuals describing the tests, directions for administering them, and norms are usually provided.

Improving Physical Fitness

After tests have been given they must be analyzed. The teacher must study them in terms of group and individual status and achievement to ascertain which of the components of fitness were not adequately developed through the

Table 10-2. Fitness Tests for Elementary School Children

NAME OF TEST	GRADE OR AGE LEVEL	TEST ITEMS	SOURCE
AAHPER Youth Fitness Test	Grade 5–College	Pull-ups Sit-ups Shuttle run Standing long jump 50-yard dash 600-yard run-walk	AAHPER, Washington, D.C.
New York State Physical Fitness Test	Grades 4–12	Posture test Target throw Modified push-up Side-step 50-yard dash Squat stand Treadmill	New York State Education Dept., Albany, N.Y.
State of Washington, Physical Fitness Tests for Elementary School Children	Ages 6–12	Standing broad jump Bench push-ups Curl-ups Squat-jump 30-yard dash 25–50-yard dash	State Office of Public Instruction, Olympia, Wash.
Amateur Athletic Union Physical Fitness and Proficiency Test	Grades 1–12 (Ages 6–18)	Sprints, walk-run Sit-ups Pull-ups Push-ups Standing broad jump Baseball throw Continuous hike for distance Running high jump	AAU, 231 West 58th St., New York, N.Y.

activities presented in the regular program. In the case of children who fail to meet minimum levels, the teacher should talk with each child and make plans for individual improvement. Children need to know that expectations for them are realistic. They should not be expected to catch up immediately with the rest of the class.

If a child is unable to achieve much success in tests, it is logical to assume that his or her attitude toward plunging into a strenuous exercise program may be apprehensive or negative. It is possible that the major reason for the poor fitness level is simply a poor attitude toward exercise or even a poor attitude fostered by parents. Motivating the child to desire a high fitness level is essential before any progress can be made.

First of all, students must have some understanding of the factors involved in fitness. A few children's books which describe fitness factors and the importance of fitness in the child's vocabulary are included in the bibliography. It would be wise for each elementary school to have copies of these books in the library. The teacher should encourage students to read books of this type, and they are excellent reference books for use in health instruction.

Many teachers fail to realize that most parents are very interested in the fitness of their children and will respond to helping their children at home if they understand the problem. Presentation of objective evidence of poor test results is quite convincing to those who may resist a general statement that their child is unfit. Together the child, the parents, and the teacher may set up a plan for specific types of exercises to be done at home as a supplement to the regular activities at school. If the child's physical condition is below par, and the program at school is adequate, it stands to reason that the child's problem is unique and that special attention is needed to help solve the problem. Task cards with specific goals, directions for exercises, and space on which to record progress may be designed and worked on at home. Periodic conferences and progress checks should be had with the teacher.

Explanation of physical fitness tests and guidelines for interpretation of the results may be made to parents at a PTA or parents' room meeting early in the year. Thereafter, if a profile chart of each pupil's scores is sent home periodically, the parents will be much more interested and aware of the meaning of specific scores. If it is found that scores of many children are lower than those of national or state norms, it may be wise to prepare group profiles and present these to the parents. It may be that facilities, equipment, time allowed for physical education or preparation of the teachers are inadequate. After the parents become aware of and interested in the problems, they may exert their influence toward the improvement of the deficiencies.

Prerequisite to a fit school population, of course, is the opportunity for children to exercise. A daily instructional physical education period of adequate length should be a part of the total school organizational plan. Thirty minutes for grades 1 through 4, and forty-five minutes for grades 5 through 8 should be allotted to instructional programs. This should be supplemented with provision for after-school activities. Special-interest groups or remedial groups provide opportunities for improving fitness. Children who need special help may feel better pursuing remedial work with others with similar problems.

Isolated exercises are not the only means of building physical fitness. In fact, isolating a specific part of the lesson as fitness exercise time may be more harmful than helpful. Children should recognize that the play activities they enjoy contribute to development of physical fitness. Apparatus work, basic movement skill work, stunts and tumbling, active games, work with small equipment, and dance activities can be planned in a progression and sequence in which all muscle groups of the body are challenged and the tempo and intensity of them are stepped up to a challenging point for everyone according to individual needs. In terms of endurance, there is hardly a more challenging activity than a vigorous folk dance.

Guidelines for Exercises

Although an elaborate program of exercises for developing fitness in the elementary school is not proposed here, there may be a need for such in some situations because of lack of time, facilities, and equipment for a well-rounded program. There may be a need to build up children who have had no previous opportunity for activity that develops fitness qualities. Learning how to do a number of exercises is valuable to children from several viewpoints.

1. An understanding of the need for a warm-up period before strenuous exercise or an all-out effort should be developed. Learning the progression of starting from slow, rhythmical stretching and swinging movements to faster, more vigorous movements can be accomplished through a guided exercise series. *Exercises for developing fitness elements and for warming up should not be confused.* Evidence as to the value of warm-up on subsequent performance is conflicting; however, there is evidence to indicate that slow, stretching movements similar to those that are to be done afterward in a strenuous fashion are helpful if done just prior to the action. To do a series of unrelated exercises and then sit down and talk about what is to be done has no value for the subsequent activity.

2. A brief exercise or calisthenic routine at the start of the period should provide exercise for all muscle groups, since the activity done in the rest of the period may not provide this opportunity.

3. If exercises are learned correctly, benefit will be gained from them.

4. Students should build a repertoire of exercises that they may do on their own when it is not possible to do more vigorous big-muscle activity owing to time, space, weather. It is hoped that this will be carried into adulthood and even that children will teach their parents the exercise habit.

5. In order that exercises be valuable, certain principles of exercise should be heeded.

   a. Exercise must be done consistently and regularly. If practice ceases, strength and endurance are lost almost as quickly as they are gained.

   b. To increase strength or endurance the overload principle must be employed. The number of times an exercise is done must be increased, the tempo at which it is done must be increased, and the resistance which is offered must be increased if gains are to be made.

   c. Exercises must be strenuous and vigorous. They must be done with purposeful movement. Children must be encouraged to make a genuine effort; they must not quit when they feel the first signs of being tired.

   d. Children must be motivated to do exercises well. Acquisition of skill is important here too, since speed cannot precede control, and lack of success does not contribute to the desire to work harder and longer. Skillful movements save energy. Knowledge that their efforts are being productive is also motivating. Retests should be given frequently enough for children to realize what gains they have made from their efforts.

   e. Exercise periods should be reasonable in length and allow for individual differences in tolerance for exercise. Feeling stiff and uncomfortable after exercises will not prove very motivating for future sessions.

6. Exercises may be presented formally or informally. If a series is to be done by the group or by the individual at the start of each lesson, it is wise to build a routine by making a formal presentation until children can conduct exercises by themselves. Specific exercises can be presented to children in an informal manner by using an indirect approach. The teacher may select an exercise and build a series of questions around the directions for the exercise. He or she must first get the children into the correct starting position, then proceed with the challenges or questions. For example: In

teaching the sit-up you might say, "Lying flat on your back, can you curl up and touch your toes? Can you touch your right toe with your left hand? With your hands clasped behind your head, can you bend your knees and then sit up and touch your right elbow to your left knee? Are your feet flat on the floor? How many times can you do this without stopping?" Caution must be taken that each child does the exercise in the way it was intended to be done and vigorously enough to be of value. Too often beginning teachers do not ascertain whether each child is benefiting from exercise taught in this fashion. They concentrate on the questions and not the answers in movement.

Activities to Develop Fitness

Activities must be selected which will provide for maintenance and development of strength in the major muscle areas, flexibility in the major joints, and general endurance. Running provides one of the best exercises or activities for the development of endurance. Since children love to run, some variation of running might be included in every lesson. Distance running may precede each lesson and serve two purposes—building endurance and releasing energy and tension. Running may be done in place, around the gym, or in a prescribed area outside. Suggestions for variations of running may be found on this page.

Jogging is also a fun way to exercise. The parents of many children may be joggers. Jogging is an easy, relaxed way of running at a personal pace which can be maintained over a long distance. The teacher should help children understand the principles of jogging (overload principle applied from day to day) and set up a program that is progressive and challenging and can be carried on by the student outside school. A jogging route may be identified around the schoolyard and the length determined so children can measure progress. The distance around the gym can be measured and converted to number of times around per mile. For those interested, a record-keeping card may be used. A distance to a certain city or local landmark may be set as a goal within a certain period of time and comparable number of times around the gym accumulated until the total distance is reached. For example, "Run across the country," "Run to the state capital," the "1000-Mile Club."

Aerobic exercises are another popular way to fitness in which pupil's parents may be or can get involved. Aerobics are based on a progressive program that stimulates circular-respiratory activity for a time period sufficient to bring about significant changes in the body. It may be increasingly longer or faster periods of running, cycling, walking up and down stairs, some type of continuous exercises, or dance movements.

Aerobic dancing involves dance movements in continuous sequences with an aim to building cardiovascular endurance and building skeletal muscles in a rewarding way. Many children and adults have found this type of dancing and exercising fun because it utilizes modern music as accompaniment. There are a number of commercial records with exercise directions on them accompanied by catchy popular tunes. The teacher can use any popular record with a good beat as background. (A few popular recordings follow. Record vendors are identified and addresses given on page 299.) Before advising or planning aerobic activities, you may want to read some of the references suggested for further information.

- "And the Beat Goes On"
  KEA 5010
- "Jumpnastics"
  KEA 6000
- "Aerobic Dancing, Elementary"
  KEA 1125
- "Fitness for Everyone"
  HPR-R-24

- "Chicken Fat"
  209 CF1000
- "Exercise is Kid Stuff"
  K2070
- "Rhythmic Rope Jumping, Elementary"
  K4001

Exercises for development of specific physical components are given in Chapter 17. Suggestions are given for making each progressively more difficult or demanding. These may serve as a source for building an exercise program for individuals or a series for warm-ups, maintenance, or building fitness for the class.

Individualized programs of exercise may be designed and children may proceed to do their own exercises at their own rate and complete their series, then move on to another activity of their choice or the activity of the class for the day.

Frequently a circuit of stations is established, and certain exercises are done at each station. Each child is to perform a set number of bouts at each station at his or her own rate, and then move on. Directions or record cards may be at each station. Usually the goal is for students to do progressively more in number or more in a set period of time, if they are increasing their fitness level. Each station would reflect exercises that develop each element of motor fitness and endurance. Consecutive stations should not make demands on the same section of the body. Figure 10-4 shows a circuit of stations with exercises to be completed at each station. Each exercise is described elsewhere in the book. The card at each station might give the directions and also indicate how many units to do or at what speed to do them, indicating high level, medium level, or low level. This can be ascertained after assessing the performance level of the class on an initial run through the circuit or from norms of previous years.

Completing an obstacle course in decreasingly less time is a way of increasing and measuring fitness that has great appeal for children. An obstacle course can be used as a medium for experiencing different movements without

Figure 10-4 Circuit training course.

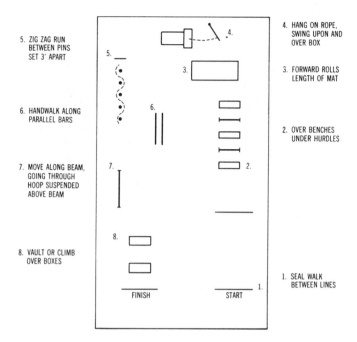

5. ZIG ZAG RUN BETWEEN PINS SET 3' APART

6. HANDWALK ALONG PARALLEL BARS

7. MOVE ALONG BEAM, GOING THROUGH HOOP SUSPENDED ABOVE BEAM

8. VAULT OR CLIMB OVER BOXES

4. HANG ON ROPE, SWING UPON AND OVER BOX

3. FORWARD ROLLS LENGTH OF MAT

2. OVER BENCHES UNDER HURDLES

1. SEAL WALK BETWEEN LINES

FINISH   START

Figure 10-5 Obstacle course.

regard for time. Many schools install permanent apparatus outdoors so that pupils can move from piece to piece, with each succeeding piece requiring an emphasis on different elements of fitness and movement. Some commercial companies sell sets of apparatus for this purpose. Figure 10-5 shows an indoor obstacle course using movable pieces of apparatus and equipment. Children love obstacle courses and can often design better ones than the teacher.

Summary

It is readily apparent that a good state of fitness is vital to the health and happiness of individuals and to the vitality of the nation. It is the responsibility of the physical education program to build a positive attitude toward fitness, a knowledge and understanding of the components of fitness, and the skills to maintain fitness. Within this program there must be provisions for identifying children who are physically underdeveloped and opportunities provided for their improvement. A well-balanced, comprehensive program of activities that provide for natural growth and development of strength and circulatory-respiratory endurance, flexibility, and other aspects of motor fitness, as well as maintenance activities, must be developed.

Not all children need a program for building fitness. Activities and several modes of programs have been suggested for those who *need* and for those who are motivated to increase their fitness level beyond that possible in the regular program. Fitness is very personal and specific; therefore personalized fitness programs must be developed.

SUGGESTED REFERENCES FOR FURTHER STUDY

AMERICAN ALLIANCE FOR HEALTH, PHYSICAL EDUCATION AND RECREATION, *Youth Fitness Test Manual*. Washington, D.C.: National Education Association, 1976.

BOWERMAN, W.J., and W. E. HARRIS, *Jogging—A Physical Fitness Program for All Ages*. New York: Grossett & Dunlap, 1967.

COOPER, KENNETH, M.D., *Aerobics*. New York: Bantam Books/Evans Co., Inc., 1968.

GREENE, LEON, and DONNA OSNESS, "Sunflower Project: Changing Lifestyles of Children," *Journal of Physical Education and Recreation*, 49, no. 2 (February 1978), 28–29.

HUNSICKER, PAUL, *Physical Fitness: What Research Says to the Teacher*, #26. Washington, D.C.: Department of Classroom Teachers, National Education Association, 1963.

JENKINS, DAVID, "Cardiovascular Fitness Education for Elementary Students," *Journal of Physical Education and Recreation*, 49, no. 5 (May 1978), 59.

JONES, K. L. et al., *Total Fitness*. New York: Harper & Row, 1972.

PRESIDENT'S COUNCIL ON YOUTH FITNESS, *Youth Physical Fitness*. Washington, D.C.: Superintendent of Documents, 1973.

SAFRIT, MARGARET J., *Evaluation in Physical Education*. Englewood Cliffs, N.J.: Prentice-Hall, Inc., 1973.

WALLIS, EARL, and GENE LOGAN, *Exercises for Children*. Englewood Cliffs, N.J.: Prentice-Hall, Inc., 1966.

11 / UNDERSTANDING AND TEACHING BASIC MOVEMENT

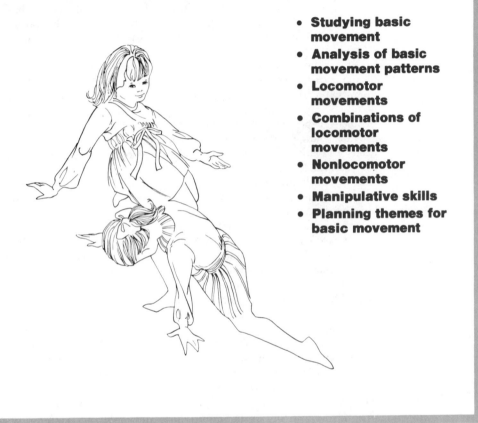

- Studying basic movement
- Analysis of basic movement patterns
- Locomotor movements
- Combinations of locomotor movements
- Nonlocomotor movements
- Manipulative skills
- Planning themes for basic movement

Studying Basic Movement

In the primary grades the focus of the physical education program is the exploration and refinement of basic movement patterns and the understanding of the environmental factors that affect movement. Emphasis is placed on the "why" of movement, on understanding one's own capacity in movement, and on acquiring proficiency in a wide range of movement skills.

Indirect styles of teaching are utilized to help children develop the processes of exploration, experimentation, simple problem solving, and evaluation. Consistent with their stage of development, children are given a great deal of freedom and responsibility for learning to adapt movements or skills to elements of space; different tempos and speeds; different levels; variations of force and intensity; different shapes of small and large objects and obstacles; and in relationship to others as they experience the joy and fulfillment that can accompany movement.

Although the emphasis is on the study of basic movement patterns and understanding the factors that affect the performance of these skills, much of the actual study and experiences to refine and enjoy them is done in structured activities such as dance, gymnastics, games, and if possible aquatics, as well as unstructured activities. Inclusion of a sequential study of basic movement gives children the background to work skills and the various games, sport, dance, and aquatic activity which are the basis of the active leisure pursuits of youth and adulthood.

Essential in the preschool, kindergarten, and primary grades is a concern for experiences that will enhance the continuing development of the sensorimotor capacities. Movement is essential to our ability to cope with the world about us. Movement stimulates perception and perception *directs* our movements. We perceive through our sensory mechanisms. Therefore, we must provide young children with a rich sensorimotor environment and the opportunity to explore and experiment with movement using the perceptual cues they receive.

The early program should stress exploratory and discovery experiences in body awareness, spatial orientation, basic body actions, form perception, eye-hand and eye-foot coordination, and rhythm, with the input designed to be received by all sensory modalities and receptors.

It is essential that the teacher allow plenty of time and freedom for exploration. The main concern should be for carefully arranging the space and equipment and providing tasks, questions, and challenges that will allow individual responses. Young children have different readiness levels for achieving efficient movement. If there is a healthy balance of pupil and teacher evaluation of ideas, the child will benefit.

Teachers of elementary school physical education must understand the basic movement patterns and be able to apply the various environmental factors which affect movement in order to analyze children's abilities and needs and to plan appropriate movement experiences for them. Following are descriptions of body awareness, the elements of movement, and basic movement patterns, along with suggestions for learning experiences. Note that these are the definitions or descriptions of the terms in the Basic Movement Glossary on page 173. All of these should be studied, used, and learned through games, sports, and dance. The ways in which each is used, and their purposes, are all different. In dance, for example, the expressive forms of the skills are used for purposes of expression.

Body Awareness

Body awareness or body image is the physical aspect of self-concept. Body awareness refers to the way children perceive their physical self: their knowledge of the body parts and their relationship to each other; their physical size; the body actions they can do; how they feel when they use their body parts; and how their bodies relate to space. Of course body awareness develops from birth on. The extent of its development by the time a child reaches school is dependent upon his or her opportunities for movement experiences.

Activities or experiences that enhance body awareness are essential for young children. One good way to assess children's body image is to have them draw pictures of themselves. After performing many activities planned to enhance body image, have them draw another picture of themselves. This time compare the relative proportions they assign to body parts; the symmetry of arms and legs, ears and eyes, etc. Have their perceptions of themselves changed? This is always an interesting and valuable experiment. Other assessment techniques are to ask children to identify and use various body parts, through question or on demand; or imitate or mimic the movements of another (see page 526 for other screening suggestions).

To enhance body awareness, tasks of varying degrees of difficulty should be designed. The tasks should include those which require identification of body parts, symmetrical movements, and laterality, as well as those which help the student understand the use of different body parts leading to movement, and the receiving, bearing, and transferring of weight. Selected examples of tasks which develop body awareness are given below. They should serve as a springboard for many more tasks.

The teacher can pose problems (notice that some involve a verbal input, some a visual input, some a combination). For example:

> Here is my head; touch your head.
> Here are my eyes; touch your eyes.

(The teacher touches each part and asks pupils to do the same, continuing to identify all parts.)

> Touch your head.
> Touch your eyes.

(This time pupils must react to the auditory stimuli alone. This would be repeated for all body parts.)

> Touch a part of your body and call it by name.
> Touch the upper part of your body. Touch the lower part of your body. Touch the middle of your body. Touch the very lowest part.

(Continue asking for awareness of different general locations.)

> Touch your head with your hand.
> Touch your foot with your elbow.

(Continue so that children see relationships of different parts.)

> Touch left elbow to right elbow.
> Touch left knee to right elbow.

(Continue with actions that develop laterality.)

Children lying on backs:

> Raise left leg, then right.
> Bring both arms above the head until they meet. Have arms glide across floor.
> Glide both arms out and above head, clasp hands. At the same time glide legs out to the side, keeping them straight.

(Continue with variations of symmetrical and assymmetrical movements with arms and legs.)

Children standing:

Arms at side, feet together, slowly bring arms above head and clap both hands together.
Jump and spread legs apart to the side; to the front.
Spread arms above head and at the same time jump and spread legs to the side.

(Repeat these and then encourage a faster pace.)

Two children facing each other or one facing a mirror:

Touch partner's right hand.
Touch partner's right shoulder.

(Continue with tasks that encourage directionality.)

One partner move and the other try to match his movements.

Explore some of the basic body actions stressing the use of specific body actions:

Walk fast with your side to the stage; when the drum sounds, walk with your back to the stage . . .
Run and raise your arms up and down while running.
Run and raise first your right arm, then your left arm, alternating them as you run.
Move across the gym with your left foot leading all the time.
Move across the gym with your body weight only on your hands.
Move across the gym with your body weight on one hand and one foot.
Move across the gym, transferring your weight from a base using an upper part of your body to one using a lower part of your body.

Play games like "Angels in the Snow," "Simon Says," "Do This—Do That," "Mirror Game." Do dances like "Hokey-Pokey," "Loopy Lou," "Did You Ever See a Lassie?"

Elements and Dimensions of Movement

In the performance of all movement skills, the body must make adjustments to the elements of time, force, pattern, and flow—all of these being dependent upon the purpose of the movement.

TIME Time refers to the speed at which a movement takes place. The extreme degrees of time are sudden and sustained. There are many instances in games and sports when a sudden explosive movement means beating an opponent on the takeoff or reaching a ball that otherwise would have been just out of reach. Sustained movement allows a person to continue moving while still in control of the body, yet capable of changing speed if necessary. There are many variations of time between these two extremes. The ability to accelerate with ease comes with an awareness of how to control the body.

Foundations of Movement

SUGGESTIONS FOR STUDY

1. Run fast.
2. Run slowly.

3. Run fast, slow down, and run fast again.
4. How slowly can you move?
5. How fast can you move your arms in a circle? How slowly?
6. How quickly can you "take off" from a standing position?
7. Move in slow motion.
8. Can you start moving on the count of one and reach the line at ten? (Teacher should give class the cadence before they start to move. Several trials should be given and then the cadence changed.)
9. Do the same with throwing a ball (force applied and angle of release will be involved here).
10. Walk (run, skip, gallop, etc.), changing your speed each time the drum beats.
11. Run in general space, slow down to avoid people but never stop your running action. (Also tests quality of flow.)

(See *Tempo*, page 279, for more suggestions.)

FORCE Force refers to the tension of the muscles of the body and the degree of strength needed for a certain movement. Experiences in moving lightly or heavily will help a child to control the tension of muscles only to the extent that is needed to fulfill the purpose of a task. For example, compare the force needed to push an empty box as opposed to that needed to push a box of sand; or the amount of force needed to get up on a high bench as opposed to that needed to jump from it. In the latter the tension of the muscles has to be slight, yet not completely absent in order to make the landing light but controlled.

SUGGESTIONS FOR STUDY

1. Let's see you move very softly.
2. Can you move like a feather?
3. Move very strongly; make lots of noise with your feet.
4. Make strong movements with your arms like a helicopter on a windy day.
5. How hard can you push against the floor? Does pushing against the floor help you when you want to jump high?
6. Be a floppy rag doll; change the tension in your muscles so you feel like a tight spring.
7. Throw the ball to a partner who is four feet from you. Now move back 10 feet and throw it with the same amount of force. What happened? How much more force do you have to use to get it there on the second try?
8. Throw a balloon to your partner. How hard did you have to throw it?
9. See if you can keep your balloon in the air but keep it below your head level. Can you sit down and do this?
10. Can you make strong swinging movements with your arms? Change to light ones. Can you make heavy stamping movements with your feet and light swinging movements with your arms at the same time?
11. Skip across the room. The next time, see if you can get high in the air each time you step. What helps you go higher?
12. Run slowly; make a sudden burst of speed, run slowly, then speed up. What kind of steps did you use to speed up?

BODY SHAPE Body shape refers to the position of the body in space. Changing shapes is movement. The body may be extended (long or wide or straight) or flexed (tucked or curled small and round). Some skills require a quick change from a tucked to an extended position; i.e., tumbling, or turning stunts on bars. The size of the space available creates a need to change shape. The child must learn what shapes it is possible for the body to take and how to control changes from one shape to another with a smooth, flowing action. For intermediate and upper-grade children, reference to different body joints and the range of their movement can be related to making body shapes (see page 194).

SUGGESTIONS FOR STUDY

1. Make yourself long and narrow; big and wide.
2. Curl into as small a ball as possible.
3. Quickly change from a ball to a bat.
4. Crawl under a wand supported low between two traffic cones.
5. Move through a very curvy obstacle course—you will have to make many changes of shape in order not to touch the objects.
6. Move with your body in a curled position.
7. Support your weight on your hands on the floor and change your body shape.
8. Hanging from a bar, make as many different body shapes as you can.
9. Be a twisted tree trunk.
10. With your body, make the first letter in your name.
11. Be a number 6; a 5; a 2; a 7; a 9.
12. In small groups spell out the name of your school.
13. Make one shape with the lower part of your body and at the same time another shape with your upper body. Hold this position until you count to 21.
14. Make a different shape, hold it 5 seconds; then make another. Develop a smooth flow from one shape to another.

FLOW Flow refers to the sequence of actions and the transition from one position to another. There can be a smooth, controlled series of movements joined together which give continuity to the pattern. *Free flow* describes movement that must continue to a controlled conclusion, while *bound flow* is movement that can be stopped and balance maintained at any time. For example, a routine on a piece of apparatus, no matter how simple or complex, calls for both free and bound flow. All exercises on the equipment must flow together in a continuous pattern; however, each exercise may involve a movement that calls for building momentum to a point at which momentum must be checked and a certain position sustained for a period of time before the movement is completed. Many experiences of work with skills and flow lead to efficient, graceful movement.

SUGGESTED ACTIVITIES

1. With arms held up in front of you, swing them from side to side.
2. *Stop* at the top of the swing; hold. Now you can start them again with the same flowing movement. Stop and start, making a nice flow. Let your body sway with your arms and hold the position when your arms stop.

3. Run or walk, touching each of the marked squares on the floor without changing your movement pattern. Then run or walk, touching each of the marked squares, holding a balanced position on one foot before running on to the next.

4. Run and go into any type of roll; come out of it into a run. Keep your flow of movement going.

5. Move on to the box or bench and as you come off keep right on moving to another bench without pausing.

6. Run, step on the box and hold your position; run right off the box and on to the next.

7. Roll on the floor, stop in a balanced position, hold for 5 seconds, and continue rolling.

8. On the bar turn over fast, hold a position over the bar for a few seconds, then continue into the roll over and off the box.

9. Run up to a horizontal bar set at eye level. Grasp it with two hands, run under the bar to an extended position, then run backward, forward, backward, and swing out under the bar and go into a forward roll coming to a balanced stand; pause, then run back to the other side of the bar again.

10. With a ball in one hand pass it to the other hand, moving it back and forth in a flowing motion. Can you do this with your arms high above your head? Let your body move with the ball. Pause and hold the ball and your body for a few seconds, then repeat.

Space

All movement takes place in space, which in itself may be quite varied. The amount of space available demands many adjustments in the performance of specific skills. There are two kinds of space. *Personal* space is the space about or around an individual which can be utilized when he is in a stationary position. The periphery of personal space is as far as one can stretch out about him. This would be the amount of space children perceive as their reaching or stretching size. The skills most pertinent to use in this situation are nonlocomotor or axial. *General* space is that area into which a person or all people in the room can move.

Movement into space can be in different *directions:* forward, backward, sideward, diagonally, upward, downward, and any combinations of these. It can be in different *levels* of space: high, low, or medium. Becoming aware of spatial elements will help a child learn to judge heights from which balls are approaching, opportunities to evade opponents, distances, and levels at which to lead passes to opponents, and distances to clear apparatus, to mention but a few practical applications.

SUGGESTIONS FOR STUDY FOR PERSONAL AND GENERAL SPACE

1. Standing still, make yourself as wide as possible, the outer edges of your body identifying your personal space. Lie down, then find the limits of your personal space.

2. Move one of your feet all around your personal space.

3. What are the limits of your personal space above you?

4. With your hands as your base, move the rest of your body around in your personal space. How many different ways can you move your body around your hands?

5. Explore all parts of the room. Touch only the farthest boundaries of the room. Do not touch or run into other people.

6. When the drum beats run and continue running anywhere in the room without touching anything or anyone (change style of locomotion).

7. With your own ball, find a personal space and see how many different ways you can bounce the ball, keeping it within your personal space (toss and catch to self in personal space).

8. With your ball, can you move into general space, bouncing the ball, and maintaining control, so you do not run into anyone or let your ball hit anyone?

9. With a partner, find a space where you can throw the ball back and forth between you without interfering with anyone else.

SUGGESTIONS FOR STUDY FOR DIRECTION

1. Move in general space and change directions every once in a while.

2. Run in general space and when the drum beats, change directions. (You may designate the direction and vary the locomotive pattern.)

3. Move sideways, with the left foot always leading.

4. Move backward, with the same foot always leading.

5. Walk in a circle, then cut across your own circle diagonally.

6. Toss your ball upward.

7. With your ball, move in general space, changing directions each time the drum beats.

8. Make a sequence of ball bouncing and moving with four changes of direction in the sequence.

9. In your personal space, move your ball in all directions around you. Keep passing the ball from hand to hand.

10. Move across the balance beam; change the direction you are facing when you move back across.

SUGGESTIONS FOR STUDY FOR LEVEL

1. In your personal space, move the lower part of your body at a low level.

2. Turn your hand around and around at the highest level you can.

3. Move into general space with your weight on your feet; move around at the lowest level you can; at medium level; at highest level.

4. Moving with a partner, one of you move at a high level, one at a low level.

5. Move at a low level sideways with your body weight on three parts.

6. Jump on the box, and come off with your front to the box.

7. Run and jump and make a low landing.

8. Jump off the box and change direction in the air.

9. Jump off the box and make a high landing.

10. Get your whole body as high off the floor as possible.

11. Move with your hands low and your toes high.

12. Keep a balloon moving at a high level within your personal space.

Relationships

In most game, dance, and apparatus activities children do not move alone in space. They must move with someone, oppose someone, overcome obstacles, or use implements of some type. In early skill learnings children must have experiences for which they must adapt skills to performance with or in opposition to a partner, then in a small group, and with a variety of obstacles and objects. When working with a partner one may *match-shadow* the other's movement pattern, do the movement *together*, *contrast-mirror* the other's pattern, or each may do his own pattern but relate it to that of the other, or *lead* the other. When working in a group one may move *following* a leader, move *with* four or five other people, move in *response* or *opposition* to another group, work with a group in solving a problem or creating a pattern together, work in the group with each doing his or her own movement but relating it to every other group member's pattern.

SUGGESTIONS FOR STUDY

1. Move across the room with a partner, with hands joined.
2. Move across the room with a partner. Keep together, but do not touch.
3. Facing a partner who is the leader, mirror his actions. Change leaders.
4. Start facing a partner; both move backward into general space but maintain an equal distance between the starting point. Move back together again.
5. Shadow a partner's movements as he moves around in general space.
6. Standing 6 feet from a partner, run and pass the ball back and forth as you run down the gym.
7. Lay a rope on the floor; move next to the rope, making the same pattern with the body as the pattern of the rope.
8. Lying on the floor with feet end to end with a partner, design a pattern with matching movements with your legs (and with other parts of the body).
9. Dribbling a ball (with hands or feet), move in and out of pins set 4 yards apart without knocking them over.
10. Do activities where the pupil moves *with*, *off*, *along*, *across*, *below*, *under*, *through*, *above*, *on*, *over*, or *around* small equipment or large apparatus for adaptations of the individual's movement patterns in respect to the relationship he or she has with the object.

Basic Movement Patterns

This factor actually involves learning what movements or skills the body is capable of doing. There are movements that can be done in a stationary position. The body may move as a whole, or various parts may move independently or together. These are the nonlocomotor skills of twisting, turning, stretching, swinging, bending, shaking, bouncing, pushing, pulling, and combinations of these. The body can move in space utilizing the locomotor skills of walking, running, jumping, hopping, leaping, and various combinations of these.

Children should realize that any part of the body may *lead* the movement into space. The weight of the body may be *supported* by different parts of the body and locomotor movements developed from many positions such as walking on the hands, hanging by the hands, and turning over a bar with the head leading down.

The body or parts of the body can *receive weight* in the form of outside objects or weight of other body parts; for example, in receiving the weight of the body as in landing from a jump or fall; in catching balls.

The body can *transfer weight* of the body itself or that of an outside object; for example, in dodging (the body weight must be transferred from one part of the body to another part as a base), in propelling the body in the air as in many gymnastic events, in throwing and/or striking objects.

Analysis of Basic Movement Patterns

The remainder of this chapter is devoted to an analysis of the basic movement patterns that are common to all physical education activities and should be developed and refined in the first three grades. Because these are essential in all activities, the teacher must become familiar with their execution and use.

The analysis of the patterns is made in the form of a description which is intended to help the teacher gain a clear concept of the pattern. It is much too detailed for the elementary school student. Following the description of all but the nonlocomotor patterns are the basic mechanical principles relative to the understanding of the different factors involved in the movement pattern. The principles are stated in a manner that should help the teacher gain an understanding of *why* the pattern is done in a specific way so that it is most efficient. The common faults children often have are related to the mechanical principles. Key words or phrases that have been found useful and meaningful to young children are suggested as aids in teaching or stimulation for correction.

The uses of basic patterns in sports, gymnastics, dance, and utilitarian efforts are described. A recognition of the many different ways in which each pattern is adapted and used serves to emphasize the importance of learning how to do each one well and in many variations at an early age. The uses should give the teacher some ideas for study of the skill through imagery or the actual actions.

Suggestions for the study of each pattern are presented. These may be utilized in a variety of ways—as ideas for exploration, self-testing projects, problems, or in whatever way the teacher may wish to present the lesson. The teacher may rephrase the suggestions and use them for an indirect technique. For example, "Jump and turn around in the air"; as a challenge, "Who can jump and turn around in the air?"; a direct technique, "Stand on a line, jump and turn in the air, and land on the same line facing the same direction"; or even more direct, "Put your two feet on a line, twist your arms to the left, swing them right, and jump in the air turning your body. When you land, bend your knees, and pull your upper body back to regain balance, put your arms out to the side. Like this . . . (demonstration)." All of these are revisions of the original suggestion to jump and turn in the air.

Because the emphasis in studying movement patterns is to learn to do them efficiently and with confidence, much time should be spent in exploring the many ways one can do them in combinations with other skills and factors of movement. The teacher should be evaluating patterns and helping individuals with the correction of errors or refinement of the skills.

The basic locomotor patterns are presented first, followed by the most frequently used actions, which are combinations of the basic patterns. The basic nonlocomotor patterns are described next, with actions that are combinations of locomotor and nonlocomotor skills following. The manipulative skills of fundamental catching, throwing, and striking patterns complete the section of analysis.

The chapter is summarized by a teacher's guide for analyzing selected fundamental skills. When a child does not reach skill goals, the teacher should look for mechanical errors in these six major areas: base of support and balance, production of force, direction of application of force, focus, follow-through, and absorption of force. The chart on page 265 is intended to serve as a quick reference for identifying errors or causes of errors in execution of skills.

In subsequent chapters, reference is made to the basic body actions as they relate to specific sport, dance, and gymnastic skills. The reader will find it helpful to refer to Chapter 9 and to this chapter for a review of elements involved in understanding and correct execution of the specific skill under consideration. The specific goals, implements, rules, and boundaries of sports and games will necessitate some adaptations in the fundamental skill patterns.

This material is intended for the improvement of the teacher's knowledge, as is evidenced by the vocabulary. How successfully he or she utilizes this information with children is dependent upon application of the learning principles and teaching methods discussed in Chapters 4 and 5.

Locomotor Movements

Walk

DESCRIPTION A natural walk is a movement that carries the body through space by a transference of weight from one foot to another. The movement is initiated with a push-off diagonally backward against the ground with the ball and toes of one foot. After the push-off is made, the leg swings forward as flexion is initiated at the hip joint, then the knee and the ankle lift the foot clear off the floor. The weight is transferred from the heel along the outer edge of the foot to the ball and to the toes as the next push-off is made. The feet point straight ahead and the inner borders fall along a straight line. As the arms swing freely and in opposition to the legs, they counterbalance the rotation of the trunk and help carry the upper part of the body forward. There is a brief period of time when both feet are in contact with the floor and a new base of support is established. The position of the body should be erect and easy.

The surface on which the walk is done influences the amount of force necessary in the push-off owing to the amount of counterforce from the surface. On soft surfaces, more force must be exerted, because much of the force is lost in pushing back the sand, snow, or whatever one encounters. When walking on ice or another slippery surface, one should reduce force and shorten the stride in order to keep a larger base of support. If a person is walking up a hill, his body must lean forward so the center of gravity is over the base of support. Walking downhill, the reverse is true. The lean should be made from the hips. In order to increase speed of the walk, the force must be increased and the stride lengthened.

BASIC MECHANICAL PRINCIPLES

1. The angle of push-off must be in the desired direction. Too much vertical push results in a bouncy, inefficient gait.
2. The period of double support allows a new base of support to be established for security. When feet are pointed straight ahead and the inner edges are placed along a line, the center of gravity may shift directly over the base of support.
3. The sequential transference of weight from heel, to outside edge of foot, to toes, allows the force to be absorbed over a longer period of time and thereby reduces the shock of the contact with the ground.
4. If the feet are moved straight ahead, the base is too wide and the weight must be shifted a great distance from side to side. Thus there is much swaying of the body and great inefficiency. If the feet are placed one foot in front of the other, the base is too narrow and unstable. There also is a loss of efficiency when each foot has to be swung out and around the other on every step.
5. An exaggerated arm-swing rotates the trunk excessively and hinders the forward movement.
6. A more forceful contraction of the extensor muscles of the leg creates greater resistance from the surface and drives the body forward at greater speed.

COMMON FAULTS

1. Too much vertical push, resulting in bobbing or bouncing motion.
2. Walking with toes turned out, resulting in "duck walk" appearance.
3. Feet placed too far apart, resulting in "duck walk" appearance.
4. Feet placed too close together, resulting in "jerky" appearance.
5. Walking with toes turned in, resulting in "pigeon-toed" appearance and weakening of arch.
6. Excessive swing of arms from side to side.
7. Head forward.

KEY TEACHING PHRASES

1. Push off with toes.
2. Swing leg from hip.
3. Land on heel and let weight roll along outside edge of foot to toes.
4. Point toes straight ahead.
5. Walk lightly.
6. Head up, look straight ahead.
7. Swing arms and hands forward easily.

USES The walk is the most basic skill, for we employ it as we move about in our daily tasks. It is learned early in life, and little heed is paid to the instruction of it. However, many children develop poor habits of walking which add stress and strain to various body parts and consume unnecessary energy through inefficient movement. Correct body alignment and mechanics of the walk add to the aesthetic values of appearance. The walking step is used in combination with other forms of movement to make up many other skills. There are very few sports which do not involve the use of the walk. Most dance steps are variations of the walk combined with other movements.

SUGGESTIONS FOR STUDY

1. Walk freely (stress good alignment).
2. Walk in place; forward; sidward; backward; zigzag.
3. Walk using various combinations of the above.
4. Experiment in walking with toes turned out; toes turned in; toes straight ahead. Contrast in terms of rotation, smooth flow, speed, feeling, and appearance.
5. Walk on tiptoes.
6. Walk on heels.
7. Walk, changing speeds from fast to slow, alternate with stopping, and then make a smooth transition from slow to fast and vice versa.
8. Walk with knees held high.
9. Walk as if in a slow processional.
10. Walk as if on ice.
11. Walk with legs held stiff.
12. Walk as if in a parade.
13. Walk while slowly lowering and raising the body.
14. Walk while turning, twisting, stretching, or curling the body.
15. Walk slowly with long steps; very tiny steps.
16. Walk fast with long steps; very tiny steps.
17. Walk as if walking up a hill; down a hill.
18. Walk in combination with other locomotor movements.
19. Walk beside a partner. Can you stay in step? Can you swing arms together?
20. Walk with a partner holding hands; change directions.
21. Walk with a partner holding hands; one walk forward at the same time one walks backward.
22. Make up a routine involving _____ factors (teacher or student can assign factors).

Run

DESCRIPTION The run pattern is much like that of the walk; however, there is a period of no support in the run. The foot contacts the ground under the center of gravity, and the weight is first taken on the ball of the foot. The knees are bent more than in the walk and are carried upward and forward. The arms are bent at the elbows and swing in a forward-backward direction alternately with the legs. In order to increase speed quickly, short driving steps are taken, and thereafter the stride is lengthened. Bending the supporting knee more as the weight is taken helps increase speed. Contrast the form

Figure 11-1 Running form.

of boy A in Figure 11-1 as he runs from his knees and swings his arms cross-wise with the good form of boy B.

BASIC MECHANICAL PRINCIPLES

1. Landing on the ball of the foot first makes it possible to give with the ankle, knee, and hip, which helps absorb the force gradually.
2. Bending the knee shortens the length of the lever to be moved and this allows the leg to be moved faster. This also applies to the bending of the elbows.
3. If the knee is bent more when the foot is pushing off against the ground, the leg muscles are able to extend more forcefully and, as a result, more speed is gained.

COMMON FAULTS

1. Taking weight on the heels first.
2. Running in an erect position.
3. Swinging arms from side to side.
4. Throwing legs in and out, rather than upward and forward.
5. Failing to lift knees.
6. Carrying arms straight down at sides.

KEY TEACHING PHRASES

1. Run on balls of feet (if child tends to run on heels, exaggerate and tell him to run on toes).
2. Bend elbows and knees.
3. Swing hands and arms forward.
4. Head up.
5. Run lightly.

USES Running is vital to many games that children play during the elementary years, as well as to many sports. Basketball, tennis, and badminton require short runs with quick changes of direction and rapid acceleration and deceleration. The field games of soccer, hockey, lacrosse, football, and speedball all demand longer runs along with quick changes of direction and sudden stops. Track events require either short sprints or long-distance running. A short but powerful run precedes some field, apparatus, and tumbling events. The run as used in dance activities is basically the same but requires a more expressive style.

SUGGESTIONS FOR STUDY

1. Run in place, then move running fast; move in slow motion; lift knees high; run lightly; heavily; vary speed.
2. Run straight ahead for specified distances; run as fast as you can (dashes).
3. Run around or between objects.
4. Run, making your own pattern of direction.
5. Run and dodge objects or people.
6. Combine run and jump.
7. Run for increasingly longer distances each day.
8. Run and stop on signal, then run again.
9. Run in relay formation.
10. Run with a partner side by side, run, holding hands with partner.
11. Run following the leader.
12. Run under a rope.
13. Run over or through a turning rope.
14. Run while throwing and catching a ball to oneself, then with a partner.
15. Run in a small group following a zigzag pattern set by the leader.
16. Run in a column of five; the last person runs around the group to the head of the line, then adjusts his speed to that of the group. The last person in line then moves up to the front, continuing pattern (interval running).
17. For expressive style use imagery and imaginative movements regarding feelings, animals, objects.

Children love the joy of running. Because running is vital to so many activities, it is wise to include some type of running in nearly every lesson. Always stress good form regardless of the variation.

Leap

DESCRIPTION The leap is much the same as the run; however, in a leap the ankle and knee actions are increased so that a more upward motion is achieved. The knee leads out and then stretches forward as the foot reaches out for the landing. The rear leg extends backward in the air after a vigorous push-off from the ground. The period of suspension in the air is greater in the leap than in the run. The arms move upward to sustain the body in the air. The takeoff is from one foot and the landing is on the other foot. Usually a leap is preceded by one or more running steps in order to gain more momentum for the lift into the air.

BASIC MECHANICAL PRINCIPLES

1. The same principles which apply to the run also apply to the leap.
2. The greater push-off from the floor adds force and momentum for the more vertical path of the body.
3. A few preliminary running steps help gain momentum for both the distance and height desirable for the leap.
4. A forward upward motion of the arms helps produce momentum to help carry the body in the desired direction.

COMMON FAULTS

1. Failing to push off with enough force to elevate the body.
2. Failing to suspend body in air.
3. Failing to stretch or reach with the legs.
4. Failing to use arms.
5. Landing on two feet instead of one.

KEY TEACHING PHRASES

1. Push up, stretch, and reach.
2. Swing arms up and forward.
3. Run, run, *leap* (accent *leap* to denote greater push or effort).

USES   The leap is usually combined with running. The leap is utilized when a slight obstacle is to be cleared without breaking the running pattern. When catching a high pass on the run, a leap is preferable to a jump since the running pattern can be continued easily. The leap is the basic hurdling pattern without the hip rotation.

SUGGESTIONS FOR STUDY   (The leap is difficult for young children and much variation in the pattern is difficult for them to control. Practice on the leap itself with variation in the distance and height to be attained are sufficient for the primary and intermediate grades.)

1. Run several steps and leap.
2. Leap over a rope on floor (raise rope off floor gradually).
3. Leap a distance between two lines (increase the distance between lines).
4. Run and leap over a small box or other obstacle.
5. Run and leap over small hurdles, 12 to 20 inches high.
6. Run and leap over a series of hurdles without breaking stride.
7. Do series of leaps without running steps between; emphasize distance and height in leap.
8. Leap like a deer.

Jump

DESCRIPTION   A jump is a motion that carries the body through the air from a takeoff from *one* or *both feet*. The body is suspended in mid-air momentarily and then drops back to the ground to a landing where the weight is taken on *both feet*. The purpose of the jump may be to gain distance forward or to gain height. For both purposes the power is produced by a quick action of the extensor muscles of the legs against the ground and a strong arm-swing in the

Figure 11-2 Jumping over a rope.

A   B

direction of the desired movement. Because the hips, knees, and ankles must be bent in order for the force to be produced through extension of the muscles, it is important that the takeoff be from a crouched position.

If the purpose of the jump is to gain distance, there is a forward lean of the body and the arms swing backward and then forcefully forward for the push-off. The legs are bent and swing forward under the body as it travels through the air. The angle of takeoff is approximately 45 degrees.

If the purpose is to gain height, the knees are bent and the push-off is against the floor straight up and the arms are swung upward. The body extends or stretches as far as possible into the air. In Figure 11-2 contrast the vertical lift and elevation of all parts of the body of the boy in B with the forward direction and lack of elevation of the boy in A.

BASIC MECHANICAL PRINCIPLES

1. The initial crouching position provides for the hips, knees, and ankles to be bent so that the extensors of the legs exert more force against the floor. (The crouching is necessary only if maximum height or distance is needed.)

2. The swing of the arms in the direction of the jump produces greater momentum to carry the body in the desired direction.

3. The forward lean of the body carries the center of gravity beyond the base of support; thus gravity aids the forward motion of the body when distance is desired.

COMMON FAULTS

1. Failing to bend the legs after taking off so that the feet touch the ground. This almost immediately causes distance loss.

2. Upper part of body leaning forward in the jump for height.

3. Failing to swing arms forward or upward in time with takeoff.

1. Swing arms back and forth, down and up.
2. Bend knees and ankles, and "blast off."
3. Stretch and reach.

USES The jump is utilized in a jump stop in all games requiring running with quick stops where one needs to maintain balance. One jumps from many objects. Landing from a jump is treated separately. Long jumping and high jumping are field events. The jump pattern is found in basketball as a jump-and-reach in rebounding, a tossed ball, and a lay-up shot. The jump-and-reach is also the pattern for the spike and block in volleyball. In any sport where an object is thrown or hit and must be caught, a jump often accompanies the throw and catch.

SUGGESTIONS FOR STUDY

1. Jump in place with an emphasis on height; make light jumping movements; heavy jumps.
2. Jump and turn.
3. Jump like a bouncing ball, continuously; vary the bounce pattern; bounce high; low.
4. Jump and move.
5. Jump and reach for various objects and at various heights.
6. Jump forward; backward; sideward.
7. Jump in and out of a hoop held at various heights.
8. Jump in and out of a circle or circles drawn on the floor.
9. Jump over a rope; a bench; a box.
10. Jump for distance.
11. Jump off benches or trampolet for height, knees bent, arms out, turn in the air.
12. Jump around obstacles.
13. Change directions while jumping.
14. Jump with a rope.
15. Jump while bouncing a ball, or throwing and catching with a partner.
16. Jump over a partner.
17. Jump with a partner.

Hop

DESCRIPTION The body is pushed off the floor from *one foot* and after a slight suspension in the air it is returned to the floor with the weight taken on the *same foot*. The knee of the inactive leg is bent, and the leg makes no contact with the floor. The arms move upward to help with the body lift. The landing is on the toes, and immediately the weight is shifted to the ball of the foot and then to the heel.

BASIC MECHANICAL PRINCIPLES

1. The upward swing of the arms adds momentum to the vertical lift.
2. The vertical lift keeps the center of gravity over the base of support.

COMMON FAULTS

1. Taking off on one foot and landing on the other.
2. Trying to go forward more than upward.
3. Landing on the whole of the foot rather than on toes first, then ball to heel.
4. Losing balance because of body sway and lack of arm-swing.

KEY TEACHING PHRASES

1. *Up* in the air on one foot and *down* on the same one.
2. Lift arms up.
3. Head held high.
4. Bend knee.

USES In dance and sports activities, a hop is usually used in combination with a jump or walk. It is used in the traditional steps in dance in the skip, step-hop, schottische, polka, mazurka. A hop-step precedes a stop in running games.

SUGGESTIONS FOR STUDY

1. Hop in place; hold position with weight on one foot for varying length of time.
2. Hop and turn; make a pattern of turning.
3. Hop forward; backward; sideward; make a pattern.
4. Hop holding free leg in various positions.
5. Hop high; low.
6. Hop covering varying distances.
7. Hop over a rope.
8. Hop with a partner.

Combinations of Locomotor Movements

Slide

DESCRIPTION A slide is a combination of a step and a leap. The individual steps to the side and draws the other foot to the side of the supporting foot and puts the weight on it. The same foot always leads. The sliding pattern may be done in a forward or backward direction; however, then it is often called a *gallop*. When the direction is to be changed, a slightly higher leap is taken, and the weight is shifted in the desired direction.

BASIC MECHANICAL PRINCIPLES

1. The momentum generated for the step sideways is checked by the upward movement of the hop; therefore, balance is maintained easily.
2. The hop, as used in the slide for most sports activities, involves gaining little height.
3. Because the body weight is always within the base of support, the sliding pattern provides a well-balanced position for quick changes of direction.

Understanding
and Teaching
Basic Movement

239

COMMON FAULTS

1. Failure to shift weight from lead to following foot.
2. Hopping too high and not gaining distance sideways.

KEY TEACHING PHRASES

1. Step to side.
2. Draw foot up toward other and hop.
3. Lead with the same foot.

USES The slide is an important element of defensive footwork in basketball. It allows one to move efficiently in a balanced manner and to be ready to move quickly in any direction. A slide movement is utilized in volleyball, tennis, badminton, softball, and baseball to gain position for subsequent play when changes in direction and actions are necessary. The slide is a basic dance step and is found in many simple folk dances.

SUGGESTIONS FOR STUDY

1. Slide sideward to the right; reverse direction.
2. Slide sideward, then forward. Make a square by changing from sideward to forward, then backward.
3. Slide slowly without much lift.
4. Slide with a big lift.
5. Slide, turning in air on hop every fourth slide step.
6. Slide, ten times right, ten times left, eight times left, eight times right, six times left . . . two times left, two times right, back and forth.
7. Slide left four times, run forward ten steps, slide right four times, continue in pattern.
8. Slide with a partner, holding hands.
9. Slide facing a partner, without holding hands.
10. Slide with a partner using a mirror effect; designate one as leader, and have other follow leader's movements.
11. In a circle with other children slide a set number of times in one direction, then change direction. Stress smooth changes of directions.

Skip

DESCRIPTION The skip is a combination of the walk and the hop. The person steps forward on one foot, then hops on the *same* foot, and then steps forward on the opposite foot and hops on it. The skip can be executed in any direction, but the pattern is always done on alternate feet with the weight shifting on each walking step. The arms should be swung in opposition to the legs to maintain balance and help gain weight, if the latter is desired.

BASIC MECHANICAL PRINCIPLES (The principles that apply to the walk and the hop apply to the skip.)

1. It is the propulsive force exerted by the one foot push-off of the hop that gives the upward movement of the skip.
2. The upward swing of the arms adds momentum in the desired direction, if height is desired.

Foundations of
Movement

240

1. Stepping on one foot and hopping on the other foot. The weight is transferred on the hop rather than the step.
2. Gaining forward distance rather than height because the leg is not lifted upward.

KEY TEACHING PHRASES

1. Step forward and hop *up!*
2. Swing arms up. (If a child has difficulty with the pattern, take his hand and skip with him.)

USES The skip pattern is an important part of footwork in most games and sports where quick stops and changes of direction are needed. A skip stop is useful for a quick stop and regaining of balance and position. A skip usually precedes a lay-up shot in basketball. The skip is a traditional dance step used in many folk dances.

SUGGESTIONS FOR STUDY

1. Skip forward; backward; in a circle; make a pattern.
2. Skip high, low.
3. Skip lightly; heavily.
4. Skip and add another movement pattern.
5. Skip around obstacles.
6. Skip with a partner.
7. Play relays with skipping as a means of locomotion.

Landing

DESCRIPTION

1. Landing on the balls of the feet with knees and ankles bent absorbs the force and helps decelerate momentum gradually.
2. The wider the base of support, the lower the center of gravity; hence equilibrium is regained more easily. (Caution: the base should not be so wide as to put strain on joints and ligaments. It should be no more than the width of the hips sideways.)
3. Holding the upper part of the body and the head erect helps keep the center of gravity over the base of support.

COMMON FAULTS

1. Landing with feet in flat position.
2. Keeping knees rigid.
3. Landing with feet close together.
4. Looking down at the floor.
5. Bending forward at the waist.

KEY TEACHING PHRASES

1. Come down on balls of feet.
2. Extend arms sidewards.
3. Bend knees.

4. Keep chest and head high.

5. Look in the direction of the next movement.

6. Rebound from the floor with a little jump into a standing position.

USES Every jump must be accompanied by a landing, a skill used in all sports and games. In basketball one lands from a jump ball, jump shot, rebound, jump stop, and after catching high passes. Landing techniques are needed after spikes and blocks in volleyball. Catching high balls in softball, football, and lacrosse all demand that one come down to the ground and quickly regain balance before the next move is made. Whenever a jump upon, over, or from a piece of apparatus is executed, a landing must be made. The jumping events in track and field all demand the ability to land properly and safely. Any dance movement that takes the body into the air requires a landing.

SUGGESTIONS FOR STUDY

1. Jump into the air, and land with knees bent.

2. Jump into the air, land, and immediately rebound into another jump.

3. Run, jump, and land.

4. Jump from benches, bleachers, tables, or boxes of increasingly greater heights, and land.

5. Jump over ropes and land.

6. Jump over a bench or box and land.

7. Jump over a partner who is in a hands-and-knees position.

8. Jump and land, preceded by and followed by another type of movement.

9. Jump, turn in the air, and land.

Stopping

DESCRIPTION There are two styles of stopping: the running stride stop and the skip stop. In the former the runner simply stops running with feet in a forward stride position, bends the knees, leans the body weight backward, and reestablishes balance. The latter employs a step and a hop before the actual stop. The weight is carried back and taken on the balls of the feet which are in a forward stride position. The hop allows the individual to gain more forward distance on the stop. The latter is dependent on the angle of take off of the hop.

BASIC MECHANICAL PRINCIPLES

1. Forward momentum must be checked and balance gained in order to stop.

2. Bending the knees helps absorb the momentum gradually and also lowers and moves the center of gravity backward.

3. The upward motion of the hop checks the forward momentum to a greater extent than the sudden stride stop does.

COMMON FAULTS

1. Failing to bend knees.

2. Letting body weight continue forward; thus balance is not regained and additional steps are required before a stop is made.

3. Taking off for the hop at too small an angle; i.e., jumping forward rather than upward.

KEY TEACHING PHRASES

1. Bend knees.
2. Lean back at waist.
3. Land with feet apart, forward and backward.
4. Head up.
5. Step, hop, and land (for skip stop).

USES The skill of stopping is used in all movement activities since one has to come to a stop whenever any locomotor movement is made.

SUGGESTIONS FOR STUDY

1. Run a certain distance and stop.
2. Run and stop on signals—whistle, drum, voice, clap; vary locomotor movement preceding stop.
3. Follow the leader, stop when the leader stops.
4. Draw a line in front of a barrier; run and stop between line and barrier.
5. Jump down from a height, run and stop.
6. Run in a circle, stop on command.
7. Make a pattern of running a certain number of steps, then stop for a certain count, and then continue running.
8. Play relays with command stops and starts.

Pivot

DESCRIPTION The pivot is used to change directions efficiently when in a stationary position. The individual uses one foot as the base of support and keeps the ball of that foot in contact with the floor as he pushes off from the floor with the other foot in the desired direction. The knees should be bent with the body weight kept low over the stationary foot. In this manner one can make a turn of any degree in all directions. The direction the turn is made is dependent on the purpose of the pivot and the proximity or position of an opponent or partner.

Another form of turning is the reverse turn. With the feet in a forward stride position the player spins to the rear on the balls of both feet while the feet remain on the floor. In this situation the turn may be made in the direction of the rear foot only. As in a pivot, the knees are bent and the body weight is low. The weight is equally distributed over both feet. The same principles are followed when other parts of the body are the base of support. One body part, such as one hand, may be the base of support.

BASIC MECHANICAL PRINCIPLES

1. The nearer the center of gravity to the base of support, the greater will be the balance; therefore, the body weight is lowered.
2. The off-center application of force by the free foot causes the body to move in a circle about the pivot foot which is the center of rotation.

3. The rotary movement around an axis is fastest when the radius is shortest; therefore, the closer the body appendages and external objects are carried to the body and over the base of support the faster the turn will be.

4. Spinning on the ball of the foot reduces the friction that would be created in turning on the whole foot without actually moving it.

5. By keeping the body weight low over the base of support, the person is in a balanced position and ready to initiate any new movement rapidly after the desired direction is assumed.

COMMON FAULTS

1. Moving the pivot foot.
2. Changing pivot foot.
3. Trying to spin on the whole foot.

KEY TEACHING PHRASES

1. Spin on ball of foot.
2. Push with the free foot.

USES The pivot and reverse turn are utilized in all sports when a quick, efficient change of direction is desired. Many dance patterns and changes of direction in dances are intially dependent upon a pivot or reverse turn. Gymnastic activities involve many pivots with a variety of bases of support.

SUGGESTIONS FOR STUDY

1. Using the pivot, change directions on command.
2. Facing a partner, learn to pivot away from him or her.
3. Run, stop, pivot or do a reverse turn, and run back to a starting point..
4. Receive a ball from a partner; pivot and pass to another point.
5. Walk and pivot.
6. Pivot around in a circle.
7. With a partner pivot around in a circle.
8. Walk forward and do a reverse turn.
9. Make a pattern of walks and reverse turns.
10. Using the hands as a base of support, pivot around in a circle.
11. Using the hips as a base of support, pivot around in a circle.

Dodge

DESCRIPTION In order to execute a dodge, the individual stops running forward and changes the direction of the motion of his body by bending the knees, dropping the weight to a low point, and shifting the weight in the direction of the dodge. The latter may be described as a *lean-away* from the original direction. The subsequent forward movement in the new direction is made by pushing off from the ground or floor with the foot which bears the body weight. One foot or both feet may be used to stop as the dodge is initiated and to push off from the ground in the new direction.

BASIC MECHANICAL PRINCIPLES

1. Dropping the weight lowers the center of gravity; consequently, better balance is gained. Also, the momentum of the forward or sideward movement can be absorbed over a greater period of time.

2. Since one of the principles involved in running is to put the body off-balance to start, the purpose of shifting the weight in dodging is to bring the center of gravity back over the base of support in order to stop and shift into a starting position again.

3. The forward motion of the body is started by upsetting equilibrium by means of putting the body weight outside the base of support and pushing off by one or both feet.

COMMON FAULTS

1. Failing to bend knees.
2. Failing to check forward momentum by not shifting weight far enough back over base of support at the start of the change of direction.
3. Holding balance too long and therefore getting a slow start in the new direction.

KEY TEACHING PHRASES

1. Bend knees.
2. Check forward movement.
3. Lean toward dodging side.
4. Push off in new direction.

USES A dodge is employed in all sports and games where evading an opponent is involved. The field sports of hockey, lacrosse, speedball, football, and soccer utilize the dodge pattern extensively.

SUGGESTIONS FOR STUDY

1. Run to a certain line, change direction.
2. Run around a series of obstacles.
3. Run to a partner and go around him (it is best to designate a line which the dodger must cross before changing direction).
4. Run to a partner who reaches out to tag dodger. Dodger tries to avoid being tagged.
5. Run to a partner who moves out to tag dodger. Dodger tries to avoid being tagged.
6. Run and dodge a ball thrown by someone else.
7. While dribbling a ball with hand or foot, follow the same series (3–6).
8. While dribbling a ball with hand or foot, dodge around pins as in an obstacle course.
9. Run anywhere trying to avoid an opponent who tries to tag dodger.

Falling

DESCRIPTION There is always the possibility of losing one's balance and falling to the ground. As a safety measure in all activities, it is important that children be taught to fall safely.

If balance is lost and one falls, the principles of absorption should be applied. The person should relax so the joints can give and force can be absorbed over a longer period of time. If possible, the fall should be taken on the padded parts of the body—the hips, thighs, buttocks, or back of the shoulders and on the greatest number of these as possible at one time. If a fall onto the arms or hands is impossible to avoid, the wrists and elbows must give. It should be stressed that a fall directly onto the head, elbows, or knees should be avoided if possible. A rolling motion or curled position should be assumed. The head should be tucked in, or a slight twist given to the area of the body about to strike the floor.

BASIC MECHANICAL PRINCIPLES

1. Absorbing the force on the padded areas of the body reduces momentum gradually.
2. The rolling motion gives a greater amount of time for momentum to decrease.

COMMON FAULTS

1. Falling onto outstretched rigid hands.
2. Failing to tuck head in.

KEY TEACHING PHRASES

1. Relax.
2. Bend joints.
3. Roll with the fall.
4. Tuck head in.

USES Skills should be taught with a positive approach so that children may move confidently and safely; however, a loss of balance is encountered in many situations for many different reasons. The mechanics of the rolls in tumbling should be related to the mechanics of falling safely.

SUGGESTIONS FOR STUDY

1. Roll in a curled position.
2. Tumble in a forward; sideward; backward position.
3. Be a ball and roll around in a circle.
4. From the end of a low box, put hands on the floor and go into a forward roll.
5. Jump from a low box and go into a roll.
6. Melt like an ice cream cone.
7. Collapse like a balloon.

Nonlocomotor Movements

Bend

DESCRIPTION A bend is a movement around a joint where two adjacent parts of the body (bones) join together. The technical term is *flexion*. Very small bending movements (bending the fingers) or large bending movements (bending at the waist) can be made. Bending and stretching often go together when the bend is a preparatory movement for greater stretching power. A number of bending actions are made at one time for some actions. For example, in making the body as small as possible a great number of joint actions are made simultaneously.

Foundations of
Movement

TEACHING HINTS   The structure of some joints determines the range of bend. The extent of bending one can do is dependent upon flexibility, and this flexibility is specific to each joint. Children are usually quite flexible but become less so as they get older. Thus the teacher should continue to provide many opportunities for bending at all grade levels. The terms "curl" and "tuck" are often used when referring to bending movements.

USES   Bending of some body parts is essential to the majority of dance, sports, apparatus, and aquatic skills as well as to daily tasks. The degree of bend of the knees and ankles in most locomotor skills helps regulate the amount of force built up from the subsequent extension of these parts. The rate of absorption of force upon landing or falling is also dependent upon the bending of various parts; and success in many rotary actions is related to the extent of the bending or tucking of the appendages.

SUGGESTIONS FOR STUDY

1. With arms outstretched, bend the lower half of the arm upward and toward the body; sideward and out; in. Do it slowly, then faster.
2. Bend the arm from the shoulder, upward, downward, sideward, in all directions, and in various combinations.
3. Standing on one leg, bend the other knee upward, bend the ankle upward, then downward.
4. Standing on two feet, bend the knees forward and downward.
5. Standing, bend the trunk forward and downward, sideward and downward, backward and downward.
6. Make various combinations of knee and arm bends.
7. Standing, touch the floor in front and to the side.
8. Lying on the back, bend knees toward chest; alternate bending knees.
9. Lying on the front, bend one knee upward, then the other; alternate.
10. Bend knees, and jump up as high as possible.
11. Bend up and down as you bounce like a ball.
12. Walk while bending the knees deep, walk without bending the knees.
13. In kneeling position with weight on lower legs, bend each upper body part until head touches knees.
14. Make yourself as small as possible.
15. Run and jump; while in flight change your shape.
16. Jump off a box; change shape while in air.

Stretch

DESCRIPTION   A stretch is the extension or hyperextension of the joints of the body. The stretching action may take place at any of the joints of the body in various combinations. Stretching may also be thought of as expanding any part of the body.

TEACHING HINTS   Precede tasks involving maximum stretching with gradual loosening-up activities. Stress good balance before maximum stretch. Using imagery with primary-grade children fosters a good concept of stretching.

USES   The ability to stretch or extend at will helps maintain flexibility of the joints. Stretching is allied with flexing or bending where the latter is most

Understanding
and Teaching
Basic Movement

247

often a preparatory movement to aid in full extension. Stretching is utilized in many daily tasks of reaching for objects. Almost all sports skills involve stretching as an aid to achieve maximum force, distance, and speed in actions. Many dance skills employ stretching in various factors of time and positions and as an expressive movement.

SUGGESTIONS FOR STUDY

1. Stretch whole body tall.
2. Stretch fingers, arms, or other isolated body parts.
3. Stretch wide.
4. Stretch like a rubber band.
5. Reach for spots, real or imaginary, on the wall.
6. Combine bends and stretches.
7. Hang and stretch on bars of some type.
8. Jump and stretch.
9. Stretch out while running.
10. Stretch one leg while bending the other.
11. Stretch in an inverted position.
12. Lie down, and be as long as possible.
13. Jump and stretch with legs apart, legs together.
14. Leap and stretch.
15. Stretch legs high and wide while weight is on shoulders and upper back.

Pull

DESCRIPTION   A pull is a forceful movement made to move or draw an object toward the body. This is most often done with the arms. Initially, the arm or arms are extended. Then, as the object is drawn toward the body, the elbows and wrists bend, and the body straightens. The body leans slightly forward, and the knees are bent. According to the resistance or weight of the object, more force may need to be developed by using the strong muscles of the legs.

TEACHING HINTS   If a heavy object is to be moved, stress a wide stable stance. Stress bending at the knees and letting the muscles of the legs do the work.

USES   The pull is a utilitarian skill needed in daily work tasks, such as pulling a wagon, a door open, a window closed, a sweater down over the head, a drawer out, oars in a boat, and so forth. Swimming requires one to pull oneself through the water. Archery depends on a strong pull on the bow string. The body must be pulled up from the floor to various positions on different pieces of apparatus.

SUGGESTIONS FOR STUDY

1. Pull an object toward body (use a real object or imagine one).
2. Pull an object from in front of body; from in back; from the side; use both arms; use only one arm.
3. Walk and pull something from behind, then from front.
4. Sit and pull an object.
5. Kneel and pull an object.
6. Pull an object while lying down.

7. Pull an object quickly, then slowly.
8. Pull a partner who is standing across a line on the floor.
9. Pull a partner who is sitting down across a line.
10. Pull a partner who is lying down up into a standing position.
11. Play Tug-of-War with four or five people on each end of a rope.
12. Lying down, have a different partner hold onto each hand and pull yourself into a standing position.

Push

DESCRIPTION   A push is a forceful movement made to move some object away from the body or a movement made against an object to move the body away from it. A push may be made by the legs, wrists, arms, feet, hips, shoulders, or a combination of these, depending upon the amount of force needed. There is usually a preparatory bend and forceful extension as the pushing motion is made.

TEACHING HINTS   If a heavy object is to be moved, all the mechanical principles relating to balance and the development of force and application of force must be applied, including the placement of feet in a forward stride position wide enough to maintain stability, the preparatory flexion efforts for building momentum, a summation of all the forces, and a direct application of the force in the direction the object that is to be moved. Stress using muscles of the legs to push heavy objects.

USES   A push is a utilitarian skill needed in daily tasks, such as pushing a lawn mower, saw, or vacuum sweeper, moving heavy boxes and other objects. Many stunts, tumbling, and apparatus activities require one to push oneself up off the floor, away from apparatus, and off apparatus. Some contact sports require that a player push the opponent out of position.

SUGGESTIONS FOR STUDY

1. Push lightweight objects across the floor, then heavy objects (use both real and imaginary objects).
2. Push with two hands, with one hand.
3. Push with feet.
4. In a kneeling position, touch forehead to floor; with hands, push body back into a straight kneeling position.
5. Lying down, push self up with hands.
6. Push partner across a line, using hands, then shoulders, then hips.
7. Lying on back, bend knees; partners put soles of feet together and push.
8. On hands and knees, push partner across line.
9. Stand one foot away from the wall, lean forward from ankles, bend arms at elbows and place hands and head against wall; push away from wall; increase distance.
10. Jump up and support weight against a box or bar, hold and push away and return to standing position.

Lift

DESCRIPTION   A lift is a movement that raises an object or a body part from one level to another. Pushing and pulling movements are involved in lifting.

Lifting is actually pushing and pulling in a vertical direction rather than in a horizontal direction. The hands and arms bend as the object is moved upward and extend as it is placed in a high position or moved to another place at a lower level. The knees bend as the object is picked up and extend as they assist in raising the object.

TEACHING HINTS If the object to be lifted is heavy, the width of the stance should be great, and the knees bent more than usual. A stooping position should be taken to get body close to the floor. The strong muscles of the leg should be utilized. The hands should be placed under the object and it should be brought up in the air close to the body.

USES The lift is primarily a utilitarian skill and is used in many household and vocational tasks. In some stunt, tumbling, and apparatus activities the body must be lifted into various positions from the floor. In sports activities balls and implements must actually be lifted into positions. The arms and legs themselves are lifted in all sports and dance activities.

SUGGESTIONS FOR STUDY

1. Lift the arm sideward to shoulder height; forward to shoulder height.
2. Lift a leg forward and upward; backward and upward.
3. Sitting, lift one leg at a time. Alternate legs, lifting and lowering slowly.
4. Lift one foot at a time.
5. Lift a basketball; a balloon; a bowling ball.
6. Lift a rock (real and imaginary).
7. Lift a box and put it on a high shelf.

Swing

DESCRIPTION The swing is a movement of arms, legs, upper trunk, head, or body as a whole in a circular or pendular fashion around a stationary center. The part to be swung is dropped into space where the power from the drop will carry it upward in the opposite direction; then it will drop downward again. The swing may be continued by adding more force to the body part at the beginning of each drop. When more force is added, a faster swing will result. If enough force is added, the swing will carry over and drop back on the other side, thus making a full-circle swing.

TEACHING HINTS Help arms or other swinging body parts move as they swing down. No more force should be added to the downward movement if the swing is to stop gradually. When swinging movements are being done on rings, swings, or bars, one should get off or drop off at the back of the swing as the momentum is temporarily halted.

SUGGESTIONS FOR STUDY

1. Swing one arm across the front of the body. Let it fall limp. Swing it three or four times, let it fall limp.
2. Swing one arm across the front of the body, keeping it going at the same speed. Make it swing faster, slower.
3. Swing one arm across the front of the body several times, then make it go in a circle. Do the same with the leg.

4. Repeat the above sequence with both arms and legs.

5. Swing one arm backward and the other arm forward in opposition to each other.

6. Standing on one foot, swing the other leg back and forth; swing it fast then slow.

7. Swing one arm and the opposite leg.

8. Lying down, swing one leg back and forth; then swing both legs.

9. Standing, swing the upper part of body, bend over, and swing it; let arms swing with body.

10. Swing head from side to side.

11. Hang by the hands from a bar and swing the lower part of body; the whole body.

12. Swing with one hand only holding the bar.

13. Hang by the knees and swing.

14. Swing on a hanging rope.

15. Swing on a rope and get off while swinging.

16. Swing on a rope and land on top of a box.

17. Swing arms, and jump high.

18. Swing arms and jump for distance.

19. Standing on one leg, swing several times, then jump; try this, and turn in the air and jump.

Turn

DESCRIPTION A turn is a rotation or circular movement of the body or body parts around in space. Joint structure restricts some body joints to twisting rather than turning. The focal point of the turn is the space in which the body or body part turns.

TEACHING HINTS When speed or force is to be gained in the turn, a preliminary twisting motion in the opposite direction of the turn will help develop momentum. Stopping after a fast turn will require regaining balance and control of weight.

SUGGESTIONS FOR STUDY

1. See how many body parts can turn all the way around. Make big circles, then little ones.

2. Turn the whole body around.

3. Standing on one foot, turn body around quickly, then slowly.

4. Sitting down, turn body around quickly, then slowly.

5. Lying on stomach, turn around.

6. Turn while walking, running, skipping.

7. Start with a small part of the body turning, then make other parts turn until the whole body is turning.

8. Turn around a chair; a ball; another person; a wand; a rope.

9. Turn with a partner.

10. Hold hands with a partner; one turn left, the other turn right.

11. Move around the room while turning with a partner.
12. Kneel with hands on ground; make hands walk around body.
13. Support weight on part of body other than feet and turn around.
14. Jump up and turn in the air.
15. Jump off a box and turn in the air.

Twist

DESCRIPTION A twist is a rotation of some body part around its own long axis. Twisting action can only take place at the spinal, neck, shoulder, hip, and wrist joints.

TEACHING HINTS Children often confuse twisting and turning. Ask them to think of the lower arm as a rod around which the muscles twist. The focal point in the twist is the action around the body part itself. In the turn, the focal point is the space in which the body part turns.

USES The twist is a utilitarian skill used in many household tasks such as twisting lids, dials, screwdrivers. Often the head must twist in order for a person to see objects at various angles, the body must twist to get into and out of small cars and through small openings. Twisting movements are used in many stunt, tumbling, apparatus, dance, and sport activities.

SUGGESTIONS FOR STUDY

1. Twist one arm around the body; both arms.
2. Standing, lift one leg and twist it as far as possible.
3. Twist one body part one direction, another in the other direction.
4. Standing on one foot twist the whole body; untwist quickly.
5. Standing with feet apart, twist right arm around the left leg and pick up an object lying between the feet.
6. Twist the head around and determine how far you can see in the opposite direction.
7. Hold the head steady and twist the shoulders around as far as possible.
8. Support weight on hands and knees and twist into a position where weight is supported on the back.
9. From a standing position, twist body and place hands on floor to the right of the body and then support weight on hands.
10. Twist trunk from right to left while walking.
11. Twist like a screwdriver.
12. Twist like a spring.
13. Put hand against wall and twist under the arm.
14. With arms out to sides, twist vigorously from side to side.

Manipulative Skills

Manipulation involves the control of objects of some type. We manipulate objects with:

The Body	HOW		Implements
*Hands	*Propel*	*Receive*	Paddles
*Feet	Throw	Catch	Bats
Head	Strike	Trap	Sticks
Shoulders	Bounce	Collect	Rackets
Knees	Kick	Block	Scoops
Hips	Roll	Stop	Others
Others	Volley		
	Dribble		

(*Primarily)

Manipulative skills utilize the fundamental patterns of throwing, catching, and striking in a variety of ways and with a variety of objects and implements in many play, game, and sport activities. Many environmental variables influence the acquisition of efficient manipulative patterns and their variations. It is essential that teachers recognize these variables or factors and arrange tasks and activities in a way that will allow children to become proficient and confident in their development and readiness. Some will be able to adjust to one variable or factor but not another. Task stations may be designed for adapting to factors affecting throwing. Charts can be used to assess individual readiness and to provide a source of individual programming. Figure 11-3 is an example of pupil planning and self-evaluation of specific factors in catching.

CATCHING PROFILE

Name_____

FACTOR	WHAT I DID TO IMPROVE	HOW I DID	DATE
Small ball			
Vertical arc			

Game(s) I made up to practice and use skill.

Figure 11-3 Profile Sheet for self-directed study on a skill.

The fundamental pattern of the catch, throw, and strike are analyzed here in detail; the factors affecting the performance of these skills are identified as a basis of sequencing of learning tasks and activities. Suggestions for study out of the context of specific activities are made. The adaptation of these manipulative skills as they are used in specific sport activities are found in the chapters on team and individual sports activities.

Catching

DESCRIPTION It is essential to be in line with, directly behind, or underneath the ball before attempting the actual catch. The palms face the direction from which the ball is approaching. If the ball is coming at a level below the waist, the hands are held with the fingers pointing downward (little fingers together). If it is to be received above the waist, the hands are held with the fingers pointing upward (thumbs together). The fingers are spread and slightly curved. The arms reach forward slightly to meet the ball. As soon as the ball comes into the hands, the arms pull it in toward the body. The feet should be in a forward stride position. The faster the oncoming ball approaches, the wider the stance should be. Young children tend to catch with the body—to gather the ball with arms as well as hands. With more experience and more opportunity to experiment with different sizes of balls, a more mature pattern emerges.

BASIC MECHANICAL PRINCIPLES

1. If one is in line with the ball, the force of the oncoming ball can be taken close to the center of gravity of the body.
2. The stride position in the direction of the oncoming ball increases the stability of the body.
3. Pulling the object in toward the body decelerates the speed of the object by increasing the time and distance over which the force can be reduced. This is sometimes referred to as a cushioning effect or as "giving" with the ball.

COMMON FAULTS

1. Reaching out to the side to catch, and therefore not being in line with the ball.
2. Failing to draw ball in toward the body.
3. Keeping fingers straight and rigid; hence the ball hits fingertips and rebounds forward, often causing injury.
4. Putting heels of hands together; thus object bounces out of hands.
5. Losing balance if the ball comes hard and fast because the feet are too close together in a side stride position.

KEY TEACHING PHRASES

1. Get in line with ball.
2. Stand with feet in forward stride position.

Table 11-1. Factors Affecting Catching

				OBJECT			
	SIZE	WEIGHT	SPEED	SHAPE	TEXTURE	TRAJECTORY	DIRECTION CATCHER MUST MOVE TO CATCH
Easy	Large	Moderate	Slow	Round	Soft	Horizontal	Front
↓		Light Moderate				Vertical	Side
Difficult	Small	Heavy	Fast	Oblong	Hard	Arc	Back

4. The trunk must rotate and the weight of the body be transferred forward in order to move the shoulder forward.

COMMON FAULTS

1. Starting the throw with the body facing square to the target.
2. Failing to rotate the trunk.
3. Holding the ball in the palm of the hand.
4. Failing to keep elbow bent and to lead the throw with the elbow (key to many girls' problems).
5. Holding elbow close to the body, resulting in a pushing motion.
6. Failing to transfer weight to forward or left foot.
7. Dropping the wrist before releasing the ball.
8. Using little or no follow-through.

KEY TEACHING PHRASES

1. Keep eyes on target.
2. Start with shoulder to target.
3. Hold left arm at shoulder level and point to target.
4. Twist body backward.
5. Keep elbow bent and shoulder high and away from body.
6. Lead throw forward with the elbow.
7. Whip arm through to target.
8. Snap wrist.
9. Release ball off fingers.
10. Reach for the target.
11. Step onto right foot.

USES   The overhand throw is used primarily for throwing an object that is small enough to be held by the fingers. The overhand pattern is commonly used for all throwing in baseball, softball, and football. It is the basis of the overhand serves in tennis and volleyball, and the smashes in the racquet games. It is the preferred pattern for throwing in lacrosse.

SUGGESTIONS FOR STUDY

1. Start with beanbags or darts with large suction grippers on the ends. Standing close to wall, throw at wall. Emphasis should be on having the elbow bent and held high. Pattern instead of distance should be stressed.
2. Using tennis balls or fleece balls, throw at wall at varying distances. (Children can grasp fleece balls in their fingers easily, and they will not rebound very far after hitting the wall. Tennis balls can be held with fingers but rebound with greater force.)
3. Move progressively farther back from wall, and throw. Teacher should point out the body rotation and shift of weight necessary to throw at increasingly farther distances.
4. Throw at targets on the wall. Use various shapes, sizes, angles.
5. Throw ball through a hoop held by a partner.
6. As catching skill improves, throw and catch with a partner.

7. Throw at a moving target, another person, a moving ball.
8. Throw a football for distance.
9. Throw a football for accuracy.
10. Throw a softball for distance. Add a preliminary run for more force.

Underhand Throw

DESCRIPTION   A child's first attempt at throwing is usually that of a two-hand toss or underhand throw. As the hands get larger and when a small ball is used, the one-hand throw develops.

With feet together, the thrower stands facing the target. The right arm is brought straight down and back. At the same time the body rotates slightly to the right, and the weight is shifted to the right foot. The arm is swung quickly forward, and at the same time a step forward is taken onto the left foot. The ball is released when the arm is at a right angle to the target. The left arm swings backward to aid in balance.

BASIC MECHANICAL PRINCIPLES

1. The amount of momentum generated by the body is transferred to the ball. The rotation of the body, the backswing, and the shift of the weight to the rear foot allows the ball to be brought back farther so that there is more time to build up momentum in the forward movement.
2. The straight arm affords a greater arc through which the ball travels to build up momentum.
3. The follow-through enables the hand to be moving its fastest at the moment of release. The object moves in a tangent to the arc the hand is traveling at the time of release; consequently, the point of release is when the arc of the hand is tangent to the target.

COMMON FAULTS

1. Using little or no rotation of the trunk.
2. Failing to use a long enough backswing.
3. Failing to shift weight backward.
4. Releasing ball too high.
5. Failing to step forward on left foot.
6. Failing to follow through.

KEY TEACHING PHRASES

1. Face target.
2. Twist body to right as ball is brought back.
3. Bring arm down and straight back, and then swing it straight forward.
4. Step forward on left foot.
5. Reach for the target.

USES   The underhand throw pattern is effective for throwing tasks involving accuracy because the throwing hand follows a straight path. It is used as a pitch and a short throw to basemen in softball; as a roll-in for hockey, and as the delivery in bowling; it is used when a pass of short or medium distance is needed in basketball. The underhand pattern is the basis of many skills—such as volleyball serve and the badminton serve—which use the hand or other instruments as striking objects.

1. Throw a ball up in the air and catch.
2. Using a beanbag or fleece ball, throw to wall, and increase distance from wall.
3. Using a large ball, throw to wall. Left hand will have to support ball on backswing.
4. Roll ball at targets.
5. Throw to a partner.
6. Throw at targets, moving and stationary.
7. Run, stop, throw a short pass to a partner.
8. Run, pivot, throw to a partner who is a short distance away.
9. Throw ball up to self, turn around and catch.
10. Run alongside partner, throwing and catching the ball.
11. Use different sizes and shapes of balls for all of the above.

Sidearm Throw

DESCRIPTION The thrower stands in a forward stride position with the right foot back. If the object is large, the palm of the hand holds it against the lower arm. A small object is held with the fingers. The body rotates or twists toward the right, and the body weight is transferred to the back foot as the arm swings back in a *horizontal* arc. When the object is small, the forward actions are the same as in the overhand throw with the exception of the horizontal arm pattern. That is, the arm moves with a whiplike action with the elbow leading, the body rotates toward the target and the object is released when the hand is at a point tangent to the target.

If the object is large, the arm moves as one long lever, and no series of joint actions is practical. The ball must be released at the moment that the arc of the throwing arm is tangent to the target.

BASIC MECHANICAL PRINCIPLES The long backswing, the body rotation, the follow-through, and the movement of weight forward all contribute to the force and speed that is transferred to the object as it leaves the hand.

COMMON FAULTS

1. Failing to rotate the body backward.
2. Failing to shift weight back, then forward.
3. Releasing ball too early (ball goes to the right).
4. Releasing ball too late (ball goes to the left).

KEY TEACHING PHRASES

1. Eyes on target.
2. Hold large ball against wrist.
3. Shift weight back.
4. Twist body.
5. Whip the ball forward with the elbow leading.
6. Follow through with the hand in direction of target.

Table 11-2. Factors Affecting Throwing

| | | OBJECT | | | TARGET | | |
	SIZE	WEIGHT	SHAPE	DISTANCE TO BE THROWN	LOCATION	SIZE	ANGLE FROM THROWER
Easy	Small	Moderately light	Round	Short	Stationary	Large	Straight ahead
↓		Moderately heavy			Moving slowly		Left of thrower
Difficult	Large	Light Heavy	Oblong	Long	Moving fast	Small	Right of thrower

USES The sidearm pattern is generally used to throw large objects for distance, such as the discus and basketballs. Deck-tennis rings are thrown with a sidearm pattern. It is also the basic pattern for drives in badminton, tennis, and paddle tennis.

SUGGESTIONS FOR STUDY

1. Throw a basketball or a soccer ball for distance.
2. Throw a deck-tennis ring from the right side, from the left side (forehand and backhand).
3. Throw a small ball to the wall, to a partner.
4. Throw at a target on the wall.

Striking

DESCRIPTION The striking pattern is utilized in many sports activities. Most of the activities involve hitting an object with some part of the body or an implement that is controlled by the hand. The object to be struck may be stationary or moving. The striking pattern is much the same as that involved in any one of the three throwing patterns.

No matter what plane the implement of striking follows, the speed of the struck object is governed by the same principles as those involved in throwing. The amount of momentum developed depends on the length of the backswing, the number of muscles brought into play, and their orderly sequence of action. The object to be struck should be contacted at the instant the maximum speed of the swing has been reached. The implement must follow through in the direction of the target. The implement should be held out and away from the body and swung in a plane that is a right angle to the object to be hit.

A stance that provides a solid base is important if fast-moving objects are to be struck and propelled any distance. The firmer the hitting surface of the striking implement, the greater the forward force becomes. Implements vary in their firmness; however, a strong grip is always essential. If the hand or foot is the striking tool, the broadest, firmest parts must be the striking surface; i.e., the top of the instep of the foot or the broad area of the fist. Specific striking patterns such as batting in softball, kicking in soccer, serving in volleyball, and so forth are described in Chapters 14 and 15.

Table 11-3. Factors Affecting Striking

	OBJECT					TOOL	
	SIZE	*WEIGHT*	*SPEED*	*TRAJECTORY*	*SIDE OF BODY TO WHICH OBJECT COMES*	*WEIGHT*	*LENGTH*
Easy	Large	Light	Stationary	Stationary	Preferred side	Light	Body part
↓			Slow	Horizontal	Non-preferred side		Short
Difficult	Small	Heavy	Fast	Vertical arc	Midline	Heavy	Long

BASIC MECHANICAL PRINCIPLES

1. As a stationary object is struck, it will move only if the force applied to it is sufficient to overcome its inertia. Therefore, it is essential to develop great speed in the striking movement. This movement is accomplished by weight shift, body rotation, length of backswing, and sequence of muscle actions.
2. The reaction of an object against a striking surface is just as great as the force that projects the object. Therefore, the striking surface should be as firm as possible and the striking tool held as firmly as possible.
3. The more nearly an object is contacted in line with its center of gravity, the greater the amount of force that is transferred to the object in the direction it should travel. Since in most striking activities encountered by young children it is intended that the object go forward and slightly upward, this may be interpreted as slightly below dead center.
4. If the object is moving, the striker must also move to get into a position in which his or her body is directly behind or "in line" with the object in order to contact the center of gravity.

COMMON FAULTS

1. Failing to use sufficient backswing.
2. Rotating body too little.
3. Keeping elbow in too close to the body (when arm action is involved).
4. Failing to grip striking implement tightly.
5. Hitting too far above center of object or "topping object."
6. If striking a moving object, not getting in line with it before contact is made.

KEY TEACHING PHRASES

1. Eyes on object to be hit.
2. Get in line with object.
3. Shift weight back and through.
4. Make a big swing.

Table 11-4. Factors Affecting Kicking

			OBJECT			KICKER	
	SIZE	*SHAPE*	*SPEED*	*POSITION*	*DIRECTION OF APPROACH*	*PART OF FOOT USED*	*DIRECTION MUST MOVE TO MEET OBJECT*
Easy	Medium	Round	Stationary	Stationary	From favored side	Toe	Stationary
↓	Large		Slow	Smooth roll		Instep	Forward
				Bouncing roll		Outside of foot	Side
Difficult	Small	Oblong	Fast	In air	From nonfavored side	Heel	Backward

5. Hit just below center of object.
6. Make a level swing.
7. Follow through in direction of target.

USES The striking pattern is used with parts of the body being tools, such as the hands in volleyball and in basketball; the head, shoulder, knee, or foot in soccer; the hand in handball. The same pattern is employed with implements such as the racquets in tennis and badminton, the sticks in hockey, golf, and softball.

SUGGESTIONS FOR STUDY

1. Hit a ball suspended from a rope with hand.
2. Hit balloons with the hands, fists.
3. Hit playground balls or volleyballs with hands and fists for distance.
4. See how high volleyballs or playground balls can be hit.
5. Use a large wooden paddle to hit a ball suspended from a rope.
6. Throw ball in air, and hit it.
7. Hit different sizes of balls thrown by someone else.
8. Use plastic fun balls, and hit them with paddles.
9. Using a batting tee, hit plastic balls with plastic bats.
10. Kick a stationary ball for distance.
11. Kick a stationary ball to a partner.
12. Stop a rolling ball with the feet and then quick-kick it to a partner.
13. Kick into a target area.
14. Walk and kick a ball, keeping it close to the body.
15. Hold a ball in the hands, drop it and kick it before it touches the ground.
16. Kick a ball back and forth with a partner while running.

17. Using a tennis ball, tether ball, or fun ball suspended from a rope, try to hit the swinging ball with a paddle, bat, or hand.

18. Vary force, direction, and aerial pathways of oncoming ball. Kick and hit with hand and various instruments.

Planning Themes for Basic Movement

Basic movement factors can be used as themes or ideas around which to build a series of lessons for an instructional unit for primary children. This conceptual framework allows progressive planning to help children learn about movement and learn to move well. For the primary level, the long-term planning should revolve around a selection of themes from the Basic Movement Glossary, p. 172. A major factor should be identified as the focus or theme. Additional elements, dimensions, and relationships will necessitate adaptations of the major theme so that the program can be refined over a period of time.

The teacher will then plan a series of lessons, bearing in mind the readiness of the children. If the major theme factor is new to the children it should first be explored. Then variations of it should be added and limitations given. There will be a range of different combinations of elements and dimensions, problems will be dealt with, and there will be repetitive experiences. Children will be given opportunities to meet their personal needs or interests, and to choose solutions to meet the demands of rules and boundaries or some particular equipment or apparatus. The movement experiences will be refined, and children will have a chance to learn more creatively. Within the theme, lessons should reveal definite progressively difficult experiences. The sequence of types of learning experiences described on p. 87 should be appropriately evident.

For example, the nature of tasks at different stages of the theme of the *Run,* with added elements of *speed* and *body shape* and the relationship to a *partner,* might be as follows:

1. Initial emphasis is on free running, with some guided exploration stressing good running form (long strides, head up, swing arms alternately straight ahead and back, land on balls of feet).

2. Add the element of time (run fast, run slow, speed up, slow down).

3. Add the element of body shape (change body shape while moving, be wide, twisted, straight and narrow).

4. Add the element of relationship with a partner (run side by side with a partner, can you run at same speed; can you hold hands and run, slow down together, etc.

5. At point 3 or beyond, running games could be played using these combinations of elements, dimensions, and relationships.

This sequence might take several lessons. It could be repeated as a theme without the initial exploratory work on the run, and perhaps more dimensions and relationships added, with the tasks becoming more challenging. Try developing a series of tasks that would fit the themes below.

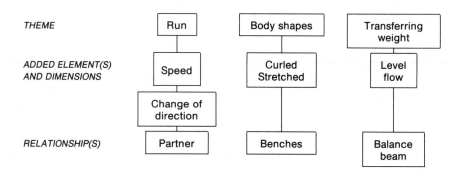

THEME	Run	Body shapes	Transferring weight
ADDED ELEMENT(S) AND DIMENSIONS	Speed	Curled Stretched	Level flow
	Change of direction		
RELATIONSHIP(S)	Partner	Benches	Balance beam

Suggested Format for Developing a Long-term Movement Theme

1. Identify from the Basic Movement Glossary the major theme factor to be studied.

2. Identify additional elements you wish to stress which necessitate adaptation of the major factor.

3. Identify what type of specific relationship(s) you will select—i.e., person-partner or piece of apparatus and relationship to it (may be more than one).

4. List the major objectives for children for the theme:

    a. What they need to understand (knowledges—cognitive).

    b. What they need to learn to do (skill—psychomotor).

    c. What they need to become (attitude and feeling—affective).

5. For each lesson (six to eight):

    a. Design the major tasks, problems, subproblems, and activities you will give children. These should reveal some progression in types of learning experiences:

    (1) *Exploratory experiences.*

    (2) *Limitation—Discovery experiences* as defined by limitations set by the teacher.

    (3) *Selective—Refinement experiences* which will help children repeat and refine solutions.

    (4) *Performance experiences* for which children will select solutions or preferences in use through games, dances, creative sequences or routines, or problems.

    b. Determine and describe organizational modes you will use within your lessons (ways in which children will be involved; circuits, teaching centers, designing games, sequences, etc.).

    c. Determine and describe any teaching aids you will need. Within the lessons indicate where and how you will use them. (Task cards, loop films, records, checklist, worksheets, etc.).

    d. Evaluation: Determine the who, what, and how of movement tasks, as related to the child, peers, teacher, partner.

Table 11-5. Teacher's Guide for Analyzing Selected Fundamental Skills

SKILL	BASE OF SUPPORT AND BALANCE	PRODUCTION OF FORCE	DIRECTION OF APPLICATION OF FORCE	FOCUS	FOLLOW-THROUGH	ABSORPTION OF FORCE
Walking	Brief period of support on both feet, weight shifted in direction and new base of single support. Feet pointed straight ahead, placed alternately along a line.	Contraction of extensor muscles of leg, ankle to push off with toes. Arms swing in opposition to the legs.	Push off horizontally and very slightly vertically. Arms swing back and forward, not across body.	Head up, eyes straight ahead.		Weight taken on heels, transferred along outside edge of foot to toes.
Running	Base: one foot. Body weight forward, lean from ankles.	Contraction of muscles of hip, knee, ankle; push off from toes.	Feet placed straight ahead; legs move upward and forward; arms swing in opposition, forward and backward. Elbows bent.	Head up, eyes straight ahead.		Land on ball of foot.
Jumping A. *Height*	Base at takeoff weight even over both feet; weight low, with knees bent, but hips must be tucked under. In flight, erect position of body. Landing, body erect, weight over both feet; use arms for counterbalance.	Hips, knees, ankles bent; force is derived from extension of these muscles. Arms swing forward and upward.	Push off directly vertical. Arms swing upward.	Head up, eyes upward.	Stretch and reach with all parts of body.	Landing, bend knees, ankles; take weight on balls of feet.

Table 11-5. Continued

SKILL	BASE OF SUPPORT AND BALANCE	PRODUCTION OF FORCE	DIRECTION OF APPLICATION OF FORCE	FOCUS	FOLLOW-THROUGH	ABSORPTION OF FORCE
B. *Distance (Standing)*	Base: Takeoff weight over both feet, forward lean of body. In flight, weight forward. Landing, weight low and forward on both feet.	Hips, knees, ankles bent; force derived from extension of these muscles. Arms swing first backward then forward, vigorously.	Forty-five degree angle upward. Legs swing forward under body.	Head up, eyes straight ahead.	Whole body stretches and reaches forward.	Land in a crouched position, weight on balls of feet.
C. *Distance from a running start*	Preliminary run demands takeoff from one foot. Same as B in flight and landing.	Greater forward momentum gathered from fast run. Push-off is from one foot. Arms swing forward vigorously.	(Same as B)	(Same as B)	(Same as B)	(Same as B)
Hopping	Base: weight on one foot, brief period of no support, weight returned to same foot. Arms counterbalance.	Contraction of extensor muscles of hip, knee, ankle. Push-off from one foot. Upward swing of arms.	Upward amount of forward movement depends on use of hop.	Head up, eyes straight ahead.		Land on toes, shift weight to ball of foot.
Landing	Base: Feet in side on forward side-stride position (no more than width of hips sideways). Weight low and over base. Use arms to counterbalance.			Head up, eyes straight ahead.	As soon as weight is absorbed, legs are extended and rebound to standing position.	Hips, knees, ankles bend, land on balls of feet.

Movement					
Leaping	Longer period of nonsupport than for run. Base shifts alternately on feet which are placed along a straight line forward. Weight forward, arms counterbalance.	Greater flexion of knee and ankle than in run to increase upward movement. Vigorous push-off from rear leg. Forceful upward movement with arms adds to vertical force. This is preceded by a run to gain more momentum for height.	More vertical push off than horizontal as in run. Forward-upward direction of arms.	Head up, eyes straight ahead. Stretch and reach with whole body.	Land on balls of feet.
Skipping	Period of nonsupport on hop, weight shifts to alternate feet. Arms counterbalance.	Propulsive force upward from one-foot push-off of hop gives upward momentum. Arms swing upward.	Forward and upward.	Head up, eyes straight ahead.	Land on toes and transfer weight to balls of feet.
Sliding	Base moves to alternate feet. Weight shifted from lead to following foot. Weight always within base of support.	Extensor muscles of leg as foot pushes vertically and horizontally.	Sideways, more vertical push-off if height is desired on hop.	Head up, eyes straight ahead.	Weight taken on ball of foot.
Stopping	Feet in stride position. Weight brought directly over both feet.	Push off with one or both feet.		Head up, eyes straight ahead.	Bend knees, ankles, land on balls of feet. Lean back from waist.
Dodging	Body weight drops low and is brought back over both feet to initiate dodge; the weight is then shifted outside. The base of support is the new direction of movement.		Push off horizontally in new direction.	Head up, eyes straight ahead.	Bend knees, land on balls of feet.

Table 11-5. Continued

SKILL	BASE OF SUPPORT AND BALANCE	PRODUCTION OF FORCE	DIRECTION OF APPLICATION OF FORCE	FOCUS	FOLLOW-THROUGH	ABSORPTION OF FORCE
Falling	Make broad padded areas of body new base—hips, thigh, buttocks, or back of shoulders.			Tuck head, eyes on landing spot.		Relax joints and muscles, land on padded areas, go into roll so there is a greater amount of time for momentum to decrease.
Pulling	Base: both feet in wide stance. Body weight low. Weight shifts in direction of pull.	Preparatory movement of extension of arms, knees bend. Object drawn to body by flexion of arms and extension of legs.	Arms toward body, legs backward at center of gravity of object to be moved.	Head up, eyes on object to be pulled.	Body straightens.	
Pushing	Base: Both feet in wide stance. Weight low, weight shifts in direction of push.	Preparatory movement of flexion of arms, hands, knees. Summation of forces in extension of legs, arms, and hands.	Directly forward at center of gravity of object to be moved.	Head up in direction object is to be pushed.	Body straightens.	
Lifting	Base: both feet in wide stance. Weight low.	Preparatory flexion of legs, arms, hands, then a summation of forces from an extension of legs and arms as object is raised and placed somewhere else.	Upward under center of gravity of object to be lifted.	Head up, eyes on spot to where object is to be lifted.	Whole body straightens.	

	Base			
Catching	Base: stride position in direction of ball. Wide stance, body weight low. Weight directly over base.	Eyes on ball.		Fingers spread, slightly curved. Reach with arms slightly forward, curl fingers around ball, pull in toward body. Whole body gives slightly.
Throwing	Base: both feet in stride position. Weight shifts to rear foot on backswing to forward foot on throw. A forward step is taken as part of follow-through to regain a stable base on both feet.	All in direct line toward target.	Preliminary movement includes backswing, trunk rotation, shift of weight to increase arc and develop greater momentum. Forward motion: Trunk rotates forward, all leg, trunk, arm wrist, hand muscles extend sequentially. Ball released with final snap of wrist and fingers as arm is straightened. Weight shifts to forward foot as upper arm passes; shoulder and lower arm are fully extended.	Head turned toward target, eyes on target. Arm and hand follow directly to the target. Step onto right foot to regain balance.

SUGGESTED REFERENCES FOR FURTHER STUDY

BILGROUGH, A., and P. JONES, *Physical Education in the Primary School.* London: University of London Press, 1965.

GERHARDT, LYDIA, *Moving and Knowing—The Young Child Orients Himself in Space.* Englewood Cliffs, N.J.: Prentice-Hall, Inc., 1973.

GILLIOM, BONNIE CHIRP, *Basic Movement Education for Children: Rationale and Teaching Units.* Reading, Mass.: Addison-Wesley, 1970.

GODFREY, BARBARA, and NEWELL KEPHART, *Movement Patterns and Motor Education.* New York: Appleton-Century-Crofts, 1969.

KRUEGER, HAYES, and JANE KRUEGER, *Movement Education in Physical Education: A Guide to Teaching and Planning.* Dubuque, Ia.: Wm. C. Brown Co., 1978.

LOGSDON, BETTE J. et al., *Physical Education for Children: A Focus on the Teaching Process.* Philadelphia, Lea & Febiger, 1977.

MURRAY, RUTH L., *Dance in Elementary Education.* New York: Harper & Row, 1976, Chapters 5, 8, and 10.

RIDENOUR, MARCELLA, ed. *Motor Development Issues and Applications.* Princeton, N.J.: Princeton Book Co., 1978.

WICKSTROM, RALPH L., *Fundamental Motor Patterns.* Philadelphia: Lea & Febiger, 1977.

Part IV
Movement Experiences

In this part of the book a wide variety of activity experiences specific to the different forms of movement (dance, games and sports, and gymnastics) are presented. These constitute the activity content through which the basic movement skills, knowledges, and concepts are developed and refined. Included are structured traditional and creative aspects of each of the forms. Activities are presented in a sequential or progressive manner so that teachers will be able to plan and select activities appropriate to the readiness level of their pupils. Activities are suggested by levels for the elementary school and for the seventh and eighth grade as guides to the inexperienced teacher. These denote when it would be appropriate to introduce specific skills or activities; however, this is all relative to the readiness of the students.

Alternatives are offered with the hope that you will select those which best fit your situation in terms of children's needs and interests; your competence and values; and time, facilities, and equipment available or obtainable. What is suggested here is intended to give the beginning teacher a good background and source upon which to build his/her *own* program and to design unique learning experiences.

In some communities there are numerous opportunities for children to participate in competitive youth sport programs and in dance instruction and performance activities sponsored by the community, service organizations, and private schools. Obviously all children will not be involved in these groups; therefore there will be considerable differences in the opportunity to learn and use skills. Since the emphasis in sport programs is usually on the competitive experience, there may be a considerable difference in your approach and that which children encounter outside school. You will have to be cognizant of who does or does not engage in outside-school programs. Experience makes marked differences in readiness within classes, particularly in upper-grade levels, and this factor makes individualization essential.

You should be reminded that all instruction in physical education for boys and girls should take place in a coed class as per federal regulation Title IX. Plans will need to be made for separation of the sexes for most competitive contact sports. Both sexes can learn the skills together, but game play should usually be separate.

12 / DANCE

- Fundamentals of dance
- Creative dance
- Structured forms of dance
- Dance steps
- Preliminary teaching
- Teaching structured dances
- The elementary school dance program

Dance activities have served many cultures as a form of art and recreation; they continue to play an important role in American life. Dance in the elementary school curriculum is vital to the child's development of body control, of expressiveness, and of creativity. Children learn what their bodies can do and how to adapt the various movements of the body to force, space, and objects through all activities, but movement affected by a time structure is learned best through dance activities.

Children usually have a sense of rhythm, a natural love for rhythmic movement, and an innate creative ability. How extensively all of these qualities are developed depends upon the opportunities a child has to express them. These opportunities are provided by a variety of dance forms.

Dance has many forms of which only four are generally studied in the elementary school—fundamentals, creative, folk, and recreational. In the primary grades the emphasis is placed on the fundamentals and the creative forms. Simple singing games and folk dances are included. The fundamentals are the foundations of a movement action vocabulary and provide an understanding of the rhythmic elements affecting movement. They also enable creative responses to be expressed, since they are the foundation on which the child may experiment, explore, and interpret.

In the intermediate and upper grades, more emphasis is placed on learning the structured folk and recreational dances. Creative dance is equally important at these levels.

Fundamentals of Dance

The fundamentals of dance include basic locomotor and nonlocomotor skills and various combinations of them, and an understanding of rhythm, space, and force. These are the basic tools for all other dance forms and, as such, are given major emphasis in the primary grades.

Actually, the movement skills and the elements of time, space, and force that must be considered are the same as those discussed in Chapter 11; however, in dance the *expressive form* of the skills is stressed. More emphasis is given to the coordination of the movements and rhythm elements. Since all movements for each individual have an internal rhythm, it is difficult to make a great distinction between dance movement and basic movement.

Many people believe that dance experiences must have musical accompaniment, but this is not so. Since each person has his own internal time organization, it is difficult for young children to develop many good movement skills within an imposed external rhythm. They must learn to match their rhythm with that of another person or with an accompaniment of some kind. Words, poetry, stories, and objects may also be accompaniment for dance. Whether the young child's experiences in exploration and experimentation with basic movement elements and patterns are called part of dance or basic movement is immaterial. The same patterns and knowledges are the bases of gymnastics, games, and sports but obviously the purposes and ways they are used are different for each form of movement. The significance lies in having experiences in using the body to make creative and expressive responses, and in acquiring the tools of movement with or without an imposed rhythm.

Locomotor Movements

Locomotor movements are those that move the body in space in any direction; the feet are the moving base. The basic locomotor movements are the walk, run, jump, leap, and hop. These are performed in an even rhythm.

Various combinations of basic locomotor movements performed in a specific space and time pattern are the traditional dance steps. The gallop, slide, and skip are the simplest of these to learn and are known by many children before they come to school. They are taught and used in first-grade dance activities. The walk and run are also used in their natural form as dance steps.

Movement Experiences

1. The gallop is a combination of a walk and a run. The same foot is always the lead foot.
2. The slide, a combination of a walk and a run, is much the same as a gallop, but it is usually done in a sideways direction.
3. The skip is a combination of a walk and a hop.

These three steps are performed to an uneven rhythm. Even though they are actual dance steps, they are considered fundamentals because they are a vital part of children's movement vocabulary before dance steps are utilized in structured forms.

Nonlocomotor Movements

Nonlocomotor or axial movements are those in which various parts of the body move in space, with one part of the body serving as an axis or base around which the other parts move. The nonlocomotor movements are the swing, sway, stretch, bend, twist, turn, rock, push, pull, and various combinations of these.

Any of the locomotor and nonlocomotor movements may be done in combinations with one another. Variations of any one should be explored after the movements are learned in their original form. All of the nonlocomotor and locomotor movements included here are analyzed in Chapter 11.

Elements of Rhythm

All dance movements are affected by the elements of rhythm because they are performed within a time structure. This structure is bound by the same elements of rhythm found in music. These elements should be studied simultaneously in music and physical education. The elements of rhythm which should be learned in relation to dance are underlying beat, rhythmic pattern, measure, tempo, accent, phrasing, and intensity.

UNDERLYING BEAT The underlying beat is the steady continuous sound that is heard or felt throughout any rhythmical sequence. It is the constant unit of measurement upon which rhythmic structure rests. It may be likened to the steady beat of the heart or the pulse. Each movement is synchronized with the underlying beat. For example, a step is taken and completed within the time limit of each beat on a drum. A new step is taken on each beat of the drum. The length of the beat may vary.

RHYTHMIC PATTERN A rhythmic pattern is a definite grouping of sounds or beats related to the underlying beat. A particular pattern of unequal sounds or beats must fit within a unit of underlying beats. For example, the uneven pattern of the skip has a rhythmic pattern fitting into units of the underlying beat as follows:

Rhythmic pattern	walk	hop	walk	hop	walk	hop	walk	hop
Underlying beat	(skip)		(skip)		(skip)		(skip)	

MEASURE A measure is an identical grouping of underlying beats. The number of beats in a measure and the time value of each beat are dependent on the meter of the measure; i.e., 2/4, 4/4, 3/4, 6/8 time.

ACCENT The accent is the force of emphasis in movement given to any one beat in a series of pulse beats in measure. In dance the accent is usually on the first beat of every measure.

TEMPO Tempo is the rate of speed of the movement, music, or accompaniment. It may be fast, slow, or moderate.

PHRASING A phrase is a group of measures that, in itself, is a complete sequence of sounds or movements. It can be likened to a sentence or an idea in itself. It is very important that children learn to recognize and identify phrases in their rhythm experiences, because phrasing is essential to learning folk dance easily. The end of a phrase usually signifies changes in direction or movements.

INTENSITY Intensity is the quality of the movement or music. It denotes the loudness or softness of music or forces of a movement.

Space Elements Whether creating a dance or following a traditional dance, an understanding of the space elements that affect movement is important. These elements are direction, level, and floor pattern. Although these are described in detail in Chapter 11, they will be reviewed briefly here as they relate specifically to dance.

DIRECTION Direction is the line of movement taken. It may be forward, backward, sideward, diagonal, upward, downward, or combinations of these.

LEVEL Movement through space may be done at a high, low, or medium level.

FLOOR PATTERN The design made by the body as it moves in space is called the floor pattern. It may take the form of a circle, square, straight line, or zigzag.

Teaching the Fundamentals of Dance

The dance fundamentals can be learned best through a progressive series of teacher-planned experiences wherein children learn to use their bodies in relation to all the factors that affect movement (Chapter 11). These must be teacher-planned to ensure the sequential, purposeful acquisition of skills. If the approach is hit or miss and poorly planned, the child's dance foundation will be deficient. The experiences should be planned by the teacher with opportunity for the class to enjoy exploration, experimentation, and problem solving. Refinement and development of movement skills can be enhanced by creative experiences.

The elements of rhythm should be taught along with the movement skills. Both can be taught in the classroom or the gym and can be integrated naturally. If there are specialists to teach music and physical education, they should work together in planning for dance and rhythmic experiences. Lessons and/or units of work are planned around themes of movement and rhythm fundamentals.

Kindergarten and first-grade objectives should include:

Movement Experiences

1. Recognition that one starts and stops when the accompaniment starts and stops.

2. Recognition of one's own space.

3. Maintenance of a general direction pattern.

It is suggested that much time in the first two grades be devoted to individual work with the basic locomotor movements in their natural form. Simple variations in tempo, direction, and level should be introduced. These variations can become more complex after a year, along with the teaching of additional uses of body parts in nonlocomotor movements. Young children perform large movements better than small confining movements. As soon as movements are done well alone and the pupil can respond to simple external factors that affect movement patterns, combinations of movements should be attempted.

Learning to move with the tempo of the accompaniment is also an early objective. In the beginning stages, the accompaniment should be a drum, hands, sticks, piano, or some other means by which the teacher can control the tempo. Young children are not accustomed to moving within an imposed time and rhythm. They progress from a consciousness of their own tempo to that of the group and finally to that of the accompaniment.

Children should be encouraged to provide their own accompaniment, since it helps them gain a knowledge of beat, tempo, accent, and phrasing. Clapping their hands may be the first experience. Sticks, shakers, and drums can be handled easily by children. Making one's own instrument is a worthwhile project. Those of the primary grades will be crude and simple, but they will be a source of pride to young children and will serve to augment their understanding of rhythmic elements.

Teaching the Elements of Rhythm

UNDERLYING BEAT

1. Using a drum, beat steadily, and have the children clap on every beat, then step on every beat. Vary means of locomotion. Change to asking for axial movements as response. Change rate of speed of beat.

2. Have children provide beat with hands, feet, sticks, or other instruments.

3. Use different instruments, and assign a different movement to each one. Children must stay with the beat as each change of instrument is made. Assign a different direction for each beat.

4. Use a march record, and step on every beat.

5. Jump rope to the beat.

6. Bounce balls to the heart.

7. Police officer: Use a drum or a record for accompaniment. Leader stands where everyone can see him/her. Using the arms as a police officer does to direct traffic, leader indicates different directions in which class should move. The object is to make the changes without losing the beat. Predetermined signals for various other changes may be made, such as changes in level and force, and changes to locomotor from nonlocomotor activities.

RHYTHMIC PATTERN

1. Make up a series of two speed patterns. Children clap out the pattern. Use a combination of walks and runs as next responses. Later, three speed patterns can be added; however, these are more difficult (Figure 12-1).

Figure 12-1 Rhythmic pattern.

Figure 12-2 Clapping names.

Figure 12-3 Clapping rhymes.

2. Clapping names (Figure 12-2). Names are selected, and the rhythm of the name is clapped and spoken. Later, one group may select names for a designated category, and the other children must guess which name it is. Movements may be added to the pattern.

3. Clapping rhymes (Figure 12-3). Select a favorite nursery rhyme. Clap out the rhythmic pattern. Divide into small groups. Each group selects any nursery rhyme. Each child in each group will clap one beat of the pattern. After this, movements may be substituted for claps.

4. Echo. Teacher claps a rhythm pattern. Children must echo the pattern with claps. Progress to having the children echo with movement.

5. Radio stations. Small groups of four or five children are stationed in each corner of the room and are given letters of radio stations. One station sends out a clapping message. The next station must pick it up and duplicate the message. The message should be in claps first, then in movement.

ACCENT

1. Select a meter and beat the drum accenting the first beat in each measure. Have children clap on accent. Change accent to different beats.

2. Clap on every beat but the accented one.

3. Vary response to accent with locomotor movements and nonlocomotor movements.
4. Combine walking on a nonaccented beat with a forceful nonlocomotor movement on accent.
5. Change direction on accent.
6. Change levels on accent.
7. Divide into groups; each group may be assigned a different beat to accent.
8. Use claps or beating instruments at first, then movements.

TEMPO

1. Play drum, changing speeds. Children change speeds as drum changes. Try walking at double time; quickly; slowly.
2. Select objects or animals which usually move at a fast or slow rate. Whenever tempo of accompaniment is like that of their chosen object or animal, they move as it does.

PHRASING

1. Listen to record. Clap at the end of the phrase. Move, changing direction at end of phrase. Change level, style of movement, alternate nonlocomotor and locomotor each time the phrase changes.
2. Use various folk dance records to identify phrases. Make several groups. Each group is assigned to move at the end of each phrase. If in a circle formation, one group may move in when the phrase changes, and the other group may move out. Try the same thing with partners.

Creative Dance

Dance fundamentals should be refined and expanded through creative experiences. Acquiring dance tools and using them are interrelated, since movement skills are needed as the tools of expressive movement, and at the same time these tools are improved and expanded through creative experiences.

The development of creativity is one of the major objectives of education. E. Paul Torrance states that people "seem to prefer to learn creatively, by exploring, questioning, experimenting, testing, and modifying ideas and solutions."[1] Too frequently children are not encouraged to learn in this way, and consequently they do not develop their creative ability. Creative dance experiences provide an opportunity for such development, since these skills are concerned with self-expression through the media of movement. Opportunities to solve movement problems and to relate their experiences and feelings in an outward expression enable children to think creatively in a rather permissive, accepting environment. Young children are naturally very expressive and readily show their feelings. If the opportunities to use powers of expression are continued in all the elementary grades, children will develop their powers of creative thinking.

Dance

[1] In his "Seven Guides to Creativity," *Journal of Health, Physical Education and Recreation* (April 1965), p. 24.

Creativity reflects one's concepts and perceptions, or, to generalize, one's experiences. Feelings or emotions, ideas, and interpretations may be expressed through exploration, improvisation (moving freely in response to various stimuli), solving a problem (usually working out a problem posed by the teacher), composition (making a dance that has a definite form, beginning, and ending), or modifying an established step, pattern, or dance.

The experiences of primary grade children are rather limited compared to those of older children. The ability to abstract grows with age. Therefore, the main themes for creative dance lessons for young children must center on their immediate surroundings and experiences. They enjoy being "like something" or moving "like something." Their reaction to moving like something is usually dramatic. The younger the children, the more apt they are to be imitative. This changes as their experiences broaden and as they develop the tools of movement. Imitation and pantomime should be channeled. For example, if after a field trip to the fire station a story play is worked out, the children should verbally and actively be a firefighter, a fire truck, or a fire hose.

As children grow into the middle grades, their experiences broaden, as do their interests in other people and the world beyond their immediate environment. They are very curious about the when, where, and how of things. Their intellectual powers and, of course, their classroom studies open new vistas of knowledge about science, history, and adventure. Their ability to reason and to abstract grows. They are less self-centered and more interested in sharing and working with others in small groups. More conscious of other people, they have emotional reactions to what other people think, do, and say. They are in need of a means to express emotions through movement.

Children need avenues of expression as they enter puberty and encounter many frustrations and feelings of insecurity. Relationships between boys and girls change at this time. Good vigorous dance activities provide social settings for boys and girls where they can work and play together and feel comfortable in their interactions.

Teaching Creative Dance

A great deal of the creative dance lesson is spent on exploration, problem solving, improvisation, and composition work. Compositions may range from a very simple individual interpretation or expression to a complex dance of many parts or sequences in time and form. The process of arriving at the final composition may involve experimentation and exploration.

Teachers must lay the foundation whenever the class as a whole—as members of small groups or as individuals—is to be given problems to solve or composition work. First the teacher may give some challenges or tasks for children to attempt or explore. Then there may be time given to refining ideas or responses. Then a simple problem is presented to the whole class so that each child must work out his/her own answer. The problem may be presented in stages so that children experience the format of working out a pattern for a dance, changes in direction, or partner relationships, before becoming a member of a small group.

Children should be taught how to approach a problem. If everyone is to work on the same topic, it should be discussed first. Possible answers or solutions may be presented, and ideas for format discussed. After dividing into small groups, the first step is discussion of the problem, then presentation of individual ideas, modification of ideas, use of them, further discussion, then final refinement. After the working period is over, the members of each group should have a chance to present their answer or composition. Observation and evaluation should follow.

Children in primary grades work best alone or with partners. As they get older, small groups of three to five provide a satisfactory working number. Larger groups become difficult, since frequently the less imaginative youngsters let the more aggressive ones do all the planning. There is apt to be disagreement among group members and much time consumed in planning verbally instead of in movement. Groups should be planned so that the most and least aggressive youngsters are scattered throughout the groups. Care should be taken that everyone is working and contributing. A chairperson may be appointed.

The same problem may be assigned to each group or a different problem to each group. Only about 8 to 10 minutes should be allowed for planning and working on most compositions. Children are most productive in the first 6 minutes. If they have not reached the acting stage or refining stage by then, chances are they will not for a long time. Polished productions should not be expected. The emphasis is on the process, not necessarily the product. Some compositions may warrant further refinement. Naturally, more time should be taken for refining the pattern if a dance is designed which may be learned by all, may be used in the future, or may be taught to others. In the upper grades larger group compositions may be undertaken, possibly for presentation to another group or a parent group.

Whenever an individual or small group presents a solution to a problem, an evaluation should be made. It might include points that were not considered in the solution, other ways to solve the problem, use of movements, quality of movements, and perhaps suggestions for refinement or further pursuance.

The teacher sets the stage, serves as a catalyst, then an audience, and finally as a mediator in evaluation and observation of the creative efforts of children. The most crucial responsibility lies in the selection of themes, problems, and activities for the creative lesson. The way the material is presented to the class is also important in terms of the children being able to understand the problem clearly. As children are working on their compositions, the teacher serves as the catalyst—asking questions, prodding, giving few suggestions but much encouragement. As children present what they have done, the teacher serves as an audience, or at least as part of the audience, and after the performance as a mediator in the evaluation.

Creative Dance Experiences

Teaching creative dance to children is as much a creative exercise for the teacher as it is for students. Developing ideas to fit a specific group, expanding old ideas, using new media, and so forth is a constant challenge. Presented here are a few ideas to use as a springboard into teaching dance. The teacher will find that ideas come rather easily. One's ideas grow and flourish from watching and listening to children as they work.

There are a number of approaches one may utilize to develop the creative efforts of children. Suggested here are some one might use as themes for creative dance lessons. The basic approaches are much the same for children in all grades; however, as children grow, more emphasis is placed on small-group compositions and subsequent evaluations. Older children become more interested in the historical and theoretical backgrounds of problems and are able to abstract better. Their experiences provide them with broader and deeper personal interpretations of problems or cues given by the teacher.

SUGGESTED APPROACHES

Music   Children can make dances to the music and the words of songs with which they are familiar or can learn easily. The type of movement and the form of the dance follows the music and spirit of the song. The words usually suggest the nature of the dance that is composed. Most songs used with primary-grade children should be short. They may be taken from the school music books or be songs that are learned before attempting to make a dance to them. Since most school music books are excellent sources of songs, and many music teachers do encourage learning a dance to songs, no particular books will be recommended here. Older children like to work with popular songs, work chants, rounds, and television jingles.

Many good records are available with selections of music which stimulate improvisation by children as a response to the mood, tempo, rhythm structure, and quality of movement suggested by the music. Older children may wish to bring their own popular records for this purpose. Some records are suggested here:

> *Elementary Rhythms.* Phoebe James, Box 134, Pacific Palisades, Cal. Four different records. Two are particularly good for work with basic movements. Two may be used for exploration and simple composition work.
>
> *Let's Play Series,* #1 and #2. Ortman Recordings, 1644 West Broadway, Vancouver, B.C. The suggestions for activities are set in story play form. Excellent for primary grades.
>
> *Listen and Move,* I, II, III, IV. McDonald and Evans Limited, 8 John St., London, England. (May be ordered from Canadian FDS, Audio-Visual Aids, 605 King St., Toronto, Canada.) These records contain interesting short pieces featuring percussion instruments, voices, and music of different moods. Excellent for use in exploration, improvisation, and compositions.
>
> *The Rhythm Program,* E71, 72, 73, Vol. I, II, III. R.C.A. Victor Record Division, 155 E. 24th St., New York, N.Y. Each volume contains short pieces of work of well-known composers. The records may be used for exploration of fundamentals, improvisation, and composition.

Poems   Poems afford an excellent source of dance making for children, since most of them have a rhythmical, rhymed pattern that is appealing and almost automatically sets one off on a movement accompaniment. Poems may be used as an accompaniment, or the poem may be read and the meaning interpreted in movement. Whichever way the teacher chooses to use the poem, it should be either learned or read and discussed before children begin to make their dances. Poems that include a moving character or object are better than those with abstract meanings or feelings.

Design   Primary-grade children should become aware of design and can easily portray their own work from the art class in movement. Simple line drawings or writing one's name in movement is challenging to them. Before doing them in movement, they should first make their designs on paper or on the blackboard.

Color Colors stimulate feelings. Children can be asked to respond to the names of colors; to the colors seen in pictures, clothes; colors of flowers, seasons, etc.

Nature Young children are discovering the sights and sounds of nature. Nature objects can suggest design, shape, texture, color, structure, sounds, etc. Examples are animals, trees, leaves, streams, waterfalls, weather, flowers.

Sensory Stimuli Words or actions associated with the senses can provide stimuli for improvisations related to actions and feelings—i.e., touch, sounds, smell, taste, sight. Examples are taste (sweet, sour, bitter, salty), smell (perfume, flowers, vegetables, meats).

Stories Stories serve as an excellent opportunity for children to be dramatic in their movements. Children should not be told to pantomime the story, but should be encouraged to move as if they were the characters in the story. Stories from readers, simple story plays, or stories that children write may be the basis for the dramatization. The story may be read prior to the class and plans made for dramatization to be done in the gymnasium. With primary children a story may be read as they interpret the action line by line. Stories which involve animals or actions that are big and bold serve best.

Descriptive Words

EXPLORING MOVEMENT WITH DESCRIPTIVE WORDS AS MOTIVATION

tall—short	sleepy—peppy	hot—cold
loud—quiet	smoky—wispy	sad—happy
dark—light	elastic—spongy	big—little
still—windy	crooked—straight	tight—loose

EXPLORING MOVEMENT AND IDENTIFYING OBJECTS AND PEOPLE FROM DAILY LIFE Everyday experiences with people and objects provide an excellent source to motivate creative approaches. Suggested experiences from which to plan for young children may include pets, animals, toys, favorite play activities, storybook characters, community helpers, home chores, nursery rhymes. Sports movements (as participants and spectators), occupations, cheerleading, transportation, mastering space, travel, moods, and emotions are just a few areas that are relevant to older children. Making dances using dance steps and formations from structured dances also appeals to older children.

SAMPLE PROBLEMS FOR SMALL GROUPS OF OLDER CHILDREN

1. Make up a dance using the schottische step and the step-hop. Include three changes of direction and three different partner relationships.
2. Using the telephone number 351-1798, make up a dance. Either the group or an individual may do the actions for each number. Use the same movement between each number to signify a change in number. Use either locomotor or nonlocomotor movements. (Each group may be assigned a different number; then each must guess the numbers of the other groups.)
3. (Each group is given an object, such as a feather, scarf, coconut, or piece of driftwood.) Show through movement how the object feels. Describe the

form or the shape of the object (e.g., use movements that denote surfaces that are smooth, rough, jagged, and so forth). (This problem is easily adaptable to work with individuals.)

4. Work in couples with a ball for each couple. Make a pattern of combinations of throwing, catching, and bouncing. Change levels and directions at some points in the pattern. Utilize phrasing in making the changes.

5. In groups of four, make a dance which combines swinging, twisting, and turning. At some point use opposing movements with half of the group, then return to movements in unison.

6. In groups of four, make a dance which combines swinging, twisting, and turning. At some point use opposing movements with half of the group, then return to movements in unison.

7. In groups of six, make a dance to go along with a social studies project in the classroom. Might be Westward Movement, Colonial Days, etc.

8. Working in couples with a ball for each couple, make a pattern of combinations of throwing, catching, and bouncing. Change levels and directions at some points in the pattern. Utilize phrasing in making the changes. (Pupils may choose their own accompaniment or one recording can be used for all. This could also be a project for a much larger group.)

9. Using jump ropes, make up a routine to music which calls for individual work on different styles of jumping, with some unison work as a chorus.

10. (Each small group is given a greeting card.) Communicate the theme or message on the card in movement. (This is appropriate at seasonal holidays.)

11. Using face masks made in art class, do interpretations of the face through movement; i.e., clowns, skeletons, warriors, etc.

12. Using lummi sticks (¾-inch dowels, 8 inches long) with a partner, make up a routine of tossing and hitting and flipping sticks to a selected record.

13. Select your favorite color then show that color in movement.

Structured Forms of Dance

The forms of dance which involve movements done in a specific pattern and sequence are *folk dances* and *recreational dances*. In these forms children learn to use the fundamental skills and formations of dance within a prescribed structure of pattern, time, and style. The major purposes for including these structured forms are to develop cultural understandings, to experience the moods they suggest, to control body movements in a defined relationship to other people, to promote social abilities and adjustments, and to fulfill the need for vigorous activity.

Folk Dance

Folk dance is a cultural art form which communicates the customs, rituals, occupations, and beliefs of the people of a country or a nation. Since folk dances have been handed down from generation to generation, the dances we know today are not entirely authentic. Nonetheless, they provide an excellent source of information about the peoples who originated them.

America's true folk dance is considered by some to be the dance steps which originated with the jazz music of 1915 to 1920, developed in New Orleans. From the basic shuffle step came the lindy, the jitterbug, and other dances. Because this style originated in America (although today it may be found all over the world), it is referred to as the American style of dance. The play/party dances—square, couple, and round dances—which became popular in pioneer times and days of westward expansion are sometimes called American folk dances; but they were really based on formations and steps borrowed from folk dances of other countries.

Because folk dance is an art form, it is a valuable part of the school curriculum in the study of other countries and peoples. Folk dances should not be taught for the exclusive purpose of learning the steps or formations. These should be learned out of context of a dance and become a part of the child's movement vocabulary. The major focus in folk dance, then, is the dance itself and the selection of it should be an outgrowth of the study of some aspect of a people or country. The folk dance can make this aspect come to life for the student and enrich learning in social studies, language, literature, music, and art.

Mere mention of the nationality of a folk dance or pointing out its origin on the map does not foster cultural understanding. This is too common a practice. Units of folk dance are often planned in which dances from various countries are selected because they are listed as appropriate for a grade level. Folk dances should be taught when the countries, peoples, and customs are being studied in other subject areas. Rather than have one or two units of folk dance a year, several short units may be planned to coincide with classroom study. Two or three dances of a country may be learned. These give the students a good background for the dance, because they may be able to put themselves in various roles of the people they are studying.

Early study of folk dance may become a foundation for a lifelong leisure activity. Many college and adult recreation groups are formed for the preservation and study of authentic folk dances, as well as for the enjoyment of the dance activity.

Recreational Dance

Recreational dance includes square, round, longways, couple, and social dances. The primary values of these types of dances are recreational and social. For the most part, the terminology of the forms is derived from the shape of the formation of the dances.

The square and longways (or contra) dances are products of America's westward expansion and provide a good opportunity for study of pioneer life. Round and couple dances are social dances usually based on combinations of walking steps, the two-step, the schottische, and polka steps. Frequently, they are of quite recent origin and are put to popular tunes played in a country style. They are usually easy to learn and often provide for many changes of partners.

Many mixers with very simple patterns based on the walking step ease the tension between boys and girls in the early pubescent years. These dances also may be used to make it less obvious that some boys are shorter than the girls. Square and longways dances have a particular appeal to boys in intermediate and upper grades because they are quite vigorous, easy to learn, and do not involve positions that require boys and girls to be close to each other for long periods of time.

Since social or ballroom dancing is a popular leisure activity of adolescents and adults, children need a good foundation in the accompanying social skills, procedures, and courtesies. Usually children have their initial contact with social dance during the seventh and eighth grades, if not earlier. Whether or not social dance is a part of physical education is dependent upon the community customs and the needs of the children. If there is no occasion or place where social dancing is appropriate outside of class, many boys are not interested in learning these skills before they reach high school.

Every year or two a new or revived dance step becomes popular and fashionable, such as disco dancing when this edition went to press. The current fad or interest may well be the highlight of the dance unit at Levels III and IV.

Dance Steps

Although the walk, run, and hop are steps used frequently in structured dances, there are a number of combinations of these basic movement patterns, which are called dance steps. All of these should be taught to children out of context of folk or recreational dance so that they become a part of their dance and movement vocabulary. When dances are introduced which require the use of any one of the steps, then it is only necessary to refer to the step or to review it before the pattern of the dance is taught. In this way the focus is on learning the dance and the associated cultural knowledge, rather than on the skills of the dance.

Teaching Dance Steps

A general format or procedure that has proved successful for teaching a new step is described here. Because some step patterns present unique problems, specific suggestions are made for each step. All the steps of the general format are not repeated but are implied, and they should be incorporated into the teaching of each dance step, especially steps 11, 12, and 13. Note: This is a very direct way of teaching but each dance step is specific and can be learned very quickly in this manner.

1. Play the music.
2. Clap the rhythm.
3. Step in place with the music.
4. Teacher performs the step.
5. When children feel ready, they should try the step. (At this point a verbal description may be necessary for some steps.)
6. Individuals work on the step; teacher helps those who are having trouble. Cue words are used.
7. Vary the direction.
8. Combine with other steps.
9. Explore the step for other variations.
10. Do the step with partner.
11. Partners try variations of the step.
12. Do a dance that uses the step.
13. Make up a dance using the step.

Movement Experiences

Those steps which are usually called traditional dance steps are (progressing to the most complex): slide, gallop, skip, step-hop, schottische, polka, two-step, waltz, and mazurka. The first three step patterns can be learned easily in the primary grades. They have been described earlier. All the others should be taught before the end of the sixth grade. Each of the last six is analyzed, and specific suggestions are given for teaching and developing each step.

STEP-HOP (record: RCA 1957) 2/4 or 4/4

Count	1	2	3	4
Cue words	step	hop	step	hop
Foot pattern	left	left	right	right

1. Standing in place, step and hop on left foot, then on right.
2. After pattern of step-hop is established, move forward with step, hop. (Sometimes children step on one foot and want to hop on the other foot.)
3. Combine four walking steps, then four step-hops; repeat.
4. Do four walking steps, then four walking steps going around in a circle.
5. Vary directions of step-hops; backward, sideward.

SCHOTTISCHE (record: Imp. 1046A) 4/4

Count	1	2	3	4
Cue words	step	step	step	hop
Foot pattern	left	right	left	left

1. Standing in place, take three steps on alternate feet and on the fourth count, lift the leg and hold. Repeat. (Left-right-left, lift right, right-left-right, lift left.)
2. Progress to hopping on the supporting foot on the fourth count as the leg is lifted and swing slightly forward. Stress *not* putting weight on the foot that was hopped on. (Some children want to leap rather than hop.)
3. Move forward around the room, changing directions. Go forward, backward, sideward, in a circle.
4. Use a light run emphasizing a light spring in the air with the hop.
5. Accent the fourth count with a lift on the arms to coincide with the hop.
6. Take two schottische steps and then four step-hops in place. Continue pattern.
7. Move with a partner; make many different space relationships with partner.
8. Using a record with a faster tempo, take light running steps rather than walking.
9. Try variations while working with three people.
10. Teacher should teach a simple folk dance with schottische steps. (Danish Schottische—World of Fun, record 102A)
11. Make up a partner dance using the schottische.

POLKA (record: RCA 25-2009) 2/4

Count	and	1	and	2	and	1	and	2
Cue words	(hop)	step	close	step	hop	step	close	step
Foot pattern	(right)	left	right	left	(left)	right	right	right

Note that the hop in the polka is on the last *and* of a measure. It comes on the upbeat. Due to this, the step has a bouncy quality. The polka step can be learned easily from the slide by following this suggested progression.

Approach from a slide

1. Everyone in a circle takes eight slides to the right. This may be done in a scatter formation also.
2. Turn back to center, and take eight slides in the same direction around the circle.
3. Turn face to center, four slides in same direction around circle.
4. Turn back to center, four slides in the same direction around the circle.
5. Turn face center, two slides in the same direction around the circle.
6. Turn back to center, two slides in the same direction around the circle.
7. Continue turning on every two slides. This is the polka.
8. In the circle facing a partner, everyone has the inside hands joined. They take one polka step starting on outside foot, turn and take another step with backs to one another, continue. This is the face-to-face, back-to-back polka.

Approach from a gallop

1. Starting with right foot leading, take eight gallops.
2. Left foot leading, eight gallops.
3. Right foot leading, four gallops.
4. Left foot leading, four gallops.
5. Right foot leading, two gallops.
6. Left foot leading, two gallops.
7. Repeat with left foot leading, then right, left, right, etc. This is the polka step.

Approach from a two-step

1. Using a two-step, make the step short and bouncy, with a quick hop at the end of each measure becoming part of the first step at the beginning of the next measure.
2. Continue with variations in directions and partner relationships.

TWO-STEP (record: WD 7621) 2/4

Count	1	and	2	and	1	and	2	and
Cue words	step	close	step	(hold)	step	close	step	(hold)
Foot pattern	left	right	left		right	left	right	

A step forward is taken with the left foot, the right foot is brought forward and placed next to the left heel with the weight put on the right foot. Another step forward is taken with the left foot, and the weight is held on it for one count. The sequence is repeated with the first step being taken with the right foot. Frequently children do not get the idea of leading with alternate feet. The cue may be changed to: *Left*, two-three, *right*, two-three, with an accent on the alternate foot leads.

1. Standing in place, clap the rhythm. Clap, clap, clap, with no clap on the fourth count. (The idea of quick, quick, slow; quick, quick, slow should be caught.)
2. Step in place. Left, right, left, hold weight on left; right, left, right, hold weight on right. Continue, and then say "quick, quick, slow."
3. Move forward step, close, step; step, close, step. Alternate cue words with "quick, quick, slow."
4. Move to side, changing directions as lead foot alternates.
5. Move forward four two-steps, backward four two-steps. Continue pattern.
6. Holding hands and facing partner, do pattern in #5 with one moving backward and one forward.
7. Alone. On the first step turn left shoulder to the left and step with left foot placing toes toward the left; bring right foot beside left and step and hold on left foot. (Dancer has made a half-turn. This may be repeated right.)
8. Try various combinations of quarter-turns, half-turns, and sequence of steps in different directions.

WALTZ (record: MG 649) 3/4

Count	1	2	3	1	2	3
Cue words	step	step	close	step	step	close
Foot pattern	left	right	left	right	left	right

1. Clap 1, 2, 3, on each beat of the measure. Accent the first beat with a loud clap.
2. Standing in place, step on alternate feet, 1, 2, 3. Accent first step of each measure with a slightly heavier step, then a deeper bend of knee; for emphasis dip the same shoulder. All notes and steps have an equal time value.
3. Step forward taking a long step on first count, a medium step on second count, and a tiny step on third. The third step should become a closing step. Move around the room with this pattern.
4. Move forward, taking a long first step on left foot, a short step sideward with right foot, and bring left foot close up to the right foot ("Forward, side, together"). Step backward on the right foot, step sideward on the left foot, and bring right foot close up to the left foot ("Backward, side, together"). These two movements done together comprise the box waltz.
5. Move forward four waltz steps, move backward four waltz steps.
6. Turn, using the first and long step as the move in a new direction and the second closing step to complete the turn.
7. Facing partner and holding hands, waltz forward, backward, do a box waltz, turn, and repeat.

MAZURKA (record: FC 1130) 3/4

Count	1	2	3	1	2	3
Cue words	step	close	hop	step	close	hop
Foot pattern	left	right	right	left	right	right

1. Clap 1, 2, 3; 1, 2, 3, accenting the first count and the second count.
2. Standing in place, step left, right, hold left. Accent counts 1 and 2 with slightly heavier step.

3. Still in place, step left, right, and hop on right.

4. Move forward step left, step right hop, on right; left, right, hop. The same foot always leads as the weight is held on the hopping foot.

5. Lead left, right, hop-swinging the free "left, right" leg down for the next lead step.

6. Do the step with a partner.

There are several dance steps frequently used in folk and recreational dances which are not referred to as traditional dance steps. These too should be a part of every child's movement vocabulary and should be learned before they are encountered in folk dances. These are the stamp, draw, bleking, heel and toe, step swing, buzz, grapevine, and a basic Indian step. The fox trot, the lindy, and if desired, a contemporary dance step should be taught if social dancing is part of the upper-grade curriculum.

STAMP   One foot strikes the floor forcibly but no weight is taken on the stamping foot.

DRAW   A step to the side is taken, the free foot is then drawn up close to the supporting foot, and the weight is usually shifted. The sideward step may be exaggerated by a body lean in the direction of the step.

BLEKING   A hop is taken on the left foot, and the right leg is extended forward with the heel touching the floor. A hop is taken on the right foot with the left leg extended. The position of the left heel and right heel are exchanged in a rhythmic sequence.

HEEL AND TOE   The heel of one foot is touched to the floor forward, the toe of the same foot is touched to the floor backward. Sometimes the heel of one foot is touched diagonally forward and a slight hop is taken on the other foot. The toe of the same foot is then touched to the floor across the other foot near the instep. A slight hop is taken on the other foot as the change is made.

STEP SWING   A step is taken on the left foot and the right foot is swung across in front of the left; a step is taken on the right foot and the left foot is swung across in front of the right leg. Toe of swing foot is pointed in the direction of the diagonal swing.

BUZZ   With weight kept on one foot, the other foot pushes against the floor as the weight revolves around the pivot foot. A pushing step is taken on each beat of the music. This is usually done with a partner.

GRAPEVINE   This is a sideways walking step. The right foot is crossed over in front of the left foot; another step is taken on the left foot; the right foot is brought behind the left foot, then a step is taken on to the left foot. Cue words may be right over, left, right back, left. The step may be done in either direction.

BASIC INDIAN STEP   A step is taken onto the ball of the left foot, then weight is dropped onto heel of left foot; a step is taken onto ball of right foot, then weight dropped onto heel of right foot. The knee bend should be exaggerated and the arm on the opposite side swung forward.

FOX TROT (record: RCA 20–3663A) 4/4

Count	1	2	3	4
Cue words	step	hold	step	close
Foot pattern	left	(hold)	right	left

1. Clap the first and third beats.
2. Standing in place, walk on first and third beats.
3. Walk forward.
4. Walk backward.
5. Step forward on left foot, hold, step to right on right foot, bring left foot up to side of right putting weight on left foot. Step forward on right, hold, step to left on left foot, bring right foot up to side of left putting weight on left foot ("Slow, quick, quick").
6. Move, using step forward and backward.
7. Combine forward and backward step to make a box pattern.
8. To turn, take first step in the desired direction, complete the turn by bringing the other foot around to a square position in desired direction.
9. Combinations with a partner.

   a. Step sideward left, close with right, taking weight on right; step sideward left, close with right but do not take weight (side step).
   b. Combine two fox-trot walks and one fox trot (step, hold; step, hold; side together).
   c. Combine two fox-trot walks and half-turn with two fox-trot turn steps.
   d. Four fox-trot steps forward, four backward, turn, walk four steps, repeat.

BASIC FAST STEP

LINDY (record: RCA 20–2421A) 4/4

Count	1	2	3	4
Cue words	slow	slow	quick	quick
Foot pattern	sideward left	sideward left	backward left	right in place

1. Step in place to learn the beat of the music.
2. In closed position, lead person steps to the left side with left foot, then steps to right side with right foot, then turns away to a semi-open position by stepping backward on left foot, putting it behind the other foot, then rocking forward in place with right foot. The knees bend slightly on each step. The two quick steps are known as the rock step.
3. After practicing the basic step the double lindy can be learned. Lead steps sideward left onto ball of foot, then brings the heel down, steps sideward right onto ball of foot, then brings heel down, backward on left, and steps on right in place. Cue words are: toe, heel, toe, heel, backward left, and step on right. This is called the dig step.

The lindy step is small and is usually done in one spot on the floor. The dancers move around each other, forward and back, and the girl moves under the boy's arm. Many variations and combinations of the dig step and the rock step can be done.

Preliminary Teaching

Directions for folk and all of the forms of recreational dances utilize a common terminology. Most frequently the terms are not explained within each set of directions, since it is assumed that the reader knows what they mean. Each of these formations, positions, and figures should be learned by children before the pattern of a dance is taught. This is termed "preliminary teaching." Then, as with the dance steps, these will become a part of the children's dance vocabulary, and they can readily respond to the directions of a new dance without interruptions in the pattern to learn a new figure or position.

Dance Formations

FREE   Couples or groups of three take a position anywhere in room.

CIRCLE

1. *Single with no partners:* All dancers stand in a ring facing the center or facing counterclockwise in the circle.
2. *Single with a partner:* All dancers stand in a ring. If facing toward center of circle, girl is on boy's right. If partners face each other, girl's right hand is toward the inside of the circle and the boy's left hand is toward the inside.
3. *Double:* Couples stand in a ring formation. Boy is on inside of circle. Usually both face counterclockwise if not facing each other.

GROUPS OF TWO OR THREE   Any combination of threes; may be in circle or free formation.

LONGWAYS OR CONTRA   Any number of couples standing in a double line, usually boys on one side, girls on the other and with partners facing. Head of the set is on end nearest the music. Foot of set is at the opposite end.

SQUARE   A set of four couples arranged in a square formation. The couple with its backs to the music is called couple number 1. The couple to their right is number 2, the couple opposite them is number 3, and the couple on their left is number 4.

QUADRILLE   A set of four couples arranged in a square formation. The couples facing the music and with their backs to the music are the head couples. The other two are side couples.

Directional Terms

CLOCKWISE   Direction in which a clock moves.

COUNTERCLOCKWISE   Direction opposite clockwise, usual direction of movement in a circle.

LINE OF DIRECTION   Direction the dance takes—usually counterclockwise.

Dance Positions

OPEN   Partners stand side by side with inside hands joined. Girl is usually on boy's right.

SKATING OR PROMENADE   Partners stand side by side facing same direction, girl on boy's right. Hands are held, right in right and left in left, with the right arms above left.

VARSOVIENNE   Partners stand side by side facing forward. Boy stands slightly behind and to the left of the girl. Boy holds girl's right hand in his right, her left hand in his left just above shoulder level.

TWO-HAND   Partners stand face to face and join both hands. May be used in place of closed position or shoulder-waist position.

SHOULDER-WAIST   Partners stand face to face; boys put both hands on girl's sides. Girl puts both hands on boy's shoulders.

CLOSED (SOCIAL DANCE POSITION)   Partners stand face to face; boy puts his right arm around the girl placing his hand just below her right shoulder blade; girl puts left hand on boy's right shoulder. The girl's right hand rests lightly in the boy's left palm which is held just below shoulder level. They look over each other's right shoulder.

Position Terms   **INSIDE FOOT OR HAND**   Foot or hand nearest the partner when side by side.

OUTSIDE FOOT OR HAND   Foot or hand farthest from partner when side by side.

HOME   The original or base position in a set or circle.

CORNER   Boy's corner is the girl on his left, lady's corner is boy on her right.

Dance Figures   **TURNS**

1. *Elbow:* Boy and girl hook elbows and walk, skip, or step-hop around each other as directions indicate.
2. *Two-hand:* Right hands and left hands clasped and walk, skip, or step-hop around each other. (A one-hand turn may be substituted.)
3. *Hungarian:* Partners stand with right sides together; right arms on each other's waist, left hand raised above head with elbow bent. (One- or two-hand turn may be substituted.)

SWINGS

1. *Elbow:* Partners hook elbows and swing around clockwise with either a running or walking step, usually two complete turns.
2. *Two-hand or one-hand:* Holding hands partners swing around clockwise with either a running or walking step.
3. *Buzz:* In either an elbow or two-hand or closed turn position weight is held on one foot, and the other foot pushes against the ground while pivoting on right foot. Movement is clockwise, and usually two complete turns are made.

PROMENADE   Partners walk or dance around the circle or set side by side in a counterclockwise direction.

GRAND RIGHT AND LEFT   In a circle or square formation, partners face one another, holding right hands. All boys face counterclockwise and all girls clockwise. All move forward passing right shoulders, reaching out for the next person's hand. When the hand of the next person is grasped, the other hand should be released and that arm extended to meet the next person. Continue around the circle in the *same* direction alternating right and left hands and right and left shoulders. The figure appears as a weaving in and out. Continue until original partners meet.

ALLEMANDE RIGHT   Partners face each other, join right hands and then walk *completely* around once in a clockwise direction, returning to their position.

ALLEMANDE LEFT   Same as allemande right, only left hands are grasped, and the walk is in a counterclockwise direction. May be done with a partner or a corner.

DO-SI-DO   Partners face one another, cross arms over chest and move forward four steps, take one step to the side and then walk backward back to place. May be done with corners.

REEL   (Usually found in longways dances.) Head couple goes to center of set and does an elbow turn one-and-a-half times around, the girl goes to the first boy in the boy's line and does an elbow swing, boy does same with first girl in girl's line. They both return to the center and do an elbow swing once around with each other; they then return to the third boy and girl respectively and do an elbow swing, and go back to the center for an elbow swing. They continue to proceed in like manner to the end of the line.

RIGHT-AND-LEFT-THROUGH OR PASS THROUGH   Two couples exchange places; both walk forward. They drop hands when they meet the opposite couple whom they pass through by passing right shoulders. The boy turns the girl around in the new position so that she is on his right.

LADIES' CHAIN   Girls walk across set and meet their opposite girl, grasp right hands, pass right shoulders, drop hands and reach out to take left hand of the opposite boy; he turns her around and the ladies repeat the same pattern back across the set back to their homes.

STAR   Four dancers go to the center of the set, join right hands high in center and walk around in a counterclockwise direction. They may reverse direction and reverse hands and go once around in clockwise direction.

Teaching Structured Dances

Because each dance has its own structure of formation, time, steps, positions, figures, and patterns, the teaching of dances must necessarily follow the nature of a direct method. The teacher who develops a technique of teaching a dance in which children may be involved in each step of a progressive sequence of the presentation will find students eager, cooperative, and absorbed in learning the dance. Thereafter they will enjoy dancing for the pleasureful satisfaction of doing it well. Children can design their own dances using their knowledge of fundamentals, steps, formations, etc. They can also make variations of known dances.

Some preliminary teaching is necessary for each dance. This may be in the form of a long-term preliminary preparation where dance steps, positions, and figures have been explored, learned, and performed in many variations.

It may be done prior to the learning of the dance itself when a new figure specific to that dance must be learned. Perfection of a step must not be demanded before it is used in a dance, but certainly familiarity and confidence in doing the step must be gained before trying to adapt it to a time and pattern structure, or there will be frustration and displeasure.

When a dance has been selected for its cultural implications, much of the discussion about the dance can take place in the classroom. A brief follow-up or review may be conducted in the dance setting. Many of the recreational dances have interesting historical backgrounds or portray a colorful incident, which makes the dance more meaningful for the children. The introduction should be brief. The real value of the dance to the child is the enjoyment derived from participation and the satisfaction gained from doing it well. The name of the dance should be made clear to the children so they can identify the dance easily.

While children are in the formation of the dance, the music should be played at least once or twice through the entire dance. Most dance patterns or sequences are repeated several times so there is no need to play the entire record. While the music is playing, the children will feel the beat. If they have a good dance background, references can be made to the beat and phrases identified. They will learn to identify fast and slow movements and recognize what steps the time and rhythmic patterns suggest. They may clap the pattern or try some of the steps in place. The teacher may guide their understanding by a few cue words such as, "What does that sound like? A skip?"

After listening to the music, the children should see a demonstration of the dance. How much of the dance can be demonstrated depends on the length and complexity of the dance and the number of people in a set. Perhaps only one part of it can be performed at a time. With the music, the teacher should demonstrate as much as possible of the dance. The teacher may select an alert pupil as a partner, quickly telling him or her the sequence, and then guiding the pupil through the dance. The children can see how the dance looks and better understand how the various parts relate to the whole.

Verbal descriptions may then accompany the demonstration. Depending on the complexity of the dance or dance part, the children may be asked to try it with the teacher when they think they see and feel the pattern. If many children cannot follow the demonstration, the class should go through the pattern without the music. The teacher should continue doing the dance with the class and give cue words when there is a change of direction, position, or step.

Long practice sessions without the music should be avoided. Music helps children feel the pattern and also holds their attention. Long practices at a tempo slower than the accompaniment should also be avoided. If a variable-speed record player is available, the speed can be decreased while the dance is learned and then gradually increased. The transition from a slow tempo without the music to the normal tempo with the music may be difficult, and all that was gained can be quickly lost.

When there are many parts to the dance, the dance must be broken down to be learned and then put together. The parts may have to be repeated several times. Each child will learn from repeating and from watching others. Often if the teacher can be the partner of a child who is having trouble for just a few trials, the youngster will be better prepared.

When individuals or couples have had a chance to work out the pattern, the whole dance should be done a few times. The teacher can quickly spot those having trouble. If the whole group or a large number lose the timing or get confused, the dance should be stopped immediately and started again from the beginning.

The teacher should continue to use cue words; however, he/she should stress listening to the music and particularly to the phrases. When children have to depend on listening to the phrases for cues, they become much more involved, and inattentiveness is avoided.

The dance should be practiced several times during subsequent periods so that children will know it well and enjoy doing it. Only after the dance pattern has been learned well should much attention be given to style. Controlled body movements, good posture, attention to neat sets, and other factors can be stressed at that stage.

The sequence of teaching a dance is summarized in these points.

1. There should be preliminary teaching of new steps, positions, figures, or review of those already learned that are included in the dance to be learned.

2. Name of the dance is given, and associated learnings discussed briefly.

3. The children should listen to the music, identify phrases, beat, etc.

4. Demonstration of dance is given in its entirety.

5. Students try the dance or parts, first with music if possible, or without music if necessary.

6. Unify the parts, dance the whole dance.

7. Refine problem spots.

8. Refine whole dance in a series of practices.

Selection of Partners

Because many dances require partners, the teacher must have a prearranged plan in order to set up partner relationships quickly. Boys in the intermediate grades frequently have anti-girl and anti-dance attitudes. In sixth and seventh grades some girls are taller than boys in their room. At both of these stages, problems arise in dancing and particularly in selecting partners.

The extent of these problems depends upon the teacher's selection of dance content and the atmosphere. If all forms of dance have been a part of the children's physical education program in each grade, they will have a wholesome attitude toward dance, and few problems will arise. Units should begin with vigorous individual work with balls, ropes, sticks, and then gradually structured work with Indian dances, line dances, longways dances, and finally with dances that call for closer partner relationships.

The teacher should not hesitate to make changes in dances if they are too difficult, or if positions call for close proximity of boys and girls and this causes problems. For example, if the directions call for a varsovienne position, and several boys would have to stretch up to hold the girl's hands at shoulder height, it would be much more practical to ask for a two-hand open promenade position.

It is desirable for everyone to have a partner of his or her own choice, but this is not always practical. There is not always an equal number of boys and girls, some would always be asked last, some would argue over the choice. Learning to choose partners quickly is a long-term process. Children should realize that it is fun to dance with different people; it is a challenge to adjust to various people's style; it is polite to accept the first invitation; it is kind to help other people learn and improve.

Mixers, where after a certain sequence in the dance everyone automatically gets a new partner, provide an opportunity for children to focus their attention on the dance and de-emphasize the importance of who one's partner is. If choices are allowed, little time should be given for choice, and an emphasis should be placed on choosing the nearest boy or girl. A few suggestions follow for arranging partners.

1. Boys form a circle facing one direction, and girls form one on the outside of it facing the opposite direction. All walk to the music, and when it stops everyone stops, turns, and faces his partner.

2. One large circle is formed with every other person a boy. Girl on boy's right is his partner.

3. Form two lines, boys on one side, girls on the other. Walk forward to the music and meet a partner.

4. In the same formation as described in number 3, each line walks around the room in opposite directions, and the two lines meet in the middle. As they meet, they pair off and walk down the center of the floor. This may be repeated, or partners may be established at this point. A grand march may be conducted in much the same manner.

5. Form a single circle with every other person a boy. Do a grand right and left around the circle. Persons who are together when the music stops are partners.

6. Move freely about the room doing whatever step the music suggests. When the music stops take the nearest person for a partner and be ready to move together when the music starts again. Do this several times before partners for dances are established.

7. Look at someone, focus on someone else's eyes. Two people should be staring at each other; they should walk toward each other and become partners.

8. When doing couple dances, have broom dances or ribbon dances in which the extra person gives the object to someone and takes that person's partner.

When there are more boys than girls and the dance directions call for boy and girl parts, do not have boys take girls' parts (and vice-versa). Extra children may operate the record player, do the steps at the side, or sit and wait their turn. There should be a definite rotation pattern so that these children will be included in the dance.

Accompaniment   One of the best and least expensive types of accompaniment for dance is a percussive instrument. A percussive instrument is one that is struck to produce sound. Included in this type of instrumentation are drums, sticks, bells, cymbals, clapping hands, tapping feet, shakers of all types, etc. A percussive instrument provides a strong, easily identifiable beat. It is especially valuable when you are working with young children and when teaching dance fundamentals. The beat can be adjusted to the tempo that dancers take. A good drum is an essential piece of equipment for the teacher of dance. Children can make many other percussive instruments.

A piano is most desirable for use in instruction; however, many schools cannot provide one. Also, many teachers can play the piano, but some find it difficult to give suggestions, directions, and help individuals at the same time. Ideally, an accompanist who enjoys children and who can improvise should be available.

A sturdy, reliable record player is another essential. It is desirable to have a three-speed player with a variable speed control so that the speed may be decreased for beginning work with structured dances. There are many good records available for accompaniment for all forms of dance. Most records or albums contain well-written directions for the dances or suggestions for the use of listening or rhythm records.

The school should have a file of current catalogs from major educational record companies. In larger cities some record shops carry educational records. Most shops will gladly order for schools or individuals and will usually have current record catalogs.

Selection of Dances

It is difficult to assign a specific grade level at which a dance should be learned, since the background of the dancers is such an important factor. However, there are certain factors that make a dance difficult or easy. Even though a grade level is assigned to a dance, the teacher should read the directions with the following factors in mind before deciding if it is appropriate for the particular group.

1. *The dance skills and rhythm skills required in the dance:* Have the children in the class learned the steps, formations, positions, figures required in the dance? Have they done them enough that they can quickly adapt to the rhythmic factors present in the dance music? If they haven't learned them, can they learn them quickly before the dance is taught?

2. *The number and combinations of dance skills required in the dance:* Can the students handle many different steps or variations or changes of formations at the same time?

3. *The number and length of parts in the dance:* Can the whole dance be learned quickly? Are there so many parts that it will take a whole period or longer to learn the complete dance?

4. *The positions and style required in the dance:* Are the positions called for consistent with the maturity level of the group? Are the movements too confined for the maturity and interest level of the group? If so, can they be altered to fit the needs of the group?

5. *The compatibility of the cultural learnings inherent in the dance with the background of the group:* Will there be value in the associated learnings in relation to classroom units? Will the cultural meanings have any significance to the group?

Suggested Dances

A variety of folk and recreational dances are suggested for the primary, intermediate, and upper grades in Table 12-1 through Table 12-5. The name, nationality, formation, skills needed for the dance, and suitable records are listed for each dance. Complete descriptions and directions for each dance are not given because they are included with the records that are suggested. Frequently timing and sequences within the same dance are different on records of different labels. For this reason, when directions are taken from a book, care should be taken that the suggested record is used. A key to the suggested records and addresses of the record companies precedes the dance list.

Table 12-1. Key to Suggested Records and Record Sources

COMPANY	CODE	COMPANY	CODE
Radio Corporation of America, Victor Record Division, 1133 Avenue of the Americas New York, N.Y. 10036	RCA	Folkcraft Records 1159 Broad Street Newark, N.J. 07114	FC
World of Fun Records, Cokesbury Regional Service Center 1600 Queen Anne Rd. Teaneck, N.J. 07666	WF	Educational Activities, Inc. P.O. Box 392 Freeport, N.Y. 11520	EA
Windsor Records 5528 North Rosemead Blvd. Temple City, Cal. 91780	W	Kimbo Educational Records P.O. Box 55 Neal, N.J. 07725	K

Table 12-2. American Square Dances

DANCE	RECORD
Birdie in the Cage	FC 1261*
Texas Star	FC 1268*
Forward Six	FC 1279*
Buffalo Gals	FC 1135
Dip and Dive	FC 1270*
Red River Valley	FC 1053
Dive for the Oyster	RCA 20592
Oh Johnny	FC 1037
Hot Time	W 7115
My Little Girl	FC 1036
Let's Square Dance	RCA 3001 Albums I and II

* Calls on one side, instrumentals on the other.

Table 12-3. Singing Games for Levels I—II

Dance	Nationality	Formation	Skills	Record
Bluebird	American	Single circle	Walking and skipping, dramatization of bluebirds	FC 1180, RCA 20214
Rig-a-Jig-Jig	English-American	Single circle	Skip	FC 1199
Loopy Loo	English	Single circle	Walk, dramatization with various body parts	FC 1184
Did You Ever See a Lassie?	Scottish	Single circle	Imitation of one person's actions	FC 1183, RCA 45-5066

Table 12-3. Continued

Dance	Nationality	Formation	Skills	Record
Farmer in the Dell	English-American	Single circle	Skip	FC 1182
The Muffin Man	English	Single circle	Skip, word dramatization	FC 1188
The Big Gray Cat	American	Circle or scatter	Dramatization of cat and mice movements	FCA WE 87
How Do You Do My Partner	Swedish	Single circle	Skip	FC 1190
Hokey Pokey	American	Single circle	Body-part identification	MC 699

Table 12-4. Folk Dances

LEVELS I AND II

Dance	Nationality	Formation	Skills	Record
Shoemaker's Dance	Danish	Double circle, partners	Skip, dramatization of shoemaker	FC 1187, RCA 45-6171 RCA 1624
Danish Dance of Greeting	Danish	Single circle, partners	Run	FC 1187, RCA 45-6183
Children's Polka	German	Single circle, partners	Draw, stamp	FC 1187 RCA 1625
Chimes of Dunkirk	French	Double circle, partners	Run, walk	FC 1187 RCA 1624

LEVEL III

Dance	Nationality	Formation	Skills	Record
Greensleeves	English	Double circle, two couple sets	Walk	WF 106, RCA 45-6175 RCA 1624
Cshebogar	Hungarian	Single circle, partners	Slide, skip, draw, turn	FC 1195 RCA 45-6182
Bleking	Swedish	Free, couples	Bleking step, hop	RCA 1626 FC 1188
Gustaf's Skoal	Swedish	Quadrille	Walk, skip	FC 1196 RCA 45-6170 WF 108
Norwegian Mountain Dance	Norwegian	Groups of 3	Running step, step-hop	RCA 6173, FC 1177
Circassian Circle	English	Single circle (mixer)	Walk	FC 1247 WF 104

Table 12-4. Continued

LEVEL III

Dance	Nationality	Formation	Skills	Record
Seven Jumps	Danish	Single circle	Step-hop, follow the leader actions	RCA 1623
Ace of Diamonds	Danish	Double circle, partners	Face to face, back to back polka, elbow swing	RCA 1622 WF 102
Danish Schottische	Danish	Double circle, partners	Schottische, step-hop	RCA 1622
Hansel and Gretel	German	Free, couples	Heel-toe	RCA 45-6182

LEVEL IV

Dance	Nationality	Formation	Skills	Record
Black Nag	English	Longways, sets of 3 couples	Running	WF 109, FC 1174
Waves of Tory	Irish	Longways	Walk, star, promenade, cast-off	WF 102
Mayim	Israeli	Single Circle	Grapevine	FC 1108
Troika	Russian	Groups of 3	Running	WF 105
Tantoli	Swedish	Double circle	Heel-toe polka, step-hop	FC 1160
Weggis	Swiss	Free, couples	Heel-toe polka, step-hop	FC 1160
Little Man in a Fix	Danish	Groups of 4 couples	Waltz, run	RCA 20449
Road to the Isles	Scottish	Free, couples	Schottische, hop	FC 1095
Horah	Israeli	Single circle	Side-step, step-swing	FC 1110
The Roberts	Scottish	Single circle, partners	Draw, heel-toe, two-step	FC 1161
Kalvelis	Lithuanian	Single circle, partners	Polka	FC 1051
Hop Morr Anika	Swedish	Double circle	Walk, skip, polka	RCA 4142
Crested Hen	Danish	Groups of 3 couples	Step-hop, stamp	RCA 45-6176
Tinikling	Filipino		Leap, jump (over 2 poles held by 2 people)	RCA 4126
Miserlou	Greek	Single circle	Grapevine, walk	RCA 1620
Cherkassia	Israeli	Single circle	Grapevine, step-hop	RCA 1623
Ersko Kolo	Yugoslavian	Single circle, partners	Schottische, side-step	FD MA 3020 A
Korobushka	Russian	Free, couples	Schottische, balance	FC 1170

Table 12-5. American Play Party—Mixers—Round—Couple Dances

LEVEL III

Dance	Type	Formation	Skills	Record
Bingo	Mixer	Single circle	Walk, grand right and left	FC 1189
Glow-Worm	Mixer	Double circle, partners	Walk	FC E1158
Patty-Cake Polka	Mixer	Double circle, partners	Heel-toe, slide, skip	FC 1124
Oh Susannah	Play party	Single circle	Walk, grand right and left, prom-enade	FC 1186
Skip to My Lou	Play party	Single circle	Walk, skip	FC 1192
Heel and Toe	Couple	Free	Slide, polka	FC 1166
Virginia Reel	Play party	Longways	Walk, skip	FC 1141
Bow Bow Belinda	Play party	Longways	Walk, skip, cast-off, do-si-do, elbow swing	FC 1189
Paw Paw Patch	Play party	Longways	Walk, skip, cast-off	FC 1181 WF 111

LEVEL IV

Dance	Type	Formation	Skills	Record
Teton Mountain Stomp	Round	Double circle, partners	Side-close-stomp, walk	WD 7615
Wrangler's Two-Step	Round	Double circle, partners	Walk, grapevine, balance turn	WD 7621
All-American Promenade	Mixer	Double circle, partners	Walk	WD 7605
Jessie Polka	Couple	Free	Two-step or polka	FC 1071
Ten Pretty Girls	Mixer	Single circle, partners	Walk, point	WF 113
Put Your Little Foot	Couple	Free	Mazurka, waltz	FC 1165
Cotton-Eyed Joe	Couple	Free	Heel-toe, polka, hop, two-step	WF 118
Rye Waltz	Couple	Free	Slide, waltz	FC 1103
Brown-Eyed Mary	Mixer	Double circle, partners	Walk, skip, prom-enade, alle-mande	FC 1186

The Elementary School Dance Program

LEVELS I AND II MOVEMENT SKILLS   Explore and refine the basic locomotor and nonlocomotor skills in expressive style with accompaniment as they are affected by speed, intensity, level, direction, and various relationships.

Dance steps: slide, gallop, skip, and step-hop.

RHYTHM SKILLS Learn and understand the use of underlying beat, measures, even and uneven rhythms, tempo, rhythmic pattern, and phrasing in relation to movement.

Rhythmic games: Clapping Names, Clapping Nursery Rhymes, Police officer.

CREATIVE DANCE

- Move expressively with accompaniment, relating sounds to movement.
- Use dramatic rhythms.
- Relate story plays.
- Create own movement sequences.
- Make simple dances.

STRUCTURED DANCE

1. *Singing games:* Loopy Loo, Bluebird, Did You Ever See A Lassie, Rig-a-Jig-Jig, Farmer in the Dell, Mulberry Bush, Muffin Man.
2. *Folk dances:* How Do You Do My Partner, Danish Dance of Greeting, Chimes of Dunkirk, Kinder-Polka, Shoemaker's Dance.

LEVEL III MOVEMENT SKILLS Continue working on combinations of movement with many variations, and stress quality of movement.

Dance steps: schottische, step-hop, polka, draw, heel and toe, Indian step.

RHYTHM SKILLS Respond in movement to accent, phrasing, note values, and rhythmic patterns.

Rhythmic games: Echo, Radio Stations, Clapping Orchestra, Lummi Sticks, ball bouncing, jumping ropes, exercises with music.

CREATIVE DANCE Move expressively with accompaniment in solving problems, improvisation, and composition.

Basic themes: Work and play ideas, poems, stories, songs, occupations, transportation, pioneer days, Indian dances, machines, props.

STRUCTURED DANCE

1. *Formations:* double circle, groups of three, longways, quadrille, square.
2. *Positions:* open, promenade, two-hand.
3. *Figures:* honor, elbow turn, two-hand turn, reel, do-si-do, grand right and left, elbow swing, two-hand swing, promenade, allemande.
4. *Dances:*
   Walk: Greensleeves, Norwegian Mountain March, Oh Susannah, Bingo.
   Slide: Cshebogar, Hansel and Gretel, Patty-Cake Polka.
   Bleking: Bleking.
   Skip: Paw Paw Patch, Gustaf's Skoal, Virginia Reel, Bow Bow Belinda.
   Step-hop: Seven Jumps.
   Polka: Ace of Diamonds.
   Schottische: Danish Schottische.

LEVEL IV MOVEMENT SKILLS Continue working on refinement and use of skills in creative work particularly. Use more difficult variations and combinations stressing quality of movement.

Dance Steps: two-step, waltz, mazurka, grapevine.

RHYTHM SKILLS Continue work on all rhythm skills with an emphasis on tempo, accent, cumulative rhythm, double time. Solve rhythm problems.

CREATIVE DANCE Do improvisation and composition work utilizing the following themes—conversation in movement, making dances based on traditional steps, historical subjects, poems, nonsense rhymes, cheerleading, sports, machines, current heroes, sensory cues.

STRUCTURED DANCE

1. *Figures:* swings, right and left through, chain, star, buzz step
2. *Positions:* varsovienne
3. *Dances:*
   Walk: Sicilian Circle, Brown-Eyed Mary, Glow Worm, All-American Promenade, Ten Pretty Girls
   Two-Step: Jessie Polka, Texas Schottische, Badger Gavotte, Ten Pretty Girls
   Waltz: Little Man in a Fix, Rye Waltz
   Grapevine: Cherkassia, Serbian Kolo
   Polka: Tantoli
   Run: Troika
   Schottische: Four-Horse Schottische, Weggis, Road to the Isles
   Square Dances: Birdie in the Cage, Dive for the Oyster, Take a Little Peek, Buffalo Gal

GRADES SEVEN AND EIGHT MOVEMENT SKILLS *Dance steps:* Mazurka, fox trot, lindy

RHYTHM SKILLS Symmetrical and asymmetrical movement, accumulative rhythm, resultant rhythm, grouping

CREATIVE DANCE Emphasis on improvisation and composition work; suggested themes for boys and girls (together) are the same as for fifth and sixth grades with expectations of compositions being more expressive and refined. Emphasis on work with themes that center on original designs, poems, mirroring, rounds, ball gymnastics, music.

STRUCTURED DANCE

1. *Social:* fox trot with variations, lindy with variations, current fad dance, jazz, disco
2. *Square Dances:* Birdie in the Cage, Texas Star, Forward Six, Dip and Dive, Solomon Levi
3. *Line Dances:* Mayim, Miserlou, Cherkassyia
4. *Folk and Round Dances:*
   Slide: Teton Mountain Stomp
   Jump: Tinikling
   Two-step: Sentimental Journey, Laces and Graces, Jessie Polka, Susan's Gavotte
   Waltz: Black Hawk
   Mazurka: Put Your Little Foot
   Schottische: Highland Schottische, Korobuscha
   Polka: Cotton-Eyed Joe, Kalvelis

SUGGESTED REFERENCES FOR FURTHER STUDY

AMERICAN ASSOCIATION FOR HEALTH, PHYSICAL EDUCATION AND RECREATION, *Children's Dance.* Washington, D.C., 1973.

BOORMAN, JOYCE, *Creative Dance in the First Three Grades.* New York: McKay, 1969.

FLEMING, GLADYS ANDREWS, *Creative Rhythmic Movement: Boys and Girls Dancing.* Englewood Cliffs, N.J.: Prentice-Hall, Inc., 1976.

JOYCE, MARY, *First Steps in Teaching Creative Dance.* Palo Alto, Cal.: National Press Books, 1973.

KRAUS, RICHARD, *A Pocket Guide of Folk and Square Dances and Singing Games for the Elementary School.* Englewood Cliffs, N.J.: Prentice-Hall, Inc., 1963.

MONSOUR, SALLY, MARILYN COHEN, and PATRICIA LINDELL, *Rhythm in Music and Dance for Children.* Belmont, Cal.: Wadsworth, 1966.

MURRAY, RUTH L., *Dance in Elementary Education.* New York: Harper & Row, 1975.

RUSSELL, JOAN, *Creative Movement and Dance for Children,* 2nd ed. London: MacDonald & Evans, Ltd., 1975.

TAYLOR, CARLA, *Rhythm: A Guide for Creative Movement.* Palo Alto, Cal.: Peek Publications, 1976.

VICK, MARIE, and ROSANN MCLAUGHLIN COX, *A Collection of Dances for Children.* Minneapolis, Minn.: Burgess Publishers, 1970.

13 / GAMES

- Cooperative and competitive games
- Components of games
- Sequencing game learning
- Self-designed games
- Teaching games
- Predesigned active games
- Relays
- Classroom and inactive games
- Individual and dual games

Games are fun, challenging, meaningful, and uniquely satisfying to everyone. People like to play games whether they are skilled, unskilled, adults, or children.

Games in the contemporary elementary program do not focus simply on the enjoyment of playing; they primarily involve the development of skillful game players. The emphasis is on teaching children to adapt their skills according to the shifting demands of the many movement situations inherent in each game; to adapt predesigned games, and design new games to meet individual needs and interests. The opportunity to create their own games lets children experiment with their movement knowledge, skills, process abilities, as well as to extend their value judgments.

The discussion in this chapter focuses primarily upon what are usually termed "low-organized games" as opposed to those associated with sports. These are games that are not played in the context of a sport, and the skills are learned and practiced out of the context of a sport. In playing low-organized games, children develop concepts of space, relationships to others (partners, teammates, opponents, objects, and implements), and this helps them develop into good game players. Of course basketball, volleyball, and other major sports usually associated with the competitive arena are games—but they are much more highly organized, restrictive, and involve more sophisticated strategies. Low-organized games can become rather highly organized as players become more skillful and socially and mentally more mature. Games with very complicated rules can be designed even though only very basic skills are used.

Games for children are of two types: *predesigned* or structured games and *self-designed* games. The latter may be teacher- or pupil-designed, and provide a natural extension of learning new skills, studying particular concepts of movement, or working in various relationships; they afford many opportunities for problem solving and creativity.

Cooperative and Competitive Games

Both predesigned games and self-designed games may be either *cooperative* or *competitive*. Traditionally, most games have been competitive, with one or several, as a team, trying to play their best to achieve mastery over their opponents. Whenever there is more than one player on a team there has to be cooperation. Cooperative games focus on working with one or more people to achieve a goal. For example, in Circle Keep It Up, the whole team tries to keep the ball in the air as long as possible. The emphasis may also be cooperative in a competitive game, such as a net game. One helps the opponent try to achieve the goals of the game and enjoy it by placing the ball in different relationships to him yet making him move to get the ball and return it.

Most active games fall into two general categories: those involving *chasing* and *fleeing*, and those involving *objects*. Chasing and fleeing games enhance development of the basic locomotor and nonlocomotor skills and body control. Running, dodging, starting, and stopping are the major skills used and various games require that these skills be adapted to specific demands of spatial arrangements, quick direction changes, acceleration, deceleration, and good control of flow movement.

Games involving objects, therefore the manipulative skills, focus on one or more of the following:

- Throwing an object
- Catching an object
- Kicking an object
- Carrying an object
- Stopping an object with body or instrument
- Dribbling an object with body or instrument
- Striking an object with body or instrument

When children attain the readiness to control their bodies and the object by means of one of these skills, they are ready to play games that are combinations of the two categories—for example, the dodgeball games, Tadpole (p. 333), or the more advanced Cricket Ball (p. 334). *Lead-up games* to sports are all of the combination type, focusing on one type of object control, but their successful play presupposes control of body and control of objects. They are not primary age games.

Components of Games

Since games have affective, social, cognitive, and physical objectives, success in them assumes that one must have achieved a certain readiness to play the particular game. When selecting a predesigned game, setting limitations for designing a new one, or modifying an old game to make it easier or more difficult, one must consider the components of games and what makes them difficult or easy. Following are some guidelines for assessing the difficulty of a game and/or game components. Note that within these, reference is made to the cognitive, physical, and social developmental factors described in Chapter 2 and the factors affecting the manipulative skills described in Chapter 11.

Assessment of Games

Although most descriptions of games suggest grade levels at which the game can be played, the teacher must analyze the game in relation to the readiness of the particular class. Guidelines for determining the difficulty of a game are discussed in the following paragraphs. The teacher may apply these guidelines when selecting new games, when creating new games, and when making an old game more challenging.

SKILLS The teacher must look first for the skills basic to the game. If a skill vital to the conduct of the game has not been taught to the class, naturally the game must be disregarded or the skill introduced, explored, and practiced before the game is introduced. Some basic skills are harder than others; for instance, skipping is harder than running, catching is harder than throwing. Beyond checking the skills involved, one needs to analyze *how* the skills are used. First-graders can run, but it is much more difficult for them to make many changes in direction while running. It is relatively easy for one student to evade being hit by a ball, but when it is necessary to do so while holding on to another, the difficulty is increased. Hitting a moving target is harder than hitting a stationary target.

NUMBER AND COMBINATION OF SKILLS The number of skills utilized in a game may increase its difficulty. Remembering how to do each skill, recovering balance after executing one skill and immediately initiating a new and different movement is difficult for inexperienced or young children. For example, in Simple Dodgeball (p. 320) one has only to dodge one ball. In Battleball (p. 339) one has to dodge the ball, pick it up after it has bounced once, throw it at another moving target, and at the same time be alert to dodging a second ball that is also in play. Obviously, proficiency in skill and mental awareness of sequence of skills and rules are involved in the latter game. Each of these skills is not difficult alone, but in combination with others under the stress of speed and competition, the game becomes an advanced game.

NUMBER AND COMPLEXITY OF RULES   Just as the number of skills compounds the difficulty of a game, so does the number of rules. Greater maturity and an increased attention span are necessary before children can remember and follow a number of directions or patterns of doing things. Using Battleball as an example again, players must remember that the ball cannot be touched before it bounces; they are not out if they are hit below the waist or if the ball hit them after it bounced; they may not take steps as they hold the ball; they may not hold it more than 3 seconds; they may throw at people on the other team or to teammates; after they are hit they go to another area and continue to play. In Simple Dodgeball, players rejoin the circle after being hit whenever the ball hits them below the waist. Both of these are dodgeball games in which the primary skills are dodging and throwing, and the object is either to hit a person with the ball or to avoid being hit, depending on the position at the time.

Naturally, the more complex the rules the longer it takes to understand and learn the game. Contrast the simple version of Squirrels in Trees (p. 319), in which the squirrels change trees upon a signal and the one who does not find an empty tree is left out, with the more advanced version, Hounds and Rabbits (p. 321), in which two people are not in the trees and one chases the other. The one chased may enter an occupied tree, whereupon anyone in the tree must leave and become the chaser. If introduced first, the latter is too complex for a first-grader.

STRATEGY AND RESPONSIBILITIES   When a game requires specific responsibilities or positions for individual players, it becomes difficult. If everyone does basically the same thing, it is easy to remember what to do, and the game pattern is learned quickly. When position responsibility calls for unique action or rules on the part of several different players, it takes more concentration and time to learn. Although all games require some strategy, the more complex the game becomes the more advanced it is. Coordinating the skills, efforts, and ideas of several people takes more maturity and concentration than primary children can handle. Even double-line games involve more teamwork than beginning first-graders can produce. Contrast the chasing and fleeing games of Cowboys and Indians (p. 317) and Prisoner's Base (p. 338), in which running, dodging, and tagging are the skills involved. In Cowboys and Indians players run away from the line and toward home base, trying not to be tagged. In Prisoner's Base, the strategy is very involved and requires group planning and cooperation to get just one person from home base to the base of another team.

DURATION AND CONTINUITY   The length of playing periods of a game may increase its difficulty in terms of physical and emotional demands due to sustained concentration and excitement. If a game is played for a long time and the attention span is short, pupils become disinterested; inattention and behavior problems will arise.

NUMBER OF PEOPLE   The greater the number of players children have to relate to on their own team and compete directly against on the other, the more demanding the game becomes. There is a definite progression of difficulty in all skill drills and games. A certain degree of competency and confidence in a skill is necessary before it is used in a game situation. Each opponent or teammate added to the game makes it necessary to use a skill in a somewhat different manner. This is obvious in the transition from the very simple games, in which most of the skills are done in an independent fashion, to the more involved team games, in which one plays with or against increasingly large numbers. For young children, cooperation with more than one person is as great a problem as is competition.

Sequencing Game Learning

Keeping the developmental factors and these criteria in mind, the teacher must *sequence* game learning. The first stage involves using *individual games* or tasks to help the child reach the basic readiness to use skills as they would be used in a particular game.

Working on the task individually, out of the context of the target game, gives one a chance to develop some proficiency and confidence in a skill. Many people do not think of individual practice as a game, but prefer to call this type of learning self-testing or just plain practicing. However, making a game out of tasks makes the tasks and practice fun and personal. In the context of the concept of sequencing game learning, it is a game. At this stage the games are usually self-designed or teacher-designed.

Stage two of the sequencing involves *partner* games, both cooperative and competitive, in which use of skills is developed working with or against one other person. This calls for a little more maturity and is more challenging to students. Again, most partner games are self-designed. (Remember that the teacher or pupil may do the designing.)

Stage three involves *small-group games,* both cooperative and competitive. In this case the learners must adjust their skills and strategies so that they can work with/against people, and accommodate to different spatial arrangements and responsibilities and other factors related to environmental aspects. Most of these games are self-designed or are a modification of a predesigned game in which number of rules and number of players may be decreased.

Stage four involves a *large-group* or *team* game in which skills and increasing social and cognitive maturity are needed. Most of these involve more rules and responsibilities and concern for group success, and are predesigned. The traditional predesigned chasing and fleeing games for the primary grades are usually large-group games; however, their design caters to the egocentric interests of children at this age. They focus on the one-to-one relationship of the tagger and the runner, and for the most part are not cooperative with respect to the group or team.

The object of large-group games is usually for the players to run and avoid being tagged by a person who has been designated as IT. In some games the team consists of only one chaser and one fleer. In others, the whole group may be fleeing from one person. Younger children love the independent vigorous running. As they grow older, competition and excitement become more important.

Readiness for these group games can be sequenced, beginning with individual self-designed games that involve running in different pathways, changing directions quickly, dodging obstacles, stopping and starting, accelerating and decelerating, tagging, or similar small-group games. Major values of most of these games have to do with learning beginning relationships with a larger number of people while moving in space. Usually, such games are sequenced with respect to social maturity and are laced with imagery that appeals to primary-age children.

Beginning predesigned games usually involve a circle formation, which provides the initial experience of staying in a confined area. Unfortunately, in this formation there is only one chaser and one fleer (Slap Jack, p. 319). Games involving a single-line boundary follow, in which the whole group may run from one line to the other trying to avoid the IT, who initially stands in the center (Chinese Wall, p. 323). This calls for more independent control, because the boundaries are larger and less confining. The next step is to utilize double-line formations in which two parallel lines are used as goals for two different groups or teams. This is the first venture into teams or two sides at play, where one player's actions affect the entire team (Blue and Gold, p. 322). A whole area boundary formation may involve one goal, or many goals, or even changing goals—i.e., a player may run anywhere within the defined play area (Squirrels in Trees, p. 319). The latter calls for independent decisions and close attention to the rules.

By following these stages of developing readiness to play a game or games, the difficulty of the games can be sequenced. Sequencing is also used when students are learning lead-up activities to sports. How long a person stays at one stage is dependent on his or her general readiness for the activity. The same concept of sequencing and readiness is utilized in teaching structured dance steps and dances.

Self-Designed Games

Students at all ages must be given the opportunity to design their own games and make up variations of known games. It is well to discuss the structure of games with children so that they will not only understand the components of games as they are learning them but also will be well prepared to design new games. The discussion earlier in this chapter on determining the degree of difficulty of a game pretty well analyzes the aspects or components that would be considered in designing a new game. These components are:

1. Defined objective(s) that can be met through the game.
2. Minimum and maximum numbers of players and their interrelationships.
3. Equipment needed.
4. Focal skill patterns or movements involved.
5. Organizational patterns—formation, relationship of players to one another and to equipment.
6. Rules and limitations—time, scoring, boundaries, infractions, penalties, procedures, etc.

Figure 13-1 is a Game Analysis Chart to help the teacher or pupil design or change games or to analyze a predesigned game. The analysis helps in determining whether or not the game will indeed meet the desired objectives, and whether the pupils are ready for the game. It clarifies any components that need to be changed, and identifies the way in which to change them. In

Figure 13-1   Game Analysis Chart used to analyze pre-designed game.

Game Analysis Chart

NAME OF GAME:	Corner Ball (page 329)

OBJECTIVES TO BE MET	# OF PLAYERS AND THEIR RELATIONSHIP	EQUIPMENT	FOCAL SKILLS	ORGANIZATIONAL PATTERN	RULES AND/OR LIMITATIONS
1. Improve long passing. 2. Intercepting passes. 3. Catching. 4. Pivoting. 5. Teamwork. 6. Dribbling.	2 teams 8 on a team	Jr. size basketball or 8″ playground ball	Throw Catch Intercept Dribble	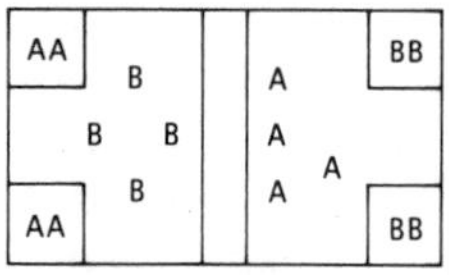 [court diagram: AA, BB in corners; B A players spread across court] 4 players from each team in corners at opposite ends of court.	1. Game starts with free toss at center court. 2. Teams try to get ball in air to corner players for 1 point. 3. After point game starts in center again. 4. Violations: a. Going out of court area, over center line or corner line. b. May not move with ball. c. May not hold ball over 5 seconds. *Penalty:* Ball given to other team. *Playing time:* 5 minutes. Change corner players, repeat.

CHANGES TO MAKE EASIER

OBJECTIVES TO BE MET	# OF PLAYERS AND THEIR RELATIONSHIP	EQUIPMENT	FOCAL SKILLS	ORGANIZATIONAL PATTERN	RULES AND/OR LIMITATIONS
Same	Same	Same	Same	Increase size of corners.	a. Add unlimited dribble. b. Passing to teammates. c. Take 3 steps.

CHANGES TO MAKE HARDER

OBJECTIVES TO BE MET	# OF PLAYERS AND THEIR RELATIONSHIP	EQUIPMENT	FOCAL SKILLS	ORGANIZATIONAL PATTERN	RULES AND/OR LIMITATIONS
Same	Same	Add a ball	Same	Decrease size of corners.	a. May not hold ball over 3 seconds. b. Roving player from each team.

introducing a new game, the teacher may use the chart on the blackboard to analyze it with the class rather than just verbally describe the game.

Simply to tell pupils to "create a game" is foolish. They need tools with which to create. They must have a background of understanding of each component, experience in variations of each component, and opportunities to make variations of known games. In other words, they have to *learn to design*. Discussion and evaluation of the designs will enhance this learning. Giving students the chance to design one component should be the initial step. Over a period of time more components may be opened for design until the whole game is open ended.

Following are some examples of problems with various limitations. Pupils may design a game just to play it themselves, to solve a problem, to present to others, to write up for a booklet of games designed by individuals or the class, etc.

PROBLEM   Design a game with these provisions:

OBJECTIVE TO BE MET	# PLAYERS	EQUIPMENT	FOCAL SKILLS	ORGANIZA-TIONAL PATTERN	RULES AND LIMITATIONS
A. Accuracy	4	2 balls	Kicking	One side, cooperative	Yours
B. Development of agility	2	None	Yours	Back-to-Back	Yours
C. Yours	6	Deck-tennis ring	Throwing Catching	Random Competitive	Yours
D. Endurance	11	None	Running Dodging	Parallel Lines	Yours
E. Flexibility	8	Beam, box, ball	Running	Random	Yours
F. Teamwork, passing	8	Ball, paddles	Striking	Yours	Winner at end of game plus yours

The limitations set are only basic requirements. The skill listed should be the focal skill used, but of course supportive skills will also be needed. Any movement factor may be shifted in or out of these categories in order to reinforce or test specific factors studied in class. Try some of the problems.

Teaching Games

PRELIMINARY PREPARATION

1. Plan for maximum participation so that everyone is busy and active.
   a. Avoid circle games in which only one or two people are active at one time.
   b. Avoid elimination-type games unless you can change the elimination rule to an active status.
   c. Break the game down into the smallest logical units of play.

2. The teacher or the pupil presenting the game should know the game thoroughly. For presentation, condense the rules into the simplest and shortest terms.

3. Have all necessary equipment ready and accessible.

4. Select playing area before class time. If lines are necessary, mark them before the class period. Use chalk, poster paint, or plastic tape indoors. Lime, ropes, or pins may be used outside. Do not ask children to imagine lines.

5. Most game rules can be changed to fit the available space, amount of equipment, or number of students. Don't hesitate to modify to adapt to the needs of the group.

6. When games call for mingling of players from opposite teams, provide some type of color identification for each team.

7. Plan to play games of varied formations but neither too many nor too different. Frequently, much time is wasted in just moving groups from one location to another.

ACTIVITY

1. Select an alert pupil to start the activity.

2. Encourage children to admit having been tagged and to raise hands when they are aware that they have made a foul or violation.

3. Enforce rules immediately. If the rule is "No stepping over the line," then follow the line rule. If the progress of the game is hindered by too many stops for rule infractions, it is possible that the rules are too difficult for the group and need to be modified.

4. Be sure that teams are of equal size or number before play begins.

5. If it is obvious that there is a misunderstanding about the rules or procedures, stop the game and straighten out the difficulty immediately.

6. The teacher may play in the game occasionally, but should not dominate the play. Children enjoy having the teacher play, but they usually will not notice if he/she withdraws gracefully as the game progresses.

7. Try to make sure that everyone has a turn and that a certain few do not dominate game play.

8. Continue teaching once the game is started. Introducing the game may be mechanical or routine, but teaching during the game is essential. Look for those who need encouragement. Look for teachable moments when the game can be stopped and a concept can be learned in light of the situation or positions of the players at the time. Watch for use of skills and space. Plan for evaluation after the game.

9. Rotate positions so that all have an opportunity to play in favored positions.

10. Once the game is apparently understood by all, regroup into smaller units, if possible.

11. When interest appears to be waning, stop the game. Do not wait until all interest is gone.

12. Check the time remaining in the period. Do not start a new game unless there is time to play it for at least a few minutes.

13. Maintain a learning atmosphere. A certain amount of noise accompanies good hard play, but screaming or uncontrolled boisterous noise should not be allowed. Establish signals for quiet and attention.

1. Culminate the game with a meaningful discussion of its procedure. Have the students make suggestions for improving game play. Evaluation need not come at the end of a game; it should come when appropriate or when a rest period or change of positions are necessary. Praise good performances and sportsmanship.
2. Make plans to play the game again. Repetition will improve skills and strategy.

SAFETY FACTORS

1. A wall must never be a goal. Lines should be 8 or 10 feet from the wall or from any other hazard. A permanent line should be painted around the entire gym at these distances.
2. Tennis shoes are the only suitable footwear on gym floors. If the floor is clean and free from splinters, children may play in bare feet, but never in socks alone.
3. Rules must be established as to where one may hit another person with the ball in dodgeball games. It is safest to hit another person on the legs or in the shoulder region. The use of a playground ball or volleyball is recommended for dodgeball games rather than the heavier soccer or basketballs.
4. Glasses should be removed when people are playing dodgeball and other games in which the player is not always focusing on the ball.
5. Traffic patterns for throwing and running should be established to avoid collisions.

Predesigned Active Games

A variety of predesigned games are described here. For the convenience of the inexperienced teacher, they are grouped by the levels (as originally introduced in the Program Objectives) at which children would be ready to learn them. The teacher should analyze each game, following the guidelines offered in the discussion on degree of difficulty of games. Each may be modified to suit the readiness level of the children for whom it is selected. The majority of games that are described, with the exception of the more advanced individual and dual games, are for small or large groups. These games should be balanced with games designed by both the teacher and pupils at all levels. Suggestions for self-designed games for individuals and partners are implied in the tasks for suggested study in the skill descriptions in Chapter 11. Additional ball skill games are described in the chapter on team and individual sport activities.

In the descriptions, the minimum number of players is suggested. When the number of players recommended is few, several games can take place at the same time. The person who starts the game is identified as the leader; this may be the teacher or a pupil. The playing area should be permanently marked with outside boundary lines and center dividing lines whose size fits most game-court dimensions—25 by 50 feet. The size of the playing area may be altered to the available space in order to adjust to ability level of the class. Usually, 8½-inch utility balls are recommended, but any ball of approximately that size may be substituted.

LEVEL I

• Call Ball

Skills: Tossing ball in the air, catching.

Equipment: 8½-inch playground ball.

Formation: Circles of four, one child in the center.

Description: The child in the center throws the ball into the air and calls out the name of one of the players, who tries to catch the ball *before* it bounces. If the person called is successful, he or she becomes the next thrower; if not, the first thrower has another try. The name must be called as the ball is thrown, and the ball must not go outside the circle.

Variations: Numbers may be used instead of names. More than one number may be called once skills are well developed. If children have trouble catching the ball in the air, they may catch it on the first bounce (use with kindergarten).

• Charlie Over the Water

Skills: Selected locomotor skills, stooping, tagging.

Equipment: None.

Formation: Single circle, one or two children in the center.

Description: One or two children are chosen as Charlie, depending on the size of the group. Charlie stands in the center of the circle. The others walk, run, skip, or hop around the circle chanting:

> Charlie over the water,
> Charlie over the sea,
> Charlie catch a blackbird,
> Can't catch me!

As "me" is said, the children stoop quickly. Charlie tries to tag as many as possible before they are in squatting position. Charlie is allowed three turns, then chooses someone he tagged to take his place.

Variation: Points may be kept for those tagged; however, the initial emphasis should be on trying to avoid being tagged.

• Circle Stride Ball

Skills: Rolling ball, stopping ball with hands.

Equipment: 8½-inch or 10-inch playground ball.

Formation: Single circles of eight, one child in the center is IT.

Description: Players stand with legs apart, but in a balanced position. Their feet should touch the feet of player beside them. One player is IT and stands in the center; that person tries to roll the ball outside the circle through the legs of the other players. The latter try to keep the ball in the circle by stopping it with their hands. If the ball goes out, the player between whose legs it went chases the ball and becomes the new IT.

• *Cowboys and Indians (or Brownies and Fairies)*

Skills: Running, tagging, dodging.

Formation: Double-line formation with goal lines at opposite ends of the playing area. Two teams.

Description: Half of the group are Cowboys and stand behind one goal line; the other half are Indians and stand behind the other goal line. The Cowboys face away from the Indians' goal line and the Indians quietly walk up behind them. The teacher or leader waits until the Indians are quite close and calls out, "The Indians are here!" The Cowboys turn around and chase the Indians back to their goal line. Any Indians who are tagged before reaching the line must become Cowboys. The Cowboys then become the chasers, and the game continues with alternating chasers and fleers.

Variation: The game may be called Brownies and Fairies, Cats and Dogs, or any combination of "enemies."

• *Gardener and Scamp*

Skills: Selected locomotor skills, dodging, tagging.

Equipment: None.

Formation: Circles of eight, one child inside the circle, one outside.

Description: One player is selected as Scamp and stands inside the circle made by the rest of the group. One is selected as the Gardener and walks around outside the circle, saying, "Who let you in my garden?" The Scamp answers, "No one," and the Gardener begins to chase him. The Gardener must use the same locomotor movements that the Scamp uses in the chase. They may cut across, in and out, and around the other players. When the Scamp is caught, he and the Gardener select replacements, and the game starts again. If the Gardener does not do the same movements that Scamp does, a new Gardener is selected by Scamp.

Variations: Players in the circle may hold hands and must raise their arms to let the runners in and out. Scamp should be encouraged to change movement patterns frequently. If the Gardener cannot catch Scamp after a short time, halt the game and select new runners.

• *Hot Ball*

Skills: Kicking.

Equipment: One soccer ball.

Formation: Single circle.

Description: One player is chosen to "set a fire" under the ball. He dramatically "heats" the ball, then kicks it into the circle and says, "The ball is hot." The players try to kick the ball away to keep from getting "burned." If the ball stops in the center of the circle or goes out of the circle, the person who kicked it last gets it and must "start the fire" again. The ball should be kicked with the side of the foot and kept close to the ground.

Variation: The ball may be thrown or pushed away.

• Jet Pilot

Skills: Running.

Equipment: None.

Formation: Lines drawn across each end of the playing area, one designated as the takeoff line and the other as the turning line.

Description: All players are considered to be Jet Pilots except for one, who is the Starter. The Pilots all stand behind the takeoff line. The Starter calls out, "Tower to pilots—take off!" All Pilots run down to the turning line and back across the takeoff line. The first Pilot back shouts, "Checking in," and then becomes the new Starter.

Variation: Pilots may be called Space Ships, the words may be: "Control center to Space Ships, blast off!"

• Old Mother Witch

Skills: Running, dodging, tagging.

Equipment: None.

Formation: A goal line at one end of playing area. Large box or circle drawn at other end of playing floor.

Description: One child is chosen to be Old Mother Witch. The Witch walks around in the box while the rest of the children walk around the outside of the box or dash across and out of the box. The children chant:

Old Mother Witch
Fell in a ditch,
Picked up a penny,
And thought she was rich!

At the end of each verse the Witch asks, "Whose children are you?" The children may answer with any name; however, when one child answers, "Yours," the Witch must chase the children back to their goal line. The first child tagged becomes the new Witch.

Variations: One child may be appointed as a Leader responsible for saying, "Yours." The Witch may catch any number of children she or he can, and gets a point for each child caught. A new Witch may be chosen by the old one.

• Red Light

Skills: Running, fast starts, fast stops.

Equipment: None.

Formation: A goal line drawn at each end of the playing area.

Description: All the players stand on one goal line. One person is selected as IT. IT stands on the far goal line and faces away from the others, counting "1, 2, 3, 4"; may say "Red Light," any time before "10." As IT is counting, the others advance as far as they can before "Red Light" is heard. Upon saying "Red Light," IT turns around. If people are caught moving, they must go back to their goal line. The counting is repeated. The first one who reaches the other goal line becomes the new IT. Players may move anytime; however, if IT sees them, he or she may send them back to their goal line.

Variation: Instead of counting, IT may say, "Green Light," pause, and then say, "Red Light," as the signal to stop.

- **Slap Jack**

Skills: Running, tagging.
Equipment: None.
Formation: Circles of eight, one child is IT.
Description: All players in a circle stand facing the center with their hands held together, palms up, behind them. One is chosen as IT, and walks around the outside. When he slaps a player on the hands, that player chases IT around the circle and tries to tag him before he reaches the empty space in the circle. The chaser becomes the next IT.
Variation: IT may run, skip, or perform any kind of locomotor movement.

- **Squat Tag**

Skills: Running, dodging, tagging.
Equipment: Colored scarf.
Formation: Large playing area with defined boundaries all around.
Description: One player is IT and tries to tag any other player. To be safe, runners assume a squat position. When one is tagged, the tagger gives the new IT the colored scarf.
Variations: More than one player may be IT, but all should carry a colored scarf so that the IT is easily identified. Other safe positions may be designated.

- **Squirrels in Trees**

Skills: Running.
Equipment: None.
Formation: Groups of three scattered about the playing area.
Description: Two players hold hands and form a "tree" for the other person to stand in. Two players are chosen as Squirrels and have no Tree. The leader gives a signal and all the Squirrels must get out of their trees and find a new one. The extra Squirrels get into a Tree, and of course two are left out again. Emphasis should be placed on finding a Tree. Rotate Trees with Squirrels until everyone has been a Squirrel.

LEVEL II

- **Boundary Ball**

Skills: Throwing, catching.
Equipment: Volleyball or 8½-inch playground ball.
Formation: Playing area divided in half.
Description: Opposing teams are scattered in each half. One ball is given to a player on each team. The purpose of the game is for a team to throw, roll, or bounce a ball across the opponents' goal line. A point is scored for a team whenever this occurs. The game continues without interruption for a set period of time or until a set number of points is reached by one team or the other. Players may stop the ball in any manner they can.

Variations: Kicking may be employed rather than throwing. Children may be prohibited from walking with the ball.

- ### *Cat and Rat*

Skills: Running, dodging, tagging.
Equipment: None.
Formation: Single circle.
Description: One player in center of circle is the Cat, one on the outside is chosen to be the Rat. Circle players hold hands. The Cat tries to chase and tag the Rat. The circle players let the Rat in and out of the circle but try to prevent the Cat from going in and out by lowering or raising their hands. When the Rat is caught or after the Cat has had ample time to catch the Rat, each chooses someone else to take his or her place.

- ### *Simple Dodgeball*

Skills: Throwing at a moving target, dodging.
Equipment: 8½-inch playground ball.
Formation: Playing group divided in half. One half makes a single circle, others are inside the circle.
Description: The players in the outside circle try to hit those inside the circle somewhere between the waist and ankles. The ball may be rolling or in the air. When one is hit, he joins the circle. The last one to remain in the circle is the winner. If the ball goes outside the circle, the last one who threw it goes after it. Players may step inside the circle to get the ball, but must return to circle before throwing it. When a winner has been declared, the game is started again with the teams changing places.
Variations: When a player is hit he may exchange places with the player who hit him. As skill increases, the rule may change; i.e., the ball must be in the air when it hits the players.

- ### *Club Snatch (or Steal the Bacon)*

Skills: Running, tagging, dodging, reaction time.
Equipment: Club or beanbag.
Formation: Two groups along parallel goal lines about 30 feet apart. Mark an X in the center of the two lines, and place the club on it.
Description: Number players; start at opposite ends with 1. The leader calls one of the numbers. The player from each team having that number runs out and tries to snatch the club and take it back across his or her goal line without being tagged by the other player. The team of the player who successfully gets the club across his goal line receives 2 points. If the other player tags him before crossing the line, 1 point is awarded to his team. The club is set back in the center, and new numbers are called. The team with the most points at a designated time wins. Stress deceptive movements in trying to snatch the club.

- ### *Crows and Cranes*

Skills: Running, changing directions, tagging.
Equipment: None.

Formation: Two lines 3 feet apart are drawn across the middle of the playing area. Goal lines are drawn at either end.

Description: Players are divided in half, one group called Crows and the other Cranes. They line up on respective opposite center lines. The leader calls out "Cr-rr-r-ows" and the Crows turn and run toward their goal line with the Cranes in pursuit trying to tag as many as possible before they cross the goal line. When a player is caught he must join the opposite team. The leader should drag out the "Cr" and mix calling the teams so there is suspense and a need for quick reaction on the part of both runners and chasers.

Variations: Children may be challenged to find sound-alike words to vary the name of the game.

• *Fire Engine*

Skills: Running.

Equipment: None.

Formation: A starting line is drawn. A parallel goal line is drawn across the playing area at the other end.

Description: Everyone stands along the starting line. Each child is given a number between 1 and 5. The numbers signify an alarm number. A child chosen to be Fire Chief stands midway down the side line. He claps loudly, stopping at any number between 1 and 5, then calling, "Fire!" All children having that number run down to the far goal line and then back across the starting line. If the Chief counts to more than 5, he calls "General alarm," and everyone runs. The first one to return to the starting line becomes the new Fire Chief.

Variations: The Chief may call, jump, or use any other signal to signify the alarm number. Fire Stations may be formed by groups, each player within the group having an alarm number. The first person back to the line wins a point for his team.

• *Hound and Rabbit*

Skills: Running, tagging.

Equipment: None.

Formation: Groups of three.

Description: Two hold hands and are called the Tree, the other is a Rabbit and stands in between them. There is an extra Rabbit and Hound. The Hound tries to catch the Rabbit. The Rabbit can be safe by dodging into a tree. The Rabbit who was in that tree must get out and then becomes the Rabbit who is chased. If the Hound catches the Rabbit, they change places. Periodically, the game should stop, and Rabbits and Trees exchange places until all have had a chance to be Rabbits. This is an advanced version of Squirrel in Tree.

• *Man from Mars*

Skills: Running, tagging.

Equipment: None.

Formation: Large playing area with end lines and defined side boundaries.

Description: One player is chosen to be the Man from Mars. The other players stand behind one end line and call, "Man from Mars, may we chase you to the stars?" The Man from Mars says, "Yes, if you are wearing green" (or any other color he wishes to call). All those who are wearing some clothing of the color called chase the Man from Mars until he is tagged. The player who tags him first becomes the new Man from Mars.

• Midnight

Skills: Running, tagging.

Equipment: None.

Formation: Large playing area with end lines and defined side lines.

Description: One end is the Roost and one the Den. One player is chosen as the Fox, the remainder are Chickens. The Chickens walk slowly up to and around the Den line and ask the Fox, who is in his Den, "What time is it, Mr. Fox?" The Fox answers with various times. When he says, "Midnight," the Chickens all run for the Roost. The Fox tries to catch as many as possible and then sends them to his Den where they join him in trying to catch Chickens the next game. No one may start to flee or chase until the Fox calls, "Midnight!" When a greater number of Chickens have been caught, the Fox chooses someone to replace him and the game starts again.

LEVEL III

• Blue and Gold

Skills: Running, dodging, quick reaction, and change of direction.

Equipment: A piece of cardboard or rubber painted blue on one side and gold on the other.

Formation: Playing area divided in half with goal lines and side lines marked off. A 3-foot space should separate the two halves. Players divided into two teams.

Description: The teams, called Blue and Gold Teams, line up along their center line. The leader throws the object up in the air between the teams. The team bearing the name of the color side of object that lands facing upward, turns and runs to its goal. The members of the other team try to tag opponents before they cross the goal line. If tagged, a player must join the other team. The team with the most players at the end of a specified time wins.

Variations: Points may be given to a team rather than having players change teams when caught. Any two color combinations may be used.

• Center Touchball

Skills: Throwing and catching.

Equipment: 8½-inch playground ball.

Formation: Single circle, one player in the center as IT.

Description: Circle players pass ball around circle and IT tries to touch the ball. If he is successful, the player who threw ball last becomes the new IT.

- *Chinese Wall*

Skills: Running, dodging, tagging.

Equipment: None.

Formation: Two end boundary lines with two parallel lines about 10 feet apart drawn across the middle of the playing area. This space is called the Wall.

Description: Two children are chosen as Defenders of the Wall. Everyone starts behind one end line. At a signal everyone tries to cross the Wall and get to the other end line without being tagged by a Defender. Everyone who is caught becomes a helper for the Defenders. New Defenders are chosen from among the last few who have not been caught and the game starts again. Defenders may not go off the Wall.

Variations: Points may be given for each time one crosses the Wall. People may cross the Wall with partners. If one gets caught, the other is considered caught also. This encourages cooperative strategy in trying to outwit the Defenders.

- *Circle Race*

Skills: Running.

Equipment: 8½-inch playground ball.

Formation: Single circle. Children number off by threes around the circle, each set of three becomes a team, and each team is given a number. (It is wise to write the team number in front of each team with chalk.)

Description: The space between children must be the same. Each player sits facing the inside of the circle, with legs crossed in front. The ball is placed in the center of a circle. A small circle is drawn around it to mark the center. The leader calls number 1, 2, or 3. Each player having the called number gets up and runs counterclockwise around the outside of the circle and runs into the circle through the spot where he was sitting. The first person to the center of the circle must pick up the ball and hold it high over his head and call out the number of his team. No one can take the ball away from anyone after it has been touched. Emphasize stooping to get ball and bringing it up high to avoid collisions in the center. The number one player on each team is charged with keeping score for his team. The team with the most points at the end of a specified amount of time is the winner.

Variations: Players may be given names of cars, animals, or planes and may win points for themselves.

- *Club Guard*

Skills: Throwing, blocking the ball with legs.

Equipment: 8½-inch playground ball, pin.

Formation: Single circle, with small circle drawn in center of circle. Place pin in center.

Description: One child is chosen to be the Guard, and he must stop the ball from knocking over the pin. He may not step into the small circle. He may kick ball, block it with legs, or if it comes above his waist, he may bat it away with his hands. The players in the circle throw at the pin. They may pass it around the circle quickly to try to draw the Guard out of guarding position. Whoever knocks down the pin becomes the new Guard. If the Guard knocks over the pin, the person who last threw the ball gets to be the new Guard. The Guard changes places with the successful thrower.

- **Exchange Dodgeball**

Skills: Throwing, dodging.

Equipment: Playground ball.

Formation: Single circle, small square drawn in center. Children number off around circle by threes.

Description: One child is chosen as IT and stands in center of circle with ball on floor in the square. IT calls a number, and all players with that number exchange places. IT picks up ball and throws it at a player below the waist who is exchanging places. If one is hit he becomes the new IT.

Variations: Names may be called instead of numbers. Players may be given names of cars, animals, or flowers rather than numbers.

- **Freeze Ball**

Skills: Throwing, dodging, running, catching.

Equipment: One 8½-inch playground ball.

Formation: Single circle, one person chosen to be IT stands in the center.

Description: IT throws ball straight up into air and calls someone's name. As the player called runs to catch ball everyone else scatters. When the ball is caught, the player calls, "Freeze," and everyone must stop where they are at that time. Then he tries to hit one of the players below the waist with the ball. If he hits the one at which he aims, he gets to be IT and throws the ball. If he misses, the person at whom he throws becomes IT. When a player is hit he receives a point. The winner is the person who has the least number of points at the end of the playing time. Limit the area into which players may scatter if the playing area is large or if players have trouble hitting anyone. The thrower may be allowed one step to get nearer to someone before he throws.

- **Last Couple Out (Figure 13-2)**

Skills: Running, dodging.

Equipment: None.

Formation: Partners standing in a file formation. One odd person is IT, and stands on a line 15 feet from the first couple. Side lines 30 feet apart.

Description: IT stands with back to the file of players and calls, "Last couple out." The last couple in the file separates and each partner runs on the outside of his respective line and tries to join hands with his partner somewhere in front of the IT, who tries to catch one of them as soon as he can see them coming. If he catches one, he takes that person's partner and the caught runner becomes IT for the next turn. If he does not catch one, he is IT again. Runners may not run outside the side boundaries.

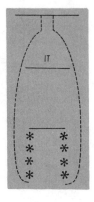

Figure 13-2 Last Couple Out.

- *Loose Caboose*

Skills: Running, dodging, tagging.

Equipment: None.

Formation: Players in groups of three, holding onto waist of one in front of him. The first player is the Engine, the second the Baggage Car, and the third the Caboose, all forming a train.

Description: One or two players are designated as Loose Cabooses, and must find a train to latch onto. The Engine tries to avoid the Loose Caboose and the rest of the train must try to dodge with him. The Loose Cabooses try to latch on to other Cabooses. If they do, the present Caboose becomes Loose or IT, the Engine becomes the Baggage Car, the Baggage Car the new Caboose and the former Loose Caboose the new Engine. If a train pulls apart in trying to be evasive, the Loose Caboose joins the train and the Caboose is IT.

- *Flinch*

Skills: Throwing, catching, reaction time.

Equipment: One 8½-inch playground ball.

Formation: Single circle with one person chosen as IT in the center of circle.

Description: IT throws the ball to each person in the circle or pretends to throw it. If the catcher makes any move to catch the ball and it is not thrown, he must sit down. If it is thrown, he must catch it or sit down. The thrower must be encouraged to move very fast. The last one standing is the new IT. With small circles, the game should go very quickly. Catchers may not hold onto their clothing in order to avoid flinching.

- *Newcomb (Figure 13-3)*

Skills: Throwing, catching.

Equipment: One volleyball or 8½-inch playground ball, 6-foot net. Rectangular court approximately 20 by 44 feet.

Formation: Group divided into teams of eight each. Each team forms two lines on a side of the court.

Description: The player in the right-hand back-row corner throws the ball over the net into the opponent's court area. This is called a serve. The ball is

Figure 13-3 Newcomb.

thrown back and forth over the net until one team misses the ball or one team throws it out of bounds. When this happens, the successful team wins a point and continues to serve or wins a point and the serve. The server remains the same until his team loses the serve. When the serve returns to the first team, the second person from the right in the back row is the server. When everyone in the back row has served, the two lines change places. A player may not walk with the ball. The ball may be thrown to a teammate before it is thrown over the net except on the serve. The team that has the greatest number of points after 10 minutes wins the game.

Variations: A shorter serving line may be designated if children cannot throw ball all the way over the net. Rotation by moving in a clockwise direction in a circular fashion may be taught. A certain number of throws per side might be established to encourage teamwork and change of direction.

- ### Numbers Exchange

Skills: Running.

Equipment: None.

Formation: Single circle, players numbered off around the circle. IT chosen to be in the center of circle.

Description: IT calls two numbers. Players whose numbers are called try to exchange places. IT tries to get in one of the vacated positions before the other gets there. The player left without a position becomes the new IT.

- ### Prisoner Ball

Skills: Throwing, catching.

Equipment: 8½-inch playground ball.

Formation: Parallel lines drawn about 25 feet apart across playing area. Players divided into teams, one on each side of center area.

Description: A leader is appointed for each team. He sees that each player has a number between 1 and the number of players on the team. This should be done so players on the other side do not know who has what number. The ball is given to one team. A player throws the ball across the center area. As he throws he must call a number. Anyone on the other team tries to catch the ball. If he misses, the player who has the number that was called becomes a prisoner of the throwing team and must stand at the side line. If the player catches the ball, he calls a number and throws the ball back to the other team. Prisoners may be released one at a time when their team throws a ball and their opponents fail to catch it. The team with the least number of prisoners at the end of the playing time wins.

• Stick Catch

Skills: Quick reaction time, running, catching.

Equipment: Stick or wand.

Formation: Small circle with players each given a number, one IT.

Description: IT stands in center and balances stick on end, calls a number and lets go of stick. The person whose number is called runs to center of circle and tries to catch stick before it reaches ground. If he is successful, he becomes IT. If the stick is not caught, the original IT calls a new number as he balances stick again.

Variation: Names may be called rather than numbers, and ball bats may be used rather than sticks.

• Trades

Skills: Running, dodging, pantomime.

Equipment: None.

Formation: Playing area divided in half with a free space of 5 feet between two center lines. Players divided into two teams, standing behind own goal lines.

Description: Team 1 selects some trade or occupation; each player will pantomime the movements that characterize the trade. As they advance toward the center line, the players call out:

Team 1 "Here we come!"

Team 2 "Where from?"

Team 1 "Detroit (or any city)."

Team 2 "What's your trade?"

Following this, Team 1 acts out its trade. Members of Team 2 call out what they think the trade is. If and when they do call the correct one, all members of Team 1 run for their goal line, and members of Team 2 chase and try to tag them. They count the number of players caught and the score is recorded. A new game is started and Team 2 becomes the tradespeople. The winners are those who have the most points at the end of the playing time.

• Up the Field

Skills: Throwing, catching.

Equipment: 8½-inch playground ball.

Formation: Entire playing area inside, or large rectangular area approximately 100 feet long and 50 feet wide outside divided in half by center line. Divide players into two teams, members scattered in their own half of playing field.

Description: Ball is given to a player on one team three-quarters of the way back toward their goal line. The ball is thrown, with intent to get it across the opponent's goal line. When the ball is caught, it must be thrown immediately; thrower can take only one step forward. Each team tries to get the ball across their opponent's end line while it is in the air and not touched by the other team. Whichever team succeeds in getting the ball across its opponent's goal line first wins a point. The ball is then put into play by the opposing team at a place similar to that at the beginning of the game.

- ## *Bombardment (Figure 13-4)*

Skills: Throwing, catching, blocking ball.

Equipment: A pin for every player, ten balls.

Formation: Playing area divided into half. A restraining line drawn across the end of each side 4 feet from the end line. The pins are set up in this area an equal distance apart.

Description: Five balls are given to each team. Players try to knock down the pins in their opponent's goal area and at the same time try to keep their own pins from being knocked down. No one may step over the restraining line. Each pin knocked down should be removed from the playing area. The team that knocks down all of its opponent's pins first or the team that has knocked down the most pins at the end of a specified time, wins. A new game is then started.

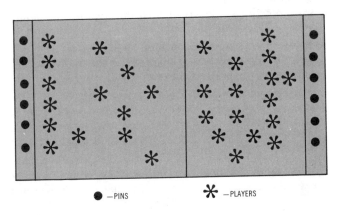

● —PINS   ✳ —PLAYERS

Figure 13-4 Bombardment.

- ## *Ball Stand*

Skills: Running, throwing.

Equipment: 8½-inch playground ball.

Formation: A wall with a restricted playing area marked out in front of it is utilized, the size of the area depending on the number of players. All players are given a number, then line up in front of the wall.

Description: The leader throws a ball against the wall and calls a number. All except the person whose number was called run as far away from the ball as possible while staying within the playing area. The one whose number was called chases the ball and when he catches it he stands still and calls, "Ball stand." Everyone must stop immediately and stand with their backs to the person with the ball, who tries to hit another player's back with the ball. If a player is hit he calls out, "Ball hit," and retrieves the ball. After gaining possession of it he calls, "Ball stand," and attempts to hit someone. After hearing the words, "Ball hit," all the other players run away again. The game continues like this until someone is missed in the hit attempt. Then the player who last tried to hit someone starts the game anew by throwing the ball against the wall and calling a new number.

• Chain Tag

Skills: Tagging, running, dodging.

Equipment: None.

Formation: Scattered. If the outside area is too large, side and end boundaries should be established. One player selected as IT.

Description: IT tries to tag someone. As soon as he does, they join hands and work together to take someone else. Each new person caught joins the chain. Only the head and end players may tag. If the tagging or chain line breaks, no one may be tagged until it is rejoined. If the group is large, two chains may be formed. Play may continue until all are caught or until a specified time elapses.

• Circle Hook-On

Skills: Tagging, dodging.

Equipment: None.

Formation: Three players join hands and make a small circle. One player in the circle is designated as the one to be tagged (tagee). A fourth player is outside the circle and is the tagger.

Description: The two players in the circle not designated as tagees try to protect the tagee by pulling and dodging the tagger. They must not let go hands. The player outside must stay outside and touch or tag from outside the circle. When one is tagged, the tagger moves into the circle and the person tagged goes outside after designating one of the other two as the new tagee.

Variations: The tagee can wear a football flag or rag in his belt and when that is taken he is considered tagged.

• Corner Ball (Figure 13-5)

Skills: Throwing, catching, dribbling.

Equipment: Junior-size basketball.

Formation: Playing area divided into halves. A 4-foot square is drawn in each of the rear corners. Playing group is divided into two teams which take scattered positions on their respective halves of the court. Two players from each team are chosen to take positions in the squares in their opponent's end of the courts.

Description: The ball is thrown high in the air at mid-court. Whoever catches it initiates an attempt to throw the ball to one of his corner players on the

Figure 13-5 Corner Ball.

other half of the court. The opponents try to intercept the ball and throw it to their own corner players. When a corner player catches the ball in the air, 1 point is awarded to his team and the ball is started in the center again. Players may not go out of their court area, may not run or walk with the ball, may not hold the ball over 5 seconds, or step into or out of the corner spaces. Violation of any one of these causes the ball to be given to the opponents. Players may take three bounces with the ball. Corner players should be changed periodically. The team with the most points at the end of a specified period of time is the winner.

- *Gangster and Guard*

Skills: Throwing, blocking ball.

Equipment: One 8½-inch playground ball.

Formation: Single circle with small 3-foot diameter circle in center. One player chosen as Guard and one as Gangster.

Description: The Gangster sits in the small circle with arms folded across head. The players in the circle throw the ball trying to hit the Gangster. The Guard tries to keep ball from hitting the Gangster by kicking or blocking the ball with his body or hands if it comes above his thighs. If the Gangster is hit, the Guard becomes the Gangster and the person who hit him becomes the Guard. The Gangster takes the new Guard's place in the circle. Encourage throwing the ball around rapidly in order to get the Guard out of position.

- *Gap Ball*

Skills: Throwing, catching while standing and on the run.

Equipment: 8½-inch ball for each circle.

Formation: Small circles of eight are formed with a leader in the center.

Description: The leader throws the ball to one person, who returns the ball to the leader, then runs in back of the circle to the next gap or between the next two people. The leader again throws the ball to the same person who likewise returns it and runs to the next gap, etc., until he is back in his original position. The next person does the same until each has completed his turn around the circle.

Variations: This can be used as a race between several circles. Leader in the center may be rotated.

- *Guard Ball (Figure 13-6)*

Skills: Throwing, catching, guarding.

Equipment: 8½-inch utility ball, junior-size basketball or soccer ball.

Formation: Two parallel lines about 20 feet apart. Two teams.

Description: One team has half its players in middle court, other team has half of its players behind either line. The players on the outside of the lines try to pass the ball back and forth to one another without letting the players in the center get it. Balls must be passed below head level. They may use bounce passes or roll the ball. The players in the center attempt to intercept or to block the passes with their arms. If they catch the ball it is returned to the other team. One point is awarded for each successful pass. Teams change places after 4 minutes. Deceptive maneuvers with the head, eyes, and arms should be stressed.

Figure 13-6 Guard Ball.

- *Jump the Shot*

Skills: Jumping, timing of jump.

Equipment: A rope about 20 feet long with a beanbag, deck-tennis ring, or tennis shoe attached to the end of it.

Formation: Single circle.

Description: One person or the teacher swings the rope around the circle so that the object is traveling no more than 1 foot from the ground. The players jump over the rope as it swings under them. If a player is hit by the rope or shot, he has one shot on him. The winner is the player who has the least number of shots at the end of the playing time. Because it takes a little practice to control the swing of the rope, the teacher may start the game and then teach the students how to swing. The one with least number of shots may be the turner.

Variations: The length of the rope and the speed of the rope may be adjusted according to the number and skill of the players. The game may be made more difficult by having the circle players walk and then run around the circle and jump on the move. A long stick or bamboo pole may be used instead of a rope. It should be swung low as the center person squats and pivots around.

- ### *Poison Ball*

Skills: Throwing at a moving target.

Equipment: As many balls 7 inches or larger that are available, and a large ball of a distinctive color; this is called the Poison Ball.

Formation: Class divided into two groups with a goal line drawn across each end of playing area.

Description: Balls are divided equally between teams. The Poison Ball is placed in center of playing area. Each team's players try to hit the Poison Ball, trying to knock it across the opposite team's goal line. Players may not hold the balls or go out into the playing area to retrieve them. They may not touch the Poison Ball to keep it from crossing their line. If many balls get stuck out in the middle, someone may be appointed to go get them and throw them back to the players of each team. When the Poison Ball crosses a goal line, play ceases, a point is awarded to the team who caused it to go across, and a new game is started.

- ### *Stealing Sticks (Figure 13-7)*

Skills: Running, dodging, strategy.

Equipment: Twelve sticks or pins, color bands.

Formation: Playing area divided in half. Two teams, one each side of playing area. At one end of each goal line is a 4-foot square area marked off as the Stick area and at the opposite end of it is a 4-foot square area marked off as the Prison. Six sticks are placed in each team's stick area.

Description: The object of the game is for one team to take one stick at a time from the opposing team without being tagged. When players cross over the

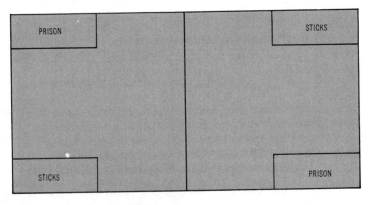

Figure 13-7 Stealing Sticks.

center line they may be tagged by members of the other team. If tagged, they are put in prison. They may be rescued by a teammate who can reach the prisoner's outstretched hand before being tagged. A rescuer and prisoner may go home free if they walk back to their side holding hands. The game ends when all the sticks have been taken from one team or, if time does not permit, whichever team has the combination of most sticks and prisoners wins. Teams should be encouraged to plan strategy in guarding sticks and prisoners and in going in platoons to get sticks or prisoners.

- **Tadpole (Figure 13-8)**

Skills: Running, throwing, catching.

Equipment: One 8½-inch playground ball.

Formation: Two teams. One in single circle, the other in file formation at one point behind a member of the circle.

Description: The ball is given to the circle team. The ball is thrown around to each member of the circle. As the ball is started, the first person in the file line runs around the circle. When he returns he tags off the next runner and goes to the end of the line. The object is to see how many trips the ball can make around the circle before everyone on the running team has gone around the circle. The game is repeated with teams changing sides. The team that had the most round trips with the ball wins the game.

Variations: Vary the type of pass required. Vary the locomotor skill used in going around the circle.

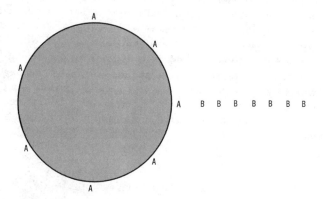

Figure 13-8 Tadpole.

LEVEL IV

- **Capture the Flag (Figure 13-9)**

Skills: Running, dodging, tagging.

Equipment: Two flags or towels.

Formation: Playing area divided into half. At each right-hand rear corner a rectangle 3 feet by 6 feet extends into the court and is known as the Jail or Prison. The flag is placed in a small circle drawn in the center of the court behind the goal line.

Figure 13-9 Capture the Flag.

Description: Once the game is started, anyone who steps over the center line into opponent's half of the court is eligible to be caught and taken to Prison. The major objective of the game is to capture the enemy's flag. A player must get through the enemy lines without getting tagged. Prisoners may be rescued by teammates who get through enemy lines without being tagged and touch the prisoner's outstretched hand. If rescued, both the prisoner and rescuer may walk back to their own court hand in hand down the sideline without being tagged. The last prisoner caught becomes the end player in a line formed by prisoners so that the first one caught is the first one released. Only one prisoner may be rescued at a time. When a player reaches the flag and holds it up high, the game is won. A new game may be started and a point given for each game won. Students are charged with planning their own strategy in getting the flag, rescuing prisoners, guarding flag and prisoners.

Variations: A player may be required to bring the flag back to his team without getting caught on the way back. All prisoners must be out of Prison before flag can be captured. This game may be adapted to a large outside play area and be considered a war game in which patrols are sent out in various maneuvers.

- *Cricket Ball (Figure 13-10)*

Skills: Throwing, batting, catching, running.

Equipment: 5-inch playground ball, 3-inch whiffleball, 2 wide bats or paddles, 2 batter's tees or batting posts, or traffic cones to set small ball on.

Formation: Teams of two. First team of two is at bat. Second team pitches and catches. All other teams are in field positions within oval playing area. Players rotate from batting team to a field position. Fielders move to pitchers and catchers, pitchers and catchers to batters.

Description: The object of the game is for the batters to hit a pitched ball into the field and exchange places at the batting tee at either end of the field before the fielders can dislodge the whiffleball, which is sitting on the batting tee. A run is scored each time the batters successfully reach the other base. A batter from Team 1 and a pitcher-catcher from Team 2 stand at the base or batting tee at opposite ends of the field. A pitcher-catcher throws the ball at

Figure 13-10 Cricket Ball—field markings and starting positions.

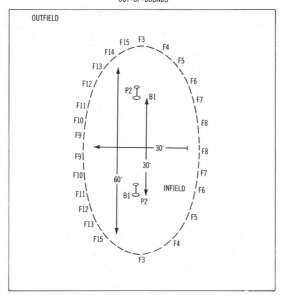

the batting post at the opposite end of the field. The batter tries to keep the ball from hitting the post by batting it. If he hits it, both batters run to their opposite base, bats in hand, and try to hit the base with the bat before the fielders retrieve the ball and throw it at the base, trying to dislodge the whiffleball. If they reach the base successfully, a run is scored. If the ball is dislodged before they reach it, an out is scored and all players rotate. Batters remain at bat until an out is made. Batters may run on a bad pitch or continue scoring runs if a fielder makes a bad throw and ball goes out of the playing area and has to be retrieved. If the ball is not hit by the batter or it does not dislodge the whiffleball, the pitcher-catcher then pitches to the batter at the other end of the field. Batter is out when: a pitched ball dislodges the whiffleball, a fly ball is hit and caught, a fly ball goes outside the playing area, a fielder throws the ball and dislodges the whiffleball, or a batter accidentally knocks the ball off the base. A ground ball hit out of the playing area scores 2 runs (automatically).

Variations: Ball may be struck by the hand rather than batted. Game may be played indoors and out. Walls may be designated as out of bounds.

- ● *Football Goal Catch*

Skills: Throwing, catching.

Equipment: Junior-size football.

Formation: Playing area approximately 40 by 50 feet divided in halves. Lines drawn parallel to each end line about 6 feet from them. This area is the goal area. Playing group divided into two teams with four players in the goal area opposite their end of the field. The rest are field players and play anywhere in their half of field.

Description: A ball is given to a goal-line player on one team. He tries to throw it to one of his teammates at the opposite end of the playing field. The fielders then try to pass the football to a goal-line player. If one catches it, the team receives 1 point. The opposing players try to intercept or knock down the pass and in turn try to throw it to one of their goal-line players. The team that has the most points at the end of 10 minutes is the winner. Rotate field and goal-line positions periodically.

- *Gym Hockey (Figure 13-11)*

Skills: Running, dodging, striking.

Equipment: Plastic hockey sticks, no-bounce 3-inch balls, goal net.

Formation: Floor area length twice the size and width with outside boundary lines 3 feet from walls; center line across width; goal net, 43 by 36 by 15 inches. Six to eight players per team (depending on size of playing area): center, two wings, two defensive players, goalie.

Description: Object is for the offensive players (centers and wings) to push or hit the ball with stick into opponents' goal net. The defensive players try to prevent ball from reaching goal and to send it out to their offensive players. Goalie guards the goal and tries to prevent ball from entering net. Players stay in their own side of court, thus covering the whole area. Only the offensive players cross into opponents' side of floor. Play begins with a face-off between centers (when ball is dropped by referee, players touch sticks to floor three times, then hit ball). Ball must be hit or deflected off a player as it enters goal

Figure 13-11 Gym Hockey skills—game and equipment adaptable for many age groups. Photograph compliments of Shield Mfg. Inc., Tonawanda, N.Y. 14150.

to count score. If it is kicked or thrown in, the score does not count and ball is returned to center line and another face-off is taken.

Playing Period: Three 10-minute periods. (If teams are rotating into play, shorter periods are desirable.)

Out of Bounds: If ball goes beyond boundary lines, last team to have contact loses possession. Play is started where ball went out.

Infractions: **Ball behind net:** if ball goes 10 feet behind net or gets stuck in net, a face-off is taken to side of net. **Goal tending:** ball must precede player across center line. If pass is made to player across line, goal tending is called, ball is given to opponents at center line. **Catching, carrying, or throwing a ball:** loss of possession, ball given to opponents at center line.

Fouls and Penalties: Kicking, kneeing, cross-checking with sticks, body checking, tripping, high sticking, slashing, falling on ball, elbowing, rough play. Penalty: free shot 20 feet from goal with only goalie guarding goal.

Scoring: One point for each goal.

Variations: Adjust number of players to size of playing area; as few as two may form a team. Play may be on blacktop as well as grass. Play may be on tabletop or in box with miniature equipment. Same game may be played on gym floor with players on scooters.

- ### *Kickover*

Skills: Kicking.

Equipment: 10-inch playground ball or cage ball.

Formation: Players divided into two teams which sit on parallel lines 8 feet apart and face one another.

Description: The ball is rolled or bounced down between the lines by the leader. Players from both teams sit with their hands palms down on their respective lines and try to get the soles of their feet under the ball and kick it over the heads of their opponents. Whichever team kicks it over the opponents' heads wins a point, and the ball is put into play again by the leader. The team with the most points at the end of a specified time wins.

Variations: The leader stands at the head of the line. When the ball is kicked over, he moves back to a distance he thinks is equal to the distance away from the line the ball travels. The end player on the team who kicked the ball over must run and touch the leader's hand and go to the head of his line before the other team's end player runs out, retrieves the ball, and brings it back to the head of his line. The first one back wins a point for his team.

- ### *Machine-Gun Run*

Skills: Running, dodging, throwing at a moving target.

Equipment: Six 8½-inch playground balls.

Formation: Players divided into three teams. Parallel lines drawn about 25 feet apart and 40 feet long.

Description: Team 1 lines up behind one of the lines, Team 2 on the other. Team 3 waits at the end of the lines. Teams 1 and 2 are each given 3 balls. At a signal, players on Team 3 run down between the two lines to one end and back. Players on 2 and 3 repeatedly throw the ball and try to hit players above the ankles or below the waist with a ball. The number who were not hit are counted, and the teams rotate: Team 3 takes Team 1's place; Team 2 becomes the running team. After each team has run the line twice, scores are compared, and the team with greatest number of people who were not hit wins.

Variations: Distances may be varied to fit the throwing ability of the groups. More balls may be added. More running turns may be allowed.

• Prisoner's Base

Skills: Running, dodging, tagging.

Equipment: None.

Formation: A goal line is marked off at each end of the playing area. Prisons 3 by 9 feet are marked off at the right-hand corners of the goal lines. Players are divided into two teams, each lining up along their assigned goal lines.

Description: The object of the game is to take as many Prisoners as possible in the time allotted for the game. Once a player steps over his goal line he can be caught by someone from the other team who must declare that he is "fresh on _____" before the chase begins. Therefore one may chase a specific player and be chased by a specific player. At any time that a player returns to his goal line, he erases the "fresh" for the person he was chasing and the "fresh" on him is eliminated. If a person is tagged, he is taken to Prison. Prisoners form a chain from the back of the Prison with the last one caught taking the back position each time. A Rescuer and Prisoner may come back to their line free if they clasp hands and hold them high. A leader should be appointed for each team and he is responsible for team strategy. Players should be very clear about their vows about being "fresh" on a certain person.

• Three-Team Dodgeball (Figure 13-12)

Skills: Throwing at a moving target, dodging.

Equipment: Two 8½-inch playground balls.

Formation: Court is divided into three equal courts lengthwise. Playing group is divided into three teams, with one team occupying each court.

Description: Play is divided into three playing periods of 4 minutes each. At the end of each period the teams rotate positions so that at the end of the game each team has been in every court once. A ball is given to each of the end court teams. The object is for everyone to try to hit someone on another team. The ball must hit below the waist, and be in the air when it hits. Once the ball has bounced, it may be picked up and thrown. No walking, or holding the ball over 5 seconds. When a player is hit he goes to the side line directly opposite his team's court and sits down until that playing period is over. The number sitting is counted each period and all players reenter the game. The team with the least number of points at the end of the three periods is the winner. The team in the center will always have the greatest number eliminated.

Variations: Add more balls if the game goes slowly. Teams may be called red, white, and blue.

Figure 13-12 Three-Team Dodgeball.

- *Agents and Spies*

Skills: Running, throwing, accuracy.

Equipment: A utility ball and a pin for each team.

Formations: Each team has four players. One-half the teams are Agents and the other half are Spies at the start of the playing time. Teams line up in single file with a team of Agents behind a line 40 feet across from a line behind which the Spies stand. Midway between each set of Agents and Spies are placed a ball and a pin. It is wise to mark a small circle in which each is placed. Upon a signal from the leader, the first person in the Agents' line and the Spies' line, respectively, run out to the center. The Spy picks up the pin and tries to get it back to his line before the Agent can pick up the ball and throw it and hit the Spy. If the Agent hits the Spy his team gets 2 points; if the Spy gets home safely his team gets 2 points. After everyone has had a turn, the teams are reversed in their actions and titles. Play may continue for a set length of time and at the end of the period the team with the most points wins. Agents retrieve the ball and the Spies must return the pin to place each time. Any number of teams may play at the same time.

- *Battleball (Figure 13-13)*

Skills: Throwing, dodging.

Equipment: One 8½-inch playground ball.

Formation: Players divided into two teams. Playing area is divided into two equal areas approximately 20 by 40 feet. The center line is extended 3 feet out to each side of the courts.

Description: Each team is scattered in its own court. A player from each team is stationed outside the boundary lines at the opposite end from his own team. This player is called the end guard and will be joined later by the members of his team who are legally hit by the ball. These players may throw the ball at the opposite team's players, but must stay outside the boundary lines and may

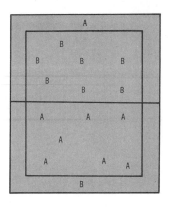

Figure 13-13 Battleball.

not cross the center-line extension. The play starts with a jump ball (in the center of the court) with a person from each team jumping and immediately returning to his own court. Players try to eliminate players from the opposite team from the center court. The team with the last player in its center court wins. The ball must be in the air when it hits a player and it must hit below the waist. A player may pick up the ball as soon as it has hit the floor or another person. A player may not walk with the ball or hold it over three seconds. He may bounce or dribble the ball three times. The ball may be passed from player to player. As soon as one is hit he goes to the outside court at the opposite end anywhere around the side lines of that court and remains active in the attempt to get balls to hit his opponents.

Variation: Use two balls.

- ### *Bronco Dodgeball*

Skills: Throwing, dodging.

Equipment: 8½-inch playground balls.

Formation: Single circle. Two sets of three people each are selected. The three must hold onto the waist of the player in front of them. Players in the circle try to hit the last person with the ball. If a player hits the last in the chain, he then becomes the head, and the tail player takes his place in the circle. The three players must work together to dodge the ball. The head player can hit the ball with his hands or kick it. If the three break their chain, they must stop and regroup.

Variations:

1. More Broncos may be added.
2. More balls may be added.
3. Scattered formation may be used.

- ### *Busyball*

Skills: Throwing, catching.

Equipment: An odd number of volleyballs, utility balls, soccer or basketballs. At least nine balls, the more the better. Volleyball net.

Formation: Volleyball court, players divided into two teams. Divide the balls equally between the two teams, with the leader keeping the odd one.

Description: The leader gives the signal to start and members of both teams throw the balls over the net into the other team's court. The leader tosses the odd ball into one of the courts at the signal to start. The object is for a team to have the least balls on its side of the court when the whistle blows at the end of 3 minutes. The game may be repeated for a set number of playing periods.

Variation: Players have to hit ball over net rather than throw it over.

• *Hemenway Ball (Figure 13-14)*

Skills: Throwing, striking with hand, running, dodging.

Equipment: Base, volleyball or 8½-inch playground ball.

Formation: A rectangular area about 90 feet by 40 feet is designated. A line is drawn down the center lengthwise. The base is placed 8 feet from the end line and on the center line. At the opposite end a batter's box is marked off on one side of the line and a pitcher's box directly across from that. Players are divided into two teams, one out in the field area, and one lined up behind the home line and to the left of the center line.

Description: The object of the game is for the batter to hit the ball into the field, run down the right side of the center line, touch the base, and run back to the batter's box on the left side of the center line without getting hit by the ball. The first person in the line tosses the ball up so the second player can hit it with his fist out in the field. If the ball is caught in the air by the fielders, the batter is out. The fielders try to field the ball and then throw it at the runner. They may not walk with the ball, hold it more than 5 seconds, or hit the runner above the waist. They may pass it to other teammates. If the runner reaches home line without getting hit, he scores a run for his team and then goes to the end of the line. Everyone else moves up a position until each has had a turn batting, whereupon the sides change. After each team has had a specified number of equal bats, the team with the most points wins. A violation of the rules gives the opposing team a point.

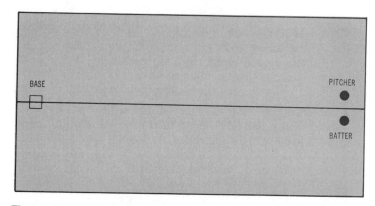

Figure 13-14 Hemenway Ball.

- *Poison Pin*

Skills: Pulling, pushing.

Equipment: A pin for every three players.

Formation: Divide players into groups of three, scattered about the floor.

Description: Players make a small circle and place pin in the center. Holding onto hands, each tries to pull the others into the circle so they knock the pin down. When the pin is knocked down, a point is given to the one who was responsible. The pin is reset, and the game is started again. This will be tiring to the arms, but it is strength-building. The player with the least number of points at the end of a specified playing period wins.

- *Wall Kickball (Figure 13-15)*

Skills: Running, kicking.

Equipment: 10-inch playground ball or cageball.

Formation: Players are divided into two teams. A line is drawn parallel to the wall and 6 feet from it. Two parallel lines, 8 feet apart, are drawn perpendicular to this line. Players of one team sit on one line and those of the other across from them on the other line. A base is established 20 feet from the ends of the team lines.

Description: The leader throws the ball between the two lines so that it hits the wall and rebounds in between the teams. Players try to kick the ball over the heads of their opponents. When the ball is kicked over, the end players next to the wall get up, run behind their lines, to their goals and back to the other end of the line. The first one back wins a point for his team. The team that kicked the ball over the heads of the others also receives a point. The game continues for a specified length of time, and the team with the most points at the end is declared the winner. Stress bending knees and kicking the ball up with the soles of the feet.

Figure 13-15 Wall Kickball.

• Basket Baseball

Skills: Throwing, catching, running, shooting baskets.

Equipment: Four bases, one basketball or soccer ball.

Formation: A home base is placed at the free-throw line of the basketball court, with the other three placed in positions as for a regular softball game. Players are divided into two equal teams. Boundary lines are the same as for a regular softball game.

Description: One team is at bat and stands along the first-base line. The fielding team is scattered throughout the playing field. One player is designated as the catcher. The first batter throws the ball into the field and proceeds to run the bases in order. The fielders attempt to catch or field the ball and relay it in to the catcher, who attempts to make a basket. If he makes a basket before the runner reaches home base, he scores 2 points for his team. If the runner returns before a basket is made, he scores 2 points for his team. Once everyone has run, the teams change sides. A new catcher should be appointed or chosen each time the sides change. The distance between bases may have to be shortened if the fielding team always returns the ball to the catcher before the runner gets home. If the runner always beats the ball, the bases may be too close.

• Basket Netball

Skills: Catching, throwing, guarding, shooting baskets.

Equipment: Basketball, volleyball net, color bands.

Formation: Volleyball net divides the basketball court into two sides. Players are divided into two teams. One member of each team is selected to play in the keyhole area of the opposite team's court.

Description: The ball is given to one team, which tries to pass the ball over the net into the keyhole area to a teammate. If the teammate gets the ball, he attempts a shot for a basket. One point is given for a completed pass to the keyhole, and 2 additional points if a basket is made. Once a basket is made, a new player is rotated into the keyhole. Whether the basket is made or missed, the ball is given to the opposite team at their end line to the right of the free-throw lanes. The ball may be passed among teammates. No steps may be taken with the ball, no bounces, and no player may hold the ball for more than 5 seconds.

• Bull in the Ring

Skills: Throwing, catching, guarding.

Equipment: One soccer, basketball or 8½-inch utility ball.

Formation: Single circle of 6 to 8 players.

Description: Players are each given a number. One player is IT. IT calls a number and tosses the ball to any player in the circle. The person whose number was called is the "Bull." He goes immediately to the center of the circle and attempts to intercept or "tie up" the ball. The circle players must pass the ball around or across the circle. They may not pass it to the player standing next to them in the circle. No player may hold the ball more than 5 seconds. As soon as the ball is tied up or intercepted by the Bull, he returns to the circle, calls a number, and starts the ball in play again.

Variations:
1. Points may be given for intercepting or taking the ball.
2. More than one number may be called.
3. More than one ball may be used.

- ### *Crab Soccer*

Skills: Crabwalk, kicking.

Equipment: Soccer ball, color bands.

Formation: Playing area approximately 40 by 60 feet with a goal line designated for each team. Players are divided into two teams.

Description: Teams line up on their own goal line. Ball is placed in the center of playing area. On signal, players from both teams advance using a crabwalk (weight on hands and feet, with seat toward the floor) and try to kick the ball over the opposing team's goal line. Hands may not touch the ball. Two points are awarded to the team that gets it across the opponent's goal line. After a goal is made, the ball is placed in the center, and play starts again. The winner is the team with the most points at the end of a designated period of time.

Variation: If scooters are available, players may sit on them and kick the ball.

- ### *Flak Dodgeball (Figure 13-16)*

Skills: Running, dodging, throwing.

Equipment: Base, 8½-inch playground ball.

Formation: A goal line drawn 15 feet from the end of the playing area and a base placed 10 feet from the other end and midway between the sides. A circle 3 feet in diameter drawn around the base.

Description: One team (fielding) is scattered anywhere in the field except in the restraining circle around the base. The other team (running) is divided in half. One group is in a line marked on the goal line 10 feet from the right side line, and the other is lined up 10 feet from the left side line. The leader throws

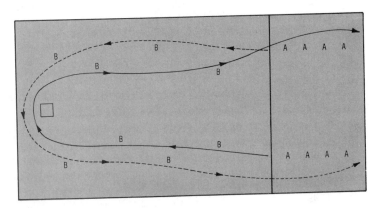

Figure 13-16 Flak Dodgeball.

the ball into the playing area, and the first person in each of the running team's lines runs out in the field and tries to circle the base and go to the end of the other line. The fielding players try to hit the runners below the waist and above the ankles with the ball. Fielders may not walk with the ball or hold the ball more than 5 seconds. They may pass the ball around to other teammates. If a runner is legally hit, he raises his arm high and immediately goes to the side line and walks back to his line. The raised arm is a signal for the runner next in line to start running. If the runner reaches the goal line safely, 2 points are counted for the running team. This is also the signal for the next in line to run. Since the running is continuous, and no signals to run other than those mentioned are given, everyone has to be alert. There are always two runners in the field. If fielders violate the rules, 1 point is added to the running team's score. After everyone has run twice, the teams exchange sides. It is wise to ask one person in each line to keep score; the scores may be added as teams are changing sides.

Variation: Two balls may be put into play when the game is understood by all.

• *Race to the Moon (Figure 13-17)*

Skills: Passing, catching, basket shooting.

Equipment: Two basketballs or soccer balls, basketball goals.

Formation: Basketball court, or parallel lines about 40 feet apart. A large new-moon-shaped line drawn in the center of the two lines. Players are divided into two equal teams, each lined up along its respective side line. Half of a basketball court may be used thus, and two games can be played at one time. A ball is placed at each tip of the moon. Each player is given a number.

Description: The leader calls a number. Players having this number run out to the center, pick up the ball closest to them and start throwing the ball to each member of their teams. When they have thrown the ball to and received it from each of the players, they dribble to the basket and attempt to make a basket. They shoot until they do, then race back and place the ball on a tip of the moon. The first one back to his goal line wins 2 points for his team. The

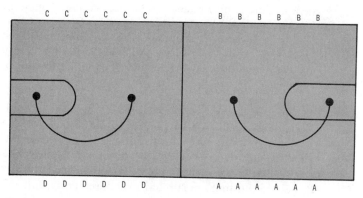

Figure 13-17 Race to the Moon.

game continues, another number is called. The team with the most points at the end of the playing time wins.

Variations:

1. A player may make only one attempt for a basket.
2. Two points are given for a basket, and 1 is given for the person who replaces his ball on the moon first.

- ## Skeet Ball

Skills: Throwing at a moving target.

Equipment: A large cardboard or stiff plastic disc, a tennis ball for each player (any other type of ball may be used if tennis balls are not available).

Formation: Two parallel lines, drawn about 30 feet apart. Players are divided into two teams. Teams line up behind their designated goal line. Players are numbered.

Description: Leader calls a number and at the same time throws the disc up in the air. Those bearing the number called try to hit the disc. A point is given to the team of the player who hits the disc. Each player retrieves his own ball; the leader, the disc. The game is repeated any number of times. The team with the most points at the end of a designated time or the first team to reach 20 points wins.

Variation: A large ball or beanbag may be used instead of a disc.

Relays

Relays are a form of games in which each child is on a team, and each team member in order performs a skill. Teams compete against each other in a race to see which team's members can complete their turns first. Relays may also be used as skill practice formations when no race is involved. This form of game is not recommended for first- or second-graders. Relays are actually a form of team game, and the confinement, cooperation, and excitement of the organization is too advanced for primary-grade children.

There are a number of formations or patterns relays may take. Several of these are described in Chapter 6. The most common one is a single-file formation. Children enjoy relays a great deal and are highly motivated. They very quickly see that their efforts are important to the success of the team. A great deal of self-control is required, since children must wait their turns, react quickly in starting their turns, and follow strict rules. It is important that skills are fairly well-developed and directions understood before the relay race is begun.

Teaching Relays

1. Divide class into teams of six or less. Be sure teams are equal. If they are not, make provision for players on the short teams to take two turns. Put slow or handicapped players in middle of the team. When a team loses, it often appears to children that it is the last player's fault, even though it may have been another player who was too slow.

2. Select skills that are familiar to children or teach the skill before the relay.

3. While teams are seated, clearly establish goal line and starting line.

4. Be definite about when a person starts, how one must tag the next person's right hand with his right hand before he may cross the line, and what one does when he returns to the end of the line. If a ball is being kicked, dribbled, or thrown, it must be in the next player's hands (or hit his feet) before he starts across the line. It is best to have everyone sit down when finished, so that it is easy to distinguish the winning team. An object or ball that is dropped must be retrieved by the person dropping it, and play is resumed at the place where it was dropped first. These rules should be enforced by setting a definite penalty for infractions.

5. Briefly describe the purpose of relays. One group may walk through relay to demonstrate the procedure.

6. If the combination of skills or the pattern is new, everyone can have a trial without the elements of racing being involved.

7. Have an object as turning point at the far goal line. This object should be easy to see in order to maintain straight lines.

8. Use an established signal to start relay. "1, 2, 3, Go!" or "Ready, (blow whistle)."

9. Recognize winning team, and second, third, and fourth places. Do each relay several times. A whole period should not be devoted to relays; however, if much of the period is concerned with this type of game, points can be kept for winners, and a final winner declared when total points are tallied. Because it usually takes only a few seconds to run through a relay, there should be several races to justify the time it takes to assume the formation.

Safety Factors

1. Have goal line 8 to 10 feet from the wall.

2. Place teams far enough apart so there is room to run between lines.

3. Establish a traffic pattern. "Run back on right side, tag right hand of next partner with your right hand, and go to the end of line." Demonstrate carefully.

4. Sit with legs crossed in order that returning members do not trip over feet of the other players. Keep lines straight.

Description of Relays

A number of relays are suggested. The teacher or students can create relays to fit the needs of the group; the same ones may be used for different grade levels, but the distances may vary. The following types of activities lend themselves well to relay games.

1. Locomotor skills and combinations.
2. Skills and stunts from self-testing units.
3. Obstacle relays.
4. Object-handling activities.
5. Specific sport skill practices.
6. Novelty stunts for parties and for limited spaces.

• *File Formation Relays (Figure 13-18)*

This is the basic relay formation for beginners to learn. The skill of walking may be utilized first to learn the format. The first player walks down to line B, goes around the object, returns to line A, touches the second player, and then

Figure 13-18 File Formation Relays.

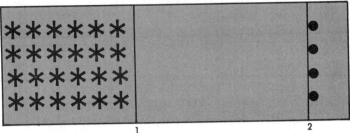

1 — STARTING LINE
2 — TURNING LINE
● — TURNING POINT OBJECT

sits at the end of his line. This is repeated by each person in turn. The first team in which everyone is sitting wins. The following skills may be utilized in this format:

1. Any one of the locomotor skills; variations in style may be designated.
2. Animal walks: bunny hop, elephant walk, seal walk, etc.
3. Bouncing the ball while running or walking.
4. Various stunts.
5. Riding scooters.
6. Skills combined inventively by students and teacher.

- *Carry-and-Fetch Relay (Figure 13-19)*

Equipment: Two blocks of wood 3 by 5 inches, beanbags, or pins.

Formation: File; objects are placed in a small circle drawn approximately 20 feet out in front of the team. Another circle is drawn at the turning line.

Procedure: Upon signal, the first person runs to the objects, takes one, and carries it to the circle on the turning line. He goes back to get the next object and places it in the circle on the running line, then tags off the next player. This player returns the objects one at a time to the first circle. This pattern continues until everyone has had a turn.

Figure 13-19 Carry-and-Fetch Relay.

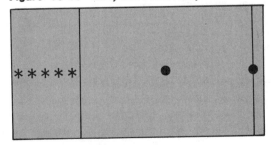

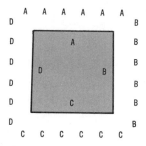

Figure 13-20 Corner Spry.

- *Corner Spry (Figure 13-20)*

Equipment: Ball for each team.

Formation: Four teams. A square formation is used, with each team forming one side of the square. A square 6 feet by 6 feet is drawn in the center. A person from each team stands in the center square and faces his team.

Procedure: On the signal the ball is thrown back and forth from leader to his teammates in order down their line. When he throws to the last player in line he calls, "Corner spry" and goes to the head of the line. The last player carries the ball into the center and becomes the new leader. This continues until the original leaders are in the center. The first one back sits and his team wins.

- *Human Hurdle Relay (Figure 13-21)*

Equipment: None.

Formation: Circle for each team. Players are in prone position. They face the center of circle; their arms are outstretched, fingers touching. One player remains standing.

Procedure: The player who is standing must run and jump over each player on his team in order. When he reaches his starting point, he exchanges places with the first person. Everyone has a turn.

Variations:

1. Players may bounce a ball over each person, do a cartwheel over him, or whatever teacher or class decides.
2. Each player may be given a number, and when a leader calls that number, the player on each team with that number will rise, hurdle over everyone around the circle, and return to his place. The first player back in place wins a point for his team.

- *Jump-the-Stick Relay*

Equipment: Stick or wand for each team.

Formation: File; stick placed on turning line.

Procedure: First person runs and picks up stick. He returns to the team, and the second person grasps one end of the stick. The two carry the stick back to the end of the team, drawing the stick under each player. Each player must jump over the stick. When they come to the end of the team, the first player remains there. The second player takes the stick to the head of the line and the third player grasps one end of the stick. It is again taken to the end. This

Figure 13-21 Human Hurdle Relay.

continues until everyone has a turn. The last player will carry the stick down and place it on the turning line and return to the line.

Variation: Each player may run down to the turning line and back after he brings the stick to the front.

- *Obstacle Relay*

Equipment: Chairs or pins are placed in intervals of 8 feet along the way to the turning line.

Formation: File.

Procedure: On signal the first person must run around each obstacle on his way down to and back from the turning point. He touches off the second player, and the relay continues until the players of one team have finished.

Variations:

1. Players may dribble the ball; another form of locomotion may be used.
2. Apparatus equipment or objects to go over and under may be used as obstacles.

- *Over and Under Relay*

Equipment: Ball for each team.

Formation: File.

Procedure: Ball is alternately passed back between a person's legs or over his head. When the ball reaches the last player, he brings it back to the front of the line and starts the ball moving back again by passing it between his legs. When all players have returned to their original places, the relay is over.

Variations:

1. Various objects may be passed.
2. In the classroom any objects may be passed under and over the seats.

• *Shuttle Relay*

Equipment: None.

Formation: File; one person standing on turning line.

Procedure: On signal, the first person in line runs down and tags off the person standing on the turning line and stays there. The other player runs to the team, tags off the second person, and goes to the end of the line. This exchange of places continues until everyone is back in his place.

Variations:

1. This makes a good style relay for track and field units for the intermediate grades. Distances between lines may be varied.
2. Ball may be dribbled either with foot or hand.

• *Star Relay (Figure 13-22)*

Equipment: Ball for each team.

Formation: Star formation, five players on a team arranged in the fashion of a five-point star. Each player is given a number.

Procedure: The number 1 player on each team throws the ball to the number 2 player and after he has thrown he runs to the number 2 position. The number 2 players throws the ball to the number 3 player and then runs to the number 3 position. This continues until everyone is back in his own position. The first team to complete their trip around the star wins.

• *Strideball Relay*

Equipment: Ball for each team.

Formation: File; players standing with feet in a wide side-stride position.

Figure 13-22 Star Relay.

Procedure: Ball is rolled down between the spread legs of the team. The last player picks up the ball and runs to the head of the line and starts the ball back again. When everyone has returned to original position the relay is over. As player is carrying ball to front, all other players should be moving back so first player will be standing behind line.

Variation: Ball may be passed under legs rather than rolled.

- **Task Relay**

Equipment: One jump rope, one ball for each team.

Formation: File; three circles are drawn equidistant between the starting line and the turning line. The rope is put in the first circle, the ball in the second.

Procedure: Upon signal the first person runs to the rope, jumps it five times, replaces it in the circle, and runs to the next circle. There he bounces the ball five times, replaces ball in the circle, and runs to the next. Here he must do five mule kicks, run to the turning point, and then tag off the next player in line. Objects must be placed in circles and the required tasks done properly the required number of times. When everyone has had a turn, the relay is over.

Variation: Any stunt or task may be utilized. Squads may be assigned the responsibility of making a relay for designated periods.

Classroom and Inactive Games

Occasionally the teacher has a need for games that involve a restricted space and little vigorous activity. In some situations the physical education class must be conducted in the classroom whenever there is inclement weather. This may be a permanent situation when there is no gym or playroom in the physical plant, or a temporary one when the usual play space is being used for another purpose. The latter is frequently true where multipurpose rooms are utilized for plays, community events, displays, concerts, and other events.

In addition to including inactive games in the regular physical education period, the teacher may use them for relaxation, indoor recess, and recreation. Most teachers realize that it is valuable to incorporate game ideas in learning situations in all phases of the curriculum. Quickly organized inactive games at the end of a stimulating and vigorous physical education lesson calm the children before they return to academic work in the classroom.

When the classroom is the only indoor play space, the teacher must plan a program composed of a great deal of vigorous activity outdoors and including adaptable activities which permit a maximum of activity in the classroom. Many dance and self-testing activities are suitable for classroom space. Consideration in selecting the activities must revolve around:

1. Space available.
2. Safety factors.
3. Noise resulting.
4. Amount of participation by all.
5. Equipment needed.

You can adapt games to classroom or limited space use by modifying the means of locomotion, using beanbags, or fleece balls for the regular balls and varying as the directions suggest:

GAMES	PAGE	LEVEL
Hot Ball	317	I–II
Numbers Exchange	326	III
Circle Stride Ball	316	I–II
Club Snatch	320	III
Fire Engine	321	I–II
Stick Catch	327	III
Trades	327	III
Gangster and Guard	330	III
Flinch	325	III

LEVELS I AND II

• *Birds Fly*

Equipment: None.

Formation: Standing anywhere in room. A leader is chosen and stands where everyone can see him.

Description: Quickly, the leader gives the name of anything that flies. When he does, the rest of the players flap their arms vigorously like wings. If the leader gives the name of something that does not fly, no one is supposed to flap arms. If someone does he must sit down. If everyone is eliminated in quick order, the last one down becomes the new leader. Otherwise a new leader is chosen after several minutes. *Example:* "Ducks fly, . . . geese fly, . . . mosquitoes fly, . . . mules fly."

• *Boiler Burst*

Equipment: None.

Formation: Everyone seated in seats or in circle. One person chosen to be the first storyteller.

Description: The storyteller begins to tell a story. He may end the story at any time by saying the words, "and then the boiler burst." This is a signal for everyone to get up and exchange seats. The storyteller attempts to get a seat. The person left standing becomes the new storyteller.

Variation: This may be done in a circle, and everyone must exchange places at least two places from his original place.

• *Fruit Basket Upset*

Equipment: None.

Formation: Everyone sitting in own seat. Class divided into four teams. A leader of each team is appointed. An IT is appointed.

Description: Leaders give each player a name of a fruit. IT calls out the name of a fruit, and each player bearing the name of the fruit exchanges seats with

Games

someone else of that fruit. IT tries to get a seat for himself. The person left without a seat is the new IT. When IT calls, "fruit basket upset," everyone gets a new seat.

• Seat Change

Equipment: Seats arranged in any fashion, one less seat than players.

Formation: Everyone seated. A leader is chosen.

Description: The leader calls out the direction that players are to go as he gives the signal to change seats—i.e., "Left change." "Front change." "Right change." When the leader says "Scramble," the players may change seats in any direction. At this time the leader tries to get a seat. The person who is left without a seat becomes the new leader.

• Simon Says

Equipment: None.

Formation: Everyone standing beside his seat; standing in a circle, or in a scattered formation. One chosen to be Simon.

Description: The person who was chosen to be "Simon" says, "Simon says, 'Stand up.' " Everyone follows his command. He continues to give commands in this fashion and the members of the group do what he says. If he omits the words "Simon says" preceding the command, they are not supposed to do the action. Those who do are eliminated or are given a point. Simon should mix commands and actions very quickly so the group must listen carefully. The one who can stay in the longest or has the fewest points becomes the next Simon.

• Beanbag Target Relay

Equipment: Four beanbags for each team; circle 30 inches in diameter drawn on blackboard in front of each team.

Formation: Seats are arranged in rows, or children sit in relay file formation in front of blackboard.

Description: Upon signal from the leader, the first person in each row throws his four beanbags and tries to hit his target. Two points are given for each target hit. After throwing the last beanbag, he gets up and retrieves his bags. Meanwhile, every other child moves up one seat. The first person places the retrieved bags on the first desk then sits in the last seat. The second person then takes his throws at the target. This process is repeated until all have had a chance to throw. The winning team is the one that has the most points.

Mental and Guessing Games

LEVELS I AND II

• Bird, Beast, or Fish

Equipment: None.

Formation: Children seated, class divided into two teams. One person is the leader.

Description: The leader points to a child and says either "bird," "beast," or "fish." Immediately he starts counting aloud to 10. The person to whom he points must say the name of a bird, beast, or fish (whichever was called). For example, if "bird" were said, the child could answer, "Sparrow." If the child cannot give a satisfactory answer before IT counts to 10, the opposite team receives a point. A member of the opposite team is selected to give the answer.

Variation: Any types of categories may be substituted for bird, beast, or fish.

• *I Saw*

Equipment: None.

Formation: Children sitting in seats or in a circle.

Description: One child chosen to start the game stands in center of circle or in front of room. He says, "On my way to school this morning I saw _____." He then portrays with body actions what he saw. The class has three guesses to say what he saw. The child guessing correctly becomes the next person to describe what he saw. If no one guesses and the portrayal was reasonably correct, he may do another one. If the portrayal was not true to form, he may be asked to choose someone to take his place.

• *Poor Pussy*

Equipment: None.

Formation: Everyone seated in seats or in a circle. One child chosen to be Pussy.

Description: The Pussy walks around and stops in front of a child. He strokes a child's face and says, "Poor pussy," three times. In between each he makes funny faces. If the child laughs or smiles before this is done three times he cannot become the Pussy. If he can stay sober-faced the three times, he becomes the Pussy.

• *Telegrams*

Equipment: None.

Formation: All seats are arranged in equal rows. Everyone is in his seat.

Description: Everyone places hands on desk and closes eyes. At a signal, the last player in each row taps the shoulder of the child in front of him. This child in turn taps the shoulder of the child in front of him. When the first person in the row is tapped, he stands up and the first one up indicates the winning team.

• *Who Has Gone from the Room?*

Equipment: None.

Formation: All children are sitting in their seats. One is chosen as IT.

Description: IT hides his eyes. The leader indicates which child should leave the room. After he has left, IT opens his eyes and guesses who has gone. If he names the child correctly, that child is IT the next time. If he fails to name the child, he closes his eyes, the child returns to the room. IT opens his eyes and guesses who has returned to the room. If he fails to do so, he is IT again.

• *Buzz*

Equipment: None.

Formation: Children are seated.

Description: A number is selected to be the Buzz number. The object of the game is for everyone in turn to count consecutively to 100. Every time the number designated to be the Buzz number comes up, the word "Buzz" must be substituted. The child who fails to do this correctly is given a letter of Buzz. If he fails the first time he gets a B, the second time a U, etc. The idea is to have as few letters as possible. *Example:* If the number 5 is chosen, the counting goes: 1, 2, 3, 4, Buzz, 6, . . . 13, 14, Buzz, 16. Fifty-five would be Buzz, Buzz. When 100 is reached, counting may start over again.

• *Cities*

Equipment: None.

Formation: Players are sitting.

Description: The first child names a city. The next child must give the name of a city which starts with the last letter of the first city—e.g., Detroit, Toledo, Owosso, etc. No name of a city may be repeated. If no name is given within 10 seconds, that player is eliminated. The object is to stay in the game as long as possible.

Variation: The category may be changed to that of states, rivers, countries, or any other topic the class is studying.

• *Concentration*

Equipment: None.

Formation: Children are sitting in a circle. IT is chosen to be number 1. IT sits at designated spot in circle, and rest of group is numbered off in order around the circle.

Description: An order and rhythm of clapping is established. Clap hands, slap thighs, and say number. IT begins by saying his number first and adding any other number. This must be done in perfect rhythm, and in the following manner: Clap hands, slap thighs, "One—four." The child numbered four must respond in rhythm with: Clap hands, slap thighs, "Four—six" (or any other number). If child does not respond in perfect rhythm or say his number first, he must go to the end of the line. Everyone who came after that number is renumbered. The object is to work up to the head of the line.

• *Human Tic-Tac-Toe (Figure 13-23)*

Equipment: Nine X's are marked on the floor about a foot apart in a square formation.

Formation: Nine players are assigned to a team. Two teams are waiting to the right of the block of X's.

Description: A member from each team steps on an X, alternating turns. The first team which has three players in a row wins the game. Row may be diagonal, across, or up and down.

Movement Experiences

356

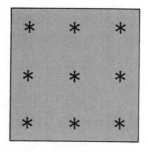

Figure 13-23 Human Tic-Tac-Toe.

• **Radio Stations**

Equipment: None.

Formation: Teams of six; each group is standing or sitting together in a corner of the room.

Description: Each group chooses to send a message of several simple combinations of claps. After practicing a few minutes, each group in turn sends its message, and the others try to catch it and repeat the message.

• **Subject Baseball**

Equipment: None.

Formation: Each player is given a position on a baseball team.

Description: Any subject may be chosen, such as arithmetic. The leader asks a question, and the first player on the first team at bat tries to answer it. If he is correct he gets a hit and goes to first base. (The game may be diagramed on the blackboard.) If he misses, he is out. If the second player answers his question correctly, the person on first moves to second. The object is to be moved around the bases by having people answer questions correctly. When a runner crosses home, a run is scored. After three outs the batting teams change, and the other team has a chance to bat (or answer questions).

Skill Games

• **Balloon Volley**

Equipment: Balloon or very lightweight ball.

Formation: A rope is strung across the room; children are standing.

Procedure: This is a modification of volleyball. Children try to keep balloon going back and forth across the net. The same skills, rules, and scoring should be used that would be used in the regular game at this stage (p. 436).

Variations:

1. Rope might be strung between two chairs and players could sit on the floor.

2. Players may sit in seats and try to hit across a stretched rope. Extra balloons would have to be readily available.

3. No net is needed. Class may be divided into two teams with every other row being members of a different team. The object is for the team to get the balloon over to a designated goal. Players may hit the balloon only with their fingers.

Games

- *Bowling*

Equipment: Plastic bowling sets (or empty plastic bottles) and playground balls.

Formation: Most rooms will afford some floor space that can be used for bowling games. If the desks are arranged in rows, the aisle space will suffice.

Procedure: The same procedure can be utilized that is suggested for bowling (p. 358).

- *Floor Table Tennis*

Equipment: Table-tennis paddles, balls.

Formation: If no table-tennis table is available, a court of similar size may be marked off on the floor. Players can stand, kneel, or sit depending on the amount of space available and consequent size of the court.

Procedure: The same rules and scoring should be followed as in regular table tennis (p. 365). Some modifications may have to be made due to the change in size of equipment, etc.

Individual and Dual Games

Individual and dual games are those that may be played by one, two, three, or four people. They are sometimes referred to as recreational games since they need so few participants, and once learned they can be played without direct supervision. They are valuable in establishing social experiences and relationships as well as in creating opportunities for skill development. Each player is active all the time.

- *Bowling*

Equipment: Plastic bowling set, regular bowling pins, or Indian clubs. One 8-inch ball. Pins should be set up in triangular fashion with five pins in the back row, three in the next, two in next, and one in the front. A space just as long as the pin should be left between the pins. It is best to mark the floor where the pins will sit, or to mark an oilcloth or paper and set pins on it. Mark a starting line 25 feet from the head pin.

Players: Two to five players.

Procedure: Each person rolls the ball in turn at the pins. If he hits all of them down on the first try he marks his score 10. If not, he gets a second ball to try to hit the remaining pins. The total number of pins knocked down on the two attempts is then recorded. The winner is the player who has the highest total after ten turns. One person is appointed pinsetter, but after the first person has bowled he becomes the pinsetter, and the responsibility continues to be rotated. Children should be encouraged to place the ball on floor as it is released instead of throwing or dropping it down hard. A cardboard may be placed behind pins so they do not fly so far.

Variation: Any number of trials may be allowed depending on the skill level.

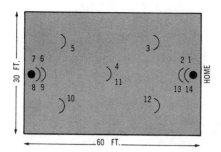

Figure 13-24 Croquet.

• *Croquet (Figure 13-24)*

Equipment: Croquet set; wickets set out as in diagram.

Procedure: Players decide on playing order. Object of the game is for a player to hit his ball through each wicket around the course and be the first to reach the home goal or stake. Players alternate turns. Each gets one hit in turn, and an additional hit each time his ball goes through a wicket. If player can hit his opponent's ball, he gets two bonus shots. One of these may be used to hit his opponent's ball out of the way. This is done by the hitter's placing both balls side by side and then putting a foot on his ball so that it may remain in place as the mallet hits it; the resulting force drives the other ball away.

Variations: The first player returning his ball to the home goal or stake may be termed "poison" after he hits the stake. Following his regular turn he may then try to hit other players' balls and thus eliminate them from the game. If four or six are playing together, teams may be formed in which all play strategically in order to get one member of the team home and "poison."

• *Deck Tennis*

Equipment: One deck-tennis ring. Court 25 feet by 50 feet. Net 5 feet.

Players: Game may be played as singles (two players) or as doubles, (four players).

Procedure: The object of the game is for one player or team to keep the ring going back and forth across the net and to try to throw the ring so the opponent will miss it. The game is started with a service by one player from behind his base line (from the right side of the court). He must deliver the ball with a forehand delivery in an upward fashion to the diagonally opposite half of the court. If the server or his teammate makes a point, the server continues to serve from the left side of the court. Server continues to alternate serving from right to left court until his side makes an error or a foul. In doubles, his partner than has a term of service, and in singles the serve goes to his opponent.

Scoring: The serving side scores a point whenever the receiving side makes an error or a foul. No point is scored if the serving side errs or fouls; the serve is won by the opponents. A game is won by the first team to win 15 points. If the score is tied at 14, one team must get two successive points to win. A time limit may be set, and the team with the most points at the end of it is the winner.

Fouls:

1. Catching the ring with two hands.
2. Changing ring from the catching hand in order to throw with the other.
3. Making a downward stroke with the ring.
4. Causing the ring to land outside the boundary lines.
5. Stepping over the line when serving.

- ### Four Square (Figure 13-25)

Equipment: Volleyball or 8½-inch playground ball. Court as diagramed.

Players: Four. Additional players may rotate into game and wait at points marked X on the diagram.

Procedure: The object of the game is to stay in square A (or move there and remain as long as possible). The ball is put into play by the player in square A who drops the ball, then hits it underhand from the bounce into one of the other courts. He must stand behind the diagonal service line. The game continues, each player hits the ball off the first bounce as it comes into his court. It may be redirected to any of the courts. The object, though, is to get the player in A to move down. If a player errors or fouls, play ceases and that player moves down to square D or to the end of the waiting line. All other players move up one square, or the first person in the waiting line moves into square D. The ball is again served by the player in square A.

Fouls:

1. Failing to return the ball to another square. Balls hitting lines are considered fouls.
2. Stepping on or over the service line when serving or the inner court lines during the game.
3. Striking ball with first or letting ball hit anything but hands.
4. Hitting ball overhand or carrying ball in the volley.

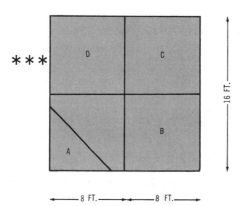

Figure 13-25 Four Square.

- ### Handball (Figure 13-26)

Equipment: One tennis ball, small rubber ball, or handball.

Players: Singles, two players; doubles, four players; or three may play, each against the other.

Procedure: The object of the game is for one player to hit the ball against the wall and have it rebound into the court area in order to cause the opponents to error or foul in trying to return it to the wall. The server, while standing in the front of the service line, drops the ball and hits it with the palm of his hand so that it hits the wall and rebounds into the court area behind the service line. The receiver then tries to hit the ball so it will hit the wall and rebound back anywhere in the court. The receiver may hit the ball on the fly or off the first bounce. Play continues with server and opponent alternating hits until an error or foul is made. The server receives a point if the receiving side is at fault. If the server is at fault it is called a "handout" and the serve goes to the opponent. When three are playing the server must play every other ball. When serving he alternates his serve with the opponents'. After a handout the players rotate on the court counterclockwise for the serve. In doubles the ball must be hit alternately by a member from each team. The server has two trials to make a good serve.

Scoring: The serving team scores a point when a foul or error is committed. The receiving team wins the serve when a handout is made. Twenty-one points constitute a game.

Fouls:

1. The server must have the service rebound beyond the service line or it is short. He receives a second trial if the serve is short. The ball must rebound within the lines of the court. A ball landing on a line is considered good.
2. The ball must be hit alternately by members of each team in doubles.
3. The ball may be hit with one hand only and may not touch any other part of the body.
4. The ball may be hit in the air or after the first bounce. The receiver may not stand in front of the service line when waiting for a serve.
5. If a player intentionally interferes with an opponent, a foul is called.
6. If the interference is unavoidable, the point is replayed.

Teaching Hints: This game may be considered a lead-up game for tennis. If it is treated as such, tennis terms and scoring may be stressed from the start.

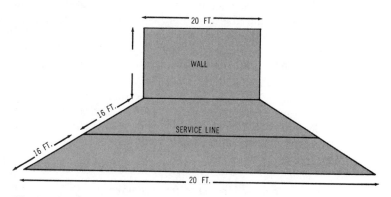

Figure 13-26 Handball.

Figure 13-27 Hopscotch.

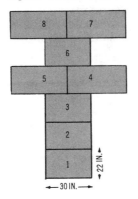

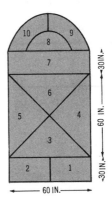

- *Hopscotch (Figure 13-27)*

Equipment: Stone, checker, button, or penny for each player.

Procedure: There are a great many forms of this game. The general rules are presented here along with a few variations. Just a few of the many styles of courts are diagramed. Players determine the playing order. In turn each player tosses his stone into space 1. He then hops into the first space, picks up the stone, and hops back to the starting space. He repeats this, going as far as he can until an error is made. Neither the stone nor a foot may touch a line. If a player loses balance and touches any part of his body to the ground, an error is declared, and the turn is over. The winner is the one who goes through the whole sequence with the fewest misses.

Variations:

1. Some games demand that the player kick the stone back to the starting place rather than carry it back.
2. Certain squares may be designated on which both feet may be placed.

- *Horseshoes*

Equipment: For outside use where there is plenty of space, regulation metal horseshoes may be used. For beginners where the space surrounding the pits may be small in area, hard rubber shoes should be used. Indoor sets of rubber stakes and shoes may be secured; four shoes and two stakes are required for each game. Stakes set 30 feet apart.

Players: Two or four.

Procedure: In singles, both players alternate turns, each throwing both shoes at a turn. In doubles, one player from each team is at each end. Play starts at one end with players from opposite teams alternating turns. The object is to get the shoe over the stake or as near to the stake as possible while standing at the stake 30 feet away.

Scoring:

1. 1 point—Horseshoe nearest stake.
2. 2 points—Both shoes of one player nearer to the stake than either of his opponent's shoes.

3. 3 points—Ringer (the horseshoe must encircle the stake far enough to permit a stick or ruler to touch both ends of the shoes and still clear the stake).
4. Game score for singles is 21 points; for doubles, 50 points.

Fouls:

1. When throwing, the instep of the rear foot must not be farther forward than the stake. If it is, the position of the thrown shoe is disregarded for scoring.
2. Shoes that are hit and displaced by an opponent's shoe are scored where they finally rest. Displaced ringers are not counted as ringers.

• *Jacks*

Equipment: A set of jacks, one small rubber ball, and a smooth surface.

Players: Two or more.

Procedure: A player throws the jacks out on the playing area. He then tosses the ball into the air, and with the same hand, he reaches out, picks up one jack, and catches the ball after it has bounced once. The jack is put in the other hand. Each jack is picked up in this fashion. After these are picked up successfully, two at a time are picked up, then three, and so on until all have been picked up at one time. When a player makes an error or foul he relinquishes his turn to the next player. Upon starting again, he must start at the beginning of the set where he made the error.

Fouls:

1. Touching a jack other than the one that is supposed to be picked up.
2. Dropping the jacks or ball.
3. Failing to catch ball on first bounce.
4. Switching hands to catch the ball.
5. Failing to pick up the correct number of jacks.

Variations: There are a great number of variations at local schools or playgrounds. Ball may be caught before it bounces once. Jacks must be transferred to other hand before ball is caught. Toss ball up, throw jacks down, catch ball in right hand. Throw ball up, pick up all jacks, catch ball in same hand.

• *Marbles*

Equipment: One marble and one shooter for each player. Ring 6 feet in diameter drawn on smooth but not too hard playing surface.

Players: Two to six.

Procedure: Each player puts one or two marbles in the center of the circle. The playing order is established by all "lagging" or throwing their shooter toward a line. The players shoot in order of closest to the line first. The first player shoots his shooter or "taw" from the edge of the circle and tries to knock a marble out of the ring. If he is successful he keeps that marble and shoots again. He continues as long as he knocks marbles out of the ring and his taw stays in the ring, or until he commits a foul. The players play in order. Whoever has the most marbles at the end of the game or playing time wins. Marbles are given back to their owners.

Fouls:

1. Failure to have the knuckles in contact with the playing surface when the taw is shot.
2. Taw leaves ring.

• *Shuffleboard (Figure 13-28)*

Equipment: Eight discs, two cues for singles, four for doubles. Court as diagramed.

Players: Two for singles, four for doubles. If two, each stand at the same end of the court and shoot together. If four, one from each team stands at opposite ends.

Procedure: The object of the game is to push one's discs into the scoring areas and at the same time try to knock out opponent's discs. Once a disc is in scoring position, it is wise to place another disc in front of it for protection. Discs are shot from within the 10-off area. Players shoot discs alternately until all are shot. Then they walk to the other end and count the score. Any disc touching a line is not counted. In singles, the two players then shoot the discs back to the other end. In doubles, it is not necessary for players to go to the other end to count, since partners may do this. If a disc is hit into the 10-off zone, 10 points is deducted from the score. Game score of 50, 75, or 100 should be declared before the game starts.

Teaching Hints: Players should be taught to place cue directly against discs and then push forward gently. There is a tendency for beginners to bring the cue back and hit the disc, thereby hindering control and accuracy.

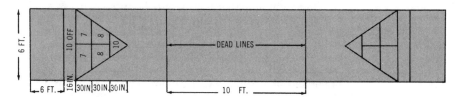

Figure 13-28 Shuffleboard.

• *Sidewalk Tennis (Figure 13-29)*

Equipment: One tennis ball or other small rubber ball.

Players: Singles, two people; doubles, four people.

Procedure: The object of the game is to bat the ball back and forth across the net line with the palm of the hand until someone makes an error or a foul and a score is made. Players stand where S is indicated in the diagram. Play is started by one of the players who serves the ball with the flat of the hand across the net line into the area in front of the base line. After the ball has bounced, his opponent returns the ball over the net line. On the return the ball may be hit while in the air or on the first bounce.

Scoring: A point is scored only by the server. When an error is made or a foul is committed, either a point is given the scorer or the receiver wins the serve.

Figure 13-29 Sidewalk Tennis.

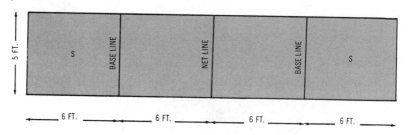

In doubles each side has two turns of service. A server continues to serve until he makes an error or foul. Game is 15 points. If the score is tied at 14-all, one person must make two consecutive points to win.

Fouls:

1. Hitting the ball with any part of hand or body but the palm.
2. Stepping over base line to serve.
3. Any ball that lands outside of the lines.

Variation: The game lines may be squares of a sidewalk. Lines may be painted or marked in chalk on blacktop or gym floor or drawn in sand. A larger ball may be utilized; however, in this case the court should be larger.

- ### *Table Tennis*

Equipment: Table-tennis table, a paddle for each player, a table-tennis ball.

Players: Singles, two people; doubles, four people.

Procedures: In singles, play starts with a serve and continues with the opponents alternately playing ball until one player misses the ball, errors, or fouls. In doubles, the serve begins from the server's right-hand court and bounces into the opponent's right-hand court. After the serve, partners alternate playing the ball until there is an error or foul committed. On the serve the ball must bounce on the server's side of the net before crossing the net.

Scoring: A point is awarded to the opponents of the player who errors or fouls. A player serves until 5 points are made. In doubles, the serve then goes to his partner or to the opponents if both partners have served. Twenty-one points constitute a game. If the score becomes 20-all, one team must then make 2 consecutive points to win.

Fouls:

1. Illegal serve—when ball does not bounce on server's side first; when a ball does not go diagonally across to opponent's service court.
2. A ball that is hit before it bounces.
3. Touching hand to table while ball is in play.
4. A ball that is hit off table or hits on receiver's side during rally.

Variation: A progressive game with many players may be played. Each player hits the ball, then lays paddle on table; the next person must pick it up and play the next ball. Player drops out if he makes an error or foul. Players must move around table and play on both sides.

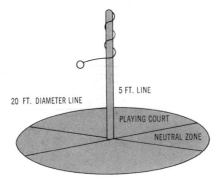

Figure 13-30 Tether Ball.

- *Tether Ball (Figure 13-30)*

Equipment: A pole 10 feet high anchored in the ground firmly or set in movable but stable base. A tether ball hanging from a rope attached to the top of the pole and reaching down 3 feet from the ground. Mark off 20-foot circle as shown in diagram.

Players: Singles, two players; doubles, four players.

Procedures: Players stand on opposite sides of pole. One player starts the game by hitting the ball in either direction all the way around the pole. The object is for either player to get the rope wound around the pole above the 5-foot mark until the ball touches the pole. The first player who succeeds in this wins the game and the winner then starts another game. If a foul is committed, the game is awarded to the opposite player. In doubles, the ball may be hit alternately by each team player or by whoever can hit it. Player who wins four games first wins match.

Fouls:

1. Hitting the ball with any part of the body except hands.
2. Stepping over the neutral zone or court lines.
3. Catching or holding the ball during play.
4. Touching the rope or pole during play.

Variation: A tennis ball and paddles may be substituted for the larger ball and the hands.

- *Volley Tennis*

Equipment: One volleyball, paddle tennis court (p. 451), 3-foot net.

Players: Singles, two players; doubles, four players.

Procedure: The game is started with a serve from the right-hand base line to the serving court diagonally opposite. The ball must be dropped and hit from the bounce. The fist or open palm may be used. The ball is returned anywhere in the court by the receiver. The ball may be hit while in the air or on the first bounce only after the serve is returned off the first bounce. The server continues to serve from alternate courts until he makes an error or a foul. Then the serve goes to the opponent. When the opponent errors or makes a foul the server scores a point. The first side to make 15 points wins the game. If the score is tied at 14-all, one side must make two consecutive points.

Fouls:

1. Failure to hit ball within the service court.
2. Failure to hit ball within the boundary lines.
3. Catching or carrying the ball in hand.
4. Stepping over base line when serving.
5. Allowing ball to hit any part of body but hands.
6. Touching the net or reaching over it to hit a ball.

Variations:

1. With four players the serving side has two terms of service.
2. Ball is hit by whoever is in the best position to hit.
3. The game may be played with six players; however, the court should be enlarged in this situation.

SUGGESTED REFERENCES FOR FURTHER STUDY

CRATTY, BRYANT J., *Active Learning: Games to Enhance Academic Abilities.* Englewood Cliffs, N.J.: Prentice-Hall, Inc., 1971.

————, *Intelligence in Action: Physical Education Activities for Enhancing Intellectual Abilities.* Englewood Cliffs, N.J.: Prentice-Hall, Inc., 1973.

————, *Learning About Human Behavior through Active Games.* Englewood Cliffs, N.J.: Prentice-Hall, Inc., 1975.

"GAMES TEACHING," *Journal of Physical Education and Recreation,* September 1977.

FLENGELMAN, ANDREW, ed., *The New Games Book.* San Francisco: Doubleday-Dolphin, 1976.

HUNT, SARAH E., and ETHEL CAIN, *Games the World Around.* New York: Ronald Press, 1950.

LAWRENCE, CONNIE, and LAYNE C. HACKETT, *Water Learning: A New Adventure.* Palo Alto, Cal.: Peek Publishers, 1975.

MORRIS, G. S. DON, *How to Change the Games Children Play.* Minneapolis: Burgess Publishers, 1976.

ORLICK, TERRY, *The Cooperative Sports and Gamesbook: Challenge with Competition.* New York: Pantheon Books, 1978.

RICHARDSON, HAZEL A., *Games for the Elementary School Grades.* Minneapolis: Burgess Publishers, 1972.

14 / SKILLS AND LEAD-UP GAMES FOR TEAM SPORTS

- General teaching considerations
- Basketball activities
- Basketball skills
- Football activities
- Football skills
- Soccer activities
- Soccer skills
- Softball activities
- Softball skills
- Volleyball activities
- Volleyball skills

As children reach Level III or the third grade and have a good background of understanding and proficiency in the fundamental skills of movement, they are psychologically and physically ready to learn specific sport skill patterns. Their yearly physical education experiences should provide opportunities to combine skill patterns into specific skills demanding the use of a variety of implements and objects.

Because children become acquainted with traditional American sports at an early age, they desire to learn how to play all types of sports and games. Therefore, the school program should include sports and games appropriate to the maturation level of the children involved.

This chapter presents the teacher with a comprehensive study of the skills, concepts, rules, and basic strategies of games which enable children to play the traditional American team sports. The emphasis in this chapter is on a progressive acquisition of these items. A progression chart for each sport precedes the content to be learned. It indicates the developmental order in which skills, rules, knowledges, and focal lead-up games for the grade level should be introduced. These are accumulative, and by the seventh or eighth grade the official sport may be learned. There are usually some modifications of official rules, playing time, and size of playing areas even at the high school level.

A lead-up game is a game that is utilized as an instrument to teach skills, rules, knowledges, appreciation, and strategies of an official sport. It must include at least one skill, rule, and simple team strategy that can be identified with the parent game. Its organization must be such that it offers an opportunity for a team or individual climactic effort such as scoring a goal, or preventing a goal, and redirecting effort to counteract the other team's achievements. These skills, rules, and strategies become more complex as children progress in physical maturity and skill. At the point when children are physically and mentally mature enough to handle official sport rules, the lead-up game they are playing should be almost identical with the parent game so the transition will be simple and smooth. One lead-up game generally is the focal point of each unit of instruction. Playing several games within a unit is sometimes distracting and can lead to confusion. Success and enjoyment of a game at the end of a unit builds enthusiasm for learning a new and more complicated game the following year.

As mentioned earlier, many children participate in sports programs outside school. The teacher should be aware of who these children are and provide relevant learning opportunities for them as well as for the other students. The progressions suggested here assume that the child has not had earlier experience outside the developmental program suggested for the younger children. The teacher should tap into the suggested progression wherever appropriate. This is another example of the need for individualization.

General Teaching Considerations

There are many general considerations common to the teaching of specific sport skills for team or individual sports. When reading the suggestions herein and subsequently selecting and/or designing learning tasks and games, remember the factors that influence readiness for particular manipulative skills (p. 252). *Sequencing* in respect to readiness factors of both maturation and experience is essential (p. 310).

The information given here is background material for the teacher who must apply knowledge gained about methods and techniques and various modalities of organization gathered from preceding chapters.

TEACHING OF SKILLS

1. Most of the sport skills are similar to one another and, of course, are based on basic skill patterns. The teacher should relate characteristics of skills already known to those of the new ones.

2. Skills can be improved only through practice. Skill practice is essential in some form—whether it be drills, skill games, or individual practice.

3. Skills do not have to be perfected before being used in a game, but some prior practice under game conditions should be provided. Game play will indicate practice needs and may motivate additional practice.

4. The cross-reference charts of drills and skill games are designed to improve specific skills. The pages on which the games are described may be found in the index. Many of the active low-organized games may be adapted in order to practice most skills. A chart for each sport precedes descriptions of games for the sports that are not described elsewhere in the book.

5. The skills are analyzed for right-handed players.

6. The teacher should use self-designed games and tasks in addition to those suggested here.

EQUIPMENT AND SPACE

1. For the most part, junior-size equipment should be used in Levels III and IV.

2. Playing areas may be modified to fit the abilities of the group or the space that is available.

3. Equipment should be improvised if what is called for in the game directions is not available.

CLASS PARTICIPATION

1. Every child should have an opportunity to participate in game play. Suggestions for team sizes should be observed as much as possible.

2. Children who must wait for turns should be practicing skills at assigned areas or involved in some other way. Specific arrangements must be made for this.

3. It is usually more efficient to divide the playing space and conduct two games instead of one if large numbers must be accommodated. For example, two games of volleyball on smaller courts with six on each team is much better than one game on an official court with eight to twelve players on each side.

EVALUATION OF SKILLS

1. Skill tests are suggested for each sport. Only skills that have been stressed should be tested.

2. Most skill tests also make good practice tasks.

3. The reader is referred to the *Sports Skill Test Manual* of the American Alliance for Health, Physical Education and Recreation for more extensive tests, detailed instructions, and norms for boys and girls ages 10 through 18 for each specific sport.

TERMINOLOGY

1. Game terms are somewhat synonymous and should be used consistently.

2. Official terms should be used as soon as the rules and concepts are introduced. For example, the terms "violation" and "foul" should be used appropriately whenever an infringement of a rule occurs.

3. The terms "offensive" and "defensive" should be introduced early and used consistently. *Offensive* refers to the team that has the ball or is in the process of attempting to score. *Defensive* refers to the team that does not have the ball and is trying to prevent the other team from scoring.

SELECTING GAMES

1. Although games are suggested which have proven to be satisfactory for children at the level mentioned, each class is different and the teacher must select games carefully. The guidelines suggested for selecting low-organized games should be utilized in the selection of skill and lead-up games.
2. The presentation of too many games within a short period of time is confusing to children and not very productive. Learning to play one game well is better than merely being familiar with three games.
3. Only one, or in some cases two, lead-up games should be played in one time unit. This game is the sport for that grade. Sometimes the lead-up game that was played the year before is played at the start of a unit to refresh memories for rules and skills. Sometimes the focal game for the following year is presented at the very end of the unit as a preview.

EXTRACLASS ACTIVITIES

1. Opportunities to play the games taught in class should be offered in the after-school program in which children may learn to enjoy playing active sports in their leisure time. The class period is an instructional period for everyone. Those who wish it can receive additional help in the voluntary program.
2. The activities of the intramural program should be drawn from those taught in the class. In addition, special-interest clubs may be formed.
3. Students can learn to use strategies and teamwork cooperatively as they play in a more self- or student-directed situation.

RULES

1. The rules of a game should always be enforced. If the game is persistently delayed for infractions and penalties, the rules are probably too difficult for the group or are not well understood and should be modified.
2. Children should be taught to call their own infractions. This is not to say they should officiate and play at the same time. The game moves faster if children hold up their hand when they make an infraction rather than waiting for the teacher to call this. Calling one's own infractions leads to good sportsmanship and a better knowledge of the rules.
3. Older children should be taught (not just assigned) to officiate. This will make them aware of the rules and prevent argument over rules when play is held without teacher supervision.
4. The rules that generally govern the official sports for girls and boys are set by the National Federation of State High School Athletic Associations and are available from The Association, 7 South Dearborn Street, Chicago, Illinois 60603.
5. The rules for the lead-up games are modifications of these rules, and if learned cumulatively, should lead to a knowledge of the official rules.

Basketball is one of the most popular American sports. It is one of the few team sports that originated in the United States. The game was created in 1892 by Dr. James Naismith in Springfield, Massachusetts.

The original game is different from the game played today. Designed for men, the game consisted of teams of nine players who were allowed to throw, bat, and pass in the attempt to get the ball into peach baskets suspended from a gymnasium balcony. The object then, as now, was for one team to make more baskets than the other.

Today boys and girls play in teams of five. Although the rules for each sex differ somewhat, the skills, knowledges, and strategies are similar.

Children seem to be fascinated by the challenge of putting a ball through a basket. The values of the game are many. Most of the skills are not complex and are all based on the fundamental skill patterns of throwing, catching, running, and jumping. Thus vigorous exercise is provided for all the participants. Few players are needed to set up a game, and the equipment is inexpensive and can be improvised.

The skill games and lead-up games suggested for the intermediate grades call for repeated use of simple skills in a controlled situation. Those for the upper grades require faster action and a mingling of players from both teams, and have a greater emphasis on strategy.

Teaching Considerations

1. Soccer balls, 8½-inch playground balls, and volleyballs may be used in the intermediate grades for ball-handling practice and lead-up games.
2. Junior-size basketballs should be used until seventh grade; if necessary at this time the official-size ball may be used.
3. Baskets should be mounted or lowered to a height of 8 feet or less until the seventh grade.
4. Color identification bands are needed for all lead-up games when players from both teams are in the same playing area.

Basketball Skills

Catching

Catching is described and analyzed on page 253. The basic principles of catching should be emphasized when catching is first used in basketball games. As proficiency develops and as the need arises, the following points should be stressed:

1. Move to meet the ball to shorten the distance it has to travel and to cut off the opponent.
2. Draw the ball in toward the body and use this motion as the backswing for a subsequent pass.

Table 14-1. Progression of Skills, Knowledges, Rules, and Lead-up Games for Basketball

SKILLS	KNOWLEDGES AND RULES	LEAD-UP GAME	LEVEL
Catching	Out-of-bounds ball		
Short passes	Line violations		
Chest	Holding ball more		
One-hand	than 5 seconds		
underhand	Traveling		
Bounce	Forwards		
Long passes			
Shoulder or	Guards	End Ball	III
overhand			
Pivot	Scoring field goal		
Reverse turn	Illegal dribble		
Dribble			
Shooting		Basket End Ball	
Unguarded set shots		Six-Court Basketball	III
Free throw	Scoring free throw		
Guarding technique	Use of terms		
Jump for tossed ball	Violation		
Passing on the move	Foul		
Catching on the move	Fouls		
Push shot	Snatching ball		
	Pushing		
	Tie ball	Toss-Up Basketball	IV
Rebound	Defense		
Lay-up shot	Offense	Alley Basketball	
Lead passes	Charging	Modified Basketball	
Cutting	Blocking		
		Sideline Basketball	
		Half-Court Basketball	

Passing

There are a number of passes, and each has specific uses. The distance the ball has to travel and the position in which the ball is caught often determine the choice of the pass. Accuracy is important in passing. All passes are based on the basic throwing patterns described on pages 255–260. The method by which they are adapted for different purposes is described here.

CHEST PASS If the ball is caught at chest height, it can be passed quickly from this position with both hands. The ball is held by the fingers, with the thumbs behind the ball. It is brought slightly downward, then upward, and pushed away from the chest and released with a snap of the wrists and fingers. Elbows should be bent and kept close to the body. The arms are pushed forward from the shoulders as the elbows straighten. More distance can be gained if the knees are bent, a step forward is taken, and the weight is transferred to the forward foot. This is a good pass to use for covering short distances.

1. Holding the ball in palms of hands; prevents quick release of ball.
2. Holding elbows away from body; thus force is lost because movement is all in the forearm.
3. Using little or no wrist or finger snap.
4. Ball is released too high, causing a high looping pass.

TEACHING PHRASES

1. Hold ball with fingers, thumb behind ball.
2. Elbows are in close to body.
3. Bring ball down, around, push upward, and then forward.
4. Snap wrist and fingers as ball is released.
5. Arms follow through toward target.

BOUNCE PASS   This pass may utilize a one- or two-hand overhand, underhand, or chest pass. The new element in this pass is that a bounce is used with the pass so that the ball may bounce into the receiver's hands. The passer must judge the spot where the ball is to bounce according to the distance to be covered and the height at which the ball is to be received. For beginners, it is helpful to suggest that the ball should strike the floor three-fourths of the distance from the passer to the receiver if it is to be caught at waist height.

COMMON FAULT   Actually bouncing ball downward rather than throwing it forward.

KEY TEACHING PHRASES

1. Bounce the ball at a point three-fourths of the way to the target.
2. Reach out as ball is thrown.

ONE-HAND UNDERHAND PASS   This pass utilizes the underhand throwing pattern (p. 258). Since the ball is large, the left hand is put on top of the ball to steady it when the ball is brought back by the right hand and arm; however, it is removed as the ball is brought forward. Only the right hand and arm follow through toward the target as the ball is released. This is a good pass for a short hand-off play on the move in advanced games in which several opponents are in the same area.

SHOULDER PASS   This pass utilizes the overhead throwing pattern (p. 255). Since the ball is large, the left hand is placed on top of the ball in the backswing as a steadying agent; however, it is removed as the ball is brought forward. Although long passes are not particularly encouraged in basketball, passes of varying distances are often necessary. Scoring passes in End Ball are usually shoulder passes.

Dribbling

Dribbling is a legal way for a player to move with the ball. The ball is bounced repeatedly; impetus is given to the ball after each bounce and the ball is not allowed to rest or to be caught in one or both hands between bounces. The bounce is controlled with the fingers and wrist actions. It must be pushed so that it strikes the floor at an angle from which it will rebound up to the player the desired distance the player wishes to move. The bounces should be low. This skill can be learned prior to its use in actual basketball-type games.

COMMON FAULTS

1. Using the flat of the hand to slap the ball rather than using fingertips to push it.
2. Bouncing ball too high so that it gets away from player as he or she moves.
3. Carrying ball because the hand is put underneath ball between dribbles.

KEY TEACHING PHRASES

1. Push ball with fingertips.
2. Use wrist to control bounce.
3. Keep ball below the waist.
4. Push ball forward slightly.

Shooting

The basic patterns for basket shooting are those of throwing. According to the height of the basket, adjustments must be made in the angle of release of the ball and in the force required to send it to the basket. The various shots are described in order of difficulty.

TWO-HAND UNDERHAND SHOT This is one of the easiest shots for children to make because the underhand motion allows for a big backswing, has the assistance of the strong leg muscles for additional force, and makes possible greater accuracy than any other shot. The ball is held high in front of the body; the fingers of both hands are under the ball and the thumbs are pointing upward so that the rim of the basket can be seen over the ball. The knees are bent and the ball is brought down between the legs, then upward as the knees straighten. The ball is released when the arms are fully extended in the direction of the basket. The follow-through should be high in the direction of the basket.

ONE-HAND PUSH SHOT The ball is balanced by the fingers of the shooting hand and partially supported from underneath by the other hand (Figure 14-1). The ball is brought up to and in line with the shoulder of the shooting hand. In this position the elbows are bent. As the ball is released, the shooting arm is extended upward and toward the basket. The wrist flexes as the fingers guide the ball. The follow-through is high and toward the basket. The amount of knee bend and subsequent extension attending the shot is dependent upon the distance from the basket. A jump from the floor should be encouraged. The shot is difficult to guard, since it starts high and can be released quickly. This shot can be executed after a two-foot jump into the air (jump shot) and thereby becomes even more difficult to guard.

TWO-HAND SET OR CHEST SHOT This shot is like the chest pass, but the angle of release is different. The ball is brought upward and released when the arms are fully extended toward a point above but in line with the basket. Because the distance to the basket will be greater than that for which a chest pass is used, more flexion and extension of the body is required than in the pass.

Figure 14-1 One-hand push shot.

— — — AIM

- - - - PATH OF BALL

LAY-UP SHOT The mechanics of the lay-up shot are similar to the one-hand push shot, but the ball is aimed at the backboard so it can rebound into the basket. Most commonly, a player approaches the basket from the side with a dribble or receives a pass from a teammate as he is running. In either event, as he jumps high in the air, the ball is brought to a position off the shoulder of the shooting hand. With the arm fully extended, the player pushes the ball, guiding with the fingers to a spot on the backboard. The jump is started with a takeoff from the foot of the nonthrowing side. The step pattern is a *step* and a *hop* high into the air. Children should practice the shot without the jump first so they get an idea of where on the backboard the ball must hit in order to fall into the basket.

COMMON FAULTS

1. Failure to bring ball up high off the bounce.
2. Stopping, then shooting.
3. Failure to extend arm fully and to release ball as high as possible.

KEY TEACHING PHRASES

1. Eyes on basket.
2. Jump and reach.
3. Lay ball against backboard.
4. Guide ball with fingers.

GENERAL CONCEPTS ABOUT SHOOTING

1. Obtain balance before attempting a shot.
2. Use fingers to hold ball and let ball roll from fingertips.
3. Bend knees and thrust body upward when more strength is needed for long shots.
4. Aim for farthest rim of basket or for the backboard.
5. Reach way up and out with arms so that the ball has an arch and will fall down into basket.
6. Do not shoot when directly under the basket. Pass to a teammate, or pivot and dribble out.

Individual Tactics

BODY CONTROL   Since basketball is a very fast game with many quick stops, starts, jumps, and changes of direction, body control is essential for every player. Many of the skills and techniques are studied in the primary grades, but as children grow older and develop more control, the same skills must be practiced in relation to the demands of the game being played.

Reverse Turn and Pivot   These skills are analyzed on page 243, and suggestions are made for practice on page 244. These two basic skills are used in every game for changing direction. The pivot is an essential maneuver in both offensive and defensive play.

Stopping   Regaining balance without taking steps is vital to retaining possession of the ball and in gaining position in basketball. Stopping is analyzed on page 242. The skip stop, for which a hop and a step are taken as the player stops, puts one in the best position for subsequent action. Children can learn this easily from skipping and stopping, then running and taking one skip and stopping.

Dodging   This is a technique used to evade an opponent. It is analyzed on page 244.

OFFENSIVE TACTICS

Passing and Catching on the Move   Because basketball is a very fast game, and the fastest way to move the ball is to pass it, a player will frequently receive the ball and pass it while running. A moving player is much more difficult to guard than a stationary player. Any pass may be made while the player is on the move, but the choice of pass is usually made on the basis of the position of the ball. If the ball is caught low as a result of a pass or a bounce, it would be inefficient to bring it up high to initiate a subsequent pass.

Children should be taught to catch a ball and make the absorption phase of bringing the ball in toward the body the backswing for the next pass. They should be taught to be alert and to throw to a player at chest level.

Lead Passes   Passes should either be passed ahead of a player or to his non-guarded side rather than directly at him unless he is absolutely unguarded and the pass is fast and direct. Although a guard is not normally in front of a player, he can easily step in front of that player by the time the ball arrives.

Cutting   This is an evasive technique a player uses to get into position to receive a pass or to shoot. He watches his teammate who has the ball, and when this player is ready to pass, he breaks for an open spot toward the basket. The pass should reach the open spot at the same time as the person who has cut. Frequently, a player will make a short pass to a teammate and immediately cut toward the basket. Speed in moving and a quick change in direction are aids to misleading opponents as to the intended direction of the cut.

DEFENSIVE TACTICS

Guarding   For the simpler lead-up games in which opponents do not play in the same area, guarding is a matter of jumping high and intercepting passes. Children should learn to keep their eyes on the ball. When two people are in the same area, the emphasis changes. The usual practice in basketball is to stay between the person one is guarding and the basket. The guarding stance is taken with feet spread, arms outstretched to the side, with one arm up and one down. A guard stays between the basket and on the inside-basket side of his opponent when he does not have the ball. The knees are slightly bent, weight slightly forward on the balls of the feet. The player is ready to move in any direction; eyes are on the ball and the opponent. If the opponent moves, the guard adjusts position with a sliding step and tries to cut off the opponent's path to the basket.

When the opponent receives the ball, the guard moves within 2 or 3 feet of him and assumes the same ready stance, then tries to deflect the ball from the opponent's hands or to deflect the pass. Frequently, beginners will want to face their opponent, whether that person is facing the basket or not. They also become overly concerned with chasing an opponent. They must understand that by staying between the basket and their opponent and by using a sliding step, they have less distance to cover and will be in a better defensive position. Since approximately 90 percent of the goals that are made are shot within an 18-foot radius of the basket, it is important for guards to cover this area rather than to be drawn out toward the center of the court.

Jump for Toss-Up   Many lead-up games are started with a toss-up between a player from each team. When two opposing players tie a ball or both cause a ball to go out of bounds at the same time, a toss-up occurs. The two opposing players stand with side to side, each facing his or her own basket. The ball is tossed up between the two players. Each should jump and reach to tap the ball to a teammate. The jump should be made when the ball reaches its highest point. While waiting, eyes must be kept on the ball, weight low and on balls of feet, knees flexed, and elbows flexed. At the right moment, the arms are brought forward and upward, feet push off from the floor, and the whole body stretches and reaches to tap the ball. The jump and return to the floor must be vertical so players do not fall into each other, thereby causing a foul and possible injury.

Rebounding   This is a jumping and positioning tactic for getting possession of the ball after it has bounced off the backboard or rim of the basket. Usually the ball will rebound at the same angle it hit. It is an advanced skill to be able to time the jump and be in the right spot to get the ball. At an early stage, children should be taught to get into position for the rebound as soon as a ball is shot and to jump and reach for the ball.

OFFENSIVE CONCEPTS

1. All players must have a constant awareness of their teammates' positions.
2. All players should be alert to chances to cut into empty spaces.
3. Players should cut following their pass.
4. When the ball is secured under the other team's basket, the ball should be brought up court quickly. Passes in front of the basket should be avoided and the ball played toward the side line.
5. Generally, the same player should always take the ball out under the basket in order to put the ball into play quickly.
6. Short passes are generally more successful than long ones.
7. Dribbling should be used only when a pass is a poor risk.
8. Players should *run* to become free.

DEFENSIVE CONCEPTS

1. Most of the guarding efforts should be concentrated in a semi-circle from the free-throw line back (toward the basket), since few goals are made from a distance beyond that.
2. Every player should know whom he or she is guarding.
3. At least one guard should always stay back to guard the vulnerable space near the basket.
4. Guards should stay between the basket and the player they are guarding.
5. Guards should *slide* to stay with their opponent.

Skill Games to Improve Basketball Skills

• *Odd and Even*

Equipment: Two balls.

Formation: Circle, players numbered around circle by ones and twos.

Procedure: Balls are started anywhere in the circle. Ones throw in sequence to each other; twos do the same. When the ball returns to the person who started, he shouts "Odds" ("Evens"), and all players on that team sit down. The first team to sit down wins.

Variations:

1. Balls can be started in opposite directions.
2. Balls can be started side by side; however, this may cause confusion as to whom they belong unless different-colored balls are used.

• *Ten Trips*

Equipment: One ball for every three players.

Formation: Players are in sets of three. Number 1 stands midway between 2 and 3, who are about 25 feet apart.

Procedure: Several sets compete against each other. A trip for the ball consists of 1 throwing to 2, who throws a long pass to 3, who throws it to 1. Each time 1 receives the ball he counts aloud then starts the ball on another trip. When the count reaches 10, the team sits down. The first set to complete ten trips wins.

Variation: Vary the style of passes used for the short passes.

Table 14-2. Skill Game Guide for Practicing Basketball

| | SKILLS | | | | | | | | |
SKILL GAMES	CATCHING	PASSING	SHOOTING	PIVOTING	GUARDING	DRIBBLING	DODGING	STOPPING	STARTING
Odd and Even	x	x							
Ten Trips	x	x							
Center Miss Ball	x	x							
Tally Ball	x	x			x		x	x	x
Leader and Class	x	x							
Center Touch Ball	x	x							
Tadpole	x	x							
Gap Ball	x	x							
Boundary Ball	x	x			x				
Poison Ball	x	x							
Corner Spry	x	x							
Star Relay	x	x		x					
Maze Relay						x			
Dribble Up, Throw Back	x	x				x			
Red Light							x	x	x
Stop and Go							x	x	x
Mirror Game				x			x	x	x
Around the World			x						
Twenty-One			x						
Pig (or Horse)			x						
Guard Ball	x	x			x		x		
Keep-Away	x	x		x	x				

- *Center Miss Ball*

Equipment: Two balls for each circle.

Formation: Single circle, leader in center.

Procedure: The leader has one ball, the person in the circle has the other. On signal, the player in the circle passes to the leader, and at the same time the leader passes to person who is standing to the right of the circle passer. If the leader misses or fumbles the ball, he or she exchanges places with the person who last threw the ball. If the pass was poor, the leader is allowed to remain in the center.

Variation: Vary the style of passes used.

• Tally Ball

Equipment: One ball. Colored pinnies.

Formation: Teams of six, both on one half of a basketball court.

Procedure: Ball is given to one team out of bounds at the center line. Team in possession of the ball tries to complete six consecutive passes. Each time a pass is completed the person who catches it calls out the number of completions so far. When six consecutive passes have been made, the last person may walk to the free-throw line and try for a basket. One point is awarded for six passes, two for each successful free throw. Players from the opposite team attempt to intercept passes. After the attempt for basket is made, the ball is put in play by the opposite team at the free-throw line. The winner is the team that has the most points at the end of a specified period of time.

Violations:

1. Walking with the ball.
2. Holding ball more than 3 seconds.
3. Batting ball from opponent's hand.
4. Pushing or holding an opponent.

Penalty: Free pass in from side lines given to opponents.

Variations: The whole court may be used, and four players from each team may be on each end of the court. They are designated as forwards at one end and guards at the other. The forwards try to tally the points, the guards try to intercept passes and throw the ball down to their forwards at the opposite end of the court.

• Mirror Game

Equipment: None.

Formation: Leader, everyone else scattered about room facing the leader.

Procedure: Leader makes sliding movements—forward, backward, sideward, moving arms up or down. Everyone else tries to match the movements of the leader. After a specified time, the leader may select someone to take his place.

Variation: The same thing may be done with couples, each taking turns being the leaders.

• Around the World

Equipment: One ball for each player.

Formation: Mark six circles at varying spots around the basket. Put a number in each circle.

Procedure: One child stands in each circle and attempts to make a basket. When he does he moves on to the next circle in order. If someone else is in that circle, he or she takes turns shooting. The first one to go "around the world," or to make a basket from each circle, is the winner. Each successive circle should present a slightly different challenge as far as distance and angle are concerned.

- ### *Twenty-One*

Equipment: One ball for each playing group.

Formation: Small groups of four to six, each given a number for shooting order.

Procedure: In turn each player shoots one ball from behind the free-throw line. If made, the shot counts 2 points. The player retrieves his own ball and tries a second shot from wherever the ball is recovered. If made, the shot counts 1 point. The first person to reach a total of 21 points wins. The total required may be altered.

- ### *Pig (or Horse)*

Equipment: One ball for each playing group.

Formation: Small groups of four to six, each given a number for shooting order.

Procedure: The first player may shoot from wherever he wishes with whatever type of shot he wishes. If the shot is made, the next player must attempt the same style shot from the same place. If the shot is missed, the player receives the first letter of the name of the game, P (or H). Then the next player may choose his style of shot and place to shoot from. As long as the shot is made, the player who follows must attempt a shot of the same style and from the same place or receive a letter. When one completes the name of the game he is eliminated or the game starts over.

- ### *Keep-Away*

Equipment: One ball for each playing group, color bands.

Formation: Small teams of three or four.

Procedure: The ball is given to one team, which tries to keep possession of it by passing it back and forth between teammates. The other team tries to gain possession of the ball by intercepting passes. Play continues for a specified length of time.

Violations:

1. Holding the ball for more than 3 seconds.
2. Pushing or holding another player.
3. Taking steps while in possession of ball.

Penalty: Opposite team is given the ball.

Variations: A point may be awarded to a team each time its members intercept a pass.

Basketball Lead-Up Games

- ### *End Ball (Figure 14-2)*

Area: Volleyball or basketball court divided in half. A line is drawn approximately 5 feet from each end line to form two end zones. Two teams of equal size. Half the players are designated as forwards and are placed in the end zone. The other half are guards and are placed in the zone farthest from their own end zone.

Figure 14-2 End Ball.

AF	BG	BG	AG	AG	BF
AF					BF
AF	BG	BG	AG	AG	BF
AF					BF
AF	BG	BG	AG	AG	BF
					BF

Procedure: The ball is given to any guard on the court; he tries to pass over the heads of the opposing team to one of his own forwards. If the ball is caught by a forward, 2 points are scored. (If the opposing guards intercept, they attempt to pass to their forwards.) After the score, the ball is given to the opposing guards. The game may be played for any period of time. Forwards and guards should be rotated several times during the playing period.

Violations:
   1. Stepping out of assigned area.
   2. Walking with the ball.
   3. Holding the ball more than 5 seconds.

Penalty: Ball is given to opposing guards.

   • ***Basket End Ball***

The rules for End Ball are followed with these exceptions:
   1. All players may use the unlimited dribble within their own area.
   2. After a forward catches the ball and 2 points are made, he may shoot for goal anywhere within the end zone. If the first attempt is not successful, the ball goes to the opposing guards. Two points are given for a successful field goal.

   • ***Six-Court Basketball (Figure 14-3)***

The rules for Basket End Ball are followed except that:
   1. Two additional lines are added to the court markings.
   2. A line of guards from one team is between the two lines of guards from opposing teams. Therefore, more interceptions and quicker passes are possible.

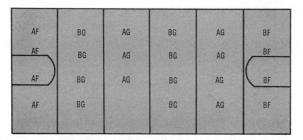

Figure 14-3 Six-Court Basketball.

Figure 14-4 Toss-Up Basketball.

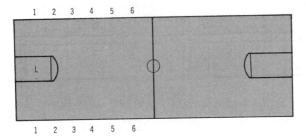

- *Toss-Up Basketball (Figure 14-4)*

Area: Half of a basketball court (allows two games on one court). Two teams of six to eight players arranged along each side line and numbered consecutively.

Procedure: The leader stands with the ball under the basket. A number is called, and the ball is rolled, bounced, or tossed up between the two teams. Players with the called number scramble for the ball. The player who gains possession of it must complete two passes with his own side-line players before shooting. After a shot for goal, the ball is dead and another number is called.

Violations:

1. Traveling.
2. Shooting before two or more passes have been made.
3. Illegal dribble.
4. Ball out of bounds.

Penalty: Ball is put in play by a side-line player of the opposing team.

Fouls:

1. Snatching ball from opponent.
2. Personal contact.

Penalty: One free throw—distance may be modified in relation to size and ability of class. Ball is dead and play resumes with leader calling another number.

Variations:

1. Increase the number of players on the court to four, two from each team.
2. Rebounding may be added.
3. A full court may be used.
4. Alternate positions of teams on each side line to allow for passes to either side.
5. Alternate boys and girls on each side so when numbers are called, boys will be playing opposite boys, and girls opposite girls.

- *Alley Basketball (Figure 14-5)*

Area: Regulation basketball court divided into three alleys lengthwise. The center alley is narrower than the outside lanes. A player from each team is

Figure 14-5 Alley Basketball.

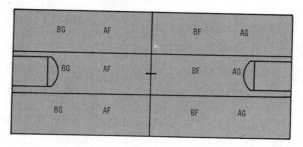

assigned to each alley. Players in the three lanes nearest their own basket are forwards; those nearest opponents' basket are guards. There should be six players on each team.

Playing Time: Two halves of equal length (6 to 8 minutes).

Procedure: Game is started with a jump ball, after which the players advance ball toward their own basket by passing and use of the dribble. Only forwards may shoot. After a field goal is made and 2 points awarded, ball is put into play under the basket by a center forward of the team not making the score. The center forward takes the free throw when a foul occurs; one point is awarded if made. Whether made or missed, the ball is put into play at the side opposite the free-throw line by a side-alley forward. Players of scoring team rotate clockwise one alley after each score is made.

Violations:

1. Stepping on or over a boundary line.
2. Traveling.
3. Illegal dribble (catching ball between bounce and pushing it with two hands).
4. Holding ball in play more than 3 seconds.

Penalty: Out of bounds at the side line for opposing team.

Fouls:

1. Snatching ball from opponent.
2. Personal contact.

Penalty: A free throw for opponents; 1 point if successful.

Variations:

1. Number of players may be increased by adding players on side lines. These players take the out-of-bounds balls. Players on court may pass to side-line players to advance ball toward basket.
2. Court may be divided into nine areas by making two lines widthwise, thereby increasing the number of players who may play at one time. The same rules can be followed as when using six courts.

- *Modified Basketball (Figure 14-6)*

Area: Court with markings as indicated in diagram.

Players: A team consists of five players with positions designated as a center, two forwards, and two guards. All players may shoot for the basket. Guards

Figure 14-6 Modified Basketball.

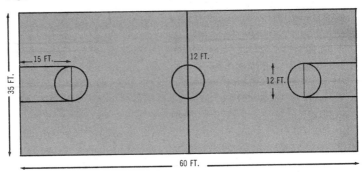

are designated as defensive players, all others as offensive players. Each team shoots at one goal and guards the other. Players may range all over the court.

Playing Time: Four quarters (6 to 8 minutes). Teams change ends of court at half time.

Procedure: Game is started with a jump between the centers from each team in the center circle. Centers may not touch the ball again until it has touched the floor or has been touched by another player. Each team tries either to advance the ball toward its own goal or to gain possession of the ball and then advance it to the goal. The ball may be passed or dribbled in order to advance it. After a field goal is made, the ball is put in play behind the end line by one of the opponents. After a foul is made, a free throw is given the player who was fouled. The other players line up on both sides of the free-throw lane in an alternate fashion. If the free throw is made, one point is awarded, and the ball is taken out under the basket by the opponents. If the free throw is missed and rebounds into the playing area, it is once again in play. If two opposing players gain possession of the ball simultaneously, a *tie ball* is called, and a jump is taken in the nearest restraining circle.

Violations:

  1. Stepping on or over the boundary lines while in possession of the ball.
  2. Traveling with the ball.
  3. Double dribble.
  4. Causing the ball to go out of bounds.
  5. Kicking the ball or striking it with the fist.
  6. Stepping into the restraining circle before the ball is tapped.
  7. Stepping over the free-throw line and lane lines before the ball hits the rim of the basket.

Penalty: Out of bounds for the other team at the side line.

Fouls:

  1. Personal fouls are those in which a player makes body contact with an opponent.
  2. Technical fouls are those in which a player commits an unsportsmanlike act or delays the game.

3. If a player accumulates five fouls during the game he is disqualified from play. One technical foul for unsportsmanlike conduct may disqualify the player if the official decrees it.

Penalty: A free throw is awarded to the player fouled or to any member of the opposing team in the case of a technical foul. A player who is fouled in the act of shooting receives two free throws if the goal is missed.

Scoring: 2 points for each field goal; 1 point for each free throw.

• Half-Court Basketball

Area: One half of a basketball court is utilized for each game. Thus two games may be conducted at one time. The free-throw line is extended all the way across the court. Both teams shoot at the same basket.

Procedure: The same rules are followed as in regular modified basketball, with the exception that the team that gains possession of the ball must throw the ball to a team member behind the restraining line before it can be passed in for a shot at the basket.

• Side-Line Basketball

Area: The same areas as used in regular modified basketball. Teams are doubled in number.

Procedure: The same rules are followed as in regular basketball. Half the players are stationed along the sideline. The ball may be passed to these players and they play all out-of-bound balls. The side-line players may not shoot for the basket. After 5 minutes of playing time, the side-line players change positions with the court players. This is repeated several times. This game is good to use with boys and girls, particularly when only one court is available. It may also be used for a co-recreational game. A team is composed of ten players (five girls and five boys). The two sexes alternate on the side line and in the court. Girls play their rules and boys theirs when they are on the court. The score is added to see which team has won; but the boys and girls never directly compete against each other.

Skill Tests

WALL PASS TEST A target 6 feet wide, 4 feet high, and 3 feet from the floor is drawn on the wall. A restraining line 4 feet from the wall and parallel to it is drawn on the floor. The subject must throw the ball against the wall repeatedly as many times as he can in 20 seconds. The ball must go in the target area, but need not be caught to be successful. The score is the total number of passes that hit the target area when thrown from behind the restraining line. Two trials are given and the best of the two scores is recorded.

SET SHOT SHOOTING A mark is made on the floor directly in front of the basket and 10 feet from it. (The distance may vary for different grade levels.) The subject shoots fifteen shots from behind this line. The score is the number of goals made from behind the line.

DRIBBLE TEST Six chairs are set in a line with a distance of 8 feet between them, and a line is drawn 10 feet from the first chair. The subject starts from behind the line on the signal "Go" and dribbles the ball going to the left of the first chair, to the right of the second, and continues to weave in and out down the line and back. A stopwatch is started on the signal "Go" and is stopped when the subject crosses the finish line. Two trials are given, and the fastest time is recorded.

ONE-MINUTE SHOOTING TEST   The subject stands at the free-throw line. Upon the signal "Go," he shoots for the basket. When he retrieves the ball he may shoot from anywhere. The object is to make as many goals as possible in 1 minute. The player must retrieve his own shots. Two trials are given, and the best of the two is recorded.

Football Activities

Football is a popular American fall sport. Official football is a contact sport and as such has been considered a male game; however there are some female football teams. In the elementary school, games are played in which no body contact is involved. Most girls enjoy Flag Football as much as boys do.

Some boys in the upper grades are involved with football leagues organized by groups outside school. Tackle football is not recommended for younger boys. It is particularly important that children know the basic skills well and learn satisfying games that do not involve contact so that their unsponsored after-school play will be safe and wholesome.

Ball-handling experiences with a football should be included in the primary grades. The skill patterns of throwing and catching are familiar to children, but much practice is required, since the shape of the ball makes the performance of these skills more difficult in football than in some other sports. Because the strategy and involvement of position responsibility can be quite complicated (even in Flag Football), prior to the sixth grade the games listed are primarily concerned with skill development.

Teaching Considerations

1. Since most children know that official football involves tackling and blocking, they should be taught that when these skills are used proper protective gear is required. They should also be helped to understand that the contact version of the game is for a later age group when the body has the ability to withstand such types of activity. It is for these reasons that Flag or Tag Football is played in school and on the playground.

2. Junior-size footballs should be used until seventh grade.

3. Some type of color identification for teams must be provided.

4. Using of flags or strips of cloth is recommended rather than tagging to signify when the runner is caught or downed. If a flag must be pulled out of a player's belt, both the runner and his opponent learn to be more evasive and the chance of body contact is lessened. It is much more objective to *see* a flag that is pulled, than to judge, if and when a player has been tagged. Flags should be worn in such a way that each player has the same amount of cloth showing.

5. Since the line and back positions require use of different skills, positions should be rotated frequently.

Table 14-3. Progression of Skills, Knowledges, Rules, and Lead-Up Games for Football

SKILLS	KNOWLEDGES AND RULES	LEAD-UP GAME	LEVEL
Passing Catching	Passers Receivers Touchdown	Football Endball	III
Centering Carrying the ball Stance Field running	Kickoff Linesmen Backs Line of Scrimmage Down	One-Down Football Kickoff Football	IV
Blocking Punting Covering or guarding	End zone Safety Touchback Off-side Penalty	Flag Football	IV
Handoff	Laterals	Flag Football	IV
	Plays Formations	Flag Football	IV

Football Skills

Passing

Learning to use the proper grip (Figure 14-7) is essential in passing a football. The fingers and thumb hold the ball between one end and the middle. The fingers are spread over the laces and the thumb is around the ball. The actual pass is made using the overhand throw pattern (p. 255). The throw should be aimed about a foot in front of the runner (who should be moving).

COMMON FAULTS

1. Holding ball in palm rather than gripping with fingers.
2. Elbow held low and close to body.
3. Failure to snap wrist on release.

Figure 14-7 Correct grip on a football.

1. Point left foot toward target.
2. Grip ball toward one end with fingers across laces.
3. Focus on target.
4. Rotate body away from target.
5. Bring ball back beyond ear.
6. Keep elbow bent, high, and away from body.
7. Cock wrist.
8. Bring ball forward past ear with elbow leading.
9. Let ball roll off fingertips after wrist snap.
10. Follow through with arm toward target.

RECEIVING A PASS   The principles of catching any ball apply to catching a football. Most passes are caught with the little fingers together. The ball should be caught with the fingers and brought into the body. As soon as the ball is secured, it should be put into *carrying position* (see carrying-the-ball position). Almost all catching is done on the move.

COMMON FAULTS

1. Failure to wrap fingers around ball.
2. Catching ball against body and arms and having it bounce off body.

KEY TEACHING PHRASES

1. Eyes on ball.
2. Reach out for ball.
3. Wrap fingers around ball.
4. Bring ball in toward body.
5. Put ball into carrying position.

Carrying the Ball

The ball is carried near the body. The hand is put under and around the end of the ball. The other end is placed in the bend of the forearm and elbow.

Centering

Centering is used to initiate play from the line of scrimmage. The ball is passed from a player on the line to a backfield player. The center takes a position with feet spread wide, knees bent. The right hand reaches down and grasps the ball as for passing. The left hand rests lightly on the opposite side of the ball to serve as a guide. The ball is tossed back through the legs with the arm and a wrist snap.

Stance

The basic stance taken before the ball is put in play has the feet shoulder-width apart (either parallel or one foot slightly ahead of the other), knees bent, the weight slightly forward and resting on the knuckles of one hand. The head is up and eyes focused straight ahead. This stance gives the player an opportunity to take a fast running start and also gives stability for linemen when they block.

Blocking

Blocking in Flag Football should only involve getting the body in front of the opposing player to block his path or to prevent him from getting the ball. Use of the hands and pushing with the shoulders and hips should be prohibited, since body contact is illegal.

Punting

Punting in football is like that in soccer, and practice in either will improve skill in both. The football must be held out in front of the right foot at shoulder height. The right hand is under the ball at the center, the left hand is on the front end and to the side of the ball. A step forward is taken with the left foot, and the right leg is brought forward with the knee bent and toes pointing. The ball is dropped just before the foot contacts the long axis of the ball with the instep of the foot. The leg straightens as contact is made and follows through high, with toes pointing toward the target.

COMMON FAULTS

1. Ball is tossed in air rather than dropped.
2. Toes are pointed up in the air rather than at target, so that ball goes straight up in the air.
3. Ball is kicked with toe rather than instep.

KEY TEACHING PHRASES

1. Eyes on ball.
2. Hold ball straight out from shoulders in front of right leg.
3. Step on left foot.
4. Bring right leg forward with knee bent, toes pointing toward target.
5. Kick ball with instep.
6. Follow through with leg in direction of target.

Handoffs

When simple plays are used in Flag Football, the ball is centered to a back who has the option of passing, running with the ball, or handing it off to someone else. On the handoff the ball is actually placed in the receiver's hand, and he quickly puts the other hand down over the ball to reduce the chances of a fumble. After the handoff the ball is put into the carrying position.

Offensive and Defensive Team Play

OFFENSIVE CONCEPTS

1. Each player must know his offensive assignment but must not reveal his intentions as he lines up using the regular stance.
2. While running, the player should hold the ball in the carrying position.
3. Dodging, feinting, and changing pace should be used to evade a defensive player when an offensive player is to receive a pass or is running down field with the ball.
4. Both hands are always used to catch the ball.

DEFENSIVE CONCEPTS

1. A player defending against a pass receiver should not let his opponent get behind him. He should play to the inside so that he can dash between the passer and the receiver and intercept the ball.

2. Defense players should keep their eye on the ball not on a particular player unless it is a pass defense; then, of course, they must watch both.
3. Defense players should watch for tell-tale moves and for the direction the feet of offensive players take in the line-up so that they are able to anticipate directions of plays.

Skill Games to Improve Football Skills

• *Pass Defense*

Skills: Passing, receiving, centering, and defending.

Formation: A line of pass receivers stands next to the center. A line of defenders stands opposite them about 5 yards apart. A passer waits in position to receive the ball from the center.

Procedure: As the ball is centered, the first receiver runs out to receive the pass. The first defender moves out and tries to intercept the pass. Afterward, both go to the ends of the opposite lines. Specific patterns, like running straight out and cutting across center, may be stated. There may be two lines of receivers and defenders. The passer throws to whichever receiver is open.

Table 14-4. Skill Game Guide for Practicing Football

	SKILLS								
SKILL GAMES	PASSING	RECEIVING	CENTERING	BLOCKING	BALL CARRYING	EVASION TECHNIQUES	PUNTING	HANDOFF	GUARDING OR COVERING
Kickover							x		
Leader and Class	x	x							
Shuttle Relay					x			x	
Keep-Away	x	x				x			x
Obstacle Relay					x	x			
Star Relay	x	x							
Corner Ball	x	x							
Football Goal Catch	x	x							x
Corner Spry	x	x			x				
Pass Defense	x	x	x			x			x
Blocking				x		x			

- **Blocking**

Skills: Blocking, evasive tactics.

Formation: Partners. Line marked off in 8-foot lengths. Partners take a football stance on either side of the line facing one another. One partner is designated as offense, one as defense.

Procedure: Upon a signal, "hike," the offense player tries to get around the defense player. He must stay within his 8-foot area. The defense player tries to contain the other player in the area. No hands or body contact may be made. Dodging, feinting, changing of pace should be used. The assignments should be changed periodically.

Lead-Up Games for Football

- **Football End Ball**

Football End Ball is played just like End Ball (page 382) except that a football is used.

- **Kickoff Football**

Area: A field space 15 yards by 20 yards, goal lines at either end, line at midfield.

Formation: Teams of six each. At the start of the game one team lines up at midfield, the other team spreads out deep in its own half of field.

Procedure: A player on the team at midfield throws the ball into the other team's area. A player there either catches or picks up the ball and tries to return it to the far goal line. He may pass the ball back (*lateral*), to a teammate or run all the way with it. Members of the other team try to tag him before he reaches the goal. If he crosses the goal untagged, his team gets 6 points. After he is tagged or makes a goal, the ball is returned to midfield, and the ball is thrown (kickoff) to the opposite team. The winner is the team with the most points at the end of a specified playing period.

Variations:

1. Once children learn to kick, this game can be used for kickoff practice.
2. When blocking is learned, blocking for teammates may be permitted.

- **One-Down Football (Figure 14-8)**

Area: Field 20 yards by 25 yards with goal lines and midfield line.

Formation: Two teams of eight. Five are line players and line up at the line of *scrimmage* (line where ball is put in play), and three line up 6 feet behind line players and are called the backs. Players on each team line up across from each other.

Procedure: The ball is put into play by one team at midfield. The ball is centered to a back, who may either run with the ball or pass it to a teammate. The object is to carry the ball over or pass to someone over the goal line. The ball may be passed any number of times from any place on the field, in any direction. Players from the opposite team try to tag the player with the ball with a two-handed touch above the waist. When a player with the ball is downed, the ball is given to the other team. Each team has only one down in which to make a touchdown. The defensive players play a player-to-player

Figure 14-8 One-Down Football.

guarding system and try to intercept passes and/or tag runners. When the ball is downed, it is put into play at various locations depending on the following situations.

1. If an incomplete pass is made from behind the line of scrimmage, the ball is given to the other team at the original line of scrimmage.
2. If an incomplete pass is made beyond the original line of scrimmage, the ball is given to the other team from the point at which the ball was thrown.
3. When a player with the ball is tagged, the ball is given to the other team at the point where he was tagged.

- ## *Flag Football*

Area: Field 60 yards by 30 yards, goal line at either end, lines drawn across field at 20-yard intervals. A line 10 yards behind each goal line designates the *end zone,* within which passes may be caught for touchdowns.

Formation: Teams may consist of six to ten players each. If less than seven are playing, four are line players and two are backfield players. Two of the line players are ends and usually go out for passes. If eight or more play, no more than four backfield players are allowed.

Procedure:

1. *Kickoff:* The game is started with a kickoff from the goal line of the team that is designated by lot or choice. If the ball is kicked out of bounds, it is brought back to the goal line and kicked again. If it goes out of bounds on the second kick, the other team starts play at its 20-yard line. The kickoff may not be recovered by the kicking team unless the other team touches and fumbles the ball.
2. *Line of scrimmage:* The ball is placed wherever a player is downed and this is called the line of scrimmage. If a pass was attempted and was not caught or intercepted, it is returned to the line of scrimmage.
3. *Downs:* A team is allowed four downs, or attempts to move the ball either by running with it or passing it 20 yards or into the next zone. If players cannot move into the next zone in four downs, the ball is given to the other team at the line of scrimmage.
4. *Huddle:* This is the term applied when a team meets in a huddle or circle to plan their next play. After huddling, the teams line up; play is started when the ball is centered.
5. *Forward pass:* The ball may be thrown forward by a player from behind the line of scrimmage. He may lateral the ball from any point. This is a pass thrown to a player behind the passer.
6. *Blocking:* A player may block only by putting his body in the way of an opponent. No hand or body contact is permitted.

7. *Tackling:* A player may only be *downed* or tackled by having one flag pulled from his belt. Players may be required to wear two flags, one on either side; or only one flag may be required, and that is worn in the center of the back of the belt. A tackler may not grab the runner and then the flag.

8. *Punting:* All punts must be announced before the ball is centered. Neither team may cross the line of scrimmage until the ball is kicked.

9. *Fumbles:* If a ball is dropped on the center pass behind the line of scrimmage, it may be picked up by a back. When a ball is dropped anywhere on the field, no one may pick it up and advance it. The first person to touch it gains possession of it for his team.

Scoring: Touchdown—6 points. Point after touchdown—1 point. After a touchdown, one play is given the team from a spot 3 yards out from the goal to make an extra point. Safety—2 points. A safety is called when the defending team causes the ball to go back over the goal line, either by fumbling it, or by catching an opponent chased over the goal line. If a player intercepts a ball behind the goal line and does not run it out, or if the ball is kicked over the goal line, a touchback occurs and the ball is taken out to the 20-yard line and given to the team that was defending the goal.

Penalties: Loss of 5 yards for the following:

1. Failure to announce intention to punt.
2. Initiating a forward pass beyond line of scrimmage.
3. Off-side (player over line of scrimmage before ball is centered).
4. Delaying the game.
5. Tucking flag too deep in the belt.

Loss of 15 yards for the following:

1. Illegal blocking.
2. Illegal tackling or use of hands on either offense or defense.
3. Unsportsmanlike conduct.

Variations: The size of the football field and number of players is dependent upon the skill level of the class and the space available. The field may be divided by 10- rather than 20-yard zones. Six downs rather than four may be allowed to go 20 yards.

Football Skill Tests

FORWARD PASS FOR DISTANCE The directions for the Throw for Distance Test may be followed for this test. Three trials are given, and the farthest throw is recorded.

FORWARD PASS FOR ACCURACY A target is painted on the wall with three concentric circles measuring 2 feet, 4 feet, and 6 feet in diameter. A point value of 3, 2, 1, respectively, is allotted to each circle. A line is drawn 15 feet from the wall. A player is given ten trials to throw at the target. His score is the total points earned on the ten trials. He must pass from behind the line. If the ball strikes a line, the highest value is given.

PUNT FOR DISTANCE The same test directions are used for the Punt for Distance as for the Throw for Distance. The subject is given three punts, and the farthest distance is recorded.

BALL-CARRYING ZIGZAG RUN Five pins are arranged in a straight line 10 feet apart with the first pin 10 feet from a starting line. The subject puts the ball in carrying position and on the signal "Go" runs to the right around the first pin, as he passes to the left of the second pin he changes the ball to his left arm, and continues in and around each pin. Each time he passes a pin, he must change the ball to the outside arm. When he reaches the end pin he turns and continues back to the starting line in the same manner. The stopwatch is started on the signal "Go" and stopped when the subject crosses the starting line again. The player is given two trials and the fastest time is recorded.

Soccer Activities

Soccer is a fall field sport that is extremely popular in many countries. In the United States it is played more frequently in some sections of the country than in others.

Young children love to play all versions of soccer since it is a fast-moving, running, vigorous game. They seem to be particularly intrigued by the fact that the ball must be handled with parts of the body other than the hands. The uniqueness of using the feet to stop and propel the ball the majority of the time makes the skills difficult to learn as well as interesting. For this reason a great deal of practice is necessary to gain control and accuracy in the use of soccer skills. A ball, some type of goal posts or markers, color bands, and a level playing field are all the equipment needed to play the game.

The official soccer rules are not included here. The field is larger and slightly different from that specified here for Seven-Man Soccer. The rules listed under Seven-Man Soccer are much the same and are adapted so there will be more opportunities for participation and for the maturation level of elementary school classes.

Teaching Considerations

1. Safety rules must be taught and maintained from the first lesson on to avoid hazardous playing habits.
   a. Kicking the ball with the instep and the inside of the foot prevents injury to the toes when soft rubber shoes are worn.
   b. Since play is vigorous and kicking is involved, pushing, shoving, tripping, dangerous kicking, and body blocking must be discouraged immediately through the enforcement of rules that prohibit this type of play.
   c. Children should be taught to protect the face (and girls, the chest) from high-kicked balls by folding arms across face or chest.
   d. Emphasis should be placed on keeping the ball low and avoiding dangerous high kicking when close to another player.
2. Most soccer games involve a great deal of sustained running and changes of directions. This is one of the assets of the game; however, some children are not aware when they are overfatigued and continue to play when they should rest. Since some positions are more demanding than others, they should be rotated frequently.

Movement Experiences

3. When soccer balls are used indoors, they should be slightly deflated so they may be controlled more easily.

Table 14-5. Progression of Skills, Knowledges, Rules, and Lead-Up Games for Soccer

SKILLS	KNOWLEDGES AND RULES	LEAD-UP GAMES	LEVEL
Kick	Free kick		
Instep	Goal		
Inside of foot	Rotation		
Outside of foot	Team positions		
Dribble	Forwards		
Trap	Side-line guards		
Sole of foot	Goal-line guards		
Place kick for accuracy			
Dribble and drive		Line Soccer	III
Dribble and pass	Forward positions		
Trap	Team positioning		
Knee:	Attacking team		
Single	Defending team	Advanced Line Soccer	
Double		Alley Soccer	III
Tackle	Kickin		
Straight	Kickoff		
Dodging	Penalty kick		
	Team positions		
	Backs		
	Forwards	Alley Soccer	IV
Tackle	Forward line		
Hook	Backfield		
Body blocking	Defensive-offensive play		
Heading	Penalty kick	Advanced Alley Soccer	IV
Punt	Corner kick		
	Defense kick		
	Goalkeeper privileges		
	Official positions	Modified Soccer	IV
Triangular passing	Marking	Official Soccer	IV

The basic skills of soccer are described under the general headings of advancing the ball, stopping the ball, and defensive tactics.

Advancing the Ball

The ball may be advanced by being kicked or by being allowed to rebound from any part of the body except the hands and arms (volleying). Because volleying is quite difficult for elementary school children to control, it will not be analyzed in detail. It should suffice to tell upper-grade children that one should get in line with the ball and stiffen the part of the body against which the ball is to rebound.

Figure 14-9 Kicking with the inside of the foot.

KICKING: INSIDE OF FOOT (FIGURE 14-9)   The ball is contacted with the inside edge of the foot. The kicking foot is turned outward, and the leg is bent at the knee diagonally backward and outward. The leg is swung across in front of the body. The knee straightens as the ball is met just in front of the body. The ball should be contacted slightly below center. The arms are used for balance, and the foot follows through toward the target. In order to increase force, a few preliminary running steps may be taken. This type of kick is used to move a stationary ball a long distance, to pass to a teammate after trapping a ball, to pass to a teammate when dribbling, or to shoot for goal.

COMMON FAULTS

1. Kicking with toes.
2. Failure to turn foot outward.
3. Contacting ball too low, causing it to rise too high in the air.

KEY TEACHING PHRASES

1. Turn kicking foot outward.
2. Bend knee.
3. Turn leg out, and swing it back.
4. Swing leg forward and across the body.
5. Contact ball slightly below center.
6. Foot follows ball toward target.

KICKING: OUTSIDE OF FOOT   The right leg is brought across in front of the left leg and swings to meet the ball slightly in front and near the outside of the left foot. Because of the limited force of the kick, this must be used for short passes to a teammate on the right side of a player. It may also be used when the player is trying to dodge and avoid a tackler.

COMMON FAULT The ball is pushed rather than kicked when it is contacted too far to the right of the left foot.

TEACHING PHRASES

1. Swing right leg across and through.
2. Contact ball in front of left foot.

KICKING: INSTEP OF FOOT The kicking leg is swung straight back, with the knee bent and the toe pointing toward the ground. As the leg is swung forward with the toe pointed, the ball is contacted below its center with the instep of the foot. The foot follows through in the desired direction. This kick is used for a long pass to a teammate, place kicking, or long kick for goal. A few preliminary steps add more force to the kick.

COMMON FAULTS

1. Ball is met too high above the center, and ball does not get off the ground or gain much speed.
2. Failing to meet ball squarely on instep.
3. Losing balance as ball is met because of lack of forward lean into the kick.

KEY TEACHING PHRASES

1. Swing leg straight back and forward.
2. Lean into kick.
3. Point toe, and contact ball slightly below center squarely on instep.
4. Follow ball with leg pointed at the target.

PUNT This skill is more advanced and should be taught later than the instep kick; however, the mechanics of the punt are much the same as those of the instep kick. The ball is held out in front of the right leg slightly above the waist. A step forward is taken on the left foot, and the right leg is brought back. The ball is dropped and the leg swings forward and upward. The leg follows through toward the sky. Only the goalie may punt the ball out of the goal area. The punt is used to clear the ball over the heads of the opponents and down the field.

COMMON FAULTS

1. Dropping ball too early, thereby missing ball.
2. Extending knee too much and kicking ball too high.
3. Kicking with toes instead of instep.

KEY TEACHING PHRASES

1. Hold ball arm's length in front of right leg.
2. Eyes on ball.
3. Step on left foot, swing right leg back from hip, drop ball, swing leg through and kick.

4. Contact ball squarely on instep.

5. Follow through toward the sky.

DRIBBLING   Dribbling is a means of moving the ball and keeping it under control. The ball is tapped gently with the inside edge of the foot. As the player runs, he should tap the ball with alternate feet. The ball should never be more than a foot ahead of the runner. The dribble is a vital but difficult skill. The dribbling pattern should be stressed first, then speed and control in moving with the ball. The dribble should be learned and practiced in a ball-handling unit before a soccer game is introduced.

COMMON FAULTS

1. The ball is kicked with the toe.

2. The ball is kicked too hard and consequently moves too far ahead of runner.

KEY TEACHING PHRASES

1. Tap ball lightly with instep of foot.

2. Tap ball with right foot then left foot when running.

HEADING   Heading is actually volleying the ball or redirecting it by hitting it with the head. Player gets in line with the ball, drops head back, maintains a good stable stance, bends knees, bends trunk backward at hips. Ball contacts forehead at the hairline. Upward and forward thrust of body is made by extending knees, and body follows through in new direction of ball. This is a difficult skill because of the need to judge the speed and position or flight of the ball. A soft ball should be used to learn this skill. The ball is tossed by self to start action, later by a partner from a short distance until the player is acclimated to the skill.

COMMON FAULTS

1. Closing eyes before contacting ball.

2. Not bending knees.

3. Not dropping head back slightly.

4. Letting ball hit or contact the top of the head.

5. Trying to hit at the ball with just the head.

6. Not extending whole body in direction of new flight of ball.

KEY TEACHING PHRASES

1. Eyes on ball.

2. Get in line with ball.

3. Bend knees.

4. Bend trunk back slightly, drop head.

5. Contact ball at hairline.

6. Let body follow ball up and forward.

Stopping the Ball

BLOCKING (BODY TRAP)   Blocking is a means of stopping the ball with the body in such a way that the ball is caused to fall to the ground in a spot near the player, where he can quickly kick the ball. The major action of blocking is absorbing the force of the ball so it will not rebound away from the body. The player should get in line with the ball and let it hit the body. The ball may be blocked with any part of the body. Just as the ball contacts the body, the player should give with it and take a slight jump backward. Children should be taught to fold their arms across their chest and hold their sides with hands to prevent reaching out to hit ball with arms and hands.

COMMON FAULTS

1. Failure to get in line with ball.
2. Reaching to meet ball.
3. Failure to give with ball or to jump back.

KEY TEACHING PHRASES

1. Get in line with ball.
2. Fold arms across chest (if ball is high) and hold onto sides of body.
3. Let ball hit your body.
4. Give with ball.
5. Jump back from ball.

TRAPPING: SOLE OF FOOT Trapping may be described as catching the ball with the feet. To use the sole of the foot in trapping, the player must first get in line with the ball. As the ball reaches the player, he raises the sole of the trapping foot with the toes upward. He quickly brings the sole down over the top of the ball and traps it between the ground and the foot. He immediately removes the foot so he can kick the ball. The weight is on the opposite foot all the time. It is best to use this trap with a slow-moving ball. Every ball should be trapped before it is kicked so direction of the kick can be controlled.

COMMON FAULTS

1. Meeting the ball too soon so that it hits the sole and rebounds off the foot.
2. Meeting the ball too late so that foot slides off the ball and presents the possibility of a fall.
3. Failing to bring foot down quickly and release it quickly so that ball is in a position for a kick.

KEY TEACHING PHRASES

1. Eyes on ball.
2. Get in line with ball.
3. Bend knee, raise toes.
4. Put sole down over ball, and trap it between ground and foot.
5. Release it quickly.

SINGLE LEG TRAP The player must first get in line with the ball. The foot of the trapping leg is brought diagonally back of the other foot. The foot flexes so that only the toes are contacting the ground. Both knees are bent. As the ball reaches the leg, the lower leg presses against the ball and traps it. The weight is held on the other foot. The ball is released immediately, and the player is ready to kick the ball. Upper torso should be erect so that balance is kept. The leg traps make it more difficult for an opponent to get at the ball than if a sole trap is used; however, it takes longer to get into kicking position.

COMMON FAULTS

1. Failure to get in line with the ball.
2. Failure to time trap properly so that ball hits leg and bounces away.
3. Leaning upper trunk forward as knees bend, and falling forward.

KEY TEACHING PHRASES

1. Eyes on ball.
2. Get in line with ball.
3. Bring foot diagonally back.
4. Bend knees.
5. Press lower leg against center of ball.
6. Keep weight on nontrapping foot.
7. Release ball immediately and get ready for a kick.

DOUBLE LEG TRAP   The player gets in line with the ball. As it approaches the feet are slightly apart and pointed outward. The knees bend deeply and quickly and trap the ball against the ground with the shins. Weight is held on the balls of both feet. Arms are used for balance. The body is quickly extended into a vertical position as ball is released from the shins. This is an effective but difficult trap because of the balance problem.

COMMON FAULTS

1. Meeting the ball off-center.
2. Bending too early so the ball is actually hit rather than trapped.
3. Leaning forward at waist and losing balance.

KEY TEACHING PHRASES

1. Eyes on ball.
2. Get in line with ball.
3. Weight on balls of feet.
4. Bend both knees quickly and deeply, trapping ball between ground and shins.
5. Keep upper trunk erect.
6. Use arms to side to keep balance.
7. Release ball quickly and get into position for a kick.

Defensive Tactics

Tackling the ball allows a player to take it away from another player or to cause that player to make a poor pass or overrun the ball.

STRAIGHT TACKLE   The tackler comes to a position directly in front of a person who is dribbling and attempts to put his foot on the ball. He then either quickly kicks it away from the dribbler or holds it until the dribbler overruns it.

HOOK TACKLE   The tackler approaches the dribbler from the front but quickly steps to one side and reaches with one leg and, using it as a hook, attempts to draw the ball out to one side. The supporting leg must be bent at the knee so that a longer reach may be made with the hooking leg. When using either tackle, the forward momentum of the body must be checked in order to avoid body contact with the opponent.

COMMON FAULTS

1. Failure to reach for ball with tackling foot and therefore running into opponent.
2. Failure to clear the ball away quickly from opponent.
3. Poor timing on the reach.
4. Failure to maintain weight on supporting leg, thereby falling into the opponent.
5. Failure to execute a dodge to avoid opponent.

KEY TEACHING PHRASES

1. Check forward movement.
2. Reach for ball with one foot.
3. Pull ball to one side.
4. Quickly clear ball to teammate.
5. Step out of the way of opponent.

MARKING In games in which there are backfield players and forward-line players, there is a responsibility for guarding a specific player. The term "marking" should be used as soon as guarding an individual is necessary. The goal line is defended, not guarded.

General Offensive and Defensive Team Play

There are a few basic concepts of defensive and offensive play which should be stressed in the first soccer experience. Additions to these are made as the games become more complex.

OFFENSIVE CONCEPTS

1. Use short, quick, controlled kicks.
2. Have ball under control before kicking it.
3. Pass diagonally ahead to a teammate.
4. Change direction of pass frequently to keep opponents off guard.
5. Clear ball out to sidelines until ball must be centered near the goal area.
6. Stay in own position area.
7. Only one player from a team should attempt to kick the ball at one time.
8. Forwards should let their own backfield players get the ball from opponents if possible, so they can run ahead to receive a pass.

DEFENSIVE CONCEPTS

1. Backs should stay behind their own forwards to pick up missed or intercepted balls.
2. Backs should attempt to intercept ball before it reaches opponent.
3. As soon as an opponent gets control of the ball, backs should prepare to tackle the ball.

Table 14-6. Skill Game Guide for Practicing Soccer Skills

SKILL GAMES	SKILLS						
	KICKING	TRAPPING	BLOCKING	DRIBBLING	PASSING	GOAL KICKING	PUNTING
Circle Soccer	x	x	x				
Mickey Soccer				x			
Soccer Goal Kick	x	x	x	x		x	
Diamond Soccer	x	x	x		x		
Circle Trap		x			x		
Kickover		x					x
Dribble Maze Relay				x			
Dribble Up and Kick Back	x			x			
Shuttle Relay	x			x			

4. When backs gain possession of ball, they should pass it ahead to their teammate immediately.

5. The ball should be cleared from in front of goal with a hard kick toward side line.

• *Circle Soccer*

Skills: Kicking, trapping, blocking.

Equipment: One soccer ball for each circle.

Formation: Single circle with a line drawn across the center. One team fills in the circle on each side. It is best if a circle is drawn on the floor or ground.

Procedure: The ball is put in play with the leader rolling the ball across the circle. The object of the game is for each team to try to kick the ball out of the circle on the opponent's half of the playing area. The ball must go below waist level and out of the circle to count 1 point. If a player touches the ball, goes into the center while kicking, or kicks the ball above waist level, 1 point is awarded to the opposing team. If the ball comes to rest in the center of the circle, a player from the team on whose half of the circle it rests may go in and kick it out to his teammates.

• *Circle Trap*

Skills: Passing, trapping.

Equipment: One soccer ball for each circle.

Formation: Single circle with one player in the center.

Procedure: The leader puts the ball into play by rolling it across the circle. Circle players keep the ball moving by passing it to one another. The person in the center tries to trap the ball. If he does, he takes the place in the circle of the person who kicked it last. If someone lets the ball go out of the circle, he must exchange places with the person in the center.

- ### Soccer Kickover

Same rules as Kickover on p. 337 except that a soccer ball is used instead of a football.

- ### Dribble Maze Relay

Skills: Dribbling.

Equipment: One soccer ball, some type of obstacles set up 15 feet apart from the starting line to the far end line. Number of obstacles varies with the skill of the children, as does the distance between obstacles.

Formation: File relay, with maze set up for each line.

Procedure: Each player in turn dribbles the ball in and out of the obstacles down the line and back. Team in which everyone completes the maze first wins. This may become a timed event and may also be used as a skill test.

- ### Diamond Soccer (Figure 14-10)

Skills: Kicking, trapping, blocking, passing.

Equipment: One soccer ball for each diamond.

Formation: Two teams line up as indicated in the diagram.

Procedure: The players nearest the middle line from each team come out to the center of their playing area. The leader rolls the ball into the center. The two players from each side try to kick the ball below waist level out of the diamond of their opponent's half of the court. The players on the outside lines try to block the ball and kick it back to their inside players. When the ball goes over the outside lines below waist level, a point is awarded the team kicking it out. Inside players take a position on either side of the far end of their half of the diamond. All others rotate one position. The team which was scored against puts the ball in play again. One point is awarded the opposite team when a player touches the ball or kicks it above waist level.

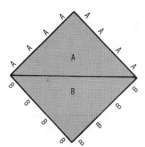

Figure 14-10 Diamond Soccer.

- *Mickey Soccer*

Skill: Dribbling.

Equipment: One soccer ball for each team placed in a small circle in the center of the circle.

Formation: Class divided into circles with even number of players, six or more.

Procedure: Each player in each circle is numbered. The ball is placed in the center of the circle. The leader calls a number. Everyone having that number runs into the center of his circle, dribbles the ball out through his place in the circle and goes to the right around the circle, back through his place, and puts the ball in the center of the circle. The player who returns to his place in the circle first wins a point for his team.

- *Soccer Goal Kick (Figure 14-11)*

Skills: Kicking, trapping, blocking, dribbling, goal kicking, goal keeping.

Formation: Two teams of six each. One team spread in semi-circular fashion in front of goal posts. The other team waits to the right of the goal posts for kicking turns. One player is first kicker, one is first goalkeeper.

Procedure: The kicker kicks the ball and runs to base. He tries to get back to the goal posts before the fielding team can kick the ball between the goal posts. The fielders should be encouraged to trap the ball, then kick for goal, dribble closer before kicking, or pass to a teammate who is closer to the goal. A point is awarded to the kicking team if the player gets back to the goal before the ball crosses the goal line. The fielding team gets a point if the ball beats the kicker across the goal line. After a point is made, the kicker goes to the end of his line, the goalie becomes the kicker and the next person in line becomes goalie.

Variations: Players may play for their own points. The procedure would be the same as for Work-Up Softball, in which each player rotates one position into the kicking spot, and no one waits in line for a turn to kick. A point would be awarded to the goalie if he blocked a goal, to the fielder if he kicked the ball through the goal, and to the kicker if he beat the ball back.

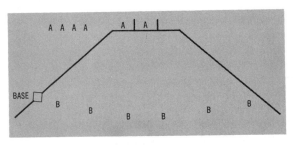

Figure 14-11 Soccer Goal Kick.

• *Line Soccer*

Area: Playing field 25 feet wide and 60 feet long divided in half by a line with a small circle in the center of it. A restraining line drawn 5 feet in from each end or goal line, a penalty mark centered 15 feet from each goal line.

Players: There are two teams of equal size. Two players from each team stand along opposite side lines on their respective half of the field. Their responsibility is to put all out-of-bounds balls into play. The other players line up between the goal line and the restraining line and are called goal-line guards. Their responsibility is to prevent the ball from crossing the goal line.

Procedure: The ball is placed in the center circle. Upon a signal, the right corner player from each team becomes a forward and runs out to the center. The forwards try to draw the ball sideward, then attempt to kick it across their opponents' goal line. The ball must pass below the shoulders of the guards to count as a goal. After a goal is made, the forward takes the place of the right side-line guard who crosses over and becomes the left side-line guard. All the other players move one position to the right. The ball is returned to the center circle and play continues with the new right corner player becoming the forward.

Fouls: Touching the ball with the hands, pushing another player, kicking ball above shoulder level. Penalty is a free kick at the point where the foul occurred. If a goal-line guard steps out over the restraining line, a penalty kick is awarded to the forward of the opposite team. This is an unguarded kick from the penalty mark.

Scoring: Field goal—2 points; penalty kick—1 point.

• *Advanced Line Soccer*

The rules for Line Soccer are used with the following exceptions. The two corner players on each team become forwards and run out to the center upon a signal. In this way the two play as teammates, passing the ball to each other and at the same time each guarding a player from the other team. This necessitates a change in the rotation system. After a goal is made, the forward who came from the right corner moves over to the right side-line guard position, the side-line guard moves to the middle of the goal-line guards, and all goal-line guards of that half of the field move one place to the right. The forward who came from the left corner moves over to the left side-line guard position, the side-line guard moves to the middle of the goal-line guards, and all goal-line guards of the left side of the field move one place to the left. It is well to mark a line on the goal line that designates the right and left division.

• *Alley Soccer (Figure 14-12)*

Area: Playing field 100 feet long, 75 feet wide divided lengthwise into five alleys 15 feet wide. There is a restraining line 10 feet in front of each goal line and a center line. There are two teams of ten players each. One player stands between goal line and restraining line of each lane and is the goal-line guard of that lane. One player stands in each lane on his team's side of the center line and is the forward-line player of that lane for his team.

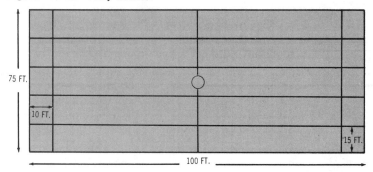

Figure 14-12 Alley Soccer.

Procedure: The object is for the forwards to dribble the ball down the field and kick the ball over the opponent's goal line. The opposite forwards try to get the ball to go toward the other goal. The team with the ball is known as the attacking team, the team without the ball as the defending team. Play is started in the center alley at the center line with the official giving the ball to one team. Forward-line players should pass the ball across alleys and down field to other forwards. After a goal, the ball is given to the nonscoring team at the center line. Players rotate one lane from left to right, starting at the left forward position. If there are more than ten players on a team, the extra players become side-line guards. In that case the right forward moves into the right side-line guard position rather than moving directly to the right goal-line position. Side-line players put all balls in play on their side of the field.

Fouls:

1. Touching the ball with the hands.
2. Stepping over alley lines.
3. Pushing an opponent.
4. Goal-line guards stepping over restraining line to defend goal.
5. Forwards stepping over restraining line to kick or retrieve ball.
6. Kicking ball for goal above shoulder height.

Penalty: Free kick from spot where foul was made (unguarded kick).

Scoring: 2 points for each field goal.

- *Advanced Alley Soccer*

The rules for Alley Soccer are used with the following exceptions. An additional restraining line is added midway between the goal line and center line of each half of the field. A line of backfield players is added. They take a starting position just behind the new restraining line. Side-line guards are omitted (if possible) and the ball is taken out by the outside alley player from the team opposite that which last touched the ball before it went out of bounds. There is only one goalkeeper, and the goal is restricted to the center alley. This alley should be marked by goal posts or pins of some type. Backfield players do not cross the center line. Fouls that occur between the 25-yard restraining line and the goal restraining line are penalized with a penalty kick from a line marked 15 feet from the goal line. Rotation must change with the left backfield player becoming the goalie and the goalie becoming the left forward. The goalkeeper may catch and throw the ball out to his teammates. He should be encouraged to throw it toward the outside-lane players.

• *Modified Soccer (Figure 14-13)*

Area: The lane lines are removed and the field is enlarged to 70 yards long and 40 yards wide. A center line and restraining lines 5 feet on either side are drawn. A semi-circle with a radius 15 feet from the goal line is called the penalty area.

Players: Players have definite positions and responsibilities and are placed on the field as is shown in the diagram.

1. *Forward-line players:* Right wing, right inner, center forward, left inner, left wing. *Responsibilities:* To advance the ball into opponents' half of field and score. Players should stay in their respective positions across the field and play the ball between them as they move forward down the field. Forward-line players should go only about three-quarters of the way down into their own defensive half of the field.

2. *Halfbacks:* Right half, center half, left half. *Responsibilities:* Play as both offensive and defensive players. They back up the forward line when on offense and mark or guard the right wing, center forward, left wing respectively on defense. They put the ball in play from out of bounds balls with a kickin.

3. *Fullbacks:* Right full, left full. *Responsibilities:* Primarily defensive. They stay in own half of field and mark or guard the inners. They drop back toward the goal line and are the last line of defense before the ball must be stopped by the goalkeeper. They should clear the ball out toward the side lines, preferably to their wings.

4. *Goalkeeper:* Guards the goal. He may use his hands to stop ball and to clear it out and away from the goal. He may punt the ball down field. He never leaves the penalty area. He takes balls that go out over the end line with a kickin (defense kick).

Procedure: The ball is started at a center circle with a kickoff by one team. The ball must roll over the distance of its circumference at least once before it may be touched by another player. No one may cross the center line before

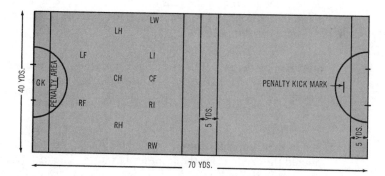

Figure 14-13 Modified Soccer.

the ball is kicked by the center forward. The forwards try to advance the ball down toward the goal area. When a field goal or a penalty kick is made, the ball is returned to the center and the kickoff is given to the nonscoring team.

Fouls:

1. Pushing, tripping, holding.
2. Touching ball with hands.

Penalty: Free kick on spot. If foul is made in the penalty circle by the defending team, a penalty kick is awarded. This is an unguarded kick 12 feet from the goal line. Only the goalkeeper and the kicker may be in the penalty area until after the ball is kicked.

Out of Bounds: Balls that cross the side line are taken by a kickin at the spot where they went out. A ball crossing the end line and last touched by the offense is taken by a fullback at the point where it went out. If it was last touched by a defense player, it is taken by a wing at the corner of the field.

Scoring: Field goal—2 points. Ball must cross line between goal posts and under them (below shoulder height of goalie, if no goal posts are available). Penalty kick—1 point.

- ### *Seven-Player Soccer*

The same general rules are used as for Modified Soccer, except the game has a different number of players and a smaller field. Three backs, three forwards, and a goalkeeper comprise the team. The field is adjusted to 150 feet long and 100 feet wide or whatever the teacher deems suitable. This makes the game somewhat simpler and allows more activity for each player. Two games with fourteen players on each team is better than one game with twenty-two and a few left over. Five-player soccer further increases the activity. Two backs, two forwards, and a goalie on a smaller court make good practice games and provide a lot of activity.

Skill Tests

DRIBBLING Four pins are set 15 feet apart in a straight line, the first being 15 feet from a starting line. On the signal "Go" a player dribbles the ball from the starting line weaving around the pins. When he gets to the last pin he starts back. A timer starts a stopwatch on the signal "Go" and stops the clock when the ball passes over the finish line. If the dribbler loses control of the ball or does not go around the pins in order, he must regain control or position and continue the course. Two trials are given and the best of the two is recorded as the score for the test.

PUNT FOR DISTANCE The same field markings and procedure can be used as for the throw for distance. The player must kick the ball from behind the starting line. He has three trials, and the best of the three is recorded as the score for the test.

PLACE KICK FOR DISTANCE The Place-Kick Test for Distance can be conducted the same as for the Punt for Distance. The distance is measured at the spot where the ball rolls dead. Three trials are given, and the best of three is recorded as the score.

Figure 14-14 Kick for goal.

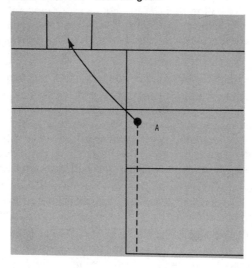

KICK FOR GOAL (FIGURE 14-14)   A line is drawn 5 yards across in front of the goal posts, and another 8 yards in front of them. Another line is drawn out from the goal line from a point 10 feet to the side of the right post (facing the goal posts), and is extended into the field 18 yards. The player must dribble the ball into area A and kick for goal from this area without stopping the ball. One point is given if the ball is kicked from the correct area and goes between the goal posts. No point is given if the player kicks from outside the area or stops the ball before kicking it. Five trials are given, and the sum of points earned in the five trials constitutes the score for the test.

TRAPPING   Two parallel lines are drawn 20 feet apart. The instructor stands on one and kicks the ball hard to the player who is behind the other line. The player tries to trap the ball successfully. Ten trials are given. One point is given for each successful trap. The score for the test is the sum of the points from the ten trials.

Softball Activities

Historically, softball is an outgrowth of the sport of baseball. Softball has been developed as a playground and recreational game because it takes less room to play, requires less protective equipment, and is a safer game than baseball. The rules and format of the two games are quite similar. Children desire to learn and play softball at an early age and continue playing the game into adulthood. The game involves the skills of running, throwing, catching, and batting. It is not classified as a very active game.

Due to the nature of the skills involved and the early acquaintance with the format and rules of the game through neighborhood play, television, and organized baseball leagues for young boys and girls, instruction in the skills and very simple lead-up games should begin in the third grade. Because children play softball in their leisure hours, it is important that they learn how to play safely, how to organize with fewer than the official number of players, how to officiate the game, and how to use the skills properly.

Teaching Considerations

1. Safety considerations are paramount whenever the first lesson is conducted.

    a. Waiting batters must wait along the first-base line in a designated area. Going out of this area may constitute an out or loss of bats. Reasons for this rule should be given. A few are described here. If a player throws a bat, it will probably go down the third-base line. More foul balls are hit off to the left than to the right. Batters crowding around the home plate can easily be in the way when the ball is thrown to home base.

    b. Players should be taught not to let go of or throw the bat after hitting. In order to avoid this, a player may be required to carry the bat to first base, or lay it down at a certain mark on the way to first. Failure to do this may constitute an out.

    c. Face masks should be provided for the catcher whenever bats are used, not necessarily because they will be hit by the bat, but the ball may be fouled off the bat into the catcher's face.

    d. Care should be taken that soft bases are used. Children should be taught the dangers of using sticks, stones, or cans for bases.

2. Games with a pitcher should be avoided until some degree of accuracy in pitching has been gained. A batting tee should be used instead. The game becomes too inactive if a ball cannot be thrown into the strike area consistently.

3. Umpires should be used in each game. This may be a rotating assignment for members of the team at bat so that no one will be inactive for a whole game. Plans to use rotating umpires should be discussed so that children will use them in their playground games and learn to accept the umpire's decision without arguing. The latter proves to be a problem because adults often provide poor models for children.

4. Since softball positions require specific actions and responsibilities, and some positions are more active than others, they should be rotated often.

5. Very soft softballs should be used in the intermediate grades.

6. The game will go faster and more people will be active if everyone on the team hits before sides are changed. If the three-outs and the change-of-sides rules are followed, one team may be up to bat all period or out in the field all period if the fielding team can get no outs.

Softball Skills

Throwing

OVERHAND THROW The overhand throw is described on pages 255–57. It is used almost exclusively in throwing to bases and returning the ball from the outfield. Balls thrown to a base from the infield or between bases should be fast and travel in as straight a line as possible.

Table 14-7. Progression of Skills, Knowledges, Rules, and Lead-Up Games for Softball

SKILLS	KNOWLEDGES AND RULES	LEAD-UP GAMES	LEVEL

Catching
Overhand throw
Underhand throw
	Outs:
	  Fly caught
	  Touch base
	Positions:
	  Fielders
	  Base players
	  Catcher
	Maintain batting
	  order		

Fielding:
  Flies
  Grounders
Batting off tee
	Foul ball
	Positions:
	  Infielders
	  Outfielders
	Outs:
		Long Base	III

	Tag runner on base	Throw It and Run	
	Throw ball ahead of runner	Tee Ball	III

Pitching
Batting a pitched ball
	Position play
	Outs:
	  Runner off base
	    on a caught fly		

	Balls Strikes	Modified Softball Work-Up	IV
Base running Stealing	Backing up Third-strike rule	Modified Softball	
	Infield-fly rule	Official Softball	IV

UNDERHAND THROW   The underhand throw is described on pages 258–59. In softball it is used more as a toss than a throw, except in pitching. The ball is usually tossed to a baseman when the ball is fielded close to the base.

Catching

Catching is done in the same manner as described on pages 253–55. However, the teacher must remember that the softball is smaller and harder than most balls.

Practice with catching thrown balls will help build confidence and skill before batted balls must be caught. Gloves will help absorb some of the force; they are, however, too expensive for some schools.

Fielding

Catching or stopping the ball after it is propelled by the batter is spoken of as fielding. If the ball is in the air, it is called a *fly ball;* if rolling or bouncing on the ground, it is called a *ground ball*.

FIELDING FLY BALLS   Basic catching mechanics are employed. The player should keep his eyes on the ball from the time it leaves the bat, watch the pattern of its flight, and then move into position to catch it. Since a batted ball comes with great force, it is essential to get in line with the ball. Beginners should be taught to catch high balls just above the chin by keeping the thumbs together. Balls that drop low should be caught between the waist and shoulders. The little fingers should be together. The stride should be forward and backward with feet spread. This helps maintain balance and also allows a good stance for the return throw to the infield.

COMMON FAULTS

1. Failing to get in line with ball.
2. Moving up too quickly to meet ball and frequently running too far under it.
3. Holding outstretched fingers rigidly to meet ball.
4. Trying to catch ball in front of eyes and face.
5. Trying to catch ball with one hand under and one hand over the ball rather than hands side by side.
6. Failing to give with fingers and elbows immediately upon grasping ball.

KEY TEACHING PHRASES

1. Watch flight of ball as it leaves bat.
2. Move into position.
3. Catch high ball with palms out, thumbs together (just above chin).
4. Catch low balls with palms up, little fingers together (between waist and shoulders).
5. As soon as fingers contact ball, squeeze it, and "give" with whole body.

FIELDING GROUND BALLS   The player should move to meet the ball and get in line with it. With the left foot forward, the player bends at the ankles, knees, and hips and gets into a semi-crouched position, keeping the upper part of the body almost erect. With the fingers pointing toward the ground, the hands are placed opposite the left foot. As the ball is met, it is picked up and brought back into a position to start the next throw.

COMMON FAULTS

1. Failing to get in line with the ball.
2. Bending from the waist and losing balance.
3. Putting hands out with fingers up, thereby letting the ball bounce off the heels of the hands.
4. Feet spread in a side-stride position (balls roll between them).

KEY TEACHING PHRASES

1. Left foot forward, move to meet the ball, and get in line with the ball.
2. Bend at the ankles, knees, and waist, with fingers pointing down; place hands opposite left foot.
3. Clasp fingers around ball.
4. Bring ball in toward body and back for the throw to infield.

Pitching

Pitching utilizes the underhand throw pattern (page 258). At the start of the pitch, both feet must be parallel, and both hands on the ball. The right arm is brought back as the body rotates. The ball is released off the ends of the fingers about hip level. The left foot is brought forward as the ball is brought forward. The right foot is brought up parallel to the left foot so the pitcher is in ready position to field the ball. Pitching arm follows ball straight toward plate.

COMMON FAULTS

1. Failing to use enough rotation and backswing to get force and speed on the ball.
2. Bringing arm across the body before releasing the ball and causing it to go from right to left.
3. Releasing ball too high or too late.

KEY TEACHING PHRASES

1. Feet together.
2. Ball held in both hands.
3. Bring arm straight back.
4. Rotate trunk to right.
5. Step onto left foot as arm is brought straight forward.
6. Let ball roll off fingertips at a point directly in line with target.
7. Follow ball with hand and arm pointing at target.
8. Bring right foot up beside left foot.

Batting

The bat is held with the left hand wrapped around the handle of the bat about 2 inches from the end, and the right hand wrapped around just above the left hand. If the bat is heavy or long, it may be held or "choked" further up on the handle. The batter stands facing home plate with feet shoulder-width apart, feet pointing straight ahead toward the plate and parallel to it. (It helps to draw a line parallel to the plate about 18 inches from it so the player has a guideline.) The player reaches out with his bat and touches the far side of the plate with the bat. This helps him judge how far away he needs to stand. (If a batting tee is used the thick part of the bat may be placed on the tee.) He holds the bat away from the body with right elbow bent and out. The bat is held at shoulder height and points diagonally upward. The knees are bent, weight is on the back foot, but hips and shoulders remain level. The batter looks over his left shoulder at the pitcher and watches the ball as it approaches the plate. To initiate the forward swing, the hips roll forward and a short step is taken toward the pitcher. The bat is swung forward level with the ground. The wrists are snapped as the bat contacts the ball and continue to roll over as the follow-through is taken. The weight is shifted to the forward foot. The bat is dropped as the first step toward first base is taken. (The trademark of the bat should be facing the batter as he holds the bat.)

COMMON FAULTS

1. Putting wrong hand on bottom of bat handle.
2. Resting bat on shoulder.
3. Facing the pitcher.
4. Elbows and arms in close to body, causing a punchy, choppy swing.
5. Swinging upward and under the ball instead of level with ground.

Figure 14-15 Batting stance.

KEY TEACHING PHRASES

1. Place left hand below right hand (right-handed batter).
2. Choke bat if necessary.
3. Face home plate.
4. Feet parallel to plate.
5. Hold bat back and up just over right shoulder.
6. Arms and elbows out and away from body.
7. Eyes on ball.
8. Weight on right foot.
9. Twist back.
10. Swing big and level with ground.
11. Shift weight to left foot.
12. Snap wrists.
13. Meet ball squarely.
14. Roll wrists over.
15. Follow through.
16. Drop bat.

Baserunning

Initially, children need only be taught to run beyond first base. When games use four bases and all of the game skills become more refined, emphasis can be placed on proper baserunning techniques. The runner should touch the inside of the bases and not run wide at each base. A runner waiting on base should assume a forward lean position, with the left foot on the base and the right foot ready to push off as soon as the ball is released by the pitcher. Until the majority of the class can hit the ball far enough to run farther than first base on the hit, to work on baserunning is a poor use of time.

Position Play

Pitcher

1. Fields balls hit near him.
2. Covers first base when first-base player must field a hit ball.
3. Backs up third-base player when a runner is on first.
4. Backs up catcher when a runner is on second.
5. Covers home on a passed ball or wild pitch.

Catcher

1. Fields balls hit or bunted near the plate.
2. Backs up first-base player when no runner is on first.

First-Base Player

1. Plays 10 feet to left of base when no one is on first.
2. Fields all balls coming toward the first base area.
3. Backs up second-base player on throws from left and center fields when no one is on first.

Second-Base Player

1. Plays between second and first base about 10 feet behind base line and 12 feet from second base.
2. Fields balls hit to the left of second base.
3. Covers second base when hits are to the right side of the base.
4. Covers second base on throws from catcher.
5. Relays throws from center fielders and right fielder to infield.

Shortstop

1. Plays about 10 feet behind the base line and halfway between third and second base.
2. Fields balls going between second and third base.
3. Covers second base on balls hit to the first-base side of second base.
4. Backs up second-base player on balls thrown from catcher.
5. Relays throws from left fielder to infield.

Third-Base Player

1. Plays about 8 feet to his left of third base and about 4 or 5 feet behind base line.
2. Fields balls hit to left side of field.

Left Fielder

1. Backs up the center fielder on hit balls.
2. Backs up third-base player.

Center Fielder

1. Backs up left and right fielders on hit balls.
2. Backs up shortstop and second-base player on ground balls.
3. Backs up second-base player on all plays.

Right Fielder

1. Backs up center fielder, second-base player, and first-base player on hit balls.
2. Backs up plays at first and second base.

Basic Offensive and Defensive Concepts

From the very first lead-up game, simple offensive and defensive concepts can be stressed once the format of the game is grasped. A few basic concepts are listed in order of presentation. The nature of the lead-up game determines whether or not these are plausible.

OFFENSIVE CONCEPTS

1. Batter runs out all hits.
2. Overrun first base.
3. Baserunners know how many outs there have been and are aware of the bases occupied.
4. Hit to empty spaces.

DEFENSIVE CONCEPTS

1. Fielders assume a ready position as soon as ball is pitched.
2. They know how many outs there are, check which bases are occupied, and plan where to throw ball.

Table 14-8. Skill Game Guide for Practicing Softball Skills

SKILL GAMES	BASE THROWING	CATCHING	FIELDING	OVERHAND THROW	BATTING	PITCHING	BASERUNNING	GENERAL RULES AND FORMAT OF GAME
Beat Ball	x	x					x	
Flies and Grounders			x	x	x			
Throwover	x		x					
Around the Bases							x	
Pepper			x	x	x			
Target Pitch						x		
Kickball								x
Leader and Class		x		x				
Star Relay		x		x				
Hit Pin								x

3. After ball is fielded they throw it to a base player or a relay player immediately; they should not hold it or run with it.

4. They throw to the base to which the runner is going.

5. They try to put out the player who is nearest to scoring a run.

6. When there are two outs, they play to the nearest base for a force out.

7. They keep eyes on ball and either get into position to catch it, or move to a covering or backing-up position.

Skill Games to Improve Softball Skills

• *Beat Ball*

Skills: Throwing, base throwing, running, catching.

Equipment: Four bases, softball diamond, one ball.

Formation: One team at bat, one in field.

Procedure: Rules for Throw It and Run or Modified Softball are followed (as far as positions and outs are concerned). A player may bat or throw the ball into the outfield. He runs all around the bases and tries to reach home before the ball does. The fielders must start the ball at second base and try to get it from second to third to home before the runner reaches home. The base player must have one foot touching the base when he throws. Teams change sides after everyone has had a batting turn. The team that scores the most runs after a specified equal number of turns at bat wins.

• *Flies and Grounders*

Skills: Batting, fielding, overhand throw.

Equipment: Bat, six balls, batting tee, for each group.

Formation: One batter; five other players scattered out in field.

Procedure: Batter hits balls into the field. Each time a player is in position to field a ball, he must yell "Mine" and attempt the play. If he catches a fly ball, he receives 5 points. If he catches a fly on the first bounce, he gets 3 points. If he catches a grounder, he receives 1 point. The first person who reaches a total of 15 points takes the place of the batter who goes into the field.

Variation: This same game may be played with throwing rather than batting.

• *Throwover*

Throwover is just like Kickover (page 337). Instead of kicking the ball, the players on one team use an overhand throw.

• *Around the Bases*

Skill: Baserunning.

Equipment: Four bases, 45 feet apart.

Formation: One squad lines up behind each base.

Procedure: The first person in each squad runs around, touching the inside corner of every base. The second player steps up on the base as his player is coming toward the base. The runner touches off the next runner by hitting his outstretched hand. The team whose members first complete their trip around the bases wins.

- **Kickball**

Skills: Kicking, throwing, catching, general format and rules of softball.

Equipment: Four bases, softball diamond, one soccer ball.

Formation: Same playing positions as for Throw It and Run (page 422).

Procedure: The same rules as Throw It and Run are followed. Instead of hitting the ball, the batter kicks the ball. The pitcher rolls the ball on the ground for the pitch.

- **Hit Pin**

The basic rules for Beat Ball apply to Hit Pin. Instead of flat bases, pins are set in the middle of 1-foot circles. The home-base circle is 3 feet in diameter. The pitcher must roll a soccer ball within the circle to make a strike. The batter must kick the ball while standing in the circle. The runner runs outside and around each base in order to try to reach home before the catcher receives the ball and knocks over the home pin. The ball must be started at first base. Whenever the ball beats the runner to a base, the base player may knock down the pin and the batter is declared out at that point.

- **Pepper**

Skills: Batting, fielding, throwing.

Equipment: One softball and bat for each team or squad.

Formation: Members of a squad line up in a single line with about 9 feet between them. They are facing the leader. The leader stands 20 feet in front of the others.

Procedure: The first person in line throws the ball or pitches it to the leader, who tries to hit a ground ball to the next player in the line. This person then pitches it back to the batter and the process is repeated. If a line player misses a ground ball, he goes to the end of the line. The first person in line takes his place, and everyone moves up one place. If the pitch is wild, the person who threw it must go to the end of the line. The object is to be batter as long as possible.

Variations: The game may be played by having someone throw grounders or flies instead of batting.

- **Target Pitch**

Skill: Pitching.

Equipment: Four softballs per target.

Formation: Targets drawn on the wall approximately 36 inches by 18 inches and 20 inches above floor. Pitching line drawn 35 feet away from wall. Two children play against one another; each represents the pitcher for a team.

Procedure: Each player in turn pitches no more than a total of seven balls. He tries to get a combination of three strikes or hits within the target to make an out. If he gets four balls or misses before he gets three strikes within the seven pitches, the other player gets a run. Players take turns. When each has had an equal number of specified turns, the player with the most runs is declared the winner.

Figure 14-16 Long Base.

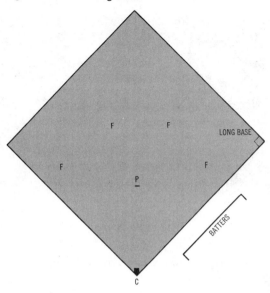

Softball Lead-Up Games

• *Long Base (Figure 14-16)*

Area: Small softball field with only one base off to the right of home plate about 30 feet away. Two teams of six. One team is at bat and stands in batter's area to the right of home plate. One team in the field, with a pitcher, a catcher, and four fielders spread over the field.

Procedure: The pitcher throws the ball to the batter, using an underhand throw. The batter catches the ball and throws it anywhere within the playing field and then runs to the long base and back trying to reach home before the fielders can field the ball and get it to the catcher, who must step on home plate when he has the ball in his hand. One run is scored if the batter gets home before the ball does. Everyone on the batting team has a turn to bat, then sides change. The distance from home to long base will have to be adjusted to fit the skills of the group. If the fielding team always gets the ball back before the runner does, the base is too far. If the runner always wins, the base is too close.

Outs: An out or no point is called if:
1. Fly ball is caught.
2. Catcher touches home with ball in hand before runner reaches home.

Variation: The runner may be allowed to stay at first base and come home on the next hit. In this case a first-base player is needed. Players can also be put out at first if the ball reaches the first-base player before the runner gets there.

Hints: Several games of Long Base may be going on at one time, since it requires so few players and a small amount of space for third-grade children. Insist that fielders return ball to catcher with an overhand throw and that they do not run with the ball.

Figure 14-17 Throw It and Run.

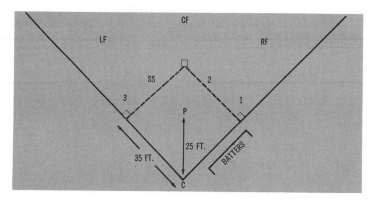

• *Throw It and Run (Figure 14-17)*

Area: Small softball diamond as diagramed. Two teams of nine players each. One team is at bat, one team takes regular softball positions in the field.

Procedure: The pitcher throws to the batter and the batter throws the ball overhand to the field within the foul lines. He then runs to first base. If he sees that the ball will probably not beat him to second base, he goes on to second and continues around to home, if possible. He stops where he must in order to prevent being put out. The fielder throws the ball to the base where the runner is going. The ball is returned to the pitcher, and another batter throws the ball. The baserunner advances, if possible. The team bats around once, then the teams change places. An inning is a division of the game during which each team has a turn at bat.

Scoring: When a batter completes the circle of bases without being put out, he scores a run. The team with the most runs after an equal number of turns at bat wins.

Outs:

1. A batter is out if he misses three well-pitched balls.
2. The batter is out if the base player steps on base with the ball in hand before the runner can get there. A force out takes place when the runner cannot go back to a base because a teammate is occupying it.
3. The batter is out if a fielder tags him with the ball before he reaches a base.
4. The batter is out if a fly ball is caught.

Strategies:

1. Base players should learn to cover their base where they are not involved in fielding the ball that has been hit.
2. Fielders should throw to the base to which the runner is running.
3. Batters should throw to an open area.

• *Tee Ball*

This is the same game as Throw It and Run; however, a batting tee is used, and the ball is hit rather than thrown. Batting should be learned and practiced before the game is played. It will be easier for children to learn the format of the game if they throw first rather than bat. The inning may last until the team has made three outs rather than until everyone has been at bat.

• *Modified Softball*

Area: Softball diamond with bases 45 feet apart, pitcher's box 35 feet from home plate. These distances may be altered according to the ability of the groups playing. One team takes the fielding positions and one becomes the batting team.

Procedure: The game starts with the pitcher pitching to the first batter, who attempts to hit the ball into the field and get on base. If he is successful, subsequent batters try to get hits and advance the runner around to home to score a run. Fielders attempt to put batters and runners out. When three outs have been made, the teams change places. A definite batting order must be maintained. A set number of innings may be specified, the usual number being seven. The team with the most runs at the end of the seven innings wins. If there is a tie, the game is extended until one team gets more points than the other after an equal number of turns at bat.

Inning: The period of time in which both teams have been at bat and have made three outs.

Strike: A pitched ball that goes over the home plate in the strike zone and which the batter fails to strike at, or strikes at and misses. A foul ball that is not caught is considered a strike if the batter has fewer than two strikes. The strike zone is the area over the plate between the batter's knees and shoulders. Three strikes constitute an out.

Ball: A ball is a pitched ball that does not go in the strike zone and is not struck at or hit by the batter.

Walk: Four balls constitute a free pass or walk to first base. If there is a runner on first base, he moves on to second. If the batter is hit by a pitched ball he is awarded a walk.

Foul Ball: A ball that is hit and settles (or is touched by a fielder) outside the base line between first and third, and between home and first base; one that lands outside of the base lines beyond first or third base. It is called a fair ball when it settles (or lands) inside these areas.

Outs: The batter is out when:

1. Three strikes are called. If the catcher drops the ball on the third strike and first base is not occupied, the runner may run for first and must be played on as usual to be put out.
2. A fly ball is caught, whether it is fair or foul.
3. The base player at first touches the base with ball in hand before the batter reaches first.
4. There is an infield fly hit and there are runners on first and second bases with less than two outs.

A runner is out when:

1. He is tagged with a ball whenever he is off the base.
2. When he is forced out at a base. This occurs when he cannot go back to the base he was on since someone else must occupy it.
3. He advances to the next base before a fly ball is caught and does not return and tag the base he left.

Overthrow: When a ball is overthrown at a base, the runner may advance as many bases as he can. If the ball is blocked or hits an obstruction behind first or third base, he may advance only one base.

Stealing Base: A player may leave the base as soon as the ball leaves the pitcher's hands. If a foul was hit, he must return to base. If there is no back-stop, it is not recommended that stealing be allowed on a passed ball. Stealing bases should not be allowed if the throwing and catching skills do not permit defensive plays to be made with any success.

• *Work-Up*

Area: A small softball diamond such as that diagramed on page 422 is used. Seven to fifteen players may play.

Procedure: The value of Work-Up is that two games may be played at the same time in a class of average size, or as few players as seven may play in a pick-up game. Rather than having two teams, each player is assigned a fielding position and three batters are designated. If twelve players are available, all fielding positions can be covered. The rules are the same as for modified softball. When a batter is out he goes to right field or some other predetermined position, and everyone rotates to a new position, working their way up to be a batter. Usually the order is: batter to right field, right to center, center to left, left to third, third to shortstop, shortstop to second base, second to first base, first to pitcher, pitcher to catcher, catcher to umpire, umpire to batter. This game has value when there are not enough players to make two teams, but it has more value in a regular class because everyone is more active, has a chance to play different positions and to bat more often. This game is recommended for all grade levels above fifth at some time during the unit. There is a need to play by sides and to learn to work as a team; however, better skills can be developed first by an exposure to different positions and when there is more opportunity for action. Work-Up may be played using a batting tee or a pitcher.

Skill Tests

THROW FOR DISTANCE   A football field marked in conventional fashion (5-yard intervals) makes an ideal area for this test. If this is not available, it is suggested that lines be drawn parallel to the restraining line, 5 yards apart. The pupil throws the ball while remaining within two parallel lines, 6 feet apart. Mark the point of landing with a small stake. If his second or third throw is farther, move the stake accordingly so that, after three throws, the stake is at the point of the pupil's best throw. It was found expedient to have the pupil jog out to his stake and stand there; and then, after five pupils have completed their throws, the measurements were taken. By having the pupil at his particular stake, there is little danger of recording the wrong score.

RULES

1. Only an overhand throw may be used.
2. Three throws are allowed.
3. The distance recorded is the distance measured at right angles from the point of landing to the restraining line.

SCORING   Record the best of the three trials to the nearest foot.

OVERHAND THROW FOR ACCURACY   A target consisting of three concentric circles with three diameters of 24 inches, 36 inches, and 48 inches is drawn on the wall 3 feet above the floor. Each circle is labeled 3, 2, 1 points, respectively. The target may be painted on oilcloth or paper and hung on wall. A line is drawn on the floor 50 feet from the wall. (This may vary in respect to age level.) Each player is given ten consecutive throws from behind the throwing line. Points are counted for the scoring area which each ball hits. Balls hitting on a line count the higher value. The score is the sum of points recorded for each hit.

PITCHING   A target 17 inches wide and 36 inches high is drawn on the wall 16 inches off the floor. A line is drawn 35 feet from the wall in front of the target. This distance should be the same as that of the usual distance from the plate to the pitcher's box. The pitcher is given fifteen consecutive trials. He must use a legal underhand pitch and must keep one foot on the pitching line before the ball is released. One point is scored for every ball that goes in the target area or touches a line.

BASERUNNING   Upon a signal, the batter swings the bat at an imaginary pitched ball, puts the bat down, and circles the bases, which are set at the distance the class is used to playing in the game. A timer starts the stopwatch when the signal to hit is given. The bat must not be thrown or carried more than 12 feet. Each base must be touched in order. The watch is stopped when the runner touches home plate. Two trials are given and the best trial is recorded as the score.

FIELDING   Fielding is more difficult to test objectively since projecting the ball for the student to field cannot be done with any great consistency. Only a test for ground balls is recommended.

FIELDING GROUND BALLS   A rectangular area is marked out on the field that is 25 feet by 60 feet with a restraining line marked 10 feet in from one end. The player stands in this 10-foot restraining area. From the opposite end the test administrator throws a hard rolling ball within the side boundary lines. The player being tested moves to meet the ball somewhere in front of the restraining line. The ball must be fielded without a bobble and returned to an assistant who is feeding the balls to the administrator. If the ground ball is outside the testing area or is a poorly thrown ball, the trial is repeated. Fifteen trials are given. Each ball successfully fielded scores 1 point. The final score is the total of points scored on the fifteen trials.

Volleyball Activities

In 1895 volleyball originated at a YMCA in Holyoke, Massachusetts. Since that time it has gained great popularity as a sport that is played by men and women of all ages. It is a good recreational game because it takes very little equipment and a small amount of space, it can be learned quickly, and it can be either a highly competitive fast-moving game or be enjoyed by those who are not highly skilled. With few modifications it can be played by boys and girls together and by just a few players; it may be played on the beach, on the playground, or in the gym.

Since the skills of volleyball are few in number and the most basic ones can be learned at an early age, there is little need for teaching many lead-up games. It is more important to modify the size and weight of the ball, the size of the court, the height of the net, and the game rules than to modify the skills and the format of the game. The game is unique in that players from opposing teams are separated by a net and are not in the same playing area. This eliminates one of the needs for modification that is necessary in most of the other team games.

The official game calls for two teams of six players. Each team occupies half of a rectangular court which is divided by a net. The object of the game is to hit a ball back and forth across the net with each team trying to earn points by placing the ball so that their opponents cannot return it.

Teaching Considerations

1. Since the overhand volley is the most frequently used skill in the game, it should be practiced extensively. It can be taught first in a basic skill lesson unrelated to volleyball, but stress must be put on correct execution and upon hitting the ball high in order to avoid forming poor habits even before the game is started. The serve can also be learned out of context of the game.

2. Nets should be adjusted to the height of the players. Too-high nets can be very frustrating and discouraging to young children who can actually perform the skill, but cannot be successful in the game because the net is too high for them.

3. Lightweight balls or heavyweight balloons can be used first, since young children can learn the skill pattern, but may lack the arm and wrist strength to hit a heavy ball.

4. Smaller balls (7-inch) should be used at first, since children's fingers are short, and they are apt to hit a large ball off-center.

5. Although volleyball is often advertised as a game that can accommodate large numbers of children and enable everyone to play, this is not always true. When more than six or eight are on a team, children experience little action. Most of them are standing and seldom have a chance to touch the ball. It is far better to make two courts out of one and have two games with six on each team in a smaller space than twelve on a team in a larger area. Control and placement of the ball should be emphasized rather than the ability to send it a long distance. Therefore, small courts with a few players will allow for more practice and participation by all. If playing space is limited, some players may practice skills against the wall or even work on different kinds of activities at various stations around the room. When there are seven players, one may stand on the side lines opposite the left front-line player. When the team rotates, he becomes the left front player and the left back becomes the side-line player. This system may be adjusted for a larger number of extra players.

6. Ropes with ribbons dangling from them may be substituted for a net.

7. Teams should be responsible for keeping their own scores in class games; the server announces the score before each serve.

8. The ball should be rolled under the net to the server. This saves a great deal of time.

9. The wall should be utilized extensively for skill practices, since the ball rebounds with more regularity than if two beginning players are returning it to each other.

10. Newcomb, Net Ball, and Deck Tennis are good active games that can be utilized in the third grade to teach scoring, rotation, and format of the game. When the latter are taught in volleyball, reference to their use in these games should be made; however, the games themselves should not be played during a volleyball unit since they all involve throwing and catching the ball (fouls in volleyball). They are not volleyball lead-up games.

Volleyball Skills

Overhead Volley The overhead volley is used whenever the ball is received at chest level or higher. The hands are held at eye level with the fingers spread and thumbs and index fingers almost touching. This gives the appearance of a triangle or window to look through as the ball is hit. The wrists are hyperextended,

Table 14-9. Progression of Skills, Knowledges, Rules, and Lead-Up Games for Volleyball

SKILLS	KNOWLEDGES AND RULES	LEAD-UP GAMES	LEVEL
Overhead volley Serve	Service Court positions Rotation Official scoring Side out Point One hit per person Unlimited hits per side	One-Line Volleyball 5-foot net Court 15 by 30 feet	III
Forearm pass (bump) Passing	Touching net foul Line violations Unlimited hits per side One, two, three attack (simple) Ready position	Modified Volleyball 6-foot net Court 20 by 40 feet	IV
High set	Backing-up Fouls: Catching Holding Pushing Body Game strategy 3 hits per side	Modified Volleyball 6½-foot net Two-Man Volleyball Court 25 by 50 feet	
Spike Block Overhand serve Recovery from net	One, two, three, attack Official rules	Modified Volleyball 7-foot net Court 25 by 50 feet Official Volleyball 7½-foot net Court 25 by 50 feet	IV IV IV

427

elbows are flexed and out at shoulder height, the knees bent. As the ball is hit, the knees and arms extend forcibly upward and forward with a complete follow-through high in the air in the direction the ball is to go. The ball is contacted by all the fingers and the thumbs simultaneously, as the wrists flex and have a flicking motion. The emphasis should be on hitting the ball high, about 15 to 20 feet off the floor, and finishing with the whole body in a fully extended position. A jump off the floor as the ball is hit should also be encouraged. The overhead volley is used (when the ball is received from the serve) to pass the ball to a teammate who then uses the volley as a set to a teammate who sends the ball over the net.

COMMON FAULTS

1. Fingers are pointed straight up, no hyperextension of wrists.
2. Ball is slapped by the palm of the hand.
3. Ball is contacted in front of the chest and pushed forward rather than upward.
4. Body is straight when ball is hit.
5. Knees, arms, and wrists do not extend; therefore little power is gained.
6. One hand is used instead of two.
7. Player reaches off to one side to hit the ball.
8. Ball goes over head because of poor positioning.

KEY TEACHING PHRASES

1. Eyes on ball.
2. Make window with hands, thumbs, and index fingers nearly touching.
3. Knees bent.

HAND POSITION

CONTACTING THE BALL

Figure 14-18 The overhead volley.

4. Elbows bent and held shoulder high.

5. Look through "window" and hit ball.

6. Hit ball high and forward, and reach high with whole body.

Underhand Serve

The player stands with the left foot slightly ahead of the right, knees bent. The ball is held on the left hand directly in front of and at the same level of the right hand as it hangs down at the side. The serving motion is like that of an underhand throw. The right hand forms a fist. The right arm swings straight back and forth in a pendular motion. The ball is contacted slightly below center and hit off the hand. The right arm follows through above the shoulder in the direction of the target.

COMMON FAULTS

1. Eyes are taken off ball.

2. Ball held too high.

3. Ball held too far to left of body.

4. Ball is tossed in air.

5. Left shoulder is lifted as right arm is swung forward, and ball is above the right fist at contact.

6. Elbow of serving arm is bent in forward swing.

7. Ball is contacted too low, therefore it goes too high in the air.

8. Backswing is too short, resulting in lack of force.

9. Arm is brought across in front of body causing ball to go to left.

KEY TEACHING PHRASES

1. Eyes on ball.

2. Left shoulder toward net.

3. Measure where ball should be held by swinging right arm straight back and forth.

4. Swing arm backward and forward.

5. Hit ball off hand.

6. Follow through in direction of target.

Overhand Serve

The overhand serve is more difficult to execute than the underhand; however, it is more effective if done well. Those children at Level IV who can use the underhand serve well and are fairly strong should be encouraged to learn and use it.

The server stands with left foot forward, side slightly to the net, knees bent. Right arm is brought back above ear, elbow is slightly bent and cocked. Ball is tossed 2 or 3 feet above the right shoulder with left hand. As ball descends, weight is shifted forward, arm comes forward and extends, wrist stays firm as ball is contacted mid-center slightly forward of the head but still high. Hips rotate slightly as body weight and arm follow through to right foot. The fist or flat of the hand may be used to contact the ball. The motion is basically an overhand throw pattern.

COMMON FAULTS

1. Ball is tossed too low.

2. Arm position too low, elbow not bent.

3. Ball contacted underneath.
4. Ball too low when contacted.
5. Wrist not firm.
6. Ball contacted in front or too far left of body.
7. No follow-through.

KEY TEACHING PHRASES

1. Eyes on ball.
2. Shoulder to net.
3. Shift weight to back foot.
4. Right elbow bent and held high.
5. Toss ball high above right arm.
6. Right arm leads with elbow.
7. Whip arm forward.
8. Contact ball high above head.
9. Step into ball on right foot.
10. Reach for the target area.

Forearm Pass (Bump)

When a ball must be received below waist level, the ball must be hit with an underhand motion. One hand is placed in the palm of the other; the thumbs are on top (Figure 14-19). The forearms are close together and parallel, elbows touching. The body must be in line with the ball, knees bent. As the ball is hit, the knees extend and the body rises upward. The ball actually rebounds off the flat side of the forearm and wrist. Little follow-through is necessary. It is essential that the body be directly behind the ball if direction is to be controlled. The ball should be sent high. The bump is used to receive most serves, to take all low balls, and to recover the ball from the net. In an emergency when the player cannot get into position for a forearm pass, a one-hand dig may be used. In this case the ball rebounds off the flat side of one forearm.

Figure 14-19 Body position and hand position for the forearm (bump) pass.

1. Body not in line with ball.
2. Failure to keep forearms close together.
3. Failure to bend knees and extend them as ball is hit.
4. Elbows bend as arms swing up to contact ball.
5. Too much follow-through.

KEY TEACHING PHRASES

1. Get directly in line with ball.
2. Grasp one hand tight in other hand.
3. Keep forearms together.
4. Bend knees.
5. Extend knees as ball is contacted.
6. Contact ball at wrist area.

The Set

The set is usually the second hit in the series of three allowed. The ball is hit to a teammate so it is in position for a spike. The overhead volley is used; however, the set must be about 15 feet high and about 1 foot from the net in a position where a teammate can spike it over the net. Even before children can spike the ball, they should be taught to set the second ball high. A ball that is high and soft is much easier to redirect, no matter what kind of a hit is used.

Spike

The spike is a ball that is sent smashing downward into the opponents' court so that it is very difficult to return. The spiker stands close to the net facing the direction from which the ball is coming. As the ball starts to come down, the spiker jumps high in the air, swings his right arm upward. The ball is hit downward when it is still above the net. The body turns in the air and the spiker lands facing the net. The ball must be set up high enough so a hit can be downward on top of the ball. The net may be lowered when the spike is first taught. Weight must be controlled so the body does not fall forward into the net.

COMMON FAULTS

1. Jumping too late.
2. Hitting ball underneath and causing it to go upward.
3. Falling forward on the jump.
4. Standing too close to the net.

KEY TEACHING PHRASES

1. Eyes on ball.
2. Jump high just as ball starts down.
3. Reach and hit downward on ball.
4. Turn and land facing the net.
5. Keep upper body erect.

Block

The block is the defense against the spike. The blocker faces the net and jumps at the same time the spiker does. He swings both arms upward so hands are about 6 inches above the net. The fingers are spread and the ball actually rebounds from the hands. This is a difficult skill because of the timing of the jump, but it can be learned by seventh- and eighth-graders.

COMMON FAULTS

1. Poor timing; jump made too early or too late.
2. Hands are apart.
3. Hands push or hit at ball.

KEY TEACHING PHRASES

1. Eyes on ball.
2. Jump with spiker.
3. Hands outstretched, thumbs close together.
4. Let ball rebound from hands.
5. Do not follow through.

Net Recovery

When the ball hits the net it will rebound in different ways depending upon how hard it hits and on what part of the net. The class should study this before attempting net recoveries. If there have been two hits or less, a player may hit the ball as it bounces off the net. He faces the net, watches where the ball hits the net, quickly gets into position, bends the knees, and uses a two-hand dig to send the ball directly upward. In desperation a one-hand dig may be tried. This is a difficult skill, because again the timing is crucial.

COMMON FAULTS

1. Failing to anticipate the rebound correctly.
2. Failing to bend and get under ball.
3. Ball is held momentarily.
4. Ball swept backward over shoulders.

KEY TEACHING PHRASES

1. Watch where ball hits net.
2. Bend knees.
3. Get under ball.
4. Hit ball upward.

General Offensive and Defensive Team Play

OFFENSIVE CONCEPTS

1. The serve should be placed into open areas and preferably deep in the court and near the side lines.
2. The three hits allowed before the ball is sent over the net should always be used. The basic 1, 2, 3, attack should be followed in the modified games as well as in the official games, even though a spike cannot be executed.
   a. *One* is the initial *pass* made to a front-line player when the ball is received.
   b. *Two* is the *set* to a front-line player.
   c. *Three* is the *spike* or the volley over the net.
3. Forward-line players never play with backs to net.
4. High passes are essential.

DEFENSIVE CONCEPTS

1. All players should be in a position of readiness. Eyes on ball, weight evenly placed over both feet, which are in a forward-stride position.
2. Most serves are received by back-line players. Front-line players should be ready to receive a pass.
3. A ball that goes above a forward-line player's shoulders should always be taken by a back.
4. The backs always back up certain players on the serve. The right back backs up the right forward and the left back; the left back backs up the left forward, the center back, and the left back; the center back backs up the center forward.
5. A player should call out, "Mine," when he intends to take a ball and when there may be some doubt as to who is going to take it.

Skill Games to Improve Volleyball Skills

• *Circle Keep-It-Up*

Skills: Overhead pass.
Equipment: One ball per circle.

Table 14-10. Skill Game Guide for Practicing Volleyball

SKILL GAMES	VOLLEY PASS	SET	BUMP	SERVE	SPIKE	BLOCK	NET RECOVERY
Call Ball				x			
Circle Keep-It-Up	x						
Zigzag Volley	x		x				
Wall Volleyball	x		x	x			
Shuttle Volley	x						
Volley by Two	x	x					
Volley by Four	x	x					
Serve to Wall				x			
Toss and Bump			x				
Wall Bump			x				
Toss and Spike					x		
Set and Spike		x			x		
Spike and Block		x			x	x	
Toss and Recover							x

433

Formation: Small circles of six. The object of the game is to see which circle can get the most consecutive hits.

Procedure: One player throws the ball up to himself, then volleys the ball to anyone in the circle. The ball is volleyed until it falls to the floor or is caught, pushed, or thrown. A leader calls out the number of hits. When a team makes a foul or the ball hits the floor, it drops out of the game. The game moves quickly, so a number of games should be played to see which team can win the most times.

Variations: The game may be played to see which team can make the most completed volleys in 30 seconds. The number may be cumulative, not necessarily continuous. If the ball hits the floor or a foul is made, the ball is put into play again with a set. It can be specified that only overhead passes may be made or that only digs can be used, although the latter are harder to control.

• Wall Volleyball

Skills: Overhead pass, bump.

Equipment: One ball, a wall space 10 feet wide and 5 feet high.

Formation: This game may be played by two, three, or four people.

Procedure: The object of this game is to keep the ball bouncing against the wall above the line. Two people oppose one another. One puts the ball into play with a serve against the wall. It must be returned by the next person, and play continues with alternate hits. When one fails to hit it above the net line or fails to return it, the other player receives a point or the serve. Only the server may win points. If three are playing, the same rules apply; players must hit the ball in order. If four play, it is a game of doubles, and partners alternate hits and serves. The first to win 15 points wins the game.

• Zigzag Volley

Skill: Overhead pass, set.

Equipment: One ball per team.

Formation: Groups of ten line up in two staggered lines so each person faces an empty space. The lines are 9 feet apart.

Procedure: The ball is started at one end. Upon a signal the first player tosses the ball up and hits it to the first player in the opposite line. The ball zigzags back and forth between the two lines to the end and back to the first player, who catches it. Everyone sits down. The first team sitting wins. The overhead pass must be used. If the ball is dropped or missed, it is set by the person who missed it, and play continues.

Variation: Lines may be moved closer together and the ball hit to the other side as if it were a set.

• Shuttle Volley

Skills: Overhead volley.

Equipment: One ball for each group, a rope stretched between two posts at a height of 15 feet.

Formation: Groups of eight. Lines drawn parallel to both sides of the rope and 4 feet from it. Four players stand behind one line, four behind the other.

Procedure: The ball must be volleyed above the rope by the first person in one line and so that the first person in the other line can volley it back across the rope to the second person in line. After a player has volleyed, he runs to the end of the opposite line. When everyone is in his original position, the team sits down. The first team finished wins the game.

Since there are few really good skill task games for volleyball, a few practice drills for the skills are suggested.

• Volley

Volley by Twos: Partners volley ball back and forth across net.

Volley by Fours: Two line up on each side of the net. The two nearest the net are front-line players, the two in the back are the backs. The first back sets the ball up to himself then passes it to the front player who hits it over the net over the head of the opposite front-line player to the back, who in turn passes it to his front-line player. Play continues with players rotating frequently.

• Serve

Serve to Wall: Individual player repeatedly serves to a point on wall 5 feet high from varying distances from the wall.

Serve to Partners: Partners serve back and forth to one another from a distance of 20 feet, then 30, depending on skill level. If there is not a ball for every two people, single-line formations on each side of the court may be used.

• Bump

Toss and Bump: Working in partners, one tosses the ball for two to dig. They alternate toss and bump responsibilities.

Wall Dig: A player tosses the ball against the wall and uses a dig to hit the ball back against the wall, continuing this until he has to set the ball up with another toss.

• Spike

Jump and Reach: Players should practice the jump and reach against the wall. Chalk lines can be used to mark how high they jump each time. This should be done at the net, so players see how high above the net they can reach.

Toss and Spike: Players are in two lines facing the net about 2 feet beside it. One person is on the opposite side of net to retrieve balls. The right-hand line is the tossing line, the left the spiking line. The ball is tossed 15 feet high and about 1 foot from the net. The spiker attempts to spike it across the net. The spiker takes the retriever's place, the retriever moves to the end of the tossing line, and the tosser moves to the end of the spiking line. The net may be lowered 6 inches below its usual height.

Set and Spike: The same drill may be used with the tosser setting the ball to himself with a toss, then setting it for the spiker.

• Block

Spike and Block: The same drill formation as for Toss and Spike may be used, only the retriever becomes a blocker.

• *Net Recovery*

Toss and Receive: Working in partners, one tosses ball into the net, the other tries to recover it. Two lines may be formed, and turns taken, playing with partners.

• *One-Line Volleyball (Figure 14-20)*

Area: A court area 15 feet by 15 feet marked as in the diagram. Two teams of four. All members stand on one line near net.

Procedure: The ball is served by the player in the right-hand corner position. The ball is returned by a member of the other team. The ball is hit back and forth until it goes out of bounds, or until a team fails to return it across net or makes a foul. The ball may be hit any number of times on a side before it is returned, but not twice in succession by the same player. Players rotate to the left when the team wins the serve. The end person goes to the head of the line and becomes the server. The serve must go over on the first try. The serving line may be adjusted to the needs of individuals or the team.

Scoring: A point is scored by the serving team if the ball is not returned over net or if it goes out of bounds on return. A team wins either a point or the serve. Ten points constitute a game. The server must announce the score before serving, stating the score of his team first.

Fouls: A player may not touch the net or step over the center line. These rules may not be necessary the first few times the game is played. The ball must be clearly batted, not caught and thrown. The teacher can introduce these rules depending on the skill level of the class.

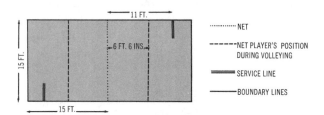

Figure 14-20 One-Line Volleyball.

• *Volleyball (Figure 14-21)*

Areas: Court 25 feet by 50 feet as marked in diagram.

Players: Six players on each team. Positions are called: left forward, center forward, right forward, right back, center back, left back.

Procedure: The ball is put into play by the right-back player from anywhere behind the end line. He must remain behind the line until he hits the ball. The ball must clear the net. The opponents try to return the serve and, if they are successful, the game continues, with the ball being hit back and forth across the net until a player misses or makes a foul. If the receiving team misses, the serving team is awarded a point and the server serves again. He continues to serve until the serving team misses, at which time "Side out" is

Figure 14-21 Volleyball.

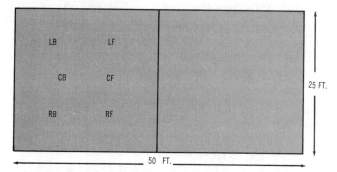

called, and the receiving team wins the serve. Only the serving team may score. When "Side out" is called, the team winning the serve rotates. Each player moves one place in a clockwise direction with the RF becoming the server.

General Rules:

1. Any ball (except on the serve) that touches the net and continues over the net is legal, and play continues.
2. The ball may be hit only with the hands and the forearms.
3. The ball may be hit three times by each team before it is sent over the net. No player may strike it twice in succession.
4. A ball touching a boundary line is considered good.
5. Balls may be hit by a player who is standing outside of the boundary lines.
6. A player must let a ball hit the floor if he thinks it is out of bounds; he may not catch it and call it out of bounds.

Fouls:

1. Hitting the ball twice in succession.
2. Hitting the ball with any part of the body but the forearms and hands.
3. Not clearly hitting the ball, catching it momentarily, pushing it, and lifting it.
4. Stepping over end line when serving.
5. Stepping over center line.
6. Touching net.
7. Reaching over net to hit a ball.

Penalty:

1. If the foul is committed by the serving team, "Side out" is called and the other team wins the serve.
2. If the foul is committed by the receiving team, point is won by the serving team.

Game Score:

1. The team that wins 15 points first wins.
2. A team must be 2 points ahead to win.
3. A time limit may be set for the game, perhaps 8 minutes, and the team that is 2 or more points ahead wins.

Further Modifications: The most common modifications are: unlimited hits per side, shorter service line, lower net, smaller courts, and shorter games. The progression chart (p. 427) indicates the modifications used at different grade levels. Rules are introduced in the order in which they are needed and can be handled by the players.

- ### Two-Player Volleyball

The game is played under the same rules as regular volleyball, with the following exceptions:

1. Playing court is 5 feet shorter than length normally used. (This can be changed to meet needs.)
2. There are only two positions, right and left area.
3. The service is always made from the right half of serving area.
4. The game is 11 points or 5 minutes of play, whichever comes first. (This can be modified.)

Two-player volleyball requires great teamwork and very fast action. It necessitates moving to meet the ball and gives each player more opportunity to play the ball.

Skill Tests

WALL VOLLEY TEST A line is drawn on the wall 6 feet from the floor. This line represents the net and may be altered to coincide with the net height that is used in the game. A restraining line is drawn on the floor 3 feet from the wall. The child stands behind this line and tosses the ball into the air, then volleys it against the wall. He continues to volley the ball back and forth against the wall from behind the restraining line. If the ball does not hit above the net line, no score is counted. Whenever the ball hits the floor it may be started with a toss up to self again. Another child counts the successful volleys. A timer gives the signal, "Go," and starts a stopwatch. At the end of 20 seconds he signals "Stop." Two trials are given, and the highest score is recorded.

SERVING TEST A volleyball court is marked as in Figure 14-22. The numbers are the point value for each area. The child serves the ball from behind the end line attempting to put the ball into the highest scoring area. He is given ten trials. His score is the total of the ten trials. It is wise to make a diagram of the court on cards and have one child record where each hit landed on a separate card for each child. Later a tally of the scores can be made.

Figure 14-22 Serving test.

SUGGESTED REFERENCES FOR FURTHER STUDY

AMERICAN ALLIANCE FOR HEALTH, PHYSICAL EDUCATION AND RECREATION, *Skills Test Manual.* Washington, D.C., current year. Manuals available for basketball, football, softball, and volleyball.

BEIM, GEORGE, Principles of Modern Soccer. Boston: Houghton Mifflin, 1978.

BLAKE, O. WILLIAM, and ANNE VOLP, *Lead-Up Games to Team Sports.* Englewood Cliffs, N.J.: Prentice-Hall, Inc., 1964.

EGSTROM, GLEN, and FRANCES SCHAAFSMA, *Volleyball.* Dubuque, Ia.: Wm. C. Brown, 1972.

KNEER, MARIAN, and C. L. MCCLURE, *Softball.* Dubuque, Ia.: Wm. C. Brown, 1969.

LITTLE, MILDRED et al., *Recreational Football: Flag and Touch.* Minneapolis: Burgess Publishers, 1977.

NATIONAL ASSOCIATION FOR GIRLS AND WOMEN IN SPORTS, *Basketball Guide.* Washington, D.C., current year.

————, *Soccer-Speedball Guide.* Washington, D.C., current year.

————, *Softball Guide.* Washington, D.C., current year.

————, *Volleyball Guide.* Washington, D.C., current year.

NATIONAL FEDERATION OF STATE HIGH SCHOOL ATHLETIC ASSOCIATIONS, *Basketball Rules.* Chicago, current year.

————, *Football Rules.* Chicago, current year.

SEIDEL, BECKY et al., *Sports Skills: A Conceptual Approach to Meaningful Movement.* Dubuque, Ia.: Wm. C. Brown, 1975.

STANLEY, DENNIS, IRVING WAGLOW, and RUTH ALEXANDER, *Physical Education Activities Handbook for Men and Women.* Boston: Allyn & Bacon, 1973.

WICKSTROM, RALPH, *Fundamental Motor Patterns,* 2nd ed. Philadelphia: Lea & Febiger, 1977.

15 / SKILLS AND LEAD-UP GAMES FOR INDIVIDUAL SPORTS

- **Badminton activities**
- **Badminton skills**
- **Tennis activities**
- **Tennis skills**
- **Track and field activities**

As children grow older, their interest in individual and dual sports increases. Most leisure activities of youth and adults are those in which only a few people participate at one time and are usually called lifetime sports. Some of the individual and dual games suggested in Chapter 13 continue to be favorites at all ages. If adequate facilities and equipment are available, upper-grade children can learn golf, archery, and bowling. There are a few individual sports which children can learn progressively through lead-up games which modify equipment and size of court, but utilize skill patterns of the official game in the same manner as those of the parent sport. Those which do not require extensive space and expensive equipment are the racket games of badminton and tennis. The skills and lead-up games for these two sports should be taught in class and offered as activities in the intramural program starting in Level III.

Track and field is categorized as an individual sport because all the events, with the exception of relays, are individual in nature. Track and field is fast becoming a popular sport in America; in part because of the success of the United States team in the Olympic Games.

Badminton Activities

Badminton is becoming a very popular recreational sport. It is a demanding, fast, vigorous sport for the experts, yet beginners can learn the basic skills quickly. Many families own badminton equipment and set up courts inexpensively in their back yards and driveways. Boys and girls enjoy playing this game together.

The long-handled badminton racquet is difficult for some young players to control. The game of paddle badminton (or aerial darts) utilizes wooden paddles and the same size court and the same rules as badminton. The handles of the paddles are shorter than in badminton and therefore easier for beginners to control.

There are commercially marketed aerial dart paddles and aerial darts. The latter are shuttlecocks made with a sponge-rubber base and heavier feathers than a regular shuttlecock. The heavier dart or outdoor shuttlecocks are best to use with the paddle. Paddles may be constructed from three-ply plywood.

The basic strokes, rules, and knowledges of badminton can be learned as early as fifth grade. These strokes can be refined and more advanced strokes learned in the seventh and eighth grades or until regulation badminton equipment is available. The skills are described as they are performed with a paddle.

Table 15-1. Progression of Skills, Knowledges, Rules and Lead-Up Games for Badminton

SKILLS	KNOWLEDGES AND RULES	LEAD-UP GAMES
Grip	Ready position	
Footwork	Home position	
Long serve	Service	
Underhand clear	Court areas	
Overhead clear	Scoring*	Modified Paddle Badminton
Smash	Faults	
	Singles	
	Doubles	Modified Paddle Badminton
Short serve	In side	
Overhead drop	Out side	
	One hand down	
	Inning	
	Setting	
	Strategy	Paddle Badminton

* See variations in Paddle Badminton.

Forehand Grip   This grip is used for all strokes that are received on the right-hand side of the body and for the serves. The paddle is taken with the small edge upward and grasped as in shaking hands. The fingers and thumb are wrapped around the handle forming a V along the handle. The handle is gripped by the fingers and not allowed to rest in the palm of the hand.

Backhand Grip   This grip is used for all strokes that are received on the left side of the body. From the forehand grip position the hand is moved one-quarter turn to the left so that the palm is directly over the handle as one looks down on the edge of the paddle. The thumb is placed along the back of the handle in a slightly diagonal direction.

Ready Position   When waiting to receive the shuttle, a player should always assume a stance facing the net, the left foot slightly ahead of the right. The weight is evenly distributed and slightly forward. The paddle is held up in front of the body and pointed at the opponent. From this position one can move quickly in any direction and have the paddle ready for overhead returns.

Footwork   In badminton, quick changes of direction, a balanced position for stroking, and a return to ready position for the next shot are essential fundamentals at any learning stage. When a shuttle is received on the paddle side of the player, he must face the right side-line and, conversely for shuttles on the nonpaddle side, he must face the left side-line.

After a shot, the player should always return to the "home position," which is slightly behind and to the left of the intersection of the service-court line in the center of the court. Moving into position for a stroke should be done by taking short diagonal sliding steps.

Serve   The badminton serve pattern is much like the underhand serve in volleyball. The serve must be an underhand stroke. As it hits the shuttle, the top edge of the paddle must be at the level of the wrist, and contact with the shuttle made below the waist.

The shuttle is held by the feathers with the thumb and forefinger well out in front of the body and slightly above knee height. The wrist is cocked, and the paddle is held against the shuttle. The arm is swung back so that the paddle extends backward at hip height. It is then brought forward forcibly, with the wrist uncocked and whipped into the shuttle just as it is contacted. The shuttle is dropped as the forward swing is started. The weight is shifted to the back foot with the start of the backswing and forward as the body leans into the hit. The follow-through is high and toward the desired line of flight.

Whether the serve is intended to be long or short, the stance and backswing are the same. For a short serve, the speed of the paddle is checked on the forward swing just before contact with the shuttle is made. The wrist is not uncocked with great force, but the shuttle is stroked gently with the uncocking wrist stopping at the point of contact. Very little follow-through is employed.

1. Dropping shuttle too soon.
2. Dropping shuttle too close to the body.
3. Full arm-swing with paddle brought too high in back of body.
4. Failing to cock wrist fully on backswing.
5. Failing to use whip action of wrist.
6. Using too much body rotation, which results in pushing shuttle rather than hitting it.
7. Using too much upward follow-through on the short serve, causing shuttle to go too high.

KEY TEACHING PHRASES

1. Hold shuttle by feathers.
2. Eyes on shuttle.
3. Take a semi-crouched position, knees bent, upper body forward, shuttle and paddle well below waist level.
4. Swing back, drop shuttle, swing forward, whip, and hit.
5. Follow shuttle with paddle.

Underhand Clear This is a defensive shot to hit shuttles that cannot be hit with a downward stroke. The bird should be hit high and deep into the court so that the player has a chance to return to home position. The mechanics of the stroke are the same as those of the serve, the only exception being that the bird is often hit when it is at a point above the waist, and the stroke may be taken on either the forehand or backhand side.

Overhand Clear The pattern for all the overhand strokes is much like that of the overhand throw. This similarity should be pointed out to the students. The overhand clear may be taken on either the forehand or backhand side. The paddle is brought back behind the head with the wrist cocked and the elbow bent and well away from the body. The forward, upward swing starts with the elbow leading. The arm whips through with a full extension of the elbow, and the wrist is whipped forward as the bird is contacted at a point high above the head. The weight is carried forward and the follow-through is forward and upward toward a point on the ceiling beyond midway back into the opponent's court. The overhand clear drives the opponent deep into his court to return the shuttle.

COMMON FAULTS

1. Failing to turn side toward the net.
2. Failing to cock wrist fully on backswing so that wrist may whip the paddle into the shuttle.
3. Contacting shuttle too low with paddle face closed too far. Shuttle flies short and low and often becomes a set-up for a smash.

KEY TEACHING PHRASES

1. Eyes on shuttle.

2. Swing back and hit all in one motion.

3. Elbow leads forward swing.
4. Reach for shuttle.
5. Follow through toward the ceiling.

Smash

The mechanics of the smash are the same as those of the overhand clear, but the shuttle is contacted high and well in front of the body with the paddle face downward. The follow-through is downward and diagonally across the body. The path of the shuttle is sharply downward, and it should just clear the net. The smash is used as an offensive stroke, since it is very difficult to return because of the speed of the shuttle and the sharp angle of flight.

COMMON FAULTS

1. Contacting shuttle too close to body with paddle face open, causing too much height in return shot.
2. Contacting shuttle too low with elbow bent, causing shuttle to go into net.

KEY TEACHING PHRASES

1. Eyes on shuttle.
2. Reach high and contact shuttle in front of body.
3. Bring paddle down on shuttle.

Overhead Drop

The mechanics of the overhead drop are the same as those for the smash except that the speed of the forward swing is checked just before the shuttle is contacted and the wrist uncocks slowly and stops when it is in line with the arm. There is little or no follow-through. The drop shot is used to catch off-guard the player who is deep in the rear court. It is a good change-of-pace stroke mixed with clears and smashes. Since all the preparatory motions and the start of the forward swing are the same for all three strokes, the use of the drop can be very deceptive.

General Concepts Students Should Learn About Badminton Play

1. Fingers, not palm of hand, should be used to hold paddle.
2. Use wrist action with all strokes.
3. Turn side toward net for all forehand and backhand shots.
4. Use sliding steps to get into position to hit shuttle.
5. Always return to "home position" after a stroke and assume "ready position."
6. Any stroke hit in a downward manner is an offensive stroke. Any stroke hit in an upward manner is a defensive stroke.
7. Reach for the shuttle and step into the hit.
8. Keep opponent on the defensive by using various shots and by placing shots up, back, and to one side or the other in different order.
9. Vary use of long and short serves to keep opponent off-guard.

- *Paddle Badminton (Figure 15-1)*

Area: Court 20 feet by 44 feet marked as in diagram. Net 5 feet high.

Players: Singles—two players, one on each side of court; doubles—four, two on each side of court. The side having the right to serve is the "in side," and the receiving side is the "out side."

Figure 15-1 Paddle Badminton.

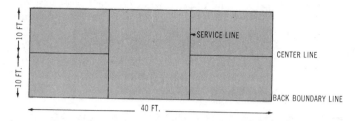

Procedure:

1. The game is started by a serve from the right side of the court.
2. The serve must go diagonally into the opponent's serving court.
3. The shuttle must be hit before it touches the ground.
4. Play continues, with the shuttle hit back and forth over the net until a fault is committed.

Singles Play: The serve starts from the right court when the server's score is 0 or an even number of points, and from the left court when the server's score is an odd number. A person alternates courts after each point is scored and continues to serve until the in side makes a fault, at which time "Service over" is called, no points are scored, and the receiver becomes the server.

Doubles Play: When a fault is committed by the in side while the first server is serving, "Second service" is called, and no point is scored. The partner of the first server becomes the server. When one of the partners has served, it is called "one hand down." When both partners have served or both hands are down, an inning is declared, and the server changes sides. Whenever a side becomes a serving side, the partner on the right-hand side serves first. The side serving first in the game has only one hand or turn of service in the first inning.

Rules:

1. On the serve the shuttle must not be contacted above the server's waist. Paddle head must not be above server's hand when shuttle is contacted.
2. Shuttle must fall into proper service court.
3. Feet of server and receiver must be in respective service courts until shuttle is delivered.
4. During play the shuttle must fall within or on a boundary line and go over net.
5. Shuttle may not be carried with paddle.
6. If a shuttle hits the net and falls into the proper boundary area, it is fair.
7. The shuttle may only be contacted once by a player and only once on each side.
8. A player must not touch net or reach over net to hit a shuttle.
9. If player completely misses a shuttle when attempting to serve, it is not a fault.

Scoring: A point may be scored only by the player on side that is serving.

Game: Singles—11 points; doubles—15 points.

Setting: If the score is tied at 9-all in singles play, the game may be set at 3 points by the player reaching 9 first. When it is tied up at 10, it may be set at

2 points. Then whoever gets 3 or 2 points respectively wins the game. If the option to set is turned down, whoever reaches 11 first wins. In a tie at 13 in a doubles game, whoever reaches 13 first may set the game at 5 points, or if it is tied at 14, the game may be set at 3 points.

Variations: The official scoring and terminology for doubles may not be advisable to introduce early in a unit. Short games of 6 or 8 points with no provision for setting are desirable in the first unit.

Tennis Activities

The modern game of tennis originated from the early game of handball as played by the Greeks and Romans. In the process of the development of today's game several different instruments, among them wooden paddles, were used until the racquet was adopted in the early 1500s. Tennis may be played by two or four people and is enjoyed by both men and women as a recreational sport. Boys and girls can learn a modified game in which wooden paddles and a small court are used. If regulation tennis courts and equipment are available, children in upper grades who are ready may play regular tennis. The games presented here can be taught and played by a larger number of pupils at one time because the court space needed is smaller and the equipment is cheaper.

The long handle of the tennis racquet extends the lever beyond the arm itself; consequently, more force and speed can be developed when a person is stroking the ball with a racquet. However, the longer lever is difficult to control. Short-handled wooden paddles may be used as a substitute for racquets when children and adults are learning the fundamentals of the game and when they are acquiring the strength and timing to control the longer lever. Some companies sell a short racquet, which is desirable because it is lighter, but it is also more expensive than the paddle.

Handball provides a beginning game in which no racquet at all is needed. Players learn the timing of the bounce of the ball as it rebounds off the floor and at the same time learn the basic ground-stroke patterns. Ground strokes involve hitting the ball after it has bounced once. Hitting the ball against the wall provides a faster and surer method of getting the ball back to a player to hit than if a larger court area were used and beginners had to rely on equally weak players to return the ball. When beginners are hitting with their hand rather than with a racquet, it seems easier for them to adjust to turning their side to the wall or the net in order to hit with greater force.

Wall paddle tennis capitalizes on the small space and the rebound from the wall to give beginners chances to hit the ball and gain confidence in their strokes before the use of the net and full court play. The games of four-wall paddle ball or racquet ball in an enclosed room or three-wall paddle ball are similar but much faster and more demanding because of the many angles of rebound possible off any of the walls. Most elementary schools do not have facilities for these games.

The game of paddle tennis utilizes a court half the size of the tennis court. Actually, it is the same size as the paddle badminton court (p. 445). The net is only 2½ feet high. The rules are the same as those for official tennis. For adults the overhand service is outlawed because of the low net.

Many experienced tennis players play paddle tennis inside in the winter as a means of maintaining physical condition and a familiarity with tennis skills. Many outstanding tennis coaches advocate using wooden paddles in the teaching of elementary strokes to people of all ages.

Paddle tennis courts can easily be set up on blacktop play areas, parking lots, and in gymnasiums. The same net that is used for all beginning net games (or a rope with strips of cloth hanging from it) may be used. Ground sleeves with removable caps can be set in the blacktop or portable weighted standards may be utilized for securing the net. Regular paddles may be purchased or made from four-ply plywood. Old tennis balls or sponge-rubber balls are suitable. Paddle tennis provides an inexpensive and fascinating game for upper-grade children.

Tennis Skills

Ready Position

While waiting for the ball, the player always assumes a position in which he faces the net, has weight evenly distributed over both feet, knees slightly bent, and weight slightly forward so he can move quickly in any direction. The racquet is held with the left hand slightly below the head and the right in a forehand grip with the racquet pointing at the net.

Forehand Strokes

The paddle is held with the small edge of the paddle facing upward, then gripped as in a handshake. There should be a V between the thumb and first finger. The fingers and thumb should be firmly wrapped around the handle and slightly separated. From the ready position the body must turn sideways to the net. The left foot steps across, and the left shoulder is then toward the net. The weight is shifted to the back foot. At the same time, the paddle is brought back horizontal to the ground. The arm should be fully extended without bending at the wrist. The paddle should be pointing to the back line of the court. All these movements should be started as the ball crosses the net. The paddle is brought forward so the ball can be hit squarely at waist height. The ball should be out in front of the left foot toward the net so one has to reach and swing into it. The body twists, and as the right shoulder comes around, the weight is shifted forward. The wrist must be firm as the paddle contacts the ball. The stroke should be continued as though the paddle is pointing to the spot where the ball is intended to go. After the stroke is completed the player should return to ready position. The forehand stroke is used to return balls that are received on the paddle side of the body. It is the most frequently needed stroke in tennis. The flight of a forehand drive should be low, long, and hard.

COMMON FAULTS

1. Failure to turn side toward net.
2. Getting body too close to ball so elbow must be bent and full extension of the arm is prevented.
3. Turning paddle and the wrist as ball is hit.
4. Too short a backswing and/or follow-through.
5. Opening paddle face, whereupon ball travels in an upward path over net rather than in a horizontal path.

1. Shake hands with the paddle.
2. Eyes on ball.
3. Side to net.
4. Swing big!
5. Step into ball.
6. Wrist firm.
7. Twist and reach for target.
8. Back to ready position.

Backhand Drive The backhand drive is used to return balls that come to the nonpaddle side of the body. The grip changes as soon as the player realizes that the ball must be hit from the nonpaddle side. The right hand is shifted to the left so the V points straight down the left side of the handle. The thumb is held behind the handle to give added support when the paddle contacts the ball. The turn and footwork are the reverse of those in the forehand stroke. The player is watching the ball over the right shoulder with right side to the net. The backswing, forward swing, and follow-through are the same as in the forehand drive. Failing to turn the side squarely to the net is one of the most common faults of beginners.

The backhand appears to be a difficult shot for many players; hence many try to avoid using it and will run around the ball so they can use their forehand. The teacher should see that every player has many chances to use and practice the backhand drive.

Serve Initially, a serve in which the ball is bounced and a forehand drive stroke is employed may be used in game play. This permits use of the forehand and backhand strokes in game play and confidence and familiarity with the game before the more difficult overhand serve is introduced. The regular serve pattern is much like that of an overhand throw and should be introduced as such.

Table 15-2. Progression of Skills, Knowledges, Rules, and Lead-Up Games for Tennis

SKILLS	KNOWLEDGES AND RULES	LEAD-UP GAMES
Using hand:	Server	
Forehand stroke	Receiver	
Backhand stroke	Rally	
Serve from bounce	Scoring	
Footwork	Faults	Handball
Using paddle:	Ready position	
Forehand stroke	Ground strokes	
Backhand stroke	Faults	
Serve from bounce		Wall Paddle Tennis
Overhand serve	Set	
Volley	Serving rules	
	Official scoring	Paddle Tennis or Tennis

The paddle is held with the same grip as that used for the forehand drive. The left foot is placed at a 45-degree angle to the base line. The right foot is parallel to the base line. The left side is to the net with the shoulder pointing directly toward the intended path of the ball. The paddle is swung down and around and makes a loop behind the right shoulder. Then the paddle swings up until the arm is fully extended and the wrist is cocked. The wrist snaps, and the paddle smashes quickly down on the ball as it is met slightly forward of the body. The follow-through is made with the paddle continuing downward and across the left side of the body. The weight is shifted to the back foot when the ball is tossed. All the weight is thrown into the downward stroke, with the right foot brought forward to take the weight on the follow-through.

The key to good serving is the timing of the toss-up of the ball. This should be practiced before the serve is attempted. The ball should be tossed straight up with the left hand in front of the left foot. The arm should reach high and the fingers guide the ball upward. The ball should go at least a foot higher than the height of the outstretched arm and paddle. The left arm initiates the throwing motion upward at the same time the right arm brings the paddle downward in a continuous rhythmical pattern.

COMMON FAULTS

1. Hitting the ball with elbow bent rather than arm fully extended.
2. Meeting ball with paddle face open because of lack of wrist action or insufficient height of toss.
3. Tossing ball too low, behind head, or too far forward.

KEY TEACHING PHRASES

1. Stand in a forward stride position.
2. Toss ball, bring paddle down.
3. Bring paddle up fast and "crash" down on ball.
4. "Throw" paddle toward target.
5. Step forward onto right foot.

Volley

When the volley is used, the ball is hit before it touches the ground. The grip, body position, and action in the volley are similar to that of the forehand and the backhand. The major difference is in the amount of backswing and follow-through employed. A punching motion is used, with the ball being hit at a point in front of the body and directly downward if the ball is received above and near the net. Less body rotation is needed. When the ball comes directly at the player's body, he can use a backhand volley more quickly than a forehand drive. The volley is used near the net where the ball can be driven deep and/or angled so that the opponent is put on the defensive. The volley is also used when one is caught mid-court, and the ball is received above the waist and below the shoulders.

COMMON FAULTS

1. Too much backswing, ball is hit too hard.
2. Weak grip.
3. Paddle face is open, ball gets too much loft.

1. Eyes on ball.
2. Punch ball.
3. Pivot from hips.
4. Keep firm grip.

General Concepts Children Should Learn About Tennis Play

1. Hold paddle firmly when the ball is contacted.
2. Keep a firm wrist in all strokes except the serve, for which the wrist is flexed.
3. Turn side toward net for all strokes taken on either side of the body.
4. Use short sliding steps to get into position to hit the ball.
5. Reach for the ball, and hit it when it is at full reach and slightly ahead of the body.
6. Keep eyes on ball.
7. Try to place shots deep and into corners of opponent's court.
8. Vary placement of shots from side to side.
9. Assume ready position between shots.

Lead-Up Games for Tennis

- *Handball*

Handball is described on pages 360–61. The principles involved in the forehand and backhand drives and footwork should be stressed when the hand is used as the implement to hit the ball.

- *Wall Paddle Tennis (Figure 15-2)*

Area: A wall space 20 feet wide and 20 feet high, and a hard surface area in front of the wall 20 feet wide and 26 feet deep is marked off. A net line is drawn on the wall 2 feet above the floor and parallel to it. A service line is drawn on the floor 13 feet from the wall and parallel to it.

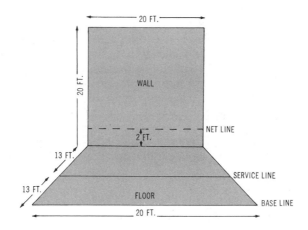

Figure 15-2 Wall Paddle Tennis.

Players: Two people.

Procedure: Singles play. Play is started by the first server standing behind the base line. He bounces the ball once and hits it at the wall within the boundary lines above the net line. The ball must rebound off the wall beyond the service line within the court boundaries. The opponent must return the ball to the wall above the net line after it has bounced. The ball may rebound anywhere within the court boundaries. Play continues until the ball is hit out of bounds or fault is made. The server continues to serve until he loses it by making a fault. Only the server may score one point when the opponent makes a fault. Game is 10 points.

Variation: Game may be played as doubles with four people. The serve alternates between teams with each team having the two terms of service.

• *Paddle Tennis (Figure 15-3)*

Area: The paddle tennis court dimensions and markings are diagramed below. Net 2½ feet high.

Players: Singles—two people; doubles—four people.

Procedure: The game is started with a serve from the right-hand court. The ball must go into the opposite service court and be returned after it has bounced once. It may be returned anywhere within the court boundaries and be hit before it strikes the playing surface. Play continues until the ball goes out of bounds or a fault is made. A point is awarded to the person who did not make the fault or hit the ball out of bounds. The same person continues to serve for a whole game.

Rules:

1. *Serve:* The ball is served from behind the base line beginning from the right court. The serve must pass over the net and hit the ground within the service court diagonally opposite the server. When the total number of points is 0 or even, the serve is from the right court. When the total number of points is odd, the serve is from the left court.
2. *Foot fault:* Server steps over the base line while serving.
3. *Let service:* Ball hits the net and continues over into the service court. Another serve is allowed.
4. *Serve fault:* Ball does not land in opposite service court. Server commits a foot fault. The server is allowed two consecutive faults before a point is declared and service changes to opposite service court.

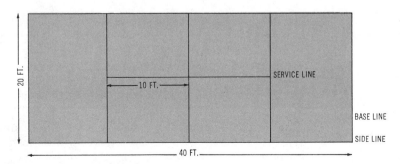

Figure 15-3 Paddle Tennis.

5. *Order of serve:* In singles, the serve changes sides at the end of each game. In doubles, partners alternate games when their side is to serve.
6. *Changing sides:* Players change sides of the court at the end of the first, third, and all odd games.

Scoring:

1. *Game:* Points made: 0, 1, 2, 3, 4. Terms used: love, 15, 30, 40, game.
2. *Deuce game:* Game must be won by two points; therefore, 40-40 would be deuce game.
3. *Advantage in:* Server makes first point after deuce.
4. *Advantage out:* Receiver makes first point after deuce.
5. *Set:* Six games comprise a set. The set must be won by two games. Same principles as apply for the deuce game.

Point Awarded:

1. If the server makes two consecutive service faults.
2. If ball, when returned, does not land within the court or on a line.
3. If ball hits surface of court twice before it is returned.
4. If player reaches across net to return ball.

Track and Field Activities

Track and field activities involve the basic skills of running, jumping, and throwing. Most children love to do these activities and are excited when track and field is in season, which is usually in the spring. This is sometimes considered a team sport, since individuals usually belong to a team, and the individual wins are recorded for a team. With the exception of the relays, all the events are individual and self-testing in nature and demand that a child have ample opportunity to practice them in order to improve.

People have competed in running, throwing, and jumping events for centuries. The relationship of track and field to Greek history and the Olympic Games makes an interesting classroom study along with the unit in physical education. A meet between classes or squads may culminate a unit and be patterned after the Olympic Games.

In recent years there has been a revival of interest in track and field for both boys and girls across the United States. Many children have an opportunity to participate in track clubs and meets outside the school.

Teaching Considerations

1. Because most of the events involve the basic skills of running and jumping, these skills are learned and performed in the primary grades but on a more informal basis. For example, the running long jump is called Jump the Brook. Children run and jump across two lines which are moved progressively farther apart. High jumping is called High Waters. A rope is held at increasingly higher levels, and more than one child jumps over it at a time. Jumping is performed on the grass, and no pits are needed.

2. Organization is important for the conduct of a track and field class. Since practice is indispensable for improvement, each child must have many opportunities to practice skills. Therefore, many stations have to be set up for small-group and individual practice. A rotation plan for squad work should be devised at the start of the unit and posted in the classroom or

Movement Experiences

gym. Squads will know where they are to start work each day and where they may take out the equipment they need. The teacher may wish to introduce new skills or emphasize important coaching points to the whole class before it is split into working groups. A great deal of the teacher's time is spent moving from station to station coaching individuals.

3. Warm-up activities should precede jumping and sprint work. Light jogging, slow bending and stretching activities should be done.

4. Younger children should run on a grassy surface free from stones, sticks, and broken glass. Older boys and girls may run on a cinder or all-weather track if it is in good condition.

5. Pits filled with loose sand, sawdust, or tanbark are necessary for jumping events.

6. Good form in all events should always be stressed.

7. Times and distances should be recorded two or three times during the unit. A child can visually and mentally record his/her progress during daily practice.

8. No skill tests are needed because the activities are self-testing. If a meet is conducted at the end of the unit, scores recorded then may serve as an evaluation of status and, if compared with earlier scores, of progress.

9. Two wooden paddles or blocks of wood clapped together make a good starting signal.

10. Table 15-3 shows the distances, weights, and heights for the different levels. This is to show increasingly more challenging tasks; however, if youngsters cannot jump an 18-inch hurdle you would not push them to jump a 24-inch one. Choice should be made for individuals based on readiness. All the events are very easy to individualize.

Track Events

The basic mechanics of the run are described on page 232. The modifications necessary for the various events are described in the following paragraphs.

DASHES OR SPRINTS The crouch start is the best method for a fast getaway in the sprints. At the signal, "Take your mark," the left or front foot is placed

Table 15-3. Sequence for Track and Field

	LEVEL I	LEVEL II	LEVEL III	LEVEL IV
Track Events				
Dashes	Informal Racing	40–50 yards	50–60 yards	75–100 yards
Relays		Shuttle	300 yards	600 yards
Distance runs	100–200 yards	300 yards	500 yards	600 yards–one mile
Hurdles	12 in.	18 in.	20–24 in.	30–36 in.
Field Events				
Long jump				
Standing	x	x	x	x
Running	Jump the Brook			
High jump	High Waters	Scissors	Roll	Roll
Throws	5 inch rubber ball	Softball	4–6 lb. shot	6–8 lb. shot

about 10 to 12 inches behind the starting line. The right or rear foot is placed approximately next to the heel of the left foot. A comfortable position is taken with hands shoulder-width apart, fingers extended and together behind the starting line. On "Get set," the hips are raised so that the back is parallel to the ground. The body weight is balanced mostly on the hands. Caution beginners to hold still until the signal "Go!" Upon the word "Go" or the sound of the whistle, the run is started by a push-off from the toes to overbalance the body weight forward. The runner keeps the body low and uses short, hard, driving steps and a powerful swing of both arms to regain balance and pick up speed. When the 30-yard mark is reached, the runner should be moving full-speed. In full stride, the knees should be lifted high and brought down forcefully, the toes pointed straight forward, and the arms bent at the elbow and moved back and forth forcefully. About 10 yards from the finish line the runner should lean forward slightly to initiate a final burst of speed. He or she should cross the finish line at top speed and run about 10 yards beyond the line.

PURSUIT RELAY In a pursuit relay, runners run in the same direction on the straight or oval track. Teams consist of four runners, each running an equal distance. It is recommended that from two to four teams compete at the same time. The first member stands at the starting line. All others are stationed at intervals of 30 or more yards around the track. The lead-off runner starts from a crouch position. The race is started in the same manner as the dash. Runners run to the next position, where they pass batons to respective teammates. The batons are passed within a 10- to 20-yard zone, and these zones should be on straightways rather than on the curve of the track. The receiver of the baton assumes a stance near the back line of the passing zone. On a signal from the passer, the receiver starts to run. He receives the baton with the right hand cupped, fingers spread to side of the body. He grips the baton tightly as it touches his hand. The baton is shifted to the left hand as quickly as possible after it is received. The passer of the baton extends the left arm and reaches as far forward as possible. He holds the baton near the end. A cue is "Give the receiver the big end of the stick." The baton must be extended at the proper height for the exchange, and some pressure exerted on the hand of the receiver so that he will know the baton is there. The passer runs near the receiver and continues to run several yards beyond the place of exchange.

SHUTTLE RELAY In a shuttle relay, runners go back and forth across the same space. The lead-off runners start from a crouch position. All the others start from a standing position with right arm extended forward at shoulder height. They must stay behind the line until touched by a runner or given a baton. Runners always pass right shoulders.

HURDLING In the primary and intermediate grades, hurdling can be taught as a leap over the hurdle while running and not breaking the run. Emphasis should be placed on bringing the lead leg high and straight out in front of the body. Very short hurdles that easily fall off their supports should be used. They may be as simple as a thin dowel laid between two cardboard boxes, or even thin cardboard boxes.

The regular hurdle is done in the following manner. The takeoff begins about 3 to 4 feet in front of the hurdle, with the lead leg kicking straight up in front of the body. At the same time the leg is kicked up, the arms thrust forward to give more lift to the body. The lead leg stretches forward as far as possible. As the lead leg crosses the hurdle, the trailing leg is bent with the knee pointing directly to the side. The toe of the trailing leg must be raised high enough to clear the hurdle. The lead leg is brought down and touches the ground as close to the hurdle as possible. As the lead leg starts down, the trailing leg comes around and takes the first step toward the next hurdle. The faster the foot touches the ground, the quicker the move toward the next hurdle. An uneven number of steps should be taken between hurdles. The first few lessons in hurdling should be conducted on the grass.

COMMON FAULTS

1. Failure to raise lead leg high enough and keep it straight.
2. Failure to use arms to add lift.
3. Failure to bring lead leg down fast once it has crossed bar.
4. Failure to keep knee of trailing leg pointed to the side.
5. Letting foot of trailing leg drop and catch bar.
6. Failure to bring trailing leg around in order to take the first step toward the next hurdle or finish line.

Field Events

The field events include jumping for distance and for height, and throwing for distance. Jumping is described in detail on p. 236. The overhand throw is described in detail on p. 255. The only new skill pattern is the shot put, which is analyzed later.

STANDING LONG JUMP The jumper achieves balance and gains momentum before the jump by rocking from heel to toe. This motion serves as a preliminary windup for the jump. A sitting position is assumed in the air with the arms and upper body reaching forward. On landing, the jumper should reach forward with the hands. The measurement is taken perpendicularly from the first break in the pit (body, feet, hands) to toe mark on the takeoff board.

RUNNING LONG JUMP A preliminary run is taken starting sixteen full strides from the takeoff board. The run is fast, and the last stride is shortened to enable the jumper to adjust his center of gravity and to step flat-footed on the takeoff board. A hard and flat-footed step on the takeoff board should be made to gain drive and spring for the forward lift. The jump is made by pushing off vigorously and extending one or both legs, depending upon the type of jump. The arms as well as the legs should be swung upward and/or forward to gain power. When the top of the jump is reached, the jumper is in a sitting, running, or layout position in the air. Upon landing, the arms are snapped back to insure forward motion. The runner should reach forward on landing.

RUNNING HIGH JUMP

The scissors jump An approach of six to eight steps is taken from a 45-degree angle to the jumping bar. The run is easy, and the last stride is usually lengthened to give more room for an upward swing of the leg. The takeoff is made from the outside foot. The inside leg is kicked up in front of the body and forward over the bar. The spring is achieved from the takeoff foot, the lift of the arms, and the vigorous upward swing of the inside foot. The landing is made on the lead leg. The takeoff must be made very close to the bar. Practice may be initiated by jumping over a pole or line on the floor.

The modified western roll or straddle roll   The approach is slower than for a scissors jump. The takeoff is begun about an arm's length from the bar by kicking the outside leg high and toward the bar. The push-off is made from the foot nearest the bar (inside foot) when the center of gravity is directly over the takeoff foot. The swing of the outside leg should turn the body so that the abdomen and chest face the bar at the height of the jump. The takeoff leg is rolled over the bar. The landing is made on the lead leg and both hands.

THROW FOR DISTANCE   Most often a softball throw for distance is included in an elementary school track and field unit. An overhand throw pattern is used. A running approach is taken from behind the restraining line. The approach adds more momentum to the throw.

SHOT PUT   Four- to eight-pound shots may be used from the fifth grade on. The shot is pushed rather than thrown. The shot is held in the right hand at the base of the three middle fingers and is balanced on the sides by the thumb and little finger. The elbow is bent and away from the body. The shot is rested against the neck and collarbone and is nestled into the side of the chin. The thrower stands with his left side to the intended target. The feet are spread about shoulder-width apart with the weight on the right foot. The left leg is swung across the body and then forward. A short hop is taken with the right foot and as the left foot hits the ground, the body rotates forward. The right arm pushes the shot forward with the body until the body weight is over the left foot. The elbow is straightened, and wrist and fingers extend to propel the shot forward and upward. The left leg and arm swing on around, and all of the body weight is taken on the left foot.

COMMON FAULTS

1. Throwing the shot rather than pushing it.
2. Failure to keep sustained movement of the whole body until shot has been released.

KEY TEACHING PHRASES

1. Rest shot in hand at base of fingers. Balance it with the thumb.
2. Tuck shot into neck.
3. Elbow bent and away from the body.
4. Swing left leg across body then forward.
5. Hop on right foot.
6. As left foot hits ground twist body.
7. Push shot forward and upward.
8. Follow around with left leg and arm. Take weight on left foot.

CROSS-COUNTRY RUNNING   The emphasis in cross-country running is to decrease the amount of time in which one can run a specified long distance on an open course. Preferably, the course should be set up on a grassy area with some variations of grade levels. Markers (flags, cones, trees) can be set to indicate the path of the course. Since most elementary schools do not have extensive acreage, the course may have to be repeated as students increase endurance and speed. This may be an interest club or intramural activity and a course on more natural terrain may be set up in a park or golf course away from school.

Jogging may precede running for fast times. Study of concepts of endurance and self-pacing must precede and accompany cross-country participation.

Track and Field Meets

A basic format is followed whether a track meet is organized within a class, between classes, or for the whole school. There are several factors that must be considered.

1. *Events:* The events for the class meet should be those which the class has practiced throughout the unit. If several classes are participating, it is wise to include dashes, a relay event, running long jump, high jump, and a throw for distance.

2. *Teams:* A class may be divided by squads, color teams, or teams named for various countries if it is called an Olympic Games meet.

3. *Competition:* Boys compete against boys and girls against girls, except in the relays, in which teams are mixed. A boy from one team runs at the same position as boys from other teams. For each event except the relays there will be places for winners for boys and for girls.

4. *Participation:* A limit is usually set on how many events one person may enter. Everyone may be in the relays and two individual events. Each team may be required to enter two contestants in each event. The number in the meet sometimes dictates how this must be done. Children may enter the events they choose, or the teams as a whole may decide who will be best in what events.

5. *Scoring:*
   First place—5 points—blue ribbon
   Second place—4 points—red ribbon
   Third place—3 points—white ribbon
   Fourth place—2 points—yellow ribbon
   Fifth place—1 point—green ribbon

   Colors for the ribbons have been designated if one wishes to award cloth or paper ribbons to winners. A card describing the event and place won may also be given as recognition of achievement.

6. *Planning the meet:* Plans must be made for participants to sign for events ahead of the meet. Once they have signed, the children can practice in earnest. Score sheets can be drawn up, and a time schedule with names of participants can be made and posted ahead of the meet. Judges must be secured to time running events and conduct and measure the jumping events. One starter begins all running events.

7. *Conducting the meet:* The referee is in charge of the meet. This may be the teacher in the class. He or she should read the events and the names of students who compete in them. The students also should know where they go for each event, and what to do when they have finished. The relays usually climax the meet. If a child is to be in a running event and a field event at the same time, he/she goes to the running event first. Field events

usually take longer to conclude than running events. If there are fewer running lanes than there are people entered in the dash, there will have to be several heats. Only winners and runners-up of each heat participate in the final dash events.

Jumping events take a long time to complete. A minimum jumping height based on class records may be set as a qualification for entering a jumping event. In the high jump each participant is allowed three trials at each height. Should a tie occur, the person with the least number of misses for all trials is declared the winner. In all other jumping events three trials are given, and the one with the longest jump wins. Scores should be reported to a master scorer as soon as events are completed so that a running score may be kept and the results of the meet announced immediately after the last event. Scores and winners should be posted on the bulletin board as soon after the meet as possible.

SUGGESTED REFERENCES FOR FURTHER STUDY

ALLSEN, PHILLIP, and ALAN WITBECK, *Racquetball and Paddleball.* Dubuque, Ia.: Wm. C. Brown, 1972.

AMERICAN ALLIANCE FOR HEALTH, PHYSICAL EDUCATION AND RECREATION, *Archery—A Planning Guide for Group and Individual Instruction.* Washington, D.C., n.d.

———, *Tennis Group Instruction.* Washington, D.C., 1972.

ATHLETIC INSTITUTE, *Track and Field for Elementary School Children and Junior High School Girls.* Chicago, n.d.

BARNABY, JOHN, *Racquet Work, The Key to Tennis.* Boston: Allyn & Bacon, 1969.

BLOSS, MARGARET VARNER, *Badminton.* Dubuque, Ia.: Wm. C. Brown, 1971.

GORDON, JAMES, *Track and Field.* Boston: Allyn & Bacon, 1972.

NATIONAL ASSOCIATION FOR GIRLS AND WOMEN IN SPORTS, *Tennis and Badminton Guide.* Washington, D.C.: AAHPER, current year.

———, *Track and Field Guide.* Washington, D.C.: AAHPER, current year.

STANLEY, DENNIS, IRVING WAGLOW, and RUTH ALEXANDER, *Physical Education Activities Handbook for Men and Women.* Boston: Allyn & Bacon, 1973.

VERNER, BILL, *Racquetball.* Palo Alto, Cal.: Mayfield Publishers, 1977.

16 / GYMNASTIC SKILLS AND ACTIVITIES

- • **Teaching gymnastic activities**
- • **Developmental stunts and exercises**
- • **Tumbling**
- • **Apparatus**
- • **Small equipment**
- • **Suggested progression for an elementary school program**

Developmental exercises, stunts, tumbling, and activities utilizing small equipment and large apparatus are the activities in the gymnastic area. These types of activities provide a setting for basic body actions in which the elements of strength, flexibility, agility, power, muscle endurance, and balance can be developed in a specific manner. The highly individualized learning situation also helps to develop determination, perseverance, courage, and self-confidence.

Children enjoy these activities because they involve the natural movements of jumping, climbing, hanging, rolling, twisting, and turning that figure in the young child's play. Youngsters, motivated to master a particular exercise or stunt, must rely on their own powers and efforts to overcome specific obstacles, such as height, time, force, or space. Although they may have to work hard to succeed, the satisfaction gained will motivate them to approach problems of even greater difficulty.

Gymnastics affords the best medium of all physical education activities by which to develop the muscles of the thorax, shoulder girdle, and arms, and flexibility in specific joint areas. Most other activities are performed with the feet as the base supporting the body weight. Isolated muscle groups or joints can be given special workloads and tasks to perform in order to correct weaknesses or deficiencies.

The emphasis in the primary grades is on *educational gymnastics,* in which children explore, experiment, learn, and adapt to a wide variety of challenges, problems, and different types of equipment and apparatus. Experiences that present progressively difficult situations have to be planned. The experiences provide the child with a chance to become familiar with many new positions and new pieces of small and large apparatus. Perfection and style in performance should not be demanded, but encouragement to do things well is always important. A knowledge of the wide variety of individual differences and stages of maturity of primary-grade children gives teachers a basis for their expectations of performance.

While still in the primary grades, children should be learning the body movements fundamental to all aspects of gymnastics; in addition, they should enjoy the physical and social values of the exercise. Basic to almost all gymnastics work are the fundamentals of jumping, landing, supporting weight on hands, transferring weight, hanging, curling, flight, rolling, and extension. All of these can be learned first and practiced on the floor or in relation to apparatus that fits the size of the youngsters.

In the intermediate grades, more specific limitations or tasks are set, and greater demands made for control and quality of performance according to each child's abilities. More time must be devoted to the perfecting of skills in order to master the fundamentals necessary for more complex tumbling and apparatus work.

One vital phase of both floor and apparatus work at any level is the development of a coordinated sequence of movements or routines. Gymnastic routines may be compared to compositions in dance which challenge both creative and physical efforts. In primary grades, the sequences will consist of very simple and limited series of stunts.

In the upper grades there should be a choice of educational gymnastics or Olympic gymnastics. The focus of study, time, and efforts center on acquisition and practice of definite movement patterns needed for safe and skilled performance in more advanced skills or stunts. For those who are interested and/or ready for Olympic gymnastics, after-school activities should be available if only educational gymnastics activities are offered in the instructional program.

Teaching Gymnastic Activities

The Lesson

Each lesson should allow for light warm-up work for the individual or for the group. Generally, the first part of the lesson should be teacher-directed; new skills are introduced and problems are solved by the group. The last part should be devoted to individual practice, problem solving, or work on routines. During this time the teacher should give individual help. The period may end with a "showoff" time. Perhaps one or two children at each station (if small-group work is being done) may be selected by their group or by the teacher to demonstrate whatever was studied during the period. If routines were to be developed, these are presented.

Achievement Charts

Young children are interested in performing and competing with others, but only for a short period. They enjoy instant challenges. Older children usually respond to achievement charts (individual or group) when a definite series of skills or patterns are to be learned. Children may check off their own skills when they are completed, or the teacher may do it in the process of evaluation. In every case, the standard and procedure for checking should be clearly established at the onset of the unit. The chart should contain some stunts that are easy enough for everyone to complete and some that are a challenge to the most highly skilled. Adequate time should be allowed to practice and to check off patterns listed on the achievement chart (Table 16-1).

Table 16-1. Group Achievement Chart for Apparatus

Group — Names	PARALLEL BARS					HORIZONTAL BARS				BALANCE BEAM				VAULTING BOX			
	STRAIGHT-ARM SUPPORT	SUPPORT SWING	HAND WALK	RIDING SEAT	ROUTINE	DOUBLE KNEE-HANG	SINGLE KNEE-HANG	PULLOVER	NUMBER OF CHINS	FRONT SCALE	KNEE SCALE	STRADDLE MOUNT	ROUTINE	KNEE MOUNT	COURAGE DISMOUNT	SQUAT VAULT	FLANK VAULT

FLOOR WORK In the primary grades, work with the basic movement skills in relation to the factors that affect movement (space, time, form, pattern, flow of movement, and the various body actions) establishes the foundation of gymnastics. It is difficult to say when one is working in the area of basic movement or in gymnastics. At the same time skills and control of the body are being developed, so are the physical elements of strength, flexibility, agility, and balance, all of which are basic to future gymnastic work.

A tumbling skill is traced here as it developed from early basic movement work.

BASIC MOVEMENT SEQUENCE

1. Walk about the room, stop and take your body weight on your hands; walk and stop, take weight on hands. Run and take weight on hands.
2. Skip and take weight on hands (hoops may be scattered on floor and hands put in hoops when weight is taken).
3. Skip and take weight on your hands, flutter your feet in the air. Repeat. Flutter higher.
4. Skip about room; change weight from feet to one hand, then the other (but not both at the same time).
5. Move about the room changing weight from hands to feet, stretching your body as you change.
6. Move about the room, changing weight from hands to feet; twist as you go so that feet come down in a different place.
7. (Rope is stretched about 8 inches off floor.) Run alongside rope; take weight on hands on other side of rope, and land on feet on other side.
8. Run on and change to other side in same manner.
9. Take weight on one hand, then the other; land on one foot, then the other.
10. Turn body as you go over rope. Repeat, stretching leg out high above you.
11. Repeat this action down the length of the rope. Do this without the rope and it is a cartwheel.

(This all would not be done in one day but over a length of time; these are only the major tasks around which the teacher can develop the sequences.) Shoulder strength will be built from the support. Placement of the whole hand flat on the floor with fingers pointing in line with the shoulders should be stressed. This series develops the cartwheel, the round-off, and the other more advanced tumbling skills in which weight must be taken on hands, body turned in air, where there is a return to floor, and an immediate movement into another pattern undertaken.

Below is a list of activities that develop agility and lead to future vaulting techniques and stunts while in the air:

1. Run and take off with two feet, and land on two feet. (Emphasize good landing techniques.)
2. Run, jump from two feet, land on two feet, take another jump.
3. Run, jump from two feet, land on two feet, do a roll (encourage performing different types of rolls), and stand up.
4. Run, take off from one foot, land on two feet.
5. Run, take off on one foot, land on two feet, and jump again onto two feet.

6. Run, jump, curl body while in air, and land with a double jump.

7. Run, stretch body in the air, land with a double jump.

8. Run, twist in the air, land with a double jump.

9. Run, jump, make a different shape in air, land with a two-foot jump.

(These can be done over a period of time. Jumps can be made free or over an outstretched rope that is lying on the floor or held at various heights from floor.)

From here the child is ready to jump on or over or off apparatus and be able to make various body shapes while in the air. If hand-support work has been done on the floor at the same time, enough strength and feeling for vaulting will have been developed. Vaulting is going over or onto an object by a run, a jump, and use of the hands on the object as a support to push off and over the object.

Many stunts done on the apparatus are done in similar fashion on the floor in order to learn the pattern and to obtain body control while the body is close to the ground and in a stable position. For example: the V sit (p. 475), single leg circles (p. 475), front scale (p. 475), upspring (p. 475) on the floor which becomes the courage vault (p. 490) off a box.

SMALL EQUIPMENT   Working with all types of small equipment develops children's manipulative abilities, their creativity and ingenuity, and their ability to use their bodies in relation to other objects. As children work with various sizes of balls, paddles, and other objects, they become familiar with them and learn to adjust their movements according to the length and weight of the tools. They are laying a foundation for acquisition of skills requiring specific sport and work tools.

The pattern of work with small equipment should be as follows:

1. Orientation to the equipment and exploratory activities.

2. Development of specific skills through problems and challenges.

3. Self-testing activities designed for practice and refinement of skills.

4. Creative routines or sequences of activity.

As children grow older and become more skilled, their interests change, and work with small apparatus becomes more specific to particular sports. Objectives in ball-handling units become more specific regarding acquisition of skills related to sports and precede or accompany work with lead-up games. Starting on page 493 is an example of this pattern as used with ball-handling skills.

APPARATUS   Children should work with large apparatus that has been scaled to their size. Many manufacturers have developed pieces of apparatus for the elementary student, and they have safe, stable, relatively inexpensive, and easily stored models of regular apparatus. Many of these pieces can be made by workers in school shops, maintenance employees, or parents. The first approach to the apparatus should be exploratory; children will find many ways in which to use different pieces. Then the teacher should emphasize the various safe ways to get on and off each piece (mounting and dismounting). Concurrently, each lesson should involve going over the equipment, going under, through, along, above, across, and various combinations of these. Work such as this should produce safe and satisfying activity for each youngster, since no specific patterns are demanded, and all can work at their own level of skill and strength. Gradually, more tasks are set up which require body actions to be modified by the factors of space, force, time, flow, and shape. Later, more specific actions are required in which proper execution and form require personal adjustments and practice.

Routines

Assignments are then made to develop a routine or a sequence in which specific movement patterns are used. The teacher sets up the general requirements of the routine, allowing each child to choose a variety of movements and positions to be performed with continuity. The movement patterns must first be learned and practiced, then put together in a creative effort by the children. All routines, no matter how simple, should be started in a good, erect, standing position, and ended in an erect, balanced, standing position. Intermediate- and upper-grade children should be taught to perform in good form, which means they must have good body control throughout the routine. They should strive for good posture and head position, point toes, hold arms and legs in position (rather than let them dangle loosely), and control the body in an easy landing position. Neither the pattern nor the routine need be complex when the children are first encouraged to become conscious of good form.

The values of individual routines are numerous, since children have specific goals. Individual work and practice is necessary, and creative thinking and movement are encouraged. All youngsters like to perform when they have mastered something and know that they are demonstrating their skills in a warm, permissive, and accepting atmosphere. From observation of performances of others, children become critical thinkers and discover ideas that can be applied to their own problems. While children are doing their routines, the teacher has an opportunity to evaluate his or her own planning and teaching methods, as well as the students' achievements.

SUGGESTED ROUTINE REQUIREMENTS

REQUIREMENTS	POSSIBLE CHOICE OF MOVEMENTS
A. 1. Forward locomotor movement	1. Run
2. Rotary movement	2. Forward roll to 2 feet
3. A jump turn	3. Jump and make 180-degree turn in air to
4. Low landing	4. Squat landing
B. 1. Balance in a 2-point contact position	1. Frog stand
2. Show strength of shoulder girdle while moving	2. Seal walk
3. Balance low on a 1-point contact position	3. V sit

REQUIREMENTS	POSSIBLE CHOICE OF MOVEMENTS
C. 1. An inverted sideward movement	1. Cartwheel
2. Two rolls	2. Forward rolls
3. Flight	3. Straddle leap
4. Inverted hand support	4. Handstand
5. One-leg balance	5. Scale
6. Flexibility in movement (spine)	6. Twist into a
7. Roll	7. Backward roll
8. Feet locomotor movement	8. Run
9. Flight	9. Leap
10. High landing	10. Extended jump to land
D. 1. Fast movement to a position for shoulder strength movement	1. (Fill in the blanks after reading further)
2. 2 rolls followed by	2. _____
3. Inverted position	3. _____
4. Hold fast full extended position to	4. _____
5. Low passive position	5. _____
6. Movements requiring abdominal strength	6. _____
7. Spring up into a	7. _____
8. Rotary motion sideward	8. _____
9. Balanced landing	9. _____
E. Balance beam	
1. Mount from standing position	1. Crotch seat
2. Travel with uneven movement on beam	2. Skip
3. One-foot balance position	3. Front scale
4. Dismount with a turn	4. Jump, half-turn in air.

Organization

Since one of the greatest values of gymnastic activities is that they require individual efforts, the class and equipment must be organized so that each person has an opportunity to be active throughout the class period. Unless mats and apparatus are used and unless there is not enough small equipment for each child, everyone can be working in his or her own space at the same time. Whenever small groups are doing different things, the class will be evenly distributed in groups and work at stations. Children may be divided into groups by size, ability, at random, or by their own preference. Groups facilitate handling equipment and moving from station to station.

Directions on problems should be given verbally to each group or written on a card that is left at each station. The directions should be very simply stated; for instance:

Gymnastic Skills and Activities

465

1. Balance beam: Move across beam, changing levels as you go.

2. Vaulting box: Mount, change body shape, dismount.

3. Low bar: Hang from four points of support, change to two and back to four, dismount.

If the directions are the same for all stations, they could more easily be given verbally. In this case, children would try to do the same type of activity at each station to which they rotate; for example, the teacher might direct, "Stretch and curl on the apparatus, then make a light landing."

If there are only one or two mats, other stations should be set up where activities that do not require mats are performed. Mats are needed for activities that involve inverted positions in which the weight is taken on the head, hands, or feet; they are needed for a landing with great force or with forward momentum; and they are required under and around apparatus pieces on which one does inverted activities or other activities at heights. For example, although a mat is not needed for a 6-inch balance beam, it is needed for a 30-inch beam. When teachers feel they must supervise work at a specific piece of large apparatus because the activity is new or requires help, they should plan other stations at which the children can work without supervision.

If mats alone are being used, they should be arranged so that the teacher is able to see everyone with one glance. If the room is small and mats must be close together, traffic patterns should be established so that a child coming off the end of one mat does not collide with one coming off an adjacent mat. Primary and intermediate children can usually use the width of the mat rather than the length; therefore, everyone is able to have a greater number of turns rather than having to wait in line for a long time.

Vary the type of activity children perform on either the apparatus or in floor work. Use an interval method of working or change the pace often. After a supportive exercise, change to running. From work in an inverted position change to an erect position; from flowing to a sustained movement; from work in a prone position change to an erect moving position. Groups should be allowed to work at each station long enough for the children to have several opportunities to improve their skill. There is no value in rotating each group to each station every day gymnastics is scheduled. It is better to be at half the stations one day and at half during the next session. A rotation chart may be made and put on the board so children know exactly where they are to go and can begin work immediately. In this way they will also realize that everyone has an equal amount of time to work at each station.

A layout for activity stations and an organization plan for rotation of squads is presented (Figure 16-1) for small-group work with both large apparatus and small equipment. Since each squad works at two stations during each period, it takes three lessons to complete the circuit. Then the order is repeated.

Safety Considerations

Common sense and logical procedures should eliminate the major safety hazards in tumbling work and work on apparatus. Too often one of the greatest dangers results from the attitude of teachers. If teachers had little experience in their own school years or are not sure of what they are doing, they tend to be apprehensive and overcautious. Care must be taken so that teachers' anxi-

Figure 16-1 Layout of activity stations and organizational plan for small-group work.

SMALL EQUIPMENT STATIONS

1. ZIGZAG FOOT DRIBBLE
2. HOOPS
3. LONG JUMP

4. BALLS (TARGET PRACTICE)
5. LONG JUMP ROPES
6. WANDS

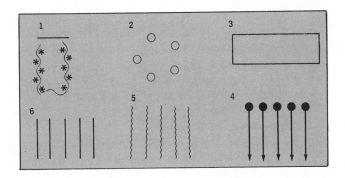

APPARATUS STATIONS

1. MAT WORK
2. HORIZONTAL BAR
3. VAULTING BOX

4. PARALLEL BARS
5. BALANCE BEAM
6. HANGING ROPES

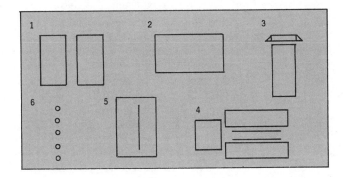

ROTATION PLAN

SQUAD	LESSON 1 STATION	LESSON 2 STATION	LESSON 3 STATION
1	1 & 2	3 & 4	5 & 6
2	3 & 4	5 & 6	1 & 2
3	5 & 6	1 & 2	3 & 4
4	2 & 1	4 & 3	6 & 5
5	4 & 3	6 & 5	2 & 1
6	6 & 5	2 & 1	4 & 3

467

ety is not transferred to the children. Proper planning and observance of the following procedures can eliminate this situation:

1. Equipment should be of good quality and inspected regularly for faulty mechanics or broken parts.

2. Equipment should be placed so that adequate space surrounds each piece so that collisions may be avoided.

3. A traffic-flow plan should be established so that no one will accidentally swing or walk into the path of another performer.

4. Use mats where performer will be landing with great force from high places or will be performing in inverted positions.

5. Set limits of how many people can work safely on the apparatus at one time for the specific types of activities.

6. Organize class so that the working groups are small enough for children to be involved in doing, assisting, or watching the stunt. If children must stand in long lines and await turns, they become restless. Frequently they become boisterous, and distract the performer.

7. Follow a careful plan of progression from simple to complex activities so that children are not required to perform skills that are too difficult for them to do well. Individual differences must be observed; consequently flexibility in the plan of progression is necessary.

8. Select activities according to the students' strength, flexibility, and endurance. If students cannot support their weight on the parallel bars, they can hardly be expected to walk on their hands across the bars.

9. Allow time for light warm-up activities at the start of the class. A brief period of time should be spent warming up whenever exercises or stunts that call for intensive muscular effort are to be undertaken. In the primary grades, there is little need for warm-ups, since the beginning activities themselves can serve as the warm-ups. Activities or exercises selected should be done rhythmically, slowly, and should include stretching, swinging, and light endurance movements. Warm-ups may be done as a group, or children may do their own series individually as soon as they come into the gym. Practice of previously learned stunts may suffice, if these stunts do not make excessive physical demands. The teacher may ask to see various body movements with no set formal pattern; however, careful observation needs to be made so that each child is doing something that fulfills the intended purpose of the warm-up period.

10. Avoid activities requiring hyperextension of and excessive strains on the ligaments and muscles surrounding the knee joints, such as knee walking, knee dips, sudden full-knee bends.

11. If activities at one station are new or are very demanding in the initial stages, teachers should plan to work with children at that particular station. They should plan activities at other stations so that little supervision is needed.

12. Place pieces of apparatus in positions so that the rotation plan may operate in such a manner that children will not be required to do stunts requiring use of the same body parts at subsequent stations. Note in Figure 16-1, the order is such that demands are made on various muscle groups in a balanced fashion.

13. Children should not be forced to do things when they are obviously frightened and display tension. Instead, they should be given alternate assignments which will increase their readiness and bolster their confidence. This does not mean they should be excused when they show disinterest. It should be made clear that their alternate assignment will help prepare them for what they are hesitant to do. Most children will operate in a conscientious manner and not overextend themselves until they are quite confident.

14. Teach children to "spot" or assist others in work on apparatus or in some tumbling stunts. "Spotting" means knowing what the other person is going to do, watching him, and being ready to assist him by helping him catch his balance, break a fall, or giving momentary support while he catches himself. It does not mean lifting or catching. Children should not be expected to catch or lift a weight greater than their own. In regard to spotting, the following should be kept in mind:

   a. *Activities in which there is potential danger to the head, such as rolls and dives.* Place hand between head and the surface it may touch. Just the motion of putting the hand there in the early stages of learning will sometimes cause the performer to tuck the head closer to the chest.

   b. *Activities on balance beam.* Walk alongside the beam with one hand upraised so performer *may* reach out and grasp hand in order to steady himself. If a child is particularly tense, just the presence of the fingertips will be assuring to him and will relieve tension somewhat.

   c. *Activities during which weight is supported on hands.* Grasp the wrist with one hand and just above the elbow with the other. This prevents the arm from collapsing and prevents a possible hard fall.

   d. *Activities in inverted position where legs may overswing, such as a headstand or handstand.* Extend arms straight out so forward swing of legs will be checked. Legs may be pushed and child told to bend knees and go down.

   These are just a few suggestions and by no means the only spotting methods that may be employed. However, they should be sufficient for most beginning activities.

15. Teach children how to land properly and how to break a fall in case of an error. The principles of absorption of force should be re-emphasized.

   a. Land on large padded areas of body. Avoid landing on outstretched hands. Tuck head.

   b. Absorb weight over a longer period of time by rolling upon contact with floor.

16. When hanging on bars, a grip should be used whereby the fingers are wrapped around the bar in one direction, and the thumb in the other (Figure 16-2). This offers a check if hands momentarily slip.

17. Children should wear clothing that will not inhibit their movements or distract their attention. Girls should wear shorts for gymnastic activities. All objects should be removed from pockets and left in the classroom.

(See the Official Manual of the United States Gymnastics Association, edited by Eugene Wettstone, listed in the suggested references for more detail on safety considerations.)

Figure 16-2 Finger and thumb position when hanging on bars.

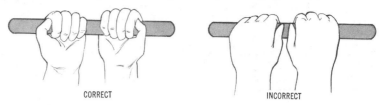

CORRECT   INCORRECT

Basic Mechanical Principles

There are a few mechanical principles operative in gymnastic activities which the teacher should recognize as essential to safe and efficient performance. Since most stunts, tumbling, and apparatus are dependent upon the proper control of balance, rotary motion, and force, a few generalizations about the principles as applied to selected activities are described.

1. The successful execution of most balance stunts depends upon a wide base of support and adjustments to keep the center of weight over the base of support.
   a. Whenever the weight is borne on the hands, care should be taken that the hands are far enough apart, that they are flat with fingers slightly spread. When supporting and hanging, the hands should be placed in line with the shoulders.
   b. Compensatory movements of arms or legs must be made in opposition to stabilize balance when body weight is shifted. Movement or weight added to one side of the body changes the body alignment, and imbalance results. When in an inverted position, the slightest movement of the feet or legs may cause instability, and a quick shift of weight is necessary for realignment. The pelvis must be stabilized over the base before the child is able to recognize automatically the need for proper compensatory movements.
   c. Whenever a roll is to be made on the floor or over a bar, balance must be lost. For example, when turning over a bar from a front rest position, the top of the body must be made heavy so that the body will go forward. Whenever an inverted position on the ropes or bars is desired, the head must be dropped in the desired direction and legs and hips lifted. Many children have trouble doing an inverted hang because it is unnatural for them to drop their head backward.
2. In rotary movements the shorter the radius of rotation is, the faster the movement becomes. The body will move faster in a tuck position (feet and knees tucked to chest) than in a layout position (body extended). The body should be lengthened to decrease the speed of rotation, and shortened to increase speed of rotation.
3. The principle of absorption of force must be applied when landing from a jump. Bending the ankles and knees provides greater time and distance over which to absorb force.
4. Force should be applied equally in the intended line of direction. A push-off in the backward or forward roll must be given equally from both hands or the performer will roll to the side. A takeoff from both feet will give a greater lift for a vault.

5. The angle of takeoff in vaulting should be great enough so that a vertical flight results rather than a low angle and horizontal flight. The takeoff should be near enough to the bar so that the body reaches its highest point in flight over the bar, rather than descending as it reaches the bar.

Activities

Suggestions are made for activities for each type of gymnastic work. They are presented in order of difficulty. Generally, they suggest a main theme or task from which teachers may construct the lesson plan. Many are activities which children will discover naturally when they are asked to give movement answers to specific questions.

Specific directions for certain stunts and exercises are given for the teacher's knowledge of how the finished skill should be executed and how it should appear. Safe and successful learning of some activities depends on prescribed movements and proper execution and leaves no room for variations. Teachers must know what is to be learned and present it to students by a method of their choice—one that will be stimulating, challenging, and motivating. For example, the teacher may describe how a push-up is done, show how it is done, combine showing and telling, or give the stunt as a challenge or task in an indirect manner. For example, "On your hands and knees, can you bend your elbows and touch your chest to the ground, keeping your back straight, then push up to your starting position? How many times can you do that? Can you do the same thing with your legs straight out behind you?" All of these can become more indirect tasks and challenges if the teacher prefaces the directions with such phrases as "can you . . ." "try to . . ." "how many times can you . . .".

Developmental Stunts and Exercises

No specific activities other than traditional stunts and exercises are suggested here for the primary grades. Exploration of basic movement skills in respect to the factors that affect them (described in Chapter 11) is the basic content of gymnastics for younger children. Suggested movement variations and combinations are also given in Chapter 11.

Particular emphasis should be placed on activities that develop shoulder-girdle strength, flexibility, balance, and agility. The body actions of curling, twisting, turning, rolling, extension, and the fundamentals of jumping, landing, transferring weight, supporting weight on various body parts, and flight should be studied and practiced in many variations and combinations. These actions can be done by the whole class at the same time; by individuals who have needs for specific areas of development either in class or at home; in circuits; or by task cards at stations of choice.

Exercises for Development of Specific Physical Elements

STRENGTH OF SHOULDER GIRDLE AND ARMS

1. *Push-ups:* Weight on knees and hands, which are placed directly under shoulders. Bend elbows and touch chest to ground, keep back straight. Straighten elbows, pushing body up. Repeat. More difficult: extend whole body, put weight on balls of feet and on hands. Raise and lower body, keeping body straight.

2. *Straddle chins:* With partner. One lying on back, between legs of other who stands with elbows straight, arms down in front of body. Clasp hands of partner, pull body up, keeping body straight, until elbows are bent; lower body to floor.

3. *Upper back:*

   a. Prone position. Arms extending in front of head. Raise and lower arms alternately keeping knees straight; raise and lower arms together. Alternate raising opposite arms and legs at same time.

   b. Prone position with hands locked behind neck. Raise head and arms slowly off floor. Continue to repeat.

   c. Same position as **b**, lift legs alternately.

ABDOMINAL STRENGTH

1. *Curl-ups or sit-ups:*

   a. Lie on back, knees slightly bent, arms at side. With head leading, curl body up into a sitting position, roll down into lying position. Exhale when going up, inhale when returning to lying position. Partner may hold feet.

   b. Vary with hands held behind head.

   c. Vary rate of speed and number of exercises to be done. Test how many can be done in a specified amount of time.

2. *Leg lifts:* Lying on back, hands at side, knees slightly bent.

   a. Raise one leg, straighten it and return it to former position. Repeat with other leg. Continue.

   b. Sit on floor leaning on elbows, knees slightly bent. Raise legs, straighten and lower to floor slowly.

   c. Vary by moving legs sideward and back as they are extended in air; describe a circle with them.

LEG STRENGTH

1. *Half-squats:* Stand erect, hands on hips. Feet flat on floor.

   a. Bend knees slightly, hold, straighten knees.

   b. Increase depth of knee bend.

   c. Bend and raise heels off floor. (Avoid sudden deep-knee bend.)

   d. Spread feet sideways and repeat.

2. *Lunge:*

   a. Assume same position as in **1.** Shift weight to side, slide leg sideways to a side stride position, bending knee. Keep other leg straight, alternate legs.

   b. Lunge forward.

   c. Lunge backward.

3. *One-leg squat:*

   a. Erect position. Lift one leg, squat on other. Return to position. Alternate legs.

   b. Hop onto foot on which squat is made.

1. *Rocker:* Prone position. With arms back, grasp ankles and make body rock forward and backward.

2. *Ostrich walk:* Bend at hips, grasp ankles. Walk forward, keeping legs fully extended, head held high.

3. *Wing flings:* Body erect, feet slightly apart, arms extended at sides at shoulder level.
   a. Bring hands together in front of chest.
   b. Fling arms back as far as possible, keeping them at shoulder level.
   c. Repeat, keeping head and trunk straight and still.

4. *Arm circles:* Body erect, feet slightly apart, arms extended at sides, slightly above shoulder level.
   a. Circle arms backward, alternate forward.
   b. Vary levels at which arms are held.

5. *Trunk twist:* Body erect, feet slightly apart, arms extended out to sides.
   a. Twist at the waist from side to side, look at some object behind body.

6. *Bobbing forward:* Erect position, feet slightly apart.
   a. With knees straight, bob several times, trying to touch floor.
   b. Try to touch floor in back of legs.
   c. Move feet closer together to make exercise more difficult.

7. *Bend sideways:* Erect position, feet slightly spread, hands at side.
   a. Bend or bob to side, alternate sides.
   b. With elbows bent, hands on shoulder, bend to side.
   c. With one hand held high and the other at side, bend to side.

8. *Pick up:* Place beanbag on floor 8 inches in front of toes. With feet just a few inches apart and knees straight, lean over and pick up beanbag. Repeat placing beanbag farther away each time.

GENERAL ENDURANCE

1. *Running in place:* Erect position. Arms at side.
   a. Start running in place, use arms (with elbows bent) in opposition with legs.
   b. Raise knees high, and use arms vigorously.
   c. Use interval pacing, run slowly, then vigorously, slowly, vigorously, etc.

2. *Jumping jacks:* Erect position, feet together, arms at sides, jump to wide stride position, fling arms up sideward and touch hands overhead, jump to starting position. Feet together, arms at side. Continue for specified number or amount of time.

3. *Grasshopper:* Assume a squat sitting position; bend forward, and place hands under shoulders just in front of knees; extend right leg backward; chest resting on forward knee. Exchange positions of the legs and continue as long as possible.

Developmental Stunts on Floor

1. *Dog walk:* Walk on hands and feet: Vary directions, vary speeds.

2. Run and stop, taking weight on hands momentarily. Run and stop and repeat weight bearing.

3. *Mule kick:* Same as 2, only kick legs up behind high in the air.

4. *Rocker:* Jump from hands to feet several times in a row without stopping.

5. *Lame dog (three-legged walk):* Weight on hands, lift one leg behind, and walk on hands and one leg.

6. *Seal walk:* Weight on hands, prone position, walk on hands, drag feet behind.

7. *Coffee grinder:* Place one hand on floor, other on hip. Straighten arm and extend body so that it is on a straight plane. Walk around a circle, hand as a pivot. Keep head back, body straight. Change hands and repeat.

8. *Crab walk:* Sitting position. Hands on floor behind hips. Take weight on hands and feet, raise weight and walk on hands and feet. Body should be straight from knee to head. Change direction of walk.

9. *Turk stand:* Sit cross-legged on the floor. Stand without using hands to help get up.

10. *Top:* Erect position. Jump into air and turn around landing facing opposite direction. Also, jump into air and turn all the way around landing in takeoff spot.

11. *Heel click:* Stand with feet about 12 inches apart, leap into air, and click heels together before landing. Try to click heels together several times.

12. *Heel slap:* Erect position. Jump up, bringing heels up behind, and slap heels with hands one or more times before landing.

13. *Thread the needle:* Erect position, hands clasped in front of body. Bend over, step over clasped hands with right foot and then with left foot. Clasped hands should be in back of body at finish. Reverse order so that clasped hands are in starting position.

14. *One-foot balance:*
    a. Standing on one foot, close eyes and balance as long as possible. Arms may be used.
    b. Hands on hips, rest left leg against right knee and maintain balance on right leg.

15. *Walk a straight line on floor:*
    a. Walk on a line 15 feet long painted on the floor.
    b. Close eyes and walk straight line.

16. *Corkscrew:* Erect position, feet slightly apart. Place beanbag in front of toes of right foot. Pick it up with left hand by passing left hand in front of body, around outside of right leg, forward between legs, and around in front of right foot. Do same with beanbag on opposite side and use opposite hand.

17. *Human ball:* Start in sitting position, knees bent close to chest. Put arms down inside legs, around outside of shins and clasp hands in front of ankles. Roll to right side, over on back, to left side and up to sitting position.

18. *Jump over foot:* Face wall, place one foot on wall about 12 inches above floor. Keeping foot on wall, jump over that leg with other foot, executing a half turn in the process.

19. *Upswing:* Sit on balls of feet in a kneeling position. Swing arms back and forward, and bring body up into a standing position.

20. *Upspring:* Kneeling position, feet extended behind, toes flat on floor. Swing arms back forcibly and then forward, and jump to a standing position.

21. *V sit:* Sitting position. Raise legs straight up and reach out with arms and grasp ankles. Try to maintain balance in this position.

22. *Knee scale:* Kneeling position, hands on floor in front of body. Raise left leg, extend behind in air. Raise arms diagonally sidewards and balance on one knee.

23. *Front scale:* Erect position. Bend forward at hips, lift and extend right leg up behind until right leg and trunk are parallel to floor; arch back. Arms extended diagonally backward and sideward to help maintain balance; head held up, eyes focused directly forward.

24. *Side scale:* Erect position. Left leg and foot pointing diagonally forward; slide left arm down left leg to point just above ankle; raise right leg upward and sideward; right arm extends over the head to the right. The right arm, trunk and right leg form one line parallel to the ground. Support may be needed at first so position may be assumed. Right leg may rest on chair or beam.

25. *Single-leg circles:* Squat position with both hands flat on floor. Left knee is between arms, right leg extended sideward. Swing right leg forward, and when it meets right arm, lift right hand and place it to right of right leg. Shift weight to right arm as right leg circles under left leg and left hand back to starting position. Make a few circles. Back should be held as vertical as possible, left knee bent.

26. *Jump and touch toes:* Jump into air, extend legs forward and upward with feet apart. Touch toes, keeping back vertical throughout jump. Extend legs downward and return to floor with two-foot landing.

27. *Jump and tuck:* Jump into air, bring knees to chest, grasp shins with hands; release, extend legs down, and return to floor with far foot landing. Keep back vertical.

28. *Jump and jackknife:* Jump into air, lift extended legs forward and upward with feet together to touch toes. Extend legs downward and return to two-foot landing.

29. *Jump and swan:* Jump into air, pull arms high over head, and pull body into an arched position. Hips forward, head and shoulders pulled back hard, legs extended to rear. Return body to vertical position for two-foot landing.

30. *Jump and turn:* As opposed to the *top,* arms should be held close to body as body turns in air. Body should be fully extended, toes pointed. (Children should be encouraged to make other changes of shapes while in the air. All jump styles should be done on the floor before they are used off various pieces of apparatus.)

31. *Arabesque:* Erect position. Raise both arms forward and upward. Lift one leg backward; bend forward at hips; arch back and maintain balanced position.

32. *Front break fall:* Erect position. Keep knees and hips fully extended and fall forward, catching self on hands. Arms flex slightly on contact with floor or mat.

33. *Forward drop:* Same as *front break fall,* only one leg is lifted off floor during fall.

34. *Fish flop:* On back, arms at side. Right foot is kicked up hard enough to bring body up on right shoulder. Turn over face downward with head pointing in opposite direction. This can be done so that body will be in almost the same place on the mat at the end of the stunt.

PARTNER STUNTS

1. *Bouncing ball:* One person squats and bounces up and down like a ball. The other person exerts pressure on the "ball's" back to make it bounce. The amount of pressure exerted determines the amount of bounce.

2. *Wring the dishrag:* (Partners) Face one another and join hands. Raise arms; turn away from each other under the raised arms and then return to face each other as the opposite arms are raised.

3. *Sawing wood:* (Partners) Face each other, standing with one foot slightly forward of the other. Place hands in each other's palms. Push opposite arms back and forward as if sawing wood.

4. *Rocker:* (Partners) Sit facing each other, legs extended (each sits on other's feet). Grasp each other's arms and rock back and forth. One leans backward and lifts other up. (Until momentum is built up, the other will have to lean forward some.)

5. *Chinese get-up:* (Partners of equal heights) Stand back to back with elbows locked. Both lower bodies to floor, then rise to a standing position by pushing against each other's backs.

6. *Leapfrog:* (Partners) One person bends over with knees slightly bent, placing hands on knees. Other runs forward, jumps with legs in straddle position, places hands on partner's shoulders, and pushes self up and over partner, landing with controlled landing on both feet.

COMBATIVES

1. *Bulldozer:* Hands and feet (not knees) facing partner, with right shoulders touching. Try to push (not bump) partner backwards. Change shoulders and repeat.

2. *Back to back:* Sit down, back to back. Using hands and feet, try to move partner without lifting seat from floor. Keep head down.

3. *Toe boxing:* Hands on hips, facing partner. Try to tap partner's toes *lightly* with foot. (Feet must be kept moving so that each cannot tap the other's toes.)

4. *Bottoms up:* Sit facing partner, hands joined, legs slightly apart with feet touching. Try to pull partner so that his/her hips come up off floor.

5. *Hand push:* Stand, face to face, feet together and exactly the length of one foot away from partner's feet. Place palms against the palms of partner and try to make him or her lose balance (move one of feet), or touch any place but on palms. Hands may be pulled away quickly or pushed, as long as balance is not lost.

6. *Indian leg wrestle:* (Two performers of equal size) Lie on the mat side by side, facing in opposite directions. Place hips at opponent's waistline. Grasp opponent's inside shoulder with inside hand. On signal "one, two, three," raise inside legs simultaneously three times. On count "three" hook inside knees and try to force opponent over into a backward roll.

7. *Indian club fight:* (Opponents face each other, arm's distance apart. Join hands. Place an Indian club an equal distance between opponents.) On signal "go," force opponent to knock over the club by pulling, pushing, or jerking him into the club.

8. *Pulldown:* (One partner on hands and knees. Other partner on knees, beside first partner.) On signal, try to get partner off hands and knees by pulling arms or legs out from under him or by turning him over. (Partner on hands and knees does not fight back, but simply tries to stay on hands and knees.) Change and repeat.

9. *Rope pull:* Four inside a circle of rope—square off and see who can pull away from his corner.

10. *Cock fight:* Partners facing, hold one foot behind you with the *opposite* hand. Try to make your partner let go of his raised foot, lose balance, or both by pushing or pulling.

11. *Elbow wrestle:* Lie on your stomach with head facing partner; legs are spread wide apart. Hold right hands together, elbows touching, with other hand behind back. Try to force partner's hand to the floor, without moving elbow off floor. (Partner will have to roll over as his hand is pressed toward the floor.)

Tumbling

Tumbling activities fall into two general categories: stands and balances, and rolls and turns. A mat should be used for most of the following activities. The activities are arranged in order of difficulty.

Stands and Balances

In all balances and stands, there should be a good base with hands under shoulders, elbows body-width apart not pointing out, hands flat, fingers slightly spread.

1. *Frog stand:* Squat position; both hands flat on floor with elbows inside and bent to press against knees; lean forward, slowly take weight on the elbows and hands until feet are clear of floor; keep head up. Hold as long as possible.

2. *Tripod:* Squat position; place hands flat on mat; crown of head about 1 foot in front of hands so the three points form a triangular base; lift body weight, resting knees on bent elbows. Maintain this position.

3. *Headstand:* Take tripod position and extend legs up over head, arch back, keep legs straight and toes pointed. Maintain balance. To come down, bend knees and let body weight come down into squat position. (A partner may stand beside and hold arm across behind other person so legs can be stopped from flying over too far. Partner should not lift legs.)

4. *Handstand:* Erect position. Push off with one leg, place hands directly under shoulders, take weight on hands and at the same time swing legs above head. Keep push-off leg slightly bent until balance can be held for more than 3 seconds; arch back, head up. (Partner should stand in front to catch thighs if legs overswing.) Bend knees, drop feet, and return to erect position.

Gymnastic Skills and Activities

5. *Shoulder balance:* Lying down, raise legs straight above hips, and balance on back of head, neck and shoulders; arms extended up the sides.

6. *Forearm balance:* Take kneeling position, with forearms on mat. Palms down, index fingers and thumbs touching, place head between them; extend right leg and swing it up overhead; at the same time spring off the left leg and bring both legs into straight balanced position.

PARTNER STUNTS

1. *Standing balance on thighs:* One partner (base) stand directly behind the other (top), facing the same direction. Base: squat, place head between top's legs, and grasp top's thighs just above knees; stand up with top sitting on your shoulders. Keep your knees bent and body erect so leg muscles are doing most of the work. Top: place your toes on base's knees with rest of feet on thighs. Base hold top's thighs just above the knees, so top can stand erect as you move your head from between top's legs. (Stunt is complete because top is in a fully extended, erect position. On signal top should jump down; base lets go of his legs.)

2. *Knee shoulder balance:* Base: lie on back with knees bent and feet flat on floor, hands stretched up and forward, ready to support top's shoulders. Top: stand in front of partner's bent knees; place your hands on partner's knees. Lean forward so your shoulders are supported by base's hands; then spring to a balance, legs extended over head, head up, body arched to maintain balance. (Caution base to keep arms perpendicular to body and not to reach forward with them.) On signal from base, top should bend knees and drop feet back to floor.

3. *Horizontal stand:* Base: lie on back, knees bent. Top: stand with feet just behind base's head, hands on base's knees. Base: grasp ankles of top. Top: spring up and shift weight to hands, while base raises arms perpendicular to floor.

4. *Angel balance:* Base: lie on back with legs raised, knees slightly bent with feet placed diagonally alongside top's pelvic bones. Take top's hands in yours and slowly raise top into a balanced position. Let hands go; top balances with arms out to side. Base: on signal, bend knees and lower top to floor, where top returns to standing position.

5. *Sitting balance:* Base: lie on mat with legs raised and knees slightly bent. Top: sit on base's feet and extend arms back, grasping partner's hands. Base: straighten legs and release top's hands. Top then extends arms to sides to help maintain balance.

6. *Three-person mount:* Two of you get down on hands and knees beside one another. Third person: get on top of the other two and place one hand and one knee on the back of each of the bases. (Care should be taken that weight is not placed in the small of base's back.) On signal, all "squash" by extending legs and extending weight on the hands.

PYRAMIDS Children enjoy designing, working out, and especially "squashing" at the end of a pyramid. Making pyramids gives a group a chance to create a design and to make up new stunts or perfect known ones to use in their design. Mounts of three, five, or more people are usually, but not necessarily, the focal point of a pyramid. Partner and single stunts form a design around the center. Some stunts that are frequently used in pyramids are the headstand, handstand, arch, tip-up, bridge, shoulder rest, knee-shoulder stand, horizontal stand, angel balance, sitting mount, standing knee mount, front rest, front scale. Hands should be placed on shoulders and on lower part of buttocks.

Rolls and Turns

1. *Log roll:* Lie across the end of the mat, arms stretched overhead. Roll over and over evenly in one direction, twisting shoulders and hips and keeping legs and arms straight.

2. *Front roll:*
   a. Stand, squat at edge of mat; place hands on mat, shoulder-width apart, fingers pointing straight ahead; lean forward; touch chin on chest; push off with feet and roll forward, hips high; take body weight on hands and carry it forward until shoulders, back, and hips touch mat. Hands may shift from mat to shins as you roll to a squat, then a stand.
   b. Start from a standing position.
   c. Do two or three continuous rolls.
   d. Take several steps, jump, and spring into a roll.
   e. Dive over a mat and into a roll (Figure 16-3).
   (It is best if the roll is first learned as one comes off the end of a box or a bench by placing hands on mat, tucking head, and hitting shoulder area first, then rolling to a stand.)

3. *Egg roll:*
   a. Stand, heels touching edge of mat; squat, rock back, placing hands beside head, fingers pointing toward shoulders. Rock forward with hand push.
   b. From squat position, roll back a little farther; place hands beside head; touch toes to floor beyond head, and rock forward to squat.

4. *Backward roll:* Start as for an egg roll, but tuck head and turn all the way over as hands push hard against the mat. Return to standing position.

5. *Backward extension roll:* Start as for a regular roll, but when hands push against mat extend feet and hold a momentary handstand position before you snap feet down into standing position.

Figure 16-3 Dive over an object into a forward roll.

6. *Eskimo roll: (Partners)* With base lying on back, partner stands straddling his head and facing his feet. Base: lift feet; then grasp one another's ankles. Top: do a forward roll, pulling partner upright. Base: do a forward roll through partner's legs, pulling him up. Continue this to the end of the mat.

7. *Cartwheel:* Place both hands in center of mat, while keeping feet just off one edge. Jump from one foot to opposite edge of mat onto other foot, keeping hands in center. Repeat movement but begin with one foot swinging over, followed by second foot. Continue, working for height of leg swing. Shift to standing position and place one hand down, as first leg swings up, then second hand and second leg. The rhythm is hand, hand, foot, foot, with no two points touching mat at the same time.

8. *Round off:* Start as for a cartwheel but when both feet are overhead, bring feet together in mid-air, twist and land on both feet simultaneously, facing direction from which you came.

Apparatus

Activities done on the various pieces of apparatus are very much alike; however, each piece provides some particular height, size, and shape to which the movements must be adjusted. Many opportunities for exploration and experimentation with different ways to climb, hang, turn over, travel, swing, jump on, jump over, jump off, and balance should be provided in the primary grades. At the same time, principles of landing and proper grip should be stressed.

Suggestions are given here for tasks for experimentation and for specific stunts and exercises which may form the basis of creative routines on various pieces of apparatus. Most pieces of equipment are rather versatile and can be utilized for many informal and exploratory activities.

A few terms and positions common to work on many pieces are explained first.

1. *Starting position:* Performer assumes an erect position, focuses both eyes and thoughts on what first movement is to be; then takes a couple of steps forward and initiates the first movement related to task.

2. *Finish position:* Performer ends the movements related to tasks and returns to a balanced, erect position; pauses a few seconds before walking away from the apparatus or mat.

3. *Mount:* Getting onto a piece of equipment or another person who will be the supporting base.

4. *Dismount:* Getting off a piece of equipment or another person who was the supporting base.

5. *Vault:* Going over a piece of equipment and using the hands as supportive assistance.

6. *Pike position:* Body bent at the hips, and legs extended at right angles to body.

7. *Tuck position:* Knees flexed; thighs held up and in toward chest.

8. *Layout position:* Body fully extended.

9. *Straddle position:* Legs extended outward from the body.

10. *Squat position:* Legs bent, seat close to feet.

11. *Front support or front rest:* Weight taken on hands, body rests on bar at a point on which body is balanced. Legs extended, toes pointed. Hands may be taken off bar and arms extended to sides.

12. *Flank:* Both legs and body move to same side of a piece of equipment, either in vaulting, mounting, or dismounting.

13. *Inverted position:* Body upside-down.

14. *Quarter turn:* Body makes a quarter-turn to right or left.

15. *Half turn:* Body ends facing opposite direction.

16. *Full turn:* Complete turn is made in the air; body ends facing the same direction in which it started.

17. *Scale:* Any stunt in which one foot serves as the base.

18. *Overgrip:* Grasp on bar with fingers pointing away from body.

19. *Undergrip:* Grasp on bar with fingers pointed in direction of body.

Horizontal Bars

Most of these activities may be done also on doorway gym bars, chinning bars, between the parallel bars, or on a medium or high balance beam. Some require various heights, and some more room under the bar and behind the bar than others.

1. *Passive hanging:* Jump and grasp bar; hold body weight as long as possible; drop and land safely.

2. *Active hanging:* As above, but contract muscles into firm position, point toes, hold head high.

3. *Flexed arm-hang:* Grasp bar, pull body up, chin resting on bar, arms flexed. Hold position as long as possible. Dismount.

4. *Hang and swing:*
   a. Swing legs from hips slowly; keep body straight.
   b. Swing from side to side.
   c. Swing and dismount at back of swing.
   d. Swing and dismount at front of swing.

5. *Hang and raise legs:*
   a. Raise legs to tuck position.
   b. Raise legs from hips, lower slowly.

6. *Front rest:* Grasp bar and balance with bar just above hips. Extend legs behind; head is up and reaching (Figure 16-4).

7. *Double knee-hanging:* Lift legs up and over bar, press feet down hard, and let the body hang from the back of the knees. Pull up to bar, disengage knees, and dismount.

8. *Skin the cat:* Grasp bar, flex knees and hips, and pull legs up between the arms and under the bar. Slowly roll over until hips are higher than head or feet touch floor. Reverse roll back to original position and dismount.

9. Grasp bar, swing and run, back and forth, back and forth, swing out and up on third run onto a box or bench.

10. Vary position of the body while inverted, from pike to lay out, tuck, etc.

Figure 16-4 Front rest on the horizontal bar.

11. *Single knee-hang:* Grasp bar, body hanging below bar with legs elevated. Pull hips up, and hook one knee over bar between hands. Unlock knee, dismount.

12. *Pullover:* Grasp bar, swing right leg forward up, hard, both legs swing around and over bar, while pulling self toward bar to finish in a front support position on the bar. (In order to get to the other side of the bar, the head must be dropped backward so center of body weight will go to the other side as the arms pull the body around.) Push away from bar from front rest position and dismount.

13. *Single knee mount:* Assume single knee-hang position; swing extended knee downward and backward, pull bar toward hips (with straight arms), and turn up into a position on top of the bar with back of one knee on bar and other leg extended.

14. *Single knee-circle:* From the straddle position assumed from the swing knee-mount, swing extended leg forward, then backward, slide other leg back so bar is in crook of knee, then swing extended leg forward, drop head and shoulders backward. Completely circle the bar, and assume straddle position. Dismount. (Leg must be straight and swung forcibly forward as head and shoulders are dropped or there will not be enough momentum to get around and on top of the bar again.)

15. *Chinning:* Grip bar in undergrip (hands toward body). Pull body up, touch chin on bar, lower body, pull up, touch chin on bar, repeat as long as possible.

Balance Beam   Initial experiences should be exploratory so confidence is gained. If the beam is too high for children to mount, a chair or stool should be provided. Most children will climb up onto a high beam from an underhang hand-foot grasp. Medium or high beams may be used for hanging, climbing, and vaulting activities as well as for balance stunts. Most balance activities can be started using a line painted on the floor or a narrow flat board on the floor and as the child progresses, the beams will be a progressively higher distance off the floor. Arms should be used to help maintain balance, and eyes should be focused forward rather than downward at feet. Balance should be attained before changes in position are made. When one wavers excessively on the beam, he should step or jump off and start again. A good exploratory activity is to move across the beam using feet as base; then using hands and feet as base; and with body under the beam, using arms and legs as support.

1. Walk forward.
2. Walk backward placing toe of foot directly behind heel of other foot.
3. Walk on toes (Figure 16-5).
4. Slide sideward.
5. Walk sideward crossing one foot over the other.
6. Hop forward, backward.
7. Vary positions of hands and arms in all of these so adjustments in weight to keep balance must be in other parts of body.
8. Hold objects of varying weights in one hand, on the head.
9. Step over and around a wand extended across beam. Go under a wand.

Figure 16-5 Walking on the low balance beam.

10. Step through a hoop held over beam.
11. Throw and catch a ball with a partner who is on the floor some distance away.
12. Change levels—sit, lie down, stoop, stretch.
13. Crawl on hands and knees across beam.
14. Squat on one foot, extending nonsupporting leg.
15. Do a half-turn.
16. Do a full turn.
17. Do a half-turn with one foot, full turn on one foot.
18. Jump up and down.
19. Jump and turn.
20. Walk on hands and feet forward; backward; sideward.
21. Skip across beam. (With musical accompaniment try other dance steps.)
22. Walk and dip nonsupporting leg down beside leg.
23. Knee scale (page 475), Figure 16-6.
24. Front scale (page 475).
25. Side scale (page 475).
26. V sit (page 475).
27. *Straddle stand:* Stand facing sideward on beam, with legs in straddle position. Bend trunk parallel to floor, arms extended sideward.
28. *Backward roll:* Lie on back on beam; reach over head, grasp underside of beam with both hands, place head to one side of beam, pull with arms, bend hips and roll over backwards; when coming out of roll, take weight on knee. (This should be done first on a low beam with a spotter.)

Figure 16-6 Knee scale on the balance beam.

MOUNTING MEDIUM OR HIGH BEAM

1. *Straddle seat:* Front support on side of beam, raise one foot to beam, put one leg over and straddle beam, push down on beam, raise body to a standing position.
2. *Side seat:* Sitting on edge of beam, push down on inside hand on beam, pull inside foot on beam, swing outside leg up and onto beam.
3. *One knee:* From end of medium height beam, push down on beam as hands swing back and forward and land on beam on one knee.

DISMOUNTING

1. Jump off side; off end.
2. Jump and quarter-turn, placing one hand on beam.
3. Straddle jump to stand; from side; from end.
4. From hand support on beam, push up and away, landing with one hand on beam.
5. Squat jump.

SAMPLE SEQUENCES

1. *Straddle mount:* Push up into front scale. Push off with hands to landing position on floor.
2. *Cross-seat mount:* Series of movements along beam from high to low. Quarter-turn dismount.
3. *Mount:* Hop into a full turn, two deep-knee bends, half-turn into a scale, change to another scale, slide into a dismount from end of beam.

Stall Bars

Many schools have stall bars. The top bar, which extends out farther than the others, can be used for chinning or free hanging. Stall bars afford opportunities for hanging and lifting body parts while hanging, yet they take little space in a room or gym.

FACING BARS

1. Climb up a few rungs. Grasp bar. Walk up until feet are as close as possible to hands; walk down.
2. With arms straight, legs at angle, bend arms and pull body up.
3. Hang with one hand.
4. Hang with two hands; swing from side to side.

BACK TO BARS

1. Hang, and pull up to flexed-arm position.
2. Hang; lift legs into tucked position.
3. Hang; lift legs into straight position.
4. Hang; lift legs and arch, jump away from bars, jump and turn in air.
5. Hang; raise feet all the way above head.

Parallel Bars

The height and width of adult parallel bars make it very difficult for small children to do stunts while supporting their weight on their hands. Unless elementary-size bars are available, only exploratory movements and stunts under or between the bars can be done safely. One bar can be used much like a horizontal bar.

UNDER AND BETWEEN BARS

1. *Inverted hang* (p. 481)
   a. Tuck position
   b. Layout position
   c. Pike position
2. *Skin the cat* (p. 481)
3. *Bird's nest:* Standing at center between bars, grasp bars with an outside grip. Lift legs to pass through the inverted hand position and backward to hook feet on bars. Extend legs, body, and arms along bars; hold head high. Bring legs back, tuck, and return to inverted position and dismount.

AT END OR MIDDLE OF BARS

1. *Straight-arm support:* Place hands on bars with outside grip directly under shoulders; jump off floor, extend arms fully and support weight (Figure 16-7).
2. *Hand walk:* From straight-arm support position, walk the length of the bars by shifting body weight from one hand to another.
3. *Straight arm-swing:* From a straight-arm support, swing the body back and forth in an extended position; push off and back and dismount.
4. *Back foot leaning rest:* At center of bars, assume straight-arm support position, bring legs up and rest feet on bars in front of body. Extend body fully. Bring legs down and dismount.

Figure 16-7 Straight-arm support on the parallel bars.

Figure 16-8 Straddle seat on the parallel bars.

5. *Front leaning rest:* From straight-arm support position, bring legs behind arms and rest feet on bar. Extend body fully. Swing legs forward and dismount.

6. *Support swing to inside cross riding seat:* From straight-arm support position bring body to a sitting position on right bar with legs between bars. Maintain an erect position, extend left leg, and bend right leg and hip. Return to straight-arm support and dismount.

7. *Support swing to outside cross riding seat:* Same as 6, but legs are on outside of bars.

8. *Support swing to straddle seat:* From straight-arm support swing both legs up and over bars resting thighs on bars in straddle position. Push up, swing legs down, and dismount (Figure 16-8).

9. *Straddle travel:* Same as 8, only rather than dismounting, make another swing and take a straddle position. These movements should be done in a flowing continuous motion the length of the bars.

DISMOUNTS

1. *Rear vault:* Straight-arm support swing. As feet rise above bar on swing, lean to right and bring both legs over right bar, flexing at hips as legs pass over bar. At the same time, grasp right bar with left hand and release right hand. Land alongside bar facing original direction. Later variations of quarter- and half-turns may be added to rear vault.

Figure 16-9 Shoulder balance on the parallel bars.

2. *Front vault:* From support swing, feet rise above bar on *backward* swing; lean to the left, shifting weight to left arm; bring both legs over left bar. At same time, grasp left bar with right hand and release left hand. Land alongside bar facing original direction. Later add variations of landing with different degrees of turns. (Older and stronger children can learn to do rolls and balances on top of the bar because they are able to lift and control body weight above the bar.) (Figure 16-9).

Swedish Boxes or Benches (Vaulting and Jumping)

Initial work on jumping and vaulting can be taught using improvised equipment. A low sturdy table, a strong wooden box, a sturdy gym bench, a sturdy stool, or springboard may be used if a Swedish box is not available.

USING A LOW BOX

1. Walk up to box, step onto it, jump off. (Stress good landing techniques, extended body.)
2. Run, jump on box, jump off.
3. Run, jump on box, vary body positions in air on jump. (Tuck, pike, straddle, twist, etc.)
4. Run, jump, land on box on two feet, jump off.
5. Run, varying takeoff foot.
6. Run, jump over box, changing body position in air.
7. Jump off box, and do a forward roll.
8. Jump on box, try a balance stunt, dismount.

Be sure children can recognize and perform with both symmetrical and asymmetrical patterns.

USING A LONG BENCH

1. Run, jump on bench, run along it, jump off.
2. Run, jump on bench, hop along bench, jump off.

3. Crab walk along bench, dismount.
4. Jump on and off alternate sides of bench.
5. Jump over and back along length of bench.
6. At end of bench, crouch vault onto knees (take weight on hands), push back and off.*
7. At side of bench, face it, vault over it with bent knees.*
8. Taking weight on one end, fence vault (one-hand support) across bench.
9. Go length of bench fence vaulting back and forth across it.*
10. Face vault (extending legs).*

Vaulting Box A higher padded box, bench, or buck may be used. Repeat many of the previous activities off higher box.

1. Climb up on box, dismount.
2. Jump up on box using hands to help dismount.
3. *Basic vault:* Approach the box, take off on one foot, bring other foot up alongside so both may land at the same spot for a double-foot takeoff in a vertical direction. Place the hands on the box; the push of them against the box helps the body gain height. Pull the feet, hips, and knees upward to clear the box. Push off with hands, but remove hands from the box as feet clear the box (Figure 16-10).

* Low box may be used.

Figure 16-10 Assisting with a basic vault.

Figure 16-11 A side or flank vault.

4. Vault atop box, landing on knees. Upswing dismount (courage dismount) (p. 475).
5. Vault to a crouch position, stand erect, jump off. Vary shape of body in air.
6. Vault to a standing position on box; jump off, varying style.
7. Vault to a standing position, turn, jump landing.
8. *Squat vault:* Basic vault approach with knees bent and brought up to chest.
9. *Flank vault:* Basic vault approach with weight taken on one arm only. Legs pass extended to one side of the box, side of body passes over box. Legs swing down over other side of box (Figure 16-11).
10. *Rear vault:* Basic vault approach—hips turn so body achieves a V position facing the side (seat passes over box). Remove right hand (if vault is executed to left) from box and place on box again after body has passed over it. Right hand leaves box and swings to the side as landing is made.
11. *Straddle vault:* Basic vault approach with both legs spread wide outside arms; push off with hands, land with feet together.

Hanging Ropes

1. Grasp rope, pull up from lying position to sitting position, and return. (Hand movements—hand over hand.)
2. Pull up from sitting position to ropes and hang—arms bent.
3. Pull up from lying position to standing position and return—legs straight.
4. Climb rope:
   a. Stand with rope between legs, wrap rope around back of calf of right leg, and over instep of right foot. Place left foot on top of rope, where it crosses instep.

b. Grasp rope in right hand above left hand and above head.

c. Bring knees up toward chest (flex knees).

d. Straighten legs. Hands should now be in front of chest.

e. Reach up as high as possible with hands.

f. Repeat knee action. Continue up rope.

g. Come down in the same manner. Do not slide. (Stress the hand-over-hand action.) (Note: Before you or the child knows his or her capacity to climb, tie ribbons at various spots on the rope to set limits or goals for climbing.)

5. Bicycling: Jump and grasp rope above height of head. Flex knees alternately, as though riding a bicycle. Count number of times you can do this before letting go of the rope.

6. Reverse hang.

7. Chin on rope, pulling self up to bent-arm position until chin is even with hands. Lower body until arms are completely extended; without touching floor, pull up again.

8. If two ropes hang side by side, various stunts can be performed.

   a. If one rope is held in each hand: tuck position, pike position, skin the cat, reverse hang.

   b. Move from one rope to another.

9. Climb rope using arms only; feet are hanging free.

Swinging on Ropes

Children must be taught to dismount or get off of the rope at the back of the swing. At this point, momentum is halted temporarily, and one can drop straight down onto the balls of the feet.

1. Swing on the rope by taking a few approach steps; jump and grasp rope so feet are free of floor. Swing and dismount.

2. Stand on box, swing off and out, and dismount.

3. Swing up and land on box, dismount from box.

4. Swing over box. (Legs must be tucked.)

5. Run and swing over cross-bar on jump standards. Raise bar at intervals.

Cargo Nets

Cargo nets come in various sizes. The number of pupils who can be on them at one time depends on their size. Some nets are secured at the bottom to the floor and some hang free. The nets provide for many climbing and hanging movements. Many of the same stunts or movements that are done on the hanging ropes or the stall bars can be done on the net. This piece of apparatus is an excellent one for free exploration and experimentation and affords some small-group work. Ribbons should be tied at various distances from the ground to the top to mark achievement levels and to have a safe place to climb for those who are not ready to go to the top.

1. Move up the net; move down.

2. Move in a circle on the net.

3. Hang on the net with different bases of support.

4. Hang on the net and make different body shapes.

5. Mirror the movements of a partner on the net.

6. Climb the net using hands and feet.

Figure 16-12 Cargo net.

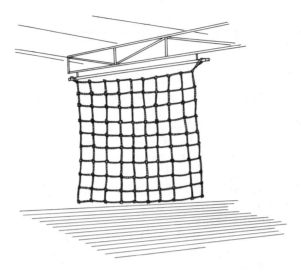

7. Climb the net using only hands.
8. Climb the net going through every other hole.
9. Climb to a designated spot in the count of 5 (8, 10).
10. One person goes to each of the designated spots. On a signal one person from the ground climbs up and passes an object to the person at the first spot; that person takes the object on to the next, with the last person bringing it down to the floor. Teams are timed as they do this.
11. Climb down the net in an inverted position.
12. Climb the net in a sideways position.
13. (Four persons) Start at the bottom at a signal; race to the top or whatever level is designated, then back to the floor.

Small Equipment

Suggestions are given here for activities using the most common types of small equipment. A creative teacher will undoubtedly include other pieces of equipment in his or her program. For the most part, major ideas or themes for work are suggested to give the teacher a springboard for planning lessons.

The suggestions for ball-handling activities are stated in an indirect manner that includes both method and content and follows the pattern of work suggested for activities with small apparatus. Lead questions are given, which would necessarily be expanded in the lesson on the basis of the children's answers and performance. The suggestions should serve as an example for the teacher to follow in implementing other activities. These could be implemented through task cards or learning packages, orally, by contracts, etc. (See also suggestions in analysis of manipulative skills, Chapter 11.)

PROBLEMS AND CHALLENGES FOR THROWING AND CATCHING

1. Throw the ball to yourself. How many different ways can you throw it to yourself?

2. How straight can you throw the ball over your head?

3. How high can you throw the ball and still catch it? How did you make it go higher? Where should you be standing in order to catch the ball easily when it comes down?

4. Starting in a sitting position, throw the ball up and catch it while you are standing.

5. How do you catch the ball most easily? With arms bent or arms straight? Do you bring the ball in toward your body?

6. At how many different levels can you catch the ball?

7. Can you stoop down to catch it and jump up and throw it while you are still in the air?

8. Can you throw the ball up in the air, take four steps, and catch it?

9. How many times can you throw the ball against the wall and catch it before you miss it?

10. Step back farther from the wall and throw. Do you have to throw harder so it comes back to you? How did you do this? Which direction was your body facing when you threw? If you twisted away from the wall as you brought the ball back, then twisted toward the wall as you threw the ball, did the ball go farther?

11. Move back. Throw again. This time try taking a step forward as you release the ball. Does this help the ball go faster or farther?

12. Pick a spot on the wall. When you throw this time, make your arm follow the ball and point to the spot. Did your ball hit that spot? How many times can you hit your target?

13. Can you throw with your left hand?

14. Who can run and throw and catch at the same time without slowing down?

15. With a partner, count the number of levels at which each can throw and catch the ball. Where do you look when you throw to your partner?

16. Throw and catch the ball with a partner while you are both running. Can you trade places without stopping the ball throwing?

17. Can you bounce the ball back and forth to a partner while you are both running?

SELF-TESTING ACTIVITIES FOR THROWING AND CATCHING

1. Throw the ball against the wall and catch it at increasingly wider distances. (The general throwing pattern may be varied.)

2. Throw at a stationary target on the wall or into a box, barrel, or basket.

3. Throw through a large hoop suspended from the ceiling.

4. Throw and catch the ball off the wall for 20 seconds (similar to wall pass test, p. 387).

5. Throw the ball over a rope, a bar, or a net; run under and catch it on the other side.

6. Throw to a moving person. Specify that the ball must reach the runner as he reaches a certain mark on the floor.

7. Set up a maze which involves going under, over, and around objects in the interim between throwing the ball into the air and catching it.

PROBLEMS AND CHALLENGES FOR BOUNCING AND DRIBBLING

1. How many times can you bounce the ball in succession?

2. Which way can you bounce it the most times before losing control of it—by catching it every time or by pushing it down each time with your fingers? Why?

3. How do you use your wrist when you bounce the ball? Is it stiff or does it bounce with the ball? Which way can you bounce the ball the fastest?

4. Can you bounce the ball best with your right hand? Left hand? Both hands? Can you switch from right to left without losing control of the ball?

5. Who can bounce the ball once and turn around before catching it again? Who can turn around twice?

6. How low can you bounce the ball? How high can you bounce it? Who can bounce it low, then high, then low, etc.? Which way do you have the best control? Why?

7. At how many different levels can you be while bouncing the ball? Who can sit on the floor while bouncing the ball? Who can be on your stomach? On your back? Can you get up while still bouncing it?

8. Can you move forward while bouncing the ball? How do you make the ball go forward? We call this dribbling.

9. Who can skip forward while dribbling the ball? In a circle?

10. Staying in your own space, in how many different directions can you dribble the ball?

11. When you move in different directions and dribble, where do you look or focus your eyes?

12. Try to "write" your initials on the floor with the ball by dribbling in the shape of letters rather than in a straight line.

SELF-TESTING ACTIVITIES FOR BOUNCING AND DRIBBLING

1. Count the number of continuous bounces in 15 seconds. Alternate hands and vary the levels for this. (Length of time may be changed.)

2. Bounce with rhythm of music.

3. Dribble with rhythm of music.

4. Move while dribbling, and change directions each time the whistle sounds.

5. Dribble through a maze made of Indian clubs. Dribble through the maze for time.

6. Dribble through a series of hoops.

7. Dribble through a maze which involves going under and over objects while dribbling.

PROBLEMS AND CHALLENGES FOR KICKING

1. Kick the ball so it travels along the ground.

2. Can you kick the ball so it travels in the air? Did you kick it differently from when it traveled on the ground? How?

3. Kick the ball as far as you can.

4. Can you kick it even farther? What did you do differently? Did your arms help? What did your other leg do? What did your kicking leg do after it hit the ball?

5. Can you kick the ball very gently, first with one foot then the other? Can you touch it with either foot each time you take a step? Why not? Don't let it get away from you.

6. Can you kick the ball up in the air so you can catch it? What part of the foot did you use to kick it?

SELF-TESTING ACTIVITIES FOR KICKING

1. Place-kick the ball for greater distances.

2. Place-kick the ball at a target.

3. Kick the ball over an obstacle.

4. Dribble the ball in zigzag fashion through a maze of chairs or pins.

5. Time the maze dribble.

PROBLEMS AND CHALLENGES FOR STRIKING BALL WITH HAND

1. Hit the ball with some part of your hands.

2. Hit it with another part of your hands.

3. Can you hit it overhand?

4. Can you hit it underhand?

5. Can you hit it very high against the wall? How high are your hands when you touch the ball? Does it help to bend your knees and stretch high as you hit it?

6. Can you hit the ball underhand with your fist?

7. How far from the wall can you get and still hit the wall? What helps you to hit it harder?

8. Hit the ball back and forth to a partner.

SELF-TESTING ACTIVITIES FOR HITTING BALL WITH HAND

1. Draw lines on wall and floor and progressively move back and hit higher on the wall.

2. Count how many continuous hits can be made on the wall.

3. Count how many times couples can keep ball going between them.

PROBLEMS AND CHALLENGES FOR HITTING THE BALL WITH A PADDLE

1. Can you hit the ball up in the air with the paddle? How did you hold the paddle?

2. Can you bounce the ball against the floor and continue hitting it with the paddle?

3. Can you hit the ball up in the air and let it bounce on the floor, then hit it up again?

4. Can you drop the ball and then hit it against the wall? Which way did you swing the paddle? Try it another way. In which direction was the paddle facing?

5. Can you hit the ball as it rebounds from the wall? Which way were you facing? What did your legs do? What did your paddle do after it hit the ball?

6. Can you hit the ball high? Low? Straight ahead?

SELF-TESTING ACTIVITIES FOR HITTING THE BALL WITH THE PADDLE

1. Count how many times you can hit the ball up in the air without missing.
2. Count how many times you can hit the ball against the floor without missing.
3. Count how many times the ball can be hit against the wall continuously.
4. Set up a large target area. Hit the ball into the target.
5. With a partner, see if you can keep the ball going back and forth, hitting it on the first bounce.

Jumping Ropes

Rope jumping contributes greatly to the development of leg muscles, endurance, and rhythmic coordination. Young girls particularly enjoy rope jumping, but boys normally do not choose it for one of their play activities. Adults often employ rope jumping as a training and conditioning device. There are a great many rope-jumping activities that can be challenging to complete at any age. Generally, short ropes are used for jumping by individuals and longer ropes by several people, with two needed to turn the ropes.

INDIVIDUAL ACTIVITIES WITH SHORT ROPES   Beginners have to learn to turn the rope as well as to jump correctly. The following means of teaching this activity are suggested. First, the student should practice turning the rope over his head (from back to front), letting the rope touch the ground in front of him. (Hands should be held out to sides and not over shoulders.) Then, the jumper should swing rope over head, let it touch ground, and jump over it with both feet. On the jump the heels are lifted first, then the push-off is from the toes. In landing the knees and ankles bend, the weight is taken on the balls of the feet first. With practice the pause between each jump can be eliminated, and jumping will be continuous. Once a child can swing the rope successfully, teach the double jump, a little jump for balance while the rope is overhead and a bigger jump over the rope as it touches the ground.

1. Jump while turning rope forward.
2. Jump while turning rope backward.
3. *Cross elbows:* cross arms at elbows and turn rope with hands far out at sides.
4. *Rock:* with one foot in front of the other. Hop on front foot, then on back foot and continue rocking motion—change feet and repeat.
5. *Heel, heel:* hop, placing alternate heels forward on ground.
6. *Feet together and apart:* alternate jumping with feet together and feet spread apart.
7. *Toe tap:* hop with free leg and ankle extended forward with little toe of forward foot tapping ground.
8. *Leg swing:* hop on one foot; swing the other foot forward.
9. *Toe tap in back:* hop on one foot, tapping in back with the toe of the free foot.

Movement Experiences

10. *Legs crossed:* jump on both feet with one ankle crossed over the other.

11. *Single hop:* hop on either right or left foot, other foot is raised and held high with knee bent.

12. *Skip:* skip in place and skip while traveling.

13. *Partners jump:* one turns rope, partner runs in and jumps with him.

OTHER USES FOR SHORT ROPES

1. Holding ropes at both ends in one hand, swing the rope in various patterns around, over, and under the body.

2. Stretch and land, holding rope tautly between the two hands.

3. Use rope for jumping marker.

4. Lying on floor, use the positions of ropes as a basis for body shapes.

5. Jumping in time with music; develop creative rhythm patterns.

ACTIVITIES WITH LONG ROPE To teach beginners, have them first stand next to the rope and jump over it. Then swing the rope slightly from side to side and have them jump it each time it touches the ground. Increase the arc of the swinging rope. Then have them stand next to the rope, swing it overhead, and have them jump over it as it touches the ground on the other side of them. Jumping off both feet should be taught first, with emphasis on jumping on toes and landing on toes and balls of feet with knees slightly bent to absorb the jar. The double jump as the rope touches the ground should be taught next. To help children get the rhythm of the double jump, call, "And jump, and jump," or "Jump, JUMP, jump, JUMP."

1. *Run in the front door:* Child runs in as the rope is turned toward him and is at its highest point, jumps, and runs out other side.

2. *Run in back door:* Child runs in as the rope is turned away from him.

3. **a.** Swing the rope over and toward the jumper and he runs through.

   b. Then two runners run through.

   c. Time it so that each turn of the rope a new couple runs through.

4. *Follow the leader:* Leader is selected, players follow leader doing whatever jump-rope stunt he chooses to do. One who misses is out.

5. For groups of four—two swing the rope, the other two jump.

   a. Join hands, turn around.

   b. Skip around each other.

6. Jump to rhymes.

7. Bounce a ball while jumping.

8. While jumping, play catch with someone who is not jumping.

9. Two ropes with two partners, each turn the ropes in opposite direction (double dutch).

10. Two ropes, two sets of partners turning ropes so they cross in the center (egg-beater).

11. *Pepper:* As a player jumps, the other players say "Salt, vinegar, mustard, pepper." On the word "pepper" the turners gradually turn the rope faster and faster until the jumper misses.

12. *Hot Pepper—H-O-T spells red hot pepper:* On word "pepper" turners turn rope faster and faster. Jumper jumps until he misses.

13. *High Water:* The turners swing the rope on a low arc while a player jumps over it each time it goes by. The rope is gradually raised higher and higher from the ground until the jumper misses.

(In jump-rope activities, verses or rhymes are used. The *italicized* word or syllable indicates when the jump should be made.)

- **Teddy Bear**

Teddy Bear, *Teddy* Bear, *turn a-round* (jumper turns while jumping),
Teddy Bear, *Teddy* Bear, *touch the ground* (jumper touches the ground),
Teddy Bear, *Teddy* Bear, *show* your *shoe* (jumper sticks one foot out to side while jumping),
Teddy Bear, *Teddy* Bear, *please skiddoo* (jumper runs out).

- **Around I Go**

On *in* I run and *around* I go (run in, turn around),
Clap my *hand* and *nod* just *so* (clap hands, nod head up and down),
I *lift* my *knee* and *slap* my *shin* (lift knee, holding it up while jumping until shin is slapped),
When *I* go *out* let _____ come in (call name of next jumper and run out).

- **Candle Stick**

_____ be nimble and _____ be quick (substitute jumper's name),
_____ jump *over* the *candle* stick,
Oh *jump,* and *jump,* and *jump* so *high,*
But you'd *better* jump *out* or _____ will *cry* (name next jumper and run out, next jumper comes in, and verse begins again).

OTHER USES FOR LONG ROPES

1. Long ropes can be held stationary between two people and used for leaping over, going under, or various combinations.

2. Lay two long ropes parallel on ground for long-jump markers.

3. Elastic ropes can be held very firmly and at an even height where the whole class can be running over or going under at the same time. One rope can be held high, one low, and children must pass between.

Wands

Wands 36 inches long may be purchased, or broomsticks may be cut down to the required size. One-and-a-half-inch doweling may also be purchased in desired lengths. Bamboo poles and long broom handles may be used for some partner work.

1. In a sitting position, grasp the wand with both hands. Put legs over it, now back again, and lower legs quietly to the floor. Extend legs over the wand without touching it.

2. Stand the wand upright in front of you. Turn around quickly and regrasp the wand before it falls to the floor.

Movement Experiences

498

3. Grasp the upright standing wand with one hand and twist around, ducking under your arm without letting go of wand.

4. Jump over the stick (hold it by yourself).

5. Hold wand in two hands at waist level; put right foot between right hand and wand, bring wand over back, twisting so that left foot can be placed back over wand and it is returned to starting position without the hands ever leaving the wand.

6. Balance wand on open palm.

7. Lie on back, pass bent legs under wand (both at the same time), stretch the legs between wand and body, pass legs back under wand.

8. Hold wand in two hands at chest height, drop wand, bend knees and catch it coming to an erect position.

9. Set wand on floor, use it to jump over. Set a series of wands in a design on the floor, and jump over with two feet. Hop over.

10. Place a wand on two boxes or chairs:
    a. Jump over wand
    b. Crawl under wand
    c. Vary height of wand

PARTNER STUNTS

1. Standing opposite partner, one person holds wand on floor vertically with fingertip. When wand is balanced, the person lets go of it and the partner tries to catch wand before it touches floor.
   a. Increase distance between partners.
   b. Each lets go of a wand at the same time, and then tries to catch his partner's.

2. *Wand wrestle:* Each holds onto one wand with an overhand grip, and tries to wrestle the stick away from his partner.

3. Face each other, each hold an end of the wand in both hands; step over and turn under the stick until returned to starting position.

4. Face each other, hold wand in both hands at arms length, lean back, pull, and make circle with small sideward steps around circle.

IN GROUPS OF THREE

1. Two hold wand between them, third jumps over wand.

2. Two hold wand between them, third uses wand as a horizontal bar.

3. Partners are facing each other with wands held between them. One is held down at thigh height, the other above head. Third person runs and jumps through "window" made by wands.

Long poles can be used also; partners hold the end of two poles. The two move the poles up and down, or in and out, in a pattern, and a third person jumps or hops over them. The dance Tinikling (Table 12-2) is a Filipino dance in which this is done in a rhythmic fashion.

Hoops

Bicycle tires and automobile tires may be utilized for some of these activities, as well as regular wooden or plastic hoops.

1. Roll the hoop straight forward, around in a circle, and backward.

2. Run faster alongside the hoop.

3. Swing the hoop like a skipping rope, and jump through it each time it comes around.

4. Roll hoop, run and cross over in front of it, let it pass on other side and catch it.

5. Roll the hoop, and run through it. Try again, and again, and again. (This may be difficult depending on size of person and size of hoop.)

6. Twirl hoop around wrist, arm, neck, waist, ankle.

   a. Change direction of twirl.

   b. Twirl one hoop on wrist, one on leg.

7. Spin hoop around its vertical axis, run around it one or more times, and catch it before it stops spinning.

8. Place hoop on floor.

   a. Jump into it and out.

   b. Go around hoop, stopping on signal to support weight on hands inside of hoop.

9. All hoops on floor arranged in pairs side by side. Run down line of hoops placing one foot in each hoop.

PARTNERS

1. Each holds one side of a hoop, pulls and leans back, taking small quick steps around a circle.

2. Using only one hoop, throw it over head of partner (who also may assume a sitting position and lift legs for target). Vary distance from target.

3. One holds hoop vertical and off floor, while the other tries to jump through it.

Scooters

A scooter is a 12 × 12-inch board set on four heavy-duty casters (Figure 16-13). It may be purchased commercially or constructed by hand for about half the price. It provides for an unlimited number of developmental exercises and means of supporting and propelling the body through space. With the body in various positions on the scooter, one has to adapt and control body weight. A child may work with the scooter alone or with a partner. All factors of movement can be studied with the body supported on a moving object. Propulsion is accomplished by hands and/or feet. The body position is prone, supine, sitting, kneeling, or on the side. The body weight is fully supported or partially supported on the scooter. Changes of directions and speeds are possible. Any type of relay may be done while the body is on the scooter. The pupil

Figure 16-13 Scooter.

may manipulate all kinds of objects, and most games and many dances can be performed while on the scooter. The scooter becomes the means of locomotion and the base of support.

Balance Board

A balance board is a square or circular board (varying from 15 to 18 inches in diameter) set on a smaller base of support about 4 inches high (Figure 16-14). The narrower the base, the more difficult it is to maintain balance on the board. The child stands on the board and balances while shifting his weight back and forth from side to side. In activities on the board the child can learn the range through which he can control his body and how to use compensatory body actions to control the center of gravity. While on the balance board, the child can

1. Stand and balance
2. Change body position or shapes
3. Balance on one foot
4. Do exercises
5. Manipulate a wand
6. Manipulate a hoop
7. Bounce a ball
8. Throw and catch to self
9. Throw and catch with a partner

Figure 16-14 Balance board with interchangeable bases.

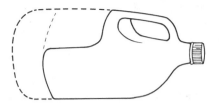

Figure 16-15 Scoop made from cut-out bleach bottle.

Scoops

Plastic scoops can be purchased commercially or constructed by cutting the bottoms from plastic bleach bottles (Figure 16-15). Scoops can be used for throwing and catching any size ball that will fit into the opening. Whiffleballs (plastic) are especially good for this. The use of scoops provides for development of eye-hand coordination and adaptations of the various throwing patterns.

Actually the ball is slung more than thrown. In order to control the ball, the scoop should be moved forward with mostly forearm control or action. The forearm extends and the wrist is snapped as the ball is rolled and thrown from the scoop. When the ball is caught in the air, it is allowed to land in the open end of the scoop. If it is rolling, the scoop can be placed so that the ball rolls into the scoop, then the wrist is snapped upward so that the ball is held in the scoop.

Many informal tasks can be designed to throw and catch the ball with the scoop by oneself, a partner, in a small group, or against the wall. Most ball games can be adapted with the scoop being used. Modifications of the game of jai alai and lacrosse, which use expensive instruments to catch and propel the ball, can be made using the plastic scoop.

Parachutes

Although parachutes surely are not small, they are not considered apparatus because for the most part children handle them rather than perform on them. The parachute can provide a large-group activity that contributes to individual development of strength, muscle endurance, coordination, and timing. One has to work with the group in order for play to be successful. A wide variety of activities for all age groups can be enjoyed using the parachute.

In the first lesson a few preliminary understandings, rules, and basic terminologies must be introduced. It is well to lay the parachute out on the floor with pupils evenly spaced about it. There are "ribs" in the parachute that each child can grasp. There are three commonly used grips in various stunts: the overhand grip (palms down), the underhand grip (palms up), and the alternating grip (one palm down and one palm up). Because a great deal of the action must be in unison, the teacher or a designated leader must give signals for starting, specific actions, and stopping. Only a few activities are presented here. Children should be encouraged to make up new stunts and uses for the parachutes. They will need little encouragement, because people of all ages seem to be fascinated by parachute play.

- *The Umbrella*

The parachute is held waist-high with the overhand grip. The center or hole of the parachute is on the floor. On the count of 1, knees are flexed to a squat position, on 2 everyone slowly raises hands and arms, count is continued to 3, 4 as the parachute goes overhead and starts to billow out. Everyone is

Figure 16-16 Parachute play.

stretched out as the parachute goes high into the air. It will stay there a short time and slowly settle back to the floor. While the parachute is ballooning, various tasks can be done under it.

1. *Numbers Exchange:* Each pupil has a number. Leader calls two numbers, pupils having those numbers run under the parachute and exchange places.
2. *Snatch the Bacon:* Pin is in the middle. Two numbers are called—those having them run in and try to snatch a club and try to take it back to their place before the others catch them. One point is given for getting the club back, if not caught; 2 points are given the catcher.
3. Class is divided into two, three, or four groups. A task is announced, then a number is called; those holding that number let go of chute and do the task, return to place, and grasp the chute again. Such tasks as the following could be used:
   a. Bounce the ball 10 times.
   b. Skip around the inside circle.
   c. Do 5 jumping jacks.
   d. Crawl over to the other side.
   e. Roll over several times.

- **Umbrella Run**

Holding onto the parachute in the umbrella position with one hand, everyone run around the room counterclockwise. On signal, change hands and run in the other direction.

- **Making Waves**

Using any grip, on signal everyone shakes the parachute up and down. Various sizes of waves can be made by the range of movement of the arms.

- **Circus Tent**

Raise the parachute into the umbrella position. As it reaches its peak, everyone steps under the rim and lowers it to the floor. Then everyone grasps the parachute from the inside and goes to a kneeling position. Everyone will be inside the tent. It can descend upon them or they can scramble out before they are completely covered.

- *Popcorn*

Place beanbags or a number of lightweight balls on the chute. Pupils shake the parachute to make the balls bounce around like popping corn.

- *Team Ball*

Use four balls of different colors. Points are given for knocking balls off the parachute by certain segments of the chute. Similarly, points may be given to the team that gets ball to go down the center hole of the chute.

- *Mushroom*

Parachute is lifted to the umbrella position and then everyone quickly walks in toward the center a few steps, keeping arms in a raised position overhead. The parachute will continue to rise in a mushroom position. When the parachute reaches its peak of inflation, everyone steps out to his original position.

EXERCISES

- *Toe Touching*

Holding the parachute with an overhand grip at waist-level, slowly lower the rim of the parachute to the floor. Keep knees stiff while lowering and then return to the starting position. Repeat several times.

Sitting with legs under the parachute, hold it tight and draw it up under the chin. Bend forward and touch the grip to the toes. Return to original position. Repeat several times.

- *Sit-Ups*

Sitting with legs under the parachute, grasp the rim with an overhand grip and slowly lie back. Contract abdominal muscles and pull on the rim. Return to original position. Repeat several times. Alternate people who go up, then down.

- *Horse Pull*

With backs to parachute, using an overhand grip and hands far apart, lean forward and pull for a count of six. Relax. Repeat.

- *V Sits*

Lie on the back. Grasping the parachute tight, raise the lower and upper body at the same time to form a V position. Keep knees straight.

DANCES A number of circle dances can be done with the parachute. Those which are easily adapted are "Oh Susanna," "Mayim," "Teton Mountain Stomp," "Seven Jumps," and "Mexican Hat Dance."

Routines to music should be designed by the pupils. Kimbo Educational Records (P.O. Box 246, Deal, N.J. 07723) has an excellent record, *Rhythmic Parachute Play* by Seker and Jones. A teacher's manual accompanies the record.

Lummi Sticks

Lummi sticks are 1-inch dowels or rolled newspapers 6 to 10 inches long. They may be purchased along with records and suggestions for routines using the sticks from Educational Activities, Inc. (P.O. Box 392, Freeport, N.Y. 11520). Lummi sticks provide an opportunity for development of eye-hand coordination and rhythmic elements. Two sticks are manipulated by the pupils or between partners, who hit them against the floor, against each other, or toss and flip them into the air in a rhythmic pattern (Figure 16-17). Accompaniment may or may not be used.

For beginners, a set of twenty-four counts may be used as a total pattern and then repeated.

With two pupils sitting and facing one another:

1. *Stick Hit*
   a. Hit ends of stick down on floor (for count of 1, 2, 3).
   b. Hit own sticks together (count of 1, 2, 3).
   c. Hit partner's right stick (count of 1, 2, 3).
   d. Hit partner's left stick (count of 1, 2, 3).

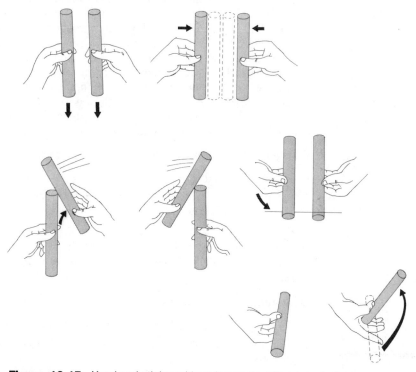

Figure 16-17 Hand and stick positions for manipulating lummi sticks.

Repeat sequence.

2. *Cross-toss*

   a. Hit stick on floor (count of 1, 2, 3).

   b. Hit partner's sticks (count of 1, 2, 3).

   c. Toss exchange right stick with partner (count of 1, 2, 3).

   d. Toss exchange left stick with partner (count of 1, 2, 3).

Repeat sequence.

3. *Stick flip*

   a. Hit stick on floor (count of 1).

   b. Flip sticks once over, catch (count of 1).

   c. Hit sticks on floor (count of 1).

   d. Flip one stick (count of 1).

   e. Flip other stick (count of 1).

   f. Toss both sticks to partner (count of 1).

Repeat 4 times.

4. Let pupils make up their own patterns.

Chinese Jumpropes

Chinese ropes are elastic and can be various lengths (6 to 8 feet) or circular. Circular ropes can be made by tying two individual ropes together. They may be purchased or made from dressmaker's elastic, $\frac{1}{4}$-inch elastic cord, or by looping a number of rubber bands together. The ropes may be used somewhat like regular ropes; to be jumped over, through, and around. They may be used as interesting props for study of extension and flexion of body parts or making various body shapes. The rope may be held or hooked over one body part and stretched into various lengths and shapes. Two people may work together with the rope stretched between them and over and under their various body parts. Force and strength may be studied in the same manner.

Activities with two ropes around the ankles of two pupils standing opposite each other about 6 feet apart are described in Figure 16-18.

With jumper standing outside ropes, side to ropes:

1. Jump in and out of ropes.

2. Jump over the far rope, hooking the one foot over the near rope and carrying it over the far rope. Touch toe and return to outside starting position, releasing the rope.

3. Do 1 and 2, making a half-turn in the air.

4. Jump rope holders move rope up to a higher position on legs and jumper repeat 1, 2, 3.

With jumper straddling ropes:

1. Jump, cross legs, and land with opposite foot outside ropes (legs crossed).

2. Shift feet by uncrossing legs with one rope behind one ankle and in front of the other.

3. Jump and let ropes fall off ankle, landing in original straddle position.

Figure 16-18 Holder's position for Chinese rope activities.

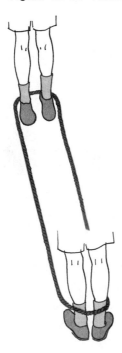

With jumper facing ropes, feet outside:

1. Jump over the far rope catching the near rope over toes; jump, letting ropes slip off, landing on the outside of the far ropes.
2. Repeat, facing the opposite direction.
3. Work with a partner, two doing the same stunts.
4. Pupils make up their own patterns.
5. Do patterns to music.

Working with Chinese ropes in this manner is much like working with bamboo poles in the dance "Tinikling." Although "Tinikling" is a Philippine folk dance, pupils may make up routines with or without accompaniment while using the poles to beat the rhythm while pupils jump in and out and over the poles.

Beanbags

Beanbags may be used much like small balls with young children. They can be grasped easily with the fingers and will not bounce or roll far away if missed or thrown at a target. Their use with older children is most valuable when working space is small.

1. Throw beanbag at various targets, up in the air, for distance.
2. Place beanbag on head and hop, run, or jump trying to keep it in place.
   a. Vary movements.
   b. Vary position of beanbag from head to shoulder, knee, foot, etc.

3. Place beanbag on foot, kick it up, and catch it with hands.
   a. Try to catch it on head.
   b. Catch it on opposite foot.
4. Pass beanbag back and forth from one hand to another.
   a. Clap between passes.
   b. Turn between passes.

Suggested Progression for an Elementary School Gymnastics Program

LEVELS I AND II FLOOR WORK

A. Exploration of basic movement skills, emphasis on development of:
   1. Elements of strength, flexibility, agility, and balance.
   2. Movements of curling, twisting, turning, rolling, and extension.
   3. Fundamentals of jumping, landing, transferring weight, supporting weight on various parts of the body, and flight.
B. Stunts: Imitative animal walks, curls, top, rocker, seal walk, lame dog, heel slap, mule kick, human ball, jumping jack, bouncing ball, sawing wood.
C. Tumbling: Forward roll, rocking chair, eggroll, frog stand.
D. Body awareness activities.
E. Exploration of basic movement skills in relationship to small equipment.
   1. Hoops, beanbags, wands, balance boards, scooters, Chinese ropes.
   2. Jumping ropes.
      a. Short ropes: Turning, big jumps, little jumps, forward, backward, jump on both feet, alternate feet.
      b. Long ropes: Turning, sequence of run in back door and in front door, jump a number of times and run out, jump on alternate feet, combine jumping and turning.
   3. Balls.
      a. Throwing with large balls and small balls. Using overhand pattern with small balls, rolling at target, throwing underhand vertically and horizontally for distance.
      b. Catching thrown ball from self, from wall, and from partner.
      c. Bouncing to self with control, to wall, and to a partner at various levels and in various combinations.
      d. Striking with flat of hand and fist against wall, kicking to wall and to partner for distance and control.

APPARATUS

A. Exploration and free use of all pieces of apparatus available.
B. Freestyle mounting and dismounting.
C. Problems and tasks involved in going over, under, through, along, above, across (and various combinations of these) all pieces of apparatus.

Movement Experiences

508

D. Simple routines.

E. Good understanding and use of correct grip on bars; understanding and use of landing techniques from high places.

LEVEL III FLOOR WORK

A. Continued exploration of basic skills.

1. Emphasis on development of shoulder girdle strength, flexibility, and balance.

2. Refinement of movements of curling, twisting, turning, rolling, extension.

3. Routines involving movements in continuity and variations in jumping, landing, transferring weight, supporting weight on various parts of the body, and flight.

B. Exercises and stunts.

1. General: Sit-ups, modified push-ups, bobbing, running in place, jump and touch toes, jump and tuck, leg lifts, half-squats, lunge, rocker, heel click, thread the needle, one-foot balance, corkscrews, wring the dishrag, Chinese get up, leapfrog.

2. Combatives: Bulldozer, back to back, toe boxing, hand push, bottoms up.

C. Tumbling: Tripod, headstand, handstand, forward roll, continuous roll, backward roll, three-person mount, simple pyramids.

D. Exploration of basic movement skills and challenge tasks in relationship to small equipment.

1. Hoops, beanbags, wands, balance boards, scooters, parachutes, lummi sticks.

2. Jumping ropes.

   a. Short ropes: Turn and jump with elbows crossed; rock; feet together; feet apart; feet crossed; skip in place, travel and skip; swing rope holding ends in one hand and make patterns; jump with a partner; create original patterns.

   b. Long ropes: partners jump, bounce ball and jump, pepper, jump the shot, helicopter, high water.

3. Balls (using tennis balls, softballs, soccerballs, volleyballs, basketballs, footballs, and playground balls of all diameters).

   a. Throwing: For distance, for accuracy, at a moving target.

   b. Catching: Ball thrown by partner from various distances and at various heights; grounders.

   c. Bouncing: Continuous dribble with either hand.

   d. Striking: Kick for accuracy, kick for distance, dribble for control, strike a volleyball with two-hand overhand pattern, serve a volleyball or 8-inch playground ball, bat a softball off a tee, bat a tennis ball against wall with paddle.

APPARATUS

A. Problems and tasks involved in going over, under, through, along, above, across (and various combinations of these) all pieces of apparatus.

B. Routines.

C. Specific stunts.

    1. Balance beam (6-inch, 24-inch): Various locomotor patterns across beam, turns, balance stands, front rest.

    2. Climbing rope: Bent-arm-hang, inverted hang (layout), sitting hang, swing and drop, climbing.

    3. Hanging bars.

        a. Bar at maximum reach: knee-hang, passive hang, active hang, flexed-arm-hang.

        b. Bar at low level: front rest, front rest somersault, skin the cat.

    4. Vaulting box: Knee mount, dismounts, jump with quarter-turn, straddle jump, tuck jump, fence vault.

LEVEL IV FLOOR WORK

A. Free exercises.

    1. Various combinations of basic movement skills.

    2. Use of stunts, rolls, and stands in combinations for creative free exercise routines.

B. Exercises and stunts:

    1. General: Straddle chins, leg lifts, sit-ups, lunge forward, backward, shoulder twist, arm circles, trunk twist, pick-up, grasshopper, coffee grinder, crabwalk, leapfrog, jump over foot, upspring, knee scale, front scale, jump and jackknife, jump and straddle, jump and turn, arabesque, routines.

    2. Combatives: Indian leg wrestle, rope pull, Indian club fight, pull-down.

C. Tumbling: Handstand, shoulder balance, standing balance on thighs, horizontal stand, Eskimo roll, cartwheel, routines.

D. Small equipment: Skills related to sports and games units; parachutes.

E. Apparatus: (a) more advanced educational gymnastic tasks and problems; (b) development and performance of routines; (c) specific stunts.

    1. Horizontal bar: Chinning, hang and raise hips, double knee-hang, single knee-hang, pullover, routines.

    2. Parallel bars:

        a. Under bars: Inverted hang (tuck, pike, layout), skin the cat, bird's nest.

        b. Between bars: Straight-arm support, support swing, handwalk, inside cross riding seat, outside cross riding seat, riding seat to seat quarter-turn dismount, routines.

    3. Climbing ropes: Climb using legs, climb using hands only, swing and drop over an obstacle, travel between ropes.

    4. Vaulting box: Knee mount, courage dismount, squat vault, flank vault.

    5. Balance beam:

        a. Mounts: Front rest, front rest to straddle seat, side seat.

        b. Balances: Knee scale, front scale, routines.

        c. Dismounts: Jump with quarter-turn, jump with half-turn, straddle jump.

A. Free exercise: Various combinations of basic movement skills, stunts, balances into free exercise routines.

B. Exercises and stunts:

1. General: Push-ups, sit-ups, trunk twister, grasshopper, arm circles, V sit, front scale, side scale, single leg circle, front break-fall, forward drop.

2. Combatives: Cock fight, elbow wrestle, rope pull.

C. Tumbling: Forearm balance, knee-shoulder balance, angel balance, sitting balance, pyramids, backward roll with extension, roundoff, routines.

D. Small equipment: Skills related to specific uses in sports and games units.

E. Apparatus: (a) more advanced educational gymnastic tasks for those who choose; (b) performance and design of routines; (c) specific stunts.

1. Horizontal bar: Chinning, one-knee mount, single knee-circle.

2. Vaulting box: Flank vault, rear vault, straddle vault.

3. Parallel bars: Back foot leaning rest, front foot leaning rest, straddle travel, rear vault dismount, front vault dismount, routines.

4. Balance beam:

   a. Mounts: Straddle seat, side mount, side seat, one knee (at end of beam).

   b. Balances: V sit, side scale, forward roll, shoulder stand, routines.

5. Climbing ropes: Climb, swing over an obstacle.

SUGGESTED REFERENCES FOR FURTHER STUDY

BELLARDINI, H. E., "A Sampling of Activities for the Cargo Net," *Journal of Health, Physical Education and Recreation,* 41 (January 1970), 32.

BILBROUGH, A., and P. JONES, *Physical Education in the Primary School.* London: University of London Press, 1963.

DIEM, LEISELOTT, *Who Can.* Washington, D.C.: Alliance for Health, Physical Education and Recreation, 1977.

DREHMAN, VERA, and ALENE HOLDAHL, *Head Over Heels—Gymnastics for Children.* New York: Harper & Row, 1967.

JACOBSEN, STAN, "Ideas—Pamphlets—Parachutes," *Journal of Physical Education and Recreation,* 46 (January 1975), 57–58.

LOGSDON, BETTE J. et al., *Physical Education for Children: A Focus on the Teaching Process,* Chap. 8. Philadelphia: Lea & Febiger, 1977.

LOKEN, NEWTON, and ROBERT J. WILLOUGHBY, *Gymnastics—The Complete Book of Gymnastics.* Englewood Cliffs, N.J.: Prentice-Hall, Inc., 1977.

O'QUINN, GARLAND, *Developmental Gymnastics.* Austin, Tex.: Texas Press, 1978.

PROVAZNIK, MARIE, and NORMA G. ZABKA, *Gymnastic Activities with Hand Apparatus for Boys and Girls.* Minneapolis: Burgess Publishers, 1965.

QUACKENBUSH, ERNEST L., "Maps and Scooters," *Journal of Physical Education and Recreation,* 47 (January 1976), 47.

WETTSTONE, EUGENE, ed., *Gymnastics Safety Manual.* The Official Manual of the United States Gymnastics Safety Association. University Park, Pa.: The Pennsylvania State University Press, 1977.

Part V
Programs for Special Needs and Interests

Chapters in this part relate to meeting the special needs and interests of children that are not necessarily met in the regular instructional class. Chapter 17 emphasizes the needs of our very special population of handicapped children and those with learning disabilities that can be associated with motor needs.

For a number of years, before the enactment of Public Law 94-142, the prevalent practice had been to isolate those with handicaps in special settings for instruction. With a greater recognition of the values of mainstreaming and the requirements of the law, teachers must learn to recognize the least restrictive environment for each handicapped child to learn in all areas. Chapter 17 helps interpret the law and gives suggestions for adopting and modifying activities, so that in fact, handicapped children are mainstreamed with other children.

The area of perceptual-motor development is put into the perspective of the regular pupil and those who have learning disabilities thought to be associated with some problem with development in this area.

Since our objectives are to help children recognize their own movement interests and to pursue them in their own way and at their own level, and develop active leisure activities, we must provide a choice of activity opportunities beyond the instructional period. Chapter 18 discusses the extraclass options usually available in the elementary school. Types of tournaments which may be used in various settings and for various purposes are presented, with a discussion of how to construct the tournaments.

17 / THE EXCEPTIONAL CHILD

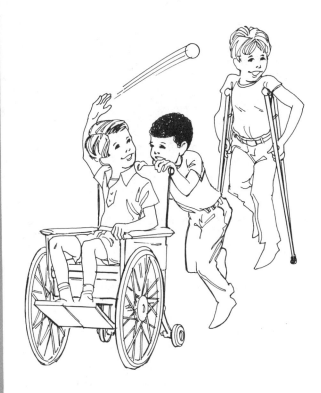

- The concept of mainstreaming
- Individualized education programs (IEP)
- Modifying activities and learning environments
- The child with learning disabilities

Current estimates are that approximately one of ten children deviates from the average in some aspect of physical, mental, social, and emotional development and behavior. Generally, a child deviates or is an exception to the average in only one of these aspects and has the normal needs, desires, and abilities in the others. Consequently, that child must engage in the same type of comprehensive school program as the peer group. Naturally, some of the learning experiences must be adapted to the individual child's limitations. Frequently, if the child does not have the opportunity to participate in the typical activities of his/her peer group, the problems and limitations grow and he or she becomes handicapped in more than one area.

For a number of years educators planned educational programs for exceptional children with varying handicaps primarily in separate and special programs. There has been no conclusive evidence that children in special classes or settings achieve more or better than do children with like handicaps who have been in regular classes.

Today the concept of *mainstreaming* pervades the planning and conduct of the educational program for exceptional children. Mainstreaming is the inclusion of children with handicaps in the instructional classes and activities with all other children in the school, as much as is possible. Mainstreaming is a commitment to concern for the individual as he or she interacts with peers and will interact in adult life with all types of people. Obviously the basis of the mainstreaming concept is a true commitment to a humanistic philosophy as well as to an individualized or personalized approach in teaching. Mainstreaming benefits both the handicapped and the normal child as they both learn to recognize, accept, and become more compassionate about individual differences as well as to see and value human commonalities.

Although the impetus for mainstreaming arose from a humanistic concern, state and federal legislation has supported the adoption of the concept by all schools. The Federal Education for All Handicapped Children Act of 1975—PL94-142—specifies that among other requirements there be

1. Free and appropriate public education which emphasizes special education and related services for all handicapped children within the least restrictive environment.
2. An annual development of an individualized program for each handicapped child after evaluation and assessment of the child's needs.
3. A statement explaining the extent to which the child is able to participate in the regular classroom.

Physical education is the only *curriculum* area included in the defined elements of special education. Recreation is identified as one of the specified related services. Provision for instruction in physical education is delineated as special physical education, adapted physical education, movement education, and motor development. It is further defined as development of (1) physical and motor fitness, (2) fundamental motor skills and patterns, and (3) skills in aquatics, dance, and individual and group games and sports (including intramural and lifetime sports). Each handicapped child must be afforded the opportunity to participate in the regular physical education program available to nonhandicapped children unless the child is enrolled full-time in a separate facility or needs specially designed physical education as prescribed in his/her individualized education program.

Implementing Mainstreaming

These particular aspects of the act have far-reaching implications for the classroom teacher and the physical education teacher. The term "least restrictive" tells us that there may be several patterns of organization wherein the handicapped pupils may receive instruction in both the classroom and the gymnasium. Handicapped children may be in the regular class all the time with modifications or adaptations of activities in respect to the particular handicap; they may receive supplementary instruction from a specialist in addition to being in the regular class all the time; they may be in the regular class for only those activities in which they can participate readily and be in a special class the rest of the time; they may attend a special class all the time; they may be in a special school; they may be in a special day school; or they may be in a residential or hospital school. In any event, physical education comparable to that in regular class must be available to the child. The goal is to help the child move toward the regular class setting and be mainstreamed with peers.

It is very likely then that in every physical education class there will be children for whom activities will have to be modified, adapted, and designed to meet varying impairments. This might range from children who have a temporary impairment because of illness or accident to those who have chronic heart conditions, impaired hearing, impaired vision, impaired speech, epilepsy, an allergy, low or exceptionally high mental ability, neurological impairment, or emotional or social maladjustment. The capability of meeting the needs in the regular class, not necessarily the severity of the handicap, will determine whether or not the regular class is the least restrictive environment and how often and how close to the mainstream a pupil can be.

Obviously teachers are going to have to know as much as they can about the individual for whom they are making adjustments as well as about the specific condition which causes the exceptionality. For many teachers this means preservice educational experiences with respect to special populations, and/or in-service experiences. The law requires that a comprehensive system of personnel development be developed in each state. Many states had already legislated similar laws or mandates and have instituted in-service plans.

It also means that physical education teachers who have received specialized education in this area must be available as resource and support teachers. Specialists will be vital in implementing the aspects of the law which state that the program must be individualized; each pupil must be assessed and evaluated annually; goals and short-term objectives and a prescription of learning experiences are needed; and there must be a means of evaluation to determine if the goals and objectives are to be met. Actually, the law is providing for handicapped children what should be done for every student in respect to personalizing education.

Individualized Education Programs (IEP)

An individualized education program must be written, evaluated, and revised annually for each handicapped child receiving special education and related services that are supported by public education funds. The IEP must be written in meetings attended by a representative of the local educational agency who is qualified to provide or supervise the provision of specially designed instruction to meet the unique needs of handicapped children; the teacher or teachers (special or regular or both) who have a direct responsibility for implementing the child's IEP; the parents or guardian of the child and, wherever

Figure 17-1 Example of Individual Education Plan **IEP** (Courtesy of City School District, Rochester, New York).

CITY SCHOOL DISTRICT
ROCHESTER, NEW YORK
INDIVIDUAL EDUCATION PLAN
(IEP)

Division of Instruction
Student Educational Services
Department of Special Education

Student's Name _____

Student's ID # _____

School _____ School Year _____ Present Program _____

Birthdate _____ Is interpreter needed for IEP conference? _____

Parent contacts regarding IEP conference arrangement: Date   Date of IEP conference _____

                                                                    Signatures of persons present:

Initial Letter _____   _____

Phone Call _____   _____

Follow up Letter _____   _____

Certified Letter _____   _____

Other _____   _____

Extent to which child is able to participate in regular class:

Present   Long Term

_____   _____

_____   _____

_____   _____

Long Term Goals:

_____

_____

Figure 17-2 Example of Individualized Education Plan (Courtesy of City School District, Rochester, New York).

INDIVIDUALIZED EDUCATION PLAN

Student's name _____ School _____ Teacher Conducting Conference _____

SUBJECT/ SKILL/ SUPPORTIVE SERVICE	CURRENT INSTRUCTIONAL LEVEL	SHORT TERM INSTRUCTIONAL GOALS	PERSON WRITING OBJECTIVES	MATERIALS AND/OR STRATEGIES	WHEN INITIATED	ESTIMATED DURATION	EVALUATION

1. Statement of present level of educational performance

1. Present level of development and performance in
   a) Physical and motor fitness
   b) Basic movement patterns and skills
   c) Sport, dance, game, and aquatic skills
   Should be an analysis and synthesis of results of assessment and reassessment in development and performance in above areas, using standardized tests, informal measures such as checklist, observations, questionnaire inventory, rating scale, conferences with pupil. Should include social behaviors, intellectual, perceptual-motor, physical attributes, and performance in basic skills. Should include analysis of results obtained by other specialists. Sherrill's Summary Diagnostic Form is recommended for use as a basis of determining present level[1]

2. Statement of annual goals

2. Based on assessment results and evaluation in #1. Should relate to areas in which child's performance is affected by handicap either physically or by virtue of special learning environmental conditions. Should be similar to Program Objectives on page 38.

3. Statement of short-term goals

3. A breakdown of goals stated in #2, which would enable one to reach annual goals over a period of time. Usually set for quarterly time period and reviewed frequently. Similar to Instructional Objectives on page 104.

4. Statement of specific educational and related services to be provided;

4. What specifically designed physical education experiences, settings, support services, special equipment are necessary—e.g., tutoring in addition to class instruction, an aide to help child dress for swimming, special flotation devices, special stretching and flexibility exercises needed in addition to class work.

   extent to which child will be in regular class

   To be mainstreamed fully. To have special instruction in addition to regular classwork upon introduction to a new activity. To be in regular class for certain activities only, in special class for others.

5. Projected dates for initiation of services and anticipated duration of them

5. Dates projected for start of special instruction or experiences; completion of annual and short-term goals. Set to help give direction and guidance. Teachers are not bound to dates or are accountable for completion of precise goals.

6. Appropriate criteria and evaluation procedures for determining whether objectives were met

6. Post-evaluation of achievement and performance based on objectives or same or similar measurements for original status statement. Objective tests, standardized procedures, norm- and/or criterion-referenced assessment. Subjective or informal techniques; checklists, observations, attitude survey, rating scales, self-evaluation; anecdotal records; pictures; diaries. Some assessment could be done during each class period or some done periodically, quarterly. Basis for revision of periodic planning meeting for revision of short-term goals and annual goals.

[1] Claudine Sherrill, *Adapted Physical Education and Recreation—A Multidisciplinary Approach* (Dubuque, Ia.: Wm. C. Brown, 1976), p. 64.

appropriate, the child; as well as other individuals, at the discretion of the parent or agency.

The law does not specifically state that physical education teachers must be involved in the planning conference; however, they must be alert to children having special needs in physical education and make themselves available for meetings or in some way see that specialized input is made into the IEP. Conversely, they must also see that a child handicapped in other learning aspects but not in physical education must not be assigned to a special setting but put into the regular physical education class. Every handicapped child does not need, want, or require a special physical education program.

The IEP must include certain information; however, the law does not specify a particular form or pattern in which the information must be gathered or presented. Many state and local agencies have developed their own forms and processes. Figures 17-1 and 17-2 show forms used in Rochester, New York. Presented here is a list of the categories of information as stated in very general terms in PL94-142, along with some pertinent remarks relative to the IEP for physical education.

Modifying Activities and Learning Environments

It is not within the realm of this book to discuss all the handicaps and the movement problems associated with them or the special needs of each population. Some modifications can be made in the majority of the regular class activities despite a child's handicap, especially in the primary and intermediate grades, in which the emphasis is on developmental activities and individualization. However, when this cannot be done logically and safely, both the teacher and the pupil must accept this. Where the adaptation or modification must be so great or demand a constant one-to-one teacher pupil ratio, resulting in interference with the normal progress of the majority of the children in the class, then it would not be logical. However, with more supportive help becoming available, the pupil may be mainstreamed into the regular class and have special help from an aide, or a specialist within the class when necessary. It is not only the physical aspect on which mainstreaming is focused but also the interaction with other children. Where the individualized program isolates children within the class, the real concept of mainstreaming is not being achieved either. There must be a blend.

Although the major objectives and activities are basically the same for all children in physical education, there are a few objectives that need to be emphasized for the exceptional child. The child must develop a positive and realistic attitude toward his or her capabilities, limitations, and potentialities in physical activities. Children must learn how to be self-directive in regulating the extent of their participation in physical activities. They must acquire knowledge and skill in a variety of games and activities in which they can participate alone and with other children in their leisure time.[2]

[2] Edna Engberg, *Physical Education Activities for the Physically Handicapped* (Springfield, Ill.: Office of the Superintendent of Public Instruction, 1963).

All the other children in the class must understand a child's handicap to a certain extent. If they do, they will be eager to help modify rules and skills and be much more accepting of any limitations. Everyone must know the special rules and limitations set for the child in the game. Handicapped children will learn that if they try hard and do their best within the limits of their capabilities, other children will accept and support them physically and socially. If teachers are personalizing or individualizing as a regular procedure, there will actually be many children performing at different levels and there will be modifications in games to meet individual needs for pupils other than those identified as handicapped youngsters in the usual sense of the term.

The teacher must modify not only the activities and equipment but also his or her methods, techniques, and procedures to meet special needs. It is essential for the regular and special teacher of physical education to have a knowledge of all aspects and techniques of individualizing and personalizing (modifying content, designing objectives, offering appropriate activity choices, matching teaching methods or styles with learning styles, organizing the learning environment and evaluation alternatives).

Modifications and adaptations are offered here for use in both a mainstreaming situation and in work with children in a special situation for a number of common handicapping conditions and/or common program activities.

1. When locomotion is a problem, children can do specific game skills which do not require mobility. For example, they can bat in softball, having someone else run for them. In volleyball, they can rotate into the game to serve. Support in the standing position may be necessary, or the child may sit. If mobility is possible but greatly inhibited, the style of locomotion may be changed and/or distances altered. For example, if a youngster cannot walk but can crawl, anyone who is chasing him may be required to crawl also. In a relay race it may be just as great a challenge for the handicapped child to go half the distance as it is for the others to go all the way, so that the race would be equal if the distance were modified for the handicapped child. Space requirements may be modified. Scooters may be used to get around on, as well as wheelchairs if one uses them regularly. (Special rules for use of wheelchairs must be made!) Children can be involved in planning special rules for specific games. When teaching team games, evaluate position responsibilities and have pupils with mobility problems play those which require the least moving around. Foam-rubber balls or cube-shaped objects are easier for a slow-moving child to control. These can be made out of sponges or chunks of foam.

2. When vision is a problem, targets must be larger, balls thrown more slowly, names called when it is the child's turn to catch, and suggestions given for adjusting direction for better accuracy. Some children may be able to throw but not catch, and vice versa. In either case, another child may do one of the tasks for the handicapped child. Balls are available that have battery-powered "beepers" inside so that visually impaired pupils can track and have some success in catching and striking activities. These are rather expensive. One can make a hole in a rubber or vinyl ball and insert small bells inside, and then repair it with tire patch to achieve similar results. Sound devices can be attached to targets also. Bells on targets

attached to a rope pulled by someone standing out of target range will also help children locate throwing, hitting, or archery targets. Guidelines or rails may be used to identify spaces, lanes, etc. Use bright-colored balls, lines, goals, targets, etc. for partially sighted youngsters. A buddy system of a sighted child and a visually impaired child should be planned.

3. When hearing is a problem, a partner might be assigned to give manual signs to the child with impaired hearing and to reinforce directions by a demonstration. Hand signals should replace or/and accompany verbal or whistle signals for starting, stopping, and officiating. Be sure hearing-impaired children can see the person giving verbal directions so that they can read lips. Don't expect them to read lips from across the floor or down the field. The teacher should learn some signs for common daily instructions used in the physical education class. (See Eichstaedt and Seiler's[3] article for a list of these.) If hearing aids are worn, they should be worn in activities except those which involve contact. When dance or rhythmics are involved, place the record player on the floor so children may pick up the vibration of the beat from the floor. Dancing in bare feet or socks will enhance this. Counting beats aloud often helps children with structured dances. Again, a buddy system should be planned, especially for pool activities.

4. When mentally retarded children are in a class, it must be remembered that their fitness level and skill level will probably be below that of the other children. With much guidance and time they often can perform simple motor tasks as well as normal children. Because their greatest deviation is in the mental realm, they do not think as fast or make decisions as quickly as normal children. Therefore, they often get confused in games that require application of a large number of rules or quick changes in direction of play, for example. Careful attention should be given to placing them in positions that do not demand too many decisions until they are comfortable in and confident of the conduct of the game. Complex skills must be broken down and sequenced very carefully for these children. When teaching new skills, a direct approach with many demonstrations and visual aids is usually more appropriate than an indirect approach. Much repetition is necessary. Retarded children often prefer more individual or couple activities than group activities, but must be integrated and encouraged to participate in the group activities. However, they should not be forced into them until they have some confidence with skills and knowledge of their responsibilities. Here again, some type of buddy system can be used.

These are suggestions for groups of children who have handicaps that are found in many classes and for whom activities may be rather easily modified or adapted in a mainstreaming situation. Of course each child will vary in his or her needs and in the extent of modification necessary. For children with other handicaps, the teacher will have to know their limitations and prescriptions for individualized programs. Where the limitation of exercise and excitement is paramount (cardiac, respiratory, asthma, emotionally disturbed, etc.),

[3] Carl B. Eichstaedt and Peter J. Seiler, "Signing—Communicating with Hearing-Impaired Individuals in Physical Education," *Journal of Physical Education and Recreation,* 29, no. 5 (May 1978), 19–21.

the teacher will have to use common sense along with special techniques to plan for integration. Remember, these suggestions are for adapting activities, techniques, equipment, and methods primarily within the regular class. They are not remedial in nature. Remedial activities must be conducted by a qualified specialist, under orders of the physician.

Ingenuity is most often the key to successful adaptation of physical education activities. You will find that in working on modifications, both you and the pupils will benefit greatly from analyzing activities in order to modify them. Anxiety and enthusiasm to do what normal children are doing may foster overindulgence on the part of some youngsters and create a problem rather than a solution. For more information about adapting activities, the reader is referred to the books listed at the end of the chapter.

The Child with Learning Disabilities

In the past few years, much concern and study have been devoted to the child who is not mentally retarded yet has difficulty learning. It is estimated that 10 to 20 percent of children in school have learning difficulties due to a disorder in one or more of the basic psychological processes involved in understanding or in using written or spoken language, and may have difficulties in listening, writing, reading, spelling, talking, arithmetic. They may have conditions variously described as brain injury, minimal brain dysfunction, dyslexia, developmental asphasia, perceptual handicaps, etc.

Perceptual-Motor Problems

A number of theories have promoted the relationship of poor perceptual-motor or sensorimotor skills to some learning difficulties. Unfortunately, not all the theories have been adequately scientifically tested. There is strong evidence, however, that links the importance of specific perceptual-motor experiences to the quality of one's intellectual performance.

Despite the variety of conflicting theories of origin and causes of perceptual-motor problems and proposals of various programs to facilitate development or remedy deficiencies, there is agreement that the acquisition of perceptual-motor skills is essential to any young child's understanding of and adjustment to the world about him—people, things, ideas, and himself; also that problems are manifested in common motor behaviors; that a rich sensory environment is essential; and that a child can be helped through similar types of motor experiences. Because the critical stages of sensorimotor adaptation are from ages 3 through 5, ideally there should be preventive or facilitating programs in the preschool, kindergarten, or early primary years. These programs should provide many opportunities for experiences to enhance development of body image, spatial and directional awareness, balance, fundamental body movements, symmetry in body actions, hand-eye and foot-eye coordination, form perception, and rhythm. Ironically, these form the framework of any physical education program and embody the goals of movement education for all children. No doubt in time we will find the perceptual-motor program in schools referred to as preschool facilitation programs or remedial programs for those who have severe perceptual-motor deficiencies. These will be in addition to the regular physical education program.

A multidisciplinary approach to the study and program aspects of present perceptual-motor activities is currently being employed in many schools with a team approach to diagnosis, prescription, and remedial programs for those who need them. However, it is still common practice in many schools for the physical education teacher and/or the classroom teacher to be responsible for both identification of problems and the subsequent necessary help. To adequately diagnose and treat children with perceptual-motor problems, one needs special training. The information applying to this subject is far beyond the scope of this book; but in order to help teachers who do not have specialists available in this area or who have not had special training themselves, a brief description of the problems and screening activities to help them detect suspected problems will be presented here.

When children come to school they are expected to have reached a certain level of readiness in skills in four areas of behavior: motor, symbolic, social, and numerical. All of these presuppose that a child has mastered certain major and minor muscle movements and combinations of such movements that enable him or her to coordinate eye-hand movements, have a sense of laterality and directionality, perceive forms correctly, and make temporal-spatial translations. These expectations give an indication of areas of motor activities in which a child will exhibit poor control and performance if he/she has not reached the readiness level to learn academic skills and understandings typical of the age group.

If slow learners have difficulty in solving movement problems that require balance, hand-eye coordination, rhythm, awareness of space in regard to their own bodies, directionality, laterality, and gross motor coordination, the teacher will be aware that retardation in motor development might underlie the lack of success in academic work. Of course, children's motor performance must be compared with that typical of their age group. Included here are a few suggestions of specific behaviors that indicate poor perceptual-motor skills. The teacher may use them as a screening device. If deficiencies are found that need to be investigated further, he or she should report the findings to the proper school authorities so that a complete diagnosis may be made and plans for improvement be undertaken.

A few words or terms must be defined to help the reader understand the discussion better. *Laterality* is an awareness of right and left within one's own body and the ability to control the two sides of the body simultaneously or separately. *Directionality* is an awareness of right, left, up, down, front, and back in space. This external awareness of direction develops from the internal sense described as laterality. The *midline* of the body refers to the vertical center of the body. *Spatial orientation* or *awareness* is the concept of the relationship between the body and the body parts with objects in space. *Posture control* is the ability to maintain balance in a static position or in a moving position. *Posture flexibility* is the ability to regain posture control after changing positions. *Body image* is the knowledge of distinguishing one body part from another and control of body parts. *Figure-ground constancy* is the ability to pick out single objects or figures from a busy or complex background. *Tracking* is the ability to monitor or follow a moving object and keep it in the center of vision. *Bilateral integration* is the ability to use both sides of the body at the same time smoothly. *Form perception* is the ability to perceive the pattern of elements of parts which constitute a whole, wherein the elements are in specific relationships to one another.

Screening
Activities
to Study
Perceptual-
Motor
Development

PROBLEMS IN BALANCE

Activities   Have children walk on a line painted on the floor; walk forward, backward, and sideward on a low balance beam; stand on one foot for 10 seconds; stand on a rocker board.

Problem Behavior   Inability to maintain balance at all. Does not use arms to catch balance. Consistent use of only one arm or one side to regulate body weight or consistent use of arms in symmetrical fashion. Need to run or walk very fast to maintain balance. Hesitancy or need to look backward to maintain balance. Hesitancy and trouble in shifting directions. Hesitancy in sideward walking. Attempts to cross over with trailing foot in sideward walking, rather than always leading with the right foot when going to right or left foot when going to the left.

Behavior such as this indicates a general lack of postural control and flexibility, lack of sense of laterality, and poor spatial orientation.

PROBLEMS IN LATERALITY AND RHYTHM

Activities   Have children jump on one foot; jump, alternating feet; hop on one foot; alternate feet; skip; hop in a pattern of right-right-left, left-left-right, left-left-right-right.

Problem Behavior   Inability to shift weight to maintain balance when jumping or hopping on one foot. Difficulty in using feet alternately. Difficulty in maintaining rhythm or flow of pattern in hopping.

Behavior such as this indicates a general lack of body control and coordination; poor sense of laterality, or inability to alternate movements across the midline; and/or poor control of rhythm or flow of movement.

PROBLEMS OF BODY IMAGE

Activities   Play Simon Says (p. 354), in which leader asks the group to touch different parts of body or to use various parts of body to do something. Play mirror game in which leader moves various limbs in various combinations but gives no verbal commands. Followers must imitate or duplicate the movements of the leader.

Problem Behavior   Errors or slowness in response to touching and using the correct body parts. Hesitancy in movements. Confusion in matching the leader's movements. Use of wrong limbs or matching behavior of opposite limbs. Reverses patterns of leader.

Behavior such as this indicates a lack of awareness of location of body parts, a lack of coordination and control of body parts, a poor sense of laterality, and a poor idea of body image.

PROBLEMS IN EYE CONTROL, HAND-EYE, FOOT-EYE COORDINATION TRACKING

Activities   Using a tether ball, or simply a ball attached to the end of a rope suspended from the ceiling, child should follow the ball with his eyes as it swings across in front of him, backward and forward, and as it swings around in a circle. He should reach out and touch ball; hit ball with hand; hit ball with large paddle; catch objects of various sizes from varying distances; kick a stationary ball, a moving ball.

Run and position body so that a tossed fleece ball hits some part of him; run and catch a ball tossed from different directions; run and hit a tossed fleece ball.

Set up a pattern of squares painted on floor or newspapers arranged on floor in an irregular pattern so that the child must use varying lengths of steps and alternate feet to step on squares as he progresses around the room.

Problem Behavior Difficulty in keeping eyes on ball as it crosses midline of body; moves head instead of eyes. Inability to touch or hit ball as it moves. Difficulty in catching ball. Reaching out for ball and moving head back. Closing eyes as ball reaches him. Hesitancy in deciding which foot to use to step on square. Always trying to use the same foot. Trouble adjusting length of step to varying distances between squares.

Behavior such as this may indicate a malfunction of the muscular system of the eye or a lack of coordination with perception and motor action. The former must be treated by a physician. If the latter is true, a lack of sense of laterality, directionality, and spatial orientation is indicated.

PROBLEMS IN SPATIAL ORIENTATION

Activities Set up a low hurdle or use a low table (or another person on hands and knees). Have children go over and under the obstacle; pass between two objects placed close together. Tell the children to throw to and at a large stationary object; throw at and to a moving object; run and throw a ball up in the air and catch it.

Problem Behavior Inability or difficulty in estimating height of obstacle and size of step needed to clear it. Difficulty in judging amount of space and necessary body adaptations needed to go under the obstacle or through a narrow space. Difficulty in judging distance target is from self. Difficulty in judging how far ahead of person ball must be thrown so ball and person meet. (This is a difficult task for a young child.) Difficulty in judging where ball is in space while one is moving.

Behavior such as this indicates that a child has problems of awareness of his body parts in space and of his body in relation to other objects in space.

Directions for the screening activities should be both auditory and visual, because frequently a child's problem may not be in the doing of the tasks but in understanding or remembering what is to be done. These suggested gross motor activities are but a few in which observations may be made of children's behavior in tasks that are basic to good perceptual-motor development. These are activities that are usually conducted within the regular physical education program. If all the children in the class do these tasks, the teacher will get a reference point as to what good control is. He or she may quickly screen children whose behaviors do not appear similar to those of the majority and later administer a more specific test and/or refer to a specialist for further comprehensive testing and diagnosis. Figure 17-3 shows a checklist the classroom teacher and the regular physical education teacher can use in a more

Figure 17-3 Checklist for Characteristics of Students Who Need Perceptual-Motor Training (with permission from *Adapted Physical Education and Recreation,* Claudine Sherrill. Dubuque, Ia.: Wm. C. Brown, 1976, p. 181–82).

Characteristics of Students Who Need Perceptual-Motor Training

Name _____ Age _____ Sex _____ Date _____

School _____ Teacher _____

This checklist is to be completed by the classroom teacher, speech therapist, or physical education instructor. The observations should be made during regular class periods without the knowledge of the student being observed. The observation should be over a period of time sufficient for an objective view of the student.

1. Fails to show opposition of limbs in walking, sitting, throwing.
2. Sits or stands with poor posture.
3. Does not transfer weight from one foot to the other when throwing.
4. Cannot name body parts or move them on command.
5. Has poor muscle tone (tense or flaccid).
6. Uses one extremity much more often than the other.
7. Cannot use arm without "overflow" movements from other body parts.
8. Cannot jump rope.
9. Cannot clap out a rhythm with both hands or stamp rhythm with feet.
10. Has trouble crossing the midline of the body at chalkboard or in ball handling.
11. Often confuses right and left sides.
12. Confuses vertical, horizontal, up, down directions.
13. Cannot hop or maintain balance in squatting.
14. Has trouble getting in and out of seat.
15. Approaches new tasks with excessive clumsiness.
16. Fails to plan movements before initiating task.
17. Walks or runs with awkward gait.
18. Cannot tie shoes, use scissors, manipulate small objects.
19. Cannot identify fingers as they are touched without vision.
20. Has messy handwriting.
21. Experiences difficulty tracing over line or staying between lines.
22. Cannot discriminate tactually between different coins or fabrics.
23. Cannot imitate body postures and movements.
24. Demonstrates poor ocular control, unable to maintain eye contact with moving objects, loses place while reading.
25. Lacks body awareness; bumps into things; spills and drops objects.
26. Appears excessively tense and anxious; cries or angers easily.
27. Responds negatively to physical contact; avoids touch.
28. Craves to be touched or held.
29. Overreacts to high frequency noise, bright lights, odors.
30. Exhibits difficulty in concentrating.
31. Shows tendency to fight when standing in line or in crowds.
32. Avoids group games and activities; spends most of time alone.
33. Complains of clothes irritating skin; avoids wearing coat.
34. Does not stay in assigned place; moves about excessively.
35. Uses either hand in motor activities.
36. Avoids using the left side of body.
37. Cannot walk sideward to either direction on balance beam.
38. Holds one shoulder lower than the other.
39. Cannot hold a paper in place with one hand while writing with the other.
40. Avoids turning to the left whenever possible.
41. Cannot assemble puzzles which offer no difficulty to peers.
42. Cannot match basic geometric shapes to each other visually.
43. Cannot recognize letters and numbers.
44. Cannot differentiate background from foreground in a picture.
45. Cannot identify hidden figures in a picture.
46. Cannot catch balls.
47. Cannot relate the body to environmental space. Is unable to move between or through objects guided by vision and an awareness of body dimensions.
48. Seems "lost in space," confuses North, South, East, and West.

extensive screening of behaviors commonly displayed by children with learning disabilities and/or mild neurological damage. It may be administered early each year. If a child has ten or more items checked, he or she should be checked more thoroughly and is a possible candidate for special physical education or remedial work in this area.

It must be remembered that within one class, few children will exhibit gross deficiencies in these areas. These few will benefit from an individualized remedial program in addition to the regular physical education program. Ideally, a specialist should be available to work with the learner at school and to help orient parents as to activities that can be done at home to help the child. Activities similar to those used in screening make good practice devices. However, it will be necessary in most cases to start with simpler concepts and tasks of balance, direction, and movement in space. There are many tasks presented in Chapter 11 which should be included in the regular program. The reader can analyze these in terms of perceptual demands.

Keep in mind that this discussion concerns the child who entered school with subnormal control of perceptual motor skills. A well-planned physical education program in the primary grades, as proposed in this book, will include the study of the factors affecting basic movement skills and much variety and variability in the exploration of skills and movement in space. These experiences will enrich a normal youngster's perceptual-motor skills and certainly improve those of children who are slightly underdeveloped in this area before they encounter great academic difficulties.

There are many books that describe theories underlying perceptual-motor programs and the programs themselves. Some of these are listed in the suggested references at the end of the chapter. The AAHPER book, *Foundations and Practices in Perceptual Motor Learning—A Quest for Understanding* (see below) includes an extensive bibliography of films relevant to perceptual-motor problems, a summary of selected perceptual-motor tests or tools, and an annotated list of eighty-five perceptual-motor tests, programs, and material sources.

SUGGESTED REFERENCES FOR FURTHER STUDY

AMERICAN ALLIANCE FOR HEALTH, PHYSICAL EDUCATION AND RECREATION, *Foundations and Practices in Perceptual-Motor Learning—A Quest for Understanding.* Washington, D.C., 1971.

————, *Practical Pointers, #6: Individualized Education Programs,* 1978; #7: *Individualized Education Programs, Methods of Individualizing,* 1978; #9: *Assessment and Evaluation in Individualized Education,* 1978. Washington, D.C., 1978.

————, *Testing for Impaired, Disabled, and Handicapped Individuals* (IRUC). Washington, D.C., 1975.

CRATTY, BRYANT, *Perceptual-Motor Behavior and Educational Process.* Springfield, Ill.: Chas. C Thomas Publishers, 1970.

EDUCATION FOR ALL HANDICAPPED CHILDREN ACT OF 1975. Public Law 94-142, 94th Congress. S-6, November 29, 1975 (20 USC 140).

FAIT, HOLLIS F., *Special Physical Education.* Philadelphia: Saunders, 1973.

"FINAL REGULATIONS OF EDUCATION OF HANDICAPPED CHILDREN. IMPLEMENTATION OF PART B OF EDUCATION FOR THE HANDICAPPED ACT," *Federal Register* 42, no. 163, Part III (August 23, 1977).

GEARHART, LYDIA, *Moving and Knowing: The Young Child Orients Himself In Space.* Englewood Cliffs, N.J.: Prentice-Hall, Inc., 1974.

LERCH, HAROLD, *Perceptual-Motor Activities*. Palo Alto, Cal.: Peek Publications, 1974.

MAINSTREAMING PHYSICAL EDUCATION. BRIEFINGS IV. National Association of Physical Education for College Women and the National College Physical Education Association for Men, 1976.

ROACH, EUGENE, and NEWELL KEPHART, *The Purdue Perceptual-Motor Survey*. Columbus, Ohio: Merrill and Co., 1966.

SHERRILL, CLAUDINE, *Adapted Physical Education: A Multidisciplinary Approach*. Dubuque, Ia.: Wm. C. Brown, 1976.

VALLETT, R. E., *The Remediation of Learning Disorders*. Palo Alto, Cal.: Fearon Publishers, 1967.

VODOLA, THOMAS M., *Individualized Physical Education Program for the Handicapped*. Englewood Cliffs, N.J.: Prentice-Hall, Inc., 1973.

18 / EXTRACLASS ACTIVITIES

- Intramurals
- Interest clubs
- Playground activities
- Extramural or interscholastic activities
- Field days
- Planning and using tournaments

Extraclass activities are a vital part of the physical education curriculum. They are an extension of the physical education instructional program and serve various purposes and needs of children. They provide an enrichment service for all. Children need more activity than the half hour or forty-five minutes the scheduled class period provides. There are athletically gifted youngsters, just as there are intellectually gifted youngsters, who desire and need more time and opportunity than is provided in class time to refine skills. Game play in student-directed activities and competitive situations is the proving ground for using skills and working together. Because extraclass activities are less teacher-directed than class instruction, opportunities for social development abound in the more informal setting. Extraclass activities take several forms: intramurals, playground activity, recess, extramural or inter-scholastic sports, playdays, field days, and clubs. Children of all skill levels should have the opportunity to pursue special interests in activities that are not offered in the instructional program.

Intramurals

Supervised play periods after school in which everyone who wishes may attend are usually called intramurals. The nature of the programs may be varied. Most frequently seasonal sports are played and teams are organized among those who attend. A tournament usually follows several nights of free play. Sometimes this is an enrichment of the instructional program where more advanced skills are taught to those who are interested and capable of learning more than regular class time permits. It may be a free-play period during which equipment and space are available for several activities and for children to do what they choose. Pupils may be surveyed to see which activities will be the most popular to schedule.

Whatever the format, intramurals should be an outgrowth of the instructional program. Everyone who is interested should be able to play.

Certain afternoons are usually scheduled for specific grade groups, depending on the organization of the school and the availability of facilities. Most often intramurals are offered starting in the fourth grade. Where play facilities are limited in neighborhoods and where many mothers work, free-play periods are often held for children in the primary grades also.

If there are several sections of each grade, interclass tournaments might climax several weeks of mixed free play. The emphasis should be on participation and recreation for all, not on intense competition. Teams are frequently formed on the basis of size or ability rather than grade level in order to equalize competition.

If a specialist is available, the after-school program should be assigned to him or her as part of the teaching load. Sometimes classroom teachers are assigned on a monthly or weekly basis. The school principal should be alert to scheduling so that after-school supervision does not become a burden to the teacher. Frequently rotation plans are worked out in which supervision of the playground before school, during recess periods, during lunch hour, and after school are shared by all on an equal time basis. Teachers who supervise intramurals should receive additional compensation if the assignments cannot be shared by all on an equal time basis. Many communities are hiring teacher aides to supervise after-school, before-school and noon-hour activities. The aides may work with the regular teachers or alone, with their responsibilities outlined under a total plan for recreation or enrichment programs. In some situations parents form a volunteer aide group. New education programs for paraprofessionals provide schools a new source of supply of trained responsible aides. Often college students who are in professional physical educational programs can be hired to work after school or can assist the regular school personnel as one of their school field experiences. This reduces the pupil-teacher ratio without additional cost to the school.

Figure 18-1 Intramural permission slip.

_____ School

Date _____

Dear Parent:

In order to satisfy the activity needs and interests of the children of _____ School, we are conducting a supervised after-school intramural play program. The activities will be an outgrowth of those regularly taught in the physical education classes. Activity will end promptly at 4:45. If you wish your child to participate, will you please sign the permission slip and have your child return it to his room teacher?

I hope you will have an opportunity to visit the school sometime during the intramural period. Any suggestions you may have for making this program more worthwhile will be greatly appreciated.

Thank you,

_____, Principal

Schedule 3:30 to 4:30	Mon.	Tues.	Wed.	Thurs.
	Boys	Girls	Boys and Girls	
	5–6	5–6	5–6	4th grade

Tear here

Date _____

(Pupil's Name)

_____ has my permission to stay after school when his class may play in the intramural program.

_____ Parent

Address _____

Phone _____

Children play a vital role in planning and implementing the intramural program. The activities are those in which students profess an interest and/or desire to learn more. This may include activities in which not everyone is interested or for which there is not enough equipment for everyone to use long enough during class to gain great proficiency. For example, some of the more mature boys in sixth grade may show an interest in weight lifting or body conditioning. It may not be prudent or practical to include this in the regular instructional period, but it might be offered after school as an interest club.

Information sheets concerning the time schedule and the nature of the activities offered in the intramural program should be sent home to parents. A slip granting permission for children to participate should be required. This also assures the school personnel that parents have been informed of the time that children are expected home from school. Figure 18-1 is a sample form including pertinent information to parents.

There is a trend toward activity interest clubs in the middle or upper grades. These take different forms. They may be an extension of study of a particular activity initiated in class. They may be formed spontaneously and be short-lived or long-term, depending upon the interest of the participants. An interest club may be initiated by a few students who wish to take part in an activity that cannot be offered in classes for some reason. Students may wish to pursue an activity actively or perhaps just cognitively and affectively through books, films, demonstrations, and so forth.

The sponsor or adult adviser may be any teacher or person in the community who has an interest or expertise in the activity. Meetings may be held at the school or at a facility in the community. For example, often children who are interested in learning to ski may be served in this way. The teacher's role would be to make the arrangements with a local ski instructor or ski facility and coordinate the financial and transportation arrangements with the children and parents who are interested.

Playground Activities

Many children do not go home at noon, but stay at school to eat lunch. There usually is free time between the eating period and the start of afternoon classes. Provision should be made for active play, semi-active play, and quiet activities. This is not an instructional period. Most often the physical education specialist is assigned to this responsibility, or shares it with classroom teachers on a rotational basis. Some schools hire adult teacher's aides for this responsibility in order to free teachers at the noon hour. Where children come to school by bus, a before-school play period with supervision may also be a necessity.

The playground supervisor's duties are mainly those of observation to foster both safety in play and the sharing of play space and equipment. Children should be free to select the type of activity they wish; however, some may need encouragement to participate or to join a group that is already playing.

The activities should be those that children can organize and conduct themselves. For the most part, there should be free play. Much equipment and play space should be available. Generally, it is necessary to designate the areas of the playground in which certain types of activity may be played. If only one part of the grounds is suitable for games requiring a large play space, the use of this part may have to be shared between boys and girls or grade levels on a rotational basis. If not, the oldest children may dominate the use of it. Areas for primary grades and upper grades are usually designated so that small children do not run into older children's playing areas and receive injuries.

Safety rules should be established for all playground areas and equipment. The student council may take a part in formulating the rules and even in maintaining them. Room representatives can relay safety information to students. An organization plan for issuing and returning equipment should be worked out at the start of the year in order to relieve the supervisor from constant responsibility for equipment and to prevent undue loss of equipment.

Extramural or Interscholastic Activities

Extramural activities are those in which play occurs between students from two schools. Interscholastic competition, where teams or individuals play a regular schedule of games with other schools, is not recommended for children under 12 in statements issued by various professional education and medical associations.[1] There has been a great deal of controversy on this subject.

Most of the criticism concerns the emotional demands put upon children when competition and the need to win are unduly stressed. Since children under 12 are prone to bone-and-joint injury because the growing ends of the long bones are not yet completely calcified, contact sports like tackle football, wrestling, and boxing are definitely not recommended. Investigation has not revealed any great proportion of physical harm from interscholastic competition. However, it has been found that the boys who are the most successful athletes before 12 are the boys who are the most physically mature.

It is common to find interscholastic athletics for boys and girls in the seventh and eighth grades and, more infrequently, in the fifth and sixth grades. The decision of whether or not to have a program of this type is not always that of the classroom teacher or even of the principal. It is usually decided by the administration of the school system, but of course each teacher and principal does have some influence in the long run, and they should be aware of the dangers inherent in overemphasis on competition and winning.

Occasionally, extramural events stem from the intramural program, and a city tournament is held, with winners in intramural programs representing each school. If there is such a program scheduled, the teachers and principal should make sure that it is conducted with neither an undue emphasis on winning nor on subsidiaries such as cheerleading exhibitions, booster clubs, fancy uniforms, awards, and admission fees. If an event of this type is planned, medical exams prior to the season, parental permission, adequate physical conditioning, and short practice periods should be required.

Field Days

Many schools devote one afternoon, usually in the spring, to an all-school or intermediate- and upper-grade field day when classes may be dismissed for a few hours. Activities are those which are learned in physical education classes. Typical activities may be running races, broad jumps, target throws, distance throws, dodgeball games, softball, volleyball, kickball, etc. Teachers and parents may serve as judges, timers, and scorers so that all students may play.

[1] American Academy of Pediatrics Committee on School Health, "Statement of Policy on Competitive Athletics," *Pediatrics* (October 1956), p. 672; and American Alliance for Health, Physical Education and Recreation, Desirable Athletic Competition for Children (Washington, D.C., 1968).

Naturally, an event such as this must be well planned so that everyone is able to participate. Scheduling in terms of space, participants, and officials must be carefully decided in advance so that everyone is aware of his or her responsibilities. Special theme days are also popular, with events centering around popular or current happenings—e.g., Olympics, Superstars, Anything Goes. See suggested references for more ideas.

Teachers should know how to plan tournaments for children in extraclass experiences as well as in class. Within instructional units of sports activities, quite frequently culminating activities are tournaments of some type. These not only have great motivational value but also give the students an opportunity to put their newly acquired skills, knowledges, and strategies to use in a student-directed activity. Teams should be charged with planning their strategy and teamwork without direct supervision of the teacher. This also gives the teacher an opportunity to evaluate the students' application of what they have learned during the unit. The three most suitable types of tournaments for class use are described in the following pages. Directions for constructing each are included.

Round Robin Tournament

The best type of tournament for class use is a round robin, in which every team or individual plays every other team or individual. In this way no one is eliminated, and the participation may be enjoyed by all. This is also a good type of tournament for intramural activities, the only disadvantage being that if there are many teams, it takes a lot of time to complete all the rounds.

In order to plan for the amount of time required to complete the tournament, it is possible to determine the number of games to be played by applying the following formula:

$$(N = \text{number of teams}) \qquad \frac{N(N-1)}{2}$$

Example with 6 Teams

$$\frac{6(6-1)}{2} = \frac{6 \times 5}{2} = \frac{30}{2} = 15 \text{ games to be scheduled}$$

The procedure for constructing the schedule of games for an even number of teams is as follows:

1. Number the teams.
2. Number the teams in sequence down the first column and up the second. Number one remains stationary, and the other teams rotate in a counterclockwise direction.
3. There will always be one less round than the number of teams or individuals in the tournament.

Programs for Special
Needs and Interests

536

Six-Team Tournament

Round 1	Round 2	Round 3	Round 4	Round 5
1 vs. 6	1 vs. 5	1 vs. 4	1 vs. 3	1 vs. 2
2 vs. 5	6 vs. 4	5 vs. 3	4 vs. 2	3 vs. 6
3 vs. 4	2 vs. 3	6 vs. 2	5 vs. 6	4 vs. 5

If there is an uneven number of teams to schedule, a bye (no play) is given to one team each round. The bye becomes the stationary point. The procedure for constructing the schedule of games for an uneven number of teams is as follows:

1. Number the teams.
2. Place the word "bye" at the top of the first column of each round. List the number of teams in sequence down the first column and up the second. The bye remains the stationary point, and all of the numbers rotate counterclockwise one place in each round.
3. There will always be the same number of rounds in the tournament as there are number of teams.

Five-Team Tournament

Round 1	Round 2	Round 3	Round 4	Round 5
Bye 5	Bye 4	Bye 3	Bye 2	Bye 1
1 vs. 4	5 vs. 3	4 vs. 2	3 vs. 1	2 vs. 5
2 vs. 3	1 vs. 2	5 vs. 1	4 vs. 5	3 vs. 4

A team is given 2 points for each win, 1 point for a tie, and no points for a loss. The winner of the tournament is the team with the most points. The winner may also be determined by the percentage of games won after the tournament is over. The percentage is found by dividing the games won by a team by the number of games the team played.

Elimination Tournament

If an individual or team champion is to be determined in a very short period of time, an elimination tournament is desirable. Since each time a team plays and loses it is eliminated, the tournament may include a great number of teams and be concluded rather quickly. However, the feature of elimination does not provide much activity for everyone. This type of tournament may climax a long season of round robin play, or it may conclude a unit on the final day.

The teacher determines the number of games that must be scheduled by subtracting one from the total number of teams in the tournament. ($N - 1$ = Number of games to be scheduled.) The procedure for constructing the schedule of games for a number of teams that is a power of 2 (4, 8, 16, 32, 64, etc.) is as follows:

1. Number or name the teams.
2. Draw the same number of lines as there are teams. Each two in ascending order are coupled together. Fill in the lines by drawing the numbers of the teams at random or whichever way is desired. Those coupled together play each other in the first round. Those who win move out into the second round and play the team coupled with them. The losing team is eliminated from the tournament. Successive rounds are played until one winner emerges.

The procedure for constructing the schedule of games for a number of teams that is not a power of 2 is as follows:

1. Number or name the teams.
2. A system of byes (no play) is used in the first round. To determine the number of byes needed, subtract the number of teams from the next highest power of 2. For example: if six teams are playing, $8 - 6 = 2$ byes. Draw eight lines for the first round. The byes are placed near the top and near the bottom of the first round. If there are more than two byes, they should be equally distributed. Sometimes the strongest teams in the tournament are given the byes so that they do not meet in the first round and they will not eliminate the weaker teams in the first round. Team names may be drawn at random and put into the first round in order of drawing.
3. The teams who drew byes are automatically put over into the second round. Other first round games are played, and the winners advance to the second round. The losers are eliminated from the tournament.

Play continues until one team is left. Figure 18-2 shows the pairings for a tournament of six teams.

Ladder Tournament

Ladder tournaments are a good means of conducting a continuous tournament during part of each period. They are particularly suited to individual activities or sports and in classes where there are not a large number of students. The objective is to climb to the top of the ladder and remain there until the tournament is declared over.

Participants are placed on a ladder and may challenge players above them. As they win they move up the ladder. This type of tournament is challenging, motivating, and encourages initiative. Because children can con-

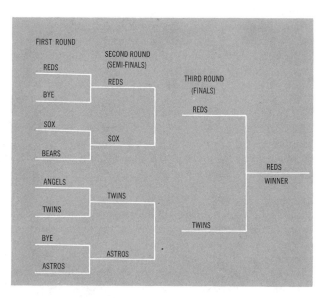

Figure 18-2 Elimination tournament.

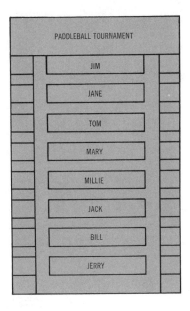

Figure 18-3 Ladder tournament.

tinue the tournament without the teacher's help, it works well for noon hours, recess, and/or after-school activities.

The procedure for constructing a ladder tournament is as follows (see Figure 18-3):

1. Use a board with hooks placed in ladder style, or a chart with movable nametags arranged one above the other.

2. Make a tag for each contestant and place one on each rung of the ladder. It is sometimes wise to place the better players near the bottom of the ladder so they have to work their way to the top.

3. Set a date for completion of the tournament. The person whose name is at the top on that date will be the winner.

4. Post a set of rules for the tournament next to the ladder. Suggested set of rules:

   a. A player may challenge people one or two rungs above him/her.

   b. Winner changes places on the ladder with the person whom he or she defeated, if he/she was the challenger.

   c. If challenger loses, he/she must play at least one other player before he/she may rechallenge the winner.

   d. Challenges must be met within a specified period (depending upon how frequently the opportunities for play arise).

   e. Established rules are used for specific types of tournaments (rules for game, what score constitutes games, set, match, etc.).

SUGGESTED REFERENCES FOR FURTHER STUDY

AMERICAN ALLIANCE FOR HEALTH, PHYSICAL EDUCATION AND RECREATION, *Desirable Athletic Competition for Children*. Washington, D.C., 1968.

———, *Youth Sport Guide for Coaches and Parents*. Washington, D.C., 1977.

CHAMBERLAIN, JAMES R., and PATRICE RYAN, "Disney World in An Open Gym," *Journal of Physical Education and Health* (September 1976), p. 43.

HYATT, RONALD, *Intramural Sports: Organization and Administration.* St. Louis: Mosby, 1977.

ODLE, LARRY, "Super Kids," *Journal for Physical Education and Recreation,* (September 1976), p. 43.

Programs for Special
Needs and Interests

Appendix

APPENDIX A

SOURCES OF EQUIPMENT AND SUPPLIES

- Cosom Sports Co.
  Plastic Play Equipment
  6030 Wayzata Blvd.
  Minneapolis, Minn. 55416

- Childcraft Education Corp.
  P.O. Box 94
  Bayonne, N.J. 07002

- Kwik Kold
  Hot and Cold First Aid Packs
  Box 695
  Moberly, Mo. 65270

- Physical Education Supply Associates
  (Specializing in Foreign Books and Equipment)
  P.O. Box 292
  Trumbull, Conn. 06611

- Program Aids, Inc.
  161 McQueston Pky.
  Mount Vernon, N.Y. 10550

- J. A. Preston Corp.
  (Equipment for Adaptative and Developmental Physical Education Programs)
  71 Fifth Avenue
  New York, N.Y. 10003

- Porter Athletic Equipment
  9555 Irvine Park Road
  Schiller Park, Ill. 60176

- Things from Bell
  12 South Main St.
  Homer, N.Y. 13077

- W. J. Voit Rubber Co.
  3801 S. Harbour Blvd.
  Anata Ana, Cal. 92704

- Wolverine Sports
  745 State Circle
  Ann Arbor, Mich. 48104

- Oregon Worsted Co.
  (Fleece Balls)
  Portland, Ore. 97202

- Nissen Corp.
  930 27th Ave., S.W.
  Cedar Rapids, Iowa 52406

- Shield Mfg. Co.
  (Gym Hockey Equipment)
  9 St. Paul Street
  Buffalo, N.Y. 14209

- J. L. Hammett Co.
  Educational and Art Supplies
  Physical Education Division
  Lyons, N.Y. 14489

- Safe and Fun
  Division of Pull Bouy
  2511 Leach
  Auburn Heights, Mich. 45807

- U.S. Games, Inc.
  1029 Aurora Rd.
  Box E G 874
  Melbourne, Fla. 32935

APPENDIX B

SUGGESTED EQUIPMENT AND SUPPLY LIST FOR AN ELEMENTARY SCHOOL

ITEM	NUMBER	APPROXIMATE COST PER ITEM	CAN BE IMPROVISED
Blackboard	1	$ 42.90	
First aid kit	1	4.00	
Instant cold pack	6	15.85 (pack of 6)	
Instant hot pack	6	15.85 (pack of 6)	
Ball inflator	1	12.00	
Color bands (4 colors)	30	2.00	x
Bags to carry balls	4	3.50	x
Safety cones	8	3.95	x
Whistles	2	1.75	
Whistle lanyards	2	1.00	x
100-foot measuring tape	1	12.50	
Stopwatch	1	21.65	
Line marker	1	12.50	x
Loop film projector			
Loop films			
Videotape recorder			
Gymnastics			
Mats 4 by 6 ft.	6	80.00	x
Balance beams (6-in)	2	72.50	x
(30 or 36 in.)	1	70.00	x
Horizontal bar	1	60.00	x
Doorway bars	2	10.95	x
Folding all-purpose unit (Horizontal bars, rings, ropes, chinning bars)	1	375.00	
Vaulting bench or box	1	70.00	x
Parallel bars	1	200.00	x
All-purpose climber	1	315.00	x
Hanging ropes	4	42.00	
Cargo net	1	150.00	
Parachute	1	75.00	
Games and Sports			
Supersoft softballs	10	21.25 doz.	
Softball bats	6	3.60	
Face masks	2	6.00	
Chest protectors	2	7.00	
Bases (indoor) set	2	12.80	x
Bases (outdoor) set	2	11.00	x

ITEM	NUMBER	APPROXIMATE COST PER ITEM	CAN BE IMPROVISED
Games and Sports			
Batting tee	4	15.00	x
Volleyballs (leather)	4	14.45	
Volleyball nets	2	36.75	x
Volleyball standards	2	63.95 pr.	x
Basketballs (intermediate)	4	13.00	
Footballs (intermediate)	4	14.05	
Kicking tee	1	2.00	
Belts for flag football	24	15.00 doz.	x
Soccer balls (rubber)	4	14.00	
Tether ball poles	2	25.00	x
Tether balls	2	13.25	
Paddle tennis paddles	12	5.25	x
Paddle tennis balls	12	.80	
Aerial tennis paddles	12	3.50	x
Aerial tennis birds	12	1.10	x
Deck tennis rings	6	2.95	x
Playground balls			
5-in.	24	2.85	
8½-in.	24	3.70	
10-in.	4	4.35	
13-in.	2	6.45	
Hurdles	6	15.50	x
Cage ball	1	42.00	
Plastic hockey kit	1	42.30	
Small Equipment			
Jumping ropes, short (16-lb. sash cord)	24	.75	x
long	24	1.00	x
Elastic rope	1	4.00	x
Chinese jumpropes	24	4.00 doz.	x
Duck and Indian clubs	10	1.25	x
Wands (dowels)	24	.90	x
Hoops	12	1.75	x
Beanbags	24		x
Plastic fun balls	6	1.25	
Fleece balls	12	2.75	
Yarn balls	12	2.20	x
Tennis balls	12	1.25	
Scooters	12	8.50	x
Frisbees	10	.90	
Dance			
Record player (with variable speed control)	1	150.00	
Dance drum	1	18.50	x
Econ. castanets	4	1.25	x
Tambourines	4	2.50	x
Maracas	2	3.25	x
Cluster bells	3	1.50	x
Lummi sticks	48	6.00 doz.	x
Adequate record supply			

APPENDIX C

DIRECTIONS AND NORMS FOR THE AAHPER YOUTH FITNESS TEST

- *Pull-up (Boys)*

Equipment: A metal or wooden bar approximately 1½ inches in diameter is preferred. A doorway gym bar can be used, and if no regular equipment is available, a piece of pipe or even the rungs of a ladder can also serve the purpose (Figure A-1).

Description: The bar should be high enough so that the pupil can hang with arms and legs fully extended and feet free of the floor. The pupil should use the overhand grasp (Figure A-2). After assuming the hanging position, the pupil raises his body by his arms until his chin can be placed over the bar and then lowers his body to a full hang as in the starting position. The exercise is repeated as many times as possible.

Figure A-1 Improvised equipment for pulling up—doorway gym bar in background, ladder in foreground.

With permission of the American Alliance for Health, Physical Education and Recreation, 1201 Sixteenth St. N.W., Washington, D.C.

Figure A-2 Starting position for pull-up.

Rules:

1. Allow one trial unless it is obvious that the pupil has not had a fair chance.
2. The body must not swing during the execution of the movement. The pull must in no way be a snap movement. If the pupil starts swinging, check this by holding your extended arm across the front of his thighs.
3. The knees must not be raised, and kicking of the legs is not permitted.

Scoring: Record the number of completed pull-ups to the nearest whole number.

- ### *Flexed Arm-hang (Girls)*

Equipment: A horizontal bar approximately 1½ inches in diameter is preferred. A doorway gym bar can be used; if no regular equipment is available, a piece of pipe can serve the purpose. A stopwatch is needed.

Description: The height of the bar should be adjusted so it is approximately equal to the pupil's standing height. The pupil should use an overhand grasp (Figure A-3). With the assistance of two spotters, one in front and one in back of pupil, the pupil raises her body off the floor to a position where the chin is above the bar, the elbows are flexed, and the chest is close to the bar (Figure A-4). The pupil holds his position as long as possible.

Rules:

1. The stopwatch is started as soon as the subject takes the hanging position.
2. The watch is stopped when (a) pupil's chin touches the bar, (b) pupil's head tilts backwards to keep chin above the bar, (c) pupil's chin falls below the level of the bar.

Scoring: Record in seconds to the nearest second the length of time the subject holds the hanging position.

- *Sit-up (Flexed Leg)*

Equipment: Clean floor, mat or dry turf, and stopwatch.

Description: The pupil lies on back with knees bent, feet on the floor, and heels not more than 12 inches from the buttocks. The angle at the knees should be less than 90 degrees. The pupil puts hands on the back of neck with

Figure A-4 Flexed arm-hang.

Figure A-5 Starting position for flexed leg sit-up.

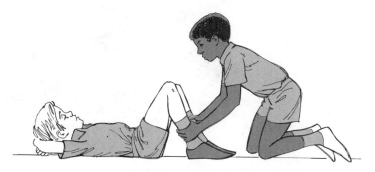

fingers clasped and places elbows squarely on the mat, floor, or turf. Feet are held by partner to keep them in touch with the surface. The pupil tightens abdominal muscles and brings head and elbows forward as he curls up, finally touching elbows to knees. This action constitutes one sit-up. The pupil returns to the starting position with elbows on the surface before he sits up again. The timer gives the signal "Ready-go," and the sit-up performance is started on the word "Go." Performance is stopped on the word "Stop." The number of correctly executed sit-ups performed in 60 seconds shall be the score.

Rules:

1. Only one trial shall be allowed unless the teacher believes the pupil has not had a fair opportunity to perform.
2. No resting is permitted between sit-ups.
3. No sit-ups shall be counted in which the pupil *does not* (a) keep the fingers clasped behind the neck; (b) bring both elbows forward in starting to sit up without pushing off the floor with an elbow; or (c) return to starting position, with *elbows flat on the surface,* before sitting up again.

Scoring: Record the number of correctly executed sit-ups the pupil is able to do in 60 seconds. A foul nullifies the count for that sit-up. The watch is started on the word "Go" and stopped on the word "Stop."

Figure A-6 Flexed leg sit-up.

Figure A-7 Starting the shuttle run.

30 FT.

- ***Shuttle Run***

Equipment: Two blocks of wood, 2 inches by 2 inches by 4 inches, and stopwatch. Pupils should wear sneakers or run barefooted.

Description: Two parallel lines are marked on the floor 30 feet apart. The width of a regulation volleyball court serves as a suitable area. Place the blocks of wood behind one of the lines as indicated in Figure A-7. The pupil starts from behind the other line. On the signal "Ready-go!" the pupil runs to the blocks, picks one up, runs back to the starting line, and *places* the block behind the line; he then runs back and picks up the second block, which he carries back across the starting line. If the scorer has two stopwatches or one with a split-second timer, it is preferable to have two pupils running at the same time. To eliminate the necessity of returning the blocks after each race, start the races alternately, first from behind one line and then from behind the other.

Rules: Allow two trials with some rest between.

Scoring: Record the time of the better of the two trials to the nearest tenth of a second.

- ***Standing Long Jump***

Equipment: Mat, floor, or outdoor jumping pit, and tape measure.

Description: Pupil stands as indicated in Figure A-8, with the feet several inches apart and the toes just behind the takeoff line. Preparatory to jumping, the pupil swings the arms backward and bends the knees. The jump is accomplished by simultaneously extending the knees and swinging forward the arms.

Rules:

1. Allow three trials.
2. Measure from the takeoff line to the heel or other part of the body that touches the floor nearest the takeoff line (Figure A-8).

Figure A-8 Measuring the standing long jump.

3. When the test is given indoors, it is convenient to tape the tape measure to the floor at right angles to the takeoff line and have the pupils jump along the tape. The scorer stands to the side and observes the mark to the nearest inch.

Scoring: Record the best of the three trials in feet and inches to the nearest inch.

- *50-Yard Dash*

Equipment: Two stopwatches or one with a split-second timer.

Description: It is preferable to administer this test to two pupils at a time. Have both take positions behind the starting line. The starter will use the commands "Are you ready?" and "Go!" The latter will be accompanied by a downward sweep of the starter's arm to give a visual signal to the timer, who stands at the finish line (Figure A-9).

Rules: The score is the amount of time between the starter's signal and the instant the pupil crosses the finish line.

Scoring: Record in seconds to the nearest tenth of a second.

- *600-Yard Run-Walk*

Equipment: Track or area marked according to Figures A-10 to A-12, and stopwatch.

Description: Pupil uses a standing start. At the signal "Ready-go!" the pupil starts running the 600-yard distance. The running may be interspersed with

walking. It is possible to have a dozen pupils run at one time by having the pupils pair off before the start of the event. Then each pupil listens for and remembers his partner's time as the latter crosses the finish. The timer merely calls out the times as the pupils cross the finish.

Rules: Walking is permitted, but the object is to cover the distance in the shortest possible time.

Scoring: Record in minutes and seconds.

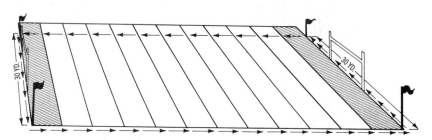

Figure A-10 Using football field for 600-yard run-walk.

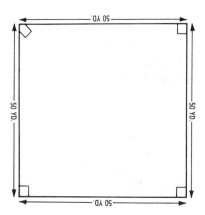

Figure A-11 Using any open area for 600-yard run-walk.

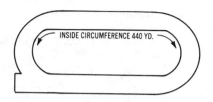

Figure A-12 Using inside track for 600-yard run-walk.

Table A-1 Flexed-Arm Hang for Girls

PERCENTILE SCORES BASED ON AGE / TEST SCORES IN SECONDS

| Percentile | Age | | | | | | | | Percentile |
	9–10	11	12	13	14	15	16	17+	
100th	78	68	84	68	65	83	69	73	100th
95th	42	39	33	34	35	36	31	34	95th
90th	29	30	27	25	29	28	24	28	90th
85th	24	24	23	21	26	25	20	22	85th
80th	21	21	21	20	23	21	17	19	80th
75th	18	20	18	16	21	18	15	17	75th
70th	16	17	15	14	18	15	12	14	70th
65th	14	15	13	13	15	14	11	12	65th
60th	12	13	12	11	13	12	10	10	60th
55th	10	11	10	9	11	10	8	9	55th
50th	9	10	9	8	9	9	7	8	50th
45th	7	8	8	7	8	8	6	7	45th
40th	6	7	6	6	7	7	5	6	40th
35th	5	6	5	5	5	5	4	5	35th
30th	4	5	4	4	5	4	3	4	30th
25th	3	3	3	3	3	4	3	3	25th
20th	2	3	2	2	3	3	2	2	20th
15th	1	2	1	1	2	2	1	2	15th
10th	0	0	1	0	1	1	1	1	10th
5th	0	0	0	0	0	0	0	0	5th
0	0	0	0	0	0	0	0	0	0

With permission of the American Alliance for Health, Physical Education, and Recreation, 1201 Sixteenth St., N.W., Washington, D.C.

Table A-2 Sit-up for Girls (Flexed Leg)

PERCENTILE SCORES BASED ON AGE / TEST SCORES IN NUMBER OF SIT-UPS PERFORMED IN 60 SECONDS

| Percentile | Age | | | | | | | | Percentile |
	9–10	11	12	13	14	15	16	17+	
100th	56	60	55	57	52	58	75	66	100th
95th	45	43	44	45	45	45	43	45	95th
90th	40	40	40	41	43	42	40	41	90th
85th	38	38	38	40	41	40	38	40	85th
80th	35	36	37	38	39	38	36	38	80th
75th	34	35	36	36	37	36	35	35	75th
70th	33	33	35	35	35	35	34	34	70th
65th	31	32	33	33	35	34	33	33	65th
60th	30	31	32	32	33	33	32	32	60th

Table A-2 (Continued)

PERCENTILE SCORES BASED ON AGE / TEST SCORES IN NUMBER OF SIT-UPS
PERFORMED IN 60 SECONDS

Percentile	9-10	11	12	13	14	15	16	17+	Percentile
				Age					
55th	29	30	30	31	32	32	31	31	55th
50th	27	29	29	30	30	31	30	30	50th
45th	25	28	28	29	30	30	28	30	45th
40th	24	26	27	27	29	29	27	28	40th
35th	23	25	26	26	27	28	26	27	35th
30th	22	24	25	25	25	26	25	26	30th
25th	21	22	24	23	24	25	24	25	25th
20th	20	20	22	22	22	23	22	22	20th
15th	17	18	20	20	20	22	20	20	15th
10th	14	15	17	18	18	20	18	18	10th
5th	10	9	13	15	16	15	15	14	5th
0	0	0	0	0	2	2	0	1	0

With permission of the American Alliance for Health, Physical Education and Recreation, 1201
Sixteenth St., N.W., Washington, D.C.

Table A-3 Shuttle Run for Girls

PERCENTILE SCORES BASED ON AGE / TEST SCORES IN SECONDS AND TENTHS

Percentile	9-10	11	12	13	14	15	16	17+	Percentile
				Age					
100th	8.0	8.4	8.5	7.0	7.8	7.4	7.8	8.2	100th
95th	10.2	10.0	9.9	9.7	9.7	9.9	10.0	9.6	95th
90th	10.5	10.3	10.2	10.0	10.0	10.0	10.2	10.0	90th
85th	10.9	10.5	10.5	10.2	10.1	10.2	10.4	10.1	85th
80th	11.0	10.7	10.6	10.4	10.2	10.3	10.5	10.3	80th
75th	11.1	10.8	10.8	10.5	10.3	10.4	10.6	10.4	75th
70th	11.2	11.0	10.9	10.6	10.5	10.5	10.8	10.5	70th
65th	11.4	11.0	11.0	10.8	10.6	10.6	10.9	10.7	65th
60th	11.5	11.1	11.1	11.0	10.7	10.9	11.0	10.9	60th
55th	11.6	11.3	11.2	11.0	10.9	11.0	11.1	11.0	55th
50th	11.8	11.5	11.4	11.2	11.0	11.0	11.2	11.1	50th
45th	11.9	11.6	11.5	11.3	11.2	11.1	11.4	11.3	45th
40th	12.0	11.7	11.5	11.5	11.4	11.3	11.5	11.5	40th
35th	12.0	11.9	11.7	11.6	11.5	11.4	11.7	11.6	35th
30th	12.3	12.0	11.8	11.9	11.7	11.6	11.9	11.9	30th
25th	12.5	12.1	12.0	12.0	12.0	11.8	12.0	12.0	25th
20th	12.8	12.3	12.1	12.2	12.1	12.0	12.1	12.2	20th
15th	13.0	12.6	12.5	12.6	12.3	12.2	12.5	12.5	15th
10th	13.8	13.0	13.0	12.8	12.8	12.6	12.8	13.0	10th
5th	14.3	14.0	13.3	13.2	13.1	13.3	13.7	14.0	5th
0	18.0	20.0	15.3	16.5	19.2	18.5	24.9	17.0	0

With permission of the American Alliance for Health, Physical Education and Recreation, 1201
Sixteenth St. N.W., Washington, D.C.

Table A-4 Standing Long Jump for Girls

PERCENTILE SCORES BASED ON AGE / TEST SCORES IN FEET AND INCHES

Percentile					Age				Percentile
	9–10	11	12	13	14	15	16	17+	
100th	7'11"	7' 0"	7' 0"	8' 0"	7' 5"	8' 0"	7' 7"	7' 6"	100th
95th	5'10"	6' 0"	6' 2"	6' 5"	6' 8"	6' 7"	6' 6"	6' 9"	95th
90th	5' 8"	5' 9"	6' 0"	6' 2"	6' 5"	6' 3"	6' 3"	6' 6"	90th
85th	5' 5"	5' 7"	5' 9"	6' 0"	6' 3"	6' 1"	6' 0"	6' 3"	85th
80th	5' 2"	5' 5"	5' 8"	5'10"	6' 0"	6' 0"	5'11"	6' 2"	80th
75th	5' 2"	5' 4"	5' 6"	5' 9"	5'11"	5'10"	5' 9"	6' 0"	75th
70th	5' 0"	5' 3"	5' 5"	5' 7"	5'10"	5' 9"	5' 8"	5'11"	70th
65th	5' 0"	5' 2"	5' 4"	5' 6"	5' 8"	5' 8"	5' 6"	5'10"	65th
60th	4'10"	5' 1"	5' 2"	5' 5"	5' 7"	5' 6"	5' 6"	5' 9"	60th
55th	4' 9"	5' 0"	5' 1"	5' 4"	5' 6"	5' 6"	5' 4"	5' 7"	55th
50th	4' 8"	4'11"	5' 0"	5' 3"	5' 4"	5' 5"	5' 3"	5' 5"	50th
45th	4' 7"	4'10"	4'11"	5' 2"	5' 3"	5' 3"	5' 2"	5' 4"	45th
40th	4' 6"	4' 8"	4'10"	5' 1"	5' 2"	5' 2"	5' 1"	5' 3"	40th
35th	4' 5"	4' 7"	4' 9"	5' 0"	5' 1"	5' 1"	5' 0"	5' 2"	35th
30th	4' 3"	4' 6"	4' 8"	4'10"	4'11"	5' 0"	4'10"	5' 0"	30th
25th	4' 1"	4' 4"	4' 6"	4' 9"	4'10"	4'11"	4' 9"	4'11"	25th
20th	4' 0"	4' 3"	4' 5"	4' 8"	4' 9"	4' 9"	4' 7"	4' 9"	20th
15th	3'11"	4' 2"	4' 3"	4' 6"	4' 6"	4' 7"	4' 6"	4' 7"	15th
10th	3' 8"	4' 0"	4' 2"	4' 3"	4' 4"	4' 5"	4' 4"	4' 4"	10th
5th	3' 5"	3' 8"	3'10"	4' 0"	4' 0"	4' 2"	4' 0"	4' 1"	5th
0	1' 8"	2'10"	3' 0"	3' 2"	3' 0"	3' 0"	2' 8"	3' 3"	0

With permission of the American Alliance for Health, Physical Education and Recreation, 1201 Sixteenth St. N.W., Washington, D.C.

Table A-5 50-Yard Dash for Girls

PERCENTILE SCORES BASED ON AGE / TEST SCORES IN SECONDS AND TENTHS

Percentile					Age				Percentile
	9–10	11	12	13	14	15	16	17+	
100th	7.0	6.9	6.0	6.0	6.0	6.0	5.6	6.4	100th
95th	7.4	7.3	7.0	6.9	6.8	6.9	7.0	6.8	95th
90th	7.5	7.5	7.2	7.0	7.0	7.0	7.1	7.0	90th
85th	7.8	7.5	7.4	7.2	7.1	7.1	7.3	7.1	85th
80th	8.0	7.8	7.5	7.3	7.2	7.2	7.4	7.3	80th
75th	8.0	7.9	7.6	7.4	7.3	7.4	7.5	7.4	75th
70th	8.1	7.9	7.7	7.5	7.4	7.5	7.5	7.5	70th
65th	8.3	8.0	7.9	7.6	7.5	7.5	7.6	7.5	65th
60th	8.4	8.1	8.0	7.7	7.6	7.6	7.7	7.6	60th
55th	8.5	8.2	8.0	7.9	7.6	7.7	7.8	7.7	55th
50th	8.6	8.3	8.1	8.0	7.8	7.8	7.9	7.9	50th
45th	8.8	8.4	8.2	8.0	7.9	7.9	8.0	8.0	45th

PERCENTILE SCORES BASED ON AGE / TEST SCORES IN SECONDS AND TENTHS

Percentile	Age								Percentile
	9–10	11	12	13	14	15	16	17+	
40th	8.9	8.5	8.3	8.1	8.0	8.0	8.0	8.0	40th
35th	9.0	8.6	8.4	8.2	8.0	8.0	8.1	8.1	35th
30th	9.0	8.8	8.5	8.3	8.2	8.1	8.2	8.2	30th
25th	9.1	9.0	8.7	8.5	8.3	8.2	8.3	8.4	25th
20th	9.4	9.1	8.9	8.7	8.5	8.4	8.5	8.5	20th
15th	9.6	9.3	9.1	8.9	8.8	8.6	8.5	8.8	15th
10th	9.9	9.6	9.4	9.2	9.0	8.8	8.8	9.0	10th
5th	10.3	10.0	10.0	10.0	9.6	9.2	9.3	9.5	5th
0	13.5	12.9	14.9	14.2	11.0	15.6	15.6	15.0	0

With permission of the American Alliance for Health, Physical Education and Recreation, 1201 Sixteenth N.W., Washington, D.C.

Table A-6 600-Yard Run for Girls

PERCENTILE SCORES BASED ON AGE / TEST SCORES IN MINUTES AND SECONDS

Percentile	Age								Percentile
	9–10	11	12	13	14	15	16	17+	
100th	2′ 7″	1′52″	1′40″	1′43″	1′33″	1′41″	1′45″	1′39″	100th
95th	2′20″	2′14″	2′ 6″	2′ 4″	2′ 2″	2′ 0″	2′ 8″	2′ 2″	95th
90th	2′26″	2′21″	2′14″	2′12″	2′ 7″	2′10″	2′15″	2′10″	90th
85th	2′30″	2′25″	2′21″	2′16″	2′11″	2′14″	2′19″	2′14″	85th
80th	2′33″	2′30″	2′23″	2′20″	2′15″	2′18″	2′21″	2′20″	80th
75th	2′39″	2′35″	2′26″	2′23″	2′19″	2′22″	2′26″	2′24″	75th
70th	2′41″	2′39″	2′31″	2′27″	2′24″	2′25″	2′29″	2′26″	70th
65th	2′45″	2′42″	2′35″	2′30″	2′29″	2′28″	2′32″	2′30″	65th
60th	2′48″	2′45″	2′39″	2′34″	2′32″	2′30″	2′36″	2′35″	60th
55th	2′51″	2′48″	2′43″	2′37″	2′36″	2′34″	2′39″	2′38″	55th
50th	2′56″	2′53″	2′47″	2′41″	2′40″	2′37″	2′43″	2′41″	50th
45th	2′59″	2′55″	2′51″	2′45″	2′44″	2′40″	2′47″	2′45″	45th
40th	3′ 1″	2′59″	2′56″	2′49″	2′47″	2′45″	2′49″	2′48″	40th
35th	3′ 8″	3′ 4″	3′ 0″	2′55″	2′51″	2′50″	2′54″	2′53″	35th
30th	3′11″	3′11″	3′ 6″	2′59″	2′56″	2′55″	2′58″	2′56″	30th
25th	3′15″	3′16″	3′13″	3′ 6″	3′ 1″	3′ 0″	3′ 3″	3′ 2″	25th
20th	3′21″	3′24″	3′19″	3′12″	3′ 8″	3′ 5″	3′ 9″	3′ 9″	20th
15th	3′25″	3′30″	3′27″	3′20″	3′16″	3′12″	3′18″	3′19″	15th
10th	3′38″	3′44″	3′36″	3′30″	3′27″	3′26″	3′30″	3′30″	10th
5th	4′ 0″	4′15″	3′59″	3′49″	3′49″	3′28″	3′49″	3′45″	5th
0	5′48″	5′10″	6′ 2″	5′10″	5′ 0″	5′58″	5′ 5″	6′40″	0

With permission of the American Alliance for Health, Physical Education and Recreation, 1201 Sixteenth St., N.W., Washington, D.C.

Table A-7 Pull-Up for Boys

PERCENTILE SCORES BASED ON AGE / TEST SCORES IN NUMBER OF PULL-UPS

Percentile	Age								Percentile
	9–10	11	12	13	14	15	16	17+	
100th	19	16	18	17	27	20	26	23	100th
95th	9	8	9	10	12	15	14	15	95th
90th	7	6	7	9	10	12	12	13	90th
85th	5	5	6	7	9	11	11	12	85th
80th	4	5	5	6	8	10	10	11	80th
75th	3	4	4	5	7	9	10	10	75th
70th	3	4	4	5	7	9	9	10	70th
65th	2	3	3	4	6	8	8	9	65th
60th	2	3	3	4	5	7	8	8	60th
55th	1	2	2	3	5	7	7	7	55th
50th	1	2	2	3	4	6	7	7	50th
45th	1	1	1	2	4	5	6	6	45th
40th	1	1	1	2	3	5	6	6	40th
35th	1	1	1	2	3	4	5	5	35th
30th	0	1	0	1	2	4	5	5	30th
25th	0	0	0	1	2	3	4	4	25th
20th	0	0	0	0	1	2	3	3	20th
15th	0	0	0	0	1	1	3	2	15th
10th	0	0	0	0	0	1	2	1	10th
5th	0	0	0	0	0	0	1	0	5th
0	0	0	0	0	0	0	0	0	0

With permission of the American Alliance for Health, Physical Education and Recreation, 1201 Sixteenth St., N.W., Washington, D.C.

Table A-8 Sit-Up for Boys (Flexed Leg)

PERCENTILE SCORES BASED ON AGE / TEST SCORES IN NUMBER OF SIT-UPS PERFORMED IN 60 SECONDS

Percentile	Age								Percentile
	9–10	11	12	13	14	15	16	17+	
100th	70	60	62	60	73	72	76	66	100th
95th	47	48	50	53	55	57	55	54	95th
90th	44	45	48	50	52	52	52	51	90th
85th	42	43	45	48	50	50	50	49	85th
80th	40	41	43	47	48	49	49	47	80th
75th	38	40	42	45	47	48	47	46	75th
70th	36	39	40	43	45	46	45	45	70th
65th	36	38	39	42	44	45	44	43	65th
60th	35	37	38	41	43	44	43	42	60th
55th	33	35	37	40	41	43	42	42	55th
50th	31	34	35	38	41	42	41	41	50th
45th	30	33	34	37	40	41	40	40	45th

Table A-8 (Continued)

PERCENTILE SCORES BASED ON AGE / TEST SCORES IN NUMBER OF SIT-UPS PERFORMED IN 60 SECONDS

Percentile	Age 9-10	11	12	13	14	15	16	17+	Percentile
40th	29	31	33	35	38	40	40	39	40th
35th	28	30	32	34	37	39	38	38	35th
30th	27	28	30	32	35	38	37	37	30th
25th	25	26	30	30	34	37	35	35	25th
20th	23	24	28	29	32	35	34	34	20th
15th	21	22	26	27	21	34	32	32	15th
10th	19	19	23	24	27	30	30	30	10th
5th	13	15	18	20	24	28	28	26	5th
0	2	0	0	2	6	4	12	1	0

With permission of the American Alliance for Health, Physical Education and Recreation, 1201 Sixteenth St. N.W., Washington, D.C.

Table A-9   Shuttle Run for Boys

PERCENTILE SCORES BASED ON AGE / TEST SCORES IN SECONDS AND TENTHS

Percentile	Age 9-10	11	12	13	14	15	16	17+	Percentile
100th	9.2	8.7	6.8	7.0	7.0	7.0	7.3	7.0	100th
95th	10.0	9.7	9.6	9.3	8.9	8.9	8.6	8.6	95th
90th	10.2	9.9	9.8	9.5	9.2	9.1	8.9	8.9	90th
85th	10.4	10.1	10.0	9.7	9.3	9.2	9.1	9.0	85th
80th	10.5	10.2	10.0	9.8	9.5	9.3	9.2	9.1	80th
75th	10.6	10.4	10.2	10.0	9.6	9.4	9.3	9.2	75th
70th	10.7	10.5	10.3	10.0	9.8	9.5	9.4	9.3	70th
65th	10.8	10.5	10.4	10.1	9.8	9.6	9.5	9.4	65th
60th	11.0	10.6	10.5	10.2	10.0	9.7	9.6	9.5	60th
55th	11.0	10.8	10.6	10.3	10.0	9.8	9.7	9.6	55th
50th	11.2	10.9	10.7	10.4	10.1	9.9	9.9	9.8	50th
45th	11.5	11.0	10.8	10.5	10.1	10.0	10.0	9.9	45th
40th	11.5	11.1	11.0	10.6	10.2	10.0	10.0	10.0	40th
35th	11.7	11.2	11.1	10.8	10.4	10.1	10.1	10.1	35th
30th	11.9	11.4	11.3	11.0	10.6	10.2	10.3	10.2	30th
25th	12.0	11.5	11.4	11.0	10.7	10.4	10.5	10.4	25th
20th	12.2	11.8	11.6	11.3	10.9	10.5	10.6	10.5	20th
15th	12.5	12.0	11.8	11.5	11.0	10.8	10.9	10.7	15th
10th	13.0	12.2	12.0	11.8	11.3	11.1	11.1	11.0	10th
5th	13.1	12.9	12.4	12.4	11.9	11.7	11.9	11.7	5th
0	17.0	20.0	22.0	16.0	18.6	14.7	15.0	15.7	0

With permission of the American Alliance for Health, Physical Education and Recreation, 1201 Sixteenth St., N.W., Washington, D.C.

Table A-10 Standing Long Jump for Boys

PERCENTILE SCORES BASED ON AGE / TEST SCORES IN FEET AND INCHES

Percentile	Age								Percentile
	9–10	11	12	13	14	15	16	17+	
100th	6′ 5″	8′ 5″	7′ 5″	8′ 6″	9′ 0″	9′ 0″	9′ 2″	9′10″	100th
95th	6′ 0″	6′ 2″	6′ 6″	7′ 1″	7′ 6″	8′ 0″	8′ 2″	8′ 5″	95th
90th	5′10″	6′ 0″	6′ 3″	6′10″	7′ 2″	7′ 7″	7′11″	8′ 2″	90th
85th	5′ 8″	5′10″	6′ 1″	6′ 8″	6′11″	7′ 5″	7′ 9″	8′ 0″	85th
80th	5′ 6″	5′ 9″	6′ 0″	6′ 5″	6′10″	7′ 3″	7′ 6″	7′10″	80th
75th	5′ 4″	5′ 7″	5′11″	6′ 3″	6′ 8″	7′ 2″	7′ 6″	7′ 9″	75th
70th	5′ 3″	5′ 6″	5′ 9″	6′ 2″	6′ 6″	7′ 0″	7′ 4″	7′ 7″	70th
65th	5′ 1″	5′ 6″	5′ 8″	6′ 0″	6′ 6″	6′11″	7′ 3″	7′ 6″	65th
60th	5′ 1″	5′ 5″	5′ 7″	6′ 0″	6′ 4″	6′10″	7′ 2″	7′ 5″	60th
55th	5′ 0″	5′ 4″	5′ 6″	5′10″	6′ 3″	6′ 9″	7′ 1″	7′ 3″	55th
50th	4′11″	5′ 2″	5′ 5″	5′ 9″	6′ 2″	6′ 8″	7′ 0″	7′ 2″	50th
45th	4′10″	5′ 2″	5′ 4″	5′ 7″	6′ 1″	6′ 6″	6′11″	7′ 1″	45th
40th	4′ 9″	5′ 0″	5′ 3″	5′ 6″	5′11″	6′ 5″	6′ 9″	7′ 0″	40th
35th	4′ 8″	4′11″	5′ 2″	5′ 5″	5′10″	6′ 4″	6′ 8″	6′10″	35th
30th	4′ 7″	4′10″	5′ 1″	5′ 3″	5′ 8″	6′ 3″	6′ 7″	6′ 8″	30th
25th	4′ 6″	4′ 8″	5′ 0″	5′ 2″	5′ 6″	6′ 1″	6′ 6″	6′ 6″	25th
20th	4′ 5″	4′ 7″	4′10″	5′ 0″	5′ 4″	5′11″	6′ 4″	6′ 4″	20th
15th	4′ 2″	4′ 5″	4′ 9″	4′10″	5′ 2″	5′ 9″	6′ 2″	6′ 2″	15th
10th	4′ 0″	4′ 3″	4′ 6″	4′ 7″	5′ 0″	5′ 6″	5′11″	5′10″	10th
5th	3′10″	4′ 0″	4′ 2″	4′ 4″	4′ 8″	5′ 2″	5′ 5″	5′ 3″	5th
0	3′ 1″	3′ 0″	3′ 2″	3′ 3″	2′ 0″	2′ 0″	3′ 4″	3′ 0″	0

With permission of the American Alliance for Health, Physical Education and Recreation, 1201 Sixteenth St., N.W., Washington, D.C.

Table A-11 50-Yard Dash for Boys

PERCENTILE SCORES BASED ON AGE / TEST SCORES IN SECONDS AND TENTHS

Percentile	Age								Percentile
	9–10	11	12	13	14	15	16	17+	
100th	7.0	6.3	6.3	5.8	5.9	5.5	5.5	5.4	100th
95th	7.3	7.1	6.8	6.5	6.2	6.0	6.0	5.9	95th
90th	7.5	7.2	7.0	6.7	6.4	6.2	6.2	6.0	90th
85th	7.7	7.4	7.1	6.9	6.5	6.3	6.3	6.1	85th
80th	7.8	7.5	7.3	7.0	6.6	6.4	6.4	6.3	80th
75th	7.8	7.6	7.4	7.0	6.8	6.5	6.5	6.3	75th
70th	7.9	7.7	7.5	7.1	6.9	6.6	6.5	6.4	70th
65th	8.0	7.9	7.5	7.2	7.0	6.6	6.6	6.5	65th
60th	8.0	7.9	7.6	7.3	7.0	6.8	6.6	6.5	60th
55th	8.1	8.0	7.7	7.4	7.1	6.8	6.7	6.6	55th
50th	8.2	8.0	7.8	7.5	7.2	6.9	6.7	6.6	50th
45th	8.4	8.2	7.9	7.5	7.3	6.9	6.8	6.7	45th
40th	8.6	8.3	8.0	7.6	7.4	7.0	6.8	6.8	40th
35th	8.7	8.4	8.1	7.7	7.5	7.1	6.9	6.9	35th
30th	8.8	8.5	8.2	7.9	7.6	7.2	7.0	7.0	30th

PERCENTILE SCORES BASED ON AGE / TEST SCORES IN SECONDS AND TENTHS

Percentile	Age								Percentile
	9–10	11	12	13	14	15	16	17+	
25th	8.9	8.6	8.3	8.0	7.7	7.3	7.0	7.0	25th
20th	9.0	8.7	8.5	8.1	7.9	7.4	7.1	7.1	20th
15th	9.2	9.0	8.6	8.3	8.0	7.5	7.2	7.3	15th
10th	9.5	9.1	9.0	8.7	8.2	7.6	7.4	7.5	10th
5th	9.9	9.5	9.5	9.0	8.8	8.0	7.7	7.9	5th
0	11.0	11.5	11.3	15.0	11.1	11.0	9.9	12.0	0

With permission of the American Alliance for Health, Physical Education and Recreation, 1201 Sixteenth St., N.W., Washington, D.C.

Table A-12   600-Yard Run for Boys

PERCENTILE SCORES BASED ON AGE / TEST SCORES IN MINUTES AND SECONDS

Percentile	Age								Percentile
	9–10	11	12	13	14	15	16	17+	
100th	1'52"	1'47"	1'38"	1'26"	1'27"	1'20"	1'21"	1'20"	100th
95th	2' 5"	2' 2"	1'52"	1'45"	1'39"	1'36"	1'34"	1'32"	95th
90th	2' 9"	2' 6"	1'57"	1'50"	1'44"	1'40"	1'38"	1'35"	90th
85th	2'11"	2' 9"	2' 0"	1'54"	1'47"	1'42"	1'40"	1'38"	85th
80th	2'15"	2'12"	2' 4"	1'57"	1'50"	1'45"	1'42"	1'41"	80th
75th	2'17"	2'15"	2' 6"	1'59"	1'52"	1'46"	1'44"	1'43"	75th
70th	2'20"	2'17"	2' 9"	2' 1"	1'55"	1'48"	1'46"	1'45"	70th
65th	2'27"	2'19"	2'11"	2' 3"	1'57"	1'50"	1'48"	1'47"	65th
60th	2'30"	2'22"	2'14"	2' 5"	1'58"	1'52"	1'49"	1'49"	60th
55th	2'31"	2'25"	2'16"	2' 7"	2' 0"	1'54"	1'50"	1'50"	55th
50th	2'33"	2'27"	2'19"	2'10"	2' 3"	1'56"	1'52"	1'52"	50th
45th	2'35"	2'30"	2'22"	2'13"	2' 5"	1'57"	1'54"	1'53"	45th
40th	2'40"	2'34"	2'24"	2'15"	2' 7"	1'59"	1'56"	1'56"	40th
35th	2'42"	2'37"	2'28"	2'20"	2'10"	2' 1"	1'58"	1'57"	35th
30th	2'49"	2'41"	2'32"	2'24"	2'12"	2' 5"	1'59"	1'59"	30th
25th	2'53"	2'47"	2'37"	2'27"	2'16"	2' 8"	2' 1"	2' 2"	25th
20th	2'59"	2'54"	2'42"	2'32"	2'22"	2'11"	2' 4"	2' 6"	20th
15th	3' 7"	3' 2"	2'48"	2'37"	2'30"	2'15"	2' 9"	2'12"	15th
10th	3'14"	3'14"	2'54"	2'45"	2'37"	2'23"	2'17"	2'22"	10th
5th	3'22"	3'29"	3' 6"	3' 0"	2'51"	2'30"	2'31"	2'38"	5th
0	4'48"	6'20"	4'10"	4' 0"	6' 0"	4'39"	4'11"	5'10"	0

With permission of the American Alliance for Health, Physical Education and Recreation, 1201 Sixteenth St., N.W., Washington, D.C.

APPENDIX D

ESSENTIALS OF A QUALITY ELEMENTARY SCHOOL PHYSICAL EDUCATION PROGRAM

A Position Paper[1]

Donald Brault,* *Madison Public Schools, Madison, Wisconsin*

Madeline Boyer,* *San Francisco State College, San Francisco, California*

Ambrose Brazelton, *State Department of Education, Columbus, Ohio*

Herbert C. Karsten,* *Willard Elementary School, Minneapolis, Minnesota*

Sal E. Abitanta, *State Department of Education, Trenton, New Jersey*

Mary Ellen Rekstad, *Towson State College, Towson, Maryland*

Elsa Schneider (liaison), *U.S. Office of Education*

Naomi Allenbaugh (liaison, Physical Education Division), *Ohio State University*

Margie Hanson (liaison), *AAHPER*

*Member of Editorial Subcommittee

A number of recommendations and position papers from the Association are represented in this document, with modifications where necessary to reflect what may be considered the contemporary thinking about physical education. Other statements were developed as new beliefs which were thought to be essential to the continuance of quality programs of physical education in the elementary school of the future.

The document was reviewed by participants at three national meetings sponsored by the AAHPER: the National Conference for Teachers and Supervisors of Elementary School Physical Education, the National Conference of City and County Directors of HPER, and the Physical Education Division Workshop which was part of the 1969 AAHPER Convention held in Boston, Massachusetts. The final document was approved by the AAHPER Physical Education Division Executive Council and by the Board of Directors of the American Association for Health, Physical Education, and Recreation.

[1] This position statement was prepared to assist teachers, administrators, and curriculum planners in general to determine direction and focus for their efforts in developing programs of physical education in elementary schools. It was developed by the Elementary School Physical Education Commission of AAHPER's Physical Education Division.

Foreword   Physical education is one of the most rapidly developing curricular areas in the elementary school program. The need of providing learning experiences in physical education to children has become universally recognized and significant changes are taking place in the content and teaching strategies of this field of study.[2]

When properly guided and developed, physical education becomes a purposeful and vital part of the children's elementary school education. It aids in the realization of those objectives concerned with the development of favorable self-image, creative expression, motor skills, physical fitness, knowledge and understanding of human movement.

In a very real measure, the degree of success the elementary child experiences in his work and play is influenced by his ability to execute movement patterns effectively and efficiently. For the child, movement is one of the most used means of non-verbal communication and expression. It is one of the important avenues through which he forms impressions about himself and his environment.

In some observable and learned form, movement underlies nearly all of man's accomplishments. The child, to become a fully functioning individual, needs many opportunities to participate in well-conceived, well-taught learning experiences in physical education. To achieve this objective, the essentials of a quality program of physical education for the elementary school need to be identified.

A Point of View   Physical education is an integral part of the total educational program. As such it must seek to contribute to the overall goals of the educational program of which it is a part.

Though these purposes and goals are often broadly conceived and include concern for the cognitive and affective fields, as well as for the psychomotor, they should serve as guidelines for determining the kind of physical education program offered in the elementary school.

In the continuing quest to make learning more relevant and personal to the child—and to realize more fully the goals of physical education—new developments in learning theories, structure of subject matter, and behavioral objectives must be constantly considered, evaluated, and implemented.

Statement of Beliefs

The Child   *We believe:*

1. Each child is a unique individual with differing physical, mental, emotional, and social needs.

2. Every child has the need and right to benefit from physical education experiences.

3. Through the teaching of carefully planned movement experiences the child:

Appendix

562

---

[2] *Promising Practices in Elementary School Physical Education,* AAHPER (Washington, D.C., 1969).

a. learns to express his understandings of himself and his environment.

b. becomes more proficient in movement skills which allow him to participate more fully in a variety of life experiences.

c. improves in muscular strength, endurance, flexibility, agility, balance and coordination, and in his knowledge and understanding of how these factors relate to life-long physical fitness.

4. Each child should have continuous learning experiences in physical education each year he is in school.

The Teacher

We believe:

1. Teachers of elementary school physical education must understand human movement, child growth and development, current learning theories, and be able to work effectively with children.

2. A qualified elementary school physical education teacher should be an involved and contributing staff member of the elementary school.

3. To assure that the most meaningful learning takes place, both the physical education teacher and the classroom teacher should work together to develop an understanding of the children and, through this understanding, should provide a program which is commensurate with the children's needs. Although the physical educator assumes the primary role in conducting the program, it is essential that he regard himself as one part of the total educational process.

   When classroom teachers teach physical education it is imperative that they be provided with regular leadership and guidance from resource people who are qualified by education and experience in elementary school physical education.

4. In schools where differentiated staffing patterns are practiced, the value of auxiliary personnel to assist the physical education teacher should not be overlooked.

   a. The use of teacher aides and paraprofessionals as supporting staff can do much to create effective and purposeful teaching teams in physical education as well as in other subject areas.

   b. The unity of purpose and program can be enhanced when staffing patterns permit all teachers, including the physical education teacher, to plan and evaluate (and sometimes teach) as a team working toward common goals.

   c. Guidelines for the utilization of professional personnel (including the use of differentiated staffing) should be developed jointly by the physical education teachers and the school administration.

Teacher Preparation

We believe:

1. Professional education background for the physical education teacher should be developed upon a liberal arts base of the humanities, social sciences, physical sciences and biological sciences. Professional preparation courses should include:

   a. study of child growth and development with an emphasis on motor development and learning.

   b. study of the nature and function of human movement.

c. study of learning processes and factors that facilitate learning, and teaching strategies as they relate to learning outcomes.

d. study of development of curriculum to include movement experiences appropriate for all elementary school children.

e. study of early childhood and elementary school curriculum as a phase of continuing education.

f. directed laboratory experiences focusing on learning to critically observe the movement of children in an elementary school.[3]

2. Preparation for the classroom teacher should include an understanding of the relationship of physical and motor development to the total learning experience of the child. Course work in movement skills, methods, and content of elementary school physical education should be required. Laboratory experiences in working with young children in physical education are essential.

3. In-service opportunities should be provided frequently for all personnel concerned with physical education programs for children.

4. It is imperative that teachers of classes concerned with preservice and in-service education in physical education have had successful recent and continuing work with children.

5. Participation in local, state, and national organizations should be encouraged as a means of keeping informed of trends, issues, and new developments in the profession.

Instructional Program

We believe:

1. A well-conceived and well-executed program of physical education will contribute to the development of self-directed, self-reliant, and fully functioning individuals capable of living happy, productive lives in a democratic society.

2. A comprehensive physical education program for all children has as its foundation a common core of learning experiences. This common core of learning is concerned with efficient body management in a variety of movement situations. It serves the divergent needs of all pupils—the gifted, the slow learner, the handicapped, the culturally deprived, and the average—and is geared to the development needs of each child.

3. The program must be planned and conducted to provide each child with maximal opportunities for involvement in situations calling for mental, motor, and emotional responses which will result in optimal and desirable modifications in behavior: skills, knowledges, and attitudes.

4. A variety of learning experiences should be planned and carried out to emphasize the development of basic concepts, values, and behaviors associated with the ultimate goal for the physically educated person.

5. Curricular content should be so organized that levels of learning in attitudes, understandings,[4] and skills are recognized and can take place in a sequential and developmental arrangement.

[3] *Professional Preparation of the Elementary School Physical Education Teacher,* AAHPER (Washington, D.C., 1969).

[4] *Knowledge and Understanding in Physical Education,* AAHPER (Washington, D.C., 1969).

6. The instructional program should be designed to: (1) encourage vigorous physical activity and attainment of physical fitness; (2) develop motor skills; (3) foster creativity; (4) emphasize safety practices; (5) motivate expression and communication; (6) promote self-understanding and acceptance; and (7) stimulate social development. It should include such experiences as basic movement, dance, games, practice in sport skills, stunts, and tumbling work with large and small apparatus. When possible, the program should include aquatics. Each must be so structured that it is interrelated with the others, permitting children to generalize from one learning experience to the next.

7. To deal effectively with the whole child, many styles of teaching must be brought to bear on the learning situation. These include both teacher-directed and self-directed learning. If learning is to be personalized and concerned with the cognitive and affective domains, problem-solving as a teaching strategy becomes vital.

8. To foster the development of generalizations and key concepts, a range of instructional aids as well as teaching styles must be employed. Innovative use of audio-visual materials, large and small group instruction, individual help, and interdisciplinary approaches must all be considered.

9. Opportunity should be provided for participation in organized intramurals and such extramural programs as play days and sports days. These should be designed to serve the purpose of the class instruction phase of the program.

Evaluation

We believe:

1. Evaluation must be a continuous and vital part of the physical education program. It is used to determine and clarify instructional purposes and to assess individual pupil progress in achieving program objectives.

   a. It is essential in the guidance of children toward the attainment of acceptable goals and in motivation of children and teachers to bring about needed improvement.

   b. It provides the basis for assessing the behavioral response of the learner in relation to the planned learning experience and the development of learning experiences to follow.

   c. It should be utilized as one means of interpreting the program to parents and the community in order to provide for a better understanding of educational values and outcomes.

2. A variety of evaluative techniques should be used for determining individual differences and needs of elementary school children. Such techniques should include the use of teacher observation, class discussion, knowledge testing, anecdotal records, motor skill, and physical fitness assessment. The results of the use of these techniques should be interpreted in light of the local situation rather than solely in relation to national norms. It is more important to compare the records of the child's progress than it is to consider the child's rank in relation to other children.

3. Children need to be directly involved in their own on-going evaluations of themselves, their groups, and of the program in relation to the realization of specific behavioral objectives.

We believe:

1. Pupils in elementary school should participate in an instructional program of physical education for at least 150 minutes per week in addition to time allotted for free and/or supervised play.

   a. To best serve the activity needs of children, a daily program is recommended.

   b. The length of the class period must be appropriate to the instructional purpose of the lesson and to the needs and maturation of the learner.

   c. The time allocated of instruction should be exclusive of time allotted for dressing, showering, recess, free and/or supervised play periods, and noon-hour activities.

2. Groupings for instruction in physical education should be appropriate to the objectives of the lesson being taught, and they should be ordinarily consistent in size with those of other subject areas and/or self-contained classes.

   a. Opportunities for individualizing instruction should be of primary concern in determining class groups.

   b. Class groupings must be flexible enough to provide for differences in interests, levels of maturity, size, abilities, and needs.

3. Consideration of the teaching load is crucial to effective, high-quality teaching. Personnel responsible for scheduling must consider the following factors:

   a. The number of different classes assigned to a physical education teacher in a day is a better criterion for determining teaching load than is the number of hours he teaches.

      For example: The teacher who is teaching 10 or 11 classes in a school day of approximately 5½ hours has a greater load than the one teaching 6 or 7 classes in the same period of time. Planning for and adjusting to a new class every 30 minutes is far more demanding than changing groups every 45 to 50 minutes.

   b. Group or class scheduling should be planned to minimize equipment changes from one class to the next (e.g., scheduling all primary classes in a block of time). It is desirable to leave several minutes open between classes to enable the teacher to talk to individual students, make teaching notes, or confer with the classroom teacher.

   c. The physical education teacher needs time to *plan* his program; *coordinate* the total program; *consult* with teachers, principals, other resource teachers, and parents; and to *work* with children needing additional help. Teachers who travel between schools during the day should be given special considerations to assure that they can function effectively as members of the teaching teams in the schools to which they are assigned.

4. Pupils and teachers should be appropriately dressed for the types of activities being conducted in the physical education class. Concern for freedeom and quality of movement, as well as for safety, should influence the type of attire worn.

Equipment and Facilities

We believe:

1. Boards of education, through their regular school budget, should provide:
   a. sufficient funds for the maintenance and purchase of supplies and equipment.
   b. adequate facilities and equipment for school and community use.
2. Standards for the purchase of supplies and equipment should be developed jointly by the physical education teachers and the school administration.
3. All children should have many opportunities to participate in physical education activities, a goal of one ball, one rope, etc., per child is realistic for a physical education class. If children are to be physically active and fully experiencing the learning situation, ample equipment and supplies for each child are as essential as pencils and books in the classroom.
4. Sufficient indoor and outdoor facilities, equipment, and supplies should be provided in each of the elementary schools (e.g., adjustable apparatus which provides for climbing, swinging, jumping, crawling, hanging, and balancing).
5. School and community facilities and programs should be planned and used to supplement each other in serving the needs of children.
6. Blacktopped areas should be properly marked with circles, lines, courts, etc., to permit participation in a wide variety of activities appropriate for various age levels. Play spaces should be designed to permit creative and exploratory types of play. Apparatus should be selected (or created) for its developmental and educational value.[5]
7. Plans for new physical education facilities are the responsibility of the community as well as the school and should be developed in cooperation with physical education teachers, principals, and other resource persons. Personnel involved in planning should be guided by recent developments in instruction as well as construction.[6]

School Related Programs

We believe:

1. The physical activity needs of elementary school age children can best be served through a program of instruction in physical education which is supplemented by other opportunities for participation that are provided by school, home, and community.
2. The school-related program should provide opportunities for further development of knowledge and skills gained in the instructional physical education program during such periods as recess, noon hour, and extended school-day programs. The program should be differentiated in content and organization to provide for the unskilled child as well as the skilled performer.
3. Extended opportunities for continued participation in sport-type games, dance, gymnastics, and other activities should be offered in the intramural program for all boys and girls. This program usually starts in grade five as the desire for competition and group identification begins to emerge.

[5] *Physical Education for Children's Healthful Living,* Association for Childhood Education International (Washington, D.C., 1968).

[6] *Planning Areas and Facilities for Health, Physical Education and Recreation,* Athletic Institute and AAHPER (Chicago, 1965).

4. Competition at the elementary school level is a vital and forceful educational tool. Properly used it can stimulate a keen desire for self-improvement as well as create environments in which children, motivated by common purpose, unite in an effort to accomplish goals in a manner not unlike the roles they will play as adults in a democratic, competitive society. However, to be beneficial, competition must be success-oriented for all children and relevant to the school program. Carefully structured competitive experiences within the school, involving individual and group opportunities and developed and conducted to achieve specific behavioral objectives, are usually more congruent with elementary education goals than inter-school competitive programs.

If there is a desire to develop a program of inter-school athletic competition for upper elementary school children, it should be considered carefully within the context of relative educational values for children of this age.[7] Such consideration should follow only after a sound physical education program has been provided for all the children in the elementary school as well as an intramural program for the upper elementary grades.

[7] *Desirable Athletic Competition for Children of Elementary School Age,* AAHPER (Washington, D.C., 1968).

INDEX TO SPECIFIC MOVEMENT EXPERIENCES

GAMES AND SPORTS

GENERAL INDEX

Field days, 535
Fielding, softball, 413
Fitness, 201
   (*see also* physical fitness)
Fitts, Paul, 71, 73
Flexibility, 209
Flow, 226
   bound, 226
   free, 226
Folk dance, 284
Football activities, 388
   lead-up games, 393
   offensive and defensive play, 391
   progressions, 389
   skill drill and games chart, 392
   skill drills and games, 392
   skill tests, 395
   skills, 389–91
   teaching, 388
Force, 187, 225
   absorption, 188
   application, 188
   basic concepts, 189
   production, 187
Forearm pass, 430
   (*see also* bump pass)
Formative evaluation, 151
Fundamental skills, teacher's guide for
      analyzing, 265

Games analysis chart, 312
Games and sports, 54, 306
General space, 227
Gentile, Ann, 73
Glossary, basic movement structure, 172
Goals, 30
   evaluation activities, 149
   humanistic education, 32
   physical education, 33
Goal setting, 69, 140
Grading, 153
Gravity, 177, 190
Grouping, 113
   forming, 114
Growth and development chart, 23
Growth and development factors, 16
   cognitive, 21
   motor, 16
   physical, 18
   social and emotional, 20
Guided discovery method, 80
Gutteridge, Mary, 10
Gymnastics, 52, 460
   achievement charts, 461
   apparatus, 463
   development of skills, 462
   developmental stunts, 471
   educational, 460
   floor work, 462
   lesson, 460
   mechanical principles, 470
   organization, 465

Gymnastics (cont.)
   positions and terms, apparatus, 480
   progression, 508
   routines, 464
   safety considerations, 466
   small equipment, 492
   teaching, 460
   tumbling, 477

Hand-eye control, 525
   problems, 526
   screening activities, 527
Hanging ropes, 490
Heading, soccer, 400
High jump, 455
Hilgard, Ernest, 21
Hoops, 499
Hop, 238
Horizontal bars, 482
Humanistic approach, 28
   curriculum, 29
   education, 29
   schools, 164
Hunter, Madeline, 65
Hurwitz, Dick, 102

"I Can" statements, 144
"I Learned" statements, 146
Incidence charts, 161
Independent study, 139
Indirect approach, 82
   examples, 84, 86, 88
   exploration, 85
      free, 86
      guided, 85
   implementing, 82
   practical suggestions, 91
   problem solving, 83
Individualized Education Programs (I.E.P.),
      517
Individualized instruction, 99
Instructional model, 126
Interest days, 135
   clubs, 534
Interest in learning, 69
Interscholastic activities, 535
Intramurals, 532

Jewett, Ann, 106
Jogging, 217
Jump, 236
Jumping ropes, 496
   long, 497
   short, 496

Kehres, Larry, 11
Kelley, Earl, 32
Kicking, 262
   factors affecting, 262
   soccer, 398, 399
Kirschenbaum, Howard, 5, 12
Knowledge testing, 162